Pat Henderson
259-3848

The Victor Handbook
of Bible Knowledge

The Victor Handbook
of Bible Knowledge

V. GILBERT BEERS

VICTOR BOOKS

a division of SP Publications, Inc.

WHEATON, ILLINOIS 60187

Offices also in Fullerton, California • Whitby, Ontario, Canada • Amersham-on-the-Hill, Bucks, England

EDITORIAL STAFF

RESEARCH AND STAFF WRITING
Ronald A. Beers
Leslie R. Keylock

PROJECT EDITOR
Lloyd O. Cory

ADMINISTRATIVE EDITOR
Arlisle F. Beers

MANUSCRIPT EDITOR
Barbara Williams

ADMINISTRATIVE

EDITORIAL DIRECTOR
James R. Adair

PRODUCTION COORDINATOR
Myrna Jean Hasse

ART AND DESIGN

ART DIRECTOR
Sam Postlewaite

PHOTOGRAPHERS
V. Gilbert & Arlisle F. Beers

PHOTO GRAPHICS
Douglas R. Beers

CONTRIBUTING ARTISTS:
Vanides Mlodock Studios
Wayne Hanna, Rene Scharli
Myrna Jean Hasse, Jack White
John Steel

Copyright © 1981 by V. Gilbert Beers

Biblical illustrations, copyright © by Scripture Press
Publications, Inc. 1971–1981.
All maps copyright © 1981 by Scripture Press Publications,
Inc.

Library of Congress Catalog Card Number 81-50695
ISBN: 0-88207-811-9

Manufactured in the United States of America

ILLUSTRATION ACKNOWLEDGMENTS

Location of illustration
on a given page is indicated by:
  L-left, C-center, R-right,
  T-top, B-bottom,
  or combinations,
  such as BLC-bottom left center,
  and BL/C-bottom left and center.

Douglas Beers: photo graphics for all black and white
  photographs except those noted in acknowledgments.
V. Gilbert & Arlisle F. Beers: all photographs except those noted
  in acknowledgments.
Dagon Collection, Haifa, Israel: 33TR, 76TL,
  81TRC/CR/BTR/BC/BR, 141L, 162CR, 237BR.
The Haifa Music Museum and Amli Library, Haifa, Israel: 151T,
  315T.
Hecht Collection, Haifa, Israel: 35B, 50-51, 54B, 64, 88TL,
  97TLC, 103BR, 169BC, 176-177, 203T, 236BL, 245CL, 250-
  251B, 265TLC, 282TL, 315BR, 321TR, 352C, 485C.
Metropolitan Museum of Art, New York: 75BRC, 77RC, 78C,
  79TR, 84-85, 93BL, 94B, 95BL, 98TR, 102TR, 105TR/TCR,
  109L, 182C, 183C, 222-223, 223CR, 265C, 275CL, 288CR,
  305BL, 321TL/TC, 338-339B, 453R, 517CL.
Museum of Fine Arts, Boston: 25BR, 75RC/BR, 102TC/C, 118TL.
The National Maritime Museum, Haifa, Israel: 88CL/CR, 160TR,
  228-229, 268B, 268-269, 402-403, 605CR/B.
The Oriental Institute, Chicago: 22TL, 23BL/R, 25T, 44BL, 49, 55,
  77B, 80B, 81CL/BL, 89TR/TCR, 91CL/B, 95C, 97TR, 102CL,
  105BL, 109C, 120B, 128TR, 129CL, 135C, 143L, 146-147,
  150TL, 168B, 198TR/C, 199C, 205C, 219T/B, 228BL, 229B,
  231B, 236TL, 239BC, 250-251B, 263C, 264R, 272CL/B, 274BR,
  275TL, 289TR, 294CR/BR, 296B, 297C, 300-301T/B, 302TL,
  303BR, 338-339C, 486CR.
Standard Publishing Company, Cincinnati: 253, 259, 278, 302, 348.
The University Museum, University of Pennsylvania: 24B, 185BL.
Scripture Press Publications, Inc., Wheaton, Illinois.
Page locations for biblical illustrations: 14, 18, 21, 22, 24, 26,
  28–29, 34, 47, 52, 57, 70, 72, 78, 84, 92, 98, 100, 104, 108,
  110, 112, 114, 116, 118, 123, 130, 132, 136, 148, 150, 162, 164,
  166, 168, 180, 184, 187, 194, 196, 198, 210, 212, 216, 222, 224,
  227, 234, 237, 238, 240, 244, 246, 249, 250, 251, 255, 256, 260,
  262, 266, 269, 270, 276, 280, 285, 288, 291, 292, 294, 296, 298,
  300, 305, 306, 316, 319, 320, 322, 324, 326, 328, 330, 332, 334,
  336, 340, 342, 344, 346, 350, 356, 362, 364, 368, 370, 372, 374,
  376, 380, 386, 388, 392, 402, 408, 414, 416, 418, 420, 422, 428,
  431, 435, 436, 439, 442, 445, 450, 454, 458, 460, 462, 464, 466,
  470, 472, 474, 476, 482, 486, 490, 492, 494, 500, 505, 514, 520,
  523, 525, 527, 530, 532, 536, 538, 546, 550, 553, 558, 560, 564,
  566, 572, 579, 580, 582, 588, 590, 594, 602, 614.

PREFACE

On your bookshelf and mine there are already some excellent Bible handbooks. We use them regularly and are grateful for them. THE VICTOR HANDBOOK OF BIBLE KNOWLEDGE is not intended to replace them, or to compete with them, but is a new, important reference work to serve another purpose.

Most Bible handbooks are arranged book by book, chapter by chapter, and verse by verse through the Bible. A few are arranged topically. When you approach Bible study with either method, these handbooks provide a direct access to the information sought.

Many people, however, approach the Bible story by story. Millions of teachers, parents, pastors, and Christian education workers focus much of their work on Bible stories. Yet, to our knowledge, there has never been a Bible handbook organized story by story through the Bible. Now THE VICTOR HAND-BOOK OF BIBLE KNOWLEDGE does this, moving through the Bible, story by story, with background information in word and picture for the 300 most important Bible stories. It provides a storehouse of authentic material relating to these 300 stories—including hundreds of drawings taken from objects or monuments of Bible times, photos of Bible lands today, archeological discoveries, full-color paintings, reconstructions, and colorful maps which show the Bible in action. Altogether there are more than 1350 illustrations, more than any other volume of its kind.

To make this treasury of materials useful to all, including children, we have written the text in an easy-to-read style, with much emphasis on interest as well as information.

Every library—home, church, and school—may find this important reference work in wide use. It will enrich Sunday School lesson preparation, sermon preparation, devotions, and Bible storytelling. It will become an important resource for all Bible study.

CONTENTS

NEW TESTAMENT

Continued on following page

CONTENTS

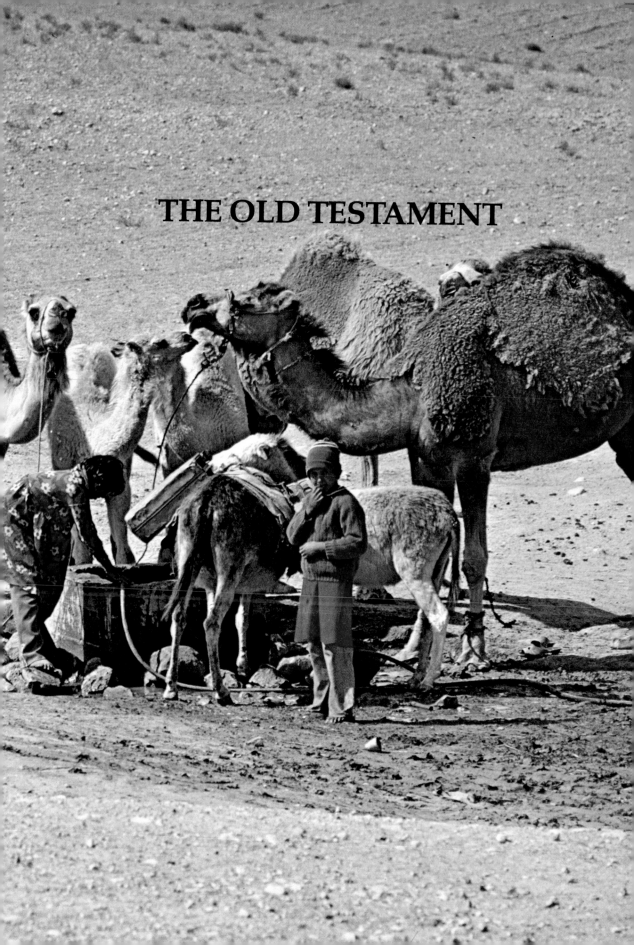

THE OLD TESTAMENT

Creation

GENESIS 1—2

Synopsis

From nothing, God made the world and all that surrounds it and all that is in it. He spoke the word, and it happened. That was Creation.

The Seven Days of Creation

Day 1

God created light and separated the light from the darkness. The light He called day, and the darkness He called night.

Day 2

God made the earth and the heavens (the universe and the skies), and separated the two.

Day 3

God separated the oceans from the dry land. He then created every kind of plant and tree, each bearing its own seed.

Day 4

God created the sun, moon, and stars. He placed them in the heavens to provide light for the earth and seasons for the year.

Day 5

God made fish and all other creatures that live in the oceans and lakes. He also made birds to fly above the earth.

Day 6

God created man and all the animals, and placed man in charge of the animals. He also told man to multiply and fill the earth.

Day 7

God rested from all the work He had done while creating the world.

The Bible World

Compared with the whole world we know today, the Bible world was small. Included in the world of Bible events is the ancient Near East, sometimes called "The Cradle of Civilization" because the earliest-known nations have been found there. Countless empires have fallen, but even today this area remains in the world's spotlight.

The Fall

GENESIS 3

Synopsis

God created the world and all that is in it and all that surrounds it. He also created a man and a woman, and called them Adam and Eve. God placed them in a beautiful garden called Eden and gave them all they needed. But Satan came, and tempted them to want more. That led to sin, and sin led to ruin.

The Garden of Eden

No one knows the exact location of the Garden of Eden, but the Bible offers a clue. It tells of a river that flowed out of the garden and divided into four branches. Two of them, the Tigris and Euphrates, flow through the modern countries of Syria, Iraq, and Turkey. The other two branches are called the Pishon and Gihon and their locations remain a mystery today. Most scholars believe that the Garden of Eden was located somewhere near the head of the Persian Gulf, at the junction of the Tigris and Euphrates Rivers.

No trace of the beautiful garden has been found and some think that it withered and died when God expelled Adam and Eve. Others believe it was destroyed by the great Flood in the days of Noah. Some think it still exists.

Cherubim

The Bible mentions two kinds of spiritual beings created by God—angels, who are in fellowship with God, and demons, who are in rebellion against God. Many believe there are different kinds or ranks of angels and that cherubim fit into one of these ranks.

The appearances of cherubim are mentioned only a few times in the Bible. Ezekiel

Far left: in the Garden of Eden, Adam and Eve had all they needed and wanted. But Satan tempted them to want more. Above: fig leaves. When they were ashamed, Adam and Eve made clothing of fig leaves to cover their nakedness. Right: pomegranate. Some have suggested this as the tempting fruit. It is common in the Middle East today and was commonly known in Bible times.

saw them in a vision, but could not express in words their actual appearance. He had to compare them to things he recognized on earth. He said that cherubim looked like men (Ezek. 1:5), but had two faces (41:18, a man and a lion), or four faces (1:6, 10; 10:14, a man, a lion, an ox, and an eagle). Some had two wings (1 Kings 6:24) and others four (Ezek. 1:6, 11). Cherubim are usually associated with fire. They and a flaming sword guarded the entrance to the Garden of Eden (Gen. 3:24). In Ezekiel's vision they walked on stones of fire (Ezek. 28:14, 16). When they accompanied God and His throne-chariot, coals of fire were seen between the wheels (10:6), and at God's command the cherubim were to spread these burning coals over the city of Jerusalem as an act of judgment (10:2, 7).

Throughout Bible times carved cherubim were used for idol-worship in pagan temples. Heathen cultures such as the Babylonians and Assyrians depicted cherubim as winged humans with an eagle's head or lion's head. Cherubim were also popular as artwork in sculptures and reliefs, but they did not follow the Bible's description of these angels.

The Israelites also made cherubim but did not worship them. Two cherubim of gold were placed on the mercy seat of the ark of the covenant. Cherubim were also embroidered into the tabernacle curtains and two large cherubim of olive wood overlaid with gold were set in Solomon's temple as a symbol of God's greatness.

15

Cain was a farmer, and probably raised wheat, such as that at the left, which grows in Bible lands today. Abel raised animals, much as shepherds have for many generations.

Cain and Abel

GENESIS 4

Synopsis

After God created the heavens and the earth, He made a man and a woman and called them Adam and Eve. He placed them in a beautiful garden called Eden and gave them all they needed. But Satan tempted them to want more, and this led to sin. They were expelled, forced to leave their paradise and work for a living. Sin continued, and one day Cain killed his brother Abel in a fit of anger.

The Family of Adam and Eve

After expulsion from the Garden of Eden, Adam and Eve started a family. Cain, Abel, and Seth were sons of Adam and Eve, and their only children mentioned by name. But the Bible points out that Adam and Eve had many other sons and daughters. Many of these married and had children of their own.

Cain

Cain was the oldest son of Adam and Eve. Early in his life he was a farmer. Cain "worked the soil" (Gen. 4:2). He was the first man to commit murder (4:8), and God condemned him to a life of wandering away from Eden.

Alienated from his family, Cain was forced to leave and traveled to the land of Nod. There

he founded the first city (4:17), and was the ancestor of the earliest musicians and metal-workers (4:21-22). But all of Cain's descendants perished in the great Flood of Noah's time.

Abel
Abel was the second son born to Adam and Eve, Cain's younger brother. Abel was a shepherd, as he "kept flocks" (Gen. 4:2). Abel's offering was accepted by God while Cain's was rejected. As a result, Cain became jealous and killed Abel. This was the first murder in history. No descendants of Abel are mentioned in the Bible, as he probably had none.

Seth
Seth was the third son of Adam and Eve and only his line of descendants was saved from the great Flood. His family tree was preserved through Noah and continued through Abraham and David. Hundreds of years later, this line reached into the home of Mary and Joseph and culminated in the birth of Jesus Christ.

The Land of Nod
After murdering his brother, Cain traveled to the land of Nod. The Bible says that Nod was located east of Eden. There Cain started his family and founded the first city. Nothing else is known about Nod and its location remains a mystery. Some think that Nod is only a play on words used to illustrate a man condemned to wander. Some scholars translate the phrase "land of Nod" into "land of wandering."

The Word "Begat"
Throughout the Bible, there are long lists of family genealogies. In some versions, each generation is separated by the word "begat." For example, Irad begat Mehujael and Mehujael begat Methushael (4:18). The word "begat" can mean either "to become the father of," or "to become the ancestor of." Therefore, several generations may be omitted between steps in a family tree. In the case above, Irad might have been the father of Mehujael, but he could also have been his grandfather.

17

Noah Builds the Ark

GENESIS 6

Synopsis
The years passed after Adam's and Eve's sin in Eden. The world grew worse until God would tolerate it no longer. Then He planned to destroy the world with a great Flood. Only Noah and his family would survive, for they alone pleased God.

The Times before the Flood
The problems we face today are strikingly similar to those before the Flood. It was a time of population explosion, crime out of control, moral decay, and rotting marriage and family life.

God was displeased with the marriages between the "sons of God" and the "daughters of men." Some think the "sons of God" were special heavenly beings. Others think they were godly men in Seth's family who married ungodly women from another family.

Noah and his family were the only people who pleased God. Thus God decided to destroy all others and begin life anew through this one family. This decision led to the great Flood.

Most Bible scholars do not give a date for the Flood, though they place it much earlier than the 2350 B.C. in some chronologies. One respected authority (*Unger's Bible Handbook*) says it was before 5000 B.C.

The Flood
The Bible says the Flood covered the earth. Some Bible scholars say this means only the populated earth known to Noah. Others say it means the entire earth.

The Test of Obedience
God's command must have seemed strange to Noah. Build a large ship, fill it with animals, but build it on dry land far from a lake or sea. But the hope for all future mankind rested

on Noah's complete obedience, even to a seemingly strange command. The key was the Commander, not the command. We must all remember that!

Noah
A descendant of Seth and ancestor of Abraham, Noah was 480 years old when God told him to build the ark, 600 when the Flood came.

Some believe that Noah was a shipbuilder and thus knew how to make a large boat such as the ark. But there is no way to be sure about this.

Noah had three sons. No others are mentioned in the Bible. Noah lived 350 years after the Flood and died at the age of 950.

Ham
Ham was probably born about 24 years after God's order to build the ark, and 96 years before the Flood came. He was the youngest of the three sons.

Ham's four sons were Cush, Egypt, Put, and Canaan. Their descendants were the Ethiopians, Egyptians, Libyans, and the Canaanites. Ham's family is listed in Genesis 10:6-20.

Shem
Abraham's lineage from Noah came through Shem, the father of the Semitic people.

Shem was born 98 years before the Flood, 22 years after God's order to build the ark. He was the oldest of Noah's three sons.

Shem's sons were Elam, Asshur, Arpachshad, Lud, and Aram. From them descended the people of Persia, Assyria, Chaldea, Lydia, and Syria. Abraham, and later Jesus, came through the lineage of Arpachshad, also spelled Arphaxad. Shem's family is listed in Genesis 10:21-31.

Japheth
The Greeks and dwellers of southeastern Europe descended from Japheth, father of seven sons.

Japheth helped Shem cover his father when Noah became drunk. Ham was cursed, and his son Canaan because of him, for looking at his father's nakedness. The family of Japheth is listed in Genesis 10:2-5. He was the second son of Noah.

How Old?
The Patriarchs—
Noah to Abraham

The time of Noah and the great Flood marked a decline in people's longevity. Noah and many of his predecessors lived from 500 to 1,000 years. This chart shows the declining years that men lived in the following generations.

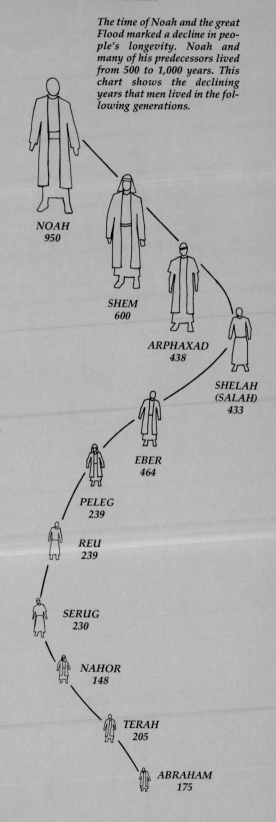

NOAH
950

SHEM
600

ARPHAXAD
438

SHELAH
(SALAH)
433

EBER
464

PELEG
239

REU
239

SERUG
230

NAHOR
148

TERAH
205

ABRAHAM
175

The Great Flood of Noah's Time

GENESIS 7—8

Synopsis

After Adam and Eve yielded to temptation in Eden, sin entered the world. It grew worse as the years passed, until the time of Noah. God decided to destroy all life on earth, except Noah and his family, and a special assortment of animals and birds. After Noah spent 120 years building a big ark, he and his family entered it. Then the Flood began.

Size of the Ark

If the ark were placed on a football field, it would stretch beyond both goal posts. Since it was 450 feet long, it was about 1½ times as large as a football field from goal line to goal line. The length of the ark, 450 feet, was about 137 meters. Its width, 75 feet, was about 23 meters and its height, 45 feet, was about 14 meters.

Time of the Flood

Noah was 480 years old when God told him to build the ark. Despite his old age, he apparently had no children yet. Then, strangely, 22 years after God's order to build the ark, Shem was born. Japheth came a year later, and Ham a year after that. No other children are recorded, even though Noah lived to be 950 years old. It is interesting that the three sons grew up around the ark, from the time they were born until they were almost 100 years old, for it took 120 years for Noah to complete the ark.

Waters of the Flood

There were two sources of water for the Flood. "The springs of the great deep burst forth" suggests a mighty upheaval of the seas or great springs under the earth. "The floodgates of the heavens were opened" suggests the heavy rains which came down (Gen. 7:4, 11).

Wood and Other Materials for the Ark

Gopher wood is not mentioned anywhere else in the Bible. Some say it was cypress, pine, or cedar. Others suggest that "gopher" did not refer to the type of wood, but rather to wood covered with pitch, the substance used to seal the cracks in the ark.

Special Features of the Ark

The ark had three decks. Larger animals or waste materials were probably housed on the lower deck. Living quarters were probably on the top deck, which was covered by a roof. Light and ventilation came from wide windows, 18 inches high, built all around the ark near the roof.

There was a great door in the side of the ark, so large that God Himself closed it when the Flood began (Gen. 7:16).

Noah's Ark—How Big Was It?

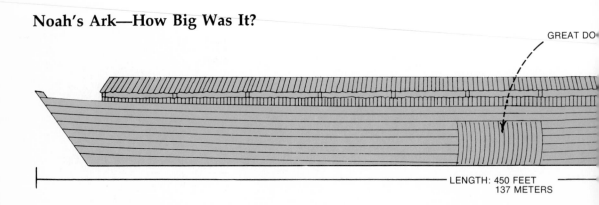

GREAT DO

LENGTH: 450 FEET
137 METERS

Purpose of the Ark

The ark had one purpose—a floating refuge for Noah, his family, and the animals during the months of the Flood. It had no sails, no oars, and no other way to power it. It had no way for Noah or his family to navigate it toward any certain place. All movement was in the hands of God.

Noah and his family within the ark are excellent examples of people totally committed to God's direction. Once in the ark, they depended completely on God to take them wherever He chose, for as long as He chose, and as fast as He chose.

The People on Board

Eight people are mentioned as passengers on the ark—Noah, his wife, his three sons, Ham, Shem, and Japheth, and their three wives. No one else is mentioned. As mentioned earlier, Noah apparently had no other children, either at this point, or later. Not only that, but his three sons, though nearly a hundred years old, apparently had no children at this time. They did, however, have children later, after the Flood.

Some say that Methuselah, Noah's ancestor (possibly grandfather) died the year of the Flood, possibly as a result of the Flood, at the amazing age of 969.

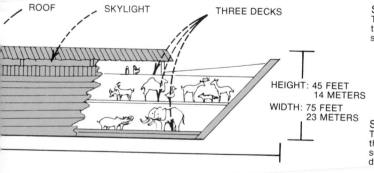

ROOF   SKYLIGHT   THREE DECKS

HEIGHT: 45 FEET
14 METERS

WIDTH: 75 FEET
23 METERS

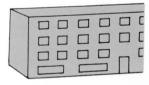

SCHOOL
The ark was taller than a four-story school building.

SCHOOL BUS
The ark was longer than a dozen big school buses or two dozen family cars.

Above: one reconstruction of the Tower of Babel as it may have appeared. Right: workmen build this enormous tower, reaching toward the heavens.

The Tower of Babel

GENESIS 11:1-9

Synopsis
After God created the universe, Adam and Eve sinned and were driven from their home in the Garden of Eden. From that time on, sin grew worse and worse. By the time of Noah, it was so bad that God destroyed all people except Noah and his family. More time passed until the incident which caused one language to become many.

Where
The Tower of Babel was built on a plain in the land of Shinar. Throughout the Bible it becomes apparent that Shinar is another name for the land of Babylon. Well-known Babylonian cities are identified as being in the land of Shinar (Gen. 10:10). When Nebuchadnezzar, king of Babylon, sacked Jerusalem, he carried the captives back to his country, the land of Shinar (Dan. 1:2). He placed the spoils in the temple treasuries and asked that certain captives be taught to serve in the king's court. This would have taken place in the capital city, named Babylon, in the land

also called Babylon. So it is almost certain that the land of Shinar and the land of Babylon are identical.

The Tower of Babel
After the Flood, the earth once again multiplied with people. A group of these people migrated east, to a plain in the land of Shinar. There they decided to build a large tower that would reach to the heavens. The Bible does not mention the name of the tower, but it is commonly called the "Tower of Babel." In Babylon's native language, Akkadian, "Babel" meant "the gate of God." A similar word in Hebrew means "to mix or confuse."

Ziggurats
The Tower of Babel was probably a ziggurat. A ziggurat was a temple tower common in the land of Babylon about this time. It marked the central place of worship for a city or region. Here the people gathered to worship their gods and perform religious ceremonies.

The architecture of ziggurats was developed by the Babylonians. Frequently they resembled pyramids, but without the smooth sides. Most ziggurats had seven stories. Each story was slightly smaller than the one below it, creating a steplike appearance. Stairways on the outside of the building connected each level.

Some ziggurats were cone-shaped, and had stairs or ramps that wound around the tower leading to the top. These were the "winding road" variety and very common in the northern Near East. Other ziggurats had four levels instead of seven. Three stairways joined at the top of the first level. From there, one stairway led to the top. Usually, this top section was the size of just one room, and the holiest place in the ziggurat.

Ziggurats were large buildings. At the base, most were 200-300 feet in each direction. Their height could reach 300 feet as well. The Tower of Babel was one of the largest ziggurats, mea-

suring about 300 feet on each side. Each level was painted a different color and the building looked like a large rainbow.

Mud-brick was the common building material for a ziggurat. It was made of either mud and straw, or clay, and then fired at high heat for extra strength. Asphalt was used instead of mortar to glue the bricks together.

The ziggurat was the focal point of a city. It was always the largest building in the area, and could be seen from anywhere in the city. Around the ziggurat were many smaller temples and towers, each devoted to the worship of a particular god.

Ziggurats Associated with the Tower of Babel

Either of two ziggurats uncovered today may have been the ancient Tower of Babel. The temple of Ishtar, built by Nebuchadnezzar II, was constructed over the ruins of an earlier tower. Some say this earlier tower was Babel. At Nimrud, a ruined temple, or ziggurat, has been excavated. According to ancient Jewish tradition, this was the Tower of Babel.

The Birth of Nations

Throughout the years, families continued to multiply. Each new generation had many more people than the previous one. These large families soon formed groups called clans. For organization and protection, different clans joined together and formed tribes. In time, these tribes grew into nations.

White

Blue

Green

Yellow

Red

range

k

Left: a reconstruction of the Tower of Babel. This tower, or one like it, appears above in a reconstruction of ancient Babylon. A drawing of the tower, showing the different colors at various levels, appears at the upper left.

23

Abraham Moves from Ur to Canaan GENESIS 11:27—12:9

Synopsis

A long time had passed since the language of mankind was confused at the Tower of Babel, perhaps more than 2,000 years. One of Noah's descendants, a man named Abraham, who was first called Abram, is found living in Sumeria, then is seen migrating northward to Haran, and then southwestward into Canaan.

Ur

On the banks of the Euphrates River stood the ancient city of Ur. Abraham spent his childhood years in this busy center of trade before migrating to Canaan. Ur was located in the southern section of the region of Mesopotamia. This section was called Sumer, and was inhabited by the Sumerians, the dominant people in Mesopotamia at that time.

Ur was an ancient city full of activity. It was surrounded by an intricate system of man-made canals and for protection, an oval wall was built around the city. The average house was a small, one-story mud-brick shelter with no windows. Its unpaved streets were muddy

24

when wet. Ur had no sewers or garbage pickup.

The marketplace was the center of activity. Here the Sumerians gathered to trade their wares and talk about the day's news. Farmers coming in from the fields offered a great variety of food including onions, barley, and apples. Traveling merchants also brought exotic goods from India and other foreign regions.

The Fertile Crescent

As Abraham journeyed from Ur to Canaan, he followed the arc of the Fertile Crescent. This is a large bow-shaped strip of land where fertile soil and plenty of water can be found in the midst of a vast wilderness.

The Fertile Crescent stretches northwest from Ur toward the area of Haran, a city where Abraham lived for a time on his way to Canaan. The crescent then turns southwest and follows the eastern coast of the Mediterranean Sea, spreading across the land of Canaan, later called Israel.

It is no wonder the early civilizations settled in this fruitful land. Cattle and other flocks thrived on the rich pastureland, where wheat, beans, and barley also grew. Numerous rivers fed the area, providing water for vineyards, fields, and gardens. The rivers were also important in travel and communication and helped to form and unify the earliest empires.

Mesopotamia's Dominant Peoples

In Abraham's time, the Sumerians were the dominant people of Mesopotamia. Later the Babylonians dominated and then the Assyrians. The Persians ruled after the Assyrians fell. Then came the Greeks and Romans.

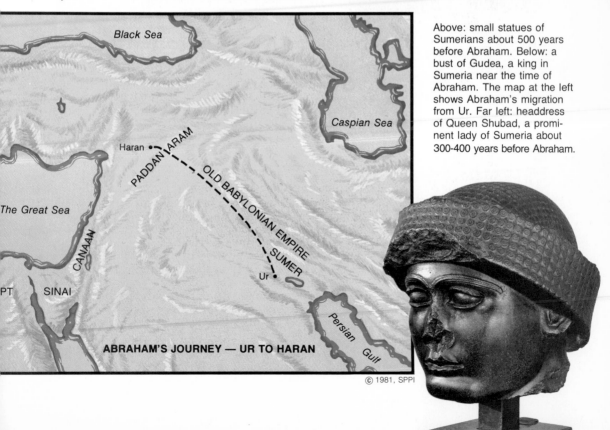

ABRAHAM'S JOURNEY — UR TO HARAN

© 1981, SPPI

Above: small statues of Sumerians about 500 years before Abraham. Below: a bust of Gudea, a king in Sumeria near the time of Abraham. The map at the left shows Abraham's migration from Ur. Far left: headdress of Queen Shubad, a prominent lady of Sumeria about 300-400 years before Abraham.

Left: Abraham and his family and servants move slowly with flocks and herds. Bottom right: the path Abraham followed from his home in Ur through Haran to Canaan and Egypt. Far right: the sphinx and pyramids of Egypt, built before Abraham's time. The power of pharaoh is seen in these three drawings, clockwise from above: pharaoh with his scepter and tall crown, pharaoh with crown offering a statue to a goddess, and servants carrying a pharaoh.

Abraham and Sarah Go to Egypt

GENESIS 12:10-20

Synopsis

From Sumeria, Abraham migrated northward and westward along the great arc of rich land known as the Fertile Crescent, and settled in Haran. Later, he migrated again into Canaan, moving southwestward along the remaining part of the Fertile Crescent. But famine came to Canaan, and Abraham was forced to migrate once more, this time to Egypt.

Abraham's Sister

When Abraham told the pharaoh of Egypt that Sarah was his sister, he was not completely lying, but he was not telling the whole truth either. Sarah was Abraham's half-sister on his father Terah's side (Gen. 20:12). In other words, Abraham and Sarah had the same father, Terah, but did not have the same mother. The Bible does not mention their mothers, but it does say they were not the same.

Famine

Imagine entering a grocery store and finding no food on the shelves, and then returning a week later only to see the shelves still empty. By that time there would be many hungry people. But what if those grocery shelves remained empty for months? Where would people get food and how would they survive?

Abraham faced this kind of problem when famine struck the land of Canaan. A famine is a critical shortage of food lasting for a long period of time. It may be caused by a number of circumstances. Drought was the main cause of famine. The land of Canaan (later called Israel) depended on two rainy seasons for its crops to grow. If there was no rain in the months when it was supposed to rain, the crops withered

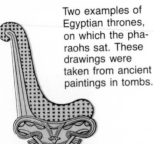

Two examples of Egyptian thrones, on which the pharaohs sat. These drawings were taken from ancient paintings in tombs.

and died, and food became scarce. Wealthy people could buy food from foreign countries, but the poor had to live with what little food they could forage from the fields or beg from the wealthy. Life would be difficult at least till the next harvest, which was months away. And some famines lasted for years.

Even with plenty of rain, famine was still feared by the people. Large numbers of insects often devoured the fields before they ripened. Armies invading the land usually attacked during harvest. After taking enough food for themselves, they destroyed the fields, leaving cities and villages without food.

Harems

In the days of Abraham, most people, and especially kings, thought nothing was wrong with having many wives. A king might have as many as 1,000 wives, plus other women who were not married to him. He built a special place for them to live and called on them whenever he pleased. This building, called a harem, was very common among ancient nations.

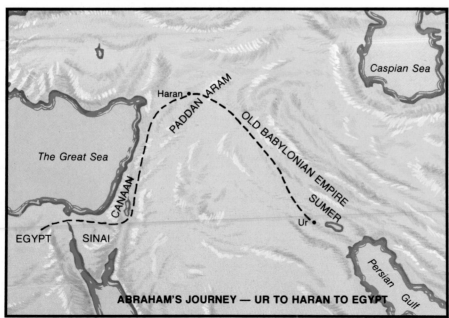

ABRAHAM'S JOURNEY — UR TO HARAN TO EGYPT

27

Abraham and Lot Part

GENESIS 13:1-13

Synopsis
After Abraham and his wife Sarah moved to Egypt, Abraham became frightened that the Egyptians would kill him so that Pharaoh could marry his wife. Because of this, Abraham lied, telling Pharaoh that Sarah was his sister. Pharaoh gave Abraham many gifts, took Sarah into his harem, and would have kept her, but for a plague which arose. Pharaoh discovered the truth and made Abraham and Sarah leave the land. Back in Canaan, the herdsmen of Abraham and his nephew Lot began to quarrel over the rich pastureland.

Lot
Lot spent his childhood years in Ur, just as Abraham had. In fact, he was the son of Abraham's brother Haran. But Haran died in Ur, and probably out of a sense of loneliness Lot migrated toward Canaan with his uncle Abraham and his grandfather Terah. He became a wealthy shepherd in Canaan with many flocks and herds. But soon his herdsmen started quarreling with Abraham's, and the two men decided to split up. Lot chose the fertile Jordan Valley. Though this was a beautiful and well-watered area, it was the home of the wicked people of Sodom and Gomorrah. When God destroyed these cities with fire, only Lot and his daughters escaped.

The Jordan Valley
Abraham and Lot decided to separate their huge flocks, because the land could not hold all of them. Abraham told Lot to choose whatever land he wanted. Lot took the fertile Jordan Valley. This area begins where the Jordan River enters the Dead Sea and stretches northward for about 25 miles. Though this area was noted for its water and rich pastureland, it was also noted for the wickedness of its people.

Canaan—Ancestor to Israel
Before the time of the Judges, the land of Israel was called Canaan. This was the land in between the Jordan River and the Mediterranean Sea, the land where Jesus lived and walked. It was also the "Promised Land," the destination of the Hebrews on their Exodus from Egypt.

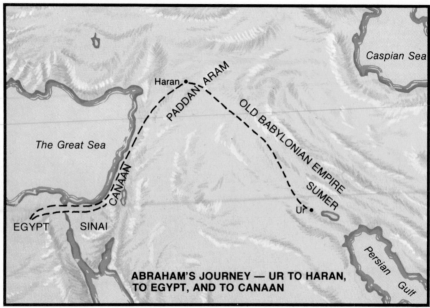

Haran

PADDAN ARAM

Caspian Sea

OLD BABYLONIAN EMPIRE

The Great Sea

SUMER

CANAAN

Ur

EGYPT   SINAI

Persian Gulf

ABRAHAM'S JOURNEY — UR TO HARAN, TO EGYPT, AND TO CANAAN

© 1981, SPPI

Left: Abraham and Lot part as Lot chooses the richest land for himself. Top: near Beersheba today, this flock of sheep grazes on land where Abraham's flocks once grazed. At one time Abraham lived at Mamre, near Hebron, which is marked today by this stone marker. Above: a map shows Abraham's travels from Ur to Haran, then to Canaan, to Egypt, and then back to Canaan. Picture just above: near Beersheba, a scene which reminds us of Abraham's time—bedouin tents, with goats and sheep.

29

The Harsh Life of Those Captured in Battle

People captured in battle in ancient times could expect the worst, and would probably find it. Torture was common, slavery was almost certain. Families were torn apart with some sold as slaves to one place, others to another place. These drawings, taken from ancient monuments and tombs, show different kinds of suffering inflicted on those captured.

WOMEN ENSLAVED: Women were especially vulnerable in captivity. They were often forced to serve as mistresses or prostitutes in a foreign land, or as slaves to serve in whatever way their captors chose. These women have been captured by Assyrians.

CHAINED: Ethiopian prisoners are chained to one another, captives of Egyptians in the time of Ramses. Note that they are chained around the neck.

CHAINED: Asiatic and Philistine captives chained to one another come before Pharaoh Ramses.

SLAVERY: Women were not the only ones forced into slavery. Men were sent into hard work, serving their captors. Children also were sent into slavery. Many died in captivity. Pharaoh's soldiers lead mothers with children to their new lives as slaves.

PUTTING FOOT ON CAPTIVE: A king places his foot on a captive king to humiliate him before his subjects. Placing the foot on the neck was also done.

BOUND: One of the first humiliations for a captive was to be bound. These two captives are secured by an ancient form of handcuffs.

Lot Is Captured

GENESIS 14

Synopsis

Abraham and his wife Sarah had migrated from Ur, in Sumeria, to Haran, then to Canaan. But a famine came and forced them to move to Egypt. Abraham lied to the king of that land, Pharaoh, telling him that Sarah was his sister, for he was afraid Pharaoh would kill him to marry Sarah. When Pharaoh learned the truth, he forced Abraham and Sarah to leave Egypt. They returned to Canaan. There a quarrel between Abraham's herdsmen and his nephew Lot's herdsmen forced the two to separate. Not long after that, the city where Lot had moved, Sodom, was involved in a war. Along with others in the city, Lot was carried away captive.

The Alliances of the Kings

In Abraham's time, almost every city in the land of Canaan had its own king and army. However, many of these cities were small, and were forced to pay tribute to a king who was much more powerful than theirs.

Around the Dead Sea, there were 5 of these small city-states, that for 12 years had paid tribute to Kedorlaomer (Chedorlaomer), a strong king from a far-north place called Elam. The following year these kings grew tired of paying their yearly tribute and formed an alliance in order to rebel. These five kings were Bera, king of Sodom, Birsha, king of Gomorrah, Shemeber, king of Zeboiim, Shinab, king of Admah, and the king of Bela or Zoar.

Together these weak kings made up a strong army, too strong for Kedorlaomer alone, for when he learned about the rebel alliance, he organized an alliance of his own.

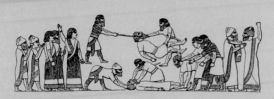

TORTURE: Assyrians were especially cruel in their torture, as recorded on this relief, and many others. They cut people until they died, tore skin off, or tortured in other ways to make prisoners suffer untold pain until they died.

BLINDED: This Assyrian king is about to gouge out the eyes of his captive, probably a king. This happened to King Zedekiah of Judah.

FLAYING AND DECAPITATING: The Assyrian at the right holds the head of a prisoner who has been decapitated. At the top left: two Assyrian torturers flay their prisoners, tearing off strips of skin one by one until the prisoners die of pain.

CUT TO PIECES: This Assyrian relief shows a prisoner being cut into pieces, as opposed to having his skin stripped off a piece at a time, as in flaying. Daniel (3:29) referred to cutting people into pieces.

FLAYED ALIVE: One of the most painful tortures was flaying, pulling strips of skin from a prisoner until he or she died. This Assyrian relief shows an Assyrian torturer flaying or cutting a prisoner to pieces.

CRUSHING WITH HAMMERS OR CUTTING WITH AXES: These prisoners are about to be cut to pieces with an ax by Pharaoh.

Not all ancient people were this cruel. But these pictures from ancient times remind us that captivity in those days was a terrifying experience. No wonder Abraham risked all to save Lot and his family!

He quickly joined forces with three other kings; Arioch, king of Ellasar, Tidal, king of Goiim, and Amraphel, king of Shinar. With their skillful warriors, Kedorlaomer and his allies easily crushed the rebel kings and carried the survivors back to their homelands in the north. Lot and his family were among these captives.

Abraham's Pursuit

When Abraham found out that his nephew Lot had been captured, he set out in pursuit. Leaving his home at Hebron, Abraham and his men traveled northward, finally catching up with the enemy alliance at Dan, a distance of about 130 miles.

A skilled warrior himself, Abraham made a surprise attack by night and scattered the enemy. He continued the chase as far north as Hobah. The exact location of Hobah is not known for sure, but most think the city was located 50 miles north of Damascus, which is about 50 miles north of Dan. This means that Abraham traveled a distance of approximately 200-250 miles north in order to rescue Lot.

Melchizedek

Returning from victory, Abraham was greeted by Melchizedek, the king of Salem who was also a priest of God. Many think that Salem was the city of Jerusalem, about 25 miles north of Abraham's home at Hebron.

Melchizedek is mentioned in other places in the Bible. "You are a Priest forever in the order of Melchizedek" (Ps. 110:4). This psalm apparently refers to Jesus Christ prophetically. Melchizedek is also mentioned in Hebrews 5, in relationship to Jesus as High Priest.

God's Covenant with Abraham

GENESIS 17

Synopsis

Abraham, whose name at this time was Abram, had left Ur to migrate with his family to the north, in Haran, then down to Canaan. But a famine in Canaan forced him to move to Egypt. With a lack of trust in God to take care of him, so unusual for Abraham, he pretended that Sarah (Sarai) was his sister. Pharaoh almost made Sarah a part of his harem, and when he learned the truth, forced Abraham to leave Egypt. Back in Canaan, Abraham and his nephew Lot parted when their herdsmen quarreled over the land. Lot moved to Sodom and was captured, but Abraham freed him in a swift battle. Now, when Abraham was 99 years old, God appeared to him and renewed His covenant with him.

Changing Names

In the Old Testament, there were a few people who had their names changed. This almost always marked a very special occasion.

Abram's name was changed to Abraham when God made a covenant with him (Gen. 17:5). Sarai became Sarah when God promised her a son (Gen. 17:15). After wrestling all night with an angel, Jacob's name was changed to Israel (Gen. 32:28). As captives in Babylon, Daniel and his three friends were assigned new names. Daniel was given the name Belteshazzar, Hananiah was called Shadrach, Mishael was named Meshach, and Azariah became Abednego (Dan. 1:7).

Miraculous Birth of Children in Old Age

Sarah was too old to have children. At least that was what Abraham and Sarah thought. But God had promised the couple a child and God does not break His promises. So, at the age of 91, Sarah gave birth to Isaac. At that time, Abraham was 100!

John the Baptist was a "miracle baby" also. His parents, Elizabeth and Zacharias, were both very old when John's birth was promised

At the time of this incident Abraham lived at Mamre, a short distance north of Hebron (see map below). The photo at the upper left shows the countryside at Mamre. The ruins above are at Mamre today. The clay tablet at the upper right is a form of an ancient contract, or covenant. It is a Sumerian account from the time of Abraham, promising to pay for day laborers with wheat.

by God. Zacharias did not believe God's promise and as punishment, God made him speechless until John's birth.

Covenants

In Bible times, there were two types of covenants. The first type was a contract or binding agreement between two people or nations. Both parties were obligated to follow the terms of the agreement which was sometimes sealed by drinking each other's blood or eating a sacrificial meal. God made a covenant with the people of Israel to be their God if they would only follow and obey Him. But Israel rejected God and did not hold up their end of the agreement. So the covenant was broken completely and the Israelites were carried into captivity.

The second type of covenant was a promise made by one person to another. The one making the promise was bound to keep it, but the one receiving it could accept or reject it. Today, an example of this covenant is a will.

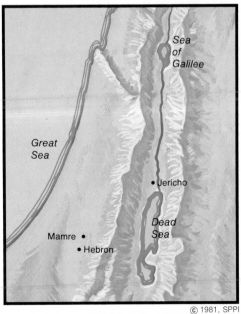

33

Abraham Entertains Angels

GENESIS 18

Synopsis

Abraham had moved from his native home in Ur to the land of Haran, and then to Canaan. After a short time in Egypt, during a famine in Canaan, Abraham returned to Canaan to live out the rest of his life. He and his nephew Lot parted ways because of quarreling herdsmen, but Lot was captured and Abraham rescued him. After that, God renewed His covenant with Abraham. One day God visited Abraham's tent in the form of angels, clothed in men's bodies.

Mamre

When Abraham returned from Egypt after the famine, he "pitched his tent" by the oaks of Mamre, very close to the city of Hebron. It was here that Abraham entertained three angels and bargained with God for the safety of Sodom. Later, near Mamre, Abraham bought the field of Machpelah from Ephron the Hittite. There was a cave at the end of the field where Abraham buried his wife Sarah. Abraham was buried there as well. The Arabic name for Mamre is Ramat el-Khalil which means "the high place of the friend of God."

Tents as Homes—How They Were Made

The first reference to tents in the Bible is in

Genesis 4:20, where a man named Jabal is called "the father of those who live in tents." A tent in Jabal's time was probably made of animal skins crudely patched together. Later, when the bedouins learned the process of weaving, tents were made by spinning cloth from camels' hair or goats' hair.

The Arabs and Israelites usually made their tents of goats' hair. Because most of the goats were black or dark brown, the tents were this color as well. When spun together, this goats'-hair made a coarse, heavy fabric. In the winter, it protected a family from the cold winds, and in the summer the sides were rolled up to let in the breeze. When dry, the goats'-hair cloth was porous and could "breathe," keeping the tent from getting too stuffy. But after the first rain, the hairs shrunk together making the tent waterproof.

Tents were usually oblong in shape. The size depended on the number of people in a family or a person's wealth. Most tents had between one and nine poles. The poles were set in the ground and the tent material was spread over the poles. Leather loops were sewn to the edge of the cloth, and long cords were tied to them. To allow more room inside the tent, these cords were stretched tight and fastened to the ground by iron or wooden pins or pegs. A woman named Jael killed Sisera, an enemy general, with one of these pegs (Jud. 4:21).

Tents as Homes—How People Lived in Them

When many bedouins lived together, they pitched their tents in a circle. Cattle, sheep, and goats were allowed into the circle at night for protection. The sheik or ruler of the tribe placed his tent in the middle of the circle. Outside the door was his spear, stuck in the ground as a symbol of his authority.

Tents were often large and heavy, and pitching one usually took more than a single person. Some tents had two or three sections. Just inside the entrance were the men's living quarters. Behind a curtain of goats' hair was the women's section, and behind that was an area for the servants or cattle.

Life was simple in a bedouin tent. Rugs made of skins or goats' hair covered the dirty ground. Sacks of grain supported the tent poles. In the center of the tent floor a hole was dug for cooking. On hot days the cooking was done outside. Each tent had a hand mill for grinding grain to make bread, and a leather bucket for drawing water from the well.

Top: bedouin tents today are much like those in Abraham's time. Many of these tents are made from the hair of goats (center picture). The butter churn in the bottom picture is from a time much earlier than Abraham, but may have been similar to one which Abraham used to churn the butter for his guests.

The Destruction of Sodom

GENESIS 19

Synopsis

When the herdsmen of Abraham and Lot quarreled, Lot moved away to Sodom, a wicked city. Not long after that some kings from the north attacked Sodom and its neighbors and carried Lot away among the captives. Abraham rescued Lot, who then returned to live in Sodom. One day the Lord appeared to Abraham as angels in men's bodies, warning him that Sodom would be destroyed. Lot would be spared for Abraham's sake.

The City of Sodom

After God totally destroyed Sodom, the city was never again mentioned in the Bible as an active city. It was probably never rebuilt, but this is not known for sure. The exact location of the ruins of the city remains a mystery. Most believe that the ancient ruins of Sodom now lie under the southern part of the Dead Sea. In Lot's time, the sea was probably much smaller, because there is no water outlet and until recently it took in more water than could evaporate.

The Dead Sea Area

There is no dry land anywhere in the world lower than the Dead Sea area. Where the Jordan River enters the Dead Sea, the elevation is 1285 feet *below* sea level.

There is no doubt as to how the Dead Sea got its name. Because of the high salt and mineral content of the water, there is no life in the Dead Sea. It is simply a lifeless body of water, too bitter to drink, often nauseating to smell, and too full of salt, bromide, and sulfur to support any fish or other water life.

The Dead Sea is almost 50 miles in length stretching from north to south. Traveling from east to west the widest point is about 11 miles. The sea appears greenish in color because of the mineral salts. There are freshwater springs on the sea floor, but not enough to affect the balance of the water. There is no water outlet, but most think that if there were, the Dead Sea would be a freshwater sea full of life. The Dead Sea loses water only by evaporation.

The surrounding land is parched and barren. In an entire year, two to four inches of rain falls. But the sea does have some benefits. With today's modern technology, large amounts of minerals are extracted from the sea and its surrounding area and used for a variety of chemicals, especially fertilizers.

The Deception of Lot

After Lot escaped from the burning city of Sodom, he fled to the city of Zoar. But Lot was afraid to live in Zoar, so he left the city and went to live in the mountains, taking his two daughters with him. Soon Lot's daughters grew tired of their lonely life. They wanted children but the only man for miles around was their father. So one night they got him drunk and had children by him. The two children, Moab and Ben-ammi, became the ancestors of the Moabites and the Ammonites, two fierce enemies of Israel who brought much trouble and destruction to the nation.

The photo at the far right shows a formation near ancient Sodom much like the form of a woman. Tourist guides often point to such a formation as "Lot's wife." The part of the Dead Sea seen in the photo below is coated with minerals.

When the angels appeared at Abraham's tent, he bowed toward the ground to greet them. The three drawings show several forms of such bowing: at the top are three forms.

37

The Patriarchs
The Family of Abraham, Isaac, and Jacob

People of Abraham's time thought it was not only right, but good to marry within the family. This chart shows the complicated relationships which developed in Abraham's family through such marriages.

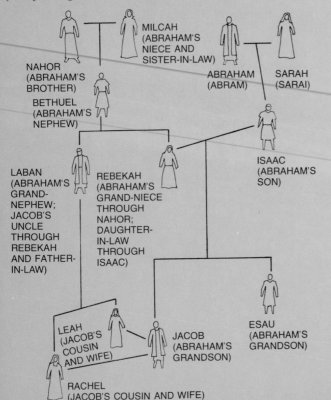

MILCAH (ABRAHAM'S NIECE AND SISTER-IN-LAW)

NAHOR (ABRAHAM'S BROTHER)

ABRAHAM (ABRAM)

SARAH (SARAI)

BETHUEL (ABRAHAM'S NEPHEW)

ISAAC (ABRAHAM'S SON)

LABAN (ABRAHAM'S GRAND-NEPHEW; JACOB'S UNCLE THROUGH REBEKAH AND FATHER-IN-LAW)

REBEKAH (ABRAHAM'S GRAND-NIECE THROUGH NAHOR; DAUGHTER-IN-LAW THROUGH ISAAC)

LEAH (JACOB'S COUSIN AND WIFE)

JACOB (ABRAHAM'S GRANDSON)

ESAU (ABRAHAM'S GRANDSON)

RACHEL (JACOB'S COUSIN AND WIFE)

Isaac Is Born

GENESIS 21:1-7

Synopsis

After Abraham and Lot parted, Lot was captured by some northern kings, but Abraham rescued him. Lot returned to his home in the wicked city of Sodom. One day the Lord told Abraham that Sodom would be destroyed, but Lot would be spared for Abraham's sake. Sodom was destroyed and Lot was spared. As time passed, God gave Abraham and Sarah a son, as He had promised, and they named him Isaac.

Beersheba

Abraham lived for a time by the oaks of Mamre, near Hebron. But after a while he moved to Beersheba. In all the land of Israel, Beersheba was the farthest city to the south. In fact, there was a saying in Israel "from Dan to Beersheba," which meant from the most northern city to the most southern city.

At Beersheba, Abraham dug a well, and made a covenant of peace with Abimelech (Gen. 21:32). According to the Bible, Abraham gave Beersheba its name which means "well of the covenant."

Some years later, Isaac had many of his wells stolen by the Philistines. Finally, the

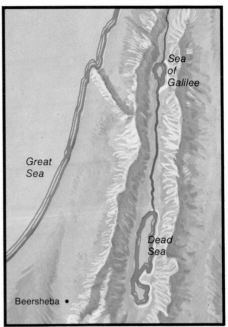

Sea
of
Galilee

Great
Sea

Dead
Sea

Beersheba •

Philistines stopped bothering him when he dug a well at Beersheba (Gen. 26:32-33).

Isaac was living at Beersheba when Jacob deceived him to get the family blessing. The two photos above show the ruins of ancient Beersheba. The map identifies its location.

The Meaning of Names

In Bible times, and especially in Old Testament times, a child's name was chosen with great care. Israelites deeply believed that names molded a child's personality and were responsible for events in their lives. A name was more than just a word to identify a person. Knowing someone's name gave a clue about his behavior and character.

Abraham's name means "father of a great number." God had promised Abraham that he would be the father of many people, more than the sand on the seashore.

Sarah's name means "princess." Isaac means "laughter," because Sarah was so full of happiness over the birth of her child at such an old age. Jacob's name means "deceiver," which turned out to be prophetic when he tricked Isaac and got the family blessing.

Isaac

Isaac was the only son of Abraham and Sarah. It was through him that God chose to fulfill His covenant with Abraham. Through Isaac came the nation of Israel, King David, and most important of all, the birth of Jesus Christ.

When Isaac was born, Abraham was already 100 years old. Isaac's birth was a miracle promised by God. But Isaac was not the oldest son of Abraham. His half-brother was Ishmael, the son of Abraham and Hagar. Per Hebrew custom, Ishmael would get the family birthright. But God wanted Isaac to be Abraham's chief heir. So Isaac received his father's blessing and inherited most of his belongings.

Isaac was an excellent example of obedience. When it appeared that he would be sacrificed on Mount Moriah, he faithfully followed his father's instructions, even when Abraham tied him on the altar.

Through the years, Isaac continued to trust his father and rely on God's guidance. When Abraham's servant Eliezer chose a wife for Isaac, he gladly married her without even seeing her face before the marriage.

But Isaac was not perfect. Like his father he lied to Abimelech, telling him that Rebekah was his sister instead of his wife. His favoritism toward Esau over Jacob caused strife in his family and fostered Jacob's deceit. But just before his death, he probably found out that his two sons had again become friends.

Hagar and Ishmael Are Sent Away

GENESIS 21:8-21

Synopsis

After Abraham settled in the land of Canaan, he and Lot separated, for their herdsmen quarreled over the pasturelands. Lot moved to Sodom, a wicked city which was soon captured by a coalition of kings from the north. But Abraham rescued Lot, who returned to Sodom. The Lord destroyed Sodom and nearby Gomorrah, sparing Lot for Abraham's sake. After that, Abraham and Sarah had a long-awaited son, and named him Isaac. But this son, and Abraham's earlier son, Ishmael, caused so much jealousy between the mothers that Abraham had to send his oldest son Ishmael away with his mother Hagar.

Ishmael

Ishmael was the son of Abraham and Hagar, Sarah's Egyptian slave. Ishmael was born because Sarah was unable to have children. It was an embarrassment for a married couple in Bible times not to have children, so Sarah gave her servant Hagar to Abraham to bear children for her.

40

Hagar gave birth to Ishmael when Abraham was 86 years old. For a long time Abraham thought that Ishmael was the son through whom God would fulfill His covenant. But when Sarah finally had her own son Isaac, the son promised by God, she saw Ishmael as a threat to Isaac, who was now the son to receive the family birthright. Sarah's jealousy forced Hagar and Ishmael to be sent from Abraham's camp and wander in the wilderness of Beersheba. But God did not neglect them. Hagar found Ishmael a wife and he became the ancestor of the Arab nations of today. Ironically, Isaac's son Esau married Ishmael's daughter.

Giving Servant Girls as Substitute Wives

In Bible times, a married woman was shamed and her husband embarrassed if they had no children. Children were a sign of prosperity and good fortune. They were also responsible for helping parents in their work and caring for them in old age. Boys were to master their father's work and carry on the family line. Girls were to help their mother around the home, and someday provide their husbands with many children.

If a wife could not provide children for her husband, she was obligated to give to the husband her servant or slave to bear children for her. According to custom, the slave's children were legally the children of the wife, and after birth, were taken into the home of the master. Often the children never knew who their real mother was.

The Wilderness of Beersheba

Expelled from the camp of Abraham, Hagar and Ishmael wandered into the wilderness of Beersheba. The city of Beersheba lies at the most southern part of the land of Israel, just on the outskirts of a vast desert stretching to the south of the city. This was probably the area referred to in Genesis as the "Wilderness of Beersheba."

The bedouin woman at the upper left reminds us of the life-style of Sarah and Hagar. Upper right: flocks of goats come for water in the wilderness area south of Beersheba, probably the Wilderness of Beersheba mentioned here. In the center are several types of "bottles" made of animal skins sewed around the edges. Hagar probably carried the water for herself and Ishmael in one of these types of animal skins.

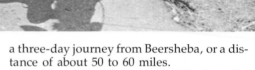

The man on the donkey at the right reminds us of Abraham. The donkey was probably Abraham's chief means of transportation, though he did have camels as well. A ram such as the one below, of the fat-tailed variety, took the place of Isaac on the altar.

Abraham Offers Isaac

GENESIS 22

Synopsis
Abraham was 100 years old when his long-promised son Isaac was born. Throughout the years he had longed for and waited for this son. Now God asked him to offer Isaac on an altar as a burnt offering.

When
Isaac and Abraham traveled to the "land of Moriah" around 2050 B.C. The historian Josephus thinks that Isaac was about 25 years old. In this story, the Hebrew text seems to imply that Isaac might have been just a bit younger, but it is impossible to know his exact age.

Mount Moriah
This mountain was one of the focal points throughout Bible history. It is located just to the north of the city of Jerusalem as it was in David's time. For Abraham and Isaac it was a three-day journey from Beersheba, or a distance of about 50 to 60 miles.

On Mount Moriah, God gave Abraham the supreme test of faithfulness, asking him to sacrifice his own son. Because of Abraham's obedience, God started a new nation with Isaac (Gen. 22:1-19).

On this same mountain was Araunah's threshing floor. It was here that God stopped a violent plague from killing the people of Israel because of David's disobedience. David bought the threshing floor and built an altar to God (2 Sam. 24:1-25).

God's holy temple was built on this mountain, first by King Solomon, then by Zerubbabel after it had been destroyed, and finally by Herod the Great. For centuries it was the center of worship for all Jews (1 Kings 5—8; Hag. 1:12—2:9; John 2:20).

The Last Supper took place a short distance down the west side of Mount Moriah. There Jesus and His disciples ate for the last time before His crucifixion (Matt. 26:17-29). Just a few weeks later, the disciples gathered in an upper room, probably this same one, and received the Holy Spirit's power (Acts 2:1-4).

The golden-domed Dome of the Rock stands today over the place where Abraham almost sacrificed Isaac. Solomon's temple once stood there, then later Herod's temple, in the time of Jesus. The map shows the route Abraham probably took from Beer-sheba to Mount Moriah, now in Jerusalem.

Other Important Mountains

There were other mountains throughout Bible lands that played an important role in Israel's history. On Mount Ararat, Noah's ark came to rest (Gen. 8:4). Moses received the Ten Commandments on Mount Sinai (Ex. 24:12). Jesus was transfigured on Mount Tabor or Mount Hermon (Luke 9:28-36). On the Mount of Olives, Jesus was arrested in the Garden of Gethsemane (Matt. 26:30-56). Later, on the same mountain, He ascended into heaven (Luke 24:50-51).

Altars

An altar was much more than a place where an Israelite offered a sacrifice to God. Stepping up to the altar symbolized communion with God and was an act of remembering His covenant. In simple terms, the word "altar" means "to approach." For the Israelites, the altar was a means of approaching God, asking forgiveness for sins, and worshiping Him.

An altar was made of stones, earth, or even metal. Certain Israelite altars could only be made from the stones found in a field. Cutting or shaping the stones for such altars with any type of tool was forbidden, and made the altars unholy and its sacrifices unacceptable to God.

Most altars did not have steps. This was to prevent the priest's body from being accidentally exposed when he walked over to the altar and presented an offering before the people of Israel.

There was a unique design to many Israelite altars. On each corner of the altar at the top, was a horn like a bull's horn. Why these horns were placed on the altar remains a mystery, but most think the idea was to symbolize God's strength and power.

Burnt Offerings

The word "offering" today has a much different meaning than it had in Old Testament times. Instead of putting money into a collection plate, the people of the Old Testament placed an animal or food on an altar and burned it before the Lord. Burnt offerings were carried out to ask forgiveness for sins, or to give thanks or praise to God.

43

Abraham Buries Sarah

GENESIS 23

Synopsis

Abraham had migrated from Ur to Haran, then to Canaan. A famine in Canaan forced him and Sarah to live in Egypt for a while. Back in Canaan, he settled down to a life of raising animals. He and his nephew Lot separated when their herdsmen quarreled, with Lot moving to the wicked city, Sodom. But Lot was captured by a raiding party of northern kings and Abraham risked his life to rescue him. Lot returned to Sodom, but then the Lord destroyed the city, sparing Lot for Abraham's sake. When Abraham was 100, he and Sarah had a long-awaited son and named his Isaac. But a few years later, the Lord tested Abraham's faith by asking him to sacrifice this son as a burnt offering on Mount Moriah. The years passed. When Sarah was 127, she died and Abraham buried her in a cave at Hebron.

The Cave of Machpelah

When his wife Sarah died, Abraham needed a place to bury her. He bought the field of Machpelah from Ephron the Hittite. At the end of the field was a cave called the cave of Machpelah. In this cave, Abraham

The scales with which Abraham's silver was weighed were balances, much like those above, taken from an ancient Egyptian painting. The clay tablet above gives the details of a mortgage on a field. It is from a period somewhat later than Abraham, about 1500 B.C. The cave at the right, not far from Hebron, is probably similar to the cave of Machpelah in Abraham's time. The mosque (far right) at Hebron covers the cave of Machpelah today.

buried Sarah. Some years later, Abraham was also buried in this cave next to his wife. Other members of Abraham's family who were buried in the cave of Machpelah were Isaac and Rebekah, and Jacob and Leah.

Abraham had returned from Beersheba to Hebron, by the oaks of Mamre, when Sarah died. Since Abraham had lived in the area before, he must have had a good knowledge of the land and known about the cave of Machpelah, which was close to, or "opposite" his home at Mamre.

Abraham Buys the Property

According to Hittite law codes and implied in Genesis, there were a large number of Hittites living in the area of Hebron when Abraham lived there. Abraham paid a high price for the field of Machpelah, and this was possibly an attempt by the Hittites to try to prevent a foreigner from acquiring too much property and earning the right to citizenship. But Abraham was aware of God's promise to give the land of Canaan to his descendants, so he was glad to pay the full price for the land. Ephron offered to give the property to Abraham, but it is likely that this was not a real offer, but rather a custom to begin the bargaining.

The City Gate

Almost all business agreements took place by the city gate. This was probably the most central place to meet, and the easiest place to find witnesses, who were necessary for the completion of any business deal.

Death

Death brought many hardships to a family in Abraham's time. There were no hospitals to take care of the sick, and no undertakers to prepare the body for burial. All of this had to be done by friends and family. When someone died, a person let out a death wail, which informed the entire neighborhood of the death. Friends and relatives came to help and console the survivors, and everyone wailed loudly for days.

A Bride for Isaac

GENESIS 24

Synopsis

For many years the Lord had promised Abraham that he and Sarah would have a son. But they had lost hope, for this son was not born until Abraham was 100 years old. As the child grew, the Lord tested Abraham's faith one day by telling him to offer this only son of his beloved Sarah as a burnt offering. When Abraham obeyed, the Lord stopped him and provided a ram for the offering instead. The years passed and Sarah died at the age of 127 and was buried at Hebron. Abraham then focused his attention on finding the right bride for his son.

Eliezer—Abraham's Servant

Eliezer was the most faithful and trusted servant of Abraham. As a result, he was placed in charge of all Abraham's household. This made him responsible for all of Abraham's belongings, as well as all the activities carried on by the other servants.

It is almost certain that Eliezer would have been the servant Abraham chose to travel to Haran and find a wife for Isaac. He was probably chosen for his faith in God, evident when he prayed to God at the well in Haran.

Isaac's Wife Is Chosen for Him

In Abraham's day, most young men and women were not allowed to "court" or go on "dates." They could not even go to each other's house for dinner! Usually, a man did not see his bride until their wedding day.

Sometimes a man could suggest his personal preferences, but usually young men and women were not allowed to choose their mates. The parents, or a trusted servant had that job. They decided when and where to look for a bride who would be suitable for the son. When she was found, gifts were sent to the woman and her parents. If the father of the woman accepted them and approved of the marriage, the wedding day was then determined.

There were probably no wedding ceremonies in Abraham's day, but great wedding feasts that lasted for days.

Wells

Every city and village had a well. The well was obviously a popular place, for in many

46

Far left: nose rings, commonly worn by bedouin girls. Eliezer gave Rebekah rings (Gen. 24:22), which may have been nose rings or earrings. He also gave her bracelets (left). Eliezer made his way to Haran by camel (the picture at the upper left reminds us of his travels). Above: stone water troughs at Haran today. The map below shows the possible route he took from Beersheba to Haran. Right: Rebekah waters Eliezer's camels.

cities it was the only source of water. They were usually dug just outside a small village in order to keep the dust and crowds of people away from homes and business activities. Larger cities needed wells inside the city as well.

Often a city or village was built next to a well that had already been dug. The well might have been built years before for watering flocks, or along a caravan route.

The well was a busy place early in the morning and just before sunset. Women came to draw cool water for household chores, cooking, and washing. Shepherds also arrived to water their flocks.

Drawing Water from a Well
In a deep well, a woman dropped a pitcher tied to a rope into the water and pulled it up when it was full. A shallow well often had steps going down to the water, and the pitcher was dipped into the well by hand.

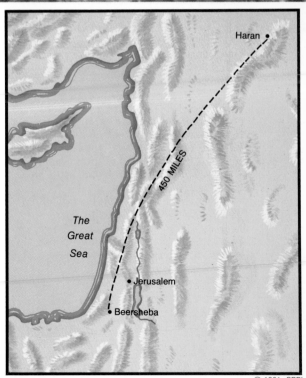

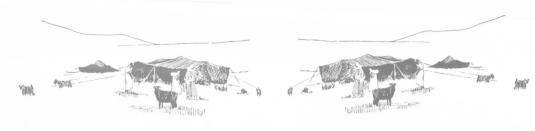

Jacob and Esau Are Born

GENESIS 25:19-28

Synopsis

After Sarah died, Abraham arranged for their son Isaac to be married. He deeded everything he owned, except for some gifts which he gave to his other children, to Isaac before he died. Isaac was 40 when he married, but he and Rebekah had no children until he was 60. Then twin sons were born—Jacob and Esau.

Marriage at an Older Age

In today's world, the average couple gets married in their twenties, hoping to spend the rest of their lives together. But in early Old Testament times, people lived much longer, and many marriages came at a much older age.

Isaac, for example, did not marry until he was 40 years old, and his two sons, Jacob and Esau, were not born until he was 60. Esau and Jacob were twins. Esau married at 40, but Jacob married years later. It would seem that Jacob was about 80 years old when he first married. But Isaac lived to be 180, and Jacob died at 147. This still gave them plenty of time after their marriages to spend with their families.

Life of Nomads

Nomads were people on the move. They lived in tents and stayed in an area only as long as there was enough water and grass for their flocks. Nomads usually were shepherds, or tended cattle. Wherever they went, they carried their belongings as they wandered through vast, uninhabited areas of land.

48

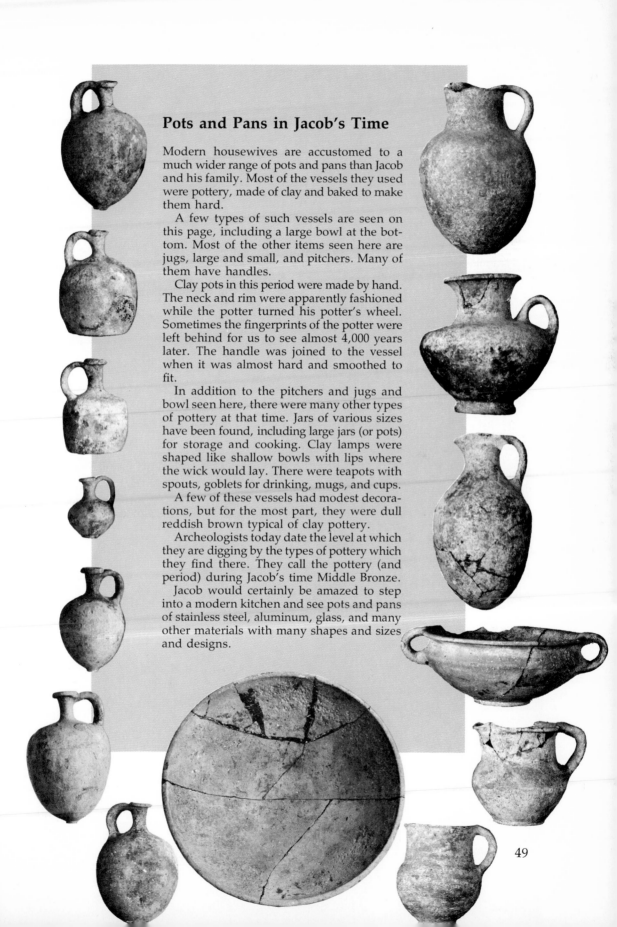

Pots and Pans in Jacob's Time

Modern housewives are accustomed to a much wider range of pots and pans than Jacob and his family. Most of the vessels they used were pottery, made of clay and baked to make them hard.

A few types of such vessels are seen on this page, including a large bowl at the bottom. Most of the other items seen here are jugs, large and small, and pitchers. Many of them have handles.

Clay pots in this period were made by hand. The neck and rim were apparently fashioned while the potter turned his potter's wheel. Sometimes the fingerprints of the potter were left behind for us to see almost 4,000 years later. The handle was joined to the vessel when it was almost hard and smoothed to fit.

In addition to the pitchers and jugs and bowl seen here, there were many other types of pottery at that time. Jars of various sizes have been found, including large jars (or pots) for storage and cooking. Clay lamps were shaped like shallow bowls with lips where the wick would lay. There were teapots with spouts, goblets for drinking, mugs, and cups.

A few of these vessels had modest decorations, but for the most part, they were dull reddish brown typical of clay pottery.

Archeologists today date the level at which they are digging by the types of pottery which they find there. They call the pottery (and period) during Jacob's time Middle Bronze.

Jacob would certainly be amazed to step into a modern kitchen and see pots and pans of stainless steel, aluminum, glass, and many other materials with many shapes and sizes and designs.

49

Esau Sells His Birthright

GENESIS 25:29-34

Synopsis
Before Abraham died, he arranged for his son
Isaac to marry Rebekah. During the last few
years of his life, Abraham also arranged for
Isaac to inherit all his possessions, except for
the gifts which he gave his other children.
After Abraham's death, Isaac and Rebekah
waited for 20 years to have children, then at
last had twin sons, whom they named Jacob
and Esau. One day, when these sons had
grown, Jacob bought Esau's birthright from
him for a bowl of lentil soup.

Favorite Sons
Many parents have a favorite son or daughter.
Often they try hard not to show their favoritism, but it is very difficult. Isaac and Rebekah
were this way. As their sons, Jacob and Esau
grew, Isaac began to prefer Esau over Jacob.
The reason for this might be that both Isaac
and Esau loved the out-of-doors. Esau was
also a hunter and enjoyed bringing venison
home to his father. The Bible says that both
Isaac and Esau enjoyed the taste of game.

Rebekah preferred Jacob. This was evident
when she cunningly helped Jacob steal the
family blessing from Esau. According to the
Bible, Jacob was a man who "lived in tents."
Because of this, he probably spent a lot of
time around the family camp, and therefore
would have spent a lot of time with his
mother. Naturally, the two would have developed a strong bond of affection.

The Birthright

In a Hebrew family, the firstborn son was very fortunate. He was treated with great respect and honor, and given the privilege of the family birthright.

The birthright was the father's special blessing to his oldest son. This gave the son leadership over his brothers, but it also gave him the responsibility of taking care of the family after his father's death. He was to manage the family property, and support his widowed mother and unmarried sisters.

When the father died, the oldest son inherited twice as much as his brothers. Israelite custom did not allow the daughters of the dead father to inherit anything, because it was the duty of the son with the birthright to take care of his sisters.

A birthright could be sold, or given away. If the father thought the oldest son did not deserve the birthright, he could give it to a younger son, or to someone else. In order to pass the birthright on, the father gave a special blessing to whomever was receiving it. Once this blessing was given, the birthright could not be taken back. This was one reason why the father waited to hand over the family birthright until soon before he was expected to die.

Lentil Soup

Jacob was making a very common soup or stew when Esau came in from the fields. This soup was made from lentils, a type of vegetable that was probably so plentiful that it was almost worthless.

In Abraham's day, it is likely that lentils were grown as crops. On the plant grow small, flat pods. Inside these pods are the lentils, which are about the size of a pea. When boiled, they turn the soup into a chocolate-red color. When Esau was famished, he asked Jacob for a bite of that "red stuff" (Gen. 25:30).

Esau

The oldest son of Isaac and Rebekah, Esau was a "hairy man" who enjoyed hunting outdoors, and bringing meat, or venison, home to his father. He was Isaac's favorite son.

But Esau did not always please his family. He sold his precious birthright to Jacob, his younger brother, for a bowl of soup. Later, Esau wanted to kill Jacob when he deceived Isaac and received the birthright, but Jacob escaped. Twenty years later however, the two brothers met again as friends.

Esau married two women who were foreigners to the people of Abraham. This showed his lack of concern for God's covenant. Esau became the ancestor of the Edomites, another enemy nation that hated the Israelites.

Lentils grow in pods, much like tiny peas (upper center). People in ancient Egypt made lentil soup, just as Jacob did. They recorded this process on the walls of their tombs. Drawings from these tomb paintings may be seen below the lentil plant. At the lower left is Beersheba today, the place where Jacob bought Esau's birthright for a bowl of lentil soup. A large pot, similar in appearance to the one in the drawing, and approximately from the time of Jacob is at the bottom center. Other cooking scenes may be seen below, drawn from tomb paintings of Old Testament times.

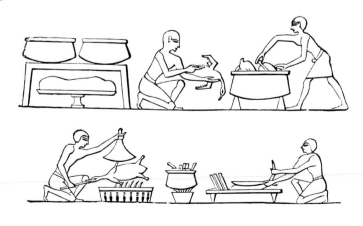

Isaac Refuses to Fight for Wells

GENESIS 26:17-33

Synopsis

After Isaac's mother Sarah died, his father Abraham arranged for his chief servant to find a bride for Isaac. Eliezer, the servant, went to Abraham's relatives in Haran, and returned with Rebekah. During the next 20 years, Isaac and Rebekah yearned for a child, but had none, until the birth of twins, Jacob and Esau. After these sons grew into manhood, Isaac moved to Gerar, in Philistine country, where his father Abraham had once lived and had dug some wells. The Philistines had filled the wells after Abraham's death, so Isaac tried to dig the dirt from them again.

The Fight over the Wells

When someone dug a well in an uninhabited area, an unwritten custom gave them the right to own a large section of land around that well. It was an act of war when enemies came and filled up the well with dirt.

Water was often hard to find, and herdsmen were always fighting over it. Digging a well was very hard work and took a lot of time. When enemies filled a well with dirt, days or weeks of time were wasted, and flocks suffered from lack of water.

But Isaac did not want to go to war, even though he was stronger than the Philistines (Gen. 26:16). He preferred peace instead. For him, it was better to dig another well than to cause strife and bloodshed.

Philistines

The Philistines were a constant threat to the Israelites until the time of David. These people first settled in the southwestern corner of Canaan before Abraham's time. Where they came from is not certain, but most think from the islands of the Aegean Sea or from the island of Crete. At that time, they were called the "Sea People."

In Palestine (Israel), the Philistines rose to their greatest power in the days of King Saul and King David. Their grip on the land finally ended when David crushed them in battle, leaving them weak and subdued.

The Philistines had five key cities, each ruled by a "lord." These five "lords" governed the entire Philistine nation, reaching important decisions by majority vote. This organized government gave the Philistines a

Without machines to dig wells, men were forced to work by hand, involving many hours (upper left). Isaac's trouble with wells began at Gerar (above). He found peace at last when he dug a well at Beersheba. The traditional "Abraham's Well" (below) stands in Beersheba today.

tremendous advantage over the Israelites before they had a king and were simply a large group of disorganized tribes.

Gerar

Gerar is near the Mediterranean Sea, below the southern border of Canaan. The exact spot is unknown, but the city was in the general area of the Philistine city of Gaza.

Abraham once lived at Gerar before Isaac. Both of them lied to Abimelech, claiming that their wives were their sisters. When Isaac was asked to leave Gerar, he settled in the nearby valley. Here he had trouble with the herdsmen in the area filling his wells with dirt.

Herdsmen

Men who tended flocks of cattle, sheep, or goats were called herdsmen. They were probably different from shepherds only because they did not watch their own sheep, but instead were hired by other men who had too many flocks to watch alone. But these herdsmen still had the same responsibilities as a shepherd—finding food and water for flocks, and protecting them from wild animals and thieves. When watching the flocks for several owners, herdsmen were especially good at knowing which sheep belonged to each owner's flock.

Jacob Deceives Isaac

GENESIS 27:1-40

Synopsis
Isaac was born when Abraham was 100 and Sarah was 91. He had been promised to them for many years, and God kept His promise in their old age. Isaac did not marry until he was 40, and had no children until he was 60, when he and Rebekah had twin sons, Jacob and Esau. Then, in later years, Isaac moved with his family to Gerar, in Philistine country, where his father Abraham had once lived. Later, he moved to Beersheba. While living there, Jacob deceived his father, Isaac, and took from him a blessing which Isaac had intended to give to Jacob's brother Esau.

Preparing the Meal before the Blessing
Before Isaac would bless Esau and pass on the family birthright, he wanted Esau to prepare for him a "savory" meal. This meal was sometimes a custom in the ancient Middle East before a covenant or a birthright would be passed on. It turned out to be Esau's undoing, for while he was out hunting for meat, Jacob had time to deceive Isaac and steal the family birthright for himself.

A "savory" meal probably meant a meal that was cooked with

Jacob cooked goat meat for Isaac in preparation for the blessing. The photo above shows a goat herd near Beersheba today, the place where Isaac and his family lived. The jar above is from the time of Jacob and may have been similar to the one which Jacob and Rebekah used to cook the meat for Isaac.

seasonings. Jacob brought Isaac a goat, along with other seasoned food, and Esau brought venison. This meat was cooked by dropping it in a pot of boiling water, or by roasting it over a fire. Meat that was boiled in water left a broth that was eaten with the meal, or saved for another meal.

A Widow and the Birthright

After the birthright had been passed on, and the man of the house had died, the wife was left with nothing. But this widow was not forgotten. Her welfare was actually a part of the birthright. Whoever inherited the birthright also inherited the responsibility of caring for the widow and her unmarried daughters. This was true regardless of who received the family birthright.

This statuette from Egypt, from the time of Abraham, shows a man butchering an animal. Jacob had to butcher a goat in much the same way before cooking it for Isaac.

Rebekah

Rebekah was chosen by Abraham's servant to be the wife of Isaac. Her father, Bethuel, was a nephew of Abraham. For 20 years she had no children, but finally gave birth to two sons, Esau and Jacob. Esau was the ancestor of the Edomites, and Jacob was the ancestor of the Israelites. It was Rebekah's idea to deceive Isaac so that Jacob would receive the family birthright instead of Esau. Because of Esau's anger, she asked Isaac to send Jacob to Haran, to live with her brother Laban.

Jacob's Ladder

GENESIS 27:41—28:22

Synopsis

When he was younger, Jacob had "bought" his older twin brother's birthright for a bowl of lentil soup. Then when it came time for his father to give the "blessing," which confirmed which son would have the birthright, Jacob pretended to be Esau, whom his father wanted to bless. Jacob received the blessing, but the family was divided. Isaac and Esau were divided from Rebekah and Jacob. To make matters worse, Esau threatened to kill his twin brother. So Rebekah persuaded old Isaac to send Jacob to Haran to find a bride.

How Far?

When Jacob left for Haran, he had a long trip ahead of him. From his home in Beersheba to Bethel, where he dreamed of the ladder to heaven, was a distance of about 60 miles. From Bethel, there was still another 400 miles or so to Haran. The total distance of his journey then, was over 450 miles. Today that might only take an hour. But then it took many days or weeks. He either walked, or rode a camel. Both were slow ways to travel such a great distance.

Bethel

Bethel is about 60 miles north of Beersheba, and approximately 10 miles north of Jerusalem. It was formerly called Luz, and today it has the name of Beitin, or Beit El.

Long before Jacob had his dream at Bethel, Abraham made a sacrifice there (Gen. 12:8; 13:3). In the days of the Judges, the ark of the covenant was kept at Bethel for a time (Jud. 20:26-28). Samuel stopped at Bethel to settle disputes and encourage people to follow God (1 Sam. 7:16).

Bethel became a center of foreign religion and idol worship. Hosea warned Bethel of its idol worship and called it Beth-aven, which means, "the House of Wickedness." King Josiah destroyed most of the idols in Bethel and led the people to follow God.

Haran

Though the city of Haran was not in the land of Palestine, it played an important role in the history of Israel. The city is located in the arc of rich land, the Fertile Crescent, about 450 miles northeast of Beersheba, Jacob's home before traveling to Haran.

Abraham and Sarah lived in Haran before coming to the land of Canaan (Gen. 11:31). Abraham's father, Terah, died there (Gen. 11:32).

When Abraham decided to move to Canaan, he must have left many relatives behind. In finding a wife for his son Isaac, Abraham sent his servant back to the area of Haran to choose a wife among his relatives (Gen. 24:4). The servant found Rebekah, the daughter of Abraham's nephew, Bethuel.

Years later, Isaac sent his son Jacob to Haran to find a wife. He stayed with Rebekah's brother, Laban (Gen. 28:2). There he fell in love with Laban's daughter, Rachel.

The Roads to Haran

In Old Testament times, the best route to a place was not always the straightest. Roads avoided mountains and deserts, and followed rivers or streams whenever possible. This added many miles. Between cities, travel was lonely and dangerous.

The three photos above show Bethel, called Beit El or Beitin today, as it now appears. The bottom picture shows ruins from Crusader times, perhaps about 700 years ago. Above it is a view of the village which stands over the ruins of Bethel today. At the upper right is another view of the village from the south, showing the rocky landscape. The map shows the possible route Jacob followed from Beersheba through Bethel to Haran.

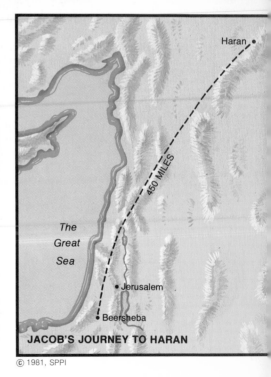

JACOB'S JOURNEY TO HARAN

Haran

450 MILES

The
Great
Sea

Jerusalem

Beersheba

© 1981, SPPI

57

Upper left: a shepherdess tends a flock near Jacob's home, Beersheba. Above: two wells near Haran today. These may be much like the wells of Jacob's time, except these two wells use a pulley to draw the water. Rachel probably drew water like the man at the right, pulling it up by hand.

Jacob Meets Rachel

GENESIS 29:1-14

Synopsis
Isaac had grown old and wanted to give his oldest son Esau the family "blessing," which would confirm that Esau would rule the family. But Jacob and his mother Rebekah deceived Isaac, so that he gave Jacob the blessing instead. Esau was furious and threatened to kill Jacob. Then Rebekah persuaded Isaac to send Jacob away to Haran, where he could find a bride and live away from home until Esau's anger cooled. Along the way, God spoke to Jacob and showed him a ladder that reached from earth to heaven. Confident that God was with him, Jacob continued on to Haran to search for his bride.

Well Coverings
A stone was often placed over the opening of a well. This stone sealed the well and helped to keep the water clean.

Most of the wells where shepherds watered their flocks were dug in wide open spaces where the flocks had plenty of room to graze. Strong winds blowing across this almost treeless countryside picked up large amounts of dirt and sand, sometimes enough to clog up an entire well. But when the well opening was covered by a stone, the water remained clean from dirt, sand, and other impurities. These simple stones saved the shepherds countless hours of time cleaning the water and digging their wells again.

Watering Flocks at the Well

In Bible times, it was usually the custom to wait until all the flocks were gathered at the well before the stone was removed and the flocks were watered. Because the land was often dry and parched, water was precious, and most shepherds wanted the well open for as little time as possible.

Some wells even had locks. This prevented thieves from stealing water that didn't belong to them. When the well was locked, the owner of the well usually sent someone to unlock it when the time came for the shepherds to water their flocks.

Women at the Well

Shepherds came to a well to water their flocks, and a weary traveler stopped to draw a cool drink of water. But women also visited the well, probably more often than men.

Men were not the only ones to tend sheep. A woman who tended sheep was called a shepherdess. Rachel was a shepherdess (Gen. 29:9). Every day she came to the well to water her father's flocks. Moses married a shepherdess. After escaping from Egypt, he stopped by a well in Midian, and fought off some evil men who were keeping several sisters from watering their father's flocks (Ex. 2:16-22).

A woman who took care of the home walked to the well twice each day, in the early morning and late afternoon. She drew water for cooking, cleaning, and washing clothes. In a family household, it was almost always the woman's job to make these trips to the well. A woman of Samaria came to draw water when she met Jesus, who had stopped by the well to rest. She was excited when Jesus told her how to find "living water" (John 4:5-42).

Men Embracing and Kissing

Today it may seem strange for men to greet each other with a hug and a kiss instead of a handshake. But in Bible times, this was the custom, and still is common today in many Eastern countries.

Jacob Marries Leah and Rachel

GENESIS 29:14-30

Synopsis
When Jacob deceived his father Isaac, causing him to give the family blessing and birthright to Jacob instead of his brother Esau, the family split. Jacob had to run away from home until Esau's anger cooled. When Jacob arrived at Haran, he met a beautiful girl, his cousin, and fell in love with her.

The Nurse
Some families had one or more nurses, or maids, to care for the daughters as they grew up. After the daughter was married, the father gave the nurse to her as a present, and she accompanied the daughter to her new home. There she continued to care for the married daughter. The two often became close friends after the husband brought them to a land of unfamiliar people.

When Rebekah left her family to marry Isaac, she took her nurse along (Gen. 24:59). At Jacob's marriage feast, his wife Leah was

The bedouin woman at the top reminds us of Rachel or Leah, who tended their father Laban's flocks. The bottom picture and the one in the center above show flocks at Haran today.

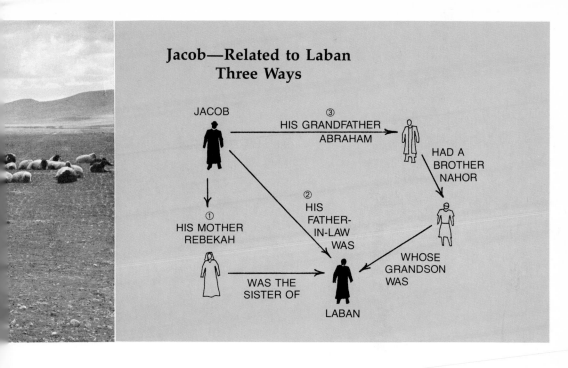

Jacob—Related to Laban Three Ways

JACOB

③ HIS GRANDFATHER ABRAHAM

HAD A BROTHER NAHOR

① HIS MOTHER REBEKAH

② HIS FATHER-IN-LAW WAS

WHOSE GRANDSON WAS

WAS THE SISTER OF

LABAN

given a nurse called Zilpah (Gen. 29:24), and his other wife Rachel received a nurse named Bilhah (Gen. 29:29).

Zilpah and Bilhah

Zilpah was Leah's nurse and Bilhah was Rachel's nurse. These two were a source of competition between Jacob's two wives.

Children were a great blessing and honor to a family. Families with none were ashamed. When Rachel could not have children she became jealous of Leah, and gave her nurse Bilhah to Jacob as a substitute wife in order to have children by her. Bilhah had two sons, Dan and Naphtali. Dan means "justice," implying that God had intervened for Rachel and given her a son. Naphtali means "wrestling," signifying that Rachel was competing with her sister.

Leah had stopped having children for a while. Leah gave Jacob her maid Zilpah as a substitute wife. Zilpah gave birth to Gad and Asher. Gad means "luck" and Asher means "happy."

The Marriage Feast

When a couple's wedding day arrived, there was often no "official" ceremony like there is today, but rather a great wedding feast that might last as long as two weeks.

The groom dressed in the best clothing he had, and was escorted by his friends to the bride's house. There he received his wife, and the entire wedding party made their way back to the groom's house for the feast.

Besides much food, there was dancing, singing, and entertainment. Heathen feasts also included games, contests, and much drinking.

The Dowry

Often the bride was not given away unless the groom could offer some compensation for her loss to the family. This might be money, a piece of land, or some animals. Instead of these, Jacob offered his Uncle Laban seven years of work.

The Veil

Parents usually decided who their sons or daughters would marry. Often the couple saw each other for the first time on their wedding day. Before the wedding feast, the woman wore a veil which covered her face. If a couple did happen to see each other before they were actually married, the woman could see the man's face from behind her veil, but the man could not see her face. Often he did not see her face until after they were married.

61

Jacob's 13 Children Came from 4 Mothers

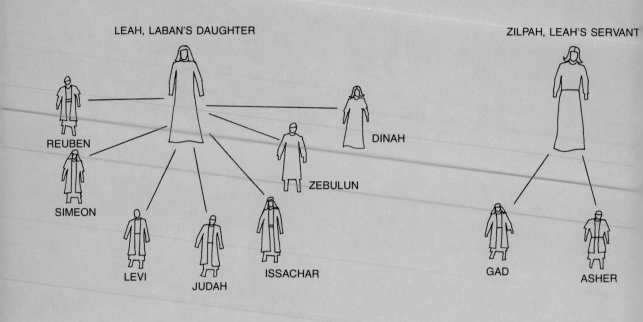

LEAH, LABAN'S DAUGHTER

ZILPAH, LEAH'S SERVANT

REUBEN

SIMEON

LEVI

JUDAH

ISSACHAR

ZEBULUN

DINAH

GAD

ASHER

Jacob's Family

GENESIS 29:31—30:24

Synopsis

When Isaac was old, his son Jacob deceived him and caused him to give the family blessing and birthright to Jacob instead of Esau, the older of the twin sons. Esau was furious and threatened to kill Jacob. But Isaac's wife, Rebekah, persuaded Isaac to send Jacob away to Haran to find a bride and to live until Esau's anger cooled. Along the way, Jacob saw in a dream a ladder to heaven. He made a covenant with God to follow Him and asked God to go with him. At Haran, Jacob met his cousin Rachel, fell in love with her, and worked seven years for her. But on his wedding night, Jacob was deceived and learned too late that he had married Rachel's older sister Leah. The following week, Jacob married Rachel and worked another seven years for her.

Leah

Leah was the older daughter of Laban and Jacob's cousin. The Bible says that Leah's eyes were "weak" (Gen. 29:17), which might be contrasting Leah's plainness to Rachel's beauty. Jacob was deceived by Laban into marrying Leah (Gen. 29:25). Jacob really wanted to marry Rachel, and Leah felt unloved when he married Rachel and

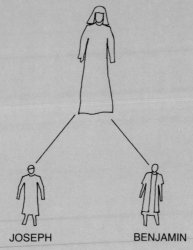

RACHEL, LABAN'S DAUGHTER

JOSEPH   BENJAMIN

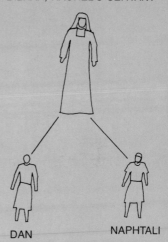

BILHAH, RACHEL'S SERVANT

DAN   NAPHTALI

preferred her to Leah. But God noticed Leah's loneliness and gave her six sons and one daughter. Through Judah, one of her sons, God chose to continue the nation of Israel.

Rachel
Rachel was the younger daughter of Laban and Jacob's cousin. She was very beautiful and when Jacob met her he fell in love. Both Rachel and her aunt and mother-in-law Rebekah were first mentioned in the Bible near a well (Gen. 24:11; 29:2). Jacob preferred Rachel to his other wife, and after he had been tricked into marrying Leah, he immediately married Rachel. For a long time Rachel had no children and became jealous of Leah who had many. But after many years, Rachel had two sons, Joseph and Benjamin. These two quickly became Jacob's favorite sons, which caused jealousy and anger among the others.

Strife in Jacob's Family
Jacob's life was not an easy one. His family was constantly torn apart by strife and jealousy. Rachel envied her sister Leah because of her seven children, but Leah was jealous of Rachel because of her beauty and Jacob's favoritism. Jacob also favored Rachel's two sons, Joseph and Benjamin. This made his other sons so blind with jealousy and rage that they sold their own brother, Joseph, into slavery.

The mandrake plant, above, was thought to have powers to increase love and produce children.

63

Top left: a shepherd tends his flocks near Haran today. Top right: camels and donkeys graze near Haran. The Astarte figurine above was one form of teraphim.

Jacob and Laban Part

GENESIS 30:25—31:55

Synopsis

After Jacob deceived his father Isaac, it was not safe for him to remain at home, for Esau wanted to kill him. Isaac sent Jacob away to his relatives at Haran to find a bride, and there Jacob married his cousins Rachel and Leah. There also he had 11 sons and a daughter, with a 12th son on the way. Jacob had worked 14 years for the right to marry Rachel, and another six years to build up his own flocks and herds. He wanted to get away from his deceitful father-in-law, Laban, for whom he had worked all these years.

Laban

Abraham and Laban were related to each other through Terah. Terah was Abraham's father and Laban's great-grandfather. Terah had three sons, Abraham, Nahor, and Haran. Nahor had a son named Bethuel, who had a daughter, Rebekah, and a son, Laban. Laban's sister Rebekah married Abraham's son Isaac. Rebekah and Isaac had a son called Jacob, who married Laban's daughters, Rachel and Leah.

Laban was a wealthy man in the region of Paddan Aram. The city of Haran, where Laban lived, was located in this region. He must have been well known, for when Jacob arrived from Canaan, he simply asked for Laban by name and the herdsmen knew where he lived.

Jacob worked for Laban 14 years for the privilege of marrying his two daughters. Jacob did not want to marry Laban's oldest daughter Leah, but Laban tricked Jacob into marrying her at the wedding feast that was supposed to be for Rachel. Over the years, Jacob's wealth increased and Laban's friendship declined. Jacob decided to leave. He and his family set out without telling Laban, afraid that if Laban knew, he would not let them go. But Laban caught up with Jacob and accused him of stealing his household idols. Jacob accused Laban of dishonesty over his wages. Finally the two made a peace agreement and parted ways.

Teraphim—Household Gods

Teraphim were small idols which were kept in the house. Many Israelites owned teraphim. It is uncertain if they adopted the idea from the Canaanites, or the Arameans, the people who inhabited the land where Laban lived. Despite the pleas of the judges and the prophets, teraphim were common in Israelite homes until the reign of King Josiah.

These house idols were believed to protect a home and offer almost any information that was asked of them. Some think that Rachel stole her father's idols for fear that he would have consulted them and learned exactly by which route Jacob and his family had escaped toward Canaan.

Teraphim were also passed on through the family birthright. Rachel could have stolen her father's idols in an effort to make Jacob the chief heir to Laban's land and possessions.

It is not known if the Israelites really worshiped the teraphim. Many Israelites who had teraphim in their homes still worshiped God. In Canaan, these household idols were a symbol of family leadership and respect. Owning a few might have made it easier for the Israelites to get along with their foreign neighbors, the Canaanites.

In the home of a wealthy man, teraphim were usually made of gold or silver. People who were not rich made teraphim of cast iron or had them molded from clay. The poor had theirs carved from wood.

Jacob in Paddan Aram

Jacob worked for Laban as a herdsman for 20 years; 14 years working without pay for his wives, and 6 years tending Laban's flocks while earning wages and increasing his wealth.

For 20 years, Jacob had been away from his homeland. Over those years he had married and become the father of 11 sons and 1 daughter. Now he realized that it was time to bring his family back to the land that God had promised to his descendants.

Wages

In Jacob's time, a man did not always work for money. Wealth was rarely determined by how much money someone possessed, but rather by the amount of land he owned, or by the number of sheep and cattle. When Jacob worked for Laban, he asked that his wages be all the speckled and spotted sheep and goats. For Jacob, owning his own flock was much more important than earning a bag of money.

Rachel may have traveled in a saddle much like the one above. The covering protected a rider from the blazing sun. The bedouin at the left reminds us of Laban or his neighbors.

Jacob and Esau Meet

GENESIS 32:1—33:17

Synopsis

Jacob had deceived his father Isaac in his old age, getting the birthright that Isaac wanted to give to Jacob's twin brother Esau. Esau was furious and threatened to kill Jacob, who ran away to Haran, married his two cousins, Leah and Rachel, and raised a family. Twenty years later Jacob started home, leaving his deceitful father-in-law Laban behind. But his great fear as he returned was whether Esau still hated him enough to kill him or whether the past was forgiven.

Edom and Its People

The nation Edom owed its existence to Isaac's son Esau, who was the ancestor, or "father" of the Edomites. But even though the nations Edom and Israel came from the same family, they were always bitter enemies.

Edom was located southeast of Israel and the Dead Sea area. Most of the region was rugged terrain, with mountain peaks, deep gorges, high plateaus, and desert landscape.

Edom grew into a nation for many reasons. On the plateaus, fig and olive trees were able to grow, as well as vineyards. The mountains supplied copper and iron ore. Herdsmen were common in the area, tending their flocks. There were also several important trade routes that crossed the country, bringing rich goods into the land.

Though Israel and Edom shared a common border, the two nations were never friendly. During the Exodus, the king of Edom refused to allow Israel passage through his country. In the time of the Kings, there were constant battles between the two neighboring lands. Centuries later, Edom was forced to pay heavy tribute to Babylon, but rejoiced when the Babylonians sacked Jerusalem. Soon afterward, the country dwindled into obscurity.

Where Did Jacob and Esau Meet?

The two brothers met near the place where the Jabbok River flows into the Jordan River, about 25 miles north of the Dead Sea.

Gifts

In many eastern countries, before two people met for business or pleasure, they often sent gifts to each other. These gifts were usually related to each man's occupation, which explains why Jacob sent sheep, goats, and cattle to Esau. Refusing a gift was a sign of hostility.

Right: the Jabboh River, near the place where it flows into the Jordan River.

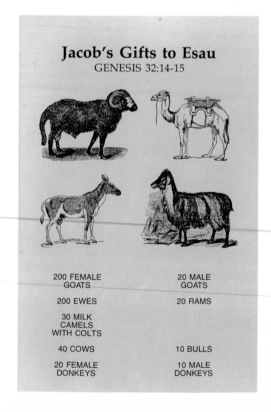

Jacob's Gifts to Esau
GENESIS 32:14-15

200 FEMALE GOATS	20 MALE GOATS
200 EWES	20 RAMS
30 MILK CAMELS WITH COLTS	
40 COWS	10 BULLS
20 FEMALE DONKEYS	10 MALE DONKEYS

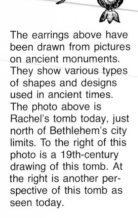

The earrings above have been drawn from pictures on ancient monuments. They show various types of shapes and designs used in ancient times. The photo above is Rachel's tomb today, just north of Bethlehem's city limits. To the right of this photo is a 19th-century drawing of this tomb. At the right is another perspective of this tomb as seen today.

Rachel Dies When Benjamin Is Born

GENESIS 35:1-20

Synopsis

For 20 years Jacob lived in the land of Haran and worked for his father-in-law Laban. He married Laban's two daughters, Leah and Rachel, and raised a family there. But Laban was a difficult man to work for, so Jacob left for his childhood home in Canaan. On the way, he feared most the meeting with his brother Esau, for Esau had once threatened to kill him. However, Esau was now loving and forgiving. Jacob moved first to Succoth, then to a place near Shechem, and then to Bethel, where he had seen a ladder to heaven. Once again he journeyed, this time to the south. Near Bethlehem, his beloved Rachel died while giving birth to their second son Benjamin.

Rachel's Tomb

Not everyone agrees on the location of Rachel's tomb or burial site. According to the Bible, Rachel died while Jacob and his family were traveling toward Ephrath. Some scholars argue that Ephrath was located about 10 miles north of Jerusalem. But the traditional view remains that Ephrath was the ancient name for the city of Bethlehem. Today, the common site of Rachel's tomb lies about one mile north of Bethlehem, which is a few miles south of Jerusalem.

Benjamin

Jacob's two youngest sons, Joseph and Benjamin, were also his favorites. Probably he liked them better because their mother was Rachel, the woman Jacob loved most.

68

Benjamin was the last son born to Jacob. Benjamin and Joseph were full brothers. All of Jacob's other sons were Benjamin's half brothers.

Jacob was protective of Benjamin. After he thought he had lost Joseph, he probably kept Benjamin at home while his other 10 sons tended the flocks. When famine struck the land of Canaan, Jacob sent all his sons except Benjamin to buy grain in Egypt (Gen. 42:3-4).

But Jacob could not be a protective father forever. The governor of Egypt, who was really Joseph, demanded to see Benjamin. If he was not brought down to Egypt, no more grain would be given to Jacob's family, and his sons would be convicted as spies (Gen. 42:15-17). Benjamin did go, and because of this Joseph was reunited with his family. Benjamin had at least 10 sons, and became the ancestor of the tribe of Benjamin.

Earrings

Since the beginning of civilization, jewelry has been a prized possession. Earrings are no exception. In Old Testament times, they came in all shapes and sizes, and were made of everything imaginable, such as gold, silver, ivory, brass, and even wood. Some earrings were very small and simple, while others were large and heavy and decorated with diamonds and other jewels.

In the Bible, earrings were often associated with idolatry. Jacob asked his family to stop their idolatry, and give up their earrings, which he buried (Gen. 35:4). The Prophet Hosea associated the wearing of jewelry with the worship of Baal (Hosea 2:13,17).

Earrings probably became connected with idolatry because heathen nations engraved strange deities and figures on their earrings and other jewelry. This was thought to ward off evil and bring good fortune to a family. They were like good luck charms, except they were taken much more seriously. Because Jacob and his family were living in a foreign land (Canaan), which was full of idolatry, he probably wanted as few distractions from the worship of God as possible.

Pillar of Stone

When Rachel died, Jacob set up a stone pillar over her grave. This was the first instance where the Bible mentions a monument erected over a burial site. This was probably done as a lasting symbol of God's goodness to Jacob and his beloved wife, Rachel.

69

Joseph's Cloak

GENESIS 37:1-11

Synopsis
After Jacob and his family returned to Canaan, they settled at first at Succoth, then moved to a place near Shechem, and finally migrated southward. Near Bethlehem, Jacob's beloved wife Rachel died while giving birth to her 2nd son, Jacob's 12th son. Jacob returned at last to Mamre, near Hebron, where his father Isaac still lived, and settled there to work as a shepherd. Of all Jacob's 12 sons, Joseph was his favorite. The family noticed this, especially when Jacob gave Joseph a fancy cloak.

Joseph's Cloak of Many Colors
In Joseph's time, most cloaks were very plain, reached to the knees, and had short sleeves or half sleeves. But the cloak that Joseph received from his father was bright-colored, probably reached all the way down to his ankles, and had long sleeves. Some think that his cloak came from Shinar, also known as the land of Babylon. The Babylonians were highly skilled at this time in making luxurious clothing and embroidery from a variety of materials and colors.

Why did Jacob give a cloak like this to Joseph? It is obvious from the Bible that Jacob favored his son Joseph over all his other sons,

including Benjamin. The beautiful cloak was a sign of Jacob's favoritism. But it was much more than that. A cloak like this was a symbol of distinction and importance. This was the type of cloak that families of royalty wore. Many think that Joseph's cloak was a sign of Jacob's desire to turn the family's birthright over to Joseph. Others believe its purpose was to ward off evil and bring good fortune. But what Joseph's cloak really did was to bring more jealousy and strife to Jacob's already troubled family.

The Variety of Uses for a Cloak
Most people owned only the clothes they wore on their backs. But almost everyone had one other piece of clothing—his cloak. This was certainly the most useful and widely used piece of clothing.

When a person had many things to carry, or when he was moving away, his belongings were wrapped in his cloak and thrown over his shoulder. The Hebrews probably carried many of their personal belongings out of Egypt in this way.

Women carried their babies in their cloaks. Farmers tied their cloaks into a sack which they hung around their necks, and then poured grain into it. From this cloak the farmer would plant his fields by throwing handfuls of grain in front of him as he walked.

When an honored guest would arrive, the host often spread his cloak on the ground as a place where the guest could sit. At Jesus'

70

Cloaks of Bible Times

*Cloaks were widely used in Bible times
by both men and women. They varied
from place to place, and especially from
nation to nation. The cloaks pictured
below are drawn from monuments of
ancient times.*

A FRINGED CLOAK

CLOAK OF AN EGYPTIAN KING

A PERSIAN CLOAK

A CHALDEAN CLOAK

CLOAKS WITH AND WITHOUT GIRDLES (BELTS)

A MEDIAN CLOAK

AN ASSYRIAN CLOAK

triumphal entry, the people of the city laid
their cloaks on the ground before Jesus as he
rode into Jerusalem on a donkey.

A cloak was also given to someone as a
pledge for a debt. When the debt was paid,
the cloak was returned. However, the Law
of Moses stated that if a cloak was a man's
only covering at night, it must be returned to
him before sunset.

At night, a person slept under his cloak,
or used it as a pillow. Some were made out
of goat or camel hair which kept out most of
the dew and rain.

In times of great grief and sorrow, a cloak
was often torn to pieces. Others would seize
the hem of someone's cloak to beg for mercy.

Dreams

Waking up from a good night of sleep often
alarmed people more than it helped them. If
they had just had a vivid dream, they would
not have laughed about it as most people do
today. Dreams in Bible times were highly respected and thought to be predictions or warnings of the future, or uncoverings of the past.

Dream interpreters were always in demand, especially in the presence of kings and
rulers. As long as their interpretations were
accurate, they were given places of honor and
prestige in the kingdom. After Joseph told
Pharaoh the meaning of his dream, he was
made governor of Egypt (Gen. 41:39-41). Daniel was promoted to a ruler of Babylon under
Nebuchadnezzar after he interpreted his
king's dream (Dan. 2:46-48).

Joseph Is Sold as a Slave

GENESIS 37:12-36

Synopsis

After returning home to Canaan with his family, Jacob was saddened by the death of his beloved wife Rachel. He had worked 14 years for the right to marry her, and now she had died, while giving birth to her second son, Benjamin. Jacob then settled down near his childhood home, living as a shepherd. As the years passed, it became clear to all that one son was his favorite. That son was Joseph. His jealous brothers brought things to a head by selling Joseph as a slave.

The Pit or Cistern

When Joseph found his brothers in the fields near Dothan, he suddenly became a victim of their jealousy. Jacob's favoritism to Joseph, along with the beautiful cloak and unpopular dreams, had fueled an intense hatred toward Joseph by his brothers. When they saw Joseph coming across the fields, they immediately wanted to kill him. But Reuben, the oldest, convinced them to throw Joseph into a "pit" until they could decide what to do with him.

The pit was probably a cistern, which is a deep hole cut down into rock or hard clay that is not porous. Cisterns were used mainly to collect and store rainwater which was used later to water flocks or quench the thirst of traveling caravans.

Cisterns were also used as dungeons when they held no water. The opening was small enough to put a cover on the top, but the bottom was much larger. This pear-shape made it almost impossible for a man to escape once he was dropped into the cistern. Centuries later the Prophet Jeremiah was also put into a cistern that had been dug in a prison courtyard (Jer. 38:6).

Dothan

Joseph left his home around Hebron to search for his brothers. He first traveled northward to Shechem, a distance of about 60 miles. There he learned that his brothers had moved on to Dothan, another 20 miles or so to the north.

Dothan is known for its rich pastureland. Even today, many shepherds still take their flocks up to the Dothan area from Jerusalem and elsewhere for good grazing.

In Joseph's time, Dothan was situated on a major trade route which connected Syria in the north with the southern kingdom of Egypt. This was probably the route the Ishmaelite traders were taking when they passed through Dothan and bought Joseph as a slave.

Caravans

Joseph's brothers sold him to Ishmaelite traders for 20 shekels of silver, which was only enough to buy one ram each.

Suddenly Joseph was a member of a caravan, on a long journey to Egypt. Caravans in Bible times were groups of people traveling a common road or toward a common destination. Traveling alone was extremely dangerous, especially when one stopped to rest for the night. Roads had no signs to direct travelers, and robbers and wild animals were frequent. For these reasons, people journeyed in groups whenever possible. The more travelers in a group, the less chance of being attacked by thieves or bands of raiders.

As a caravan made its way along the road, some joined the group, while others left it, having reached the end of their journey. Some caravans had as many as 3,000 people, but most were much smaller. Poor people walked or rode on donkeys, while the rich sat on camels. Because of the dry and dusty roads, those who had to ride at the end of the caravan were breathing clouds of dust for the entire trip.

At nightfall, caravans offered protection from the perils of the dark. Often they stopped at wayside inns, which were usually just empty buildings in which to sleep, or walled courtyards that protected people and animals from robbery or attack.

Caravans caused much excitement when entering a city or village. Often they had come from places far away, and brought with them fascinating goods from foreign lands or news that was unknown to many.

A Slave's Life in Egypt

A slave usually lived a hopeless life, full of despair. Most slaves had no "days off" or vacation. They knew that the rest of their lives would be filled with endless chores, and probably difficult, exhausting work.

Joseph was a fortunate slave. Because of his intelligence and good attitude, he was chosen to be a steward. His job was to supervise the activities of a wealthy household.

But most slaves were not so fortunate. Many had to work in copper mines, which meant certain death. Others were oarsmen on Egyptian warships. Some women were forced to be prostitutes. Other slaves were brickmakers or metalworkers.

> Upper left: Joseph travels to Egypt by caravan. The mound where ancient Dothan once stood is at the top right. Below, a camel caravan today, a reminder of the caravan which took Joseph to Egypt.

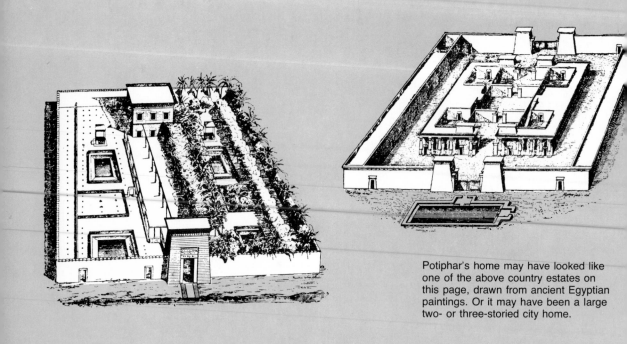

Potiphar's home may have looked like one of the above country estates on this page, drawn from ancient Egyptian paintings. Or it may have been a large two- or three-storied city home.

Joseph in Potiphar's House

GENESIS 39

Synopsis

Joseph was clearly his father Jacob's favorite son. This, of course, made his brothers jealous. Joseph aggravated this by telling about two dreams, in which his father, mother, and brothers bowed down before him. Jealousy overcame the brothers and they sold Joseph as a slave. He was taken to Egypt by caravan and sold to an official named Potiphar. There Joseph remained faithful to the Lord, even after he was wronged and thrown into prison.

Potiphar

Potiphar was captain of the bodyguard, an official of Pharaoh who bought Joseph from the Ishmaelite traders in Egypt. The Bible mentions little about Potiphar except that he bought Joseph as a slave (Gen. 39:1), noticed his intelligence and made Joseph steward of his house (39:4), and later threw him into prison thinking that Joseph had dishonored his wife (39:20).

As captain of the bodyguard, Potiphar was ultimately responsible for the protection of

Pharaoh's life. He was also in charge of important prisoners and was often given the job of sentencing them to be executed.

Steward

Joseph was bought as a slave by Potiphar, then taken to Potiphar's house, probably a wealthy home. Joseph's wisdom and attitude soon earned him the job of steward.

A steward in ancient Egypt was in charge of all the activities in his master's house. Joseph ran Potiphar's house so smoothly that the man worried about nothing (Gen. 39:6).

The home of a man like Potiphar would have been very large, with many slaves. Joseph's job was to make sure that each slave was doing his work. As supervisor, Joseph made sure that Potiphar's meal was served on time. He was also responsible for having materials on hand for spinning and weaving, and enough grain for bread and feeding the animals. Disputes among slaves were to be quickly corrected, and work performed efficiently.

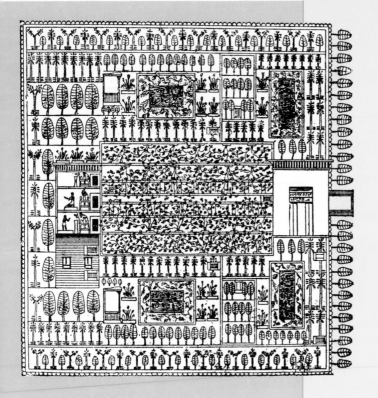

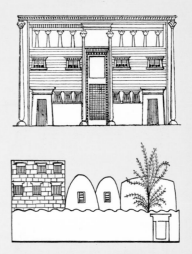

Two other Egyptian homes are shown above. The bottom one has a granary within (domed buildings). At the left is a layout of the house and gardens of a wealthy Egyptian's estate.

The comfort of the master and his family was a top priority. The house was really to be run like a business, smoothly and efficiently, with excellent service and a minimum of problems.

Prisons

"Guilty until proven innocent." That was the system of justice in ancient times. When a person was suspected of committing a crime, he was thrown into prison until his trial. Often the trial never took place, or it did not come up for years. Until then, the accused person stayed with robbers, murderers, and the insane.

A respected man or official who was accused of wrong might be kept in a room of the palace or a house. But most people were thrown into prison cells or dungeons. The rooms were dark and clammy. There were no toilets, and prisoners had to remain in their cells. The stench was unbearable, and sickness and disease were common.

Many prisons offered no food or water. Whatever food the prisoner's family could bring was all that was eaten. Many men thrown into prison far from home starved to death.

Above: three forms of Egyptian "pillows" or headrests. The top is made of alabaster. The center is made of wood. The bottom is a block headrest made of wood and inscribed with hieroglyphic characters.

75

Baker and Cupbearer

GENESIS 40

Synopsis

Joseph was clearly Jacob's favorite son. This aggravated a growing jealousy among his brothers, until they sold him as a slave. He was taken to Egypt in a caravan and sold to an Egyptian official named Potiphar. Joseph's faithfulness caught his master's eye and he promoted him over the entire household. But his faithfulness also angered Potiphar's wife. She lied about Joseph and he was thrown into prison. There he met Pharaoh's baker and cupbearer, who both dreamed strange dreams and told them to Joseph.

The Baker's Job in Ancient Egypt

When Joseph was alive, bread was the most common food in Egypt. It was popular, not because it tasted so good, but because its ingredients were easy to find and bread was inexpensive to make.

But baking bread was no easy job. Baking utensils were awkward compared with today's modern appliances. All of the work was done by hand as there were few, if any, time-saving devices.

Bread was made from wheat or barley, and since the methods for refining the flour were limited, almost all of the grain was left in the bread when it was baked. This probably kept this bread full of calories, fiber, and nutrients, making bread one of Egypt's staple foods.

The first step in breadmaking was to separate the grain from the stalks of wheat or barley. This was done

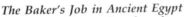

Various breadmaking scenes above, counterclockwise from top center: carrying ingredients to a confectioner, kneading dough with feet, mixing dough, making a form of macaroni, an oven, and a baker carrying bread to an oven.

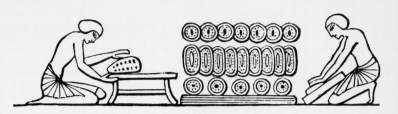

by the farmer. The baker bought this grain from the farmer and then put it into a stone pot called a "mortar." Taking a "pestle," which was a hard stone or wood bar with a large, round end, he crushed the grain into a coarse flour. Running the grain between two millstones produced a much finer flour.

After the flour had been sifted to remove dirt and sand, it was mixed with water and honey to make dough. Yeast was added if the baker wanted the bread to rise. This dough was shaped into loaves and baked in ovens of preheated rocks, or cooked on the outside of heated pottery jars called "tannurs." It is obvious that a baker had a hot and tiring job.

The Cupbearer's Job in Ancient Egypt

Also called a butler, the cupbearer stood before the king every day. His job was to serve the king his drinks, probably wine, though many think that the ancient Egyptians drank no wine.

The cupbearer was also responsible in part for the king's life. Because he was so frequently in the company of the king, the cupbearer had to be a highly trusted man. He was usually an important official with great status and respect in the kingdom.

When offering the king a drink, or refilling the king's drinking cup, the cupbearer first poured the drink into the palm of his hand and tasted it as proof that it was not poisoned. Ancient Egyptian cups usually had no handles, so the cupbearer placed the king's drinking cup directly in the palm of his hand. For this reason, Joseph told the cupbearer that he would "put Pharaoh's cup in his hand," when he had regained his old job (Gen. 40:13).

Various breadmaking scenes above, clockwise from top center: kneading dough with hands, making cakes, drawings of ancient Egyptian breads, a bread stamp, and a model of an ancient Egyptian bakery (about the time of Abraham).

77

The finery of Egyptian women of noble birth, such as Asenath, may be seen in the rich embroidered garments above.

Joseph Becomes Governor

GENESIS 41:1-45

Synopsis

In a jealous mood, Joseph's brothers sold him as a slave and he was taken to Egypt. There an official named Potiphar bought him and when he saw that the Lord was with Joseph, made him the highest officer over his household affairs. But Potiphar's wife lied about Joseph and he was thrown into prison. There he met Pharaoh's baker and cupbearer and interpreted their dreams. The baker was hanged and the cupbearer was restored to Pharaoh. Later the cupbearer told Pharaoh what Joseph had done, for Pharaoh desperately wanted his dreams interpreted. When the Lord, through Joseph, revealed Pharaoh's dreams to him, Pharaoh made Joseph governor of all Egypt.

Dreams throughout the Bible

In ancient times, dreams were a serious matter, treated with respect. God often used dreams to tell of some future event, or warn people of approaching trouble. Those who were able to interpret dreams quickly rose to positions of importance within the kingdom.

Often God talked directly to people. There is some disagreement as to whether He really conversed with them, or if He spoke to them in visions or through dreams. However, there are many instances where dreams are specifically mentioned in the Bible.

Jacob dreamed of a ladder to heaven when he stopped to rest for the night on his long journey to Haran (Gen. 28:12). Because of this dream, he made a covenant with God. Joseph interpreted the dreams of the butler and the baker (Gen. 40). With God's help, his interpretations were correct, giving him a chance later to interpret Pharaoh's dream. Once again God gave Joseph success in telling Pharaoh the meaning of his dreams. Because of this, Joseph was made governor of Egypt (Gen. 41:1-45).

Above: Joseph is led before Pharaoh, where he will interpret the king's dreams. Before Joseph entered Pharaoh's presence, he was required to shave. Ancient Egyptian razors and accessories may be seen immediately above.

Joseph's wife, Asenath, was the daughter of an Egyptian priest, such as those above.

An ancient Egyptian signet ring, probably much like the one which Pharaoh gave to Joseph. Note the hieroglyphics carved on it, which became a "signature" when pressed on clay.

Many years later, Gideon's courage was renewed when he stole into the Midianite camp and heard a soldier tell his friend of a dream in which their entire army was defeated by Gideon's men (Jud. 7:13-15).

King Nebuchadnezzar was greatly troubled by a dream. He searched his kingdom for a man who could unravel its meaning. When Daniel was able to interpret the king's dream, he was promoted to ruler of Babylon under Nebuchadnezzar (Dan. 2). Later, Daniel had a strange dream about the four winds, the four beasts, and the great sea (Dan. 7).

After Jesus was born, God warned Joseph in a dream to flee to Egypt to escape Herod's anger (Matt. 2:13). Joseph was also told in a dream to return to Israel after Herod's death (Matt. 2:19-20). When Jesus was on trial, Pilate's wife had a traumatic dream which led her to beg Pilate to release Jesus (Matt. 27:19).

Signet Rings

When Pharaoh gave Joseph his royal signet ring, all the people of Egypt knew that Joseph had been given enormous power in the land of Egypt. Handing over the signet ring symbolized the great authority that had been transferred to Joseph by Pharaoh. Next to Pharaoh, Joseph was now the most powerful man in Egypt.

Signet rings were used also to sign documents. Impressing a signet ring into clay or wax was like signing one's signature today. Many men owned signet rings, and each ring had a different mark or symbol engraved on it.

Centuries after Joseph, King Ahasuerus' signet ring marked death for the Jews when used by Haman, but life and hope when used by Mordecai (Es. 3:10-13; 8:2, 8, 10).

One of Joseph's symbols of authority, granted by Pharaoh, was his fine chariot. Two chariots of ancient Egypt may be seen above, drawn from ancient tomb paintings.

Joseph Rules as Governor

GENESIS 41:46-57

Synopsis

After Joseph's brothers sold him as a slave, he was taken to Egypt, where he became steward over Potiphar's household. But this official's wife lied about Joseph and he was thrown into prison. There he met Pharaoh's baker and cupbearer and interpreted strange dreams for them. The cupbearer returned to Pharaoh and when Pharaoh needed dreams interpreted, told him about Joseph. When Joseph told Pharaoh what his dreams meant, Pharaoh made him governor of all Egypt. Joseph's biggest task lay ahead, though. It was to keep people from starving in the coming famine. Joseph organized the land and set up a system for collecting grain.

Egyptian Storehouses

Before the great famine in Egypt came seven years of abundant harvests. During this time, Joseph, as governor, collected a tax from the people in the form of grain. Joseph knew he had to collect enough grain to carry the people through the seven years of scarcity that lay ahead.

The grain was stored in storehouses or granaries until there was so much of it that it could no longer be measured (Gen. 41:49). Most granaries were buildings with beehive-shaped domes, divided into a series of rooms. Grain was poured into each room from the top, and taken out through a small door near the bottom.

Grain—Planting and Harvesting

In Israel, farmers depended on two rainy seasons for

Harvesting scenes, counterclockwise from the top: plowing and sowing the grain, cutting ripened grain with sickles, binding sheaves, treading grain to separate kernels from stalks, winnowing (throwing mixture into the air for the wind to separate), and scribes recording the harvest.

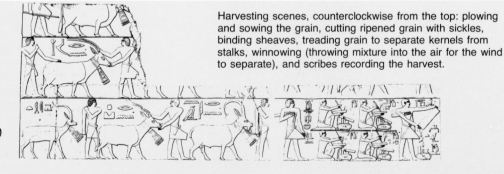

80

a good harvest. By contrast, Egyptian farmers relied on the Nile River. During the months of September, October, and November the Nile overflowed its banks, and the river flooded the surrounding land. When the waters receded, a fertile layer of silt was left behind.

While this new soil was still moist, the farmer quickly plowed his land with a clumsy wooden plow pulled by oxen. Many farmers, however, did not have animals to do their heavy work, and were forced to pull their plows themselves.

After the plowing and hoeing were done, the farmer began sowing, or planting his seeds. He walked through the fields, throwing the seeds from his hands onto the rich soil. Pigs, sheep, or other animals walked behind him, trampling the seeds into the ground. Then the farmer waited until March or April, the time of harvest.

The job of cutting the stalks of grain and tying them into bundles was given to men and women called reapers. These bundles, or sheaves of wheat, barley, or corn, were then taken to the threshing floor where oxen or donkeys plodded over the stalks, separating the grain from them.

Next the grain was strained, or sifted through a sieve, then thrown into the wind with long wooden forks. The heavier grain fell to the ground, while the chaff was blown away in the wind. This process was called winnowing. The sieve removed the heavier pieces of dirt and sand, while the wind carried away the light and useless chaff.

Now the grain was ready to be stored, until it was needed for making bread or other uses. An official arrived to make sure that some grain went to the temple granaries, for the priests' food, and some grain went to the royal granaries, for the king's food. In Joseph's day, farmers paid a tax of one fifth of all their grain, to prepare for the coming famine.

Harvesting scenes, clockwise from the top: plowing and sowing the grain, treading grain at threshing floor, woman grinding grain on stone grinder, second woman grinding grain on stone grinder, stone grinder similar to the one the woman uses, a mortar and pestle, three types of granary models.

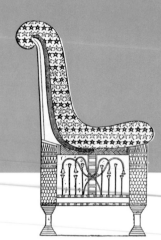

Joseph's Brothers Buy Grain

GENESIS 42—44

Synopsis
Joseph's older brothers were jealous because their father Jacob favored Joseph above them all. The jealousy grew to hatred until they sold Joseph as a slave. In Egypt, Joseph was bought by Potiphar, an official who placed him over all his household when he saw that the Lord was with Joseph. Potiphar's wife lied about Joseph and he was thrown into prison, where he interpreted some dreams for Pharaoh's baker and cupbearer. When Pharaoh had strange dreams, his cupbearer told him about Joseph, who told Pharaoh a famine was coming. Pharaoh placed Joseph in charge of the land, to prepare for the famine. In time, the brothers who sold Joseph came to buy grain.

Joseph as Governor
Joseph was second-in-command over the entire land of Egypt. Only Pharaoh himself had more power and authority. Pharaoh had great trust in Joseph, for he told the people to do whatever Joseph asked (Gen. 41:55). Joseph may have been in charge of Egypt's army, finances, agriculture, and justice system.

Just as Joseph was once a steward in the house of Potiphar, now he had a steward of his own (Gen. 43:16). When Joseph's brothers arrived in Egypt to buy grain, he remembered being sold as a slave. Now, with the power of Egypt at his fingertips, Joseph could send his brothers into a life of slavery.

Joseph must have lived in an expensive home, even larger and more beautiful than Potiphar's. It was probably three stories tall and surrounded by a walled courtyard. Slaves kept the house in order, prepared the meals, and looked after Joseph's comfort. Joseph's wife also had many slaves. Some even helped her dress and put on make-up.

Inside, Joseph's home must have been filled with elegant wall hangings and colorful rugs. Decorations of gold, silver, and alabaster

Beside the photo of the Great Pyramid above, which was standing when Joseph was governor of Egypt, is an elegant Egyptian chair, drawn from an ancient monument. The other chair and stool above are from Old Testament times.

82

were everywhere. The furniture, elaborately carved, was also made of alabaster, or an imported wood like ebony, which was inlaid with ivory.

Joseph's Silver Drinking Cup

Gold was quite common in the land of Egypt, but silver was considered a more precious metal because it was harder to come by. Joseph's personal drinking cup was made of silver. But this kind of cup was used for more than just drinking.

The cup was called a "divination" cup. Skilled craftsmen engraved symbols, spells, and religious phrases on the cup. Often the owner's name was also inscribed on the cup. When drinking from it, all of the liquid had to be drained from the cup in order to repel evil and bring the god's blessings.

In divination (looking into the future), pure water was usually poured into the cup. People thought that the cup answered questions about the future through bubbles, reflections, or calmness. Sometimes hot wax was poured into the water, and predictions were made from the shapes of the hardened wax.

Joseph's Brothers Travel to Egypt with Donkeys

The long journey to Egypt could have taken Joseph's brothers many weeks. The Bible says they made their trip with donkeys (Gen. 42:26). It does not say whether they rode their donkeys or used them only for carrying baggage and grain, while the men walked on foot.

But why didn't they take camels, so well suited for long distances? Jacob's family were mainly herdsmen, tending sheep and goats, while living in hilly country. They had little need for camels and probably owned only a few. Camels also sway when they walk, making an inexperienced rider "seasick."

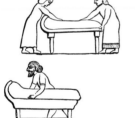

The three items of furniture are, top to bottom: a bed with headrest, making a bed, and a headrest. At the top, an Egyptian household of a wealthy family, such as Joseph's. The furniture on these pages is similar to that which Joseph had.

83

Joseph Reveals Himself to His Brothers

GENESIS 45:1-15

Synopsis

Sold as a slave by his own brothers, Joseph was taken to Egypt, where his faithfulness to the Lord became apparent to his new master. He was placed over Potiphar's household until Potiphar's wife lied about Joseph and he was then thrown into prison. But there he interpreted dreams for Pharaoh's baker and cupbearer. The cupbearer told Pharaoh about Joseph when Pharaoh desperately wanted to know what his dreams meant. Joseph told of a coming famine, and Pharaoh made him governor so that he could prepare Egypt for the famine. In time, Joseph's brothers came to buy grain. But they did not recognize Joseph until he revealed himself to them.

The 11 Brothers of Joseph

Though Joseph's brothers were not always kind or honest, God chose to continue the nation of Israel through them. Their descendants became 10 of the tribes of Israel.

Below, Joseph tells his brothers that he is not only Egypt's governor, but the brother they sold into slavery. A silver cup of Egypt, from about the time of Joseph, is seen below. To the right of it are a pistachio plant (on the left side) and a plant bearing the balm of Gilead. Balm and pistachio nuts were among the gifts which Jacob sent to Joseph as governor of Egypt.

Reuben was the oldest brother of Joseph. He persuaded his other brothers not to kill Joseph, but to throw him into a pit instead (Gen. 37:12-22).

Simeon was kept in an Egyptian prison by Joseph, while the other brothers returned to Canaan to get Benjamin (Gen. 42:18-24).

Levi was the ancestor of Moses and Aaron. Through Levi came the Levites, Israel's religious leaders and caretakers of the tabernacle (Ex. 32:25-29).

Judah had the idea of selling Joseph into slavery instead of killing him (Gen. 37:26-28). He was an ancestor of King David and Jesus (Matt. 1:1-16).

Issachar was born in Paddan Aram, as were all of Jacob's sons except Benjamin. Descendants of Issachar included Deborah and Barak (Jud. 5:15).

Zebulun was Leah's last son (Gen. 30:19-20). His name meant "dwelling" or "abiding."

Gad was Zilpah's first son (Gen. 30:9-11). His descendants settled east of the Jordan River.

Asher was Zilpah's second son (Gen. 30:12-13). His descendants received the territory that borders the Mediterranean Sea, west of the Sea of Galilee.

Dan was Bilhah's son (Gen. 30:4-6). His descendants eventually settled farther north than any other tribe.

Naphtali was Bilhah's second son (Gen. 30:7-8). The land along the western edge of the Sea of Galilee was given to his descendants.

Benjamin was born to Rachel. His descendants, the tribe of Benjamin, were almost destroyed by the rest of Israel (Jud. 19—21). King Saul and Paul the apostle came from the line of Benjamin (1 Sam. 9:1-2; Phil. 3:5).

Above: two processions, bearing gifts to Egyptian leaders. At the top, a tribute of elephant tusks is brought to Pharaoh Thothmes III (Thutmose III or Thutmosis III). The lower procession also brings tribute. These remind us of Joseph's brothers, bearing gifts to him.

When Joseph's brothers came, he invited them to dinner. Above top, servants cook such a dinner, including geese and other meat. Above bottom two panels, dinner is served and eaten. Note the small tables and foods on them.

Joseph's Family Moves to Egypt

GENESIS 45:16—47:31

Synopsis

When he was a young man, Joseph was sold into slavery by his brothers. Taken to Egypt, he was bought by an official, Potiphar, who placed Joseph in charge of his household, but later threw Joseph into prison because of Potiphar's wife's accusations. There Joseph met Pharaoh's baker and cupbearer and interpreted dreams for them. The cupbearer later told Pharaoh about Joseph, who interpreted two important dreams for Pharaoh, warning of a coming famine. Pharaoh made Joseph governor and placed him over the land to prepare for the famine. In time Joseph's brothers came to buy grain and he revealed to them who he was. Then Joseph sent them back to Canaan to return with the entire family.

Egypt—A Contrast in Living

Arriving in Egypt from the land of Canaan, Jacob and his family faced a new lifestyle. Egyptian customs were very different from those in Canaan, and the landscape was unfamiliar too. Crossing the borders of Egypt, Jacob's family would have noticed the flat and desolate land, quite a contrast to the hills and lush valleys of Canaan.

Giant monuments, such as the Great Pyra-

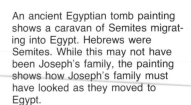

An ancient Egyptian tomb painting shows a caravan of Semites migrating into Egypt. Hebrews were Semites. While this may not have been Joseph's family, the painting shows how Joseph's family must have looked as they moved to Egypt.

Jacob and his family moved their belongings to Egypt in wagons, provided by Joseph. At the right, and above, are three styles of ancient Egyptian carts and wagons, drawn from Egyptian paintings. Joseph's family must have been awed by the sight of the pyramids (far right), built many years before they arrived in Egypt. Abraham had seen these same pyramids when he visited Egypt 200 years earlier.

mid of Cheops, must have been a strange sight. Compared with the small Canaanite villages, the sprawling Egyptian store-cities were certainly awesome and frightening.

Family life was different as well. Egyptian women were allowed to own property, and accompanied their husbands to most social functions. This was forbidden in Israelite culture. Hebrew boys learned their father's trade, while Egyptian boys started school at the age of four, and trained as scribes or government officials.

Hebrews—An Uncultured Society

Egypt operated a highly skilled and sophisticated society. They considered foreigners from the area of Canaan to be a crude and backward people.

Hebrews grew beards, while Egyptians were clean-shaven. The unsettled life of a herdsman was vulgar to Egyptian men and women, who preferred to live in houses and cities, learning jobs as craftsmen, scribes, or officials. Music and the arts were popular entertainment among Egyptians, but the Hebrews enjoyed gathering in their tents to talk and eat.

Goshen

Jacob's nationality and occupation were loathsome in the eyes of the Egyptians, so Pharaoh gave Jacob his own area of land in which to live. This region was in the eastern section of the Nile River delta, and was called the land of Goshen. It was a rich land due to the many river branches that watered the area.

The land of Goshen was in the northeastern corner of Egypt. It was one of the first sights in the land of Egypt seen by Jacob's caravan.

Goshen is also called the "land of Ramses." The city of Ramses, found in the Goshen area, was once the capital of Egypt, built by Hebrew slaves.

When Jacob and his sons moved to Egypt, they must have been struck by the different appearance of their strange new neighbors, the Egyptians. Hairstyles and head coverings such as those above, drawn from ancient Egyptian paintings, were completely different from those worn by the Hebrews. Hebrew men wore beards while Egyptians were clean-shaven.

Jacob Dies and Is Buried

GENESIS 48—50

Synopsis

After Joseph revealed himself to his brothers, he sent them home to Canaan to bring his father Jacob and all the family to live in Egypt during the remaining years of the famine. Joseph asked Pharaoh to give his family the best land in Egypt where they could live and work as shepherds. In time Jacob died, and was buried back in Canaan, in the cave of Machpelah, where his ancestors were buried.

Egyptian Embalming—Preparing a Body for Burial

When a wealthy person died in Egypt, the funeral sometimes did not begin for more than two months. During this time, a long and expensive process of preparing the dead body for burial took place. It was called embalming, and was available only to the elite in Egyptian society.

The embalmers began their work by first washing the dead body, and then removing all of the internal organs through an incision made along the abdomen. The brain was taken out with a long hook inserted through the nose. The organs were washed and preserved in small jars called "canopic jars," and the brain was thrown away.

The body was soaked in a salt-like solution called natron for a period of 40-70 days. It was then dried out and stuffed with spices, gums, or a substance that hardened like cement. Then the body was ready to be wrapped with cloth or bandages of fine linen. Ointment was rubbed over the body, and the linen strips, coated with gum on the underside, were wrapped around each hand, finger, leg, and toe separately. Next, six to eight-inch-wide strips were wrapped around the entire body which was then sewn inside a large cloth called a shroud. Embalmers used anywhere from 450-700 feet of linen wrap-

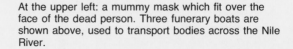

88

At the upper left: a mummy mask which fit over the face of the dead person. Three funerary boats are shown above, used to transport bodies across the Nile River.

pings during the process.

Now the body was almost ready for burial. Strips of cloth, soaked in lime, were wound in layers around the body. When the exact shape of the body had been achieved, the layers were removed in one piece, and allowed to harden into a tough case. This was the mummy case, in which the body was sealed. It was sometimes put into a larger coffin of wood or stone that was painted with religious messages.

Why did the Egyptians go through this long and expensive process? Many of them believed that as long as one's body existed, so did his soul. Some also believed that at a future time the soul would return to the body. Therefore, the body was preserved, awaiting the soul's return.

When Did Joseph Rule in Egypt?

The exact Pharaoh under whom Joseph governed is not known for sure, but most think that it was an Asian Pharaoh, for an Egyptian Pharaoh would not have tolerated a Hebrew in a position of high authority. Joseph probably ruled as governor sometime between the Middle Kingdom of Egypt (2200-1800 B.C.), and the New Kingdom of Egypt (1600-1000 B.C.). This was the period called "Between the Kingdoms" (1800-1600 B.C.), when Egypt was ruled by "Hyksos" kings from Asia.

A Funeral in Ancient Egypt

When the embalming was finally finished, the funeral procession began. The mummy was carried to the banks of the Nile by an ox cart, then boated across the river to a cemetery on the western bank. Professional mourners wailed and cut themselves with knives. Servants carried personal belongings of the deceased to make him comfortable in his life after death. The body was then buried with prayers and spells to usher it into the world of the dead. After the body was sealed in the tomb, everyone went to a great feast.

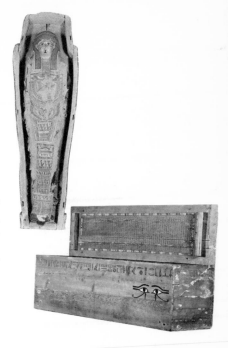

Above top: an Egyptian mummy in a coffin shaped like a body. The coffin below it was a rectangular chest with messages carved or painted on it. Jacob was embalmed, so his body was mummified.

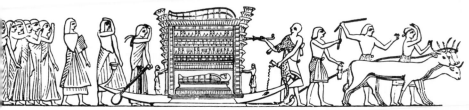

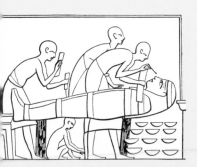

At the top: an Egyptian funeral caravan, perhaps much like that of Jacob's funeral. Below it, right, are mourners. The two drawings at the bottom show men busily making mummy cases and wrapping mummies.

89

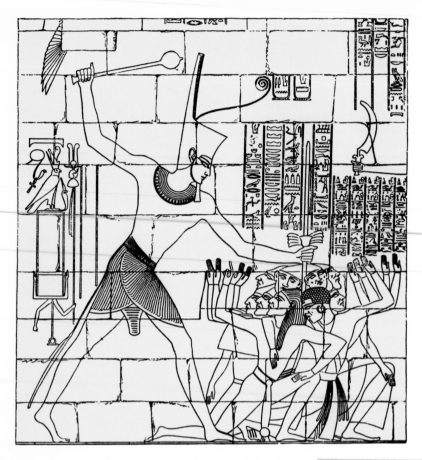

The harshness with wh[ich]
a Pharaoh could handl[e]
his prisoners is seen in
the drawing from a tem[ple]
at Karnak, Egypt, show[ing]
Seti I striking prisoners [of]
war.

Hebrews Become Slaves

EXODUS 1

Synopsis

When Joseph was still in his teen years, his brothers sold him as a slave and he was bought by an official in Egypt. The official's wife lied about Joseph and he was thrown into prison, where he interpreted some dreams for Pharaoh's baker and cupbearer. Later, the cupbearer told Pharaoh about Joseph, who warned Pharaoh of a coming famine. Pharaoh placed Joseph over the land to prepare for this famine. In time, Joseph's brothers came from Canaan to buy grain. They did not recognize Joseph, but after he tested their loyalty to their family, he revealed who he was and ordered them to bring the family to Egypt. Throughout the remaining years of the famine, he cared for his family. As the years passed, Joseph died, and a new Pharaoh came to the throne. More years passed, and more new Pharaohs came until the time when Joseph was almost forgotten. One Pharaoh decided to make the Hebrews, descendants of Joseph and his brothers, his slaves.

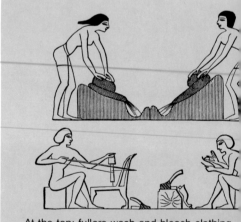

At the top: fullers wash and bleach clothing. Below it, carpenters made furniture as well a[s] other objects of wood. Right, top: potters made pottery. Below them, tax collectors flog[ged] those who failed to pay, while scribes record[ed] payments. These figures show some types o[f] work performed in ancient Egypt.

Brickmaking in Egypt

The name of the Pharaoh of Egypt who ruled the land at Moses' birth is not known, but he must have been interested in the wealth and power of Egypt. This Pharaoh started many building projects. But before the buildings could be constructed, bricks had to be made. This was probably the main job given the Hebrew slaves. Pharaoh pushed the Hebrew slaves to the brink of death.

Bricks were made by mixing together clay, straw, and water. This mud mixture was poured into wooden molds in the shape of bricks. The mixture was pressed firmly into the molds, and placed in the sunlight to dry. The hardened bricks were removed from their molds and carried to the building site, ready for construction. Because the climate of Egypt is hot and dry, with very little rain, these bricks lasted for centuries.

Taskmasters

The men in charge of supervising the work of the Hebrew slaves were called taskmasters. The word means "chief of the burden" or "oppressor." Their job was to keep the slaves working at a rapid pace and subdue their spirits by oppressing them with beatings and whippings. They were also ordered by Pharaoh to kill as many slaves as necessary to keep their numbers down.

The taskmaster was used not only to ensure that Pharaoh's building projects were carried out, but to see that the Hebrew population did not grow large enough to start a rebellion against Egypt.

The two figures at the left depict servitude in ancient Egypt. At the far left is a slave bearing a burden. The servant girl at the left carries a market basket.

Moses Is Born

EXODUS 2:1-10

Synopsis

Almost 400 years before Moses' time Joseph was sold as a slave and taken into Egypt. When he interpreted dreams for Pharaoh, warning of a coming famine, Pharaoh placed him over the land to prepare for this time. But the years and centuries passed and a Pharaoh arose who did not know about Joseph. He enslaved the descendants of Joseph and his brothers. One child born into a Hebrew slave family was Moses.

The Basket

Pharaoh's decree that all Hebrew baby boys were to be killed was put into effect throughout the land. Moses' mother, Jochebed, quickly made a wicker basket, her only hope of hiding Moses from the king's soldiers.

The basket would have been made of papyrus, a hollow reed that grows in abundance along the banks of the Nile River. Most baskets were made by weaving the papyrus reeds together. Egyptian baskets were sturdy as well as beautiful.

The basket in which Moses was placed had to be waterproof because Jochebed hid it on the river among the bulrushes. To keep the water out, the basket was covered with tar and pitch (Ex. 2:3). This tar was similar to the tar we have today, except that it was probably natural, not man-made.

The Bulrushes

Some Bible versions say that Moses was hidden among bulrushes in the Nile River. These bulrushes were large reeds also known as papyrus. They were probably the same reeds that Jochebed, Moses' mother, used to make the basket in which Moses was hidden.

Bulrushes grow from 10-15 feet tall and are as thick as 3 inches. They grow along the banks of rivers and lakes, with their roots under the water. They were used in ancient times for paper and boats.

Who Was the Pharaoh's Daughter?

Who was the princess who rescued baby Moses from the waters of the Nile? Her identity, as well as that of her father, the reigning Pharaoh, remain a mystery. But there are a few clues.

In sorting out the mystery, two main theo-

Above: papyrus reeds, such as those used for Moses' basket. Right: the princess finds Baby Moses among the live papyrus reeds growing along the Nile River.

ries have come to light. The first theory is that Moses grew up under the reign of Ramses II, a very cruel Pharaoh. Merneptah, the next Pharaoh, would have been the king when Moses led the Hebrews out of Egypt.

The second popular theory says that the princess who rescued Moses was Hatshepsut, the daughter of Thutmose I who lived about 200 years before Ramses II.

Hatshepsut was a strong woman who married her half-brother, Thutmose II. When Thutmose I died, his son Thutmose II took over as Pharaoh, but it was really the iron hand of Hatshepsut that ruled the land. Hatshepsut had no children, and there must have been bad feelings between the two, because Thutmose II wanted to make one of his sons, born to a woman from his harem, the next king of Egypt. If this happened, Hatshepsut's power would be stripped from her and her descendants. With no children of her own, Hatshepsut could have raised Moses to be the next Pharaoh as an act of revenge against her husband.

Later, Hatshepsut had another motive for raising Moses. After her husband, Thutmose II, died, she seized the throne and became ruler of Egypt for 22 years. With no children,

finding Moses would have seemed like a gift from the gods. She would have carefully raised Moses to become the next Pharaoh of Egypt.

When Was Moses Born?
Moses was born in Egypt approximately 300 years after the death of Joseph (1550-1500 B.C.). He led the Hebrews out of slavery about 400 years after Jacob and his family had first come to Egypt during the famine (Ex. 12:40). Forty years passed from the time Moses escaped from Egypt until the time he led his people from slavery toward the Promised Land.

Moses' Parents
The father of Moses was Amram, and his mother was Jochebed. They were also the parents of Aaron and Miriam. Amram was a Levite, an ancestor of the line of priests which began with Aaron.

When Pharaoh started killing Hebrew baby boys, Jochebed made a basket for Moses and hid him in the Nile River. When Pharaoh's daughter found Moses, Jochebed was given the job of caring for her son until he was old enough to live in the palace (Ex. 2:3-9).

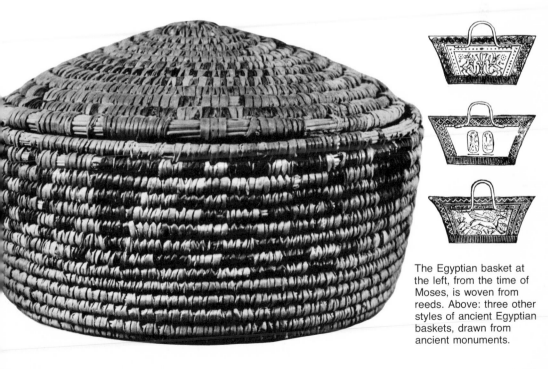

The Egyptian basket at the left, from the time of Moses, is woven from reeds. Above: three other styles of ancient Egyptian baskets, drawn from ancient monuments.

93

Moses Kills an Egyptian and Flees to Midian

EXODUS 2:11-20

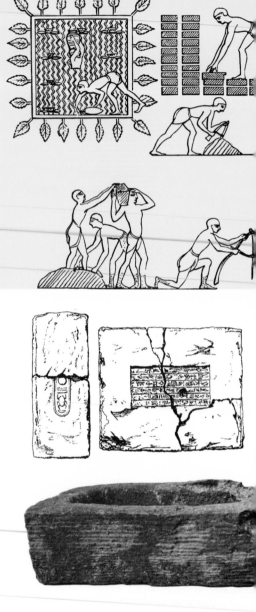

Synopsis

Almost 400 years after Joseph's time, a Pharaoh arose who did not care about the Hebrews, descendants of Joseph and his brothers. Pharaoh made slaves of them and forced them to work for him. Moses was born into one of these Hebrew slave families. One day his mother placed him in a basket and laid it in the Nile River. Pharaoh's daughter found the basket and claimed the baby for her own. Moses grew up as her son with all the benefits of the best of Egypt. But when Moses was grown, he saw an Egyptian taskmaster beating a Hebrew. In anger, he killed the Egyptian, and was forced to flee. He escaped to Midian.

The Storage Cities of Egypt

Each year the Pharaoh of Egypt collected a tax from the people in the form of grain, animals, or other produce. These taxes were collected to provide for the king and his government. During years of a large harvest, taxes were also collected to prepare the country for a "lean" year, or famine.

A place was needed to store all this food, so large cities were built for this purpose. Workmen were necessary, and the Hebrews were forced into slavery to construct great store-cities such as Pithom and Ramses. These two cities were located in the delta of the Nile River, in or near the land of Goshen.

Building these cities was backbreaking work, and none of the Egyptians wanted the job. As slaves, the Hebrews worked hard, provided cheap labor, and were no longer a threat to the Egyptian people. It is easy to see why Pharaoh did not want to let them leave Egypt.

The Land of Midian

After Moses knew that his life was in danger, he escaped from Egypt and fled across the desert to the land of Midian. This region was about 200 miles southeast of Egypt and probably north and east of the Gulf of Aqaba, an arm of water extending northeast from the Red Sea.

After Abraham's wife Sarah died, he married a woman named Keturah. They had a

The famous brickmaking scene above was drawn from an Egyptian monument of about the time of Moses. It shows the various steps of making bricks while task-masters watch over the slaves who do it. Below it are two inscribed bricks, the left from ancient Egypt, the right from Babylon. Immediately above is a brick mold of ancient Egypt, into which the clay mixture was poured and molded.

94

son called Midian, who became the ancestor of the Midianites.

Moses escaped to the land of Midian and was taken in by Jethro, the priest of Midian. There he married Zipporah, one of Jethro's daughters (Ex. 2:15-22). But despite Jethro's kindness, the Midianites and the Israelites became hostile enemies.

Jethro

Jethro was Moses' father-in-law, and the "priest of Midian." His duties as a priest are not certain, but he probably served the different tribes in the area of Midian as a religious leader and a judge.

Jethro was also called Reuel (Ex. 2:18). This name might have been given him by a Midianite tribe.

When Jethro learned that Moses had protected his daughters from a band of evil shepherds, he invited Moses to stay and live with him. Moses stayed, and married Jethro's daughter, Zipporah. They lived in the land of Midian for the next 40 years. After Moses had brought the Hebrews out of Egypt, Jethro visited him in the wilderness, and helped set up Israel's first judicial system (Ex. 18:14-27).

An Egyptian Settles with Shepherds

Born in Egypt, Moses was raised as a prince in the palace of Pharaoh. Here he was fully trained in the skills and customs of the land.

Though Moses was a Hebrew, he was raised as an Egyptian, and would have been taught that Hebrews were a crude and backward people, and that shepherding was a degrading occupation. What a humbling experience then for Moses, a prince of Egypt, to settle in the land of Midian, where he took a job tending sheep. Later he led the Hebrews, people he had been taught to despise, out of Egypt, his homeland.

Bricks in ancient Egypt and Babylon were stamped or inscribed with the name of the Pharaoh. Likewise, clay jars were also stamped (sealed) to show that the contents were as indicated. The clay stamp below is Hebrew; it sealed jars of wine to verify their contents. Brick stamps were similar to this.

The bricks below have been stamped with the symbol for Thutmose III, possibly the Pharaoh during Israel's enslavement in Egypt (1490-1445 B.C.). Israelite slaves of Moses' time may have made and stamped these bricks. At the right: the map shows Moses' journey from Egypt to Midian.

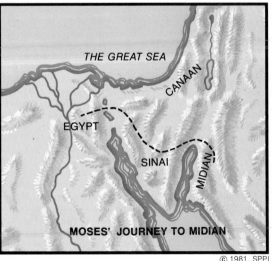

THE GREAT SEA

CANAAN

EGYPT

SINAI

MIDIAN

MOSES' JOURNEY TO MIDIAN

© 1981, SPPI

95

Zipporah was a shepherdess much like the girl at the left and the one above. Her harsh lifestyle was much different from that of the lovely ladies of Egypt.

Moses Marries Zipporah

EXODUS 2:21-25

Synopsis

Moses was born as a son of Hebrew slaves. But, to escape Pharaoh's soldiers, his mother placed him in a basket and laid it in the Nile River. Pharaoh's daughter found him and adopted him as her own. Moses grew up as her son, enjoying all the riches and good education Egypt could offer. Then one day he killed an Egyptian who was beating a Hebrew slave. Moses was forced to run away. At Midian he met and married Zipporah, a shepherdess. He became a shepherd, caring for the flocks of his father-in-law Jethro.

Zipporah

Moses lived in the land of Egypt 40 years, but he did not marry. When he escaped to Midian he met Jethro, a man who had seven daughters. In the Bible, no sons of Jethro are mentioned, so he might have been eager to take Moses into his home as an adopted son, making him the heir to the family birthright.

Zipporah was one of Jethro's seven daughters. When Moses settled in Midian, he married her (Ex. 2:21). She had two sons, Gershom and Eliezer (Ex. 2:22; 18:3-4). She traveled to Egypt with Moses when he returned to free the Hebrews. Along the way, she circumcised

96

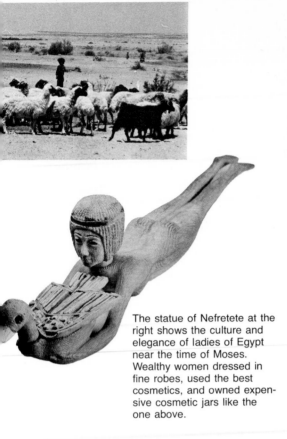

The statue of Nefretete at the right shows the culture and elegance of ladies of Egypt near the time of Moses. Wealthy women dressed in fine robes, used the best cosmetics, and owned expensive cosmetic jars like the one above.

her son, Gershom, because of God's anger at Moses for not doing so (Ex. 4:24-26). Later she returned to her father in Midian, and then rejoined Moses in the wilderness.

Moses' 40-Year Periods

Moses' life is divided into three 40-year periods. The first stretches from his birth in Egypt until his escape to Midian (Acts 7:23-29). During that time Moses was a prince of Egypt, highly trained in language, art, military, and other skills.

Moses' second 40 years begins on his arrival in Midian. During those years he lived in this country, where he tended Jethro's flocks, married Zipporah, had two sons, and met God on Mount Sinai.

After 40 years in Midian, God told Moses to return to Egypt and free His people from slavery. After Pharaoh finally released the Hebrews, they spent 40 years in the desert.

Shepherds Who Wander Far from Home

Midian was probably located east and north of the Gulf of Aqaba, a northern arm of the Red Sea. Mount Sinai was west of this same gulf near its southern end. So how could Moses, while living in Midian, talk to God on Mount Sinai, so far from home?

In ancient times, shepherds commonly traveled for weeks or months at a time looking for good pastureland. Joseph's brothers did this years earlier (Gen. 37:12).

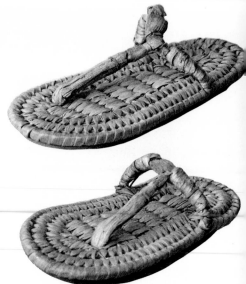

As Moses listened to God speak from the burning bush (left), he removed his sandals, as God commanded, for this was holy ground. The Egyptian sandals above are woven from papyrus, palm leaves, and grass and are from the time of Moses.

The Burning Bush

EXODUS 3:1—4:17

Synopsis

Born in a Hebrew slave household, Moses was condemned to die with all other Hebrew baby boys. But his mother hid him in a basket in the Nile River, where Pharaoh's daughter found him and adopted him. Moses grew up as a prince in Egypt until the day when he killed an Egyptian taskmaster for beating a Hebrew slave. Afraid, Moses ran away to Midian, where he married Zipporah, daughter of a shepherd and priest, Jethro. Moses then became a shepherd and cared for Jethro's flocks. One day he noticed a strange sight—a bush that burned but did not burn up.

Mount Sinai

As a shepherd, Moses wandered through the wilderness looking for good pasture in and around the land of Midian. While searching for a good grazing area for his flocks, he came to Mount Sinai, or Mount Horeb as it is sometimes called. Here God met him by a burning bush, telling him to return to Egypt to free the Hebrew slaves.

Mount Sinai was probably not in the land of Midian. Many shepherds traveled for weeks into the wilderness looking for good pastureland for their flocks and herds. Moses must have been doing this when he came to Mount Sinai.

Though the exact mountain that was called Sinai is not known for certain, tradition says that it is a mountain known today as Jebel Musa (Mountain of Moses). This mountain lies in the southern tip of the Sinai Peninsula, located just north of the Red Sea, between the Gulf of Suez and the Gulf of Aqaba.

The mountain is barren, rugged, and steep, and lies in the midst of other stark and difficult terrain. By the slopes of Jebel Musa a monastery called St. Catherine's was built at the traditional site of the burning bush. From there, a good climber can reach the top of the mountain in an hour and a half.

After the Hebrews left Egypt, they camped

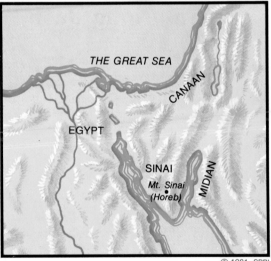

By the slope of Mount Sinai is the Monastery of St. Catherine's (above). A bush grows in one courtyard (right), and is pointed out as "the burning bush," supposedly the type of plant which Moses saw burning.

at Mount Sinai (Ex. 19:1-2, 18). Moses climbed up the mountain to receive the Ten Commandments from God (Ex. 19:20). Centuries later, Elijah visited Mount Sinai and there God encouraged him (1 Kings 19:8-18).

Sandals

In Old Testament times, sandals were often considered a luxury, for most people went barefoot, especially the poor. But when traveling long distances, or for walking over rocky terrain, sandals were helpful.

Egyptian sandals were made of reeds, papyrus, or leather. Other sandals had wood or leather soles, with leather thongs wrapped around the feet and ankles to keep the sandals in place.

Today, when men enter a house or place of worship, they remove their hats. In Bible times, they removed their sandals. In a place of worship, it was a sign of respect. Roads were hot and dusty, so removing a guest's dirty sandals and washing his feet was a way that a host made the guest to feel welcome.

© 1981, SPPI

The location of Mount Sinai, as it relates to Egypt and Midian, may be seen on the above map.

99

Above top: Rameses II, who may have been the Pharaoh who oppressed the Hebrews when Moses was young. Above bottom: Merneptah, who may have been the Pharaoh of the Exodus.

The Plagues

EXODUS 4:18—10:29

Synopsis
Many years before Moses' time Joseph had been sold as a slave and taken to Egypt. There he became governor and saved the land from famine. But many years passed and new Pharaohs came to Egypt. One did not know about Joseph and made the Hebrew people slaves. One boy born as a slave was Moses, whom Pharaoh's daughter adopted and raised as a prince. But Moses killed an Egyptian taskmaster and fled to Midian, where he married a shepherdess named Zipporah. For the next 40 years Moses lived in Midian as a shepherd until the Lord spoke to him from a burning bush and ordered him to return to Egypt and lead His people from their slavery. Moses reluctantly returned. Through him the Lord worked 10 mighty miracles, 10 plagues on the land of Egypt.

Bricks for the Egyptians
One of the primary jobs for the Hebrew slaves was making bricks for the construction of buildings, store-cities, and monuments. These bricks were made of clay mixed with water and sometimes straw.

Egyptian bricks were usually 14-20 inches long, 6-9 inches wide, and 4-7 inches thick. Often they were stamped with a seal which had the name of the reigning Pharaoh.

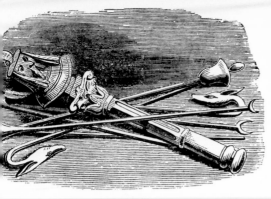

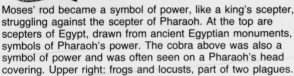

Moses' rod became a symbol of power, like a king's scepter, struggling against the scepter of Pharaoh. At the top are scepters of Egypt, drawn from ancient Egyptian monuments, symbols of Pharaoh's power. The cobra above was also a symbol of power and was often seen on a Pharaoh's head covering. Upper right: frogs and locusts, part of two plagues.

The Nile River—Lifeline of Egypt

In a great freshwater lake called Victoria, the Nile River begins its 3,000-mile journey northward to the land of Egypt. Until recently, the Egyptians had no idea where the Nile River came from. All they knew was that their lives depended on it, and that every year it kept flowing, emptying itself into the Mediterranean Sea.

In summer, the land of Egypt gets no rain, and throughout the entire winter rain may fall only three or four times. The Nile River provides the main source of water for Egypt. Almost everyone in the country lives near the river, for the lands farther east and west are barren wastelands and deserts where life is impossible.

Each year the Nile overflows its banks, leaving a rich layer of silt. When the river recedes, farmers quickly do their planting, and a good harvest is assured. The river is so much a part of everyone's life, that for centuries people worshiped it as a god, always grateful for the prosperity it brought.

The God of Moses against the Egyptian Gods

In Egypt, the people worshiped many different gods and goddesses. Each resembled an animal, an object, or a part of nature. God sent most of His plagues to show the Egyptians that He was more powerful than their lifeless gods.

God's plague of frogs proved to the Egyptian people that He was far greater than the frog itself, which was thought to be a god in Egypt. Egyptians also worshiped a cattle-god, and when God's plague struck these animals with disease, He showed His great power once again. God's plague of darkness proved that as the Creator of sunlight He was more powerful than the Egyptian sun-god, Amon-Ra.

Above: some of the gods of Egypt subdued by the plagues, from top to bottom—Hapi, god of the Nile; Hathor, cow goddess; another cow deity, the cow of Isis; Amon-Ra or Ra, gods of the sun.

101

The four royal Egyptians above may have figured in the life of Moses and the Hebrews in bondage: Rameses II, 1299-1232 B.C. (left), may have been the Pharaoh who oppressed the Hebrews; Amenhotep II, 1445-1425 B.C. (top), may have been Pharaoh during the enslavement of the Hebrews; Thutmose III, 1490-1445 B.C. (bottom center), may have been another Pharaoh during the enslavement of the Hebrews; and Hatshepsut, 1570-1490 B.C. (right), may have been the princess who drew Moses from the water.

The Passover

EXODUS 11:1—12:50

Synopsis

Moses was born into the home of Hebrew slaves in Egypt, but when Pharaoh's daughter found him in a basket in the Nile River, she adopted him and raised him as a prince. One day Moses killed an Egyptian taskmaster who was beating a Hebrew slave, and had to flee. At Midian he met and married Zipporah and worked as a shepherd for his father-in-law. Later the Lord called Moses to return to Egypt. Through Moses, the Lord sent 10 plagues. The last, the death of all firstborn sons, convinced Pharaoh to free the Hebrews. That night, when the angel of death went through Egypt, it passed over the Hebrews' firstborn sons. That first Passover is still celebrated.

When

Hebrew culture was loathesome to the Egyptians. So how did Joseph, a Hebrew, come to be governor of Egypt? Who would have permitted this?

From approximately 1800-1600 B.C., Hyksos invaders occupied Egypt, and Asian Pharaohs sat on the throne. These leaders did not possess the Egyptian blood and culture. Being foreigners themselves, they probably saw nothing wrong with a wise Hebrew ruling as governor. It is almost certain that Joseph ruled sometime during this period.

Moses was born about 300 years after Joseph's death. Eighty years after Moses' birth, he led the Hebrews out of Egypt. The Exodus probably occurred between 1500 and 1400 B.C., or according to another popular theory, between 1300 and 1200 B.C.

Which Pharaoh?

Who was the Pharaoh who oppressed the

102

Hebrews at the time of Moses' birth, and who was his successor who finally let the slaves go free after watching his country groan under God's plagues? No one knows for sure, but there are two popular theories.

The "early" theory claims that Moses' birth and the Exodus occurred between 1500 and 1400 B.C. According to this, Thutmose III was the Pharaoh at Moses' birth, and his successor, Amenhotep II was Pharaoh of the Exodus.

The "late" theory puts the Exodus somewhere around 1300-1200 B.C. It says that Rameses II, a wicked and brutal Pharaoh, oppressed the Hebrews, and that Merneptah, the weak ruler who succeeded him, let the people leave.

The Passover—When It Began

The Passover was instituted on the same night that God's angel of death moved across the land of Egypt killing all Egyptian firstborn sons. But death did not enter any Hebrew home that had followed God's instructions.

The Passover—What It Is

In the spring of every year, the Passover is still celebrated. This special day is set aside to remember the Israelites' freedom from slavery in Egypt. Over the centuries the Passover has changed, but still involves a time of festivity and a ritual meal.

The Ritual of the Passover

In the first month of the Jewish year, on the night of the full moon, the Passover begins. In Moses' day it lasted for just 24 hours.

Shortly after sunset, a lamb was killed by the father or head of the household. Its blood was sprinkled on the doorpost of the house. The lamb was then roasted and eaten along with unleavened bread and bitter herbs, symbolizing the bitterness of slavery in Egypt.

The family was to eat quickly, as the Israelites did that night before they left Egypt. Traveling clothes were worn.

To give meaning to the ritual, the youngest son asked his father about the Passover. The story of the Israelites in Egypt was then told.

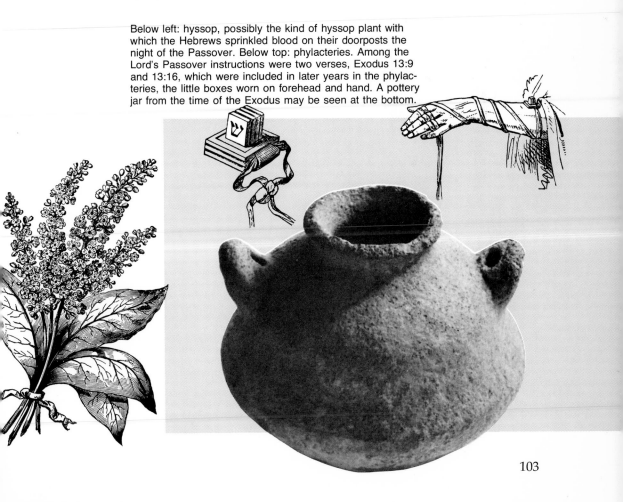

Below left: hyssop, possibly the kind of hyssop plant with which the Hebrews sprinkled blood on their doorposts the night of the Passover. Below top: phylacteries. Among the Lord's Passover instructions were two verses, Exodus 13:9 and 13:16, which were included in later years in the phylacteries, the little boxes worn on forehead and hand. A pottery jar from the time of the Exodus may be seen at the bottom.

Above: the Exodus from Egypt. Above right: ancient Egyptian women with their finery and wigs. Egyptian women gave the Hebrew women their jewels, mirrors, and treasures to encourage them to leave Egypt.

The Exodus

EXODUS 12:51—13:16

Synopsis

Though Moses was born as a Hebrew slave, he was adopted by Pharaoh's daughter and raised as an Egyptian prince. But because he killed an Egyptian taskmaster who was beating a Hebrew slave, he had to flee. For 40 years he worked as a shepherd in Midian, until the Lord spoke to him from a burning bush and sent him back to Egypt to lead His people from slavery. Through Moses, the Lord sent 10 plagues, including the last, the death of firstborn sons. But the angel of the Lord, who brought death throughout Egypt, passed over the Hebrew firstborn. This was the first Passover. After that, the Egyptians were anxious for their Hebrew slaves to go.

The Jewish Calendar

To celebrate the Exodus, the Israelites began their year with the Passover month (Ex. 12:2; 13:4). Canaanites called this month "Abib," and Babylonians named it "Nisan." The following months of the Jewish religious calen-

dar, beginning with the first, correspond to the months of our calendar. Tishri marks the beginning of the Jewish civic calendar.

Nisan (Abib)	March—April
Iyyar (Ziv)	April—May
Sivan	May—June
Tammuz	June—July
Ab	July—August
Elul	August—September
Tishri (Ethanim)	September—October
Heshvan	October—November
Kislev (Chislev)	November—December
Tebeth	December—January
Shebat	January—February
Adar	February—March

Unleavened Bread

During the Passover feast, the Israelites were forbidden to eat any bread that contained leaven, or yeast (Ex. 12:19-20). Without yeast, their bread did not rise. When baked, it was much flatter than the loaves of bread found in grocery stores today.

There were two varieties of unleavened bread. One kind was crispy and very flat, like a cracker. The other type resembled date or nut bread, thick and heavy.

104

The Feast of Unleavened Bread

Originally the Feast of Unleavened Bread began the day after the Passover, and lasted seven days. The unleavened bread symbolized Israel's haste to leave the land of Egypt. When leaven was added to the dough it sometimes took hours for the dough to rise before it could be baked. The night before the Exodus, the Hebrews did not have time to wait for the rising dough, so God commanded them to leave the next day with unleavened bread.

Like the Passover, the Feast of Unleavened Bread celebrated the Israelites' escape from Egypt and their freedom from slavery. Over time, the Passover and the Feast of Unleavened Bread gradually joined together until they became one feast, which lasted seven or eight days. Today the Passover is called a "seder" and the unleavened bread is "matzos."

Slaves—Egypt's Loss and Israel's Gain

Overnight, the Egyptians lost the services of about 600,000 men, and probably a million women and children (Ex. 12:37). These people were all slaves, responsible for the functioning of Egypt. In Egypt, the Israelites had probably learned construction, brickmaking, weaving, farming, music, metalworking, leather-making, and glass blowing.

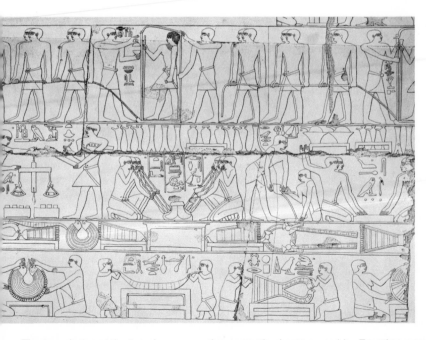

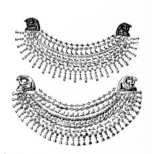

The two photos at the top show expensive cosmetic chests owned by Egyptian women of about Moses' time. Note the polished bronze mirrors in each photo. Later, the women of Israel would donate these mirrors to make a laver for the tabernacle. Some of the jewelry the Egyptian women gave the Hebrews may have been like that at the right. Jewelry-making is shown above.

105

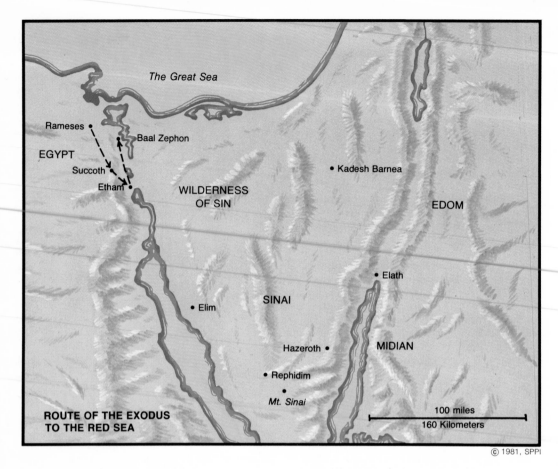

Map labels:
The Great Sea
Rameses
Baal Zephon
EGYPT
Succoth
Etham
WILDERNESS OF SIN
Kadesh Barnea
EDOM
Elath
Elim
SINAI
Hazeroth
MIDIAN
Rephidim
Mt. Sinai
100 miles
160 Kilometers
ROUTE OF THE EXODUS TO THE RED SEA

The Pillars of Cloud and Fire

EXODUS 13:17-22

Synopsis
When the Lord spoke to Moses in a burning bush, He sent Moses back to Egypt to free His people, the Hebrews. Through Moses, the Lord sent 10 plagues. The last, the death of the firstborn, caused the Egyptians to anxiously rush the Hebrews from their land. The Exodus began, with the Hebrew slaves leaving Egypt for the Promised Land. But who would lead them and how would they find their way? The answer became clear—the Lord would lead them with a pillar of cloud by day and a pillar of fire by night.

The Wilderness
The Israelites were leaving the lush Nile Delta region of Egypt, and heading for Canaan, another beautiful area which God said flowed with milk and honey (Ex. 3:17). But between these fertile areas lay a vast desert with little water and almost no trees.

Nomads lived in the desert, wandering from place to place searching for food and water for their flocks. In years of severe famine, many of these nomads grouped into bands and raided the small villages lying on the edge of the wilderness. Providing for their families' survival led them to a life of thievery.

When the Hebrews crossed this great desert, they had to deal with these nomadic tribes, as well as desert outlaws, lack of water, sparse vegetation, and serpents and wild animals. It was a frustrating experience, and a lesson in trusting God's guidance.

In a few places small springs of water rise to the surface of the desert, and give enough moisture for plants and trees to grow. Such a green island is called an oasis, a most welcome sight to a weary traveler.

106

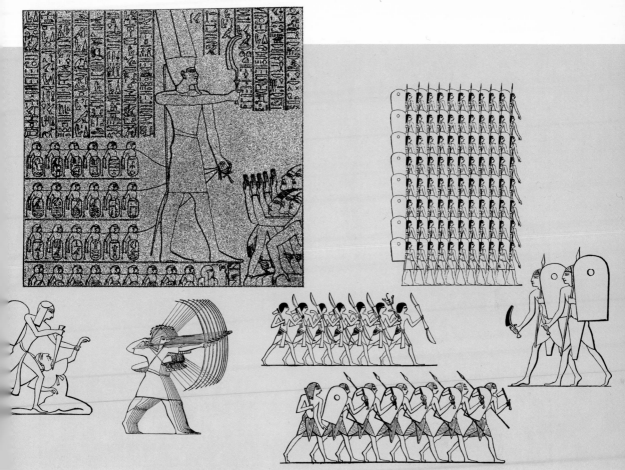

On the map the route of the Exodus may be traced from Rameses to Succoth to Etham and then to Baal Zephon. Above, top left: an ancient Egyptian drawing of Pharaoh taking Jews captive. Various scenes of Egyptian soldiers and combat may be seen above: top right a phalanx of infantry; center from left to right: Egyptian swordsmen, soldiers with axes and bows, spearmen; bottom, left to right: Egyptian archers, spearmen.

The Wealth of an Ancient Pharaoh

The Pharaoh of the Exodus lost all of his Hebrew slaves, but he was still one of the richest men in all the world. The life of an ancient Pharaoh was filled with the finest of everything the world had to offer.

The reason for a Pharaoh's riches lay in the position of Egypt as one of the wealthiest and most powerful nations of civilization in the days of Abraham and Moses. Some Pharaohs not only owned their entire country, but all of the people and animals as well.

Gold, silver, and alabaster were common items to an Egyptian ruler. In fact, they were so plentiful that one visiting king once exclaimed that there was as much gold in the land of Egypt as dust.

But a Pharaoh's wealth included much more. Hundreds of slaves attended to him. There were even slaves who dressed and fed him. The finest horses and chariots were his, along with private ships and river barges.

When a Pharaoh died, many of his personal belongings, worth millions of dollars, were buried with him in a magnificent tomb or pyramid. But the next Pharaoh of Egypt had no worries, for he still had more wealth and riches than he could count.

What the Israelites Left in Egypt

As slaves and laborers for Egypt, the Hebrews received no wages for their hard work. But the Egyptian government had the huge task of feeding all of its slaves. When the Hebrews escaped Egypt, they left behind the fertile land, the life-giving water of the Nile River, and a surplus of food and bread (Ex. 16:3).

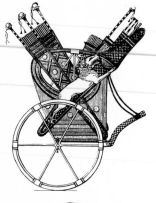

While Pharaoh led his chariot force against the people of Israel, Moses held out his rod to part the Red Sea (above). At the upper left: two Egyptian chariots of Old Testament times. Left: a chariot horse.

Crossing the Red Sea

EXODUS 14

Synopsis

Through Moses, the Lord sent 10 plagues to show the Egyptian king, Pharaoh, that He was mightier than all Egyptian gods, and that Pharaoh should obey Him and set His people free. The last plague, death of the firstborn sons, hit all Egyptians, from Pharaoh's palace to the humblest home. After that Pharaoh and his people were anxious to get rid of the Hebrews. The Exodus began, with the Lord leading His people with a pillar of cloud by day and a pillar of fire by night. But trouble came when the Hebrews were caught between Pharaoh's pursuing chariots and the Red Sea. Only a mighty miracle could save these people from certain death. Would the Lord send one?

Where Did the Israelites Cross?

The Red Sea is a great body of water that stretches north-south for nearly 1,200 miles. At its northern tip the sea divides into two arms, the Gulf of Aqaba which extends northeast, and the Gulf of Suez, which reaches to the northwest. Between these two arms of water lies the Sinai Peninsula.

Even farther north, the Gulf of Suez empties into the Bitter Lakes. The Great Bitter Lake is separated from the Little Bitter Lake by shallow straits of water. Continuing north is another lake called Ballah, about 30-40 miles south of the Mediterranean Sea.

Most believe the Israelites did not cross the Red Sea itself, but one of the bodies of water just to the north. Some of these lakes actually dry up at certain times of the year, making it possible to walk across them. However, the Bible clearly says that the waters parted as a miracle from God.

108

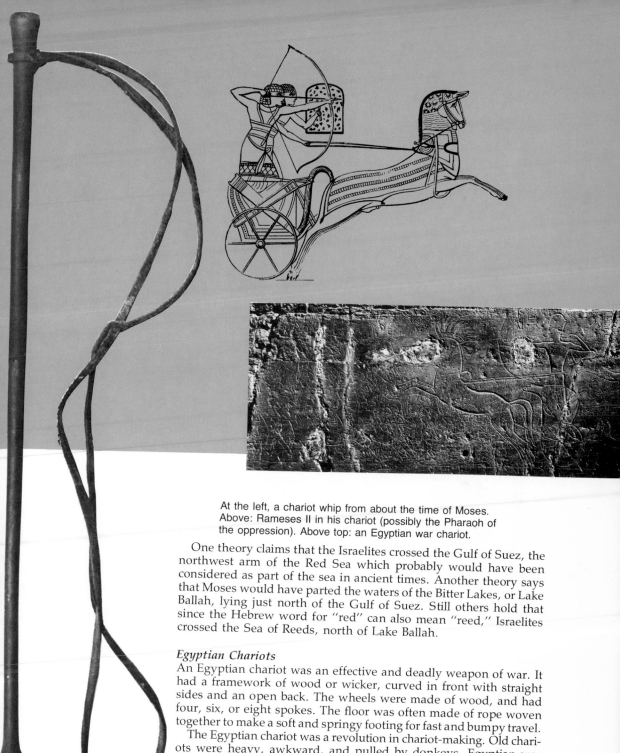

At the left, a chariot whip from about the time of Moses. Above: Rameses II in his chariot (possibly the Pharaoh of the oppression). Above top: an Egyptian war chariot.

One theory claims that the Israelites crossed the Gulf of Suez, the northwest arm of the Red Sea which probably would have been considered as part of the sea in ancient times. Another theory says that Moses would have parted the waters of the Bitter Lakes, or Lake Ballah, lying just north of the Gulf of Suez. Still others hold that since the Hebrew word for "red" can also mean "reed," Israelites crossed the Sea of Reeds, north of Lake Ballah.

Egyptian Chariots

An Egyptian chariot was an effective and deadly weapon of war. It had a framework of wood or wicker, curved in front with straight sides and an open back. The wheels were made of wood, and had four, six, or eight spokes. The floor was often made of rope woven together to make a soft and springy footing for fast and bumpy travel.

The Egyptian chariot was a revolution in chariot-making. Old chariots were heavy, awkward, and pulled by donkeys. Egyptian war chariots were made as light as possible, had lower bodies for better stability, and were pulled by swift horses.

Two people, a driver and a warrior, rode in a chariot. Attached to the wheels were long knives that cut up foot soldiers as the chariot sped along. In flat open spaces, it was a deadly weapon, but in hilly regions, the chariot was useless.

Food in the Wilderness

EXODUS 15—16

Synopsis

Through Moses, the Lord sent 10 plagues to convince Pharaoh to free His people. After the 10th plague, the death of the firstborn, Pharaoh and his people were anxious for the Hebrews to leave. The Exodus began, with the people leaving for the Promised Land. The Lord sent a pillar of cloud by day and a pillar of fire by night before them, to lead them through the wilderness. He parted the sea to let them cross safely on dry ground. And on the other side, He proved that He could give them food and water to fill their needs.

When the Lord sent manna in the wilderness, it was compared to coriander seed. The coriander plant is the top picture above. The bottom picture is of quail, the meat which God gave.

110

Foods of Egypt the Israelites Desired

Though the Lord provided manna in the wilderness, the people of Israel desired some of the foods which they had enjoyed in Egypt. Some of these foods are pictured at the left, as drawn from ancient Egyptian monuments. From left to right: Egyptians trap fowl with a net, which would be used for meat; cucumbers grow on a vine; melons, which the Israelites mentioned.

Manna

The Israelites were familiar with the good foods of Egypt—the fish, meat, melons, and a variety of vegetables. But soon they found themselves in a desolate wilderness, hot and thirsty, with no food and little water.

But God did not forget the grumbling Hebrews. He provided yet another miracle for His people. It was a food called manna. The manna looked like a gum or resin, and resembled a coriander seed, which was a pearl-shaped seed that grew throughout Palestine.

The manna must have been similar to bread (Ex. 16:12), and tasted like wafers mixed with honey (Ex. 16:31). Each morning, except on the Sabbath, when the dew evaporated, fine flakes of manna covered the ground (Ex. 16:14).

During their 40 years in the wilderness, the Israelites received manna six days a week. They added variety by boiling it, grinding it, and making cakes of it.

Oasis

For those who have been sailing across an ocean that seems endless, a small tropical island appearing at the horizon is a cause for celebration. Here is a place of rest, to escape the bright sun and hot winds.

The Israelites felt the same way when they spotted an oasis in the hot and barren desert. Springs of water reached to the surface of the sand, and around them grew date palms and other vegetation. Some oases were small, providing only enough water for a brief stop. Others were very large, like Kadesh Barnea, where the Israelites camped for months.

Measures—Omer and Ephah

When God sent manna, the Israelites were allowed to collect only one omer each per day (Ex. 16:16), which was slightly more than two quarts. An omer was one tenth of an ephah (16:36), about two thirds of a bushel.

Fish were important in the Egyptian diet. There were no fish in the wilderness and the Israelites longed for them.

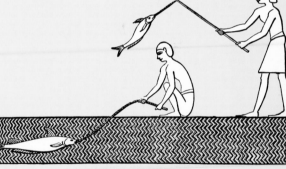

The ever-popular fishing with hook and line was used in ancient Egypt as well as in modern times.

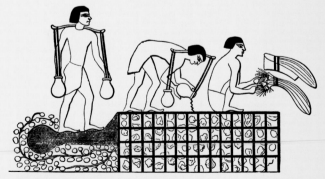

The Israelites longed for onions. Above: Egyptians water a garden and tie their onions.

111

Water from the Rock

EXODUS 17:1-7

Synopsis
God sent 10 mighty miracles to prove to Pharaoh that He is God, and that the king of Egypt should free the Hebrew slaves. At last Pharaoh realized this and the people left Egypt for the Promised Land. At the Red Sea, God sent another miracle, parting the waters of the sea for the Hebrews to cross, but drowning Pharaoh's cavalry and chariots. God sent a pillar of cloud by day and a pillar of fire by night to guide His people through the wilderness. When the Hebrews got hungry, He sent manna to feed them. When they grew thirsty, He gave them water, even from a rock! Once more God's rod in the hand of Moses proved that God was with His people and would not fail them.

The Grumblings of Israel
God performed many mighty miracles in the sight of all the Israelites. But despite these wonders, the people largely remained a group of grumblers and complainers.

Many years of brutal slavery had just ended, thanks to God's miracles of the 10 plagues. But no sooner had the Israelites left Egypt, than they started complaining.

Pharaoh and his army were bearing down on the Israelites who were trapped by mountains and the Red Sea. Since Moses had arrived in Egypt the Israelites had seen God's great miracles and listened to His promises to bring them to their own land. But instead of trusting God, they turned on Moses, bitterly complaining that the Egyptians would soon kill them (Ex. 14:11-12). But God was patient with His people and parted the Red Sea, again proving His guidance.

Soon after, the people grumbled about bitter water at Marah. Once again God provided them with a miracle (Ex. 15:22-25).

Arriving at Rephidim, the Israelites complained that there was no water, not trusting in God's promises (Ex. 17:1-7).

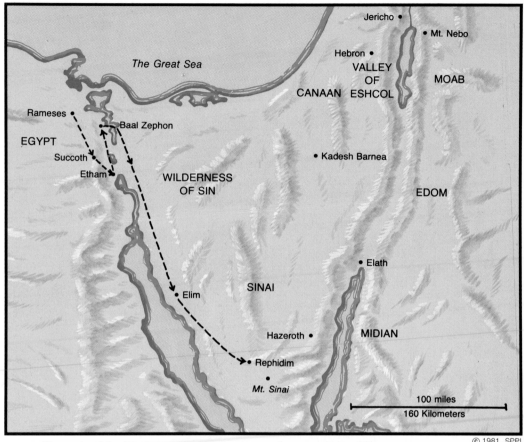

The route of the Exodus so far may be seen on the map above. After the Israelites crossed the Red Sea, supposedly at the point shown, they headed south to Elim and then to Rephidim.

When Moses spent 40 days on Mount Sinai talking with God, the people thought he was dead, and molded a golden calf to worship. For this they were severely punished (Ex. 32).

Forgetting their hopeless life in Egypt, the Israelites again complained about their surroundings. This time God punished them with a plague of fire (Num. 11:1).

Grumbling continued over lack of meat. God sent flocks of quail, but He also sent a plague (Num. 11:4-33).

Most of the spies sent into the Promised Land brought back a fearful report of giants and walled cities. They forgot that their God had just humbled the mightiest nation in the world. Even the sea obeyed His command.

After seeing miracle upon miracle, and being punished time and again, one would think the Israelites would have learned to trust God. But they grumbled and complained many more times (see Num. 16:1-3; 21:4-9). Despite God's promises, this disobedience and complaining persisted until centuries later God allowed His people to be utterly defeated and carried off once again into lives of slavery.

Rephidim

Today it is probably called Wadi Feiran, or Wadi Rufaid, but in Moses' day it was called Rephidim. The exact location is unknown, but most think this oasis was in the southern part of the Sinai Peninsula. Here Moses got water from a rock (Ex. 17:6), fought a battle against Amalek (Ex. 17:8-16), and received advice from his father-in-law Jethro (Ex. 18). It must have been a large oasis, for the people of Israel camped here for a while.

113

On Mount Sinai, God wrote with His finger the Ten Commandments on tablets of stone. Moses descended from the mountain with these stone tablets, which he broke in anger when he saw the Israelites worshiping a golden calf. Later the stone tablets were replaced and were carried for many years in the ark of the covenant.

The Ten Commandments

EXODUS 20

Synopsis

With a mighty show of miracles, God persuaded Pharaoh to free His people, the Hebrews. With another mighty miracle, He helped them cross the Red Sea on dry land. With a pillar of cloud by day and a pillar of fire by night He led them in the wilderness, and with more miracles He fed them and gave them water. Now, they had arrived at Mount Sinai. He would perform another mighty work through Moses, sending Laws for His people to obey. With His own finger, God wrote the Ten Commandments and gave them to His people. These, and His other laws, would be guides to His people for generations to come.

God's Ten Commandments

Moses spent much time on Mount Sinai talking with God. Up on the mountain, God wrote 10 basic Laws for the Israelites to follow and apply to their lives:

1. Nothing should be more important than God. He should be first in everyone's life.
2. Only God is to be worshiped, not idols. Making any kind of idol is forbidden.
3. Use God's name reverently, never foolishly. Taking God's name in vain (swearing) is wrong.
4. Remember God on the Sabbath and worship Him. Give Him special honor on this day.
5. Treat your parents with respect. Honor them with obedience and listen to their wisdom, for God chose them to be leaders

114

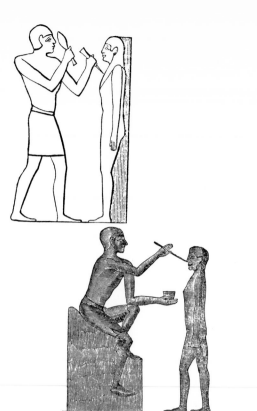

One of the Ten Commandments had to do with idols. Never were the Israelites to carve an idol. Above: at the top, an Egyptian is carving an idol, and below, one is painting it. Right: from St. Catherine's Monastery, one may see the traditional site of the Israelite campground near Mount Sinai.

of the family.

6. Never murder a person, for this is a terrible sin.
7. If you are married, commit yourself to each other. Do not become involved with someone else's husband or wife.
8. Do not steal from anyone.
9. Telling a lie is wrong. Speaking the truth brings trust and respect from others.
10. Don't desire things that other people have. Coveting breeds unhappiness and greed and is wrong in God's eyes.

Law Codes of Other Lands

While the Israelite law relied on the power and authority of God, law codes of other countries depended on the power of men.

In Egypt, Pharaoh was supreme ruler. His word was the law, and people worshiped him as a god. During this time, there were few written laws, so Pharaoh acted as a judge, using his opinions as the final verdict.

The Medes and Persians had a similar justice system. The king was thought to be divine and infallible. When a law was sealed with the king's signet ring, it was irreversible. Not even the king himself could revoke his laws, even if he later wanted to. This would contradict himself, which would embarrass a king who was supposed to be perfect. However, the king could make a new law, which neutralized the old one (Es. 3:13; 8:5, 11).

How did these ancient law codes develop? Thousands of years ago, the earliest nations had no system to stop the wrongs of society. People who were robbed or abused had nowhere to turn for help. Laws were written in an attempt to stop this widespread evil. The first law codes developed in Samaria, and were inscribed on clay tablets.

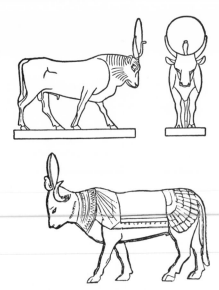

When the Israelites turned away from the Lord to worship a golden calf, they were doing what their former Egyptian neighbors had done many times before. The Apis bull figures above were among several cow and bull deities worshiped by the Egyptians.

The Golden Calf

EXODUS 32

Synopsis

After the people of Israel, the Hebrews, crossed the Red Sea, they went to Mount Sinai, where God gave His Law through Moses. There also God gave the plans for His house, the tabernacle. But while Moses was up on Mount Sinai, receiving the Law from God, the people of Israel were making a golden calf to worship.

The Bull—A Symbol of Worship

The bull has been worshiped throughout history as a symbol of strength, rich crops, and fertile harvests. Even today, in countries such as India, the bull is considered sacred, and is never killed.

In Bible times, the bull was set up as an important god in many countries. One of Egypt's most powerful gods was Hapi, the bull god of the Nile River. The Babylonians, Syrians, and Canaanites also worshiped bulls.

The Apis bull was another bull or calf highly revered by the Egyptians. This animal was very rare, and had several strange markings. A square mark on the forehead and a beetle-shaped marking on the tongue were its trademarks. All of Egypt celebrated when one of these bulls was found. It was killed, embalmed, and buried in a coffin of solid granite.

The Israelites lived in the midst of this bull worship for over 400 years. They must have felt afraid and insecure as they camped in the middle of an unknown wilderness, while their leader, Moses, was gone for so many days. Still unfamiliar with God's laws, bull worship was something they were familiar with, something which gave them comfort.

Some think the Israelites did not really worship the golden calf itself, but wanted something physical to represent God whom they could not see. But on Mount Sinai, God was forbidding graven images.

Metalworking

The golden calf was fashioned from the golden jewelry and utensils of the Hebrews (Ex. 32:2-4). But how was this done?

Some Hebrew slaves learned the art of metalworking while in Egypt. They must have

At the right is the traditional site where the Israelites set up the golden calf. Of course, no one can be sure, even though it is near the traditional Mount Sinai. The Israelites who molded the calf had learned metalworking in Egypt. In the Egyptian metalworking scenes below, the workers are melting metal with a bellows (top) and a blowpipe (center). At the bottom, workmen heat the metal (left) and pour it into molds (right).

helped Aaron make the golden calf. This bull, or calf, was probably made by first carving a wooden image of it. All of the gold was then melted and allowed to partially harden into flat sheets. These sheets were laid over the wooden bull, then molded and hammered to fit the shape of the wood.

Where Did the Jewelry Come From?

Where did the Hebrews, slaves of Egypt, get all of their gold jewelry? After God's 10th and final plague, the death of the firstborn, the Egyptian people hurried the Hebrew slaves out of Egypt. The Egyptians gave the Hebrews whatever personal belongings they asked for, in an effort to speed them out of the country (Ex. 12:35-36). The Israelites took anything they wanted, plundering the jewelry and vessels of gold and silver from Egypt. The golden calf was made from this gold, as were parts of the tabernacle and its furniture.

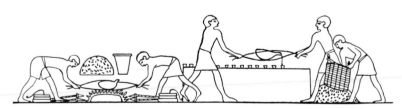

Egyptian mirrors, such as the one above, were melted to obtain the bronze for the tabernacle laver. Craftsmen who wove the fabric for the tabernacle learned their art in Egypt, as seen in the drawings at the right. In the painting above, the people are glad to give their valuables for the tabernacle.

The Tabernacle

EXODUS 35—36

Synopsis

While the people of Israel camped at Mount Sinai, the Lord God gave Moses His Law, which His people were to obey. But the people sinned, for at the very time Moses was on the mountain, receiving God's Law, they were making a golden calf below, to worship it instead of the Lord. Part of the Law which the Lord gave Moses involved a beautiful tent, called the tabernacle, which would be God's house in the wilderness and in the Promised Land for many years. The people remained at Mount Sinai until it was built.

The Tabernacle—Arrangement and Construction

Gifts of gold, silver, and bronze were used in making God's dwelling place. Fourteen raw materials were used to complete the tent of worship, including animal skins for the roof, insects for the colored dyes, acacia wood for the beams and carrying poles, and precious metals for its stunning appearance.

The Israelites journeyed from place to place in the wilderness, so the tabernacle was made easy to dismantle. Around the tabernacle was an outer court. Inside the tent itself were two rooms, the Holy Place where the priest entered each morning, and the Holy of Holies, which he entered only once each year.

Tabernacle Furniture

The table of showbread was on the north side of the Holy Place. Twelve loaves of bread were kept here at all times. The golden candlestick, or menorah, was on the south wall of the Holy Place. It lighted the room. The altar of incense was in the center of the Holy Place, just in front of the veil which separated the Holy Place from the Holy of Holies. Each morning Aaron burned incense on the altar. Inside the Holy of Holies was the ark of the covenant, which contained the Ten Commandments.

118

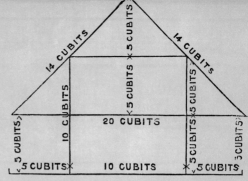

The four 19th-century drawings show: the outside view of the tabernacle (above), its dimensions (above right), the courtyard (right), and the arrangement of tribes around it (below).

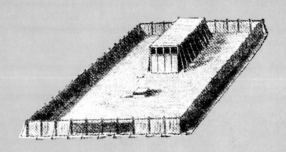

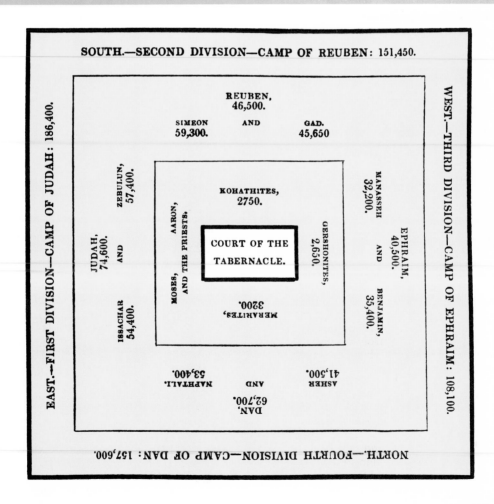

119

Priests and Offerings

EXODUS 39:1-31; LEVITICUS 1—9

Synopsis
While the people of Israel camped at Mount Sinai, the Lord gave His Law to Moses. This Law was to guide His people and their nation from that time on. God's instructions to Moses included plans for His tent-home and for a group of people, His priests, and for a system of offerings through which the people would worship Him.

The Priests
Only men who were descendants of Aaron, thus born into the tribe of Levi, were eligible to become priests. These men took care of the tabernacle and performed the daily sacrifices along with other services. The priests made a living by taking a share of the temple tax, and eating part of the meat of the daily sacrifices. The high priest wore a beautiful embroidered robe with a dark blue tunic and a breastpiece of precious jewels.

The Offerings
Man's sin destroyed his relationship with God. In Old Testament times, a man could once again come into good standing with God through an offering, or sacrifice. There were many different ways to offer a sacrifice. Often the priest made a sacrifice for the people.

Below: a high priest in full garb. Right: his breastpiece. Below it, the incense altar. Bottom center: a cluster of pomegranates, used as a pattern for the bottom decoration of the high priest's robe. Far right, top to bottom: ark of the covenant, table of showbread, altar of burnt offering, and the laver.

At the right is a photo of the traditional mountain thought to be Mount Sinai. No one is sure that this is the exact mountain, for there are four possible sites. This one is called Jebel Musa, the Mountain of Moses. By its base is St. Catherine's Monastery.

120

Twelve Spies

NUMBERS 13—14

Synopsis

From Mount Sinai, the people of Israel moved onward. Behind them lay the wilderness. To the north lay the Promised Land. To the east and south lay still more wilderness. The time had come to test their faith, to see if they were ready to enter the land of promise. But first they would send spies into the land to see what they faced.

Kadesh Barnea

Trudging wearily across the desert, the Israelites moved north toward the Promised Land, finally coming to an oasis with four springs, called Kadesh Barnea. Here the people camped for a long time.

Kadesh Barnea was south of the land of Canaan, the Promised Land, about 50 miles from Beersheba. Fifty miles to the west lay the Mediterranean Sea.

The Lord told Moses to send 12 spies into Canaan from Kadesh Barnea (Num. 13:2, 26). Ten of the spies returned afraid, and the peo-

ple lost hope. As punishment for refusing to accept God's guidance, the Israelites of that generation lived the rest of their lives in the wilderness, perhaps much of the time at Kadesh Barnea (Num. 14:26-38).

At Kadesh, the springs dried up. Moses disobeyed God in the way he provided water (Num. 20:1-13). Miriam and Aaron also died at this oasis (Num. 20:1, 22-29).

The Promised Land

God called it a land flowing with milk and honey (Ex. 3:8). Moses spent a third of his life trying to get there, but never made it. Joshua spent many years fighting for it. Where was this land and why was it so special?

The Promised Land was also called the land of Canaan. Later it became the nation Israel. It was the land that God chose to give to the descendants of Abraham, Isaac, and Jacob (Gen. 12:7).

Traveling from north to south, the country stretches from Dan to Beersheba (1 Sam. 3:20), a distance of about 150 miles. The nation is bordered on the west by the Mediterranean Sea and on the east by the Jordan River, a width that is close to 50 miles.

122

Canaan—A Promised Land of Plenty

When the spies returned from their mission in Canaan, they brought back a giant cluster of grapes. But this was only a small evidence of the riches of the Promised Land.

Thirty-eight years after the spies' return, the Hebrews were finally allowed to enter the land God had promised them. This was a land watered by the Jordan River and fed from the gentle rains that formed over the sea and moved inland. There fruits, vegetables, and grain grew in abundance.

After living in the wilderness for over 40 years, the people were filled with delight when they entered a land plentiful in cucumbers, dates, figs, walnuts, lentils, barley, onions, pomegranates, grapes, and olives.

Vineyards and olive groves were a familiar sight in this fertile country, along with valleys full of abundant harvests, rippling streams, and lush grass. After barren, windswept hills and a horizon of only sand and rocks, this land looked like a garden paradise.

Grapes

Grapes, also called wine grapes, were a common fruit in Bible times. The Bible mentions grapevines more than any other plant. The grape harvest usually begins in September. They were eaten raw, dried into raisins, and pressed into wine.

Left: when the spies returned from the Promised Land, they confirmed that it truly was a "land flowing with milk and honey." But they were afraid to trust the Lord to help them conquer it. At the time they were camped at Kadesh Barnea (upper left). From the Valley of Eshcol the spies brought enormous bunches of grapes. The exact location of this valley is not known, except that it was near Hebron, like the valley above, and was filled with vineyards.

The Bronze Serpent

NUMBERS 21:4-9

The Bible says the spies went through the Negev (some versions call it the way of the south) to investigate the Promised Land. The Negev (Negeb) was the desert region south of Judah (photo above). The map at the right shows the route of the Israelites thus far.

Synopsis

From Mount Sinai the people of Israel journeyed through the wilderness to Kadesh Barnea, where they sent 12 spies into the Promised Land. But 10 of the spies gave a negative report and the people were afraid to go into the land. So the Lord punished them for their lack of faith and sent them back into the wilderness. For the next 38 years, they would wander, unable to claim the land of promise until a new generation arose. Soon both Aaron and Miriam died. Later the people again complained against the Lord, who sent a plague of fiery serpents. Only the people who looked at a bronze serpent would live.

Serpents

The Egyptians and Hebrews had something in common—fear of snakes. From Egypt to Palestine there were a variety of these creatures. Most kinds were harmless, but a few struck quickly, with deadly venom.

As the Israelites trudged through the wilderness, they were most afraid of sand vipers and carpet vipers. The carpet viper is sometimes two feet long, and it often hides in the sand, attacking people without warning. At first the victim feels no pain, but already internal bleeding has started. After a day or two, the person actually feels better, but death soon comes. These carpet vipers might have been the serpents God sent to punish the Israelites for complaining (Num. 21:4-9).

The Egyptians had great respect for snakes. The cobra was their national symbol and worshiped as a goddess named Wadjet or Udjet. Most Pharaohs attached cobra figures to their headdresses.

The Negev

This barren desert land stretches south from the land of Canaan. At times during Israel's history, it was included within its borders. Most settlers in this mountainous area took jobs breeding and tending sheep. Later, a major trade route was carved through the region, opening commerce and increasing population.

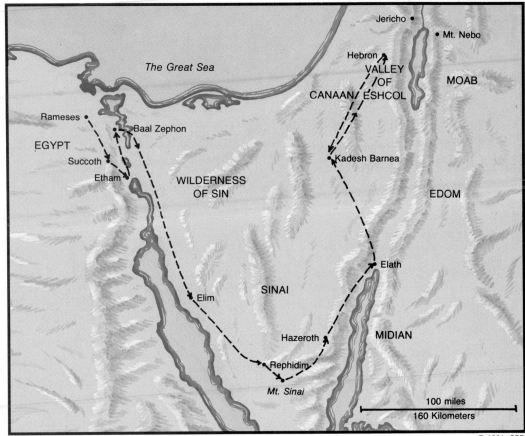

Jericho •

• Mt. Nebo

The Great Sea

Hebron

VALLEY
/OF
CANAAN/ ESHCOL

MOAB

Rameses •

Baal Zephon

EGYPT

Succoth

Etham

WILDERNESS
OF SIN

Kadesh Barnea

EDOM

Elim

SINAI

Elath

Hazeroth

MIDIAN

Rephidim

Mt. Sinai

100 miles

160 Kilometers

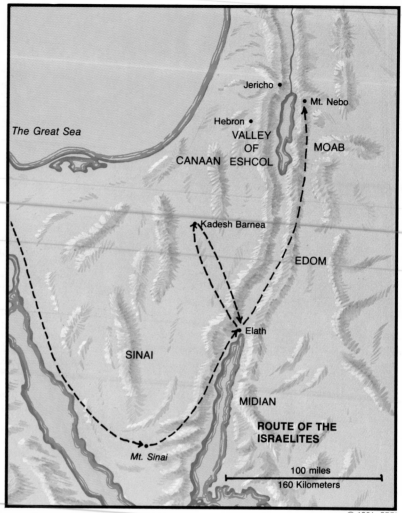

The route of the Israelites from Sinai onward may be seen on the map at the right. The route shown is one possibility, though we do not know for certain the exact way they followed. The donkey rider at the far lower right reminds us of Balaam, on his way to confer with Balak.

© 1981, SPPI

Balaam's Donkey

NUMBERS 22

Synopsis

After the people of Israel refused to enter the Promised Land, the Lord sent them back into the wilderness, where they would live for the next 38 years. Once when they grumbled against the Lord and Moses, God sent fiery serpents that killed many. But overall, the Lord remained with His people and gave them victories over their enemies. This made neighboring kings, such as Balak, king of Moab, nervous. He sent for a prophet in the north, named Balaam, to curse these Israelites. But on the way, Balaam's donkey spoke to him.

Curses

In Bible times, people believed in the powerful force of a curse. When a curse was pronounced, it was believed that a supernatural power or deity would carry it out. A curse was not just a wish, but an effective power. To the Israelites, it was God's judgment for disobedience to His covenant.

When Balak realized he could not defeat Israel with his army, he asked Balaam to place a curse on the people, to render them harmless (Num. 22:6). Moses warned that God's curse would follow disobedience (Deut. 27:10-26). Jeremiah believed in this curse, and claimed that Israel's captivity was unavoidable because the people had not obeyed God (Jer. 23:10). Jesus cursed a fig tree as a warning to those who are not fruitful in their work

126

From Abraham to the Judges

The period from Abraham to the time of the Judges involved parts of nine centuries. Each century is given at the right, with the highlights of prominent Bible history and events during that century. It is interesting that approximately nine more centuries remain in the entire Old Testament history. Almost half of those centuries (four) that remain were in the dark period of the Judges.

CENTURY BEGINNING WITH	EVENT APPROXIMATELY WITHIN THAT CENTURY
2200 B.C.	• Abraham born, moves to Haran
2100 B.C.	• Abraham moves to Canaan
2000 B.C.	• Isaac
1900 B.C.	• Jacob • Joseph
1800 B.C.	• Israelites move to Egypt
1700 B.C.	• Israelites live in Egypt
1600 B.C.	• Israelites live in Egypt
1500 B.C.	• Pharaoh makes Israelites slaves • Moses born • Exodus from Egypt and wilderness wanderings
1400 B.C.	• Conquest of Canaan • Early judges

and service for God (Mark 11:21).

A common custom in the ancient East was to curse a man's mother instead of the man himself. This was considered more painful. If a poor product was made, the man who made it would not be cursed. Instead his mother, wives, sisters, and daughters were cursed.

Donkeys

Everyone from slave to master and king to beggar understood the importance of the donkey. Before the time of King David, it was ridden by almost everyone as a means of transportation. It was also used for grinding grain, plowing, and carrying baggage. The donkey was a symbol of peace, and also a sign of prosperity.

127

When the spies entered Old Testament Jericho (ruins at far left) they found a Canaanite people occupying the city. Today the marker at the left guides the English-speaking tourists as well as the local Arab inhabitants.

Rahab

JOSHUA 2

Synopsis

Forty years passed since the people of Israel had left Egypt. One generation had died, and a new one had grown. The time had come for the people to enter the Promised Land and to claim it for their own. But before they went in, spies were sent into the land to see what the people faced. At Jericho these two spies found someone to help them, a woman named Rahab.

Windows

The king of Jericho came to Rahab's house looking for Joshua's spies, but they were well hidden in the stalks of flax on her roof. Later she helped the spies escape through a window of her house.

One of the walls of Rahab's house was actually the city wall (Josh. 2:15). There was a window in the wall that looked out of Jericho and into the surrounding countryside.

Most Bible-time houses had few windows. When they did, the windows were usually near the top of a wall or in an upper story to keep out thieves. Windows did not slide up and down like the windows of today, but often opened and closed like a door. Heavy bars of wood were pulled across a window to lock it from the inside.

A screen of latticework was sometimes a part of the window. The lattice was usually made of small wooden strips laid at right angles to each other. From the street, it was difficult to see into a home through the latticework, but from inside activities on the street were easily seen.

Spies

Spies were frequently used before a battle, to explore the enemy's weaknesses and its cities. Before attacking a city, Joshua often sent spies to scout the enemy in advance.

Where the Spies Came From

When the spies were sent to scout Jericho,

The three ivory combs at the left and below were once worn by Canaanite women. Rahab, a Canaanite woman, may have worn combs similar to these, made of ivory. She hid the spies under flax (below right) on her roof. Flax was used to make linen, which the Israelites used in the garments of the priests who served at the tabernacle.

the Israelites were still camped east of the Jordan River at a place called Shittim. This was their last stop before entering the Promised Land, just a few miles from the river.

Plants Made into Clothes

When Joshua's spies came to Jericho, they found a woman named Rahab, who took them into her house, and hid them under stalks of flax drying on her roof. Flax was an important crop in Bible times, and still is today.

From flax comes yarn which is woven into linen clothing. Each spring flax seeds are planted and grow well in the warm climate of Palestine. The key to reaping a good harvest is to keep the fields free from weeds, which might easily choke the tender plants. This was hot and toilsome work in ancient times.

The flax was harvested by hand in Joshua's

day. One pound held about 100,000 seeds. The stalks were then placed in water and allowed to partially rot for a few days. This loosened the gums that held the fibers to the stem.

The stalks of flax were then put out in the warm sun to dry. Many women, like Rahab, spread them out on their rooftops.

When dried out, the stems were broken apart, and the plant fibers separated in a process called "scutching." The coarse yarns were used for making twine, rope, or everyday work clothing. Fine yarns were spun into elegant linen cloth, from which beautiful clothing was woven.

Rope

Rahab helped the spies escape from her window by letting them climb down the city wall on a rope. This was probably woven from the coarse yarn fibers of flax.

When leaving, the spies told Rahab to hang a scarlet cord out her window. She might have made this from the finer fibers of flax. The scarlet color was taken from dyes made from the juices of insects or plants.

129

Above: Joshua directs the people of Israel as the priests carry the ark of the covenant across the Jordan River, now dry land. The ark is described in the Bible. At the left are three artists' views of how it looked, based on the description in Exodus 25:10-22; 37:1-9.

Crossing the Jordan

JOSHUA 3—4

Synopsis

Under Joshua's wise and courageous leadership, the people of Israel were ready to enter the Promised Land. Before they entered, Joshua sent two spies into the land to see what it was like. There they met a friendly woman named Rahab who helped them. At last the day came to enter the land. This time preparations included the Lord.

The Jordan River

The Jordan River is a landmark of Bible history. It begins near the slopes of Mount Hermon, and flows south into the Sea of Galilee. South of Galilee, the River Jordan runs through the Plain of Zor and the Ghor Valley. Growing wider with each mile, the

river meanders close to the Mount of Olives and finally empties into the Dead Sea.

Near Jericho, Joshua parted the waters of the river, and the entire company of Israel crossed into the Promised Land without getting their feet wet! (Josh. 3:14—4:18)

Elijah escaped from King Ahab across the Jordan (1 Kings 17:3, 5). Naaman, a Syrian general, was healed from leprosy when told by Elisha to wash in the Jordan seven times (2 Kings 5:1-15). Elisha also made an axhead float in its waters (2 Kings 6:1-7).

John the Baptist baptized believers in the River Jordan (Matt. 3:6), and later baptized Jesus there (Matt. 3:13-17). In Jesus' day, Jews traveling from Galilee to Jerusalem who wished to avoid the hated Samaritans probably crossed and recrossed the river to keep from walking through Samaria.

The Ark of the Covenant

The most treasured and sacred article in the

nation of Israel was the ark of the covenant, a symbol of God's covenant with Israel.

It was made when the tabernacle was first constructed in the wilderness (Ex. 25:10-22; 37:1-9). The framework was made of acacia wood, a strong and durable wood that resisted insects and rot, then overlaid with pure gold. Fastened to each corner was a gold ring which held the carrying poles.

Resembling a large chest, the ark was about 3¾ feet long by 2¼ feet wide. The height was about 2¼ feet. Inside the ark the Ten Commandments were kept, along with a jar of manna and Aaron's rod that had budded.

The lid of the ark was called the mercy seat. Once each year, the high priest entered the inner room of the tabernacle called the Holy of Holies, to sprinkle blood on the mercy seat, asking God to offer mercy for the people's sins.

Across the top of the ark, two winged cherubim of gold faced each other. It was believed that God dwelt between these wings, living among His people.

Gilgal

After crossing the Jordan River, the Israelites first camped at Gilgal, about two miles northeast of Jericho (Josh. 4:19). There all of the males were circumcised. The word Gilgal means to "roll away." At this place, God rolled away the waters of the Jordan and rolled away the bad memories of Egyptian slavery through the covenant of circumcision (Josh. 5:9).

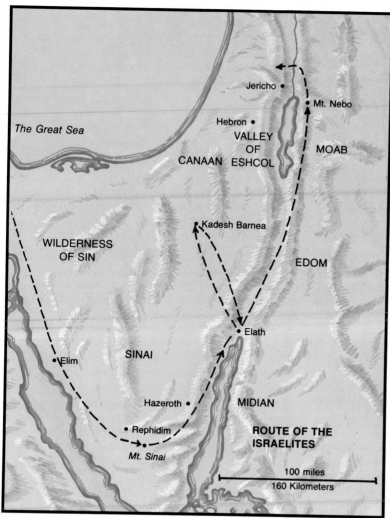

ROUTE OF THE ISRAELITES

100 miles
160 Kilometers

© 1981, SPPI

The route of the Israelites from Sinai through the crossing of the Jordan River is seen on the map at the left. Above: the Jordan River, where it flows from the south end of the Sea of Galilee. The Jordan flows from this point southward until it empties into the Dead Sea.

131

Seven priests blowing seven trumpets walked before the ark of the covenant. Seven times they walked around Jericho (left). When the people shouted at the sound of a trumpet, the walls of Jericho fell outward. Part of these ruined walls have been excavated (above).

Jericho Captured

JOSHUA 6

Synopsis

When at last the people of Israel reached the Promised Land, they waited across the Jordan River from Jericho for a report from two spies. The spies returned and encouraged Joshua to lead the Israelites into the land. Thus, while the priests carried the ark of the covenant toward Jericho, the waters of the Jordan River held back and the people crossed on dry land. The people of Jericho shut up the city, afraid of the Israelites and their God. Then Joshua gave the order for the strange silent battle to begin.

Jericho—A Fortified City

From the cold winter hills of Jerusalem, one can find a tropical paradise in the warm climate of Jericho, just a six-hour hike on foot. The city of Jericho lies about 17 miles northeast of Jerusalem, yet is close to 3,000 feet below

it. At 800 feet below sea level, the summer climate is almost unbearably hot, while the winter months are warm and pleasant.

In Joshua's day, Jericho was by no means the largest city in Canaan, but it was located in a strategic area. It lay a few miles west of the Jordan River, where most nomads and travelers crossed to enter Canaan.

Jericho was a city with walls. Excavations have uncovered ruins that prove it was an ancient city when Joshua arrived. As a fortified city, it was constructed to repel enemy attack. Many fortified cities had walls up to 20 feet thick and over 25 feet high.

On top of these walls soldiers could see for miles, and were constantly on guard, watching for the enemy. Some cities even had a moat, a large ditch filled with water, that circled their walls. Often another wall was built just outside the moat.

Jericho was a strong city, able to defend itself against a large army. But it could not be built strong enough to stop God's army, and the walls collapsed at His command (Josh. 6:20). Joshua then placed a curse on Jericho

(Josh. 6:26), which was fulfilled centuries later (1 Kings 16:34).

Jericho was (and still is) 800 feet below sea level. Thus the weather contrasts with that of Jerusalem, about 3,000 feet above it, but only 17 miles southwest. Jericho was often called the city of palm trees (see Deut. 34:3) because so many grew there (see photo below). Gilgal was about two miles northeast of Jericho. The photo below right shows the probable site of Gilgal.

Trumpets

Music was strongly woven into Israelite culture. Feasts, festivals, war, worship, and death were just some of the events where music played an important role. Music was also associated with God's supernatural power when the priests blew their trumpets and God destroyed the walls of Jericho (Josh. 6:20).

The trumpet was one of the most popular and important musical instruments in Israel. There were probably two distinct kinds. One was called the *chatsotserah*, which was long and straight, beginning with a very narrow tube at the mouthpiece, and opening at the end into the shape of a bell. It was similar to trumpets today, except that it did not have valves, so it was really a bugle.

The other type of trumpet was called the *shophar*. It was probably made from an animal horn and was bent or curved in shape. Many think this horn had a clearer, brighter sound than the *chatsotserah*.

Both of these trumpets were used to announce the beginning of feasts, signal a call to battle, proclaim a victory celebration, and inform people of important events.

Achan's Sin and the Conquest of Ai

JOSHUA 7—8

Synopsis

After the people of Israel had crossed into the Promised Land, they followed every instruction carefully and the Lord gave them a great victory over the city of Jericho. Triumphantly, they expected an equally great victory over Ai, the next target of their conquest. But their defeat caused them to search for a reason.

The Spoils of Battle

Booty, plunder, and spoil are all words that mean the same thing—useful or valuable items taken from a defeated enemy. The victors had the right to take anything they wished from the land and cities of the losers. This included animals, women and children, precious metals, jewelry, weapons, clothing, and a long list of other things.

But at times, God did not want the Israelites to take the spoils of battle. It was sometimes a test of the people's obedience. This was the case at Jericho, where everything was to be utterly destroyed except the precious metals which were to go into the Lord's tabernacle (Josh. 6:18-19, 21, 24).

When a battle had ended, those who had killed someone or even touched a dead body had to follow purification rites which lasted for a week. During this week, the soldiers stayed out of the camp with all the booty. Both the men and booty were sprinkled twice with a special water mixture called the "water of impurity." Soldiers washed their clothes, while the precious metals were "purified" in a hot flame. The booty was then divided among the soldiers, priests, tabernacle, and other people of the camp. One captive of every 500 was often given to the tabernacle service, and the very finest articles were given to the Lord.

The ruins at the left and far left are thought to be those of ancient Ai. It lies about two miles southeast of Bethel. The land where Ai was built was abundant with stones.

During the early years of the Judges, a Canaanite prince or king led an expedition and brought back captives, probably to become his slaves. The bearded prisoners may well be Israelites, brought before the royal figure, who celebrates his victory with drink from a bowl and music of a lyre. The same royal figure is shown in his chariot at the right. The ruler of Ai may have had a similar victory celebration when at first the Hebrews were defeated in battle.

Ai

The city's name means a "heap of stones," and today it still lies in ruins. Joshua totally destroyed this city. Years later it was probably rebuilt (1 Chron. 7:28; Neh. 11:31; Isa. 10:28), but once again it must have died off or been destroyed.

No archeologist can say with certainty they have found the site of the ancient city, but most would agree that it probably stood about two miles southeast of Bethel, where a large heap of ruins lies today. Recent excavations seem to show that Ai was a beautiful and prosperous city over 1,000 years before Joshua arrived there.

When Joshua first tried to capture the city, his forces were soundly defeated. Achan's sin was the reason for the Israelites' loss. After Achan was punished, Joshua easily destroyed Ai (Josh. 7:1—8:29).

The Shekel

After confessing his sin, Achan went into his tent and uncovered the stolen spoil—a beautiful robe, 200 shekels of silver, and a gold bar weighing 50 shekels (Josh. 7:21).

The shekel was the standard weight used in the ancient countries around Palestine. But this "standard" weight seems to have been different from country to country and time period to time period. Kings sometimes used a shekel of a different size and weight from ordinary people. A variety of symbols have also been uncovered, each thought to represent the shekel. Because of this, it is impossible to know the exact weight or amount of Achan's spoil.

Throughout Bible times, the shekel weighed anywhere from 8-16 grams, which is about .3 to .6 ounces. If this were true, then Achan would have stolen from 60-120 ounces of silver, and 15-30 ounces of gold, a value today of between $10,000 and $25,000. In Joshua's day, the silver alone would have bought Achan 10 slaves.

Gibeonites Trick Joshua

JOSHUA 9

Synopsis

When the Israelites entered the Promised Land at last, weary from their 40 years in the wilderness, their first conquest was Jericho. This victory was easy, for they followed the Lord's instructions completely. But when they tried to conquer Ai, defeat came as easily as victory at Jericho. Sin had come into the camp, for one man, Achan, had disobeyed the Lord's instructions. With Achan executed, they returned to an easy victory at Ai. By this time, neighboring cities were afraid. Gibeon, for example, sent men to trick Joshua into making a truce with their city.

A Long March—From Egypt to the Promised Land

After Joshua led the Israelites to victory against Jericho and Ai, the people became known as a strong nation, feared by others. Just 40 years earlier, they walked out of Egypt as a disorganized group of Hebrew slaves. But now they were learning the strength and guidance of God. Their journey to Canaan was an important testing ground. Here is a short summary of their travels:

After the first Passover meal, the Israelites left the Egyptian city of Rameses (Ex. 12:37; 13:17-18), and traveled through Succoth to Etham, where the pillar of cloud and fire is first mentioned (Ex. 13:20-22).

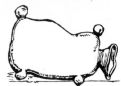

When Joshua failed to ask the Lord for wisdom, he was deceived by the men from Gibeon (top). These men came with "bottles" made to appear cracked and old. These leather water, or wine, containers were sewn animal skins (above).

136

When the Israelites appeared to be trapped by the Red Sea, God parted the waters, and the people crossed to safety (Ex. 14:5-31). The journey continued to Marah, where Moses sweetened the bitter waters of the oasis (Ex. 15:22-26).

At Elim, the Hebrews found 12 springs of water. On leaving, the wilderness of Sin lay ahead, where God sent quail and manna, but it was a long time before water was seen again. Finally, the people cried out for water, which gushed from a rock when it was struck by Moses' staff (Ex. 17:1-7). From here, it was a short distance to Mount Sinai, where Moses received the Ten Commandments from God as well as instructions for the tabernacle. The Israelites sinned by molding a golden calf to worship (Ex. 19—40).

From Mount Sinai, the company traveled northward across the great wilderness, where God sent plagues of fire and serpents because of the people's complaining and disobedience. After a long journey, they arrived in Kadesh Barnea, a beautiful oasis just south of the Promised Land. But when spies sent into the land returned afraid, the people lost hope. As punishment, they wandered in the wilderness 40 more years.

An Arab village is built over part of the ruins of ancient Gibeon (bottom). A pool from Old Testament times has been excavated there (below).

When that generation had died, Israel's new generation, under Joshua, moved to the edge of the Promised Land. Moab was afraid of them, for Joshua had conquered the powerful kingdoms of Sihon and Bashan (Num. 20:14-21; 21:21-35; 22—24). Soon Joshua and the rest of Israel crossed the Jordan River. With renewed faith in God, they entered the land with convincing victories over Jericho and Ai (Josh. 6—8). As long as the people remained faithful to God, the rest of their enemies melted before them.

Gibeon

The Israelite army was like a great wave rolling across Palestine, and the residents of Gibeon were in their path. Fearing for their lives, they deceived Joshua into making a peace covenant. Their city was about six miles northwest of Jerusalem. Years later, Solomon sacrificed at Gibeon and was given the gift of wisdom.

Above: two views of the Valley of Aijalon today, about 15 miles west of Jerusalem on the road to Joppa (Jaffa today).

The Sun and Moon Stand Still at Aijalon

JOSHUA 10:1-28

Synopsis

Victory had come easily at Jericho, the first conquest in the Promised Land, for the people of Israel had followed the Lord's instructions completely. But Ai was next, and there the Israelites suffered utter defeat. Sin was in the camp. Achan had disobeyed the Lord. With Achan executed, Ai was conquered. Gibeon, a nearby city, was afraid and sent men to trick Joshua into a truce. Before long, Joshua was forced to defend this city, even with a great miracle.

Hand-to-Hand Battle

In Joshua's day, there were no high-powered rifles, grenades, or fighter jets. In battle, each man looked his opponent in the eye and the more powerful man usually won. This was hand-to-hand combat, and even with the invention of chariots, soldiers still fought this way.

When God was with Joshua's army, it made no difference how skilled the enemy was. But years later, the Israelites did not follow God with such enthusiasm, and ran into deep trouble when faced with war.

After settling in Canaan, the Israelites were a disorganized people. Farmers and shepherds fought with hammers, axes, sticks, and hunting knives. They were no match for the skilled and organized armies of the Philistines and other Canaanites, who fought in mobilized units with horse-drawn chariots, spears and swords of bronze or iron, and powerful bows with arrows made of metal instead of stone or wood.

A soldier of Israel went into battle with everyday clothes, while Canaanite soldiers wore metal armor, with helmets and shields of iron or bronze instead of wood or leather.

The only way for Israel to win a battle was to keep their army small and disciplined. Without heavy armor, they moved quickly and fought in the hills where chariots were useless. Wise tactics and faith in God were keys to a successful battle in Israel.

Military Alliances

Joshua marched through Canaan, destroying each city he met along the way. These cities were called city-states, and many were actually small nations in themselves. Alone, they were powerless against Joshua, but united, they formed a strong army with the hope of victory.

The Bible mentions another great alliance where two large groups of kings banded together to fight a great battle in Abraham's time (Gen. 14). But Abraham, like Joshua, was able to defeat four of these kings.

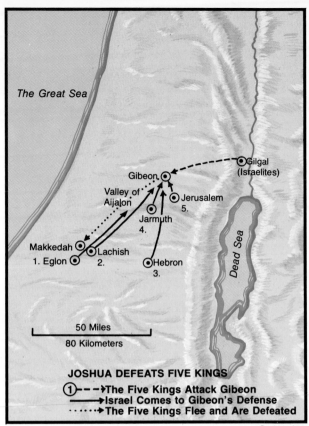

JOSHUA DEFEATS FIVE KINGS

①- - ->The Five Kings Attack Gibeon
——>Israel Comes to Gibeon's Defense
· · · · ·>The Five Kings Flee and Are Defeated

© 1981, SPPI

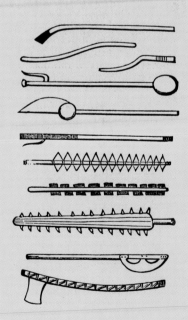

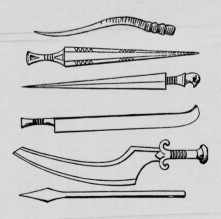

Joshua's battle strategy that resulted in victory over the five kings may be seen at the upper right. Below: various swords and other battle weapons from Old Testament times, drawn from various scenes on ancient monuments.

The mound where ancient Hazor once stood may be seen at the right. Extensive excavations have been made at Hazor, revealing much of its history.

The Conquest of Hazor

JOSHUA 11

Synopsis

The conquest of the Promised Land began at Jericho. That was an easy victory, for the Israelites followed the Lord's instructions completely. But Ai was their downfall, for they had sin in the camp. After Achan, the focus of that sin, was killed, Ai was defeated. Gibeon, a nearby city, became frightened and sent men to trick Joshua into a treaty. Thus when they were attacked, Joshua was forced to defend them, and even called on the sun and moon to stand still to give them victory. The conquest of many southern cities followed quickly. Now the kings of the northern cities became alarmed and formed an alliance to defeat Joshua and the Israelites. But the Lord gave Joshua the victory, including the conquest of the important city of Hazor.

Hazor

Hazor was the largest city in Palestine in the days of Joshua. It was a bustling center of business activity and foreign trade. Up to 40,000 residents might have lived in Hazor in Joshua's time.

Hazor was located at the junction of two important highways, about 10 miles northwest of the Sea of Galilee. One of these roads was the northwest branch of the vital international trade route called the Via Maris, which connected the countries north and south of Israel. The other road ran mostly east-west, crossing the Jordan River and intersecting the Via Maris branch at Hazor, before continuing toward Damascus. Both of these highways contributed to Hazor's prosperity, bringing rich trade and new ideas into the city.

Though Hazor was the largest city in the area, King Jabin needed more help in his attempt to stop the Israelite forces. He called together an alliance of kings that formed an army of thousands. They camped by the Waters of Merom, about 10 miles west of Hazor.

Joshua knew that a victory over this alliance would defeat many cities with just one battle. Though far outnumbered, Joshua made a sur-

140

prise attack, destroying Jabin's forces and burning Hazor to the ground.

When

The exact time period of Joshua's conquest into Canaan is still unsolved. Two main ideas are popular. The first suggests that Joshua entered the Promised Land around 1406 B.C. This date is reached by counting backward in time from the birth of David (known to be around 1040 B.C.), through the time of the Judges.

Excavations of the Tell el-Amarna tablets are also used in this theory. In these tablets, Canaanite vassal-kings are writing to Pharaoh Amenhotep III (1408-1372 B.C.), asking for military assistance in stopping the invasion of people known as "Habiru," thought by many to be the Hebrews.

The second theory places the conquest around 1200 B.C. In the year 1215 B.C., a large cliff near the city of Adam (Josh. 3:16) fell into the Jordan River and stopped the flow of water for a short while. God may have caused this to happen at just the right time so the Israelites could cross the river. Some think that the rule of some judges overlapped, shortening the period of the Judges by many years. They claim the judges ruled tribes, not the entire nation.

Canaanite Chariots

Egyptian chariots were probably the finest in the world in Joshua's day, but the Canaanite chariots were just as effective against the Israelite foot soldiers. Many were made of iron (Jud. 4:3), or wood plated with iron. They were pulled by swift horses.

On the open plain, the chariot was a deadly weapon, trampling down warriors as it sped along. Many had razor sharp knives attached to the wheel hubs. Any soldier caught in the path of these spinning blades was quickly cut into pieces.

Whenever Joshua's army was victorious, they crippled all of the chariot horses. The Israelites also learned to fight in the hills, where the chariot was ineffective.

One of the objects found in the excavations at Hazor was the large storage vessel above. It dates back to the 13th century B.C., the century when Jabin of Hazor overran Israel, and Deborah and Barak defeated him (Jud. 4—5).

One of the cities which joined with Hazor and was defeated was Kedesh (Josh. 12:22). The ruins of this city are pictured below.

141

Hebron Given to Caleb

JOSHUA 14:6-15

Synopsis
After Joshua led the people of Israel into the Promised Land, he conquered Jericho, then Ai, and then made a foolish treaty with Gibeon. This forced him into a battle to protect Gibeon, but through his victory, Joshua moved on to conquer many of the cities of the south. This alarmed the kings of northern cities, so they went to war against the Israelites. But God gave the Israelites the victory over these cities, including Hazor. The conquest of the land continued, but not all of the land was captured. When there was sufficient territory, Joshua began the task of dividing the land among the tribes. Caleb, who with Joshua many years before had wanted the Israelites to enter the land, was given Hebron.

Hebron
The city of Hebron still exists today, resting in a high valley about 25 miles southwest of Jerusalem. The nearby valleys are rich in fruits and vegetables of all kinds including figs, melons, grapes, pomegranates, and plums.

In Abraham's day, the city was called Kiriath Arba. It was named after Arba, the ancestor of the Anakim, a race of giant men who lived in the area.

When Abraham and Lot decided to separate, Lot was given his choice of land. He chose the fertile Jordan River valley, which included the evil cities of Sodom and Gomorrah. Abraham took what was left, which included part of the land of Canaan along with Hebron.

Abraham then moved to the oaks of Mamre, which tradition says was located one mile north of the city. Over the years, Abraham and his wife Sarah, his son Isaac, and grandson Jacob were all buried in the cave of Machpelah, near Hebron.

142

When Joshua and Caleb went from Kadesh Barnea with 10 other men to spy the Promised Land, they brought large bunches of grapes from the Valley of Eshcol. This rich valley was near Hebron. It is not known exactly where it was located, but was much like this valley of vineyards south of Hebron.

Hebron, upper left, is still an important city in Israel. Today it is occupied mostly by Arab peoples, though some people of Israel have moved into surrounding settlements. Above: pottery from about the time of Joshua.

After the Exodus, Joshua, Caleb, and 10 other men spied out the Promised Land and brought back a huge cluster of grapes from the Eshcol Brook near Hebron.

After Israel's conquest of Canaan, Joshua gave the area around Hebron to Caleb, because years earlier Moses had promised it to him. In the days of the Judges, Samson carried the gates of Gaza all the way to Hebron.

David lived in Hebron after Saul's death, where he was anointed king over the tribe of Judah. From the same city, Absalom organized a revolt against his father David.

Anakim

The city of Kiriath Arba, which was later known as Hebron, was named after Arba (Josh. 14:15). Arba was the father of Anak, who became the ancestor of the Anakim.

The Anakim were a race of very tall people, so tall that the Israelites called themselves grasshoppers when next to them. These great men were known as giants, and were one of the main reasons why 10 of the spies sent by Moses returned with such a fearful report.

Kiriath Arba was the home of these giants. When Caleb was given this area for his inheritance, he drove the Anakim out of the city and into the land of the Philistines.

Joshua and Caleb—Leaders of God's Land

Hundreds of thousands of Hebrews joyfully left the land of Egypt, bound for the Promised Land. But only Joshua and Caleb made it. After spying out the land, these two men were the only ones certain of victory under God. The rest of the Israelites smelled defeat, and as punishment, God did not let them set foot in the rich land. Only their children could enter.

143

Shiloh once occupied this beautiful valley about 20 miles north of Jerusalem. The tabernacle was set up here for almost 400 years, so Shiloh became Israel's center of worship during that time, much as Jerusalem did later when the temple was built there.

The Tabernacle at Shiloh

JOSHUA 18:1; 19:51

Synopsis
After Joshua had conquered most of the Promised Land, he began the task of dividing it among the tribes. The tabernacle, which had been carried through the wilderness, was now set up at Shiloh, where it remained for many years.

Casting Lots—Dividing the Conquered Land
When the land of Canaan was mostly conquered, the Israelites were eager to settle there. Caleb was given the area of Hebron because God promised him the land for his obedience (Num. 14:24), and Joshua was given Timnath Serah (Josh. 19:49-50). The rest of the land was divided among the 12 tribes by casting lots.

Lots were often cast to determine God's will. The Bible does not explain the method of casting lots. Some think that each tribes' name was written on a small piece of wood, then placed into a jar with a neck so narrow that only one piece could be shaken out at a time.

A lot might have been two small pebbles with one saying "yes" and the other "no," or they might have looked like dice, with different names inscribed on each side.

Shiloh
Year after year the Israelites had gone through the wilderness. When the pillar of cloud moved, the tabernacle was taken down, and when the cloud stopped, it was set up. But after entering the Promised Land, the tabernacle was finally set up permanently at Shiloh.

Shiloh became Israel's center of worship, lying in a quiet, uninhabited valley about 20 miles north of Jerusalem.

The tabernacle remained at Shiloh until the days of Samuel, when the Philistines invaded Israel and attacked Shiloh, probably destroying most of God's beautiful sanctuary.

Like many of the surrounding hills, those near Shiloh (below) are abundant with stones. But the broad meadows, as in the picture at the lower right, show places where the tabernacle (right) could have been set up.

The tabernacle set up at Shiloh must have been much like the one constructed by Moses at Mount Sinai. However, some more permanent features developed, such as the posts mentioned in 1 Samuel 1:9.

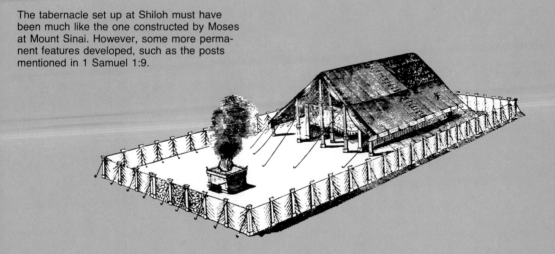

145

Harosheth, sometimes called Harosheth of the Gentiles, was the home of Sisera, captain of King Jabin's army. It has been identified with Tell 'Amer (above), near Mount Carmel. Deborah held court under a palm tree, probably much like the date palm at the right.

Deborah and Barak

JUDGES 4—5

Synopsis
After Joshua had led the people of Israel in a victory over many cities in the Promised Land, he began the task of dividing the land among the tribes. Parts of the land were never conquered, and the Israelites mingled with the inhabitants, often absorbing their heathen ways. By the time of the Judges, Israel had turned far from the Lord. Only a faithful few, like Deborah and Barak, were strong enough in their faith to lead the nation.

The Period of the Judges
Under Joshua, the Israelites followed God, finally entering the Promised Land. But after Joshua died, it didn't take long for many people to begin worshiping other gods. Soon some of the nations that the Israelites had failed to conquer turned against them and started to oppress them by destroying their

fields, killing their children, and leaving them poor and helpless.

Afraid, the people remembered God and cried for help, so God raised up judges to rally Israel behind God, and drive the other nations from the land. This period of the Judges lasted over 300 years. Whenever there was a judge, Israel united behind God, but after that judge died, they slipped back into idolatry.

Tent Pegs

Tent pegs, or pins, fastened a tent to the ground. They had to be sharp to penetrate the rocky soil of Palestine. Leather cords, attached to the tent walls, were pulled out to give the tent more room inside. These cords were also held in the ground with tent pegs.

King Jabin, a Canaanite king, had 900 iron chariots. The ivory furniture inlay (above) which once decorated a chair in a Canaanite palace, shows their chariots and drivers in a battle scene. This inlay was found at Megiddo. Below is a view of the Kishon River near Mount Carmel, where the Lord gave Israel the victory over Jabin and Sisera.

With the tip of a staff, the angel of the Lord touched the food Gideon brought, causing fire to consume it (Jud. 6:20-21). This was a sign that the Lord was with Gideon.

Gideon's Call and Tests

JUDGES 6

Synopsis

The conquest of the Promised Land was never complete. Though Joshua had been a mighty leader, the Israelites did not conquer all of the cities. So they lived among the Canaanites, the people who had inhabited the land before them, absorbing many of their heathen ways. By the time of the Judges, the people of Israel were far from the Lord. Occasionally the Lord raised up a mighty leader to rule as a judge, someone like Gideon.

Baal Worship

Coming from Egypt, the Israelites were used to the worship of numerous gods and goddesses. Canaan was no exception, except that in this land, one particular god, Baal, was much more important than the others. He was a symbol of strength and fertility to the Canaanites, and the one whom they thought brought life-giving rains to Palestine.

The people of Canaan believed fervently in this god. He was usually represented as a bull, the strongest animal known to them.

They were certain that famine was caused when Baal was worshiped improperly. To win back Baal's favor, the heathen priests of this god might offer hundreds of sacrifices, while dancing around the altar slashing themselves with knives and sharp rocks. Hopefully, Baal would feel sorry for them and once again send his gentle rains over the land.

If this failed, priests urged families to sacrifice their own children, the ultimate expression of devotion and worship to their god.

Over the years, many of the Israelites turned from God to worship Baal. This was strictly forbidden when God had made His covenant with the people. As punishment, God let other nations invade Israel, making life as difficult as it had been in Egypt.

Beating Out Wheat

When Gideon was a young man, the Midianites were in control of his people. Periodically, they swept through the land, destroying crops and livestock in order to keep the Israelites weak.

148

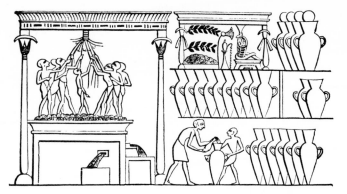

Gideon threshed his wheat in a wine-press to hide from the enemy. The four drawings above and below show a winepress in operation. These are drawn from Egyptian monuments. The process is described at the right. The drawing immediately above shows one method of squeezing juice from the grapes. Note the large storage jars in other drawings. Note also how the men treading the grapes held onto ropes attached above.

Gideon was fortunate enough to harvest some wheat before it was burned or trampled. He "beat it out" in a winepress, trying to cover up what he was really doing in case the Midianites rode by. In beating out the wheat, Gideon was separating the grain from the stalks of wheat. He did this by trampling on it or by pounding it with a heavy club. Animals usually did the job of beating out the wheat, but Gideon's livestock were probably taken by the Midianites, or possibly the plodding animals would have made Gideon's job obvious.

After the grain was separated from the stalks, it was strained in a sieve to remove the dirt, and then thrown into the wind, where the useless chaff blew away, and the heavier grain fell to the ground. The grain was ground into flour and used in baking bread.

The Winepress

A winepress was usually built on the edge of a vine-yard. Women picked the grapes from the vines and carried them in large baskets to the winepress, which resembled a large stone tub. The grapes were emptied into the tub, while men trampled on them with their bare feet, keeping their balance by hanging onto ropes tied to a wooden crossbeam. The juice from the squeezed grapes was then stored in wineskins or jars.

149

The pitchers, or jugs, at the upper left were perhaps similar to those used by Gideon to cover the torches. They were found at Megiddo and date to about 1550-1479 B.C. The paintings on the jugs include a bird.

Gideon's 300

JUDGES 7

Synopsis

The people of Israel had been victorious in conquering much of the Promised Land. But they never conquered it all. Thus they settled among the Canaanites and absorbed many of their heathen ways. Through the years they turned from the Lord, and by the time of the Judges, the nation was far from Him. Occasionally the Lord raised up a great man or woman to lead the nation as a judge. One such man was Gideon. And one of his great battles required 300 dedicated soldiers.

The Middle Watch

When danger was present, armies, cities, and even family homes kept a watch throughout the night. In Joshua's day, this watch was divided into three four-hour periods. The first watch, also called the beginning of the

watches, lasted from 6 P.M. to 10 P.M. The middle watch continued from 10 at night until 2 in the morning. The morning watch started at 2 A.M. and ended at 6 A.M.

The first watch began at sunset, and the morning watch ended at sunrise. Gideon attacked the Midianite army at the beginning of the middle watch (about 10 P.M.). This was a big surprise, because armies rarely fought after dark.

Gideon's Trumpet

Gideon's men surprised the Midianite army by blowing trumpets and breaking pitchers, uncovering flickering torches.

The horns blown by Gideon and his men were called *shophars*, which means "trumpets," or *kerens*, which means "horns." The *shophar* was usually made from an animal horn that was curved in shape. It sounded only two or three different notes, but these were bright and shrill. The *shophar* was mainly used for announcements of war, rebellion, or some of the great Israelite feasts.

At the upper left: Gideon and his men break their pottery jugs to reveal the torches beneath, while blowing on their trumpets. Above are some trumpets of ancient times, both the curved animal-horn type and another type made of a conch shell. Gideon's trumpet was probably the curved animal-horn type. The Spring of Harod, where Gideon's men drank the water (Jud. 7:1-6) is pictured at the left.

Pottery and Pitchers

Gideon and his 300 men threw the Midianite army into confusion when together they broke their pitchers, exposing hundreds of burning torches. In the dead of night, the sound of 300 breaking pitchers must have made quite a noise. But where did these pitchers come from and how were they made?

Before Abraham's day, all pottery was made by hand. It was rough and awkward. But by Gideon's time, most pottery was fashioned on a potter's wheel. This important invention gave pottery a smooth and symmetrical look. There were even tools designed to hide the seam and impress beautiful patterns.

The pitchers used by Gideon's army were probably made of clay. This was the most common material used in pottery, as well as the cheapest. After the vessel was shaped, it was dried for a few days, and then heated in an oven called a kiln. This gave the piece of pottery extra strength, preventing the clay from becoming too brittle as time passed.

Torches

Suddenly in the dead of night, 300 brilliant torches sprang up from the darkness. Gideon's men had used the torches as an effective weapon of war, scattering and confusing the Midianite army.

In Bible times, torches were also used as lights when the smaller oil burning lamps did not give off enough light.

Above: an ox grinds grain. Note the two millstones, with the top rotating on the bottom. At the right: an olive tree, mentioned by Jotham in his parable.

Jotham's Parable

JUDGES 9:1-24

Synopsis
When the Israelites entered the Promised Land, after 40 years in the wilderness, they set out to conquer it. Under Joshua's leadership, they were victorious over many cities, but never completely captured the land. Thus, they were forced to live among the Canaanites who had inhabited it, and absorbed many of their heathen ways. By the time of the Judges, the Israelites had turned far from the Lord. A few judges rose to lead them, and some were strong, such as Gideon. But sons of strong men are not always strong, such as Abimelech, son of Gideon.

Millstones
Baking bread in ancient times was a long and slow process. Bread was really made from "scratch." Even the flour had to be made before the bread could be baked. In making the flour, millstones were an important tool.

After the grain was separated from the stalks of wheat, barley, or corn, it was rubbed or rolled between two stones into flour. Together, these two stones were called millstones.

Over the centuries, grinding the grain into flour became much easier. At first, a millstone was only a narrow flat rock called a base stone, and a smaller rock, held in the hand, called an upper or rubbing stone. A handful of grain was placed on the base stone, and the rubbing stone was used to slowly crush the grain by hand into a coarse flour.

Later the millstone progressed into two round stones, one on top of the other. The lower stone did not move, but the upper stone had a hole in the center and turned around a wooden peg. Grain put into this hole dropped in between these two stones. As the upper stone was turned by hand, it ground over the surface of the lower stone, crushing the grain into a fine flour.

Much larger millstones, just like these, were also made. While the normal millstone was about 1½ to 2 feet in diameter, these larger stones had a diameter of 4 or 5 feet.

152

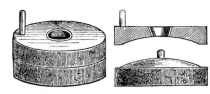

The millstones drawn at the left are similar to those which women used. Shechem's ruins are seen in the left photo above. The right photo above is of Mount Ebal (right) and Mount Gerizim (left).

They were too large for people to turn, so oxen were used, their yoke attached to the upper stone, and as the oxen walked in circles the millstone ground out large amounts of grain, often enough to supply an entire city.

Shechem—What Happened There?

Many Bible events occurred around the town of Shechem. Lying in a pass at the northern foot of Mount Gerizim, the village sits on the edge of a fertile plain. It is located about 31 miles north of Jerusalem.

When Abraham journeyed to Canaan to make a new home there, one of his first stops was near Shechem, where God promised to give the land to his descendants (Gen. 12:6-7).

Abraham's grandson, Jacob, lived near Shechem for a while. The king of the city had a son named Shechem who dishonored Jacob's daughter, Dinah. Simeon and Levi, two of Jacob's sons, took revenge on the entire city by killing all of the men who lived there (Gen. 33:18-19; 34).

Joseph went to visit his brothers, who were tending their flocks near Shechem (Gen. 37:12). When Joseph died in Egypt, his bones were carried back to Canaan during the Exodus and buried at Shechem (Josh. 24:32).

At Shechem, between Mount Gerizim and Mount Ebal, Joshua read God's laws to all the Israelites (Josh. 24). At this time, Shechem was probably the military center of Israel, while Shiloh was the religious center.

In the period of the Judges, Abimelech persuaded the people of Shechem to crown him as king. Later, the city rebelled against Abimelech, who attacked Shechem and destroyed it. Jotham also gave his famous parable here (Jud. 9).

The kingdom of Israel divided between north and south at Shechem when the 10 northern tribes rejected Solomon's son, Rehoboam, as their king. For a short time, the city became the capital of the northern kingdom of Israel (1 Kings 12:1-19, 25). Centuries later, Shechem became an important city of the Samaritans.

Watchtowers

Throughout Bible times, towers were built in all shapes and sizes. The towers where Abimelech trapped the residents of the cities of Shechem and Thebez (Jud. 9:46-52), were giant stone or brick structures used as fortifications for the city as well as watchtowers to spot an approaching enemy. These buildings could hold hundreds of people.

Vineyards used small watchtowers built of mud or field stones. As the grapes ripened, men sat in these towers day and night, constantly watching for thieves who might steal their valuable crop.

153

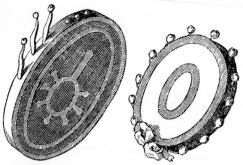

When Jephthah's daughter came to meet him, she was dancing to the sound of tambourines, sometimes called timbrels. This was a form of percussion instrument (pictured above) in which small bells on a drumlike surface beat a rhythm for dancing.

Jephthah's Foolish Vow

JUDGES 11

Synopsis

The time of the Judges was a time of trouble, for Israel had turned from the Lord. Only now and then did the Lord raise up a strong judge to lead the nation, such as Deborah or Gideon. After Gideon's death, his son Abimelech tried to rule, but his leadership was based on murder and foolish conflict. Nothing much is known of Tola and Jair, the next two judges. Then came Jephthah, a mighty warrior, but careless with his vows.

Vows

Israelites took vows very seriously. A vow was a promise to God, a solemn oath that could not be taken back. Even if the vow was regretted later, it could not be broken under any circumstances.

A vow could also be a bargain with God. Hannah, Samuel's mother, promised the Lord that if He would give her a son, she would dedicate that son to a lifetime of service in the tabernacle.

Sometimes people made vows foolishly, without thinking first. Jephthah was a mighty warrior, but he made a foolish vow with God, promising to sacrifice the first thing that met him at home, if God gave him victory over the Ammonites. Jephthah was victorious, and when he arrived home his daughter ran out to greet him.

If a woman made a vow, her husband or father could cancel it. Anything obtained

The Judges

For some 300 years, from about 1400 to 1100 B.C., these 13 judges ruled Israel. Samuel is sometimes called the 14th.

1. OTHNIEL
Judged: 40 years
From: Kiriath Sepher in Judah
Bible ref.: Judges 3:9-11

2. EHUD
Judged: 80 years
From: tribe of Benjamin
Bible ref.: Judges 3:15-30

3. SHAMGAR
Judged: ?
From: ?
Bible ref.: Judges 3:31

4. DEBORAH & BARAK
Judged: 40 years
From: Deborah: Ephraim;
   Barak: Naphtali
Bible ref.: Judges 4—5

5. GIDEON
Judged: 40 years
From: Manasseh
Bible ref.: Judges 6—8

6. ABIMELECH
Judged: 3 years
From: Manasseh
Bible ref.: Judges 9

7. TOLA
Judged: 23 years
From: Issachar
Bible ref.: Judges 10:1-2

154

JAIR
Judged: 22 years
From: Gilead, in E. Manasseh
Bible ref.: Judges 10:3-5

9. JEPHTHAH
Judged: 6 years
From: Gilead, in E. Manasseh
Bible ref.: Judges 11:1—12:7

10. IBZAN
Judged: 7 years
From: Bethlehem, in Judah
Bible ref.: Judges 12:8-10

11. ELON
Judged: 10 years
From: Zebulun
Bible ref.: Judges 12:11-12

12. ABDON
Judged: 8 years
From: Ephraim
Bible ref.: Judges 12:13-15

13. SAMSON
Judged: 20 years
From: Dan
Bible ref.: Judges 13—16

The period of the Judges was a dark period for Israel. No truly great leader, devoted to God, was to be found. Thus the people often turned from the Lord. In their weakness, they were constantly oppressed by surrounding peoples.

Other percussion instruments which figured significantly in Israel's history were cymbals (above). These were used in bringing the ark to Jerusalem (1 Chron. 15:16, 19, 28), at the dedication of Solomon's temple (2 Chron. 5:13), and the dedication of the wall of Jerusalem (Neh. 12:27). Cymbals were also used in worshiping God (Ps. 150).

against God's laws would not be accepted by God in a vow. Whatever was promised to God in a vow (such as an animal), had to be in perfect condition, as well as valuable.

Who Were the Ammonites?

The nation of the Ammonites was conceived through the sin of Lot's younger daughter (Gen. 19:30-38). They were always enemies of Israel, reaching their greatest strength during the period of the Judges.

The land of the Ammonites was situated east of the Jordan River, even with the land surrounding the city of Jerusalem to the west. Just to the south lay the nation of Moab, almost always an ally to the land of Ammon, possibly because the seed of Moab came from Lot's older daughter, making the two nations related by blood.

Jephthah fought a courageous battle against the Ammonites and defeated them (Jud. 11:32). But it wasn't until the days of King David that the Ammonites were completely crushed and reduced to an insignificant tribe.

Warriors

Jephthah was not just an ordinary soldier. He was a mighty warrior possessing exceptional bravery and courage. Warriors seem to have been a step above ordinary soldiers because of their fearless attitude and tremendous skill in battle.

King David had a group of these mighty men in his army who were fiercely loyal to him. Many of the warriors were so strong and skilled in battle that singlehandedly they killed entire troops of enemy soldiers.

155

The Birth of Samson

JUDGES 13

In the photo at the top, Zorah is at the left and Beth Shemesh at the distant right. Zorah is described at the far right.

Synopsis

When the Israelites set out to conquer the Promised Land, they had many victories. But they could not take all of the land, so they were forced to live with the Canaanites. In time, they absorbed many of their heathen ways, especially by the time of the Judges. Israel then was far from the Lord. Judges arose to lead the nation, and a few were strong, such as Deborah and Gideon. Others were weak. Samson was physically strong but morally weak.

Idol Worship in Canaan

Smoke rose in Canaan during certain times of the day called "prayer times." The Canaanites worshiped many different gods and goddesses in the form of idols. This idolatry was gradually absorbed by the Israelites as they lived among the people of Canaan.

Daily the Canaanites burned incense to their gods on incense altars. Many chose to worship on their roofs or on hilltops called "high places," believing that their gods could hear them only if the smoke from their altars reached up to the gods.

The two most popular deities in the land were Baal, the god of rain and harvest, and Ashtoreth, the goddess of childbirth and fertility. Metalsmiths were kept busy making idols to represent them. Baal was usually cast as a bull, and Ashtoreth was often made to resemble the figure of a woman.

Incense stands, or altars, came in all shapes and sizes, and were made of pottery or metal, usually bronze. Some were stones, with a small depression carved out to hold the incense. Others were large and elaborate,

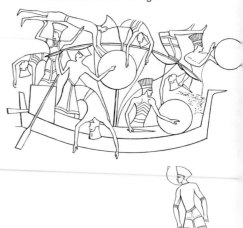

The Valley of Sorak is pictured at the right, just to the east of Samson's childhood home. Delilah, who figured in his later adventures, was from this valley (Zorah, Samson's home, was in the hills seen in the upper part of photo). Philistines are pictured above in two Egyptian drawings.

156

The Nazirite vow could be taken for as little as 30 days, or for an entire lifetime. Parents could take the vow for their children before they were born, and the children were bound by it. Samson was a lifetime Nazirite because his mother and father had made this promise to God (Jud. 13:5, 7).

A Nazirite was often punished for any of the vows he deliberately broke. If by accident he touched a dead body, he had to shave his head and face, bury the hair, and start his vow all over again. His vow was increased by 30 days if his hair was cut by mistake.

When the vow had ended, a special sacrifice was made at the tabernacle. The hair was shaved and burned in the fire.

Samson broke some of the conditions of the Nazirite vow. He killed 30 Philistines and touched their dead bodies when he stole their robes (Jud. 14:19). Later, he told the secret of his strength to Delilah who then cut his hair (Jud. 16:19). His carelessness made him a slave to the Philistines for the rest of his life.

Zorah
Samson's parents lived in Zorah, and Samson was probably born there. He was also buried near the village (Jud. 16:31).

Zorah lay in the territory of the tribe of Judah, about 15 miles west of Jerusalem. Originally, the city belonged to the tribe of Dan, but they moved to the north, driven out by intense pressure from the Philistines, who occupied the land directly west of the city.

shaped like houses or temples.

Israel's judges and prophets were always reminding and begging the people to stop their idolatry, but nobody listened. Patiently God waited for His people to turn back to Him, but when it became obvious they would not, He let them be captured and carried captive from the land He had given them.

The Nazirite Vow
Whoever took the Nazirite vow was forbidden to cut his hair or shave his beard. No wine or other strong drink was to touch his lips, and he was not allowed to touch or go near a dead person, even if it was a member of his own family. The vow was taken to set aside one's life in total devotion and service to God.

Delilah

JUDGES 16:1-22

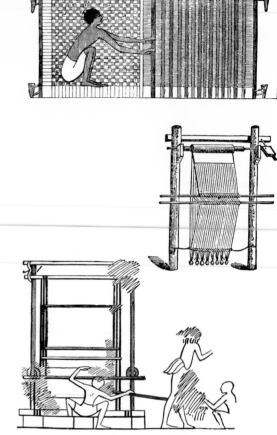

Synopsis

During the time of the Judges of Israel, the nation had turned away from the Lord. Even the judges were not always good people, as can be seen in the life of Samson. Here was a mighty man, more powerful than any other. But he let Delilah take him down the road to ruin.

The Lords of the Philistines

Samson was the strongest man on earth. The Philistines were afraid of him, for he had killed countless numbers of their people. When Samson fell in love with Delilah, who was probably a Philistine, the leaders of this nation saw a way of ridding themselves of their hated and feared enemy.

These leaders, or lords, of the Philistines came to visit Delilah one day, each offering 1,100 pieces of silver if she could find the source of Samson's strength. These lords took their offer seriously, for this was a large amount of money.

In the land of Philistia, there were five key cities, Ekron, Ashdod, Ashkelon, Gath, and Gaza. Each of these cities was ruled by a "lord." Together, these five lords made up the Philistine government. These men handled small matters on their own, but large decisions were reached by majority vote. This system of government gave the Philistines an advantage over the Israelites, who were now a group of weak, disorganized tribes.

Above: three drawings from ancient monuments, showing looms of Bible times. The loom at the top and the one at the bottom were Egyptian. The one in the center was Roman. Delilah wove Samson's hair on a loom.

Delilah tied Samson with seven new thongs, or bowstrings (Jud. 16:8). Bows of Old Testament times are shown in the drawings at the left and below. The men at the left and the one below are stringing their bows. The photo at the bottom is of the Timnah area, where Samson was married to a Philistine woman (Jud. 14).

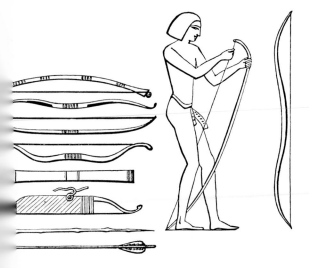

Gouging Out the Eyes

Kings and other important people captured by the enemy often had their eyes gouged out. Samson had his eyes put out after he was seized by the Philistines (Jud. 16:21). He had already inflicted great damage on the Philistine nation, and they didn't want any more trouble from him if he escaped.

When captured, most kings and great warriors were not killed, because the enemy found greater joy in humiliating these once great and powerful men. They gouged out their eyes, turning them into helpless creatures, and then forced them to do the work of slaves. For this reason, many kings wounded in battle killed themselves rather than be subjected to the ruthless humiliation of their captors.

Weaving on a Loom

Delilah wove Samson's hair in a loom, hoping to sap his strength (Jud. 16:14). How was this weaving done in ancient times?

The first step in weaving cloth was called spinning. Fibers taken from cotton, flax, wool, or goat's hair were twisted together with a spindle to form yarn or thread. A spindle looked like a small stick with a hook on the end. A whorl was a small weight tied to the fiber, to help it twist into yarn faster.

When the weaving began, long rows of yarn were tied to the loom, all going in the same direction. This was called the warp. Across the warp were laid other strings of yarn which were passed over and under the strings of the warp. The strings of yarn were then pushed together for extra strength, and the new piece of cloth was ready for sewing.

Samson grew up near Zorah and Eshtaol (photo above). His last days were spent in Gaza (photos at the right and at the upper far right). Much of his life was spent in struggling with the Philistines. The ship at the upper right is a Philistine ship of about 1200 B.C., probably still in operation in Samson's time. Gaza, Samson's last "home," was on the seacoast.

Samson the Prisoner

JUDGES 16:23-31

Synopsis

The Lord had promised the land to Israel, so when Israel entered after 40 years in the wilderness, the conquest began. Joshua led his people to many great victories, but even so, the land was never completely captured. Thus Israel settled among the remaining Canaanites and adopted some of their heathen ways. By the time of the Judges, Israel was far from the Lord. Even its leaders, the judges, were not examples of the Lord's power at work. Samson's bitter end is a sign of the times, showing how far Israel had gone from the Lord.

Grinding Grain as Punishment

Samson was a strong and mighty man in Israel. When captured, he was humiliated before the Philistines when they gouged out his eyes. Suddenly this great hero was a helpless creature. To degrade him further, he was forced to grind grain, a job usually given to women and slaves.

Other countries, such as Greece and Rome, also gave many of their prisoners the job of grinding grain. Samson probably ground grain on a small hand mill made with two round stones, one on top of the other. When the upper stone was turned in a circle, it moved over the surface of the lower stone, grinding the grain into flour. Samson may have pushed the larger type of mill usually pushed by oxen, but no one knows if this kind of mill had been invented then.

160

Samson's last days were spent in grinding for the Philistines at Gaza. Grinding grain with a small mill was usually assigned to women. But a large mill, as above, was usually powered by an animal. Samson may have been forced to turn a large mill like this. The olive press is similar in principle, except that it was used to extract olive oil from the olives instead of grinding grain into flour.

Gaza

Gaza was an important city along a major caravan route that stretched all the way to Egypt. Located 50 miles southwest of Jerusalem and just 3 miles inland from the Mediterranean Sea, the city held a vital strategic position for armies marching from Egypt in the south, and from Syria and Mesopotamia in the north.

Looking south, the city lay near the edge of a vast and dry wilderness. Gaza had 15 wells, making it an essential stopping point for those who had just come from the desert, and for those who were just entering it.

In the days of the Judges, the Philistines controlled Gaza. It was one of the five key cities of the Philistine government where one of their five ruling "lords" lived.

When Samson visited Gaza, he pulled up the city gates and carried them all the way to Hebron, a distance of over 30 miles (Jud. 16:1-3). Later, when Samson was captured, he spent the rest of his days grinding grain in the Gaza prison (Jud. 16:21).

The Temple of Dagon

Dagon was the national god of the Philistines. Many cities built large temples to this god. One of these temples was built in Gaza, the city where Samson was a prisoner.

Most of these temples were constructed after a simple design, where large porch pillars provided the main support for the roof, commonly made of mud or stone.

Inside, heathen priests sacrificed many things to Dagon, even children. Sporting events or the humiliation of prisoners was often carried out in the courtyard, while hundreds of people watched from the roof. It was during one of these times that Samson pulled down the pillars, destroying the temple and killing 3,000 Philistines who were making fun of him.

161

The Story of Ruth

The Book of RUTH

Synopsis

The time of the Judges was a dark period in Israel's history. Unable to conquer the Promised Land completely, the people of Israel settled among the Canaanites and absorbed many of their heathen ways. By the time the judges ruled Israel, the nation had gone far from the Lord. But a few bright spots shine out of this period, such as the story of a loyal girl named Ruth.

Some Important Descendants of Ruth and Boaz

After Ruth and Boaz were married, they had a son named Obed. Obed grew up and married and had a son called Jesse. Jesse became the father of King David and the grandfather of King Solomon, two of the mightiest and richest kings of Israel.

Centuries later, another descendant of Ruth and Boaz was born in the town of Bethlehem, the same small village where Ruth and Boaz were married hundreds of years before. His name was Jesus, and His birth marked man's freedom from sin and death.

Widows

Ruth, Orpah, and Naomi were all widows. Ruth and Orpah became widows at an early age. In ancient times, women depended much on their husbands. If a husband died, all of his property and belongings went to the man who owned the family birthright. The widow was left with absolutely nothing. If no one was willing to help her, the widow spent the rest of her life in extreme poverty. With no one to depend on, she was often taken advantage of.

Israelite law recognized the plight of widows and made some specific laws to help them. If the widow had sons, it was their responsibility to take care of her. But Ruth, Naomi, and Orpah did not have sons.

If a widow had no sons, she could return to her parents as Orpah did. Ruth decided to stay with her mother-in-law, Naomi, but Naomi could not care for her for she also was a widow.

If a widow's husband had brothers, they were required to take her in as their wife, beginning with the oldest. A son born from this kind of marriage was given the name of the widow's husband. But Elimelech, Naomi's husband, apparently did not have any brothers.

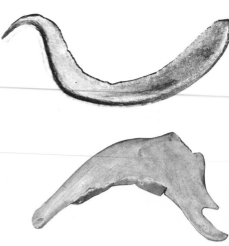

Above: two types of early sickles used to cut grain. The one at the top was made of bronze. The other was carved out of bone. At the left, Ruth brings grain which she has gleaned to help feed Naomi. Ruth was not obligated to do this, but chose to as an act of love.

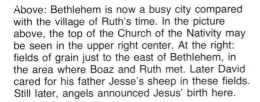

Above: Bethlehem is now a busy city compared with the village of Ruth's time. In the picture above, the top of the Church of the Nativity may be seen in the upper right center. At the right: fields of grain just to the east of Bethlehem, in the area where Boaz and Ruth met. Later David cared for his father Jesse's sheep in these fields. Still later, angels announced Jesus' birth here.

In some cases, the closest relative was then obligated to marry the widow. Boaz was the closest relative to Ruth except for one man who could not marry her without jeopardizing his own inheritance. Boaz willingly married Ruth, more out of love than obligation. Naomi was then probably cared for by Ruth and Boaz.

Gleaning

When the fields of wheat and barley were ready to be harvested, reapers were hired to cut the stalks of grain and tie them into bundles. According to Israelite laws, any loose stalks that were dropped in the fields were to be left for the gleaners.

Gleaning was done by poor and helpless people such as widows, who without the scraps from the field would have died of starvation. Each day during harvest, the poor walked through the fields and gleaned or picked up any loose stalks that were left behind. Ruth, a widow, was gleaning in a field when she met Boaz, the owner of the field.

Giving Away One's Sandal

By the city gate, in the sight of many witnesses, Boaz bought the property of Elimelech, which included the right to marry Ruth, as well as the obligation to care for both her and Naomi. The other relative removed his sandal and gave it to Boaz. This was a custom in Israel then, symbolizing that he gave up his right to walk on the land to possess it. Boaz probably returned the man's sandal, though we do not know for sure. The Bible said this legalized the transaction in those early days in Israel (Ruth 4:7).

163

Left: Hannah pours out her heart to the Lord at the tabernacle at Shiloh. Eli sits on a "chair," actually more like a priestly throne, at the entrance to the tabernacle. The structure of the building had changed since Moses had it made in the wilderness (drawings below). The front of the tent, covered curtains in Moses' time, was now a permanent porch with posts.

The Birth of Samuel

1 SAMUEL 1:1-20

Synopsis

When the people of Israel were slaves in Egypt, the Lord promised to deliver them, which He did under Moses' leadership. He offered them the Promised Land, but when they arrived at Kadesh Barnea, they were afraid to enter. For 38 more years they remained in the wilderness, entering at last under Joshua's leadership. The land was theirs, but they had to conquer it. Joshua led his people to victory over much of the land, but not all. During the time of the Judges, Israel sank low, going far from the Lord. This

dark time in Israel's history lasted about 400 years. At last, a baby was born who became a spiritual leader for Israel. His name was Samuel.

The Yearly Sacrifice

Samuel's parents, Elkanah and Hannah, traveled to the tabernacle at Shiloh each year to worship God and attend the "yearly sacrifice" (1 Sam. 1:3, 21). This time of celebration was called the Feast of the Passover, or the Feast of Unleavened Bread, the most important religious event of the year in Israel.

All Israelites were commanded to observe this eight-day feast, and many, especially the men, journeyed to Shiloh each spring to celebrate the feast at the tabernacle.

The Journey to Shiloh

Each spring, many of the Israelites went to the Feast of the Passover at the tabernacle in Shiloh, 20 miles north of Jerusalem. Samuel's parents made the trip each year from Ramah, a small village 5 miles north of Jerusalem. They had a 15-mile walk or donkey ride, which would have taken them a day or two at the most. Other Israelites came from the outer borders of the land and beyond, taking a week or more to arrive in Shiloh.

Ramah

Five miles north of Jerusalem lie the ruins of Ramah. This ancient village is known as the home of Samuel's parents and the birthplace of Samuel, the prophet.

When Samuel was weaned, his mother brought him to Shiloh, to serve God in the tabernacle. But after the Philistines destroyed Shiloh and the tabernacle, Samuel moved back to Ramah. Here he set up his religious headquarters.

Each year Samuel rode on a circuit through the land, settling disputes, and encouraging the people to follow God, and always returning to Ramah, his home.

Hannah's Bargain with God

Hannah and Peninnah were the two wives of Elkanah. Peninnah had children, but Hannah did not. In Old Testament times, a married woman with no children was ashamed before her husband. She was thought to be under a curse from God. So Hannah prayed to God, vowing that if God would give her a son, she would dedicate him to full-time service in the tabernacle. Soon afterward, Samuel was born, and Hannah fulfilled her promise to God, bringing Samuel to Shiloh.

Below: Ramah, Samuel's birthplace and later, during his ministry, his home. The upper photo below shows a Moslem mosque in the center. In the lower photo the view is toward the west, with Ramah in the foreground. In the distance, at the left side of the picture, is Nebi Samwil, traditional tomb of Samuel.

Among the articles of clothing which the high priest wore were the breastpiece (top) and the ephod (bottom). The breastpiece (breastplate) had pockets in which the Urim and Thummim were placed, which helped decide God's will. The breastpiece had 12 stones on it, representing the 12 tribes of Israel. The ephod was something like an apron in appearance. Samuel wore one as a boy.

Samuel Serves at the Tabernacle

1 SAMUEL 1:21—2:11

Synopsis

Almost 400 years had passed since the Israelites entered the Promised Land and began its conquest under Joshua's leadership. These years had been dark and discouraging, for Israel had turned far from the Lord, mingling with its Canaanite neighbors and adopting many of their heathen ways. But a godly woman prayed for a son, and dedicated that son to the Lord. Samuel, while still very young, went to live at the tabernacle and served the aged priest Eli and the Lord.

Eli—His Duties as High Priest

As a young child, Samuel was taken to the tabernacle at Shiloh and dedicated to lifetime service for God. There he grew up under the instruction of Eli, the high priest.

From Aaron, the first high priest, the office was passed down from father to son, and assumed for a lifetime. Eli was, therefore, a direct descendant of Aaron.

As high priest, Eli was ultimately responsible for all of the sacrifices and services offered by the tabernacle. Under him were the priests

The high priest in full dress must have been a splendid sight. He wore seven articles of clothing, including the ephod and breastpiece mentioned at the far left. In addition to those two, he wore a robe, an embroidered cloak or coat, the belt of the ephod, the mitre, and the diadem or cap. Special underclothing was prescribed also. The high priest's clothing was made of the finest linen. Above: a sacrificial hook, which may have been similar to the one mentioned in 1 Samuel 2:13.

and Levites, to whom Eli gave the responsibility to carry out most of the work.

The high priest represented the people before God. Each morning and evening, he entered the holy place of the tabernacle and burned incense on the incense altar, which stood in front of the veil. Sometimes the high priest gave this job to other priests.

Once a year, on the Day of Atonement, the high priest alone entered the holy of holies to offer up the sins of the people to God. This was a sacred ceremony, where the high priest begged forgiveness for the people's sins in the presence of God.

Offerings at the Tabernacle

The priests at the tabernacle were kept busy caring for the building and preparing the great variety of daily sacrifices, or offerings.

Each day, the priests killed two male lambs. One lamb was burned on the altar of burnt offering in the morning, and one in the evening. Anything that was burned with fire on the altar, including animals, plants, or food, was called a burnt offering. But burnt offerings were called by many different names. The daily offering of the two lambs was called the continual burnt offering.

Burned along with the continual burnt offering was the grain offering, a mixture of fine flour and oil, probably olive oil. The drink offering was usually included at this time as well. It consisted of different amounts of wine, varying when a lamb, goat, or bull was sacrificed.

On the Sabbath, and on feast days, many other offerings were included. People approached God with sin offerings, guilt offerings, and offerings of thanksgiving and praise.

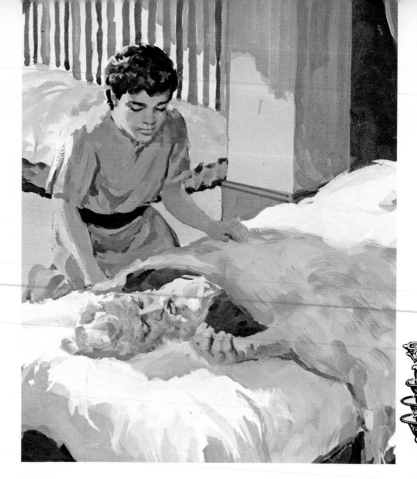

Four times the Lord spoke to the boy Samuel. Three times he went to Eli, thinking it was the voice of Eli that he had heard. The beds shown in this painting were probably far more luxurious than the actual beds used by Samuel and Eli.

God Speaks to Samuel

1 SAMUEL 3

Synopsis
As the long, dark period of the Judges came to a close, Israel's hope lay in Samuel. His mother Hannah had prayed for a son, and when he came, dedicated him to the Lord's work at the tabernacle. One night, the Lord spoke to the boy Samuel.

The Menorah—The Golden Lampstand of the Tabernacle
Samuel slept in the sanctuary of the tabernacle, by the golden lampstand known as the menorah. This was a very important piece of furniture to the Israelites, and today is still one of the major symbols of the Jewish faith.

Originally, the menorah was carved from a single piece of acacia wood, the same strong and durable wood used to make the other tabernacle furniture. It was then overlaid with 96 pounds of pure gold.

The menorah had a long straight stand. Six branches curved out and up from its center, three on each side. There were seven branches in all, including the center stand. At the tip of each branch was a small cup. Each morning a priest or Levite filled these seven cups with the finest olive oil, then lighted the wick that floated in the oil. All day the menorah burned, and into a part of the evening. These flames were an expression of God's presence.

168

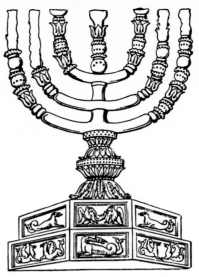

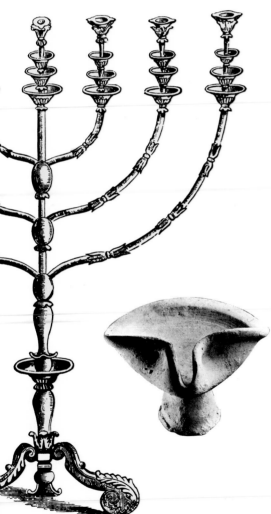

The lampstand, or candlestick, appeared many times in Jewish art in different styles. The mosaic at the upper left is from the floor of a second or third century A.D. synagogue at Hammath, just east of Tiberias. The drawing above is taken from the Arch of Titus, showing the menorah, or lampstand, as it appeared in Herod's temple in A.D. 70. The large drawing at the left is a 19th-century artist's version. The lamps in Samuel's time, shown below left in two places, were shallow and deeper dishes. Their wicks lay in their spouts.

In the morning, the three right-hand branches were lit first, followed by the three left-hand branches. The center branch was always the last to be lit. An outside branch could be relit from the center branch, but the center branch could only be relit from the altar where the burnt offerings took place.

Many think the menorah was designed to represent the tree of life. Others say the lampstand was patterned after any normal tree, symbolizing fruitfulness and peace in Israel.

Beds

In ancient times, beds were merely mats or blankets, light enough to carry from place to place. In the morning they were easily rolled up and stored in a convenient spot until evening. Samuel probably slept on this kind of bed in the tabernacle sanctuary. Poor people used only their coats, or cloaks, as their beds.

For the wealthy, beds were more comfortable, but still nothing like those enjoyed today. Rich people could afford quilts or even mattresses that were stuffed with soft cotton. Kings slept on elevated beds or couches called divans, with two or three mattresses.

169

Dagon, chief god of the Philistines, was often shown as part fish. The drawing of Dagon at the right was taken from a bas-relief at Khorsabad, a city of ancient Assyria (modern Iraq). The photo below is a beautiful mosaic on the wall of the Dagon Hotel in Ashkelon.

The Ark Is Captured

1 SAMUEL 4:1—5:12

Synopsis
The time of the Judges had been a dark period in Israel's history, a time when the people suffered many defeats because they had turned from the Lord and thus the Lord had turned from them. But as Samuel grew up, people began to recognize that he was a prophet, a truly godly leader who could help them return to the Lord. During this time, when Eli was still the high priest of Israel, the Philistines were a constant threat. On one occasion the Israelites were so desperate for victory that they took the ark to the battlefield, hoping it would turn the tide of battle. Instead, the Philistines captured the ark and took it home with them. When news of this reached Eli, he died.

Dagon
The chief god of the Philistines was Dagon. He was the god of rain, who brought forth a rich harvest. Later, he was known also as the god of grain.

Throughout the land of the Philistines, many temples were built to Dagon. Ashdod and Gaza were two cities with Dagon's temples, which were quite large, capable of holding hundreds or thousands of people.

Dagon's temples were used for religious and social activities. In years of famine, when

little rain fell, the priests of Dagon offered strange sacrifices to their god, hoping to gain his pity. In extreme cases, they even sacrificed children on the altar in an attempt to get some attention from Dagon. When all seemed to be going well, the temple was used for sporting events, or for the humiliation of captives and prisoners (Jud. 16:23-25).

Against the power of God, Dagon proved ineffective and lifeless. At Gaza, Samson pulled Dagon's temple to the ground, killing 3,000 Philistines inside (Jud. 16:23-30). A few years later, the ark of the covenant was captured by the Philistines and placed in the temple of Dagon at Ashdod. But Dagon's idol could not stand before the ark. Two times it fell before the ark, and the second time it broke into pieces (1 Sam. 5:1-7).

170

When the Philistines captured the ark, they took it first to Ashdod (above) where they put it in the temple of Dagon.

Plagues

Waves of sickness and disease often spread quickly throughout a country in ancient times. This was called a plague, and was one of the people's greatest fears.

Plagues moved quickly, and seemed to come from nowhere to inflict pain and death on both rich and poor, slave and master. The most common plague in Bible times was the bubonic plague carried by swarms of rats. When the rats died, the fleas left them, and carried the disease to humans. This highly contagious disease then swept across the land, often killing entire families.

Some plagues, sent by God for a specific purpose, may have been this disease (Num. 14:37; 16:47; 25:9). But other plagues of various types also appeared.

The Loss of the Ark

When the Philistines captured the ark of the covenant, they took Israel's most-prized possession. In fact, it was so sacred that many believed it alone would provide victory in battle.

The ark was not destroyed when captured because the Philistines understood its importance to the Israelites and wanted to show off this prized treasure to their own people. It was first seized at the battle of Ebenezer, about 25 miles west of Shiloh, and brought to the temple of Dagon in Ashdod. When God struck the city with a plague, the ark was moved to Gath, but disease spread to the Philistines there as well. Next it was sent to Ekron, but when the plague broke out again, the Philistines quickly sent the ark back to the Israelites at Beth Shemesh, about 15 miles west of Jerusalem. From there it was brought to Kiriath Jearim, where it stayed until David's time.

171

The Return of the Ark

1 SAMUEL 6:1—7:2

Synopsis
While Eli was still high priest of Israel, and Samuel had not yet begun a widespread ministry, the Philistines and Israelites fought a battle. But the battle went against the Israelites so much that they brought the ark of the covenant to the battlefield, hoping it would turn the tide for them. Instead, the Philistines captured the ark and took it back to their home territory. However, they had nothing but trouble as long as the ark remained with them, so they made plans to send it back to Israel.

Oxcarts
The Philistines lived along the flat coast of the Mediterranean Sea, and in this region, carts and wagons were very useful. But in Canaan, the land was hilly and rocky. Without roads, travel by cart or wagon was difficult, if not impossible, in many places.

In earliest times, wagon wheels were made from large pieces of wood, carved into a circle. Later, spokes were invented and metal rims added. The ordinary cart of Palestine was made of wood, but some were made of reeds, bronze, or iron. The axles turned smoothly in grease made from fish fat or oxen fat.

172

Top: Beth Shemesh and its nearby fields. Above right: Philistine wagons (carts), drawn from an Egyptian sculpture. The oxcarts above and above left remind us much of the one on which the ark (left) was returned to Israel.

From Beth Shemesh to Kiriath Jearim

When attacked by plague, the Philistines put the ark of God in an oxcart, and sent it back to Israel, to the town of Beth Shemesh, located about 8 miles east of Ekron and 15 miles west of Jerusalem. But when God killed many of the people of Beth Shemesh for looking inside of the ark, they became afraid. They sent the ark to Kiriath Jearim, about 10 miles west of Jerusalem.

The ark stayed here in the house of a man named Abinadab until the days of David, when the king brought the ark to Jerusalem. There it stayed until the days of the Captivity.

173

Saul chose Gibeah (upper left), only a few miles north of Jerusalem, as the site for his palace. From Gibeah the city of Jerusalem is easily seen today (above). Saul was made king at Mizpah (left). The map at the right shows Gibeah and Mizpah (sometimes spelled Mizpeh) and the entire nation that Saul ruled.

Saul Is Made King

1 SAMUEL 8—10

Synopsis
Samuel was a godly man, but a poor father, so his sons were unworthy to rule after him. The people of Israel recognized this and demanded a king. Saul was their choice.

Why Did the Israelites Want a King?
For years the Israelites had wanted a king, but when Samuel grew old, they were especially demanding. The people gave Samuel three reasons why they thought a king was needed.

First of all, Samuel's sons were evil and corrupt men, unfit to follow in the godly footsteps of their father. Secondly, nearly every nation around Israel had a king as the country's ruler, and the Israelites wanted to be like them. Lastly, they wanted a military commander to make them stronger in the eyes of their enemies (1 Sam. 8:5, 20).

What a King Would Do
The Israelites wanted a king, but were they willing to accept the responsibilities of one?

A king gave the people better organization and strength, but he also took much of their food, animals, and money in the form of taxes.

A king also gave the nation a military commander, but in return he took the people's sons to fight in his army, and he took their daughters to work in the palace and support him, his servants, and his army. A king also used their horses to pull chariots, and demanded more of their crops to feed his soldiers.

174

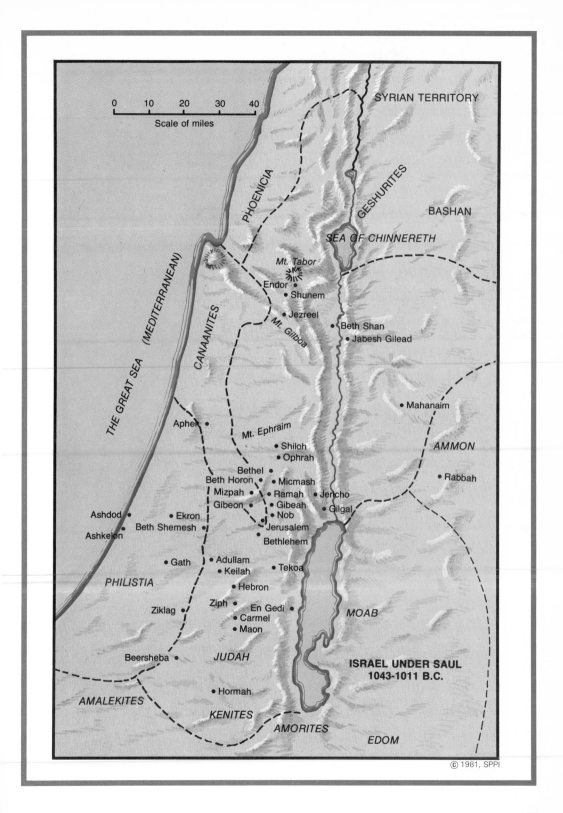

SYRIAN TERRITORY

0 10 20 30 40
Scale of miles

PHOENICIA

GESHURITES

BASHAN

SEA OF CHINNERETH

Mt. Tabor

Endor
• Shunem

• Jezreel

Mt. Gilboa

• Beth Shan
• Jabesh Gilead

THE GREAT SEA (MEDITERRANEAN)

CANAANITES

• Mahanaim

Apher •

Mt. Ephraim

AMMON

• Shiloh
• Ophrah

Bethel •
Beth Horon •   • Micmash
Mizpah •   • Ramah   • Jericho
Gibeon •   • Gibeah
• Nob   • Gilgal

Ashdod •   • Ekron
Beth Shemesh •

Ashkelon

Jerusalem

Bethlehem

• Rabbah

• Gath   • Adullam
• Keilah   • Tekoa

PHILISTIA

• Hebron

Ziph •
Ziklag •   • En Gedi
• Carmel
• Maon

MOAB

Beersheba •   JUDAH

AMALEKITES

• Hormah

KENITES

AMORITES

EDOM

ISRAEL UNDER SAUL
1043-1011 B.C.

© 1981, SPPI

175

Saul Sacrifices Wrongly

1 SAMUEL 13

Synopsis
During the days of the Judges of Israel, the nation turned away from the Lord. This was still true when Eli led the nation as high priest. But about that time the Lord appointed Samuel to follow Eli, for Eli's sons were unworthy to do this. Samuel served well, leading the nation back to the Lord. But he was also a poor father, and his sons were unworthy to do his work. So the people demanded a king. Saul was made king and served well at first. But when the Lord told Saul to wait for Samuel, he would not do it.

Saul's Sacrifices
When Saul would wait no longer for Samuel, he went ahead on his own and sacrificed the burnt and peace offerings. Peace offerings were usually not required, but were a voluntary act of worship and devotion to God.

Burnt offerings often accompanied peace offerings, showing additional devotion to God. They were sometimes given before a battle to uncover the people's sins and ask for God's mercy, as well as to unite the soldiers in preparing for war. Saul disobeyed by offering these sacrifices himself, for God had commanded that Samuel was supposed to offer them.

Gibeah
Saul was born into the tribe of Benjamin, and lived in the city of Gibeah.

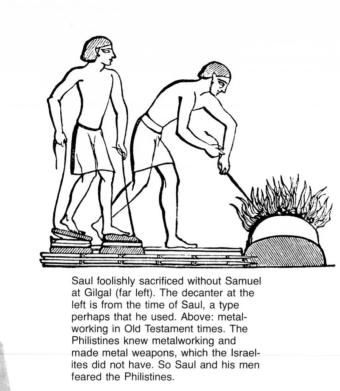

Saul foolishly sacrificed without Samuel at Gilgal (far left). The decanter at the left is from the time of Saul, a type perhaps that he used. Above: metalworking in Old Testament times. The Philistines knew metalworking and made metal weapons, which the Israelites did not have. So Saul and his men feared the Philistines.

This was Saul's first capital, only three miles north of Jerusalem. It was the headquarters of Saul's military campaigns.

The city was occupied on and off through the centuries until Titus, a Roman commander, destroyed it along with Jerusalem in A.D. 70. No one has lived there since. Excavations of the ruins have uncovered a large fortress, thought to be King Saul's palace.

Philistine Garrisons or Outposts

Garrisons or outposts were military fortresses built by an army near the borders of enemy territory. They were occupied by groups of brave men, usually for defensive purposes. They were also used as a headquarters for sending spies into enemy land. In times of war, they kept food and supplies for friendly soldiers.

Philistine Oppression

Years before the Israelites arrived in Canaan, the Philistines had moved in. At that time they were called the Sea Peoples, because they came from across the Mediterranean Sea. With their skilled and powerful warriors, they easily swept into the land of Canaan and occupied the territory along the seacoast.

In the days of Samuel and Saul, the Philistines were especially strong. Their government was run by five rulers called "lords," who reached decisions by majority vote. Along with this organized government was a highly organized army of skilled warriors. Only the Philistines knew the secret of making iron, which put the Israelites at a great disadvantage in battle. With their disorganized and bickering tribes, the Israelites were no match for the skilled Philistines, who constantly oppressed Israel until King David united that kingdom and conquered the Philistines.

Jonathan's Bravery

1 SAMUEL 14

Synopsis

When Saul became king, Israel was a rather weak nation. There was no organized army, so Saul formed one. The army had no weapons, for their enemies, the Philistines, were the only ones nearby who knew how to work iron. So when the Philistines came to fight, the soldiers of Israel were frightened. They were outnumbered and poorly armed. However, Jonathan, Saul's son, trusted the Lord more than weapons. With only his armor-bearer, he attacked the Philistine camp.

Jonathan's Victories at Micmash and Geba

These two towns were the scenes of Jonathan's brave attack on the Philistines. First, he defeated the Philistine garrison at Geba, located on a hill a few miles northeast of Jerusalem. As news reached the Philistine rulers of this defeat, King Saul moved his army from Micmash to Gilgal. Micmash lay on another large hill, and a steep gorge separated it from Geba, just to the southeast. Gilgal was at the foot of these two hills, near Jericho.

The Philistines gathered their entire army on the ridge of Micmash. From Gilgal, Saul and his men could look up to the ridge and see the vast numbers of the enemy army. It must have been a frightening sight.

But Jonathan was not afraid. Along with his armor-bearer, he slipped through the gorge that wound its way below Micmash and began the steep ascent to the Philistine camp.

178

animal gut were stretched across a curved piece of wood, or between a sound box and a piece of wood attached at a right angle to the box.

Harps were very important instruments in ancient orchestras. They provided gentle music for quieting the heart and soothing the mind and soul. There were as many different kinds of harps and lyres as there were countries. Many had elaborate carvings of bulls, cows, and stags, which may have represented the different musical sections of a choir.

Music and Musicians

Music was a language understood by everyone in ancient times. Monuments and writings dating from Bible times show that music was greatly loved and appreciated. Musicians were respected, and in constant demand.

Rarely did a day slip by without the rhythm of music in some homes. Feasts, parties, rituals, wars, celebrations, and even funerals were filled with music and song. Kings and wealthy families had their own musicians. Orchestras often performed while walking through the streets, similar to the marching bands of today.

Many men and women became musicians to fight loneliness. David, as a shepherd, must have spent many weeks alone in the quiet hills of Canaan. The pleasant sound of his harp pushed back the fears of the night, and was also effective in keeping wild animals back in the shadows.

Messengers

David was well-known as an excellent musician, and when Saul was troubled, the king sent messengers to quickly bring David to the palace. A king's messengers were reliable men and fast runners, who could be trusted to relay the king's messages correctly. Some messengers to foreign lands served as spies, while others brought back news of battles to the king.

At the left and above are two lyres of Old Testament times, one a 12-string and the other a 6-string. These particular lyres are from the time of the Exodus, earlier than David's time. But one found at Megiddo, dated near to David's time, was much like the lyre above. At the top: Gibeah, where David played at Saul's palace.

183

David's victory weapon against Goliath (above right) was the common sling of that time. Slingers were respected warriors in some nations. Assyrians carved them on their monuments (top), as did Egyptians (bottom). Goliath foolishly ignored the fact that a young man could have such skill.

David and Goliath

1 SAMUEL 17

Synopsis

When Saul, first king of Israel, became disobedient to the Lord, it became obvious that he would not be a lasting king. The Lord told Samuel to anoint David, a young man of Bethlehem, to become the next king. Meanwhile David went to Saul's palace to live and to play music for the troubled king. About that time the Israelites and the Philistines went to war. David took food to his older brothers, who served in the army of Israel. David found the soldiers of Israel terrified by a giant, Goliath. Though David was probably a teenager, he challenged Goliath and killed him. This immediately made David a hero.

184

The decisive battle between David and Goliath was in the Valley of Elah (above). Goliath may have been buried in a Philistine coffin similar to the one below. Goliath's Philistine helmet was probably like the center one below, fifth row from the top. The helmets below are as follows, left to right: first row, Assyrian; second row, Assyrian and Sassanian; third row, all Assyrian; fourth row, all Egyptian; fifth row, Philistine in center, others unknown; bottom row, Greek, Persian, and Greek.

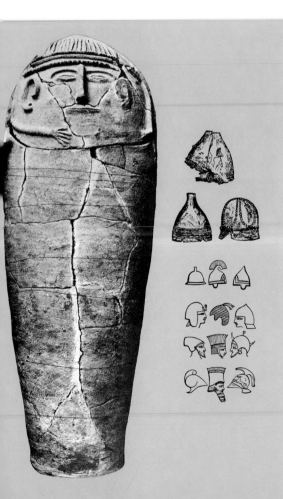

The Weapon that Won the Battle at Elah

What kind of weapon did David use to defeat the giant Goliath? It was a common sling, but it was not a boy's toy, for armies had been fighting battles with slings for centuries.

In the days of the Judges, some Israelite soldiers were excellent slingers in battle. The tribe of Benjamin had 700 left-handed warriors who could sling at a hair and never miss (Jud. 20:16).

The center of a sling, sometimes called the pan, was a wide piece of leather which held the stone. A long strip of leather, or a cord made of goat's hair, was tied to each side of the pan. Sometimes one cord had a loop at the end, for the slinger's wrist. The slinger held the end of the other cord in his hand.

With a stone in place, the slinger whirled his weapon around his head several times, then released the end of the cord from his hand, sending the stone to its mark. Goliath's people learned too late that David's sling was a deadly weapon of war, and not a boy's toy.

Goliath, a Walking Arsenal

For years, the Israelites had looked up to their King Saul as a giant. He was head and shoulders taller than anyone else in Israel, perhaps six and one half to seven feet in height (1 Sam. 10:23).

But Saul didn't come close to Goliath, who was over nine feet tall. He was half again as tall as nearly every Israelite soldier!

Goliath was as powerful as he was tall. On his shoulders and chest he wore a coat of mail that weighed 125 pounds. The iron point of his javelin alone weighed 15 pounds. With bronze leggings, bronze helmet, and his great shield and sword, Goliath must have carried 200 pounds of armor. He was a walking arsenal.

But Goliath was a deadly soldier too. He was a champion of all the Philistines, a giant who used every piece of armor with the precision of a modern pro football player. No wonder the Israelites feared him!

185

David and Jonathan

1 SAMUEL 18:1-4

Synopsis

King Saul had failed as king, not because he ruled poorly, but because he would not obey the Lord. Thus the Lord told Samuel to anoint David, who was still quite young, as the next king of Israel. David went to Saul's palace to live and played music to soothe the troubled king. In time, David challenged giant Goliath in a battle and killed the Philistine. Jonathan, Saul's son, was so impressed with David that the two became lifelong friends.

A Rare Friendship

Jonathan was not only a mighty warrior, but the prince of Israel. As the son of King Saul, he was next in line to inherit the throne of Israel. According to the custom of the day, Jonathan had every right to become Israel's next king.

But because of Saul's sin, God had taken the kingship away from Saul's family, and given it to David. Jonathan did not know this at first, and after David killed Goliath, the two young men became inseparable. Together, Jonathan and David made a lifelong covenant of friendship (1 Sam. 18:3).

Later, Jonathan learned that David, and not he, would be the next king of Israel. But an unusual thing happened. Jonathan loved David even more, and their friendship grew

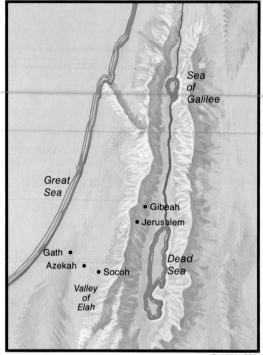

© 1981, SPPI

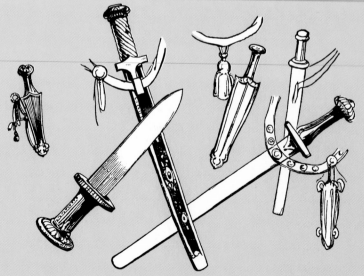

The map at the upper right shows the relationship of Jerusalem to Gibeah (Saul's palace), Gath (Goliath's home), and the Valley of Elah (where David fought Goliath), near Socoh and Azekah. Among the gifts Jonathan gave David was his sword. At the right are Bible-time swords, drawn from ancient monuments.

186

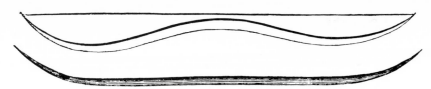

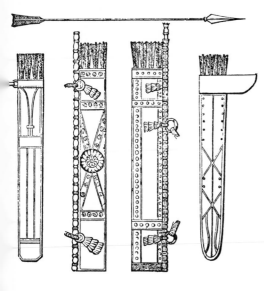

stronger. Recognizing God's will, Jonathan preferred
to lose the throne of Israel, than to lose his companion
David. What a rare friendship!

Jonathan's Gifts for David

When David and Jonathan met, they became lifelong
friends. Jonathan was so serious about their friendship
that he made a covenant with David and sealed it by
giving him his robe, tunic, sword, bow, and belt
(1 Sam. 18:4).

The word robe as used in the Bible meant an expensive and elegant cloak worn by royalty. It was made
from the finest cloth. Some were imported from faraway countries like Babylon. This in itself would have
been a valuable gift to a trusted friend.

But Jonathan gave his friend more. In all Israel, only
Saul and Jonathan had swords and spears of iron
(1 Sam. 13:22). The Philistines alone knew the secret
of forging the strong metal. Since the Israelites' weapons were made only of wood and stone, Jonathan's
iron sword was probably the most highly prized
weapon in Israel. But without a second thought, he
gave it to his friend David.

Jonathan's gifts to David included
his sword, bow, belt, and robe. Goliath's weapons included sword,
spear, and javelin (1 Sam. 17:45).
At the top are Bible-time bows and
quivers and arrows, drawn from
monuments. Below are spears and
a javelin, also drawn from monuments. The painting at the left shows
Jonathan giving his gifts to David.

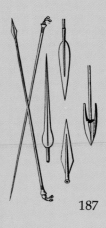

187

Saul Tries to Kill David

1 SAMUEL 18—19

Synopsis
Saul was a strong king in many ways, but he did not like to obey the Lord. So the Lord chose David to be the next king instead of a member of Saul's family. After David killed Goliath, the people praised David much more than Saul. This made Saul so jealous that he wanted to kill David.

A City Celebrates after Victory
Victorious in battle, David and Saul must have ridden back to the palace together. When entering a city on their homeward trip, throngs of happy people greeted them in the streets, shouting and dancing.

Women sang a special song as they circled around their heroes. Musicians shook their tambourines, symbolic of victory.

Often the song leader shouted a verse and the other singers repeated it in an exaggerated form. As David and Saul moved through the city, the song leader praised Saul for killing thousands of men, and the singers repeated by praising David for killing tens of thousands. Though this was a common custom in Israelite songs, Saul grew angry and jealous of David's greater praise. After this, Saul kept a suspicious eye on his popular commander.

The Spear that Missed Its Mark
What did Saul's spear look like? Though some spears looked more like short knives, Saul's spear probably had a long wooden shaft, almost as tall as he was. The spearhead was made of stone or metal, and the tip often had two hooks or barbs which left a mortal wound when the spear was pulled from a wounded soldier. These long spears were sometimes called javelins. Just the spearhead of Goliath's javelin weighed over 15 pounds! Some of these long spears were designed to spin through the air, inflicting even greater injury.

Many of the events surrounding David and Jonathan, as well as King Saul, happened at Gibeah, where Saul's palace was located (left). David lived here with the king and Jonathan for a while. Gibeah is only a few miles north of Jerusalem. The map at the right shows the kingdom during the time of Saul and David.

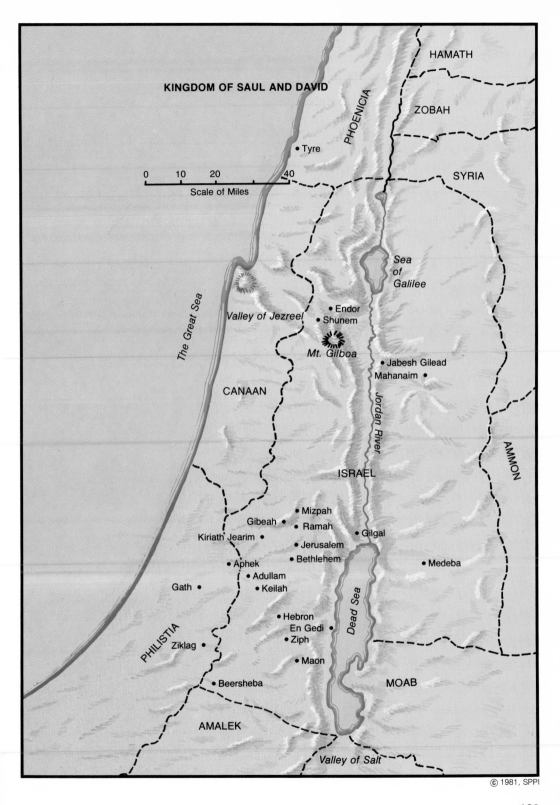

KINGDOM OF SAUL AND DAVID

HAMATH

ZOBAH

PHOENICIA

SYRIA

• Tyre

0   10   20   40
Scale of Miles

Sea
of
Galilee

Valley of Jezreel

• Endor
• Shunem

Mt. Gilboa

• Jabesh Gilead
Mahanaim •

The Great Sea

CANAAN

Jordan River

ISRAEL

AMMON

• Mizpah

Gibeah •   • Ramah

Kiriath Jearim •   • Gilgal

• Jerusalem

• Aphek   • Bethlehem

• Medeba

• Adullam

Gath •   • Keilah

Dead Sea

• Hebron
En Gedi •
• Ziph

PHILISTIA

Ziklag •

• Maon

MOAB

• Beersheba

AMALEK

Valley of Salt

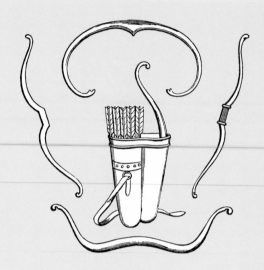

Weapons figured prominently in the life of David. With a sling he killed Goliath, who had come against him with sword, spear, and javelin. Jonathan pledged his friendship with David by giving him his sword and bow.

Jonathan Warns David

1 SAMUEL 20

Synopsis

After David killed Goliath, Jonathan became his best friend. Jonathan admired David's courage and grew to love him more than a brother. So when Saul, Jonathan's father, grew insanely jealous of David and tried to kill him, Jonathan remined loyal and friendly to David. He would not betray his friend, even for his father.

The Deadly Bow and Arrow

Jonathan used his bow and arrow to warn David of Saul's anger. But bows and arrows were mainly used in battle during war times, and for hunting in times of peace.

On the battlefield, an archer's bow and arrows was one of his most deadly and effective weapons. Instead of fighting in hand-to-hand combat, an archer with a sharp aim could pierce the heart of an enemy soldier from a distance of 40 yards or more.

The ancient Egyptians used the simple reflex bow, a curved piece of wood or bone, with a taut string of animal gut tied between the ends. These bows were often as tall as a man, and powerful enough to send a flying arrow completely through a man's body.

Canaanite hunters and soldiers used more complicated bows of wood, bone, metal, or a combination of these materials. They made a bronze battle bow so powerful that even a mighty warrior had trouble pulling the bowstring.

The arrows had a long shaft, usually about three feet, made of reed or wood. One end was notched to fit into the bowstring. The arrow-

190

The weapons on these pages have been drawn from scenes on ancient monuments. At the far left, an Egyptian archer with bow drawn and arrow in place. A quiver filled with arrows hangs at his side. Next to him is a picture of bows, quiver, and arrows. At the left are an Assyrian archer (left side) and a Persian archer (right side). Above, an archer with full armor and sword hanging by his side.

head, attached to the other end, was sometimes tied to the shaft with a cord of leather. Most arrowheads were made from flint, bone, iron, or bronze. Some were dipped in poison before battle to make sure the enemy died, even if he wasn't mortally wounded. Arrows were kept in a quiver, a leather bag strapped over one's shoulder.

Sitting at the King's Table

Few people earned the privilege of eating with the king. Persian kings often ate alone, while Israelite kings usually ate only with their closest friends and advisers. During large feasts and festivals, kings sometimes ate with a crowd of people.

The king's table was the place of highest honor. Guests were seated according to their rank or importance. If an unimportant guest took a seat too close to the king, he would be asked to move to a lower position. The Greeks and Romans thought the middle of the table was the greatest place of honor. Other nations made the head of the table the most prominent place. King Saul's seat was at the back of the room against the wall, where he could easily see everyone who was eating with him. To his left was Abner, his army general, and to his right was his son Jonathan.

The Festival of the New Moon

The Israelites were festive people. Almost every moment of the day was filled with hard work, so the people eagerly looked forward to the days set aside for feasting and festivity.

One of these festivals was always celebrated at the time of each new moon. It was called the Festival of the New Moon. Though it included religious ceremonies, it was primarily a time for the community to get together and rejoice over the fruits of the land and its bountiful harvests.

Above: a small village stands on the site thought to be ancient Nob, where the priests of Israel lived and where David visited Ahimelech. The cave at the left, within 10 miles of the supposed site of Adullam, would hold hundreds of men comfortably.

David Runs from Saul

1 SAMUEL 21—22

Synopsis

From the day David killed Goliath, the people of Israel praised him more than King Saul. This made Saul jealous, to the point of insanity, so that he often tried to kill David. At last David had to leave the palace and run from Saul, who pursued him with soldiers.

Where Was Nob?

David soon realized that Saul wanted to kill him. To save his life, David escaped from Saul's capital at Gibeah, and fled to Nob, a small town where many of the priests lived, just a few miles to the southeast.

After Shiloh was destroyed, Israel's religious headquarters were probably set up at Nob. It is likely that the tabernacle was destroyed along with Shiloh, and a temporary building might have been set up at Nob to replace it. As the new religious center of Israel, Nob was the home of many priests and Levites.

David knew he would not be safe so close to Saul's capital. He asked Ahimelech, the high priest who lived at Nob, for Goliath's sword and some of the holy showbread. Then he ran farther into the wilderness.

When Saul found out that Ahimelech had helped David, he killed that high priest along with 85 other priests. He also killed the women and children and ransacked the city (1 Sam. 22:6-19).

The Showbread

Inside the tabernacle was a table on which 12 round loaves of special bread were placed. This holy bread was called showbread, and symbolized that God was the Bread of Life for the nation of Israel.

Each Friday afternoon before the Sabbath, certain priests carefully baked the loaves of bread. Only the priests from the Garmu family knew the secret recipe, which contained only the finest flour and the purest oil.

On Saturday morning, the day of the Sabbath, eight priests took part in a special ceremony and replaced the week-old loaves with the freshly baked ones. The bread was arranged in two stacks of six loaves, with a golden bowl of sweet frankincense placed on the top of each stack.

The old bread was divided between the high priest and the other priests, and was to be eaten and not thrown away. The old frankincense was poured out over the altar and burned before God. The fresh bread remained on the table until the next Sabbath, when the ritual ceremony was performed again. There was never a day when the showbread was not present in the tabernacle.

Masada

On the eastern edge of the Judean desert, the high mountain fortress of Masada stands alone near the edge of the Dead Sea. Isolated from the surrounding cliffs, it made a perfect stronghold for David and his men when they were hiding from Saul.

For centuries, armies and outcasts have sought this mountain refuge as a means of defense. On all four sides the ascent is very steep, making an attack almost impossible. In ancient times, the only way to the top was by climbing the "snake path," a very narrow footpath that wound back and forth as it rose to the summit. Anyone attempting to scale this rugged path was defenseless to the people above. Years later, the Romans built a ramp that reached to the top on the west side.

On the summit is a 20-acre plateau, where Herod the Great built himself an impressive retreat, with garrisons, bathhouses, storerooms, and a palace.

But how did Herod get enough water to supply all of his buildings on this hot and barren mountaintop? At the foot of the mountain were two small streams, bone-dry most of the time, but rushing torrents when it rained. Herod dammed these streams up, and the excess water flowed into great cisterns built nearby. Hundreds of slaves then carried the water to the summit in pottery jars, dumping it into rock cisterns dug on the top for storing all of the water.

When Jonathan warned David to flee, he went first to Ramah to visit Samuel (Naioth is thought by some to be Samuel's home in Ramah). On the way to his next stop at Nob, David waited in a field while Jonathan returned to Gibeah to find out if Saul meant to kill David. When he found it was true, Jonathan warned David with arrows, and David went on to Nob, where Ahimelech gave David bread and Goliath's sword. From there, David went to Gath, and pretended to be insane before the Philistine King Achish. Then David escaped to Adullam, where a large number gathered with him.

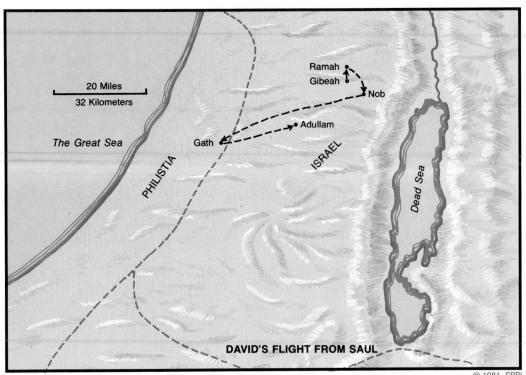

DAVID'S FLIGHT FROM SAUL

193

The Ziphites Betray David

1 SAMUEL 23

Synopsis

Saul became insanely jealous of David. Since the day when David had killed Goliath, he had been more popular than Saul, and this made Saul want to kill him. David had to flee from the palace and hide in the wilderness. Gradually a number of loyal men joined him as he moved from place to place, but Saul and his army continued to search for David. In one instance, David saved the people of Keilah, only to learn that they would betray him to Saul. Not long after that, the people of Ziph did betray him, reporting his hiding place to Saul.

Who Were the Ziphites?

While David was hiding in the hills of Judah, men from the town of Ziph, called Ziphites, discovered David's hideout and reported it to Saul.

A small town, Ziph was probably located about four miles southeast of Hebron. It lay on a large hill overlooking the surrounding countryside, just west of the hills and strongholds of En Gedi, another one of David's hideouts from Saul. This was the same area

194

where David later crept into Saul's camp by night, and took the king's spear and water jug (1 Sam. 26:5-25).

The Wilderness of Maon

The Ziphites learned that David and his men were hiding in the wilderness of Maon, a wasteland beginning about five miles south of Ziph. Saul chased David east from there, toward the region near En Gedi.

Threshing Floors

A threshing floor was the combine of the ancient world. Here, the grain was separated from the stalks of wheat, barley, and corn. But instead of sophisticated instruments, the farmer let the wind do most of his work.

Because the wind played such an important role on the threshing floor, most were built outside of the city walls, away from obstructions. During the harvesttime, farmers slept next to their floors to protect the crops from thieves or other enemies.

The threshing floor was often made in the shape of a large circle, where all of the dirt was removed down to the bedrock. A low wall of stones was built around the circle to keep the grain inside the threshing floor.

Sheaves, or stalks of grain, were thrown onto the threshing floor. Animals, usually oxen, walked around the floor, or pulled a wooden sled, crushing the stalks and separating the kernels of grain from the stalks. This was called threshing.

Men and women then entered the threshing floor with long pitchforks, and tossed the broken sheaves into the air. The broken pieces of stalks, called chaff, blew away, while the important and heavier grain fell back onto the threshing floor. This was called winnowing. The grain was gathered into baskets or bags and taken to the marketplace or storehouses.

En Gedi

Fleeing from Saul, David found a refuge at En Gedi, a place where a spring of water bubbles up in the midst of a wilderness that holds only rocks, sand, and oppressive heat.

Lying in the wilderness of Judah, En Gedi is about 15 miles east and slightly south of Hebron.

While David was fleeing from Saul, some Ziphites came to tell Saul where to find him (upper left). Saul came after David and was about to close in on him when news came of a raid back home by the Philistines. Saul rushed home and David and his men went to En Gedi to stay. En Gedi is a beautiful oasis among the mountains in the desolate land to the west of the Dead Sea (left). It is a series of waterfalls and pools, with lush plants growing around them. From these pools in the mountains, one may look eastward over the Dead Sea (right).

195

Shepherds and sheep are still a common sight in the area where ancient Maon and Carmel once stood (above). In this area Abigail once brought food for David and his men (left). David's flight from King Saul took him through the various places shown on the map at the right.

Abigail Shares Her Food

1 SAMUEL 25

Synopsis

While Saul pursued David with his army, David and his loyal followers moved from place to place. Naturally, David and his men had to find food, so they often asked local farmers and shepherds to share theirs. When they asked Nabal, an incident took place that led to David's marrying Abigail.

Carmel and Maon

In this incident, Nabal was shearing sheep at Carmel, about seven miles south of Hebron. His home in Maon was about a mile farther south of Carmel.

These two places lie in an area of gently rolling hills and rich pastureland, ideal for Nabal's work of tending sheep. Years later, King Uzziah of Judah might have planted his many vineyards on this good soil (2 Chron. 26:10).

Sheep

Life in Palestine and the presence of sheep always seemed to be woven together. In some way, these animals played a very important part in the life of almost every Israelite.

Many men and women made their living tending sheep. Shepherding is one of the best-known occupations of Israel. This was because of the many uses of the sheep and their products.

From the sheep came wool, which was spun into yarn, woven into fabric, and then made into clothing. Sheepskin was used to

make tents, providing an excellent cloth that kept out the biting winds, and resisted the cold and dreary rains.

Even more important was the food provided by sheep. Since they were considered by the Hebrews as "clean" animals, their meat and milk became staple foods in the diet of Israel. Meat for the evening meal and milk to drink kept many of the Israelites well fed. A lamb was also a major part of the Passover meal (Ex. 12:3-11). In addition, the Israelites' worship often called for offering a sheep or a lamb. They were sacrificed in burnt offerings, and in sin, guilt, and peace offerings.

Sheep are often quite particular about what they eat, and usually need richer pastureland than goats or cattle. Because of the spotty winter rains in Palestine, the shepherds wander through the countryside, searching for the better grazing areas.

As quiet and nonaggressive animals, sheep willingly follow their shepherd wherever he leads. Sheep are also defenseless, unable to cope with the dangers of attacking animals or thieves. For this reason, the shepherd must always be on the lookout, watching his flock at all times. He alone can save his sheep from approaching disaster.

Shearing the Sheep

Once each year, in the middle or end of spring, all the sheep were gathered into pens. One by one they were caught and their thick, warm wool coats were shorn off. One sheep might have up to 10 pounds of wool removed. After the shearing, a large festival was held, celebrating the prosperity of another good year.

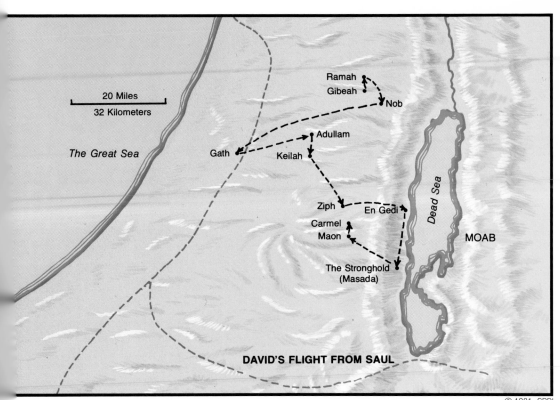

DAVID'S FLIGHT FROM SAUL

© 1981, SPPI

197

David Spares Saul

1 SAMUEL 26

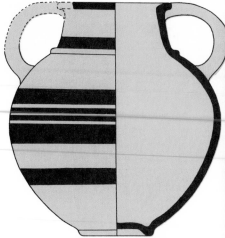

Synopsis
Because the people showed more favor to David than to him, Saul was insanely jealous of David. After Saul tried to kill David at the palace, David fled, and Saul pursued him from place to place. Once David could have killed Saul in a cave, but did not. Now, a second time, David found Saul unguarded and could have killed him, but spared him instead.

The Army Encampment
After a hard day of marching, an army stopped to set up camp. Often the soldiers stayed in their camp for more than one night, and some-times for as long as a month or even a year, when besieging a city.

In late afternoon, as the sun was slipping in the western sky, the army commander started to look for a good place to stop. He halted when he found two important things—plenty of water and a natural barrier of defense such as a long ridge or hillside.

When the right place was chosen, the soldiers pitched their tents in a large circle. Any animals they had brought with them or had captured were driven inside the circle after sunset for protection. Sometimes the commander's tent was pitched in the center of the circle. It was larger than the others, and just outside the tent door his spear was stuck in the ground as a symbol of his authority.

David and his nephew Abishai (son of David's sister Zeruiah) take Saul's spear and water jug while Saul sleeps. From this, Saul will realize that David could have killed him, but did not. The jugs shown on these pages are from the time of David and Saul. The area near Ziph, where this happened, is seen at the upper right.

198

The tabernacle in the wilderness was set up much like this, with the 12 tribes of Israel camped in a circle around the sanctuary.

Watchposts were set up on all sides of the army encampment, and throughout the night, men peered into the darkness, looking for any sign of the enemy.

Some armies, like the Assyrians, went to great lengths to protect their camps. Large walls of stone and mud were built around the tents, and tall earthen watchtowers looked out over the surrounding countryside. These elaborate encampments must have taken days or weeks to build, and were usually set up near a spot where a long battle was anticipated.

The Hill of Hakilah
Saul and his army set up camp by this hill when pursuing David. As Saul slept, David and Abishai crept into the camp and stole the king's spear and water jug, but did no harm to Saul himself.

The exact site of the hill is not known today, but it was somewhere in the wilderness of Ziph, a barren wasteland stretching south and east of Hebron.

David Moves to Ziklag

1 SAMUEL 27

Synopsis

Saul was insanely jealous of David, for he feared that David would replace him as king. This insane jealousy drove Saul to pursue David from place to place to try to kill him. At last, David realized there was no safe hiding place in all Israel. So he and his men moved to the land held by the Philistines, the enemies of Israel. The Philistines gave them Ziklag where they could settle with their families.

Ziklag—A Refuge for David

Driven with consuming jealousy, Saul would not rest until David was killed, ending the threat to his kingdom. Knowing this, David finally escaped to the city of Gath, in the land of the Philistines. After gaining the trust of Achish, the king of Gath, David was given Ziklag, a Philistine city where he could find refuge from Saul.

Ziklag was probably located about 12 miles north and slightly east of Beersheba, on the eastern fringes of Philistine territory. David was far enough from the large Philistine cities to avoid most of their influence, yet as a resident in their country, gained their confidence so that Philistine spies probably stopped trailing him.

From Ziklag, David conducted raids on the desert tribes to the south, who were mainly enemies of Israel. But David convinced Achish that he was actually raiding Israel.

David's home among the Philistines was at Ziklag, thought to be the area seen at the top. When Ziklag was destroyed, David pursued the Amalekites, who had captured his and his men's families. Some became exhausted and had to wait at the Besor Brook, above (see 1 Sam. 30:21). The route of David's flight from Saul is seen at the right, including his move to Ziklag.

The drawing of the Philistine warrior above was taken from an Egyptian painting. Note that the Philistine is a prisoner of the Egyptians. In Saul's time the Philistines were stronger militarily than the Israelites. Saul was about to be defeated by them.

Once David and his men returned to find their city plundered and their families taken captives by the Amalekites. Quickly they chased the enemy and destroyed them, recovering their families and possessions. Later, David received news of Saul's death at Ziklag.

David's Raids

Behind every successful raid by David and his men were hours of secret planning and quiet watching. Quickness and surprise decided the outcome of a desert raid, so David's men spent many days spying out the camp of an enemy tribe, searching for its weaknesses.

If spoils or valuables were all that were wanted, the camp was usually attacked when the men were away tending flocks or conducting their own raids. But if revenge was the main reason for attacking, the raiders waited until everyone was inside the camp, and then descended quickly on the people, often during the evening meal, or early morning while everyone was still asleep.

Some of David's Wives

Before David became king, he already had three wives. Michal, his first wife, was taken away by Saul. Abigail, his second wife, was Nabal's widow. Ahinoam was David's third wife. Later these and other wives would bring David great distress through their jealousy and the fighting of his many sons.

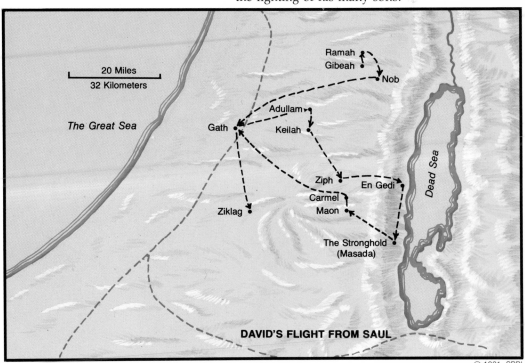

DAVID'S FLIGHT FROM SAUL

© 1981, SPPI

The Witch of Endor

1 SAMUEL 28

Synopsis
Saul had pursued David with his army, hoping to kill him. David went from place to place, but finally decided to move into the land of the Philistines to hide, for Saul would not pursue him there. When the Philistines went to war against Saul, they refused to let David go with them, for they feared that he would side with Saul in battle. Saul, in the meantime, grew frightened and went to a witch at Endor to see how this battle would go and what would happen to him.

Mediums—Their Magic and the Occult
Though forbidden by God, magicians, witches, sorcerers, and wizards continued to be popular among the Israelites. Many people sincerely believed that evil spirits and supernatural powers dictated their lives. By looking into the future, they hoped to change the course of their lives to avoid approaching disaster. Clever people were sensitive to these people's pagan beliefs, and became wizards or sorcerers to supply their demand.

These wizards, sorcerers, and magicians

Above is the mosque built at Nebi Samwil, traditional site of Samuel's tomb. The photo at the top of the page is of the cenotaph inside, an empty tomb honoring Samuel. From this hill Jerusalem is clearly visible about six miles to the south.

202

The pomegranate-shaped strainer at the left is from the time of David, Saul, and Samuel. It may have been used in cooking, possibly in preparing food as the witch of Endor did for Saul and his men. Endor is pictured below, with Mount Tabor in the background.

Nebi Samwil

On a high hill overlooking Jerusalem from the north is a mosque, covering a traditional site of Samuel's tomb. In Arabic it is called Nebi Samwil. But this place is filled with controversy.

Samuel's birthplace and home was at Ramah, thought by many to be modern Er Ram, only a few miles east of Nebi Samwil. The Bible says that Samuel was buried at Ramah (1 Sam. 25:1). If Er Ram was Ramah, then Samuel was buried there.

During the time of the Crusades, some pilgrims moved bones from a place called Ramle, which they thought was Ramah, to the place now called Nebi Samwil. After that time, pilgrims came to Nebi Samwil to honor it as the burial place of Samuel.

Like many places in Bible lands, the exact location is unknown. But Nebi Samwil remains one traditional site of Samuel's tomb.

Endor

The village where the witch of Endor lived was a small town seven or eight miles northeast of Mount Gilboa, where Saul fought his last battle the next day.

The Urim and Thummim

In times of great trouble, the ephod was often consulted to determine God's will. It was a beautiful sleeveless vest worn by the high priest. Attached to it was a breastpiece containing 12 precious stones, 1 for each tribe of Israel. Inside the breastpiece were the Urim and Thummim, which might have been two more precious stones that were probably used like lots to receive a yes or no answer to a question asked of God.

were called mediums, and were supposedly able to communicate with demons, evil spirits, and the spirits of the dead. By speaking with them, they could learn of future events. There was a big business for this, but more often than not the customers were fooled by the trick of ventriloquism. In ventriloquism, the wizard uttered sounds without moving his mouth, making noises that sounded like spirits coming up from the ground.

Reading the future, also known as divination, was practiced in other ways as well. "Magic potions" were poured into a cup, and the bubbles and reflections were read as a prediction of what lay ahead. Casting lots was done frequently as well.

God warned the Israelites through His prophets and judges that magic and sorcery were evil and dangerous. Anyone caught using these occult practices was supposed to be stoned to death. But despite God's warnings, the mystery of this evil magic continued.

Saul died in battle at Mount Gilboa, at the right. This range of mountains is about 12 miles south of the Sea of Galilee. Beth Shan, where Saul's body was hung, was at the eastern edge of the mountains. Endor was only a few miles, perhaps three or four, north of Gilboa.

Saul Dies

1 SAMUEL 31

Synopsis
While David was hiding among the Philistines, the enemies of Israel, the Philistines went to war against Saul. Terrified by the thought of defeat, Saul consulted a witch to see what would happen. Through her, he learned that he would die in battle the next day.

Gilboa—Saul's Last Battle
Saul fought his last battle on the slopes of Mount Gilboa. The Philistines killed him, along with three of his sons, including Jonathan.

Mount Gilboa rises from the Jezreel Plain. Saul wanted to avoid fighting on the plain itself, because his troops were no match for the sophisticated Philistine weapons and chariots. The battle occurred about 60 miles north of Jerusalem or close to 20 miles southwest of the Sea of Galilee. It probably started because the Israelites were threatening to close off a major trade route of the Philistines called The Way to the Sea, which ran from Egypt to Damascus.

Treatment and Torture of Prisoners of War
It is little wonder that Saul fell on his sword and killed himself when faced with the prospect of being captured by the Philistines, enemies who hated the Israelites. As a prisoner of war, and especially as a captured king and commander in chief, Saul would have been humiliated before all of the Philistines, and brutally tortured.

The Philistines enjoyed humiliating their captives by making them dance or sing before crowds of people. But the Babylonians and Assyrians were known for their brutal tactics of torture. When a city was captured, most of the men were killed, and the rest of the people were carried back to Babylon or Assyria with rings hooked through their lips or noses. Over the long trip, many died from exposure and

204

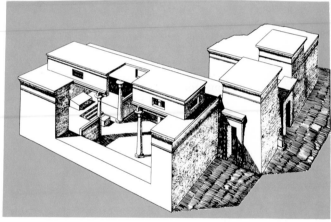

When the Philistines found Saul and his three sons on Mount Gilboa, they stripped their armor and put it in the temple of Ashtoreth in Beth Shan. At the right is a reconstruction of a temple at Beth Shan, thought to be the one mentioned in 1 Samuel 31:10. Several styles of ancient armor, drawn from monuments, are seen at the left.

starvation.

Some captives were bound alive to a table and had their skin stripped off. Others, especially great warriors, had their eyes gouged out and lived the rest of their lives as helpless creatures. Still others were thrown into small prison cells, each chained to the body of a dead man.

Not all captives were tortured. Some were killed instantly with axes or spears, while others were thrown into furnaces. Those not killed or tortured were forced into lives of slavery.

In Babylon, however, a slave's life was not all misery. He could own property and run his own business. If he earned enough money, he could even buy back his freedom!

Beth Shan

Sifting through the plunder on the day after battle, the Philistines found the dead bodies of Saul and his sons. With great rejoicing they carried their bodies about 10 miles southwest along the Jezreel Valley to the town of Beth Shan, later called Beth Shean, where they hung the corpses on the city walls. They remained there until brave men from Jabesh Gilead, a small village 15 miles farther southwest, recovered the bodies of their king and princes and buried them.

205

David Becomes King of Judah

2 SAMUEL 2:1-11

Synopsis

While David lived at Ziklag, a city which the Philistines had set aside for his home, the Israelites and Philistines went to war. Saul, king of Israel, was killed in battle with his son Jonathan. After this, David became king of Judah, and Saul's son Ish-Bosheth became king of Israel.

When

Dating Bible events in Israel's history becomes much more accurate at the start of David's reign than previously. Most authorities agree that David was crowned king of Judah between 1011 and 1000 B.C.

But how was such an accurate date determined? Archeologists have uncovered ancient Assyrian texts which mention every year in Assyrian history from 891-648 B.C., and the important events which occurred in these years.

For example, ancient Assyrian texts inscribed on stone or clay tell of the battle at Qarqar, where Ahab, king of Israel, clashed with Shalmaneser III, king of Assyria, in 853 B.C. They also mention that Jehu, the third Israelite king after Ahab, paid tribute to Shalmaneser III in 841 B.C. The Bible mentions all of the kings of Israel and the lengths of their reigns, as well as the kings of Judah who were ruling during their reigns.

The Assyrian texts provide a fixed date, and the Bible tells how long each king ruled. By combining the two, Bible events in the time of the Kings can be estimated closely.

David Chooses His Capital

Why did David choose to make Hebron his capital when crowned king of Judah? As one of the first cities built in the land of Palestine, Hebron was already old and well established when David arrived there as king.

Lying on gentle slopes and surrounded by rich vineyards and fertile olive groves, Hebron had an abundant food supply. There was also plenty of water from the many springs which bubbled up around the city.

But the most important reason David chose Hebron was for its central location in the tribe of Judah. His hometown of Bethlehem was too far north.

Hebron was also the largest city in Judah when David became king, and the most secure against enemy attack. Located at the intersection of many vital trade routes, the city was bustling with business activity.

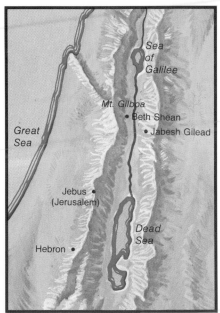

© 1981, SPPI

Hebron, located on the map at the left, is still a thriving city today. The view above is from the west. At the far left, this view of Hebron emphasizes the rocky, rolling hills on which the city is built, and which surround the city. In Hebron is the site of the cave of Machpelah, where Abraham and his family were buried.

207

David Captures Jerusalem

2 SAMUEL 5:1-16; 1 CHRONICLES 11:1-9

The Jebusite city of Jebus, which later became Jerusalem, was just south of the area where the temple was built. That area, with the remains of the Jebusite walls, is seen at the top and in the two photos on the opposite page.

Synopsis
After Saul died in combat, the people of Judah made David their king. But the other Israelites, prompted by Saul's army commander, Abner, made Saul's son Ish-Bosheth their king. Before long, fighting broke out between the two factions, and as time passed, David's forces grew stronger while the forces of Ish-Bosheth became weaker. One day Ish-Bosheth insulted his army commander, Abner, and this caused Abner to change his loyalties to David. But Abner was quickly murdered by David's army commander, Joab. Soon after that, Ish-Bosheth was murdered. The people of Israel then turned to David and made him king over all Israel. As king of all the people, David wanted to move his capital to a more central place than Hebron, so he led an expedition against Jerusalem, held at that time by the Jebusites.

Jerusalem in David's Day
During the period of the Judges, and until David's time, the city of Jerusalem was called Jebus, and occupied by the Jebusites, who were a mixed Canaanite people. The city had stood for hundreds of years and was well fortified when David marched toward it.

It was a very imposing sight commanding the summit on the hill of Ophel with its fortified walls of stone and sturdy battlements that looked down over miles of surrounding countryside. David quickly realized that his small army was no match for the strong defenses of the city. He probably looked back to his days as a desert raider in Philistine country, remembering that surprise was often the most effective weapon. With that in mind, he attacked Jerusalem through the underground water tunnel built to bring water into the city in times of a siege.

When David was anointed king over all Israel, he chose Jerusalem as his new capital. It was centrally located among all of Israel's tribes, and almost impervious to enemy attack. No tribe of Israel owned the city, because David had captured it from the Jebusites. And no tribe could really lay claim to it, because it was on the border between the tribes of Judah and Benjamin.

In David's day, Jerusalem was much smaller than it is today. The king began extensive building projects, beginning with his palace and a strong fortress. He hired skilled craftsmen from Phoenicia to help with the work.

Carpenters at Work for David

When David started the work on his palace, there were probably few if any Israelite carpenters. So David made friends with Hiram, the king of Tyre, a nation to the northwest on the coast of the Mediterranean Sea.

Hiram sent David skilled carpenters to construct the palace and perform the detailed woodworking. Their tools, some of the best in the world, were quite primitive in light of today's power equipment. Everything was done by hand. Wooden mallets were used as hammers, flax and reeds passed for rulers, and crushed sandstone was the ancient world's sandpaper.

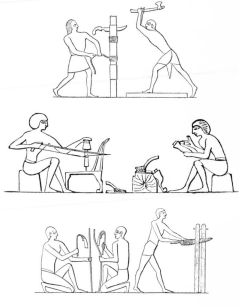

When David captured Jebus and made it his capital, he began an extensive building program. The drawings on these two pages show activities of Bible-time carpenters, recorded on the walls of Egyptian tombs. The top drawing shows carpenters splitting a beam. Center left: drilling with a bow drill. Center right: planing or polishing. Bottom left: planing with adze. Bottom right: sawing. Opposite page: gluing wood together.

When David brought the ark of the covenant to Jerusalem, he danced for joy at the head of the procession (left). His wife Michal, Saul's daughter, saw him and expressed her disgust at his dancing. For this she was no longer treated as his wife, and thus remained without children throughout her lifetime.

The Ark Is Moved

2 SAMUEL 6; 1 CHRONICLES 13; 15:1—16:3

Synopsis
After King Saul died, David was made king over Judah and Saul's son Ish-Bosheth was made king over the rest of Israel. But two years later Ish-Bosheth was murdered and the people of Israel joined in making David king of all the nation. After that, David captured Jerusalem and made it his capital. Then he made plans to move the ark of the covenant to Jerusalem.

Kiriath Jearim
Kiriath Jearim was built over a large hill. Looking east from the city one can see the golden walls of Jerusalem about eight miles away, gleaming in the late afternoon sun.

The Philistines, plagued by disease after capturing the ark of the covenant, sent the ark back to Israel, to Beth Shemesh, a town on the northern border of Judah about 15 miles west of Kiriath Jearim. When a group of men looked inside of the ark, God struck them

dead and the rest of the town begged the men of Kiriath Jearim to take the ark from them.

In Kiriath Jearim, the ark was kept in the house of a man named Abinadab. Today, a church called the Church of the Ark of the Covenant stands over the traditional site of Abinadab's house. Years later King David retrieved the ark from Kiriath Jearim and brought it to Jerusalem.

Celebrating in Song and Dance
The Israelites loved to come together and celebrate during times of feasts, festivals, and other important occasions. A joyful and natural part of these grand occasions was singing and dancing.

Song and dance were used as an expression of worship, praise, and thanksgiving to God. Much of Israel's history was also passed down through the years in songs. The Book of Psalms is a collection of songs, with many telling of the nation's history.

As the ark was brought from Kiriath Jearim to Jerusalem, David danced ahead of it, making a joyful noise to the Lord. David was also a musician. As a young man he played the harp, or lyre, to soothe King Saul, and probably sang many songs to please the king. When David was king, he started and organized the tabernacle music program, making sure that each day there were priests and Levites singing to God in praise and worship.

The Bible contains many beautiful songs. Moses and Miriam sang songs of praise to God after crossing the Red Sea to safety (Ex. 15:1-18, 21). After Deborah and Barak had routed the forces of Sisera of Hazor, they sang together a song of victory (Jud. 5). Hannah praised God in a beautiful song of thanksgiving when God gave her a son after years of prayer (1 Sam. 2:1-10). Mary, Jesus' mother, sang of the fulfillment of God's promises to Abraham (Luke 1:46-55).

The Music of the Tambourine

The timbrel, or tambourine, was a popular musical instrument in ancient times. It was not allowed in the temple, but was used in festivals and other celebrations. It was played mostly by women.

The tambourine was shaped like a circle, often hollow in the center. Pieces of bronze were set in the rim and rattled when the instrument was shaken.

The ark of the covenant was brought to Jerusalem from Kiriath Jearim. Today, the Church of the Ark of the Covenant stands over the traditional site of Abinadab's house (above). From this place, Jerusalem is clearly seen to the east (below). The ark is pictured at the near left. A cart, perhaps similar to the one on which the ark was transported, is seen at the far left.

211

At the left, Mephibosheth bows before King David, afraid that David will kill him. Normally a new king would kill any grandson of the previous king, if they were enemies, so that the young man could never claim his throne. But Mephibosheth was not only King Saul's grandson, but Jonathan's son. Jonathan and David were close friends and had pledged to each other that they would be kind to each other's descendants.

David Is Kind to Mephibosheth

2 SAMUEL 9

Synopsis

After the death of King Saul, David was made king, first of Judah, and later of all Israel. He brought the ark to Jerusalem and showed his desire to build a temple for the Lord. David also firmly established his kingdom by conquering surrounding nations. At last, with his kingdom well established, David turned his attention to a long-standing promise to Jonathan, Saul's son, and David's closest friend when Jonathan was alive. David sought out Jonathan's surviving son, Mephibosheth, and treated him like a close friend too.

Enemies of David

When David became king of Israel, he was surrounded by enemies. To the west lay the Philistines, formerly David's allies. They considered David's kingship an act of revolt, and were determined to remove him.

To the east and southeast were the Moabites and Edomites. Important trade routes ran through their lands, and often they refused Israel passage.

The Ammonites and Syrians lay to the north. The Ammonites had seriously insulted David's nation, Israel, and were doomed to feel the edge of his sword.

Finally, in the center of Israel itself, the Jebusites occupied Jerusalem. David began here in subduing his enemies. Relying more on God than military might, David was able to overthrow all these enemies.

Ziba—An Example of a Servant

There were many different kinds of servants in ancient times. Some were actually slaves, captured prisoners of war. But others were people who were hired for wages.

Ziba was a servant to King Saul, and probably a slave, for after Saul's death, David ordered Ziba to serve Mephibosheth, Jonathan's crippled son. As a slave, Ziba and his family faced a lifetime of servanthood.

Over the years however, the hard work of a servant like Ziba might have earned him the job of steward. A steward was still a servant, but was given the special responsibility of looking after the master's household and supervising the work of the other servants.

A hired servant was paid wages for his work. By displaying loyalty and excellent service, the servant was given food, shelter, and protection in return. Some servants grew to be so admired that they were asked to choose a wife for the master's son (Gen. 24), inherit property (Gen. 15:2), or marry into the master's family (1 Chron. 2:35). Female servants sometimes acted as substitute wives when their master's wives were unable to bear children (Gen. 16:2; 30:3-5, 9).

Lame Mephibosheth

Mephibosheth was born into the world as a normal and healthy child, heir to the throne of King Saul.

But when he was five years old, news reached the palace that the Philistines had routed the Israelites in battle, and Saul and Jonathan lay dead on the battlefield. Struck with fear, a nurse picked up the child and fled, possibly hoping to save the boy who someday might become king. But as she ran, she dropped Mephibosheth, crippling him in both feet (2 Sam. 4:4).

When David became king, Mephibosheth was a young man living in Lo Debar. He probably still feared for his life, for David had been Saul's enemy. Mephibosheth might not have known about his father Jonathan's covenant of friendship with David (1 Sam. 20:42).

But David remembered his covenant with Jonathan, and brought Mephibosheth to the palace. The king showed him kindness, treating him like a son. David's friendship and vow with Jonathan spared Mephibosheth's life, for he was a possible enemy heir to the throne. Many kings would have executed him.

Lo Debar

When Saul was killed in battle, some members of his family fled to Lo Debar, taking Mephibosheth with them. This city, also known as Debir (not the Debir southwest of Jerusalem) was probably located in the land of Gilead, directly east of the Jordan River.

Lo Debar itself was about 3 miles east of the Jordan River, and over 60 miles northeast of Jerusalem. At that distance, Saul's family hoped to be safe from anyone who wanted to harm them. Mephibosheth lived there with a man named Machir until David called him to the palace.

Kings of Israel and Judah
Two Centuries—Saul to Joash

ᗰ **Good King**   ᗰ **Bad King**

(40)—Years of Reign
931-913—Approx. time of reign (years B.C.)

The First Century—The Kingdom United
About 1025-931

ᗰ **Saul**
(15) mostly

ᗰ **David**
(40)

ᗰ **Solomon**
(40) mostly

The Second Century—The Kingdom Divided
About 931-800

Judah	Israel
ᗰ **Rehoboam** (17) 931-913 mostly	ᗰ **Jeroboam I** (22) 931-910
ᗰ **Abijah** (3) 913-911 mostly	ᗰ **Nadab** (2) 910-909
ᗰ **Asa** (41) 911-870	ᗰ **Baasha** (24) 909-886
ᗰ **Jehoshaphat** (25) 873-848	ᗰ **Elah** (2) 886-885
ᗰ **Jehoram** (8) 848-841	ᗰ **Zimri** (7 days) 885
ᗰ **Ahaziah** (1) 841	ᗰ **Tibni** (5) 885-880
ᗰ **Athaliah** (6) 841-835	ᗰ **Omri** (7) 880-874
ᗰ **Joash** (40) 835-796 mostly	ᗰ **Ahab** (22) 874-853
	ᗰ **Ahaziah** (2) 853-852
	ᗰ **Jehoram** (12) 852-841 mostly
	ᗰ **Jehu** (28) 841-814 mostly
	ᗰ **Jehoahaz** (17) 814-798

David and Bathsheba

2 SAMUEL 11—12

Synopsis
After David became king over all Israel, he strengthened his power by conquering the nations around him and making Jerusalem, a central city, his capital. But during one of these conquests, David foolishly had a loyal officer killed so that he could marry Bathsheba, the officer's wife.

How a City Was Captured
Invading armies and war were common events in ancient times, so before a city was built, careful attention was given to its location, which often meant the difference between defeat and victory.

Most large and important cities were built on natural barriers of defense, like hills or ridges. Huge walls of stone reaching as high as 25 feet and as wide as 20 feet also defended the city. Warriors commanded the tops of the walls, spraying a deadly shower of arrows onto the enemy below. Gates were overlaid with iron and bronze, and great wooden beams locked them shut.

With all this defense, how did an enemy army ever hope to conquer a city? David's army used their wits when besieging the city of Jerusalem by crawling through the city's underground water system and surprising the enemy.

Other armies far outnumbered the soldiers defending the city and used brute force. Thousands of warriors streamed up to the city walls

The Assyrians of Old Testament times left many drawings of warfare. While we cannot assume that the Israelites did things exactly the same way, we may find in these drawings some glimpses of warfare at that time. Top: a city wall, this one at Jerusalem. Middle: a king besieges a city while inhabitants defend it from city towers. Bottom: another siege. Opposite page: from drawings such as these, a 19th-century artist reconstructed a city siege. David's forces conducted such a siege against Rabbah.

214

with ladders and battering rams. The casualties were many, but the city was helpless against such great numbers.

At other times the invading army surrounded the fortified city and kept its people inside until they were weakened by starvation. Sometimes the city held out for a year, but finally they had no strength left to resist the attacking enemy.

Bathing
Water was hard to find in ancient times, even for a great king like David. There was no indoor plumbing, and any water had to be drawn from deep wells or saved from the rain in rock cisterns.

Baths were not taken often, for it was a long process that was considered a luxury. Soap was made mostly from the ashes of certain burnt plants. In between baths, people rubbed themselves with olive oil to cover up their bad odors and stay "clean."

David's Palace
David had built a palace for himself (1 Chron.
15:1). He saw Bathsheba while he was walking on his roof. Though it may seem strange to us, walking on one's roof was not unusual in Bible times, for most buildings were made with flat roofs, and many of the day's activities were carried out there.

Another Wife for David
When King David made Jerusalem his capital, he already had seven wives. Bathsheba became his eighth. She was formerly the wife of Uriah the Hittite, one of David's mighty warriors who was killed in combat through David's sin.

David's Other Wives
Before David became king at Hebron, he had married Michal (1 Sam. 18:27), Abigail (1 Sam. 25:42), and Ahinoam (1 Sam. 25:43). At Hebron he married Maacah (who became the mother of Absalom) (2 Sam. 3:3), Haggith (1 Chron. 3:2), Abital (1 Chron. 3:3), and Eglah (1 Chron. 3:3). David married Bathsheba, who became the mother of Solomon, at Jerusalem (2 Sam. 11:27).

Though David was the most respected of all Israelite kings, he had many enemies during his lifetime. When Absalom rebelled, David's enemies became quickly known. Shimei seemed unafraid to curse the king. But as soon as Absalom's rebellion was crushed Shimei begged for mercy (right). David refused to execute Shimei, but when Solomon became king, he put Shimei to death.

Absalom Rebels

2 SAMUEL 15—18

Synopsis
Peace had come to the land at last, for David was king. He had risen in power, conquering his enemies and establishing his capital in Jerusalem. But trouble was brewing in David's own family, as his son Absalom made plans to rebel and steal the kingdom from his father.

Absalom at the City Gate
Unknown to David, Absalom was plotting to seize his father's throne and become the new king of Israel. Absalom carried out his plan with patience, knowing that the best place to begin winning people over to his side was at the city gate, the busiest and most popular place in the city.

The city gate was always bustling with activity. Early each morning, merchants set up their wares just inside the gate. That is where the city elders gathered, to settle small disputes and witness business transactions.

Absalom spent much of his day around the city gate (2 Sam. 15:2). Here he boasted about his wisdom and ability to carry out the people's concerns. Gradually King David's support began to fade.

The Mountain of Tears
David left Jerusalem by way of the Mount of Olives when he learned of Absalom's plot to take over the kingdom. As he climbed over the summit of the mountain, he looked back over his shoulder across the Kidron Valley and cried as he gazed down on his city (2 Sam. 15:30).

One thousand years passed, and Jesus, probably standing near that same spot, wept for the sins of Jerusalem and predicted its coming destruction (Luke 13:34).

En Rogel—Hideout for Spies
Not everyone defected to Absalom's side during his revolt. Many brave and loyal men stayed with David and followed him into the wilderness. Two of David's loyal followers remained behind by a spring of water named En Rogel, to learn Absalom's plans and report them to David.

En Rogel is a deep spring lying just south of Jerusalem in the Kidron Valley. It was

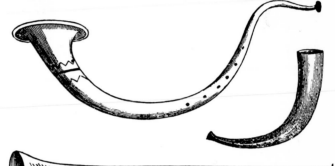

opened when men cut down into the solid rock and found an underground stream of water. Over the centuries, the valley has filled in considerably from the erosion of the surrounding hills. Today, builders have had to add their own water shaft to reach down to the stream, now many feet below the soil.

"As soon as you hear the sound of the trumpets, then say, 'Absalom is king in Hebron.'" Thus trumpets, probably like those above, drawn from ancient artifacts, heralded Absalom's rebellion. Absalom's monument (where Absalom was probably never buried) is above. En Rogel, described at the left and right, is pictured at the upper right.

Where Was Absalom Defeated?
David fled from his son Absalom across the Jordan River to a town named Mahanaim, about 45 miles northeast of Jerusalem. Absalom gathered the entire army of Israel and marched in pursuit of his father. The battle took place in the forest of Ephraim, just north of the Jabbock River and about three miles northwest of Mahanaim. But some of David's loyal followers were the greatest warriors in all Israel, and Absalom's forces were soundly defeated.

Watchman
David waited nervously in Mahanaim while the battle against his son Absalom raged on. Standing on top of the city wall was a watchman, whose duty it was to warn the king of anyone approaching the city (2 Sam. 18:24).

The Family of King David

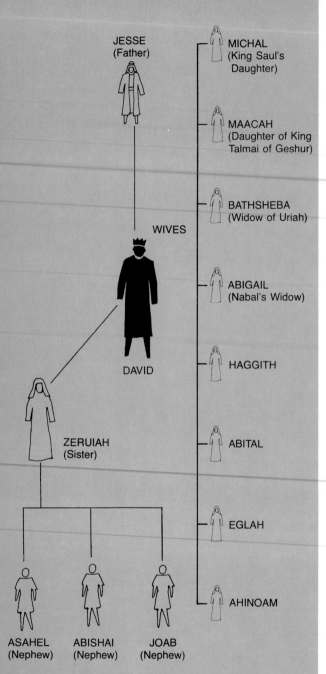

JESSE
(Father)

WIVES

DAVID

ZERUIAH
(Sister)

ASAHEL
(Nephew)

ABISHAI
(Nephew)

JOAB
(Nephew)

MICHAL
(King Saul's
Daughter)

MAACAH
(Daughter of King
Talmai of Geshur)

BATHSHEBA
(Widow of Uriah)

ABIGAIL
(Nabal's Widow)

HAGGITH

ABITAL

EGLAH

AHINOAM

David's mighty men won their way to fame as warriors. Their swords, spears, and other weapons were basic tools of their trade, just as a hammer and saw are for a carpenter or a typewriter for a writer. The swords above were drawn from various ancient monuments and represent authentic swords of Old Testament times.

Water from Bethlehem

2 SAMUEL 23:13-17

Synopsis
When victories are won and peace is at hand, it is time for brave men to remember brave deeds. So when Absalom's rebellion was crushed and David was king once more in Jerusalem, a story was remembered about a brave deed by David's "mighty men." The time was during the wars with the Philistines, a time when David was in hiding and longed for his childhood home, Bethlehem, or even a drink of water from one of its wells. The mighty men risked their lives to get him that drink.

The Mighty Men of David
King David commanded one of the most capable and valiant armies of his time. The strength of his army lay in a close group of 600 brave warriors. These fearless men were walking heroes, incredible fighters who formed the core of David's troops.

Before he was king, David escaped from Saul into the wilderness. Many of these rugged men joined him there. They were already impressive fighters, but David turned this group into highly trained warriors, enhancing their fighting ability even further. When David moved into the land of the Philistines, and then to Hebron, more valiant men joined him, strengthening this elite group.

218

The 30

Though David's army was built on a nucleus of 600 valiant men, there was an even more elite group, 30 of the bravest and most fearless heroes of war that Israel had ever known. The men became members of this prime group, known as the 30, by displaying unequaled courage and skill in battle.

One of the warriors was named Josheb-Basshebeth. He was the bravest of all the 30 and once came on 800 Philistines by himself and killed them all.

Abishai, Davids' nephew, the leader of the 30, once killed 300 enemy warriors by himself. He was the brother of Joab, the commander of Israel's entire army.

Benaiah was chief of David's bodyguard and a member of the 30. One day when he had no weapon, he was attacked by an Egyptian with a large spear. But Benaiah wrestled the spear from the man and killed him with it. Another time he killed two giants, and later killed a lion barehanded on a snowy winter day.

Bethlehem—David's Hometown

Nestled in the hills of Judah was the small town of Bethlehem, about six miles southwest of Jerusalem. David was born here, and grew up in the fertile hills near the town, tending his father's flocks.

David's descendants continued through to Jesus, who was born in this same little town which time had barely changed in over a thousand years.

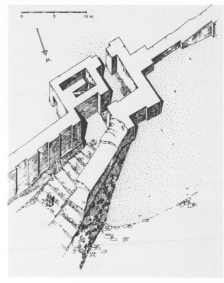

"Oh, that someone would get me a drink of water from the well near the gate of Bethlehem!" said David. At the time he was hiding with his men. Three men heard him and broke through the Philistine troops to get David's water. Drawings above and below show what a stronghold a city gate often was. It was difficult to penetrate such enemy lines.

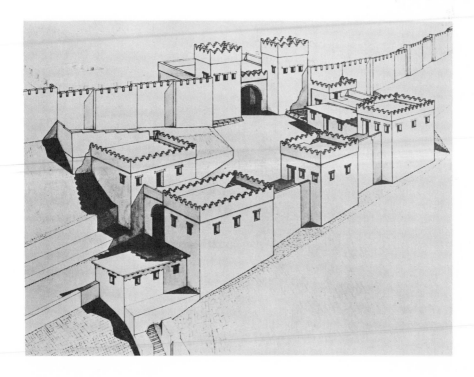

219

Araunah's Threshing Floor

2 SAMUEL 24

Synopsis

Toward the end of King David's reign, he decided to count his fighting men. We are not sure why, but this displeased the Lord. Even Joab, David's hardened army commander, knew that this was wrong and told David so. But David insisted, the count was taken, and the Lord punished David by sending a plague. When the plague ended, David bought Araunah's threshing floor and built an altar. Later Solomon's temple, and still later, Herod's temple, stood at this place.

From Dan to Beersheba

From Los Angeles to New York is a phrase that includes all land in 48 of the United States. In Israel it was the same way. When talking about the entire country, the popular phrase "from Dan to Beersheba" was often used (Jud. 20:1; 2 Sam. 3:10; 24:2). Dan was a city located at the extreme northern border of Israel, and the city of Beersheba lay on the southern border. When messengers were instructed to deliver news "from Dan to Beersheba," it meant that the message was intended for all 12 tribes of Israel.

Araunah's Threshing Floor—
A Landmark of Bible History

Long before the judges led Israel and the kings ruled the land, God asked Abraham, the ancestor of the Israelites, to sacrifice his only son on Mount Moriah. The man was puzzled,

but faithfully made the trip to the mountain, ready to sacrifice the only heir to the nation that God had promised through him.

But God was merely testing Abraham's faithfulness to Him, and at the last moment stopped Abraham from killing his son. In gratitude, Abraham made an offering to God. This was the first worship service on Mount Moriah, but over the centuries it would see more services than could be counted. For on this same site David bought Araunah's threshing floor, and Solomon built God's holy temple.

Throughout the years to follow, hundreds of thousands came from all over the world to worship God here. In Old Testament times, priests offered daily sacrifices to God, and musicians sang His praises. Planned by

Araunah's threshing floor would become one of the most hallowed spots on earth for many people—the site of the temple built by Solomon, and later by Herod. While it was used as a threshing floor, many of the activities seen on these pages were carried out there. Far left: winnowing, throwing grain into the air for the chaff to blow away. The man at the left also is winnowing.

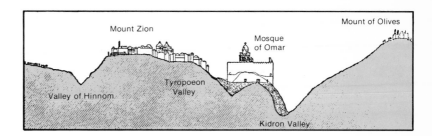

At the far left, the man is sifting grain from coarser broken straw. At the left, the threshing sledge is pulled over the grain. A closer view of the sledge may be seen below. Above is a cross section of the hills on which Jerusalem is built, showing Mount Zion, three famous valleys, the Mosque of Omar, where the temple, and Araunah's threshing floor, once stood. Threshing floors were usually built on high hills so the wind could blow away the chaff.

David, and built by his son Solomon, the temple was the focal point of Jerusalem. It remained the worship center for the Jews of the world until after the time of Jesus. Today a Moslem mosque, called the Dome of the Rock, rests on the same spot.

The Threshing Sledge

On his threshing floor, the farmer separated the kernels of grain from the stalks of wheat, corn, or barley. To do this he often used a threshing sledge. It was made of wood planks, and looked like a sled or toboggan, only heavier. On the bottom were attached sharp stones or metal. After the stalks were thrown onto the floor, the sledge was hitched to oxen and dragged over the crops while men or children sat on top of it for extra weight.

221

When David was old, he planned the temple carefully with his son Solomon, the next king, who would build it (left). Later that temple was destroyed, rebuilt, and then destroyed again. Today, where the temple once stood, stands the Muslim mosque known as the Dome of the Rock (below right).

Plans for the Temple

1 CHRONICLES 22—29

Synopsis
During the later years of King David's reign, he foolishly ordered a census of his fighting men, against the better judgment of his commander. The Lord was not pleased with this and sent a plague to punish David. When the plague ended, David bought a threshing floor on which he built an altar. This would become the site for the new temple which he planned with his son Solomon, the next king.

The People who Worked at the Temple
With God's help, David planned the temple at Jerusalem to the finest detail. One of the things he needed to think about was the wide variety of jobs required to ensure smooth operation in the big building project.

Priests and Levites were the busiest workers at the temple. The priests were in charge of all offerings and their preparations. They also made the holy showbread.

All priests were Levites, descendants of the tribe of Levi, but not all Levites were priests. Most Levites did not enjoy the special privileges of priests, but served in the temple by maintaining the building, playing music, and aiding the priests at religious ceremonies. They were also in charge of the temple treasury.

Other workers at the temple included singers, musicians, servants, guards (also called gatekeepers), and judges, who were responsible for extending some of the temple services to other regions of Israel.

Where Was the Temple Built?
In David's day, Jerusalem was much smaller than it is today. The king probably took little time in deciding just the right spot for the beautiful building, because there was one place that fit its character perfectly.

David's city of Jerusalem rested on the hill of Ophel. North of the city rose a high ridge that led up to Araunah's threshing floor, which made a platform on Mount Moriah. It seemed fitting that God's holy temple should be higher than the rest of the city. Also a great plague stopped here in David's time.

Carpentry work was an important part of temple plans and construction. The people of Israel left no pictures of their carpentry, but the people of Egypt did. In the painting at the top, from the time of Moses, carpenters drill, saw, plane, hammer, and perform many other woodworking tasks. Above: a carpenter's chest from 1800 B.C., also from Egypt, shows chest and tools. Below: the Western Wall, sometimes called the Wailing Wall, is all that remains of Herod's temple, where Solomon's temple once stood.

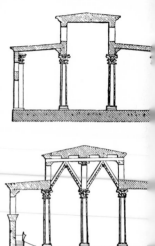

The above diagrams show two alternatives of an artist's concept of a cross section of Solomon's palace, based on the Bible record.

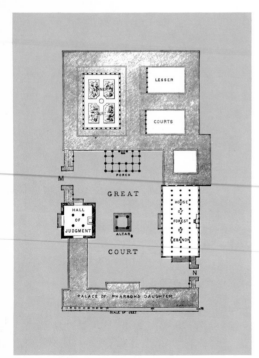

The above diagram shows the floor plan of Solomon's palace, as described in 1 Kings 7. Top: Solomon dreams at Gibeon, where the Lord offered him his choice of gifts, and where Solomon chose wisdom.

Solomon's Wisdom

1 KINGS 3; 2 CHRONICLES 1:3-12

Synopsis

After King David died his son Solomon became the new king. After Solomon removed his enemies, he made an alliance with Pharaoh, king of Egypt, and married his daughter. While Solomon made plans to build his palace and the temple, he moved his Egyptian princess to the city of David. Then Solomon went to Gibeon to offer sacrifices to the Lord. While there, he had a dream in which the Lord offered him whatever he wanted. Solomon chose wisdom above all other gifts. His wisdom was soon revealed, when two women came to him with a seemingly impossible problem.

Solomon's Palace

After the temple was finished, Solomon built his own palace. It was a magnificent structure, made of stone and cedar and called the Palace of the Forest of Lebanon. Extensive details are given in 1 Kings 7. It took 13 years to construct, and was about 150 feet (46 meters) long, 75 feet (23 meters) wide, and 45 feet (about 13.5 meters) high. The roof was cedar and the walls were

224

Solomon's Temple

David wanted to build the temple himself. But the Lord refused to let him, for David was a bloody warrior. The task of building God's house went to David's son, King Solomon.

David drew up extensive plans, gathered materials, and arranged for the people who would conduct the temple services. But he could not begin its construction. In fact, he did not live to see any construction begin, for Solomon did that after his father's death. This is an example of how God uses the talents of one person for one job and the talents of another person for a different job.

The Altar of Burnt Offering

The focal point of the temple services would be the altar of burnt offering, for on it sacrifices were made to the Lord. This altar was made of bronze, 30 feet wide and 15 feet high.

Sacrifices were placed on a bronze grating that stretched across the inside of the altar and burned before the Lord. Sacrifices were usually animals, such as sheep, goats, or bulls. But grain and wine were also put on the altar for certain offerings.

stone. The high-quality stone was cut into blocks.

This palace was located just south of the temple, and was connected to it by a gate of some sort. It is thought that the palace was destroyed by Shishak, Egyptian ruler, when he came against Jerusalem. Today the El Aksa mosque stands on the site where it is thought Solomon's palace once stood.

At the top is a photo of the El Aksa mosque, built today over the site commonly accepted for Solomon's palace. Below: a drawing of Solomon's palace on the inside. Right: a drawing of the outside, both drawings are based on the description in 1 Kings 7.

Solomon Builds the Temple

1 KINGS 5—8; 2 CHRONICLES 2—7

Synopsis

King David wanted to build a temple for the Lord. But the Lord told him not to do it, for he was a warrior. Instead, David's son Solomon would build the temple. Before David died, he made plans for the temple and helped gather many materials for it. After he died, Solomon built it.

The Temple Area

Since the time of Solomon, the temple area has remained a place of worship. Three times the Israelites built, or rebuilt, a temple on this site and each time it was destroyed. In A.D. 691, the Muslims built a mosque over the temple ruins. During the days of the Crusaders, it was converted into a Christian church. Today, it is under Muslim control again and is called the Dome of the Rock.

The Cedars of Lebanon

The precious wood from cedar trees was the finest in the Middle East. It had an elegant dark-red color, a sweet fragrance, and a durability that made it an ideal building material.

Solomon bought these beautiful trees from King Hiram of Tyre, in the north. The logs were tied into rafts, and floated down the

From the Mount of Olives today, one looks west toward the old city of Jerusalem. Across the Kidron Valley is a long stone wall, built about A.D. 1522 over earlier foundations. Beyond this wall is clearly seen the area where the ancient temple stood (below).

The Israelites did not believe in images, so they carefully avoided leaving pictures of their daily lifestyle, as Egyptians and Assyrians did. From Egyptian pictures at the left, we see how stone was brought from a quarry on ox-drawn sledges. At the lower right: Egyptians also showed us how their stonecutters worked. Workmen involved with Solomon's temple probably used many of the same techniques.

seacoast to a port city in Israel. From there, the cedar logs were dragged overland to Jerusalem, then cut into attractive wood panels.

Quarrying Stones for the Temple

Cedar wood, magnificent and expensive, was used for the inside of Solomon's temple, but the structure itself was built of stone. Solomon got his stone from large quarries just north of Jerusalem. Here, stonecutters and stonemasons toiled for years in the stone pits, cutting and shaping the white limestone for the temple.

The rock was usually cut along natural cracks or grooves, and then smoothed and squared with chisels, mallets of wood, and plumb lines. The cut stones were then moved to the building site and lowered into place with pulleys, rollers, and sledges. Skilled craftsmen squared the stones so perfectly that mortar was seldom used.

Stone for the temple was taken from quarries a few hundred feet north of the temple site. These are now called Solomon's Quarries and may still be entered today through the entrance pictured at the top. Above: Solomon dedicates the completed temple.

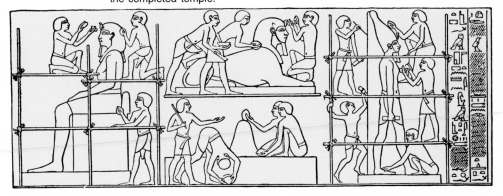

Solomon's Glory

1 KINGS 10; 2 CHRONICLES 8:17—9:28

Synopsis

David had been a great warrior and had brought peace to the land by military might. Solomon's way to keep peace was to marry the princesses of surrounding nations. With no wars to wage, Solomon concentrated on trade and wealth, making himself and his nation famous.

Solomon's Wealth—What He Had

With David on the throne, Israel had established itself as one of the strongest military nations in the Middle East. When Solomon became king, his desire was to make Israel one of the richest nations. With few enemies left, the king focused his energy on bringing new wealth into the land.

Solomon built a beautiful temple to God, an elaborate palace for himself, and a mighty fortress called the Millo. He built his own fleet of ships and established trade with other countries, which brought in millions of dollars of gold, silver, rare ivory, fine linen, precious woods, spices, and even monkeys and peacocks.

Solomon's Wealth—How He Got It

Solomon became wealthier than any other king in the world. But how did he acquire such riches?

The king opened trade to new and unfamiliar lands. Fleets of ships were sent to faraway countries loaded with copper from Solomon's mines, and they returned to Israel's ports laden with millions of dollars in gold.

Due to Israel's central location, numerous

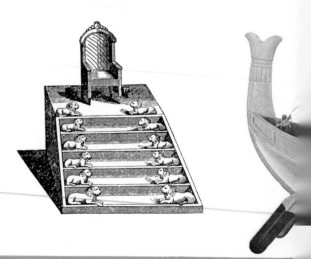

trade routes passed through the country, connecting lands to the north and south. Solomon charged huge excise taxes for goods passing through his kingdom.

Solomon's enemies brought him even greater wealth. Nations defeated by his father David paid tribute into Solomon's treasuries to avoid further conflict.

But the high cost of supporting an empire that stretched from Egypt in the south to Mesopotamia in the north was staggering. Solomon levied heavy taxes on his people to help offset these costs. The men of Israel had to work for the king one month out of every three, building his cities, supervising the work of slaves, or serving in the king's army. In addition, they still paid high taxes of grapes from their vineyards, sheep from their flocks, grain from their fields, and of course money.

Solomon's Stables
Solomon's wealth helped him build a strong army. His trade with numerous countries, including Egypt, brought many horses and chariots into the land.

To house all these horses and chariots, the king built "chariot cities" throughout Israel. It is said that these cities together held 40,000 stalls and housed 12,000 trained horsemen, or charioteers.

Megiddo, about 60 miles north of Jerusalem, was one of these cities. Ancient stalls, mangers, and hitching posts have been uncovered. Some, however, claim these stables were built in King Ahab's time, not Solomon's, and others think these were not stables, but storehouses.

Where Was Sheba?
When the queen of Sheba arrived at Solomon's palace, her caravan had traveled more than 1,000 miles! Her country, in southwest Arabia, southeast of Palestine, gained great wealth from trade of perfumes and incense, important items in the daily life and religious worship of the ancient world.

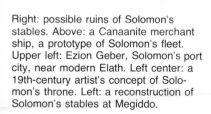

Right: possible ruins of Solomon's stables. Above: a Canaanite merchant ship, a prototype of Solomon's fleet. Upper left: Ezion Geber, Solomon's port city, near modern Elath. Left center: a 19th-century artist's concept of Solomon's throne. Left: a reconstruction of Solomon's stables at Megiddo.

Items associated with worship varied greatly in Solomon's kingdom. In the temple which he built were beautiful furnishings, designed to glorify the Lord who created man and his world.

Solomon Turns from God

1 KINGS 11; 2 CHRONICLES 9:29-30

Synopsis

To keep peace with neighboring kings, Solomon married their daughters. Who would wage war against his son-in-law? But when these foreign women came to live in Jerusalem, they brought their foreign gods with them. In time, his wives persuaded Solomon to build shrines for their gods. Then he permitted his people to worship them too. Eventually, Solomon turned far from God himself.

The Beginning of Solomon's Troubles—
A Multitude of Wives

Polygamy, marrying more than one woman, was tolerated in the Law of Moses, but not advised.

Kings were given special warnings in God's law against marrying a great number of wives (Deut. 17:17). But, like other kings of his day, Solomon followed the custom of marrying numerous wives for pleasure, political alliances, and prestige. In fact, King Solomon had 700 wives and 300 concubines, who lived as wives without full privileges.

Most of Solomon's wives did not follow the Lord, but worshiped idols of stone, wood, or metal. Trying to make them feel comfortable away from home, the king did not stop this idolatry. Soon it spread across Israel, and before long, Solomon himself accepted these foreign gods.

The age of peace and prosperity, often called Israel's "golden age," was about to end.

Above, and at the left top: two concepts of the laver, where priests washed in preparation for their part in the offerings made to the Lord. Left center: the ark of the covenant, focus of the Lord's presence. Far left: altar of burnt offering. Left: incense altar.

230

The nation and its ruler had turned far from God, and that meant trouble.

More Polygamy in the Bible

Solomon was not the only man to run into trouble with more than one wife. Jacob had two wives, Rachel and Leah, who were constantly at odds with each other (Gen. 30:1-24). This intense rivalry was continued by their sons and resulted in Joseph being sold as a slave into Egypt (Gen. 37).

Elkanah, Samuel's father, had a wife named Peninnah who had many children. She taunted his other wife Hannah for having none. Elkanah loved Hannah more. But her inability to bear children caused her much grief (1 Sam. 1:1-18).

The Idol-Gods of Solomon's Wives

Ashtoreth. This was the goddess of love and fertility, known as the giver of life. Ashtoreth was worshiped throughout Palestine and other countries. She is thought by some to be Athtar, or Ishtar, a universal goddess named after the Planet Venus.

Chemosh. Solomon built a shrine for Chemosh, the Moabites' national god. Some think Chemosh and Molech were the same god. King Josiah later destroyed Solomon's shrines to Chemosh, Ashtoreth, and Molech (2 Kings 23:13).

Molech. Molech was the national god of the Ammonites. He was called "king," and children were sacrificed in his worship. According to Moses' law, any Israelite who worshiped Molech should be put to death (Lev. 18:21; 20:5).

The lampstand, sometimes called the candlestick or menorah, on which a light was kept burning before the Lord. This and other objects of worship in the temple were associated with holiness and forgiveness of sin.

By contrast, the heathen objects of worship, usually shrines or idols, pointed to gods of wood or stone, made with human hands, and not to the Lord who created life. Heathen worship led to sinful practices such as child sacrifice and sexual rituals. The worship of God pointed to righteousness, prayer, and the forgiveness of sin.

When the kingdom divided, Jeroboam, king of the Northern Kingdom, Israel, established himself at Shechem (left). Rehoboam went to Jerusalem, his capital city, after he foolishly told the people he would tax them more than his father Solomon had done ("My father scourged you with whips; I will scourge you with scorpions"—see scorpions above). After Pharaoh Shishak of Egypt invaded Judah during Rehoboam's reign, he carved an image of a captive Jew on a wall at Thebes (below) with the inscription "The kingdom of Judah." Some think this is a picture of Rehoboam himself who, while not captured, was humiliated, especially since he was the son of Solomon.

The Kingdom Divides

1 KINGS 12:1-24; 14:21-31; 15:6-8; 2 CHRONICLES 10—11

Synopsis

King Solomon had supported his luxurious living with high taxes. When he died, his son Rehoboam was advised to lighten the tax load. He refused, and the nation rebelled, dividing into a Southern Kingdom, Judah, under his rule, and a Northern Kingdom, Israel, under the rule of Jeroboam, one of Solomon's officers. The split weakened the people militarily and spiritually. Idolatry was widely accepted in the land and under most of the kings, evil was common.

When

In 931 B.C. the kingdom of Israel split, dividing the tribes of Judah and Benjamin to the south from the 10 northern tribes. The two sides were never again united into one nation.

Shishak Invades Palestine

Inscribed on the walls of the Amon temple in Karnak, Egypt is a description of Pharaoh Shishak's invasion of Palestine. He marched his armies into Judah and Israel just five years after the kingdom was divided. King Rehoboam of Judah could not repel Egypt's forces, and Shishak broke into Jerusalem, stripping the temple and palace of all the wealth that David and Solomon had acquired.

Shishak was not strong enough to defeat Israel and Judah, but his invasion crippled the already weakened and divided kingdoms.

The Golden Calves

The revolt of the 10 northern tribes which suddenly separated them from Judah also separated them from Jerusalem, their center of religious worship. Jeroboam quickly set up two golden calves in Bethel and Dan to prevent his people from worshiping in Jerusalem, where they might change their allegiance back to Judah. The calves were made to represent God, but were confused with the Canaanite bull god Baal, and were worshiped as idols.

232

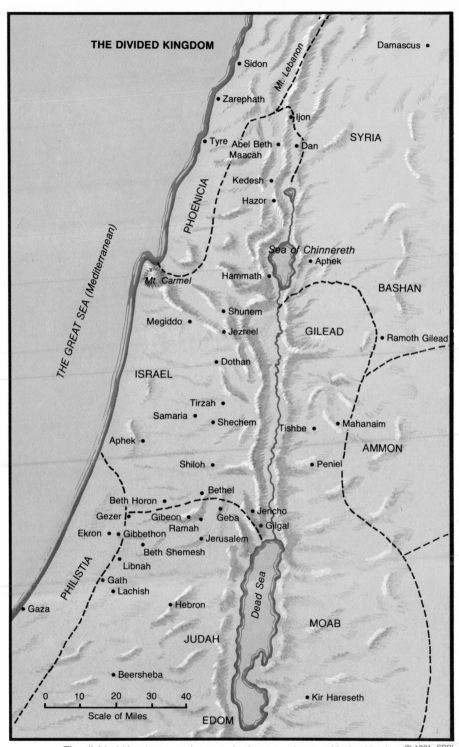

THE DIVIDED KINGDOM

Damascus •

• Sidon

Mt. Lebanon

• Zarephath

• Ijon

SYRIA

• Tyre   Abel Beth • · Dan
        Maacah

PHOENICIA

Kedesh •

Hazor •

THE GREAT SEA (Mediterranean)

Sea of Chinnereth
• Aphek

Mt. Carmel

Hammath •

BASHAN

• Shunem

Megiddo •

• Jezreel

GILEAD

• Ramoth Gilead

• Dothan

ISRAEL

Tirzah •

Samaria •   • Shechem

Tishbe •   • Mahanaim

Aphek • •

AMMON

Shiloh •

• Peniel

• Bethel

Beth Horon •

Gezer •   Gibeon •   Geba •   • Jericho

Ekron •   • Gibbethon   Ramah •   • Gilgal

• Jerusalem

PHILISTIA

• Beth Shemesh

• Libnah

• Gath

• Lachish

Dead Sea

• Gaza

• Hebron

MOAB

JUDAH

• Beersheba

0 10 20 30 40

• Kir Haresheth

Scale of Miles

© 1981, SPPI

EDOM

The divided kingdom may be seen in the map above, with the Northern Kingdom called Israel and the Southern Kingdom called Judah.

During the early part of the famine which swept the land, ravens fed Elijah at the Brook Kerith (right). One traditional site of the Brook Kerith is at the lower right, though some say it was located farther east, beyond the Jordan River. The site pictured here is a few miles south of Jericho, in the gorge known as Wadi el Qelt.

Ravens Feed Elijah

1 KINGS 17:1-7

Synopsis

To keep peace in the land, Solomon married the daughters of foreign kings. These women brought their foreign gods and before long, corrupted the land, enticing many Israelites to worship their gods. Solomon himself turned from the Lord. He lived a life of luxury, supported by heavy taxes on the people. When Solomon died, the land was ripe for rebellion. It split into two kingdoms, the Southern Kingdom, Judah, ruled by the heirs of David and Solomon, and the Northern Kingdom, Israel, ruled by others. Both kingdoms had a succession of many kings, mostly evil. The kingdom divided in 931 B.C. Fifty-seven years later, an evil king named Ahab began to rule the Northern Kingdom. During his rule a godly prophet named Elijah spoke to the conscience of Israel. On one occasion,

Elijah said there would be no rain until the Lord spoke through him. Elijah then went away to hide from Ahab and his evil wife Jezebel. While hiding during the famine, Elijah was fed for a while by ravens.

The Names of Judah and Israel

Solomon's kingdom, consisting of the 12 tribes who descended from the 12 sons of Jacob, was called Israel. These tribes entered the Promised Land with Joshua, who gave them specific land boundaries.

When the kingdom divided after Solomon's death, the 10 northern tribes wanted their land to be ruled by Jeroboam. They kept the name Israel for their new nation. Samaria became their capital in the days of Ahab.

The tribe of Judah to the south gave its own name to their new kingdom. They and Benjamin were the only tribes to remain loyal to Rehoboam, who was a descendant of Judah. Jerusalem, once the capital of Israel, was now Judah's capital.

234

The raven was like a large crow. Noah sent a raven from the ark, but it did not return (Gen. 8:6-7) for it was strong enough to fly back and forth until the waters went down. Ravens fed Elijah at God's command. Ravens are mentioned by Job (38:41—God feeds them) and Isaiah (34:11—they dwell in places previously inhabited).

The tribe of Levi owned no land, but lived in designated cities, so they were not included in the revolt.

The Reason for Famine

The Israelites do not divide their year into the four common seasons. Instead, the weather cycle of Palestine is separated into the rainy season and the dry season.

Early October marks the beginning of Israel's rainy season. The summer months from June to September produce little or no rain. By the end of September the ground is too dry and hard to plow or plant. The first rains of October, called the "early rains," are welcomed with joy and celebration. If October and November bring no moisture, the planting is delayed, and the harvest will be slim.

Rain often falls during the winter months, watering the growing crops and returning the land to life. The heaviest rainfalls occur in December and January. Often the deluge is so strong that dry riverbeds swiftly change into wild torrents of moving water, washing away everything in their path. Without these winter rains, the country would remain withered and parched from the intense summer heat. Planting could not begin and with no harvest, famine would strike the land.

By the end of April, the rains have usually stopped. May is harvesttime, a month of beautiful flowers and rich crops. But the arrival of June completes the cycle, and once again the land simmers under the summer heat.

The Brook Kerith

Elijah hid from Ahab's anger by the Kerith Brook, a small stream of water near the Jordan River, possibly in the land of Gilead.

235

The Widow of Zarephath

1 KINGS 17:8-16

Synopsis
During the days of King Ahab, the Prophet Elijah warned that there would be no rain until he said so. Without rain, the land soon dried up and crops failed. Famine came and water was scarce. Elijah hid for a while by a brook, where ravens fed him. Then the Lord sent him to Zarephath, where a miracle provided oil and flour for a widow and Elijah until the famine ended.

Zarephath—Glassmaking and Dyes
Many towns are well known for the unique products or services they produce. The small town of Zarephath became famous for its beautiful glass industry. The brightly colored glass vessels looked like ice or shiny still water, an exciting change from the objects of wood, metal, and stone that most people were used to.

Elijah the prophet moved to Zarephath after the brook where he was hiding from Ahab dried up. The village lay huddled by the Mediterranean Sea, north of Israel, between the cities of Tyre and Sidon. Zarephath lay within the borders of Phoenicia, and like other towns of this region, it probably produced deep purple dyes which were harvested from sea snails or murex seashells. Dyes were also extracted from certain plants in the area.

When Elijah visited the widow at Zarephath, she said, "I don't have any bread—only a handful of flour in a jar and a little oil in a jug." Above: jugs of Elijah's time.

Breadmaking at this time involved grinding grain into flour. Above: a mortar and pestle used to grind grain into flour, from Elijah's time. Right: women grind grain with millstones.

236

Widows—The First to Suffer

When a country was struck with hard times, widows were often the first to suffer the effects. When the severe famine struck Palestine in Elijah's day, the poor widow who lived in Zarephath was certainly one of the first to feel the pinching fingers of starvation. She was gathering firewood for her last meal when she met Elijah (1 Kings 17:12).

In ancient times, most women were left with nothing when their husbands died. The average man worked long hours every day just to put enough food on the dinner table. Israelite law called for the dead husband's sons or brothers to take the widow in and care for her. But life was difficult and short in Bible times, and often the husband's sons or brothers had also died. The widow at Zarephath had a son, but he was probably too young to care for her.

In those days, few women had the strength or skill to make a living on their own. Plowing fields required the strength of a man, and only a few women were fortunate enough to learn the art of dyes and dyemaking, or the skill of sewing fine clothing. But in hard times, even these jobs paid little. Left alone in life, greedy men took advantage of widows, offering help, but providing none.

Baking Bread in an Oven

The widow might have baked her bread on an oven called a "tannur." It was shaped like a pottery jar. Sticks were placed inside the jar and lit. The dough was plastered on the outside and baked.

Top drawing above: a man prepares an oven for bread baking. Center: another oven, lighted, with a man probably carrying bread to it. The small clay oven (bottom picture above) is from the time of Elijah and is from Israel. Left: Elijah meets the woman who has only a handful of flour and a small jug of oil.

237

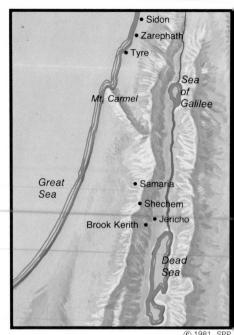

© 1981, SPP

Elijah and the Prophets of Baal

1 KINGS 18

As Elijah prays, the Lord sends fire on the altar, proving that He, not Baal, is God (above). The map at the upper right locates Mount Carmel, Zarephath —where the widow's flour and oil never ran out, and one traditional place for the Brook Kerith. Others locate this brook farther east, across the Jordan River. Right: part of the long Mount Carmel mountain range. The term Mount Carmel refers to a range of mountains, not to a single peak only.

Synopsis

During the days of King Ahab of Israel, the Prophet Elijah warned that there would be no rain until the Lord said so, through him. For a while, Elijah was fed by ravens, but then the Lord sent him to Zarephath, where He provided for both Elijah and a widow who lived there. Elijah challenged the priests of Baal to a contest on Mount Carmel one day, to determine whether their god or his God could send fire to an altar. The priests of Baal cried out and cut themselves, but nothing happened. Elijah prayed to the Lord and He sent fire in a miraculous way.

The Rich Life of a Heathen Priest

The Israelites were not the only nation to have priests as leaders of religious worship. Nearly every country around Israel had their own priests who made sacrifices and performed religious ceremonies to their gods.

Egyptian priests had immense wealth and power. These heathen priests demanded large sums of money for maintaining and protecting temples built by pharaohs and other wealthy people. For this service, they also inherited large amounts of people's property, money, and livestock when the people died.

The Canaanite priests of Baal did not have this kind of wealth, but those Elijah challenged were supported by Queen Jezebel and influenced the affairs of the nation through her. These priests often performed strange dances while slashing themselves with knives or stones. Sometimes they sacrificed children.

Elijah and Elisha—God's Prophets

We are familiar with most of the prophets in the Bible because of the books they wrote. But two of God's greatest prophets, Elijah and Elisha, did not write a book of the Bible. However, many chapters in other books of the Bible are devoted to their lives and ministries (see 1 Kings 17—19; 21; 2 Kings 1—9).

The Importance of Rain

Life in Egypt depends on the ceaseless flow of the Nile River, for almost no rain falls in the land. But the region of Palestine would wither into a desert without the arrival of the winter rains. The people rejoice when the first rains begin to fall, for farmers can begin their planting, and wells and cisterns fill again after becoming dangerously low over the hot and dry summer months.

The traditional site where Elijah and the prophets of Baal met is at the Carmelite Monastery of St. Elijah. The statue at the upper right is in the courtyard of the monastery. Below right: a bronze statuette covered with gold leaf, said to be one representation of Baal.

Above: the Kishon River, near the site where Elijah and the prophets of Baal met. Elijah executed the false prophets in this valley (1 Kings 18:40).

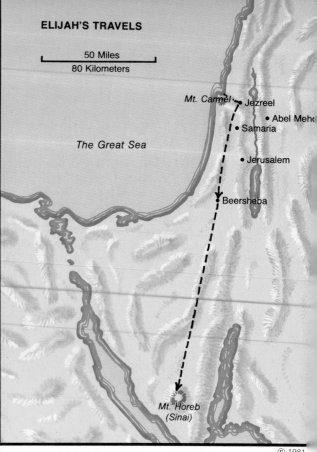

50 Miles
80 Kilometers

Mt. Carmel • Jezreel
• Abel Meh[o
• Samaria

The Great Sea

• Jerusalem

• Beersheba

*Mt. Horeb
(Sinai)*

© 1981

At Mount Horeb (Mount Sinai) Elijah hears
God speak, not in wind, earthquake, or
fire, but in a quiet whisper. Elijah's travels
from Mount Carmel to Mount Horeb may
be seen on the map above.

Elijah and
the Still, Small Voice

1 KINGS 19:1-18

Synopsis
When Elijah challenged the priests of Baal to
a contest on Mount Carmel, the Lord sent
fire on the altar there, proving that He, not
Baal, is truly God. After that, rain fell and
the drought was broken. But Ahab's queen,
Jezebel, was furious. Elijah had not only humiliated her prophets, but had executed
them. She vowed to murder him. Afraid, Elijah ran away to Mount Horeb to hide. There,
the Lord spoke to him, not in wind, earthquake, or fire, but in a still, small voice.

Elijah's Long Journey
Israel's wicked Queen Jezebel, Ahab's wife,
got furious when she learned that Elijah had
killed all of her heathen priests of Baal. She
vowed to kill Elijah, who escaped to Mount
Horeb, also called Mount Sinai. But his journey was not an easy walk, for Mount Horeb
stood over 200 miles south of Mount Carmel,
where Elijah destroyed the priests of Baal.
To get to Mount Horeb, the prophet had to
cross a wild, barren wilderness.

Rain and Harvest
Some things never change with time. Today,
as in ancient times, people frequently talk
about the weather. In Elijah's day, famine
became the main topic of conversation as each
new morning dawned clear and dry.

People's lives depended on the rain.
Storms that rolled across the land from the
sea watered the crops growing in the fields,
assuring a bountiful harvest.

In summer, rain rarely fell. Gentle showers

240

At the foot of Mount Sinai (left) the Israelites camped almost 600 years before. There Moses received the Ten Commandments and there the people built the tabernacle.

marked the beginning of the winter months. If these "winter rains" did not come as expected, the ground turned hard as stone. Plowing and planting were impossible, and in a few months famine arrived. Without a harvest, food became very scarce, and many people died of starvation. Even a king's table was not as plentiful as he would like it.

Baal

Wicked Queen Jezebel worshiped a god named Baal, the most popular and supposedly the most powerful Canaanite god. Baal was the god of rain and abundant harvests. Idols of Baal sometimes looked like bulls, animals which symbolized strength and fertility.

Ancient mythology tells how Baal's worst enemy was Mot, the god of famine and sterility. Each spring, Mot searched for Baal and killed him, leaving the land without rain through the summer months. But Anat, Baal's sister, raised him back to life, and he arrived just in time to prevent a famine by spreading his life-giving rains on the land. The farmers could then plant their seeds and later reap a rich harvest.

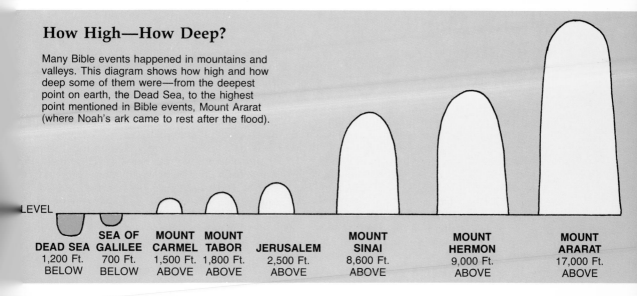

How High—How Deep?

Many Bible events happened in mountains and valleys. This diagram shows how high and how deep some of them were—from the deepest point on earth, the Dead Sea, to the highest point mentioned in Bible events, Mount Ararat (where Noah's ark came to rest after the flood).

LEVEL

DEAD SEA	SEA OF GALILEE	MOUNT CARMEL	MOUNT TABOR	JERUSALEM	MOUNT SINAI	MOUNT HERMON	MOUNT ARARAT
1,200 Ft. BELOW	700 Ft. BELOW	1,500 Ft. ABOVE	1,800 Ft. ABOVE	2,500 Ft. ABOVE	8,600 Ft. ABOVE	9,000 Ft. ABOVE	17,000 Ft. ABOVE

241

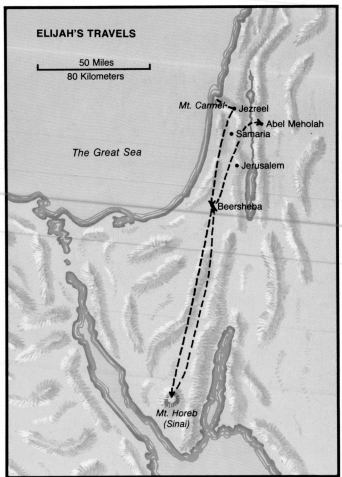

ELIJAH'S TRAVELS

50 Miles
80 Kilometers

Mt. Carmel
Jezreel
Abel Meholah
• Samaria
The Great Sea
• Jerusalem
Beersheba
Mt. Horeb
(Sinai)

© 1981, SPPI

The map at the left shows Elijah's travels in this and surrounding Bible events. It begins at Mount Carmel, where he defeated the prophets of Baal. From there he ran away to Mount Horeb (Sinai), stopping at Beersheba. Then he returned again to Beersheba (the way he came—1 Kings 19:15). From there, he went north, to Abel Meholah, where he called Elisha to leave his farming and become God's prophet.

Elijah's Mantle to Elisha

1 KINGS 19:19-21

Synopsis
Samuel, Saul, and David lived about the time of the 11th century B.C. (approximately 1035-970 B.C.). During part of the 10th century B.C. Solomon ruled. Then the kingdom divided (approximately 970-931 B.C.), followed by the rule of Rehoboam and Abijam in Judah and Jeroboam I in Israel. During the ninth century B.C., a series of evil kings, and a few good ones, ruled in the divided kingdom, while the prophets Elijah and Elisha ministered, especially in Israel. Elijah was first, but when it was time for him to choose a successor, he placed his mantle on Elisha.

The Cloak or Mantle
Almost everyone owned a cloak, but most people had just one. Cloaks were similar to the outer coats of today, but much more versatile, and taken almost everywhere.

A cloak was difficult to make. It was made by hand, and the process took time and patience. Most cloaks were made from animal hides, goat or camel hair, or from wool.

To make a cloak, a woman spun the fibers of animal hair into thread or yarn. This thread was woven on a loom into cloth, which was then sewed into a cloak. Because this took so much time, cloaks were valuable and were not thrown away until completely worn out. It was a common sight to see a cloak that had been patched many times.

The Important Uses of a Cloak
A cloak was worn as protection against the

242

When Elijah called Elisha to become a prophet, Elisha was plowing with 12 yoke of oxen. Two oxen were yoked together so they would pull equally. A wooden yoke may be seen at the right. Above: an ancient wooden plow and a man plowing with a yoke of oxen.

burning sun, and for warmth in the cold night. But these were just two of its uses.

On a warm night, a cloak made a soft pillow. At a meal, it was laid on the ground and represented a special seat for an honored guest.

A bundle of goods was carried home from the village in a cloak. A farmer tied his cloak into a bag, emptied his seeds into it, and planted his fields by hand.

A cloak was also used symbolically. By spreading his cloak over a woman, a man was announcing that he would care for her. Throwing a cloak over another's shoulders represented a transfer of power or position. Sometimes it meant a call to discipleship.

A cloak was sometimes given to a lender as a pledge for a debt. And when torn into pieces, a cloak symbolized great sorrow or grief.

Differences between Elijah and Elisha

Elijah and Elisha were two of the greatest prophets Israel had ever known. But the two men's personalities were quite different. Elijah liked to live outdoors in the wilderness. Elisha lived in homes and liked the city. Elijah was rugged and forceful in speech, while Elisha was more diplomatic. Elijah wore a cloak of camel's hair, but Elisha usually dressed like other people.

Plowing and Plows

After the first winter rains in Palestine, it was time once again for the planting season. Plowing and planting were back-breaking work.

Ancient plows were crude. The earliest were simply a light tree trunk with two strong branches forking at the end. Later, the plowshare was developed. This was a piece of wood carved into the shape of a large chisel and attached to the plow. It was the part which moved through the ground and broke up the soil. In the time of the Kings, plowshares were made of iron.

When war broke out, the Israelite farmers hammered their plowshares into swords and went into battle (Joel 3:10).

The plow was pulled by oxen. Often a farmer put his entire weight on the wooden plow handles in order to keep the plowshare down in the soil.

In contrast to modern tractors with their plows, the plow of the ancient farmer only scratched the surface. Thus the roots of his plants could not penetrate as deeply into the soil.

243

Ahab's palace and Naboth's vineyard were located at Jezreel (two photos above). Naboth's ancestors had owned the vineyard here and he was entitled to keep it. But Naboth was executed so that King Ahab could claim his vineyard. For this sin, Ahab's 70 sons were later beheaded and their heads heaped beside the gate at Jezreel (2 Kings 10:1-11). Jezebel was thrown from her palace window when Jehu came. While Ahab was alive, many of the meetings between him and Elijah took place here.

Naboth's Vineyard

1 KINGS 21

Synopsis
King Ahab of Israel was a wicked king, but his wife was even more wicked. Jezebel did not want her people to worship the Lord, so she tried to force Baal on them. When Ahab wanted a nearby vineyard, his wife Jezebel was not afraid to murder its owner. Naboth was the victim.

Ahab—An Example of a Wicked King
After the nation Israel divided into the Northern and Southern Kingdoms, God was often forgotten. Until its captivity, the Northern Kingdom of Israel was ruled by a succession of evil kings. Ahab was probably one of the worst.

During the 22 years of Ahab's reign, sin and idolatry went unchecked in Israel. Ahab's greatest mistake was his marriage to Jezebel, a wicked woman who worshiped Baal and tried to force this god on the rest of the Israelites. King Ahab was not strong enough to subdue his wife's evil habits, and soon found himself following her sinful practices.

Ahab was a strong military leader and a great builder, but he rarely listened to God. He finally died in battle against the Syrians.

244

Vineyards—Peacetime Plants

When Elijah lived in the land of Israel, life was closely woven to the land and its products. Most people worked outdoors, and their work depended on favorable weather. Famine affected everyone, from farmers to shepherds.

Vineyards were one important industry in Israel. When the rain was plentiful, clusters of grapes grew plump and delicious on the vines which covered the valleys and mountain slopes.

Vineyards yield their best crops during times of peace, because the vines require constant care and pruning if they are to be fruitful. When men went to war, the vines grew shabby and were picked over by birds and thieves.

When the grapes began to ripen in July, there was never a minute when the vineyard watchtower was not occupied. Day and night, a man stood in the tower that was built on the edge of every vineyard, and searched for any sign of approaching thieves.

September was the month of the grape harvest. If the crop was good, the month was filled with joy and feasts of celebration. As the grapes ripened, women picked them from the vines, and men trampled them with their bare feet to squeeze out the juice, which was fermented into wine. Grapes were also eaten from the vine as food, and dried under the sun to make raisins.

The King's Seal

Seals took the place of signatures. A seal might be a piece of metal shaped like a ring, or a cylinder-shaped lump of hard clay. A special marking was engraved on each seal. When pressed into wet clay or warm wax, the seal left a "signature." The king's seal was a royal order demanding swift action (1 Kings 21:8-14).

Upper left: Naboth refuses to sell his vineyard to King Ahab. Above: a seal imprinted in a jar handle during the time of the kings. The king's seal, which Jezebel used, made an imprint something like this, forming a "signature" which only King Ahab had. At the right, a rich vineyard, reminding us of the one Naboth owned.

245

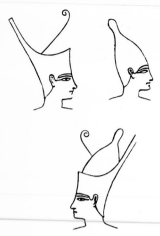

"Dressed in their royal robes, the king of Israel and Jehoshaphat king of Judah were sitting on their thrones at the threshing floor by the entrance to the gate of Samaria" (2 Chron. 18:9). Part of royal attire included the crown, symbol of authority. Above are three Egyptian crowns. At the right are five other types of crowns, the first three, Assyrian. The fourth is Syrian, and the fifth, Persian.

Micaiah's Prophecy

2 CHRONICLES 18

Synopsis
While Ahab was king in Israel, Jehoshaphat ruled in Judah. Jehoshaphat was a good king, but foolishly formed an alliance with the evil King Ahab by marriage of children. Later, Jehoshaphat visited Ahab, and Ahab asked him to help with a military campaign. Jehoshaphat agreed, but first wanted a prophet of the Lord to assure them that this was all right. The prophet Micaiah foretold Ahab's death during this battle.

Assyria Rises to Power
The nation Assyria began to grow quickly during the ninth century B.C. Soon it grew powerful, and started conquering lands to the west. Israel, though hundreds of miles to the southwest, was soon threatened.

Ashurnasirpal II, one Assyrian king, was particularly interested in the lands bordering the eastern coast of the Mediterranean Sea. These countries, especially Israel and Syria, were too busy fighting among themselves to notice the approaching danger. The Assyrians entered the region by surprise and demanded a heavy tribute of wealth in return for sparing their cities and people from destruction.

The Great Battle at Qarqar
Ashurnasirpal had died and his son, Shalmaneser III, wanted to preserve Assyria's strength. In 853 B.C., the new king marched west toward Palestine with his mighty army.

When he arrived at Qarqar, about 200 miles north of Samaria, a great alliance of kings was waiting for him, including King Ahab of Israel. The bloody battle seems to have been a draw, and the Assyrians retreated.

The four thrones at the upper left are Egyptian. The one at the upper right is Assyrian. All are drawn from ancient monuments. Below: from the high mound where Samaria once stood, one looks east toward Sebastiye, a small village surrounded by the rolling hills that once was the region which was also called Samaria.

False Prophets

The Israelites believed that a prophecy, whether good or bad, had a better chance of happening when spoken aloud. The people who worshiped idols hated God's prophets, because the punishments they proclaimed came true. These people did not understand that their troubles came from their disobedience to God.

Soon, many false prophets sprang up to counter God's prophets. By prophesying good times, they hoped to bring back the peace and prosperity Israel had once known. They claimed to be God's messengers, but their words didn't make sense, because they encouraged the people to continue in their evil ways.

Samaria

Three hundred feet above the surrounding plain stood Samaria, the capital city of the Northern Kingdom of Israel. Standing on the city walls, a watchman could see westward a full 25 miles to the coast of the Mediterranean Sea. Looking south, he could see halfway to Jerusalem, 40 miles away. Omri, Ahab's father, built the city and made it Israel's new capital. Ahab added many buildings to the city, including a temple to Baal for his wicked wife Jezebel.

247

Elijah Is Taken in a Whirlwind

2 KINGS 2

Synopsis
Elijah served for quite some time as the Lord's prophet. At the right time, he chose Elisha to be his successor, and Elisha served as Elijah's helper after that. At last God's appointed time came for Elijah to leave the earth and leave his work in the hands of Elisha. While Elisha watched, Elijah went to heaven in a whirlwind.

Kings and God's Prophets
The kingdom of Israel divided because King Solomon had turned away from the Lord and led the nation deep into idol-worship. The kingdom remained divided because most of the succeeding kings from both north and south continued these evil ways, disobeying God.

As a result, God chose special men and women to be prophets. Some were called into a lifetime of service to God, like Elijah and Elisha, while God asked others to perform one simple, yet important job. But every prophet of God was filled with a desire to tell kings and ordinary people God's messages of warning.

Kings often turned to prophets in times of trouble or danger, after all of their idols seemed to fail them. Sometimes kings grew very angry when God's proph-

Jericho, the City of Palms, (Deut. 34:3), still lives up to that name (top photo). The photo above shows the so-called Elisha's Springs, where traditionally Elisha sweetened Jericho's water (2 Kings 3:19-22).

ets predicted terrible events, for people in Israel believed that when someone prophesied a bad event in public, there was a greater chance of it happening.

But God's prophets were not out to make friends or earn positions of importance in the kingdom. Good or bad, they told God's messages to the people, sometimes at the risk of losing their lives.

The Kings of Elijah's Time
Jehoshaphat (873-848 B.C.) was the king of the Southern Kingdom of Judah when God called Elijah to be a prophet. Jehoshaphat was a good king for the most part, obeying the laws of the Lord.

But the Northern Kingdom of Israel was a wicked nation at this time, so Elijah's ministry was concentrated there almost completely. The Bible first mentions Elijah prophesying to King Ahab (874-853 B.C.), predicting that no rain would fall until Elijah said so (1 Kings 17:1). This was a result of Ahab's continued idol-worship.

Elijah also dealt with Ahab's son Ahaziah (853-852). Sometimes God's prophet had to escape from the anger of these wicked kings, and especially from Ahab's evil wife Jezebel.

After Jehoshaphat died, his son Jehoram took the throne (848-841). He was a very evil king, and not like his father. Elijah sent him a letter, predicting that calamity would strike because of his failure to obey God.

The Kings of Elisha's Time
Many kings came and went during Elisha's ministry. Both Judah and Israel had many wicked kings at this time, but Elisha spent almost all of his time as a prophet to Israel.

In the Northern Kingdom of Israel, Elisha worked under the reigns of Ahaziah (853-852 B.C.), Joram, or Jehoram (852-841), Jehu (841-814), Jehoahaz (814-798), and Joash, or Jehoash (798-782). Only Jehu and Jehoash showed a desire to serve the Lord, but later even they turned from God to worship idols.

In the Southern Kingdom of Judah, Elisha lived during the reigns of Jehoram (848-841), Ahaziah (841), Queen Athaliah (841-835), Joash (835-796), and Amaziah (796-791). At times, Joash and Amaziah brought the nation back to God, but later worshiped idols.

Chariots were an important means of transportation for dignitaries in Elisha's and Elijah's time. They also symbolized power and might. The chariot below is redrawn from an ancient monument. Elijah was taken to heaven in a whirlwind, accompanied by a chariot of fire (right).

A Poor Widow's Oil

2 KINGS 4:1-7

Synopsis
In the days when Elisha ministered in Israel, there was a school for prophets, and Elisha was a leading figure. One of the young men associated with this school got too deeply into debt, then died, leaving his debts with his young widow. In those days, creditors could force a debtor to pay in money or sell the wife and children into slavery. This poor widow faced the terrible problem of finding a large amount of money or giving up her two boys as slaves. Elisha performed the miracle of oil to provide the money for her to pay her debts. The woman was part of the miracle, to the extent that she believed that it would happen. The results were limited only by her faith—and the size of her vessels!

When the widow could not pay her debts, it seemed that she would have to give up her two sons to become slaves. But Elisha had an answer. She must borrow all the empty jars she could find. God would fill them with oil from her small jar. The woman (above) was overjoyed with the hope that her sons might be spared. The jars on these pages are from the time of Elisha.

250

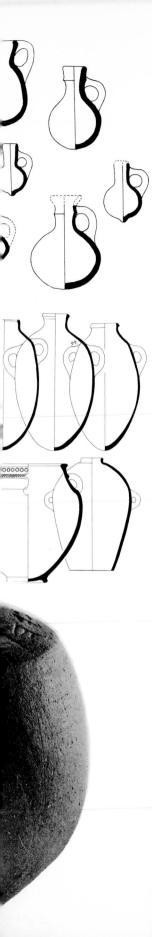

How Oil Was Made

In Palestine, oil was used as a luxury and a necessity. The ancient Egyptians used a variety of oils extracted from vegetables and animal fat. But the most common type of oil in Palestine was olive oil. The ripe olives were first partially squeezed to remove the seeds, and then pressed with a heavy stone, trampled by foot, or beaten with a small club in order to remove the remaining oil.

Almost everyone used olive oil each day, but it was usually expensive and time-consuming to make. An olive tree yielded about 10 gallons of oil a year, so each olive was pressed two or three times to make sure that every drop of oil had been squeezed out. But each time the olive was pressed, the oil lost some of its purity.

Uses of the Widow's Oil

Olive oil was an essential ingredient in the home of every family. But it was also found on the dressing table of the richest queens.

In cooking, olive oil was poured into a pan to prevent meat or bread from sticking. Oil was also mixed with flour to make bread dough.

The lamps of most Bible-time houses burned with a wick, which soaked in a small clay bowl of olive oil. The golden lampstand of the tabernacle burned with small cups of pure olive oil.

Cuts and scrapes were rubbed with olive oil to promote healing. Wealthy people took baths in warm oil, hoping to be cured of a disease. Women rubbed oil into their skin to keep it moist and soft in the hot dry climate. When there was little water, olive oil cleansed the skin and partially covered up bad odors.

The kings of Judah and Israel were anointed with the finest olive oil. Offerings made use of this precious oil as well.

The door was closed and the woman poured oil from her small jar into the borrowed ones. As long as she poured, the oil kept flowing. Only when she stopped did the oil stop flowing.

A Room for Elisha

2 KINGS 4:8-17

Synopsis
For almost a hundred years Elijah, and then Elisha, ministered for the Lord in Israel. The exact dates of their ministries are not known, but correspond with the reigns of King Ahab through King Joash, approximately 874-782 B.C. Elisha moved about through the land, ministering from place to place. At Shunem, a kind woman prepared a guest room, where Elisha and his servant could stay while in that area.

A Room on the Roof—A Sign of Prosperity
The man and woman who took care of Elisha might have been a prominent couple in their town of Shunem. The husband was probably a wealthy landowner, for he had many workers to help him in the fields. A farmer working alone could not make enough money to be rich.

The couple made friends with Elisha, who frequently passed through their village. They had no children. One day they decided to build Elisha a room on the rooftop of their house. This would be a cool and delightful place, secluded from the busy street activity.

Privacy was rare in Israelite houses, which were not built for comfort, but for shelter and protection during the night. Most houses had one main room where the entire family slept on reed mats. It took much time and money to build a house, and only a wealthy man could afford to add another addition to his home.

Stone, or bricks made from mud and straw, were the chief building materials for the average house. Windows were small and high up to keep out thieves and the hot afternoon sun. Many wealthier homes were protected by a walled courtyard.

The Perfect Gift
The Shunammite couple showed Elisha great kindness each time he passed through their village. They invited him in for a meal, and asked him to stay in their home. Because they built a room for him on the roof of their house, Elisha wanted to repay them for their kindness. But they refused.

But Elisha knew what the man and woman wanted, for they had no children. In Israel, children were considered the greatest joy and blessing a husband and wife could have. A woman who bore no children was deeply ashamed, and her husband was embarrassed. In fact, Israelite law gave husbands

Shunem (top) was in a rich agricultural area in the Jezreel Valley, in the land belonging to the tribe of Issachar (Josh. 9:17-18). The Philistines camped here in preparation for the battle in which King Saul was killed (1 Sam. 28:4). The room which the wealthy couple made for Elisha may have looked like the one at the upper right. The drawing above shows the courtyard of a Bible-time home, with stairs leading to the roof, where a room was sometimes added.

the legal right to divorce wives who could bear no children. The Shunammite woman knew this law well, and might have been afraid. So Elisha gave her the perfect gift in payment for her kindness. He promised her a son, and within a year, the baby was born.

Ancient Household Furniture

The difference between the furniture of an ordinary house, and furniture in the houses of kings and wealthy officials, was staggering.

The average house was simple and had only one or two rooms. Curtains woven by hand separated the main room into a side for men and one for women. The family often sat on reed mats to eat and slept on them at night. If a table was used for eating, it was plain, wooden, and very low, for the family always ate while sitting on the floor. On the table was a lamp, a small clay bowl filled with olive oil. Along the wall stood a few clay jars for cooking and storage, and a primitive hand mill for grinding grain into flour.

A king's house was filled with elegant furniture inlaid with ivory. Gold and silver decorations gleamed everywhere. Curtains of the finest linen separated the many rooms.

253

The bedouin woman below reminds us of the Shunammite woman. The Shunammite woman saddled a donkey and went to find Elisha (right). The route which she took is seen on the map at the far right. Elisha often ate with the Shunammite woman and her family (lower right).

Elisha Raises the Shunammite Boy

2 KINGS 4:18-37

Synopsis

Elisha, prophet of the Lord, traveled through the land of Israel. While in Shunem, he and his servant stayed in a guest room prepared for him by a kind couple. One day this woman's son became violently sick and died. Elisha was called, and raised the boy to life.

Shunem

Many farmers lived in the Jezreel Valley. The fertile soil grew rich crops and gave abundant harvests. The town of Shunem stood at the edge of this fruitful valley, about 20 miles north of Samaria, Israel's capital city.

Saul, Israel's first king before the nation divided, was killed in battle on the slopes of Mount Gilboa near Shunem (1 Sam. 28:4). David's nurse, Abishag, was a Shunammite.

A married couple from Shunem treated Elisha the prophet with great kindness each time he passed through their village. When the son he had promised them died, Elisha raised the boy from the dead (2 Kings 4:18-37).

A Woman's Daily Life in Palestine

From country to country a woman's lifestyle was vastly different. In Egypt, women were generally more sophisticated and independent, owning businesses and property. But in Palestine, both women and men worked long days just to stay alive.

An Israelite woman spent almost all of her time working around the home. She had no time or money to spend on beauty care. Baths were rarely taken, and olive oil was rubbed liberally into the skin as a perfume and deodorant. The fragrant oil was also used as a skin moisturizer. Only a few women were wealthy enough to own makeup. Hair was seldom cut, for long hair was a symbol of womanhood in Israel. Ointment was combed through the hair to repel the swarms of insects.

A woman spent most of her day preparing food and spinning cloth for clothing. It took hours to grind grain into flour by hand, or on a primitive hand mill of stone. After the flour was made, it was baked into bread. Everything had to be done by hand. Even the oven was lit by building a fire inside or under it.

Each morning and evening, it was the woman's job to walk to the well and draw water for the family's needs. On the way home, she gracefully balanced the large water jar on her head. At night, she awoke several times to refill the lamp that kept burning till morning.

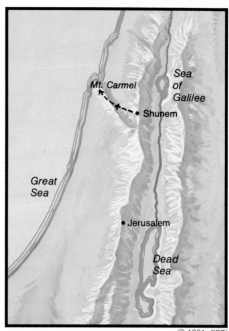

Often a slave girl was mistreated, depending on her owners. But the girl who served Naaman and his wife seemed to have a relationship with them much like child and parent. Evidently they had a special fondness for her and she for them. When Naaman's wife was sad, the girl was quick to suggest a remedy. Thus, it seems entirely possible that the girl was quick to welcome Naaman home, a healed man, especially when she had been instrumental in his healing.

Naaman Is Healed

2 KINGS 5:1-19

Synopsis

The Prophet Elisha, who ministered during the reigns of Jehoram, Jehu, Jehoahaz, and Joash, worked numerous miracles. By these, people knew that he was truly God's prophet. One of his great miracles involved a Syrian general named Naaman, a leper who came to Israel for healing.

The Life of a Leper

A leper was often driven from town and forced to live in caves or "leper" villages. This seems cruel, but it was the only way a community thought it could protect itself against the disease. Until healed, a leper lived as an outcast from society, not hated, but greatly feared.

Although the Syrian general Naaman was a leper (2 Kings 5:1), he was not treated as an outcast. This suggests that he had the milder of two types of leprosy. With this type, the skin forms white or pink patches which often do not spread over the whole body. Within one to three years, the victim is usually healed completely, though the disease might reoccur later. This type was apparently not contagious.

The contagious type of leprosy can be fatal. The skin forms white or pink patches, but they spread quickly over the entire body. A leper with this type cannot feel burns or cuts in these areas. Large boils appear, and the hands and feet become deformed. During this stage the disease is the most contagious.

It takes from 10 to 20 years for a leper to heal if he is fortunate enough to survive. The body becomes so weak from sickness that when other diseases strike, there is not

256

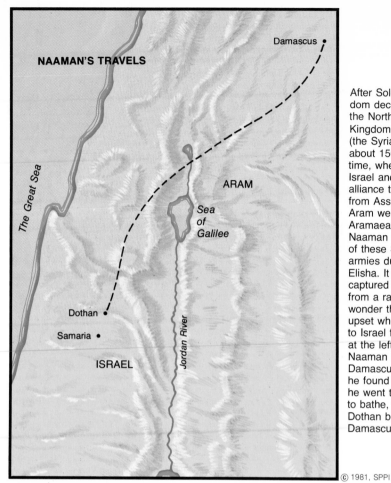

NAAMAN'S TRAVELS

Damascus

ARAM

Sea of Galilee

The Great Sea

Dothan

Samaria

ISRAEL

Jordan River

After Solomon's great kingdom declined and split into the Northern and Southern Kingdoms, Israel and Aram (the Syrians) warred for about 150 years. But at one time, when Ahab was king, Israel and Aram joined in an alliance to protect themselves from Assyria. The people of Aram were known as Aramaeans, or Syrians. Naaman was general of one of these Syrian, or Aramaean armies during the time of Elisha. It is clear that he had captured the little slave girl from a raid on Israel. No wonder the king of Israel was upset when Naaman returned to Israel for healing. The map at the left traces the path Naaman followed from Damascus to Dothan, where he found Elisha. From there he went to the Jordan River to bathe, then back to Dothan before returning to Damascus.

enough strength to fight back.

In the Law of Moses, a leper had to be declared "clean" by a priest before returning to the community. Special offerings went along with this ritual of purification. It must have been a wonderful feeling to return to normal after so many years!

What Did a Servant Girl Do?

When a battle had ended, it was common for winners to take anything they wanted from the cities and villages of the losers. This included people, who were taken from their homes to be slaves in a new land.

Naaman captured a girl from an Israelite village. As a slave, she performed household chores, cooked the meals, and even helped Naaman's wife dress and bathe.

Letters

The king of Syria sent a "letter" to the king of Israel, seeking a cure for Naaman's leprosy. What did these ancient letters look like?

The king's letter may have been written on any of several different materials. A scribe, who was a professional writer, might have inscribed the king's message into a tablet of wet clay. Instead of a pen, he would use a "stylus," a short stick with a sharp triangular point. In neighboring lands, the words were written in cuneiform, a language developed by the Canaanites. Writing was also scratched on clay pottery fragments, used mainly by the poor.

Papyrus was used in letter writing too. The material looked like paper, and was made from reeds which were beaten flat, and then rubbed smooth with a shell or with a piece of ivory.

Ink was used on papyrus. It was made from black soot, resin, and olive oil. Reeds with frayed tips were used as pens.

Elisha's Greedy Servant

2 KINGS 5:20-27

Synopsis
Naaman, general of the Syrian army, had captured a little girl on one of his raids in Israel. When Naaman's wife told her he was a leper, the little girl suggested that he go to Elisha for healing. Naaman went, and was healed, but Elisha refused the rich gifts he offered. However, Elisha's servant became greedy and tried to get these rich gifts for himself. For this, he was punished with Naaman's leprosy.

Ancient Pottery Tells a Story
Over the years, styles change. Clothing becomes shorter or longer, brighter or duller. And everyone can recognize a very "old" car when it passes by.

Ancient pottery was a timepiece of history. Over the centuries, styles changed and new pottery-making techniques were invented.

Archeologists have learned to identify when these styles were popular and which countries developed them. Of course, they are sometimes deceived. A colorful vase found in Babylon might have been made by the Babylonians, or it might have been carried to the land as part of the spoils from a distant battle.

Before the days of David and Solomon, Israelite pottery was often painted with bright colors. Animals and geometric shapes were the common design. But during the time of Solomon, a new technique called "burnishing" was developed, which gave the pottery a more subtle, softer appearance. Before the clay was dry, it was rubbed with a stone or piece of bone, and baked in an oven called a "kiln." When the vessel cooled, it looked glossy, which enhanced the original color of the clay.

Pottery also had a distinct style during the period of the kings after Solomon. Vases and jars had long necks, and the sides were often angled instead of curved. Handles were attached in a variety of places. Before this time, handles were molded on opposite sides of the vessel and called "ears."

Rimmon—God of Syria
The country of Syria, just north of Israel, worshiped a god named Rimmon. In other parts of Syria and Canaan, probably this same god was called Baal or Hadad, and is known as the god of storms and rain. Rimmon was sim-

"Is this the time to take money, or to accept clothes, olive groves, vineyards, flocks, herds, or menservants or maidservants?" Elisha asked his servant. Gehazi had seen Naaman's riches offered to Elisha (right) and had coveted them. Flocks and herds (above) were one sign of riches.

ply a local name for this popular god that was worshiped throughout the Middle East.

There was a temple to Rimmon in Damascus, the capital of Syria. Namaan, the Syrian army commander, worshiped there with his king (2 Kings 5:17-19). The god is usually pictured as a thunderbolt or a bull.

A Talent of Silver

When kings ruled the land of Israel, money was weighed instead of counted. The basic unit of money was called the shekel, which weighed between 8 and 16 grams, or .3 to .6 of an ounce. A talent was worth 3,000 shekels, or about 1,500 ounces. In Bible times, one talent was usually the price of a good ox.

Over the years, the shekel's weight varied, so its exact value remains uncertain.

Damascus

Damascus was the capital of Syria, located about 100 miles northwest of Samaria. The two capital cities were always fighting in order to keep important trade routes open.

The Syrians at War—Elisha Shows His Servant an Angel Army

2 KINGS 6:8-17

Synopsis

During the time of Elisha's ministry in Israel, the Syrians went to war against the Israelites. Elisha often warned the king of Israel about the whereabouts of the Syrian army. This angered the king of Syria, who determined to capture Elisha. When Elisha's servant woke one morning to find their city, Dothan, surrounded by Syrian forces, he was frightened. But Elisha prayed and the Lord revealed an angel army, waiting to come to aid them, if necessary. The servant knew then that the Lord's army was greater than the Syrian army.

Who Were the Syrians?

The Syrians lived just to the north of Israel, and should not be confused with the Assyrians, another powerful nation.

Most of the Syrian provinces paid tribute to King David, but after his death, they regained their independence under Rezon. For years Syria and Israel remained enemies. Only a few times did they unite in battle.

When Ahab was king of Israel, he fought against the Syrians three times. Ben-Hadad, the Syrian king, started the conflicts by laying siege to Ahab's capital of Samaria. After two victories, Ahab died in battle.

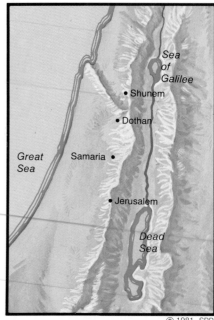

© 1981, SPPI

When Elisha prayed, the Lord revealed an angel army to his servant. Elisha was then in Dothan. He prayed for the Lord to send blindness to the Syrians, and then led them to Samaria. See map above for these cities, as well as Shunem, where Elisha had a room in the home of a wealthy couple.

Top: Dothan, where Elisha and his servant saw the angel army. Above: Samaria with ruins of Roman columns. Elisha led the blinded Syrians here.

Angels as Warriors

Artists often depict the angels of heaven as gentle and docile creatures, wearing long white robes and playing sweet music on their golden harps. But many times the Lord calls His angels to be fearless warriors.

In the Book of Revelation, John sees a mighty angel with feet that look like pillars of fire, and a voice that sounds like thunder (Rev. 10:1-3).

When Jesus was arrested, He told Peter that He could call 12 legions of angels at an instant if He wanted (Matt. 26:53). A single Roman legion was made up of 3,000-6,000 trained and valiant soldiers.

God revealed to Elisha and his servant the vast multitudes of His army, with its fearless angel warriors and their chariots of fire (2 Kings 6:17).

Jacob wrestled with an angel (Gen. 32:24-30), and cherubim guarded the entrance to the Garden of Eden with a flaming sword (Gen. 3:24). These cherubim were probably not angels, but other heavenly creatures.

Seeing the Unseen

This story suggests that all around us, supernatural events are happening which are invisible to the human eye. At times, God "opens" the eyes of certain people and lets them witness these remarkable incidents.

God showed Elisha and his servant the army of heaven to calm their fears over earthly enemies. Years later, Bethlehem shepherds witnessed a great choir of angels praising God at Jesus' birth (Luke 2:8-15).

261

Elisha and the Syrians

2 KINGS 6:8-23

Synopsis

While Elisha was a prophet in Israel, the Syrians warred against his people. The Syrians would plot a move against Israel, but the Lord would reveal it to Elisha, who would then tell the king of Israel. This angered the Syrian king and he tried to capture Elisha by sending his army to Dothan, the city where Elisha was staying. Elisha's servant was frightened, but when the prophet prayed, the Lord opened the servant's eyes to see a vast army of the Lord, ready to fight for them. Elisha then prayed for the Syrian soldiers to be struck blind and led them to Israel's king. After the Israelites fed the enemy soldiers, they sent them home in peace.

The Struggle between Syria and Israel

There was a good reason why Syria and Israel were always locked in a power struggle. Damascus, Syria's capital, wanted to increase its trade, but Israel controlled all of the important caravan routes to the southern countries of Egypt and Arabia.

On the other hand, Israel's trade to the north was limited due to the strategic location of Syria's capital. Through Damascus ran all of the vital trade routes from the wealthy countries of Mesopotamia. When Ahab defeated Ben-Hadad for the second time, he forced the Syrian king to allow Israelite traders into Damascus.

The Politics of Peace

Elisha was a diplomat. He understood that peace is not always achieved through war. After God struck the Syrians blind, Elisha led

When the Lord answered Elisha's prayers and blinded the Syrian soldiers, Elisha led them to Samaria (left). The western entrance to ancient Samaria is seen at the upper right. There Elisha told the king of Israel to give a feast for the soldiers, a diplomatic move to establish peace between the two nations for a while. Three feasts of Bible-time peoples are seen above and at the right, drawn from monuments. Top: an Assyrian feast. Bottom: an Egyptian feast. Right: a Canaanite feast.

the enemy army into the city of Samaria. When the soldiers received their sight once again, they found themselves prisoners of war.

It is likely that most of the Israelites wanted to kill the Syrian soldiers and claim a great battle victory. They must have been astounded when Elisha and the king prepared a great feast for the enemy instead! But the plan worked. When the Syrians were freed, they returned to their homes and didn't bother the Israelites for several years.

Samaria—The City and Region
After the division of the kingdom, King Omri and his son Ahab built the city of Samaria, capital of the Northern Kingdom of Israel. After the Captivity, the entire region of the Northern Kingdom was called Samaria. The Assyrians populated the Israelite cities with captured foreigners from other lands and called them Samaritans. Over the years, the Samaritans and Israelites became bitter enemies.

Why Banquets Were Given
Feasts, or banquets, were used for celebrating religious festivals (Ex. 12:14), anointing kings (1 Sam. 9:22-24), and showing kindness (2 Kings 6:23).

Jehu Overthrows Jezebel and Destroys Baal

2 KINGS 9—10

Synopsis

King Ahab ruled Israel from about 874-853 B.C. He was an evil king who married Jezebel, a woman even more evil than he. During Ahab's rule, the Prophet Elijah ministered in Israel and was often in conflict with Ahab and Jezebel. Jezebel especially hated him and tried to kill him. Ahab was killed in battle against Ramoth Gilead, going to war against the counsel of a prophet named Micaiah, and Ahab's son Ahaziah became king. But Ahaziah fell from a second-story window and injured himself. He died of his injuries and another of Ahab's sons, Jehoram, ruled instead. During his rule, Elisha anointed Jehu to be the next king of Israel, and Jehu drove his chariot to Jezreel, where he executed Jezebel, and the kings of Israel and Judah. Jehu then ruled as king and tried to rid the country of Baal worship.

The Zealous Reign of Jehu

Jehu was a very intense, high-strung man. He even drove his chariot "like a madman" (2 Kings 9:20). While he was still an army commander, Elisha anointed him as Israel's next king.

At the beginning of his reign (about 841 B.C.), Jehu listened to the advice of Elisha. Only Jehu had the zeal to carry out the bloody job of killing Ahab's entire family, including wicked Queen Jezebel. After this, the new king executed all of Baal's ministers, trying to regain the Lord's favor. But as a ruler, Jehu was a weak king. He was forced to pay tribute to the Assyrian king, Shalmaneser III. Later, Jehu turned from the Lord and Israel declined even further.

When Jehu was anointed king, he immediately went to Jezreel (lower right) to execute wicked Queen Jezebel and her son King Jehoram. Jezebel saw Jehu coming and quickly put on cosmetics (2 Kings 9:30). At the top right are kohl jars (kohl was like mascara). Below them is a cosmetic bowl. Right center: women using cosmetics (from left to right, top panel: maid brings mirror, mirror basket, and ointment jar; lady looking in mirror puts on rouge; and woman has her hair fixed. Bottom panel: attendants bathe woman.) At the right, the black obelisk of Shalmaneser III. Below, a drawing from it, showing Jehu bowing before Shalmaneser.

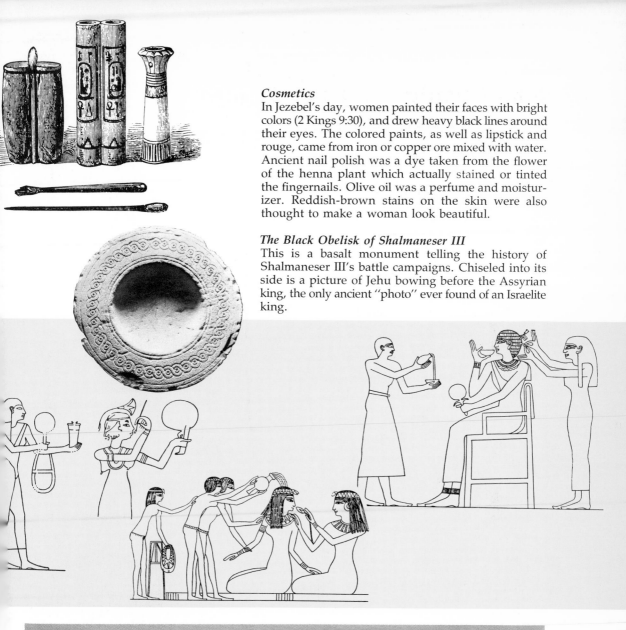

Cosmetics

In Jezebel's day, women painted their faces with bright colors (2 Kings 9:30), and drew heavy black lines around their eyes. The colored paints, as well as lipstick and rouge, came from iron or copper ore mixed with water. Ancient nail polish was a dye taken from the flower of the henna plant which actually stained or tinted the fingernails. Olive oil was a perfume and moisturizer. Reddish-brown stains on the skin were also thought to make a woman look beautiful.

The Black Obelisk of Shalmaneser III

This is a basalt monument telling the history of Shalmaneser III's battle campaigns. Chiseled into its side is a picture of Jehu bowing before the Assyrian king, the only ancient "photo" ever found of an Israelite king.

At the left, people bring their gifts to help rebuild the temple, as the Israelites had done for the tabernacle in the wilderness some 600 years before. The high priest (drawing below from description in the Bible) was the spiritual head of Israel. Jehoiada was the high priest who hid Joash in the temple until he was seven years old, at which time he proclaimed Joash king. Jehoiada was married to Jehosheba, or Jehoshebeath, a sister of King Ahaziah.

Joash the Boy King and the Money Chest

2 KINGS 11—12; 2 CHRONICLES 22:10—24:27

Synopsis
While Jehu was ruling in the Northern Kingdom, Israel, seven-year-old Joash was made king of the Southern Kingdom, Judah. He had been hidden since he was a baby in the temple, safe from his wicked grandmother Athaliah, who had killed all her other family members so she could rule. Joash was brought from hiding by the high priest, proclaimed king, and set before the people. Athaliah was executed. In his early years, Joash tried to serve the Lord. At one time, he collected money to repair the temple.

Financing the Temple Operations
The priests and Levites were in charge of the services and sacrifices offered at the temple, but the king often had control of the temple treasury. The operations and maintenance of the temple required much time and money. These funds came from a variety of sources.

Part of the spoils taken in battle were placed in the temple treasuries. A temple tax was levied too, though this was frequently forgotten during the kingdom's decline. Voluntary donations by worshipers also went into the treasury. These included sheep, cattle, and grain. The king often reached into the temple treasury to help pay the expenses of his kingdom.

Gifts for the Temple

In the wilderness, the Hebrews gave Moses a large freewill offering so that the tabernacle of God could be built (Ex. 35:5-10, 21-29). Over the years, the Israelites gladly contributed countless gifts toward the tabernacle and temple.

After making the blueprints for God's temple, David donated vast sums of wealth for its future construction by Solomon (1 Chron. 22). A yearly tax of a half shekel per person maintained its operations.

After the Captivity, many of the Israelites returned to rebuild the destroyed temple. Once again the people gladly gave an abundant offering for the temple construction (Ezra 1).

Chaos in the Family of Joash

Joash's great-grandfather Jehoshaphat was a good king, obeying the Lord. But Jehoram, Jehoshaphat's son, started Judah's decline by marrying Athaliah, a daughter of Israel's King Ahab and Queen Jezebel. Athaliah brought Baal worship into the land.

All of Jehoram's sons were killed by invading Arabs except Ahaziah, who became king after his father's death. But that same year, Ahaziah was killed by King Jehu of Israel, and Athaliah seized the throne. She promptly killed all her grandsons and became Judah's ruler. But the wicked queen had missed baby Joash, who was rescued by Ahaziah's sister Jehosheba, and hidden in the temple.

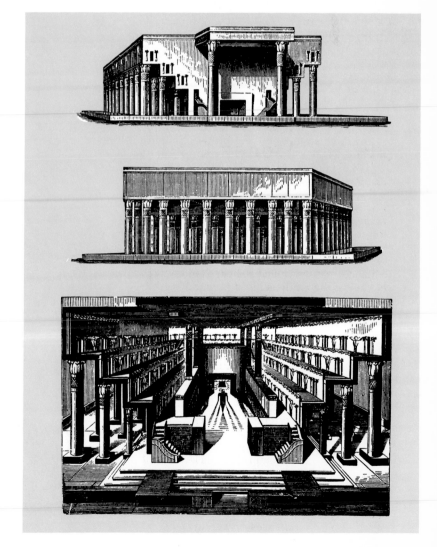

Until Joash was seven, the temple was his home. This was the same temple King Solomon had built about 100 years before. No one knows exactly how this temple looked, but many artists have tried to reconstruct its appearance from the descriptions in the Bible. At the right is a 19th-century artist's concept of the way this temple looked. From top to bottom: front view, west end, and interior.

The Story of Jonah

The Book of JONAH

Synopsis
Jonah became a prophet of God not long after the time of Elisha, perhaps even overlapping Elisha's ministry during the reign of King Joash. Jonah tried to run away when the Lord told him to preach to the people of Nineveh. Jonah was afraid, so he took a ship headed toward Tarshish, possibly in southern Spain. But the Lord sent a storm at sea and the sailors realized at last that Jonah must be thrown into the sea, where a great fish awaited him. The fish took him to land, and Jonah then went obediently to Nineveh to preach.

When
God told the Prophet Jonah to travel to an Assyrian city called Nineveh and preach against their idolatry. Nineveh was destroyed by the Babylonians in 612 B.C., so Jonah's ministry must have been before this, probably during the reigns of Jehoash, or Joash (798-782) and Jeroboam II (793-753) of the Northern Kingdom. At this time, Assyria was a serious threat to Israel,

Numerous ships sailed the waters of the Mediterranean Sea in Jonah's time. From Joppa, Jonah may have sailed on a Phoenician merchant ship such as the one below. Another ship of Jonah's time is the Phoenician warship, above.

Jonah was born at Gath Hepher, seen at the top (2 Kings 14:25). A building stands there today as a monument to him, and is said to be his tomb (top right). In Arabic it is called Nebi Yunes. The village is present-day Mashhad, some 3 or 4 miles north of Nazareth.

and Jonah's message might also have been an appeal for peace.

Nineveh

Just east of the Tigris River in modern-day Iraq, lie the ruins of Nineveh. In Jonah's day, it was one of the world's largest and most impressive cities. Since it was the capital of the Assyrian empire, it is little wonder why Jonah was afraid to go there.

In 700 B.C., King Sargon moved the capital to Khorsabad, 13 miles to the north, and Nineveh's importance declined. But his son, Sennacherib, restored the city to its greatness with a grand palace and mighty walls. Zoos and exotic gardens surrounded the city.

Ships and Sailing

Ancient ships were fragile vessels. Their styles varied little from country to country. A ship sailed only during the fair-weather months between April and October. Merchant ships were wide and made of pine.

Large sails caught the wind, while stars guided their paths.

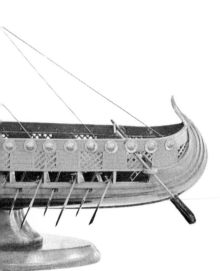

When the Lord told Jonah to go to Nineveh to preach, Jonah tried to run away. He boarded a ship headed for Tarshish (below), thought to be in southern Spain. Nineveh was in the opposite direction, toward the east across the desert. The plant below is one idea of what Jonah's gourd looked like. Its technical name is Ricinus communis. But no one knows the plant's identity for certain.

About 800-7(

Judah

   👑   Amaziah (29) 796-767

mostly
   👑   Uzziah (52) 791-740

   👑   Jotham (16) 750-735

   👑   Ahaz (20) 736-716

   👑   Hezekiah (29) 716-687

During the time when Isaiah was a prophet in Judah, the Southern Kingdom, the Assyrians swept down on the Northern Kingdom, Israel, conquered its capital, Samaria, and took many of its leading people as prisoners back to Assyria. The drawing at the left shows Assyrians leading captives, perhaps Israelites. It is taken from an Assyrian monument. Above: God calls Isaiah to serve Him as prophet. The map at the right shows the world in which Isaiah ministered.

The Story of Isaiah

The Book of ISAIAH

Synopsis
One of the great prophets of the Southern Kingdom, Judah, was a man named Isaiah. It has been said that he was of royal blood, that his uncle was King Amaziah of Judah and his cousin was King Uzziah. In the year King Uzziah died, Isaiah was called to minister as a prophet. His ministry is thought to have lasted 50 years.

When
Isaiah was a prophet of Judah during the reigns of Jotham (750-736), Ahaz (736-716), and Hezekiah (716-687).

Isaiah the Prophet
Isaiah was a prophet who was obedient to God. During his lifetime, the Assyrian Empire was a world threat, but it is interesting to note that as long as Isaiah advised Judah, it was the only nation throughout the Middle East that was not conquered by the powerful Assyrians. However, Judah did have to pay tribute to the Assyrians.

Judah in the Days of Isaiah
Uzziah restored some of the military and economic strength to Judah. But King Ahaz was evil and ignored Isaiah's warnings. With Israel and Syria ready to attack, Ahaz allied with Assyria, and was forced to accept their religion along with their military help. Judah turned to idol-worship until Hezekiah's reign.

A drawing taken from the photo at the lower left shows King Sargon II in his chariot. Another drawing of an Assyrian chariot is below it. Below: an inscribed prism of Sargon II, telling of his exploits.

Below, top: Assyrian soldiers with spears, bows, arrows, and shields. Bottom: Assyrian soldiers with drawn bows, a battering ram before them, and prisoners impaled on stakes.

Unlike Israel, it depended on the Lord from time to time. As a result, the weaker and more evil nation of Israel was destroyed first (722 B.C.).

Judah's Later Captivity Pays Off

The Assyrians earned a reputation for their brutal treatment of captives. They enjoyed flaying people alive, leading them with hooks fastened through their lips and noses, or just watching them starve to death. The captured Israelites were subjected to this torture.

Judah was not conquered for another 136 years because of the godliness of such kings as Jehoshaphat, Uzziah, and Hezekiah. By this time, Assyria had crumbled, and the Babylonians were in power. They were much more merciful to their captives, and even elevated captives such as Daniel to positions of authority.

Kings of Assyria

Shalmaneser III (859-824 B.C.) was a strong Assyrian king, the first to battle against Israel at Qarqar. The kings who followed him were Shamsi-Adad V (824-815), and Adadnirari III (808-783). These men were weak rulers, setting the stage for the long and prosperous reigns of Jeroboam II of Israel, and Uzziah in Judah.

Tiglath-Pileser III (745-727) attacked Israel in 734 B.C. and carried many people into exile. His successor, Shalmaneser V (726-722) began the siege of Samaria. Many think his son Sargon II (722-705) destroyed Samaria, ending the existence of Israel.

273

Sennacherib Goes against Hezekiah

2 KINGS 18

Synopsis
For more than 150 years, Assyria had been growing as a world power in the north. Israel and Judah, weakened spiritually and militarily, became increasingly attractive to Assyria. By 722 B.C. the Assyrians had swept down into Israel, the Northern Kingdom, and had conquered it. They destroyed Samaria, Israel's capital city, and took its important people back to Assyria as captives. A few years later, the Assyrian King Sennacherib came against Judah. But he found a king there, Hezekiah, who depended on the Lord.

Between the Captivities
The Northern Kingdom of Israel ended as a nation in 722 B.C., when the Assyrians carried the people into captivity. But Judah survived for another 136 years, until the Babylonians captured them in 586 B.C. In United States history, this represents the length of time between the Revolutionary War and the invention of the automobile at the turn of the 20th century.

As you can see, God gave Judah plenty of time to turn from its evil practices of idolatry. Godly kings such as Hezekiah and Josiah had long and prosperous reigns while uniting the nation behind God. But their efforts were soon forgotten, and God's anger fell on Judah, as it had on Israel.

The Reign of Hezekiah
No king of Judah had been able to match the religious reforms of David and Solomon until King Hezekiah took the throne in 716 B.C. His father Ahaz was a wicked ruler, but Hezekiah must have noticed that Israel's destruction was a result of its disobedience to God.

Within 16 days, the temple was reopened, repaired, and swept clean of heathen idols. The daily sacrifices were started once again, and the temple was filled with singing and

At the right, Sennacherib sits on his throne by the city of Lachish. A Judean prisoner is brought before him while attendants fan him, or possibly shoo flies from him.

Above: an Assyrian groom, who cared for Sennacherib's horses. Right: an Assyrian battering ram with archers attack a fortified city.

music. The king also brought back the Passover Feast and invited all of Judah and the remaining Israelites to attend.

Some years later, Sennacherib surrounded Jerusalem. Faithful Hezekiah did all he could to prepare his city for the attack (2 Kings 18:19-20; 2 Chron. 32:1-5). But he also trusted God for the amazing victory which He gave. (Isa. 36—37)

Later the king let his son Manasseh rule along with him. But Manasseh was not like his father. After Hezekiah died, Judah sank into the worst idolatry it had ever known. In fact, one tradition says that Manasseh murdered the Prophet Isaiah.

Sennacherib—A Mighty King who Couldn't Defeat God

At their height of power, the Assyrians defeated everyone in their path, including Egypt. In about 701 B.C., Sennacherib marched into Palestine, conquering many cities of Judah, and demanding heavy tribute from Hezekiah, who stripped the temple of its silver and gold.

To prepare for an attack on Jerusalem, Hezekiah dug an underground tunnel through 1,777 feet of solid rock, bringing plenty of fresh water into the city. But just as Sennacherib was about to advance on Jerusalem, he received news that Merodach-baladan had revolted in Babylon. One view claims that Sennacherib was forced to leave, but returned around 689-686 B.C. to continue the siege. Afraid of defeat, Hezekiah prayed to God, reminding Him of his faithful reign. God answered by sending a plague which destroyed 185,000 of the Assyrian soldiers. Though Judah was a relatively weak nation at this time, the mighty Assyrian king was no match for the power of God.

Sennacherib's prism, upper center, records events of his reign. Left: Sennacherib's cavalry on the march. Below: Assyrian bowls and drinking cups, probably like those used by Sennacherib's forces which came against Hezekiah.

Prisoners of war come before Sennacherib, probably Israelites who were captured in battle.

275

Hezekiah's Prayer—An Angel Destroys the Assyrians

2 KINGS 19

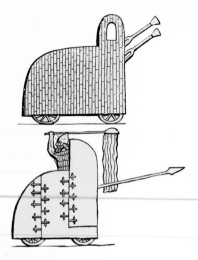

Synopsis

While Israel and Judah grew weaker spiritually and militarily, Assyria was growing stronger. By the time of King Hoshea of Israel, the Assyrians were powerful enough to sweep down and capture Israel, destroy its capital city, Samaria, and take many of its people back as captives. A few years later, Sennacherib attacked Judah and tried to capture Jerusalem. But he found a king named Hezekiah who trusted the Lord and prayed earnestly for the Lord's help. That help came. The Assyrian army was defeated, not by the army of Judah, but by the angel of the Lord, who destroyed 185,000 Assyrian soldiers in a night. Sennacherib broke camp and headed home. But not long after he arrived, his own sons came on him while he worshiped in a heathen temple and cut him down with a sword. Esarhaddon, one of his sons, then sat on the Assyrian throne.

Above: Assyrian battering rams were considered frightening weapons of war, for they could break down a mighty gate or wall. But Hezekiah had a more powerful weapon. He prayed for the Lord's help (below) and trusted Him to save Judah, which the Lord did.

The Assyrian War Machine

As the Assyrians grew in strength, they developed clever battle tactics and weapons which seemed unstoppable. So they extended their borders in all directions.

When the Assyrians first marched against a city, they surrounded it and set up camp. In a few days, they built great walls of earth around their tents, along with towers, ramps, and roads.

With their camp well fortified, the Assyrian soldiers started to tease the enemy with small raids and fires near the city walls. Any captured soldiers from the city were impaled on sharp poles which stood between the Assyrian camp and the besieged city. Death took two or three days, as friends and families watched them suffer from the city walls.

When the attack began, the Assyrians struck quickly. Iron-capped battering rams ceaselessly pounded the city walls and gates. Soldiers scaled the walls with numerous ladders. When the gates were broken, the rest of the army poured into the city and destroyed it.

Sennacherib and other Assyrian Kings

Sennacherib (705-681 B.C.) destroyed Babylon, but could not take Jerusalem. His youngest son, Esarhaddon (681-668) foolishly rebuilt Babylon, which later conquered the Assyrians. After the death of the next Assyrian king, Ashurbanipal (669-626), the Babylonians rose to power.

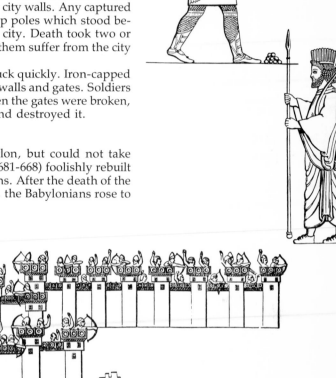

Left: Assyrians record the number of heads of battle victims. Upper right: an Assyrian slinger, using a sling much like the one David had used against Goliath many years before. The man below him is a spearman. Right: the city of Lachish fights Sennacherib. Below: Assyrians attack a city. Note the numerous things happening. Authentic drawings such as these help us see what Hezekiah faced.

Josiah Repairs the Temple—The Book of the Law Found

2 KINGS 22:1—23:30;
2 CHRONICLES 34—35

Synopsis
The Northern Kingdom of Israel had fallen. The king of Assyria had conquered it, taken its capital city, Samaria, and deported many of its finest people to Assyria. A few years later, King Sennacherib of Assyria came to Judah to do the same thing. But King Hezekiah, a godly man, trusted the Lord completely to save them, and an angel of the Lord struck 185,000 Assyrian soldiers dead in one night. Sennacherib broke camp and returned to Assyria, only to be murdered there by his sons. For a time, Judah was spared. Two evil kings followed Hezekiah. Then Josiah came to the throne and ruled as a godly king. A key event was finding and using the Book of the Law.

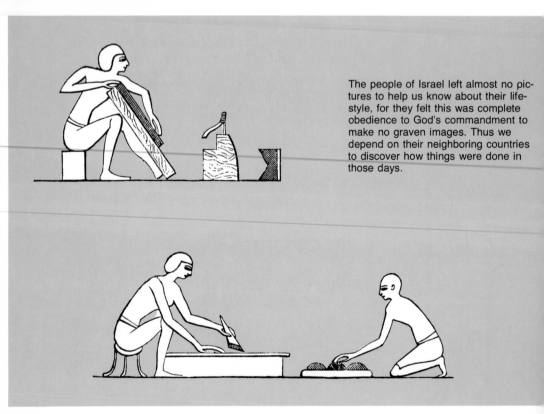

The people of Israel left almost no pictures to help us know about their lifestyle, for they felt this was complete obedience to God's commandment to make no graven images. Thus we depend on their neighboring countries to discover how things were done in those days.

Judah's Last Good King

Josiah was the last of Judah's godly kings. Like Hezekiah, he instituted sweeping reforms throughout the land, abolishing idolatry and demanding that worship be directed only toward the Lord.

The Assyrian Empire was declining at this time. Josiah took advantage of its weakness to expand his borders. His military victories included recapturing territories around Samaria and Megiddo.

Josiah was killed in battle by Pharaoh Necho of Egypt. After his death, the kingdom of Judah declined rapidly until soon it was destroyed by the mighty nation of Babylon.

The Book of the Law

When Moses and the Israelites camped at Mount Sinai, God gave them many important laws to live by. These laws were guidelines for the lifestyle of people who were obedient to God.

Moses wrote these laws in a book, and frequently read them to the people to remind them how to live. The Ten Commandments formed the core of this Book of the Law.

Where Was the Book of the Law Found?

The Book of the Law was probably not found on a dusty shelf, or in a forgotten corner of the temple. In ancient times, it was common for important documents to be placed in the cornerstone of a new building. In Josiah's day, his workmen were making extensive repairs to the temple. The old cornerstone that Solomon had laid over three and one half centuries before was probably cracked or broken, and when the workmen arrived to fix or replace it, they found the important book.

Josiah Collects Money for the Temple

When Josiah began his great religious reforms, one of his first jobs was to repair the temple and restore its services. But this required a large amount of money, so the king asked all temple-worshipers to contribute.

In Josiah's day, money was measured by weight. Coins had been invented by the Lydians just a few years before Josiah's reign, and probably were not used in Judah yet. Gold or silver ingots, or broken pieces of gold or silver jewelry, valued by weight, were likely the "money" which the people gave.

The work of carpenters and masons was vital in the temple repairs of Josiah's time. At the lower left, carpenters plane (top), glue, and grind. Below: stonemasons hammer and chisel stone, while one measures. Techniques used by these craftsmen of Egypt were probably much the same as those used by the carpenters and masons who worked for Josiah.

The Book of the Law Is Read

2 CHRONICLES 34:14-32

Synopsis
After the death of King Solomon, his son Rehoboam tried to squeeze unreasonable taxes from the people, hoping to support a life of luxury like Solomon's. But the people had had their fill of such things and rebelled, forming a Northern Kingdom, Israel, with 10 tribes, leaving only the tribes of Judah and Benjamin for a Southern Kingdom, which Rehoboam ruled. This happened in 931 B.C. For the next 209 years, both kingdoms declined spiritually, and with that decline weakened militarily. The Northern Kingdom was conquered in 722 B.C. Judah, the Southern Kingdom, held on for another 136 years, mostly because godly kings such as Hezekiah and Josiah depended on the Lord instead of military might. Josiah ruled from 640 to 608 B.C. During his reign he led a major campaign to rebuild the temple. While doing this, the workmen found a copy of the Book of the Law, which King Josiah read to the people.

Reading the Book of the Law
The Book of the Law was God's blueprint for successful living. It was the Word of God written by Moses, who first read this book to the Israelites (Ex. 24:7). On entering the Promised Land, Joshua again read this book before all the people as a reminder of God's blessings to those who obey Him (Josh. 8:32-35).

The Israelites were instructed to think about the book's message every day (1:8), and to obey its words (23:6).

Scrolls—Books of the Ancient World

Most ancient books were called scrolls. They looked nothing like the books of today. In fact, books were not bound into pages until after the time of Christ, and paper was not invented until the 10th century A.D.

In Josiah's day, most writing was done on sheets of papyrus, which came from papyrus reeds, that grew along the Nile River. The Egyptians had used papyrus for over 2,000 years, but the Israelites had just started using it to replace the clay tablet.

Sheets of papyrus were made by weaving papyrus stems across each other, much like cloth was woven on a loom. The strips were then beaten until flat, and dried in the sun. One side was rubbed smooth with a piece of ivory or a shell. The finished sheet of papyrus looked similar to paper.

These sheets were then sewed or glued into long rolls called scrolls. Some scrolls found in Egypt have been unrolled to a length of over 100 feet! Handles were fastened to each end of a scroll, to make rolling it easier. The "book" was now ready for the pen of a trained scribe.

Scribes and Writing

Reading and writing were skills learned by only a select few in Bible times. Scribes were the writers of the ancient world, and an Israelite man was usually trained for 15-20 years to become one.

Scribes were in great demand. They kept records for the kingdom and wrote letters for the king, who often could not read or write. Scribes also sat by the city gate and recorded business transactions for the people.

Public Reading of the Bible

When the Book of the Law was found, it was the only "Bible" in the entire land of Judah. It would take months for a scribe to write a few extra copies, and even so, most people could not read or write. For this reason, the Book of the Law was read aloud by a scribe at the temple or in a public square.

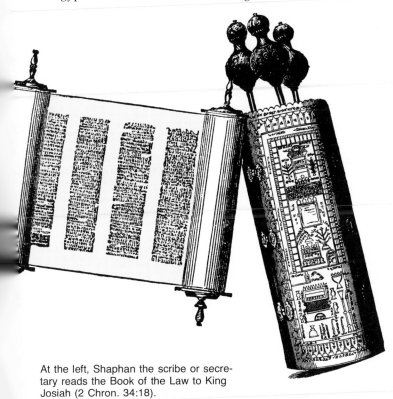

At the left, Shaphan the scribe or secretary reads the Book of the Law to King Josiah (2 Chron. 34:18).

The Book of the Law was in the form of a scroll. On these pages are pictured six scrolls, some with two rollers, others with three. The cluster of three scrolls shows two unrolled slightly for reading—one with two rollers and one with three. Writing on scrolls was done in narrow columns, which were read from the right end of the scroll to the left. Early scrolls were made of papyrus. Later, perhaps after the Exile, they were made of animal skins. The Hebrews were careful that these skins were from "clean" animals.

281

Above left: an Astarte figurine from the time of the Kings of Israel. Astarte was also known as Ashtaroth or Ashtoreth, a fertility goddess in the Middle East. Israel forsook the Lord to worship Ashtaroth and Baal. The Valley of Hinnom (above and right), or Hinnom Valley, had many pagan shrines when Josiah became king, but he tore them down.

Josiah's Reforms— He Destroys Idols

2 KINGS 23:1-29; 2 CHRONICLES 34:29-33

Synopsis

King Josiah was Judah's last hope. Judah was spared for 136 years more than its northern neighbor, Israel, before it fell. Why? Because of the good kings Hezekiah and Josiah, who depended on the Lord instead of military might to defend their nation. Josiah's rule was Judah's last golden moment before the end. He rebuilt the temple, read the Book of the Law to the people, renewed the covenant with the Lord, and encouraged his people to pledge themselves to the Book of the Law and to the Lord. Josiah tore down idols and did many other things to bring his people back to the Lord. While he lived and ruled, Judah was safe. But his death in 608 B.C. brought the beginning of the end for Judah. Within 25 years, Jerusalem would fall, and with it the Southern Kingdom, Judah.

The Different Kinds of Idols

Idols came in many different shapes and sizes. Some were giant statues set up as public places of worship. Smaller idols, called teraphim, were kept in homes. Others were small enough to be worn on a chain around people's necks.

The Hinnom Valley

In Josiah's day, the Hinnom Valley was a center for heathen cults and worship. Countless statues and shrines were set up to honor pagan gods. As king, Josiah ravaged this valley by tearing down the monuments and burning the idols.

The Three Temple Buildings

Over the years, the temple in Jerusalem was built and destroyed three times. Solomon's temple was the finest, but it was destroyed by King Nebuchadnezzar. When the Israelites returned from captivity, they built a less impressive temple under the leadership of Zerubbabel. This was dismantled in about 20 B.C. by Herod the Great, who built a more elaborate one. The temple was the focal point in Jerusalem during Jesus' day. When the Romans sacked Jerusalem in A.D. 70, the temple was destroyed and never rebuilt.

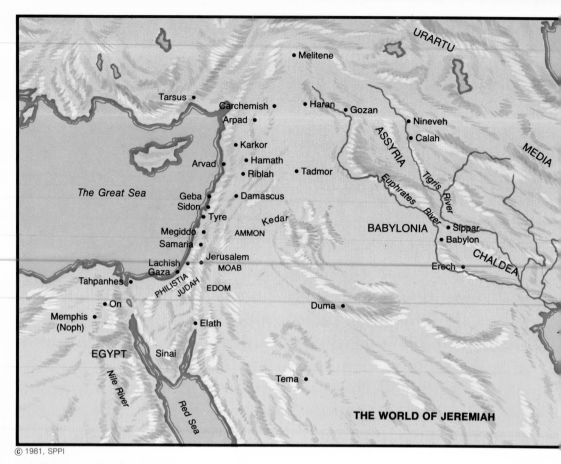

THE WORLD OF JEREMIAH

© 1981, SPPI

The Story of Jeremiah

The Book of JEREMIAH

Synopsis
After the Northern Kingdom, Israel, and its capital, Samaria, were conquered in 722 B.C., the Southern Kingdom, Judah, held on for another 136 years, until 586 B.C., when it fell. During this time, Judah was ruled by eight kings. Hezekiah (716-687 B.C.) was a godly man who did much to keep Judah alive. The next two kings, Manasseh (696-642 B.C.) and Amon (642-640 B.C.), were evil. Josiah followed (640-608 B.C.) and was a godly king, returning his nation to the Book of the Law and worship in the temple. After he died, Jehoahaz ruled for three months, followed by three evil kings, Jehoiakim (608-597), Jehoiachin (597), and Zedekiah (597-586 B.C.). During the reigns of Josiah through Zedekiah, a prophet ministered in Judah, counseling kings and religious leaders, often under persecution. His name was Jeremiah. His name remains today on the book of the Bible he left for us.

The Rise of the Babylonian Empire
The great kingdom of Babylon enjoyed its position as a world power for less than a century (605-539 B.C.). Nabopolassar, the governor of Babylon (625-605), overthrew the Assyrians and gained independence for the Babylonians. But his son, Nebuchadnezzar II, is really given the credit for founding the empire.

284

Nebuchadnezzar was the only strong king his nation ever had. Under him, trade and culture blossomed and the economy grew prosperous. The city of Babylon was strengthened and became known as a world leader.

The Fall of Assyria

In 689 B.C., Sennacherib, king of Assyria, destroyed the city of Babylon. The king immediately wrote a law demanding that Babylon remain in ruins for 70 years. But Sennacherib's son Esarhaddon revoked the law and rebuilt the city. This was a fatal mistake, for the city soon grew into an empire which was to destroy the Assyrians.

During the 18-year reign of Esarhaddon, Assyrian might was declining rapidly. Heavy taxes were forced on the people, to pay for the nation's building projects and military expeditions. The leaders neglected their country, spending most of their time trying to conquer the world. Soon rebellion broke out, weakening the country further. In 612 B.C., the Babylonians took advantage of this weakness and sacked the Assyrian capital of Nineveh, marking the end of the Assyrian Empire.

Jeremiah the Prophet

The Northern Kingdom of Israel had been destroyed for over a century because of its failure to obey God. Jeremiah was called as a prophet to try to prevent this from happening to the Southern Kingdom of Judah.

Jeremiah saw the decline of Assyria and the rise of Babylon. At this time Judah was weak. The prophet knew that obedience to God was their only hope of withstanding the Babylonians.

Jeremiah was understanding and sympathetic, but his book is bold in predicting Judah's destruction at the hands of Babylon because of its continued sin, especially idolatry.

The book of the Bible which Jeremiah gave to us was dictated to his scribe Baruch. Scribes were highly trained in reading and writing, which few people could do in those days. At the left are three drawings of scribes, from ancient monuments. Assyrians are in the center. The others are Egyptian.

The world shortly after Jeremiah's death is pictured on the map at the upper left. Jeremiah continually warned King Zedekiah of Babylon's coming invasion and conquest of Jerusalem. Left: Jehoiakim burns Jeremiah's scroll as it is read to him. Below: Memphis, Egypt, sometimes called Noph, where Jeremiah sent a message to fellow Jews (Jer. 44:1).

Judah Falls, Jerusalem Is Destroyed, and Zedekiah Is Blinded

2 KINGS 24—25; 2 CHRONICLES 36:5-21

Synopsis
After the death of King Josiah of Judah, the Southern Kingdom declined quickly. Within 25 years, four kings had ruled and the nation was ripe for conquest. Babylon, now the world power in the north, swept down and conquered Jerusalem and with it, Judah. King Zedekiah was forced to watch the murder of his sons and was then blinded. It was the sad end of a once-great nation under Kings David and Solomon.

Destruction of a Great City
Over the centuries, Jerusalem was the heartbeat of Israel's life and history. Abraham first journeyed there when the city was called Salem, to honor its King Melchizedek (Gen. 14:18-22). Later, Abraham almost sacrificed his son Isaac on Mount Moriah, the future site of the temple (Gen. 22:1-19).

In the days of the Judges, Jerusalem, then Jebus, was conquered by Joshua (Josh. 10:1-27). But over the years, the city returned to the control of the Canaanites.

King David finally brought Jerusalem back under Israelite control. He defeated the city, and proclaimed it his capital (2 Sam. 5:6-12). David made Jerusalem strong and prosperous, and drew plans for God's house.

When Solomon built God's temple, Jerusalem became the focal point in the nation of Israel. Many times each year Israelites traveled to Jerusalem from all parts of the nation to observe various feasts and festivals and to worship at the temple. The city had beauty and wealth, and soon came to be known as one of the finest cities in the ancient world.

But when Israel split in two, Jerusalem lost much of its importance. Evil kings outnumbered good, and the city became wicked. After numerous warnings from God's prophets, the once-beautiful city was totally destroyed by the Babylonians. The greatest landmark of Israel had faded into desolation.

Treatment of Enemy Kings
A captured king was a prized prisoner. A victorious king placed his foot on his enemy's neck to symbolize his dominance. The prisoner king, often a mighty warrior, was sometimes blinded, leaving him a helpless creature for life. He often faced more torture or humiliation, or was sentenced to a cruel death, or to a life of slavery.

The Babylonian Empire
The kingdom of Babylon rose as quickly as it fell. Within a century, it had overthrown the Assyrians, risen to a world power, and crumbled into extinction by the might of the Persians.

Nebuchadnezzar was Babylon's mightiest ruler. Three times he carried captives from Judah to suppress their revolts. The last time, in 586 B.C., Jerusalem was completely destroyed, and Judah lost its existence as a nation.

But Nebuchadnezzar's successors were weak, and soon Babylon began to decay. Its vast army and great capital city cost too much to support, and rebellion broke out. Within a few short years, King Cyrus and the Persians overthrew Babylon, in 539 B.C.

But Cyrus was a merciful man, and one of his decrees allowed the Israelites to return to their homeland. In captivity, the people had learned much about obedience to God.

In the times before the Exile the land we remember as Palestine looked something like this (map at right). Israel fell in 722 B.C. when the Assyrians conquered it. Judah fell in 586 B.C. when the Babylonians conquered it. Zedekiah, king of Judah, was blinded as is shown in this Assyrian picture at the right. The practice of placing the conquering king's foot on the neck of the conquered king is seen above, in another Assyrian picture.

286

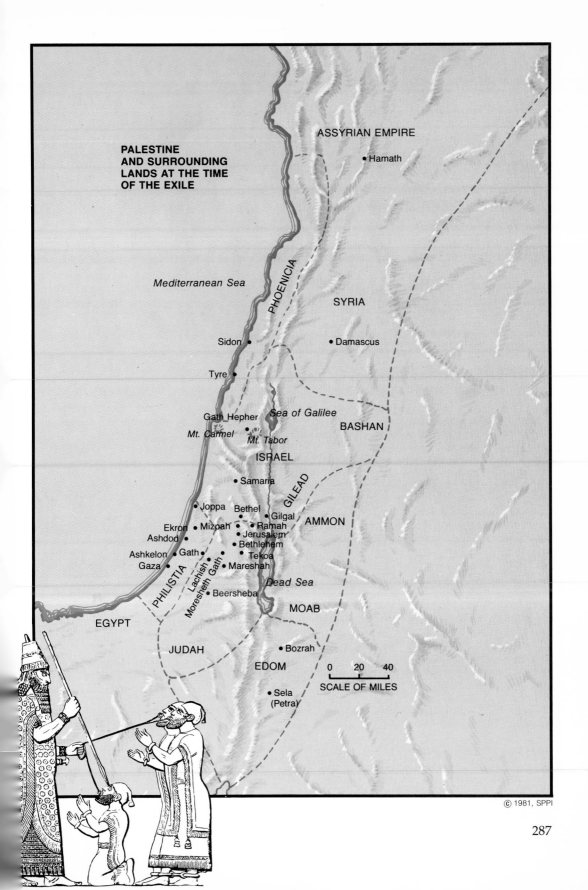

PALESTINE
AND SURROUNDING
LANDS AT THE TIME
OF THE EXILE

ASSYRIAN EMPIRE

• Hamath

Mediterranean Sea

PHOENICIA

SYRIA

Sidon •

• Damascus

Tyre •

Gath Hepher   Sea of Galilee

Mt. Carmel   Mt. Tabor   BASHAN

ISRAEL

• Samaria

GILEAD

• Joppa   Bethel
            •   • Gilgal   AMMON
Ekron • Mizpah • Ramah
Ashdod •   • Jerusalem
            • Bethlehem
Ashkelon • Gath   • Tekoa
Gaza •   Lachish • Mareshah
        PHILISTIA   Moresheth Gath
                • Beersheba   Dead Sea

EGYPT   MOAB

JUDAH   • Bozrah

        EDOM   0   20   40
                SCALE OF MILES

        • Sela
        (Petra)

© 1981, SPPI

Daniel and the King's Food

DANIEL 1

Synopsis
Nebuchadnezzar's army swept down from Babylon against Jerusalem. In one final conquest, they took the city and the land of Judah surrounding it. They burned the city and took the people of Jerusalem and Judah as prisoners. Many were taken into exile in Babylon; among them, Daniel and his friends, who were placed in special training. But these four friends had a problem. Some of their food consisted of meat offered to heathen idols and strong wine, which Daniel and his friends knew would not please the Lord. But what should they do?

King Nebuchadnezzar of Babylon
"Nebuchadnezzar" is perhaps the Aramaic form of the Akkadian word *Nabu-kudurri-usur,* which means "Nabu has protected by inheritance" (Nabu was one of Babylon's deities). Nebuchadnezzar was the eldest son of the founder of the Neo-Babylonian Empire, which succeeded the Assyrian Empire. As crown prince in 605 B.C. he led the Babylonian armies in their victory over Egypt at the Battle of Carchemish. This may have been the time when Daniel and his companions were captured and taken to Babylon. Just before Nebuchadnezzar had returned to Babylon, he learned of his father's death. He immediately made a 23-day journey across the desert to establish his kingship. He remained king for the next 43 years. In 601 B.C., and again beginning in 599 B.C., the Babylonians clashed with Egypt. Judah was inevitably involved in this international warfare. In 597 B.C. and more completely in 587 B.C. Judah became a vassal of Babylon. Historical sources for the later years of King Nebuchadnezzar's reign are completely lacking. We do know, however, that he was a great builder. Among the great

Upper left: Daniel and his friends refuse the king's food and wine. Top: a drawing of King Nebuchadnezzar, from an artifact of his time. Lower photo above: a clay cylinder of King Nebuchadnezzar, proclaiming the rebuilding of the sun-god temple.

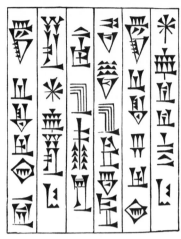

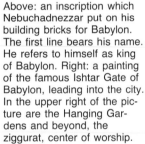

Above: an inscription which Nebuchadnezzar put on his building bricks for Babylon. The first line bears his name. He refers to himself as king of Babylon. Right: a painting of the famous Ishtar Gate of Babylon, leading into the city. In the upper right of the picture are the Hanging Gardens and beyond, the ziggurat, center of worship.

structures he built were the new half of the city on the west bank of the Euphrates River, a new palace, a rebuilt Procession Way that led from the Ishtar Gate south into the city, and, if tradition is correct, the famous "Hanging Gardens" that helped remind his Median wife of her homeland. He died in 562 B.C.

Babylon

Once the great and lavishly wealthy capital of the foremost empire of its day, Babylon today is only a series of excavated mounds extending over several square miles near the village of Jumjummah, about 50 miles southwest of Baghdad in Iraq. The proximity of the Euphrates River has made excavation extremely difficult, but over the last two centuries the upper levels have been uncovered. Earlier travelers mistakenly identified the city with the remains of ziggurat towers west of Baghdad.

In the ancient Akkadian language Babylon means "the gate of the gods," but in the Old Testament it means "confused" (Hebrew = babel). Its name reminded the Jews that confusion is the spiritual result of idolatry.

Ancient Babylon was a rectangularly shaped city bisected from north to south by the Euphrates River. About 50 miles of double walls, the inner one 21-feet thick, the outer 11, surrounded the city. They rose 300 feet into the air and were reinforced by 420-foot-high towers at 60-foot intervals. The waters of the Euphrates River were diverted to form a moat around the walls. The most important of its eight gates was the Ishtar Gate on the north. Made of glazed brick covered with lapis lazuli blue tiles, it gave access to two citadels and an enormous palace.

289

The Fiery Furnace

DANIEL 3

Synopsis

After Jerusalem was destroyed and the people of Judah were taken captive, Daniel and his friends were forced to go to Babylon to live. There they were trained to be leaders in the new kingdom. But when Daniel's three friends refused to bow to the king's golden statue, he sentenced them to be burned alive in a fiery furnace.

The Plain of Dura

The word "dura" is a common word used in naming ancient Babylonian places. It means "the wall" and probably refers to the walls built around cities to protect them.

We do not know for sure where the Plain or Valley of Dura was. In 1863, a French archeologist, Jules Oppert, discovered the pedestal of an enormous statue a few miles southeast of Babylon. Ever since then that area has been called Tulul Dura (the Tells of Dura).

The Image of Gold

What did the image of gold set up by King Nebuchadnezzar of Babylon look like?

The Bible doesn't say. But from the way the inscriptions of Nebuchadnezzar glorify the Babylonian god Marduk, it may have been an idol of that god.

Marduk was one of the chief gods in the kingdom of Babylon. Each spring the Babylonians celebrated a New Year's Festival. At that time Marduk was officially honored. The statues of all other Babylonian gods were transported to the city of Babylon by ship or wagon and brought before the statue of Marduk in the great hall of Marduk's temple. Together, these gods were supposed to help determine and shape each man's life for the coming year.

The Furnace

King Nebuchadnezzar's fiery furnace was more like a giant oven called a kiln. Mud bricks were baked inside the kiln. These bricks were used for the numerous building projects undertaken across the city of Babylon.

Most furnaces, or kilns, had both a top open-

"As soon as you hear the sound of the horn, flute, zither, lyre, harp, pipes, and all kinds of music, you must fall down and worship the image of gold," the herald warned. Daniel's three friends refused to do this, so they were thrown into a fiery furnace. The drawings at the right and below show musicians of the Assyrian-Babylonian peoples. Names of these instruments have been translated in many different ways. In the picture at the right, from right to left: the flute or pipe, sackbut or lute or trigon, and the harp or lyre. Below, the instruments from right to left are: harp, double flute or pipe, dulcimer or bagpipe, and harp.

ing and a side opening. King Nebuchadnezzar probably talked with the three men in the
furnace through the side opening.

Obeying the King's Command

King Nebuchadnezzar in his rage ordered the
great furnace to be heated to a temperature
seven times hotter than normal. Next the king
commanded several of his strongest and bravest soldiers to tie up Shadrach, Meshach, and
Abednego and throw them into the flames.

Without a second thought, his soldiers
obeyed the king's order, knowing that the
heat of the flames would almost certainly kill
them too. Why then did they do it?

In Babylon, the king was the supreme ruler.
To disobey a king's command meant death,
not always a quick death from the flames of
a furnace, but sometimes a slow and painful
death at the hands of torturers.

More musicians of Nineveh are pictured
above. The large upright stringed instruments
are harps. The wind instrument is the double
flute or pipe, and the horizontal instrument is
the dulcimer or bagpipe. Below: the sackbut,
lute, or trigon, a horizontal stringed instrument.

Below: from left to right, timbrel,
psaltery or harp, cymbals, and
another psaltery or harp. Left: Daniel's three friends are thrown into a
fiery furnace, but a fourth Person
appears with them.

מְנֵא מְנֵא
תְּקֵל וּפַרְסִין

The Handwriting on the Wall

DANIEL 5

Synopsis

Born into a Judean nobleman's family, Daniel was probably only 16 when captured by Nebuchadnezzar's forces and taken from his conquered land to Babylon. There he and a select group of friends were trained to be leaders in this new land. Daniel became one of the Hebrew leaders in Babylon and rose to the highest levels of power. When Daniel was about 70 years old, Belshazzar became king of Babylon. About 10-15 years later, Daniel was called into one of Belshazzar's drunken feasts to explain some mysterious handwriting on a wall.

King Belshazzar of Babylon

In the six years after King Nebuchadnezzar's death in 562 B.C., Babylon had many rulers: his son Evil-Merodach, his son-in-law Nergal-Shar-Usur, and his grandson, the young Labashi-Marduk. Then Nabonidus became king in 556 B.C. His son Belshazzar ruled by his side from about 550 until Nabonidus' death in 539. The Bible says that Nebuchadnezzar was the father of Belshazzar, but this simply means that he was an earlier Babylonian king.

Nabonidus was peace-loving, and much preferred to build temples and learn to read and write. This gave Belshazzar the opportunity to be a co-ruler with his father. These two rulers explain why Daniel was proclaimed the *third* highest ruler in the kingdom.

The Medes

The Medes were a people who lived in Media, a region some distance northeast of Babylon and the Tigris River. Little is known of this ancient people. Only a few words of their language have survived and their origins are almost totally unknown. One of their rulers, named Cyaxares, rose to power and extended the borders of his kingdom,

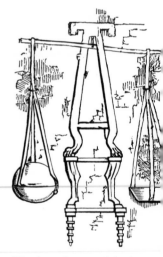

"You have been weighed on the scales and found wanting," Daniel interpreted the handwriting on the wall for the king (Dan. 5:27). Some versions translate scales as balances, a form of scales in ancient times. The four drawings above and at the right show various balances, or scales, from ancient times.

including Persia. His granddaughter, Amytis, married King Nebuchadnezzar. But in 550 B.C., Cyaxares' successor, Astyages, was betrayed by his own army to King Cyrus, and the Median empire fell to Persia.

The Persians
Persia lay to the east of both Babylon and Media. In 559 B.C. King Cyrus of Persia joined forces with Nabonidus (Belshazzar's father) to conquer much of southwest Asia. In 550 Media's ruler was betrayed and turned over to Cyrus. Then in 539 Cyrus overthrew the weak King Belshazzar of Babylon.

Cyrus was a competent and greatly admired ruler. He instituted a system of "satraps," or governors, who had considerable freedom but were nevertheless responsible directly to the king. He built an impressive capital at Pasargadae, north of Persepolis.

Purple Clothing
Purple was a sign of wealth and importance in Bible times. Most purple dye was patiently extracted from the murex shellfish found in the Mediterranean Sea. This slow process made the purple dyes rare and expensive, but in great demand. A purple robe was a symbol of status and considered to be very valuable.

The Babylonian Feast
A banquet was always prepared in elaborate fashion with meat, fish, and fruits of all varieties. Wine of the best vintage was the favorite drink, and the Babylonians enjoyed drinking.

When using balances, or scales, a person in ancient times put a fixed weight, of stone or metal, on one side, like those above. The goods to be weighed were put on the other side. Weighed and wanting meant that the king did not measure up to the gifts God had given him.

Below: a Mede and a Persian, drawn from a sculpture of ancient times. Daniel warned King Belshazzar (upper left) of the meaning of the handwriting on the wall, that "your kingdom is divided and given to the Medes and Persians" (Dan. 5:28).

293

Daniel in a Lions' Den

DANIEL 6

Synopsis

Daniel was an old man when he was called into a drunken feast, hosted by Belshazzar, king of Babylon. Daniel interpreted mysterious writing on a wall, which told Belshazzar that his kingdom would be taken from him and given to another. That night the army of Cyrus entered the city and took over without a struggle. Darius the Mede took over the rule of Babylon for Cyrus and ruled about two years until Cyrus could do it. During this time he appointed presidents, including Daniel, to help him rule. But the other presidents grew jealous of Daniel and tricked Darius into signing a law prohibiting prayer to anyone other than him. Daniel was found guilty and sentenced to die in a den of lions.

The Lions' Den

As a means of execution, hungry lions were kept within a small enclosed area. On top of the walls was a space built for spectators. A small entrance near the bottom of the wall was probably the opening which Darius sealed with a stone (Dan. 6:17).

Darius the Mede

Darius the Mede should not be confused with Darius I, a Persian king who ruled some years later. When King Cyrus took Babylon in 539 B.C. he appointed Darius the Mede to rule there as the "governor." The Book of Daniel calls Darius the Mede a "king." This was a natural title to call any ruler of a city or province.

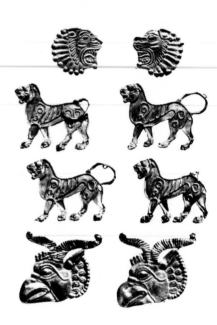

Above: gold jewelry from the time of Daniel and Esther. Note the lions' heads and the full figures of lions, part of the jewelry of the period. The lion was also shown as a mighty animal attacking a bull (below), carved on the stairway of a great hall at Persepolis, capital of the Persian Empire from the time of Darius I on. Maps at the right: the four great empires from Daniel's time until the time of Christ.

Under Nebuchadnezzar, the Babylonian Empire reached its peak (during the time of Daniel, about the 6th century B.C.).

The Medes and Persians took control the same night Daniel interpreted the handwriting on the wall. Esther was part of the Persian Empire (about 481 B.C.).

During the time of Queen Esther the Greeks began to defeat the Persians. The Greek (Macedonian) Empire was from about 359-323 B.C. From then until 63 B.C., Ptolemaic, Seleucid, and Hasmonean kings ruled in Palestine.

The Roman rule in Palestine began in 63 B.C. and continued until long past New Testament times.

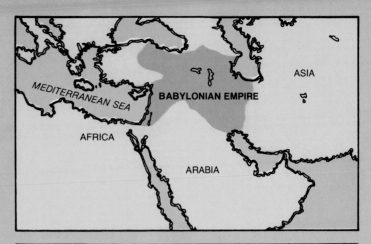

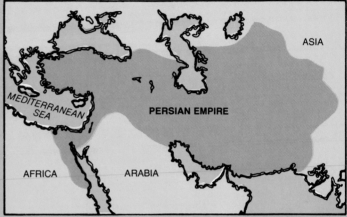

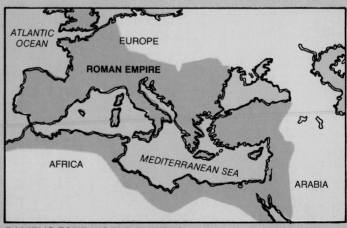

DANIEL'S FOUR WORLD EMPIRES

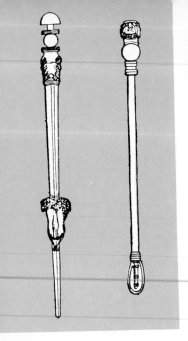

The Story of Queen Esther

The Book of ESTHER

Synopsis
After the time of King Solomon, the nation of Israel began to weaken. As the people turned away from God, He permitted the gradual destruction of the nation. First, Israel divided into Northern and Southern Kingdoms. Then wicked kings began to rule over the divided land. At last, from 745 B.C. until 587 B.C. the Assyrians and Babylonians captured large numbers of the Israelites and forced them to leave their homes and live in new lands. Assyria was the great world power until 612 B.C. Then Babylon ruled as the world power until 539 B.C. when Cyrus the Great, king of the Persian Empire, conquered it. The story of the handwriting on the wall (Dan. 5) tells of the night when Cyrus' army took the city without a fight. Cyrus ruled the Persian Empire for nine more years until he died in 530 B.C., with Darius the Mede ruling the first two years for him. During those nine years he permitted about 50,000 Jews to return to their homeland and lay the foundation of the temple.

During the reign of Cyrus' son, Cambyses II (530-522 B.C.), work on the temple was stopped. But when Darius I (not Darius the Mede) became king in 522 B.C. he permitted the work on the temple to continue. During his reign Haggai and Zechariah ministered to the Jews. By 515 B.C. the temple was completed by Zerubbabel.

Above: King Ahasuerus welcomes Esther b▮ holding out his scepter. Above left: scepter▮

The stone relief at the left pictures King Ahasuerus standing behind his father, Dari▮ who sits on a throne. This is an actual ima▮ the two kings found at Persepolis, one of t▮ royal Persian cities.

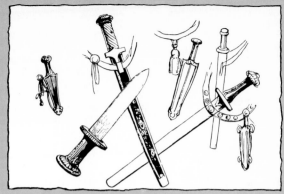

Above: Persian chariot. Esther probably rode in a chariot similar to this. Above right: Persian weapons. The battles between the Jews and their enemies involved such weapons.

The harem (left) at Persepolis, was used by the Persian kings, including Esther's husband Ahasuerus, or Xerxes. The winter palace was here at Persepolis while the summer palace was at Susa.

When Darius I died in 486 B.C. his son Xerxes (Ahasuerus) became king of the Persian Empire and ruled until 465 B.C. It was this king who became dissatisfied with his queen Vashti and banished her, marrying Esther.

Xerxes was a warrior king. After he put down a rebellion in Egypt, he invaded Greece. For a while the Persians seemed to be winning. But in a battle at Salamis, the Persians lost their fleet. Sensing defeat, Xerxes turned over his army to a general and went home. Later Xerxes was killed by one of his guards.

Esther's Name
Esther had two names. Her Hebrew name, Hadassah, meant "myrtle." Her Persian name, Esther, meant "star." It may have come from the goddess "Ishtar," or may have simply referred to Esther's sparkling beauty.

Xerxes' Name
The king also had two names. Ahasuerus is the Hebrew name for Xerxes, which was the king's historical name. Actually Xerxes is the Greek form of his name. The meaning of the name is unknown.

Shushan Palace
The kings of Persia had more than one royal city. Shushan Palace was at Susa, in what is now southwestern Iran. Persepolis was another royal city. Esther probably lived from time to time in each of these cities.

The Name of God
The name of God is never mentioned in the Book of Esther. Nor is the Book of Esther referred to in the New Testament. But the book speaks clearly of God's care for His people.

Mordecai
Esther's cousin who raised her as a daughter was probably a lower official at the king's royal palace. Both Esther and Mordecai were Jewish exiles who lived in Persia.

Time
Esther lived during the time of Xerxes, who reigned from 486-465 B.C.

297

Ezra and the People Return

The Book of EZRA

Synopsis

Daniel was a young Judean nobleman when he was captured by Nebuchadnezzar's army and taken to Babylon. There he was trained and became a leader in Babylon for many years. When he was an old man, he interpreted handwriting on a wall for another king, Belshazzar, which told how the army of Cyrus, king of the Persian Empire, would take over the land. After he did take over, Cyrus immediately gave an edict that the captured Hebrews could return to their native land and rebuild their temple.

Cyrus

Cyrus II of Persia (559-530 B.C.) began his reign over Babylon in 539 B.C. In the first year of his reign Cyrus gave the Jews the temple valuables Nebuchadnezzar had brought to Babylon in 586 B.C. He allowed them to return to their homeland. With the support of their neighbors, the Jews gathered offerings for the journey to Jerusalem. Cyrus founded a dynasty that was to last until Alexander the Great conquered Persia, in 336 B.C.

Zerubbabel

It is easy to miss the name of Zerubbabel as you read Ezra 2 and 3. He was the heir to the throne of Judah, but when he arrived in Jerusalem with about 50,000 of his people around 539 B.C. he only became governor. With Jeshua's help he began the second temple, but those who had seen the splendor of Solomon's temple wept when they saw how infe-

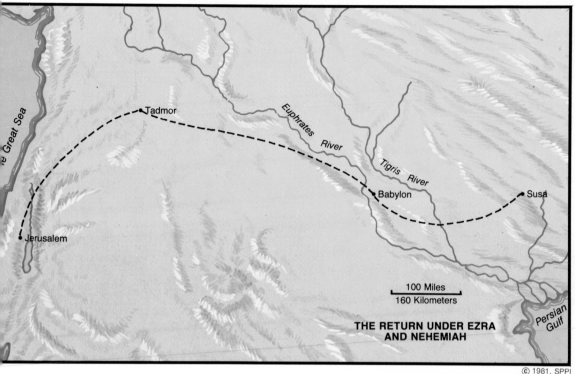

© 1981, SPPI

"There, by the Ahava Canal, I proclaimed a fast, so that we might humble ourselves before our God and ask Him for a safe journey" (Ezra 8:21). At the upper left, Ezra and his people fast and pray that the Lord will take them safely to Jerusalem. Above: the general route they followed on their journey. The exact location of the Ahava Canal (River) is not known.

rior the new temple was going to be (Ezra 3:12).

Zerubbabel's Enemies

Zerubbabel's enemies were Jews who had not been carried into exile in 586 B.C. They had remained in the land and intermarried with the people the Babylonians had brought there to settle. Sanballat is mentioned in the Elephantine Papyri of 407 B.C. as governor of Samaria. Josephus says he built the Samaritan temple on Mount Gerizim (see John 4:20). To Zerubbabel and his companions Sanballat and his associates were no longer God's people because they had married non-Jews and worshiped their gods.

King Darius I (522-486 B.C.)

When Zerubbabel's enemies, the Samaritans, tried to stop the activities of the returned exiles, King Darius searched for the decree of his predecessor, King Cyrus. He found it at Ecbatana, the old capital of Media. Zerubbabel finished the second temple in 516 B.C., the seventh year of Darius' rule.

Tattenai

Tattenai was the military governor of Judea. He reported to the king of Persia. Zerubbabel reported to him.

Xerxes and Artaxerxes I

After the death of King Darius (the Great), Xerxes became king of Persia. Also called Ahasuerus, he is known to Bible readers as the husband of Queen Esther. Though he was a weak king, he ruled from 486-464 B.C.

Artaxerxes I was Xerxes' son and heir. He helped Ezra and Nehemiah. He ruled the Persian Empire from 464-424 B.C.

Ezra

Ezra took silver and gold from the province of Babylon and with the blessing of Artaxerxes went to Jerusalem in 458 B.C., the seventh year of Artaxerxes' rule. The temple had been rebuilt. Now Ezra taught the Law of God and ended the people's pagan marriages.

299

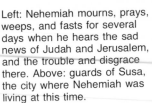

Left: Nehemiah mourns, prays, weeps, and fasts for several days when he hears the sad news of Judah and Jerusalem, and the trouble and disgrace there. Above: guards of Susa, the city where Nehemiah was living at this time.

Nehemiah Prays for His Homeland

NEHEMIAH 1

Synopsis
Belshazzar was ruling Babylon when it was captured by the armies of Cyrus, who absorbed Babylon into the Persian Empire which he ruled. Cyrus appointed Darius the Mede to rule in his behalf for a few years. Cyrus immediately gave orders for the Jewish people, the Hebrews, to be permitted to return to their native land and rebuild the temple. Work on the temple began, but was halted under the reign of Cyrus' successor, Cambyses I. When Darius I became ruler, Haggai and Zechariah resumed the work and the temple was at last finished about 515 B.C. About 34 years later, Esther became queen, with Darius' son Xerxes as her husband. After Xerxes died, his son Artaxerxes I became ruler. Nehemiah was his cupbearer, and when he made his request known to Artaxerxes, the king let him go to Jerusalem to rebuild its walls. Nehemiah worked on the walls about 445 B.C.

Homes of Persian Kings

The kings of Persia had great power and wealth. Many of them were not content to live in just one home, or palace. Others, on taking the throne, named a different city as the Persian capital, or built an entirely new city to be the chief center for the kingdom. Some did this simply because they did not like to rule from the same city where the former king had ruled. In any case, kings moved around quite a lot, and built palaces in many important cities.

One Home of Darius the Great

When Darius the Great became king in 522 B.C. he made the city of Susa one of his royal homes. There a beautiful palace was built which became the center of royal activity for Xerxes (Ahasuerus), Darius' son. Esther was the wife of Xerxes, and lived in Susa as queen. The events in the Book of Esther take place in Susa.

Another Home of King Darius

Darius the Great was not content with just one royal city or royal home. The king built Persepolis, which was about 200 miles southeast of Susa. The city was built near a hill, and to keep most of it flat, Darius placed huge stone blocks together and joined them with iron staples covered with lead. On this flat terrace he set 72 great columns, some as high as 65 feet, topped by carvings of bulls and horned lions.

The magnificent palace and the city surrounding it were enclosed by three separate walls along with many watchtowers. Many walls with their stairways may still be seen, with the elaborately carved figures of leaves and people bringing tribute to the king.

Homes of Xerxes and Artaxerxes

Susa was probably the principal capital for King Xerxes and his son Artaxerxes. But both kings carried out many of their activities from Persepolis. Queen Esther probably made many trips to Persepolis with Xerxes.

The return of Ezra and Nehemiah and their people to Judah and Jerusalem raises questions about travel in the Persian Empire at that time. The sculpture below depicts such travel, with chariots and dignitaries walking in procession. Persians wear the ribbed hats and Medes the rounded ones.

Nehemiah Goes to Jerusalem

NEHEMIAH 2—3

Synopsis

The Northern Kingdom, Israel, was conquered in 722 B.C. and many of its people taken to Assyria. In 586 B.C. Judah, the Southern Kingdom, and its capital city, Jerusalem, fell and many of its people were taken to Babylon. By this time Assyria had faded as a world power and Babylon had taken over. Daniel and some friends were among the noble young men deported to Babylon. They were trained as leaders. During Daniel's time Babylon was conquered by the Persians and was swallowed into the Persian Empire. Esther was queen about 481 B.C., married to the Persian Emperor Xerxes I (Ahasuerus). Xerxes' successor was Artaxerxes I (464-424 B.C.). Under his rule Ezra went to Jerusalem. The king's cupbearer Nehemiah also went and rebuilt the walls of Jerusalem (about 445 B.C.).

The Gates of Jerusalem

Ancient cities had walls to keep out the enemy. The only way to enter was through gates in those walls. To understand Nehemiah 2 and 3, think of the walls of Jerusalem as shaped like a golf tee. The east and west sides of the tee represent the east and west walls of Jerusalem. The top of the tee represents the north wall. If you start from the bottom tip and go along the west side, then across the top and down the east side, you pass the following gates:

At the right, Nehemiah begs the king (Artaxerxes I), to send him to Jerusalem to rebuild the walls. Nehemiah was the king's cup-bearer, an important official. The bottom figure above is a royal cup-bearer, presenting a cup to his king, and shooing flies away with a fly-flap made of palm leaves. Two other important officials are seen above: the royal sword-bearer (upper left) and the royal scepter bearer (right).

The Royal House of Persia—The Achaemenids

After the fall of Babylon, the Jews in exile were under the power of the Achaemenids, descendants of Achaemenes. Under their control, the Jews were permitted to return to their land, rebuild the temple, and were afforded numerous other acts of generosity. To the Achaemenids, the Jews owed their future as a nation. All dates below are B.C.

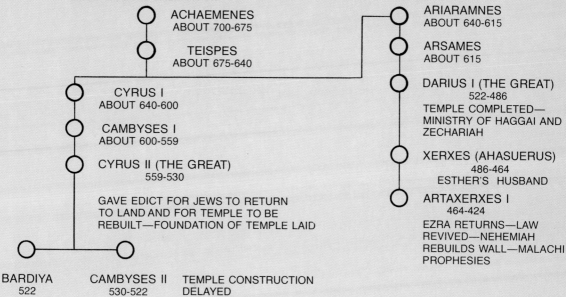

ACHAEMENES
ABOUT 700-675

TEISPES
ABOUT 675-640

CYRUS I
ABOUT 640-600

CAMBYSES I
ABOUT 600-559

CYRUS II (THE GREAT)
559-530

GAVE EDICT FOR JEWS TO RETURN
TO LAND AND FOR TEMPLE TO BE
REBUILT—FOUNDATION OF TEMPLE LAID

BARDIYA
522

CAMBYSES II
530-522

TEMPLE CONSTRUCTION
DELAYED

ARIARAMNES
ABOUT 640-615

ARSAMES
ABOUT 615

DARIUS I (THE GREAT)
522-486
TEMPLE COMPLETED—
MINISTRY OF HAGGAI AND
ZECHARIAH

XERXES (AHASUERUS)
486-464
ESTHER'S HUSBAND

ARTAXERXES I
464-424
EZRA RETURNS—LAW
REVIVED—NEHEMIAH
REBUILDS WALL—MALACHI
PROPHESIES

Darius I transferred the main capital of the Persian Empire to Persepolis. At the far left is the Xerxes Gate at Persepolis, now in modern Iran. Xerxes was the son of Darius I, and Esther's husband.
Artaxerxes I, the king who permitted Nehemiah and Ezra to return, was son of Xerxes. See chart above for more complete information.

ON THE WEST WALL: (1) Dung Gate, (Neh. 2:13; 3:13-14); (2) Valley Gate, (2:13, 15; 3:13). ON THE NORTH WALL: (1) Old or Jeshanah Gate, (3:6); (2) Fish Gate, (3:3); (3) Sheep Gate, (3:1, 32). ON THE EAST WALL: (1) Inspection, Muster, or Miphkad Gate, (3:31); (2) East Gate, (3:29); (3) Horse Gate, (3:28); (4) Water Gate, (3:26); (5) Fountain Gate, (2:14; 3:15).

King Artaxerxes
King Artaxerxes was the son of Xerxes I, also known as Ahasuerus. This means that Queen Esther could have been Artaxerxes' mother, though it is doubtful that she was his natural mother. Artaxerxes was kind to the Jews, and issued the decrees that allowed Ezra and Nehemiah to return to Jerusalem. The king hoped that his helpful attitude to these Jews would keep peace in that corner of his empire.

Workers on the Walls
Rebuilding the Jerusalem wall was such a success because all types of people willingly helped. Priests and Levites, perfumers, goldsmiths, merchants, and many women worked in repairing the walls.

In these rock-hewn tombs at Naqsh-i-Rustam (Pictures of Rustam), Darius I, Xerxes, Artaxerxes I, and Darius II were buried. The tombs are in present-day Iran.

Nehemiah Builds Jerusalem's Walls

NEHEMIAH 4—7

Synopsis
Daniel had been brought to Babylon during the days of King Nebuchadnezzar. He lived throughout this king's reign, then beyond into the reign of Belshazzar. When the army of Cyrus, ruler of the Persian Empire, conquered Babylon, Daniel was appointed one of three presidents. About 50-60 years later, Esther married Xerxes I (Ahasuerus), who was ruler of the Persian Empire at that time. His successor was Artaxerxes I, under whose rule Ezra and Nehemiah went to Jerusalem. Nehemiah led the rebuilding of the city's walls.

The People in the Story: Sanballat the Horonite
Sanballat was the leader of Nehemiah's opponents. In the Elephantine Papyri of 407 B.C. he is called governor of Samaria. He probably came from Beth Horon, northwest of Jerusalem. That is why he was called a Horonite. His name was Sin-uballit in Babylonian, meaning "May Sin give him life." Sin was a Babylonian moon god. Sanballat probably wanted to add Judah to his governorship and Nehemiah's arrival threatened that possibility. The fact that both his sons, Delaiah and Shelemiah, had Jewish names and his daughter later married the high priest's son may mean that he later became reconciled to Nehemiah's people.

Tobiah the Ammonite
Tobiah was probably an official employed by the Persian government. Both he and his son married Jewish women. The high priest, Eliashib, welcomed him into his rooms in the temple, but Nehemiah later expelled him.

Nehemiah is remembered most as the king's cupbearer who rebuilt the walls of Jerusalem. The old city of Jerusalem today still has large stone walls, but these shown here were built about A.D. 1542, on earlier foundations (above two photos).

Geshem the Arab

With Sanballat and Tobiah, Geshem was an opponent of Nehemiah. His description as "the Arab" may mean that he was the governor of Edom for the Persians. Or it may mean that he was the governor of Dedan, across the Gulf of Elath east of Mt. Sinai, in the ancient land of Midian.

Nehemiah

The hero of the book, Nehemiah, was the cupbearer of King Artaxerxes I of Persia (464-424 B.C.). This was a position of great trust and importance. Everything we learn about Nehemiah from the Book of Nehemiah shows he was a wise, prudent person who studied matters carefully before he acted. Notice how astutely he dealt with his opponents, both those from the surrounding area and those under his leadership, such as the wealthy Jews who charged too-high interest and even enslaved fellow Jews who could not pay back their debts.

Nehemiah's name possibly means "the compassion of the Lord."

The Story of Jerusalem's Walls

The story begins around 1800 B.C., when Jerusalem's walls were first erected. Walls were a symbol of strength and prosperity in Bible times. They were a sign that a city was thriving and important.

Over the centuries, Jerusalem's walls were built and destroyed many times. Sometimes the walls were not rebuilt in exactly the same place, and the new walls never looked just like the old. They varied most often in the size and shape of the stones used. One can still walk along the old Jerusalem walls today and notice many different types of stones which mark periods of the city's history.

When King David captured Jerusalem around 1000 B.C., he rebuilt the old walls and added some of his own to make the city larger. Three hundred years later, enemy invasions forced King Hezekiah to make extensive repairs to the walls. These didn't last long, for in 586 B.C., the Babylonian army destroyed Jerusalem and tore down its great walls. They remained in ruins for over a century, until Nehemiah began his amazing rebuilding program.

Since that time, Jerusalem has seen countless battles and skirmishes, with the walls being in on the activity. Now Nehemiah's walls lie far below those that stand today. If the walls could speak, what a story they could tell!

Little remains today of the Israelite building tools. The mason's float below is from Egypt, but was probably much like those used in Israel. Mortar may not have been used much in Nehemiah's walls. The construction is pictured at the right.

Above: a scroll, later than the time of Ezra and Nehemiah, but showing the form in which "books," and especially the Book of the Law were made at that time. Right: Ezra reads the Law to the people.

Ezra Reads the Law

NEHEMIAH 8—10

Synopsis
About 30-40 years after Queen Esther, Nehemiah served as cupbearer to the successor of Esther's husband, whose name was Artaxerxes I. This king permitted Ezra and Nehemiah to return to Jerusalem, where Nehemiah governed and rebuilt the city walls. Ezra established certain religious reforms which had been seriously neglected, and read the Law of Moses to the people.

The Water Gate
Along the east wall that Nehemiah rebuilt and about two thirds of the way down that wall, south of the Hill of Ophel, is the Water Gate, one of the many gates listed in the Book of Nehemiah. On each side of it was a projecting

tower. Here in an open square Ezra assembled the people and read the five Books of Moses in 444 B.C. For this occasion, people built booths on the roofs of their houses and lived in them to remind them of life during the Exodus.

Ezra the Scribe
Ezra was the priest who led about 5,000 people back from Babylon to Jerusalem in 458 B.C., several years after Zerubbabel had led the first group back and started to rebuild the temple. By 444 B.C. Nehemiah had finished the walls and Ezra was able to rekindle the people's devotion to God. He put an end to the practice of Jews marrying non-Jews and made a list of all those who had married pagans. Ezra's name means "The Lord helps."

Though Ezra is called "the second Moses" because he reintroduced the Law after the Jews returned from their exile in Babylon,

306

Left: when synagogues became popular, one major part of their services was the reading of the Law. The drawing at the left gives an insight into this reading. Above: a 19th-century drawing of one traditional tomb of Ezra. However, many such tombs are based on hearsay rather than historic fact.

little is known about him. He was not called governor of Judah, but he played a prominent leadership role.

Sackcloth

As a symbol of repentance for sins, the Jews wore sackcloth and put dust on their heads; these were traditional signs of mourning.

Sackcloth was a rough cloth made from camel or goat hair. When made into a sack, it was used to hold grain, much as gunny sacks are used today. But in the ancient world sackcloth was most frequently used for clothing, especially on such solemn occasions as funerals. It was especially common in undergarments. Because it was rough and scratchy, it came to be seen as an appropriate cloth for self-punishment and repentance.

Scrolls

When Ezra read from the "Book" of the Law of Moses, he was not reading from a book like those today. Instead he was reading from a scroll. A scroll was a sheet of leather, papyrus, or parchment. It was usually about a foot high and as much as 35 feet long. Both ends were wound on wooden rollers. Since writing went from right to left in columns, the right roller was wound and the left one unwound to read a book. The wooden rollers were most interesting. The bottoms were round to make them easier to hold in the hands. The middle parts were wrapped in the scroll. The tops were ornately decorated knobs and balls. A scroll was usually kept in a container. The Book of the Law of Moses from which Ezra read (what we know as Genesis, Exodus, Leviticus, Numbers, and Deuteronomy) was probably five scrolls.

The Tithe

The people promised to bring a tithe of their crops to the Levites, the assistants to the priests. The Levites, under the supervision of priests, traveled from city to city to collect the tithe. They in turn paid one tenth of what they received to the temple treasury to support the priests and help care for the poor. A tithe means one tenth.

The tithe was known in other countries too. Sometimes it was religious, but often it was a tax. Egyptians, for example, paid a fifth of their crops to the pharaoh.

The Story of Job

The Book of JOB

Synopsis

Somewhere back in Old Testament times, perhaps as early as the time of Abraham, lived a wealthy man named Job. This man was severely tested, and his story is recorded in a book of poetry bearing his name.

The Good Man and the Evil Man

Most people in Bible times believed that God blessed good people and punished bad ones. Our everyday experience confirms the fact that usually a person who lives the way God wants him to live is happier and better off than one whose life is spent breaking God's laws.

But what about the exceptions? Sometimes people who are corrupt get rich. And sometimes good people experience much suffering. Jesus is the best example of a good person who suffered persecution, and ultimately crucifixion, from wicked men.

The author of the Book of Job seeks to give us God's answer to this problem.

The Book of Job: Plot

The Book of Job begins and ends with a story in prose (chapters 1—2 and 42:7-17). But almost everything between is in poetry.

The first two chapters tell us that Job was a good man who lost his seven sons and three daughters, his servants, and all his livestock when Satan was given the right to test Job's faith. The Lord then allowed Satan to further test Job by afflicting this good man with painful sores, from the top of his head to the bottom of his feet. Job's three friends then came for a week's visit to comfort him in his loss and suffering.

The long poem (chapters 3—31) contains the discussions between Job and his friends concerning his losses and why he is suffering. Eliphaz the Temanite, Bildad the Shuhite, and Zophar the Naamathite argue that since God blesses good people and punishes those who are wicked, Job must have sinned. Job insists that he has not sinned, and the three friends stop talking when they find that Job is righteous in his own eyes.

When a younger man named Elihu sees

Job's self-righteousness and the inability of Job's three friends to answer him, he jumps angrily into the discussion (chapters 32—37), but he is no more successful than they were in proving his point.

In the climax of the book, the Lord speaks from a storm (chapters 38—41). When Job hears God speak, he bows in humble submission to God's omnipotence and wisdom.

The book concludes with an epilogue in which the Lord criticizes Eliphaz and his friends and tells them to make a sacrificial offering. God also restores Job's family and wealth.

The Land of Uz

Job and his family lived in the land of Uz. This area, somewhere in "the East" (Job 1:3), was named after one of the three people named Uz in Genesis (10:23; 22:21; 36:28). Bible scholars believe it was located in the Wadi Sirhan, a valley some 200 miles long and 20 miles wide, about 50 miles east of Edom, the country south of the Dead Sea.

The story of Job shows the measure of a man's wealth at that time, which may have been as early as Abraham. Flocks of sheep and goats (upper left) and camels and donkeys (above) were as important, perhaps more so, than silver and gold. The bedouin (top right) reminds us of Job, who led a similar lifestyle.

THE PROPHETS
and the Kings Who Reigned
During Their Lifetimes

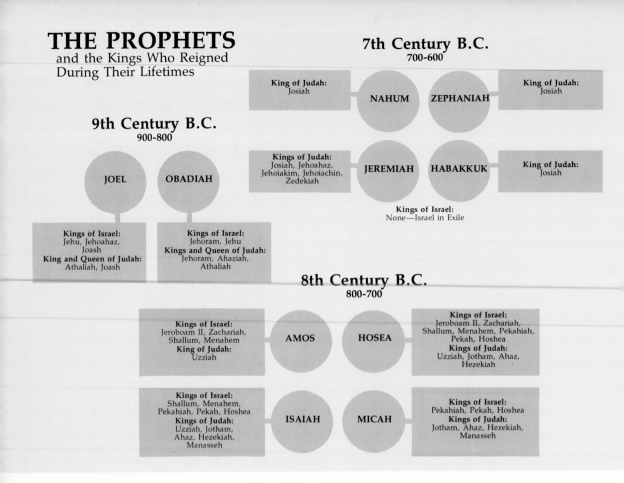

7th Century B.C.
700-600

| King of Judah: Josiah | NAHUM | ZEPHANIAH | King of Judah: Josiah |

| Kings of Judah: Josiah, Jehoahaz, Jehoiakim, Jehoiachin, Zedekiah | JEREMIAH | HABAKKUK | King of Judah: Josiah |

Kings of Israel:
None—Israel in Exile

9th Century B.C.
900-800

JOEL   OBADIAH

| Kings of Israel: Jehu, Jehoahaz, Joash King and Queen of Judah: Athaliah, Joash | Kings of Israel: Jehoram, Jehu Kings and Queen of Judah: Jehoram, Ahaziah, Athaliah |

8th Century B.C.
800-700

| Kings of Israel: Jeroboam II, Zachariah, Shallum, Menahem King of Judah: Uzziah | AMOS | HOSEA | Kings of Israel: Jeroboam II, Zachariah, Shallum, Menahem, Pekahiah, Pekah, Hoshea Kings of Judah: Uzziah, Jotham, Ahaz, Hezekiah |

| Kings of Israel: Shallum, Menahem, Pekahiah, Pekah, Hoshea Kings of Judah: Uzziah, Jotham, Ahaz, Hezekiah, Manasseh | ISAIAH | MICAH | Kings of Israel: Pekahiah, Pekah, Hoshea Kings of Judah: Jotham, Ahaz, Hezekiah, Manasseh |

The Prophets
and the Coming King

VARIOUS PROPHECY BOOKS

Synopsis

Jacob, son of Isaac and grandson of Abraham, was a shepherd with 12 sons. Joseph, one son, was sold as a slave by several of his brothers. In Egypt, where he was taken, he became governor and brought Jacob and his brothers to that land to save them from a long famine.

In time, Jacob and his sons died in Egypt. But their children remained, and their children after them. As the years passed, these families had many children and grandchildren and were known as the Hebrews.

Many years after Joseph, the pharaoh who ruled Egypt at that time made the Hebrew people slaves. He gave orders that every Hebrew baby boy must be killed.

One of these boys, who later was named

Moses, was placed in a basket in the Nile River. Pharaoh's daughter found him and adopted him. For the next 40 years Moses was trained as a prince of Egypt.

Moses had to run from Egypt when he killed an Egyptian slavemaster. For the next 40 years he worked as a shepherd in Midian. Then God called him to lead His people from their slavery. During the last 40 years of his life, Moses led the Hebrews, the descendants of Jacob's 12 sons, from Egypt, through the wilderness, and then to Canaan.

Moses died and Joshua became the new leader. Joshua led his people against the Canaanites and defeated many cities. The Hebrews, or Israelites (named after Jacob's second God-given name Israel), settled in Canaan and mingled with the Canaanite people who were never completely conquered.

During the time of the Judges, following Joshua's death, the people of Israel began to worship the idols of their heathen neighbors. They fell into sin and went far from God. This went on for about 400 years. Then God raised

310

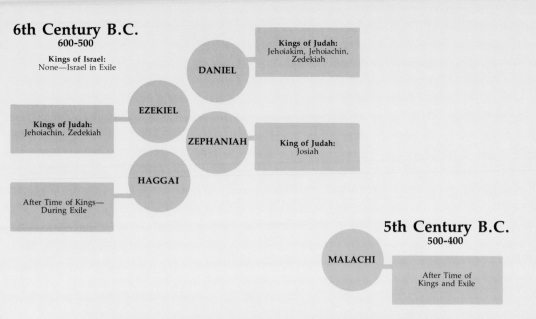

6th Century B.C.
600-500

Kings of Israel:
None—Israel in Exile

DANIEL

Kings of Judah:
Jehoiakim, Jehoiachin, Zedekiah

EZEKIEL

Kings of Judah:
Jehoiachin, Zedekiah

ZEPHANIAH

King of Judah:
Josiah

HAGGAI

After Time of Kings—
During Exile

5th Century B.C.
500-400

MALACHI

After Time of
Kings and Exile

What the Prophets Said about Jesus

Malachi 3:1; 4:5 (Announced by John the Baptist); Micah 5:2 (Born at Bethlehem); Isaiah 7:14 (Born of a Virgin); Jeremiah 31:15 (People Weep at the Massacre of the Infants of Bethlehem); Hosea 11:1 (The Flight to Egypt); Zechariah 9:9; 11:12-13; 12:10 (Triumphal Entry, Bought for 30 Pieces of Silver, Pierced at Crucifixion); Isaiah 53 (Crucified, A Lamb for Our Sins, Buried in a Rich Man's Grave).

up Samuel, a godly man, to lead the people.

Samuel led his people well. But he neglected his own sons, so when he grew old the leaders of Israel rejected them. Instead, they wanted a king over Israel. Saul was first. Then David, the greatest king of all. He was a mighty warrior and a man of God. He built Israel into a strong nation.

David's son Solomon kept Israel strong, but his love of riches caused him to tax the people heavily. To keep the peace with his neighbor nations, he married a princess from each. These women brought their foreign gods and idols to Israel. Before long, the people of Israel worshiped idols also.

When Solomon died, the nation split into two kingdoms—the Northern Kingdom, Israel, and the Southern Kingdom, Judah. It never united again as a strong nation.

From this time on, most kings over these two kingdoms led their people to worship idols and strange gods. When a few kings of Judah brought the people back to God, their nation prospered. But when a new evil king arose, the nation sank into sin and weakness.

During this time of the divided kingdom, God raised up prophets. These were men of God who spoke out against the sin of the people and warned of God's judgment. They also told of a new King who would come some day to rule. This King would be the Messiah, the Saviour.

Israel became so weak as a nation that it was finally conquered and many of its people were carried away to foreign lands. The Northern Kingdom fell in 722 B.C. The Southern Kingdom fell in 586 B.C. Even while the people were exiles in strange lands, and later when they returned, God continued to raise up prophets.

With the exception of Elijah and Elisha, the great prophets we remember wrote books contained in our Bible. Four prophets—Isaiah, Jeremiah, Ezekiel, and Daniel wrote long books and were therefore called major prophets. Twelve others wrote shorter books and were called minor prophets.

311

THE NEW TESTAMENT

John's Birth Announced

LUKE 1:5-25

Synopsis
The aging priest Zacharias burns incense in the holy place of the temple in Jerusalem. While there, he sees the angel Gabriel, who appears to him and tells him that he and his wife Elizabeth, both too old to have children, will have a son and will name him John. Zacharias doubts the angel's message, and for this becomes speechless until John is born.

When
Jesus' birth was announced to Mary 6 months later, approximately 6-5 B.C. John's birth was 9 months after the announcement to Zacharias, and Jesus' birth was 15 months after it.

The Temple
The temple was built by King Solomon in 949 B.C. on land which King David bought from Ornan or Araunah (1 Chron. 21:18-30). When the Kingdom divided, King Jeroboam, of the Northern Kingdom, Israel, set up golden calves in Bethel and Dan, so the temple at that time ceased to be the central place of worship for the northern 10 tribes. As the kingdom of Judah weakened, part of the temple treasures were captured by Shishak, king of Egypt; then later part were given to Benhadad, king of Syria, to purchase his help. When Judah fell, Jerusalem was burned and

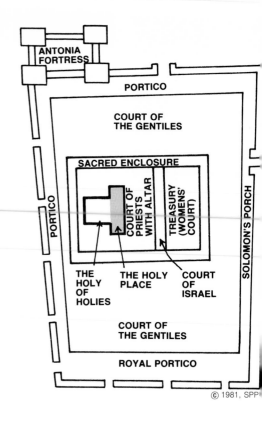

ANTONIA FORTRESS

PORTICO

COURT OF THE GENTILES

SACRED ENCLOSURE

COURT OF PRIESTS WITH ALTAR

TREASURY (WOMENS' COURT)

PORTICO

SOLOMON'S PORCH

THE HOLY OF HOLIES

THE HOLY PLACE

COURT OF ISRAEL

COURT OF THE GENTILES

ROYAL PORTICO

© 1981, SPPI

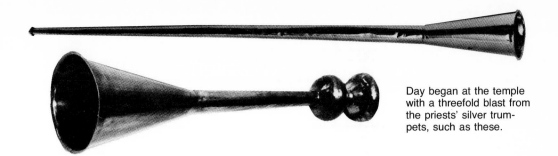

Day began at the temple with a threefold blast from the priests' silver trumpets, such as these.

its people were taken to Babylon. In 520 B.C. the temple was rebuilt by Zerubbabel and other Jews who returned from Babylon. But it was far less than the one Solomon had built. Five hundred years later, when the Romans ruled the land, Herod the Great began to rebuild the temple (about 20-21 B.C.), a task that continued for more than 80 years, until about A.D. 64.

The Order of Abijah (Abia)

During the time of David, when plans were made for the temple, the priests who had descended from Aaron were divided into 24 divisions. The eighth of the 24 was named for Abijah (1 Chron. 24:10). Zacharias served in this order, still in service almost a thousand years later. He was probably not a direct descendant of Abijah, for many records were lost during the captivity. But his order was on duty at the temple that day, taking turns with the other 23 orders. Lots were cast among the 50 or so priests on duty to see who would be highly honored to burn incense in the holy place. A priest was fortunate if he had this honor once in a lifetime, for he was only one of some 20,000 priests in the 24 orders.

The Holy Place

The holy place, pictured on the map at the left, was the second most holy place in the temple, with only the holy of holies above it. Separating the two was the veil. In the holy place was the seven-branch candlestick, or lampstand; the golden incense altar, on which red coals glowed; and the table of showbread.

Zacharias and Elizabeth

Both were descendants of Aaron, a double honor for a priestly family. But the honor was marred by the shame of Elizabeth's childlessness, a shame so great that some rabbis said that separation was a religious duty.

Above: a brown incense altar from the time of Christ. The one in the temple was probably covered with gold.

At the left: the golden domed "Dome of the Rock" covers the place where the temple once stood. Far left: a model of the temple of Jesus' time.

Left: the angel Gabriel appears to Mary. Above: a coin showing the image of Cyrenius (Quirinius), governor of Syria when Jesus was born (Luke 2:1). Below the coin of Cyrenius is the front and back of a denarius of Tiberius Caesar, emperor during most of Jesus' life, and adopted son of Augustus Caesar, emperor when Jesus was born.

From left to right, the three photos below are: Mary's Well today, in Nazareth; Gabriel's Church, built over the spring which is channeled down to Mary's Well, where traditionally Gabriel appeared to Mary; and Mary's tomb in Jerusalem.

Jesus' Birth Announced

LUKE 1:26-38

Synopsis
In the sixth month after Elizabeth conceived, the angel Gabriel appeared to Mary at Nazareth, announcing to her that she would become the mother of the Messiah, God's Son, and this child's Father would be God Himself. Mary was already betrothed to Joseph, but not married. Though this would be viewed by some as having a child out of wedlock, Mary willingly agreed to do it.

When
Approximately 6-5 B.C. It was probably October when Gabriel appeared to Zacharias, so it would have been April when he appeared to Mary.

Nazareth
The hometown of Joseph and Mary was a small unimportant village, one stop on a caravan route from the seacoast to Damascus. Nazareth is not mentioned by name in the Old Testament, though some think it may have been Sarid. The town must have had a weak reputation, for Nathanael asked, "Can

any good thing come out of Nazareth?" (John 1:46) The village is known primarily as the place where Jesus lived throughout His childhood and early life. During His early ministry, Jesus was rejected by the people of Nazareth, so He moved to Capernaum.

Gabriel
Gabriel's name is mentioned in the Bible four times: Daniel 8:16 and 9:21, and in Luke 1:19 (announcement of John's birth to Zacharias) and Luke 1:26 (announcement of Jesus' birth to Mary). In Daniel, Gabriel is called "the man Gabriel" and his voice is called "a man's voice." He flew swiftly (Dan. 9:21) and promised the coming of the Messiah (Dan. 9:24-27). Gabriel was a supernatural messenger, an angel who, as he said, stood in the presence of God (Luke 1:19). Gabriel was sent from God to both Zacharias and Mary, to bring God's special news to them.

Betrothal
When Gabriel appeared to Mary, she was betrothed to Joseph. At this time, betrothal

316

was a serious matter, a legally binding promise to marry. It was essentially marriage without living together. The actual wedding ceremony marked the time when the husband took his wife home with him. There were three ways to become betrothed at this time: (1) with a piece of money in the presence of witnesses; (2) with a written contract; or (3) by living together. The third way was not approved of in Jesus' time. A breach of vows during betrothal was considered adultery and was dissolved only by divorce. Thus, when Mary expected a child, Joseph considered divorcing her privately, though he could have shamed her publicly.

Mary and Elizabeth, Two Miracles

The two pregnancies were miracles. Elizabeth was too old to have children, and so was her husband Zacharias. Physically, there was no hope that two older people could have a child. Mary was quite young, perhaps still in her teen years, so her miracle was not age, but that she had not yet lived as a wife with her husband-to-be. She was a virgin. Thus her Child had no earthly father, because His true Father was God. Upon this truth is based one important point, that Jesus is the Messiah, God's Son.

The Name of Jesus

Jesus was named, not by Mary or Joseph, but by the angel Gabriel, probably under orders from God. The name "Jesus" is the Greek form of the Hebrew name "Joshua," which means "God saves," or "Saviour." Many men at this time were named Jesus, for it was a common name. Thus Jesus is often called Jesus Christ in the Bible, probably to distinguish Him from others who were named Jesus. The word "Christ" means "anointed one," and referred to the One anointed by God to be the Saviour. Jesus had many other names throughout the Bible, such as Wonderful, Counselor, the Mighty God, the Everlasting Father, the Prince of Peace (Isa. 9:6), Son of man (Matt. 8:20), Son of God (2 Cor. 1:19), King of kings, Lord of lords (1 Tim. 6:15), the Lamb (Rev. 17:14). He is also called the Bread of life (John 6:48), the Light of the world (John 9:5), the Good Shepherd (John 10:11), the Resurrection and the Life (John 11:25), the true Vine (John 15:1), and the Way, the Truth, and the Life (John 14:6).

Jesus' name is more than just a name. Demons were cast out, and sick people healed, in the name of Jesus (Acts 3:6; 4:10); and sins were forgiven and salvation given in His name (Acts 4:12; 10:43; 22:16).

317

At the right is a view of Ein Karem from the south. The Church of the Visitation, which commemorates Mary's visit to Elizabeth, dominates the center of the picture. The map below the picture locates Ein Karem. At the lower right, Mary and Elizabeth are together.

Mary Visits Elizabeth

LUKE 1:38-56

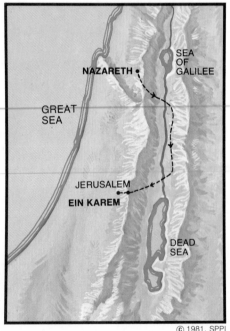

Synopsis

When Mary heard the news that she would become the mother of the Messiah, she traveled from her home in Nazareth to visit Elizabeth, who lived in a small village west of Jerusalem, traditionally Ein Karem. When Elizabeth saw Mary, she was filled with the Holy Spirit and greeted her with a beautiful "song" which recognized Mary's child as the Messiah, God's Son. Mary responded with another beautiful "song" which has come to be known as The Magnificat. For three months, Mary remained with Elizabeth.

The Relationship of Mary and Elizabeth

Mary and Elizabeth were closely related. Some Bible versions say cousins (Luke 1:36). Other sources say that Elizabeth was actually Mary's aunt, for she was probably about 40 years older than Mary. It is likely Elizabeth was around 60 at this time, while Mary was probably in her late teens or early 20s. However the ages of these two women are uncertain.

© 1981, SPPI

318

The Times to Which John and Jesus Came
Approximately 400 years had passed since the last great Old Testament figure, Malachi, had lived. During that time the land which Israel called home was ruled by the Persians (430-332 B.C.); then the Greeks (331-167 B.C.), including a group of Greek kings of Egypt called the Ptolemies. Then a group of Greek kings of Syria called the Seleucids ruled, followed by a little more than a century of independence, called the Maccabean, Asmonean, or Hasmonean period.

In 63 B.C. the Roman general Pompey took over the old Seleucid Empire of Syria, and then laid siege against Jerusalem. Thousands of Jews died before Pompey broke through the city walls and rode to the temple, where he walked into the holy of holies, flinging aside the veil to see what was inside. Finding nothing, he went out, and ordered the Jewish worship continued.

Antipater, governor of nearby Idumea, was appointed ruler of Palestine under the Jewish high priest. He was an Edomite, a descendant of Esau.

Almost 20 years passed before Antipater was poisoned and his sons struggled for his power. Then Antigonus, son of the last Macca-bean king, tried to revolt. In 40 B.C. Herod the Great, one of Antipater's sons, was appointed king of Judea, which at that time was most of Palestine. By 37 B.C. Herod executed Antigonus and ruled all the land.

These were difficult times for the Jewish people, for they were now ruled by an Idumean under Roman domination. Gentiles were everywhere throughout the land, ruling and taxing the people.

A movement began to search the Scriptures to see what the future held. Many believed that the time had come for the Messiah. The fullness of time was ripe for God to bring forth His Son.

Ein Karem
Many Christians believe that Ein Karem, now at the western edge of Jerusalem, was the birthplace of John the Baptist, the home of Elizabeth and Zacharias, where Mary visited for three months. The road from Jerusalem winds down into a terraced valley with olive trees and vineyards. Ein Karem means "Spring of the Vineyard." Four churches have been built here to commemorate John's birth. Some consider the surrounding countryside as the "desert" in Luke 1:80.

John the Baptist Is Born

LUKE 1:57-80

Synopsis

Eight days after John the Baptist was born the relatives and neighbors gathered with Elizabeth and Zacharias to circumcise and name him. They wanted to name the baby Zacharias, for his father. But Elizabeth said no, that he would be named John. The relatives and neighbors were surprised, for no family member had that name, so they motioned to Zacharias if this should be his son's name, for Zacharias hadn't been able to speak since the angel Gabriel had announced John's birth to him. Zacharias called for a writing tablet and wrote, "His name is John." Then Zacharias could speak again, and he began to praise God, prophesying John's work as the forerunner of the Messiah. The people who had gathered were afraid, for they wondered what kind of child this would be.

Circumcision

The ceremony of circumcision was a time of great joy and sacredness, for it symbolized the son joining the covenant relationship of his people, to live under the Law of God. In a sense, the father acted as a high priest, offering his child to God with love and gratitude.

For the parents of a miracle child, this was an especially meaningful time, for their childlessness had ended.

Zacharias' Loss of Speech

Zacharias had been struck dumb when he doubted the message of the angel Gabriel nine months earlier (Luke 1:20). But he also could not hear, for they had to make signs or motions to him concerning the child's name. Doubt had caused Zacharias' speech to leave. It returned with a hymn of praise.

Nazirite

John the Baptist was a Nazirite (Luke 1:15), not by choice, not by his parents' choice, but by God's appointment. A Nazirite was to refrain from three things: grapes and their products, including wine, raisins, grape juice, vinegar, and even grape seeds; cutting one's hair; and touching a dead body. Usually a person was a Nazirite because he had made a vow to be one, but sometimes, as with John the Baptist, he had no choice. The main purpose was not merely to abstain from certain things, but to consecrate himself to holy service to God.

320

The wax-covered wood tablet at the left was often used by school children learning to write. Above is an ink pot from the time of Christ, and at the left is a reed pen which was used with ink.

The Nazirite vows appear first in Numbers 6:1-21, revealed to Moses by God. Samuel and Samson were also Nazirites, given to God from birth.

Forerunner of the Messiah

John's chief purpose in life was to pave the way for the coming Messiah. For that he was born. Mark (1:2-4) tells of John's role as the forerunner, which was also prophesied in Malachi (3:1). Isaiah (40:4-8), who also spoke of John the Baptist, is quoted in Luke 3:1-6. John clearly proclaimed Jesus as the Messiah, the Lamb of God, the Son of God, and placed Jesus far above himself (John 1:29-34). John told also that he himself was not the Messiah, but only the forerunner of the Messiah (John 1:19-27). On another occasion, John said that he must decrease while Jesus must increase, for Jesus had come from above (John 3:25-36). "Forerunner" meant simply that John's work was to tell the world that this Man was truly the Messiah and in other ways prepare people to receive Jesus.

John and Jesus, Relatives

Elizabeth was either Mary's cousin or her aunt. Thus Jesus was either John's first or second cousin. Some believe that James and John were also cousins, pointing to John 19:25 (compared to Matthew 27:56 and Mark 15:40), where it appears that Salome, the mother of James and John, was Mary's sister.

Writing Tablet

Paper was not in use at this time, so writing was done on papyrus (reeds hammered together to make a form of paper), wax-covered wood tablets (pictured above), broken pieces of pottery with scratch marks or ink on them, or animal skins. Papyrus and animal skins were too expensive for general use, so broken pottery (called potsherds) was often used. Wax-covered tablets made of wood could be erased by smoothing the wax again.

Ink was dry ink, moistened when it was time to write. Black ink was a mixture of lampblack and gum. Red ink was made of sikra, a red powder also used in women's cosmetics.

Pens were made of reeds, not goose quills, which became common much later. These reeds were cut at a curve and split at the end to let the ink flow. A brush or stylus was also used to apply ink to the writing surface.

321

Above: front and back of two coins of Caesar Augustus. Each coin is called a denarius, though in some versions of the Bible it is translated "penny." The denarius was the usual payment for a day's labor in New Testament times.

Jesus Is Born

LUKE 2:1-7

Synopsis

Caesar Augustus, emperor of the entire Roman world, ordered a census to be taken. In Palestine, the Jews were to return to their ancestral homes, which for both Mary and Joseph was in Bethlehem in Judea. Leaving Nazareth near the time when Mary was to have her baby, they traveled south to Bethlehem, where their ancestor King David had lived as a lad. But they arrived too late in the day to find lodging, so they were forced to stay in the stable with the animals. That night, Mary gave birth to her baby, who was already named Jesus by the angel Gabriel.

When

Our traditional Christmas fixes the birth of Jesus on December 25. The calendar would suggest the year 0—neither A.D. (Anno Domini, in the year of our Lord) nor B.C. (before Christ). However, through the years, research into the census has shown that the birth of Christ was actually somewhere

around 4-5 B.C. No one is sure of the day of the year. During the 4th century A.D., the Western Church settled on December 25 and the Eastern Church settled on January 6. However, some point out the sheep were still on the hillsides and usually would not be in midwinter. This was true of most sheep, but the temple sheep near Bethlehem usually did stay out all year. Since no one knows for sure, December 25 or January 6 is as good a date as any.

A Winter Night

Winter in Palestine is the cold, rainy season while summer is the hot, dry season. The heaviest rainfall is between December and February, sometimes with hail, thunder, and lightning. The coldest temperature recorded in Palestine is 19°F (7°C), much colder than a normal winter night, which on the Bethlehem hills was probably not down to freezing temperatures. However, a 40° night on a lonely hillside in a rainy season can be

322

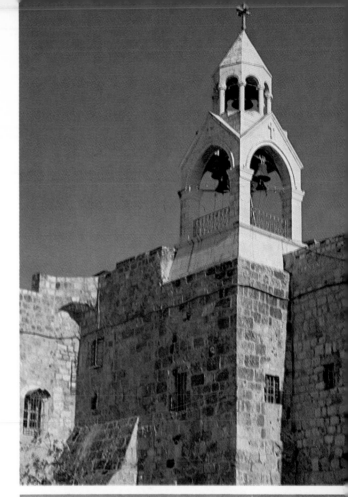

quite cold. The rain was almost more unpleasant than the cold. Rainfall in Palestine averages from less than an inch in the south at Eilat to about 40 inches per year in the north at Metulla. Jerusalem averages about 25 inches per year with only slightly less in Bethlehem.

The Inn and the Manger
Bible-time inns were not at all like our modern motels. Along caravan routes there were some public buildings in New Testament times, where travelers could stop for the night with their animals and find safety with others. In some cases, these inns had a lower courtyard for the animals, with upper space for the travelers to sleep—certainly not with private room, bath, and restaurant! In some places "inns" were little more than guest rooms adjoining a private home. Such may have been the inn of Bethlehem. The manger may have been a stone feeding trough such as the one below.

Bethlehem of Judea
There were two Bethlehems, one in Judea and one in Galilee, only seven miles northwest of Nazareth. Luke writes that Joseph and Mary went "into Judea, to the city of David, which is called Bethlehem." This leaves no doubt concerning which city became Jesus' birthplace. Boaz and Ruth met in the fields near Bethlehem and when they married lived there. David cared for his father's sheep, perhaps in the same fields. Micah (5:2) prophesied that Bethlehem would become the birthplace of the Messiah. The name Bethlehem means "house of bread" or "house of food," perhaps because of the rich fields east of the town where sheep grazed and wheat and barley grew.

Top right: the Church of the Nativity, traditionally located over the cave where Jesus was born. The church seen here was built about A.D. 527-565 by Justinian on the same site where an earlier church (built A.D. 325 by Helena) had stood. Center: Bethlehem from the north. Note the Church of the Nativity at the upper center. Bottom: a stone manger at Megiddo, perhaps much like the one where Jesus was laid.

323

Angels Appear to the Shepherds

LUKE 2:8-14

Synopsis
On the night when Jesus was born in Bethlehem, shepherds watched over their flocks on the nearby hills. Suddenly an angel of the Lord appeared to them and the glory of the Lord shone about them. The angel told the frightened shepherds the good news that the Messiah, Christ the Lord, had been born in nearby Bethlehem. Then a great heavenly choir praised God. When the angels departed, the shepherds went to Bethlehem to see the baby. Then they told the news to others, glorifying and praising God for what they had seen. The large photo, below right, shows the shepherds' fields east of Bethlehem, the traditional place where the angels appeared.

The Shepherds and Their Sheep

The Mishnah, the traditional Jewish doctrine collected before the third century A.D. suggests that these were not ordinary shepherds and their sheep. They were shepherds appointed to care for the temple flocks, destined for sacrifices. These flocks stayed in the fields throughout the year, even during the winter.

The Messiah, whose birth was announced to these shepherds, would someday die at the time of the 3 o'clock afternoon sacrifice, making it no longer necessary for sheep such as theirs to die for people's sins. The Lamb of God had come to die once and for all, so that lambs such as these would not need to die again. No wonder the angel announced the birth of the Messiah to these shepherds!

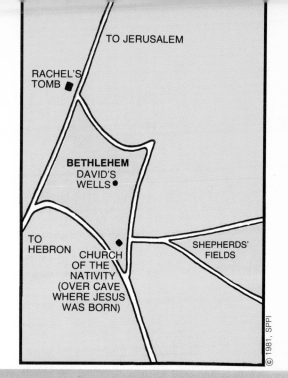

© 1981, SPPI

Shepherds Worship Jesus

LUKE 2:15-20

Synopsis

When the angel of the Lord announced the Messiah's birth to the shepherds, a host of angels sang or spoke praise to God. After they left, the shepherds went to Bethlehem to see this Baby for whom their people had waited so long. No one knows what happened there when they visited with Joseph and Mary, but they returned to their flocks, "glorifying and praising God for all the things that they had heard and seen." They also told others what the angels had said, perhaps even at the temple when they took their next sheep for sacrifice, stirring the hearts of people like Anna and Simeon.

Swaddling Clothes

The shepherds found Jesus in the swaddling clothes which Mary had wrapped around Him at birth (Luke 2:7). This was an ancient form of clothing for newborn infants. Sometimes this was called a "swaddling band." It was a square piece of cloth on which the infant was laid with its head at one of the four corners and its feet at the opposite corner. The corner at the head was tucked under the head, and the one at the feet was folded over the feet. The other two corners were folded together over the midsection, then the whole thing was wrapped with bands of cloth.

Announcement of the Messiah

The angel visit was the first public announcement that the Messiah had come. It could have been made to King Herod's court, or Caesar Augustus' throne room, or even to the high priest and temple dignitaries in Jerusalem. It could have been made to the Pharisees or Sadducees, the religious leaders, or to other high-ranking men. But God chose to make His first announcement to the small band of shepherds caring for the temple sheep which would be sacrificed in the temple. He had already privately announced to Mary and Joseph that this Son would be the Messiah. Elizabeth and Zacharias knew this. John the

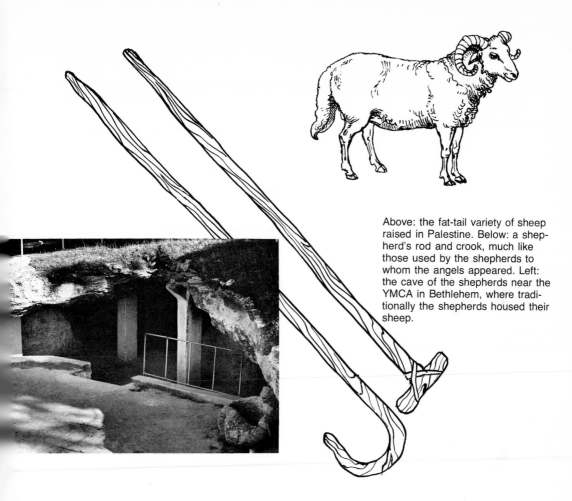

Above: the fat-tail variety of sheep raised in Palestine. Below: a shepherd's rod and crook, much like those used by the shepherds to whom the angels appeared. Left: the cave of the shepherds near the YMCA in Bethlehem, where traditionally the shepherds housed their sheep.

Baptist would know it someday, but at this time he was still an infant. Other than these, few at that time had heard the wondrous news that the Messiah, for whom these people had waited so long, had at last come to the world.

Prophecies Concerning Jesus' Birth

The place of Jesus' birth, Bethlehem, was prophesied in Micah (5:2).
The fulfillment was given in Matthew (2:1) and Luke (2:4-7).
The tribe into which Jesus would be born, Judah, was prophesied in Genesis (49:10).
The fulfillment was given in Luke (3:33) and Matthew (1:2-3).
The fact that Jesus would be born of a virgin mother was prophesied in Isaiah (7:14).
The fulfillment was given in Matthew (1:18) and Luke (1:26-35).
The murder of the babies of Bethlehem was prophesied in Jeremiah (31:15).
The fulfillment was given in Matthew (2:16-18).
The flight into Egypt was prophesied in Hosea (11:1).
The fulfillment was given in Matthew (2:13-15).
The fact that Jesus would be heir to the throne of David was prophesied in Isaiah (9:7).
The fulfillment was given in Matthew (1:1).

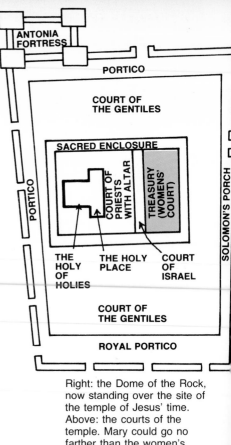

Right: the Dome of the Rock, now standing over the site of the temple of Jesus' time. Above: the courts of the temple. Mary could go no farther than the women's court or treasury.

Simeon and Anna Honor Jesus

LUKE 2:21-38

Synopsis
On the eighth day after His birth, Jesus was circumcised and named. A little more than three weeks later, Mary and Joseph took Him to the temple in Jerusalem for two ceremonies. The first was to redeem the firstborn. The second, to "purify" the mother ceremonially. While in the temple Anna and Simeon, who lived there and ministered to the Lord, saw Jesus and praised God that they had seen His Son.

Circumcision
During the time of Jesus, circumcision was an important ceremony, filled with both joy and solemnity. Relatives and neighbors gathered with the family for circumcision and to name the son on the eighth day after his birth. At Jesus' ceremony, it is likely that Zacharias and Elizabeth were there with their new son John. The ceremony was held either in the home or at the temple, and with it, the child entered symbolically into the covenant rela-

tionship of his people, to live under the Law of God. In this ceremony the father acted as a sort of high priest, offering his child to God with love and gratitude. Often his father-in-law, the child's maternal grandfather, performed the circumcision itself. Some suppose the ceremony began with a benediction as it did in later times, and closed with the naming of the child in a prayer over a cup of wine. The prayer may have been much like one of later times: "Our God, and the God of our fathers, raise up this child to his father and mother, and let his name be called in Israel Jesus" and so on. No one is sure that this part of the ceremony went all the way back to Jesus' time, but it may have been one of the many traditions that have persisted for generations. Circumcision set a Jewish male apart from his Gentile neighbors, who were often considered "uncircumcised heathen."

Redemption of the Firstborn
The second ceremony which the Baby Jesus

328

had took place at least 31 days after His birth. Like all other firstborn sons of a household, He was to be taken to the temple and was to be "redeemed" by the priest at a price of five "shekels of the sanctuary," as specified in Numbers 18:16. At the time of Moses coins were not in use, so "shekels of the sanctuary" were units of weight for silver, acceptable at the tabernacle. In Jesus' time, a shekel was a silver coin.

Purification from Childbirth

There were numerous ceremonies of purification. One was to be held after childbirth, which was thought to make a woman unclean. If the baby was a boy, the woman was considered ceremonially unclean or defiled for seven days, and on the eighth day the boy would be circumcised. Then for another 33 days she was still considered unclean and must not touch anything sacred or enter the tabernacle (or temple later). This law was found in Leviticus 12:2-5. If the baby was a girl, the time of uncleanness was twice as long. The law continued (Lev. 12:6-8): (1) when the 40 days were ended, the mother was to bring to the temple a yearling lamb and a young pigeon; (2) present them to the priest to offer for her; and (3) if too poor, bring two turtledoves or two young pigeons instead, which Mary did (Luke 2:24) for she was poor.

Wise Men See a Star

MATTHEW 2:1-8

Synopsis

In a land to the east of Palestine, some wise men, or Magi, saw a star, or arrangement of stars, which told them that the Messiah had been born. Leaving their homes, they traveled to Jerusalem, where they inquired about the newborn king. Naturally King Herod was curious about a new king and jealously called for his own religious leaders, inquiring about the place where this Messiah should be born. When he learned it was Bethlehem, Herod called for the wise men privately and asked when the star appeared. He apparently learned that it had been almost two years earlier, so he sent them on their way, pretending to want to worship this new king also, telling them to let him know when they found Him.

The Magi, or Wise Men

King Herod's fear of the newborn king was more than personal fear for his own job. It was fear of another serious revolt against himself and Rome, one which could shift the balance of power in Palestine for years to come. The story goes all the way back to the time of Daniel, who was a powerful ruler in the Babylonian Empire. Some think that the Jews at that time helped the Medians overthrow Babylon and place Cyrus in control of the ancient world. This would explain, of course, why Cyrus was so generous in helping the Jewish people rebuild their land and capital city of Jerusalem.

A religious group had great power in the Persian Empire at that time, and had held these political powers for years before. They were known as Magi, and while religious leaders, also exerted powerful influence in government. During the time of Christ's birth, they had the power to choose the king over their realm, which was then known as the Parthian Empire.

The rivalry between this Parthian Empire and the Romans had been intense for a number of years. Palestine itself had been the scene of a number of skirmishes between them, including one Parthian invasion when Herod's father, Antipater, was defeated in 40 B.C. Three years later, Mark Antony gained control of the land, but then tried to go farther against the Parthians. When he was defeated, the Parthians swept across the land and forced the Romans to retreat. Herod himself had to flee to Rome and could not return until three years later when Rome finally gained control again.

Herod ruled for the next 30 or so years between two competing empires—Rome, whom he served, and the Parthians, who were still unfriendly and could at any time launch another invasion, aided by the Jews under Herod's control.

Thus in 4-5 B.C., when the small band of Magi came to Herod asking about a newborn king, Herod accepted them in an uneasy peace. They were probably Parthian king-

At the left, wise men follow the star. Some think there may have been as many as hundreds of these Magi, traveling as a large band for protection over the thousand or so miles.

makers, asking about a new Jewish king who had just been born. At this time, Herod was a very sick man, suffering from a disease which would claim his life within a year. He would soon execute his own son Antipater, so it certainly would not trouble him to execute a few Jewish babies in Bethlehem, which he did. By doing this, he hoped to kill that one baby who was "born king of the Jews." If not, that one baby might swing the balance of power from Rome to the Parthians.

How Many?
Traditionally three wise men, or Magi, are shown in pictures. This is only a tradition, for the Bible does not say. It could have been three, or more, or fewer.

Camels
The Bible does not say the Magi rode on camels. But this would have been the logical means of transportation for important men of that time. Donkeys or horses were not as suited for long travels through the desert country as camels were.

The Star
Strange that Balaam (Num. 24:17) should refer to the coming Messiah as "the Star out of Jacob." Balaam later led Israelites astray, but at this time God must have revealed to him the Messiah, God's Son, who would come some 14 centuries later. Thus, while Christ was a star, so also was the sign in the heavens which led the wise men first to Jerusalem and then to Bethlehem.

Some say this star may have been a conjunction of Jupiter, Saturn, and Mars in 6 B.C. Others think it was a nova, or exploding star, which burns with intense heat and light for a short time. But could not the God who made the heavens make one more special star to announce the coming of His Son, the Star of Jacob?

At the top right, camels roam in the wilderness area of the Negeb. Camels such as these were probably the only logical transportation for the Magi. Center: a model of Herod's palace during the time of Christ, showing the three towers Phasael (left, named after Herod's brother), Hippicus (center, named after a friend), and Mariamme (right, named after Herod's queen). A chart showing Herod and his seven sons is at the right.

HEROD'S CHILDREN

Herod the Great ordered the murder of many children in and around Bethlehem. Did Herod hate children? Probably not, for he himself had seven sons. The four most well-known sons are shown below. This execution was for one purpose — to destroy the baby Jesus, so that He might not replace Herod or his sons as king.

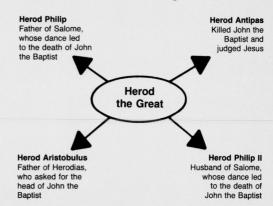

Herod Philip
Father of Salome, whose dance led to the death of John the Baptist

Herod Antipas
Killed John the Baptist and judged Jesus

Herod the Great

Herod Aristobulus
Father of Herodias, who asked for the head of John the Baptist

Herod Philip II
Husband of Salome, whose dance led to the death of John the Baptist

Frankincense is obtained from the resin of the tree Boswellia. The bark is peeled back in the summer and the tree is cut with a knife. From this wound the gum exudes as a white substance which turns amber color.

Wise Men Visit Jesus

MATTHEW 2:9-12

Synopsis

From the East, in the Parthian Empire, came a group of Magi to seek the newborn king of the Jews. When they arrived in Jerusalem, they inquired about Him. This attracted the nervous attention of King Herod, who feared that this new king might not only take his throne from him, but might swing the control of Palestine from Rome to the Parthians. Herod quickly inquired of his own religious leaders where the Messiah would be born, and learned that it would be Bethlehem. Then he privately talked with the wise men and asked when the star had first appeared, which had been almost two years earlier. When Herod learned these things, he sent the Magi to Bethlehem, pretending to also seek the new king so that he might worship Him. The star that had brought the Magi from the East led them to Bethlehem, and stood over the house where the Child Jesus now lived. They worshiped Him, and presented to Him gifts of gold, frankincense, and myrrh. Then, warned by God in a dream not to return to Herod, they went home another way, a thousand or so miles back to their homeland. The Magi, powerful men in their own empire who helped put kings on their thrones, had traveled almost two thousand miles through the desert country to worship a newborn baby!

The Gifts of the Magi

The Magi brought three types of gifts to young Jesus—gold, frankincense, and myrrh. How much of each we are not told. Nor are we told what these men expected the Infant Jesus to do with these treasures. But we may guess that these financed the flight to Egypt for a family so poor that they could not afford a lamb for an offering in the temple.

The Magi's Gift of Gold

Gold was the gift of royalty. Most people in Jesus' time, other than royalty and the very wealthy, could not afford to own gold. As far back as the patriarchs, gold and silver were standards of money, as they still are throughout the world today. Of all the standards of wealth, gold is perhaps supreme, a gift fit for any king.

Myrrh comes from a small tree, almost like a thorny bush. Sometimes it exudes naturally, but usually, like frankincense, it comes from a wound made in the tree. Like frankincense, myrrh also gives out a fragrant smell when crushed.

The Magi's Gift of Frankincense

While gold adorned the crowns and palaces of kings, frankincense mingled with the offerings of priests. It was the gift of worship, for in the many references to frankincense in the Bible, it is almost always associated with worship (see Lev. 2:1-16; 6:15; Ex. 30:34-38; Num. 5:15; and Neh. 13:5, 9). In the Song of Solomon it is mentioned as a perfume of love, the adoration of a king for his bride (Song 3:6; 4:6, 14). Frankincense was a gum exuded from a tree in Arabia.

The Magi's Gift of Myrrh

While frankincense was a gift of worship, myrrh was a gift of suffering. Gold represented the King of kings, frankincense the offering of the Saviour, and myrrh the suffering Saviour. It was this same gift of myrrh which was mixed with vinegar and offered to the suffering Saviour on the cross to ease His pain (Mark 15:23). It was also this same gift of myrrh which Nicodemus brought to anoint the body of Jesus after He had died, an offering for sin (John 19:39-40). The process of obtaining myrrh suggests suffering, for the skin or bark of the plant is pierced so that the plant will "bleed" a white gum which turns red on contact with the air.

A view of Bethlehem from the north (below) shows modern buildings with the old. The tower in the center of the picture projects from the Church of the Nativity, built over the site where traditionally Jesus was born.

Above: two coins of Herod the Great, showing front and back of each. The Romans did not let subject nations coin gold, and only a few could coin silver. Herod's coins were made of copper.

The Flight to Egypt

MATTHEW 2:13-18

Synopsis

Warned by God in a dream, the Magi returned home secretly, instead of returning to Jerusalem to tell Herod the Great where the Child Jesus could be found. Herod was angry when he learned that he had been avoided. He had hoped to murder this newborn King. Now all he knew was that this King was under two years old and had been born in Bethlehem. Taking no chances, he planned to murder all baby boys in Bethlehem and the surrounding countryside who were two years or less. But before he could put his plan into effect, an angel of the Lord appeared to Joseph in a dream and warned him, ordering him to take Mary and Jesus to Egypt. Joseph obeyed immediately, leaving by night, and remained in Egypt until Herod the Great died. After they were gone, Herod put his plan into effect, murdering the baby boys of Bethlehem. This fulfilled the prophecy in Jeremiah 31:15, as the flight into Egypt fulfilled the prophecy in Hosea 11:1.

The Angel of the Lord

The Bible does not name the angel, but it may well have been Gabriel, for it was he who seemed to be entrusted with the care of the Baby Jesus. Gabriel had announced the birth of John the Baptist, the forerunner of the Messiah, and had announced the birth of Jesus to Mary. He probably was also the angel of the Lord who announced to Joseph that Mary's Child was God's Son.

Jesus' Home in Egypt

For a year or perhaps slightly more, Jesus lived in Egypt with Joseph and Mary. The Bible does not tell where in Egypt, but tradition says it was at On, or Heliopolis. If so, the father-in-law of Joseph (Jacob's son) served there as a "priest of On" (Gen. 41:45, 50; 46:20) many centuries earlier. Heliopolis was located only 10 miles from the place where modern Cairo, Egypt is built. It was the center of the worship of the sun god Re or Ra, and thus took its name "City of the Sun" from this.

334

The Road to Egypt

When Joseph and Mary left Bethlehem for Egypt, how did they travel? There were no numbered highways as we have today. Nor were there paved roads, except in certain places where the Roman Empire had built roads with large stones.

Usually people joined a caravan which was traveling on one of the many caravan routes through the land. Joseph and Mary left Bethlehem by night, so they probably risked the dangers of the road to join a caravan in another town.

A caravan route which went north and south from Bethlehem was the way to Ephrath. The next stop to the south was Hebron and the next Beersheba. They may have joined a caravan at one of these places.

At Beersheba they had a choice of continuing south on the way to Ephrath until they reached another major route, going east and west, which went westward to Egypt and eastward to the King's Highway, or of going westward on a minor caravan route to join the busy Via Maris, a major trade route from Egypt to the north. The Via Maris followed the coast of the Mediterranean Sea from Egypt as far north as Joppa, then angled inland. Southward it went to Zoan, in Egypt, then on to Heliopolis, or On, where traditionally Joseph and Mary stayed with Jesus.

Travel Conditions

Traveling with a caravan was hot, dirty, and tiring. But at least it was much safer than traveling alone, for bandits lurked along the way to steal from anyone foolish enough to travel without the safety of large numbers. Joseph and Mary had to be especially careful, for they had the rich gifts which the wise men had brought, which probably financed their trip to Egypt and back up to Nazareth.

Caravan leaders often paid local rulers or sheiks for protection through their territory, who provided armed guards to go with the caravan. At night, a caravan stopped at an inn, a crude structure with a well in a central courtyard, a place to keep the animals safely, and a second floor where the people slept and traded goods with one another.

Merchants were the nucleus of a caravan, carrying goods from place to place, including spices, incense, gold, silver, wine, oil, food, cloth, jewelry, and slaves. Since they carried many valuable items, they were of course, always subject to bandits or raiding parties, so even a caravan was not a completely safe place to be.

The distance between Bethlehem and Heliopolis, Egypt was between 300 and 400 miles, a trip of some 2 to 3 weeks. During this time, Jesus' family was taken to a very different type of lifestyle in Egypt.

At the left are two tombs, Rachel's tomb on the right side and Herod's family tomb on the left side, Rachel's tomb is at the outskirts of Bethlehem; Herod's is in Jerusalem. Herod's evil murder of the babies of Bethlehem caused Rachel to weep for her children (Matt. 2:18).

The Return to Nazareth

MATTHEW 2:19-23; LUKE 2:39

Synopsis

When Magi came from the East, seeking a newborn king, Herod the Great was frightened. He believed a truly Jewish king would cause a revolt against Rome. The Parthians to the east would join the Jewish people and the balance of power would be upset. Herod knew he would surely be deposed and executed. Thus Herod killed all the baby boys of Bethlehem two years old and younger, hoping to kill that one Baby. But an angel of the Lord had warned Joseph to take Mary and Jesus to Egypt, where they lived during the year or two while Herod the Great still reigned. When Herod died, the angel returned, instructing Joseph to take Jesus and Mary back to Israel.

Time

Herod's death is said to be around 4 B.C. If so, Jesus' birth, trip to Egypt, and return from Egypt took place within a year, or slightly more. However, these dates are still not known for certain.

Archelaus

The Bible tells us that Joseph learned Archelaus ruled over Judea in place of his father, Herod the Great. Joseph was therefore afraid to return to Judea, but God told him to take Mary and Jesus to Galilee, to the town of Nazareth.

Before Herod the Great died, he changed his will a number of times. Altogether, he made six wills. In the last, he made his son Archelaus king, his brother Antipas tetrarch of Galilee and Perea, and his other brother Philip tetrarch of four other areas.

As soon as Herod the Great died, Archelaus took charge, but was reluctant to be crowned king, for his brother Antipas had challenged Herod's will. When Passover came Archelaus was overly anxious to keep a revolution from starting, so he killed 3,000 of the Jewish people.

Antipas and Archelaus traveled to Rome to settle their dispute over the will. Caesar Augustus settled it by making Archelaus ethnarch with a promise that he would become king if he proved a good ruler. Antipas and Philip remained in the position their father had chosen for them.

But Archelaus was brutal with the Jews and Samaritans. Perhaps this is why Joseph was afraid to settle once more in Bethlehem, under

Above: a coin of Archelaus, showing front and back. Far right: a view of Nazareth today. The Church of the Annunciation is in the center, built over a traditional site where the angel Gabriel appeared to Mary. Nazareth remained the home of Jesus and Mary until the people there rejected Him as the Messiah. Joseph probably died when Jesus was between 12 and 30.

Archelaus' rule, but went back home to Nazareth, under Antipas' rule. Some 30 years later this same Antipas would murder John the Baptist and judge Jesus.

In A.D. 6, ten years after he began to rule, Archelaus was deposed and banished. His brothers, Antipas and Philip, had gone to Rome to complain about his leadership, along with a delegation of Jews and Samaritans who complained about his cruelty. Rome recognized that when the Jews and Samaritans, bitter enemies, sent a joint delegation, something was seriously wrong. After Archelaus was banished, his territory was placed under the control of procurators. Pontius Pilate was the procurator during the time of Jesus' judgment, while Herod Antipas was still tetrarch of Galilee.

The Trip Home to Nazareth

Normally a traveler from Egypt to Nazareth would follow the caravan route called the Via Maris, a direct route from Egypt through Nazareth to the north. But Jews tried not to travel through Samaria, so Joseph and Mary may have crossed the Jordan River east of Jerusalem, then traveled north through Perea, then back westward into Galilee, as shown on the map at the right. For safety reasons, they may also have avoided the main highway.

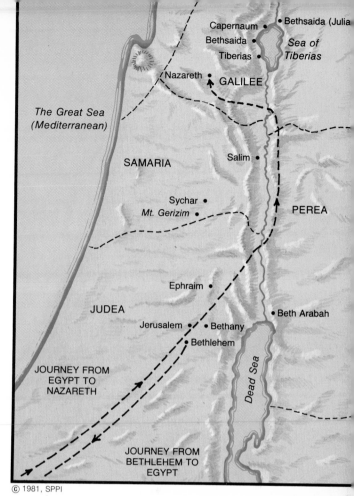

© 1981, SPPI

The Carpenter's Shop

LUKE 2:40; MATTHEW 13:55; MARK 6:3

Synopsis
When Joseph and Mary returned to Nazareth, Joseph set up his carpenter's shop again. Through the years, he trained Jesus to be a carpenter, as all good Jewish men trained their sons for a trade, usually their own. Thus Jesus' neighbors knew Him as "the carpenter, the son of Mary." Joseph must have died somewhere between the time when Jesus was 12 and the time He began his ministry around the age of 30. Jesus evidently took over Joseph's work as a carpenter until the time for His ministry to begin.

Time
The timetable seems to be this: 6-5 B.C.—Jesus was born; 4 B.C.—Jesus was brought from Egypt to Nazareth; 4 B.C.-A.D. 26—Jesus grew up in Nazareth, learned Joseph's trade as a carpenter, and after Joseph's death, took over the carpenter's shop. Jesus' public ministry began in A.D. 26. Almost nothing more is known about Jesus' childhood except His visit to the temple at age 12.

Tools for a Bible-time Carpenter
Pictured below are a number of tools used by carpenters in Bible times. Jesus probably used each type. *Mallets* (four at bottom) were used for hammering. *Adze* (center) was used for shaving wood, much like a modern plane. *Drills* (far right) were used to drill holes in wood. In the collection of tools at the lower left, numbers 1 and 3 were hand drills, to make shallow holes or punch holes in wood; number 2 was a chisel to cut off small pieces of wood in shaping it; number 5 was the bow of a bow drill; number 4 was the drill used in the bow drill; numbers 7 and 8 were saws; number 9 was a horn of oil; number 10 was a mallet, like those at the bottom of the page; number 11 was a basket of nails; and number 12 was a basket to hold these tools.

What a Carpenter Made
Many things in Bible times were made of wood, including carts, wagons, wheels, bowls and other utensils, some tools and tool handles, and furniture. Houses were usually made of stone, which was plentiful, so carpenters were not primarily house-builders and cabinetmakers. Jesus must have made many of the items listed above.

Tools shown at the left are listed above. At the right is an adze with a bronze blade bound to a wooden handle with leather thongs. The four items at the bottom are mallets, used to hammer or pound.

The Church of Joseph, near the Church of the Annunciation, is built over the site where some believe Joseph's carpentry shop was once located. Below, two carpenters work, the one at the left, with a bow drill, and the one at the right with a small tool, planing or polishing the leg of a chair. An adze rests on the wood block before him. Another chair leg leans against the wood block.

339

At the lower left, the courts of the temple, showing the sacred enclosure, separating the court of the Gentiles from the more sacred courts. It was probably here that Jesus talked with the teachers. Above: ancient Beeroth, the first stop on the caravan route going north from Jerusalem. Mary and Joseph probably discovered Jesus missing while camped here.

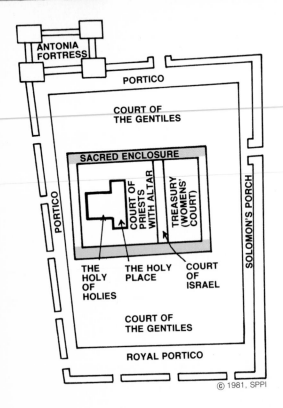

ANTONIA FORTRESS

PORTICO

COURT OF THE GENTILES

SACRED ENCLOSURE

PORTICO

COURT OF PRIESTS WITH ALTAR

TREASURY (WOMENS' COURT)

SOLOMON'S PORCH

THE HOLY OF HOLIES

THE HOLY PLACE

COURT OF ISRAEL

COURT OF THE GENTILES

ROYAL PORTICO

© 1981, SPPI

Jesus and the Teachers

LUKE 2:41-52

Synopsis
After Jesus returned from Egypt with Joseph and Mary, He grew up in Nazareth, learning Joseph's trade as a carpenter. At the age of 12, He went with Joseph and Mary to the temple to celebrate the Passover feast, as most Jewish men did every year. On this occasion, however, He entered into a discussion with the teachers in the temple, astounding them with His knowledge. Mary and Joseph left for Nazareth, thinking He was among their friends and relatives, but when they discovered that He was not, they returned to find Him teaching the teachers.

Who Were the Teachers?
During the time of Jesus there were few remaining authorities on the Law of Moses, but those who remained were apparently there in the temple. Jesus may have found them teaching in the sacred enclosure (see map) and began to ask them questions.

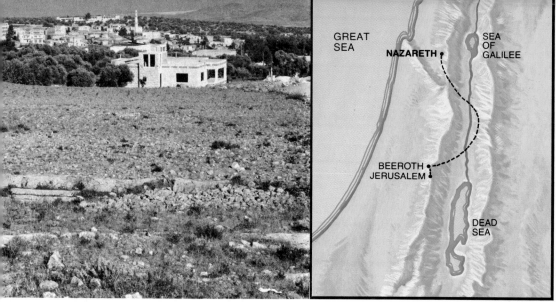

A Jewish Boy's Education

In Jesus' time, a Jewish boy was taught the Law at age five, including catechetical instruction in synagogue schools. By the age of 12, he was expected to obey the Law, and at 13 wore the phylacteries as he recited his daily prayers. At the age of 12, Jesus was on the threshold of manhood, more like a boy of 18 today.

The Passover

At the time of the Exodus, the angel of the Lord struck down the firstborn of Egypt, while passing over the firstborn of Israel. To commemorate this, the Israelites set up the Passover feast. A lamb was slain, and its blood was sprinkled with hyssop on the doorposts of the house, as it was the night before the Exodus. The whole lamb was roasted and eaten by the family, without breaking a bone of its body. The time when the lamb was killed was between 3-6 P.M., the exact time of the day when Jesus, the Lamb of God, died for the sins of the world.

Every male Israelite was expected to travel to Jerusalem three times each year to the great festivals, of which one was the Passover. When Jesus, or any Jewish boy, reached the age of 13, He became "of age," and was expected to begin these pilgrimages. Jesus began His a year early.

About 21 years later, Jesus would eat another Passover feast, this time with His disciples in an upper room. This Passover feast has come to be known as "The Last Supper." The Passover was considered the most important of the three great annual festivals of Israel.

Traveling by Caravan

Mary and Joseph, and thousands of pilgrims like them, traveled to and from the great festivals in Jerusalem by caravan. Some rode on donkeys or camels, but most walked. People traveled together in caravans for protection, for numerous robbers lay in wait along the way. At night, they stopped at crude inns, completely unlike our modern motels, without any form of luxury, with a well in an open courtyard, places for the animals at the ground level, and places for people on the second-floor level. Sometimes these inns had bazaars where traveling merchants traded their goods.

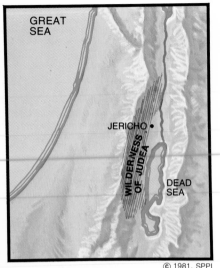

© 1981, SPPI

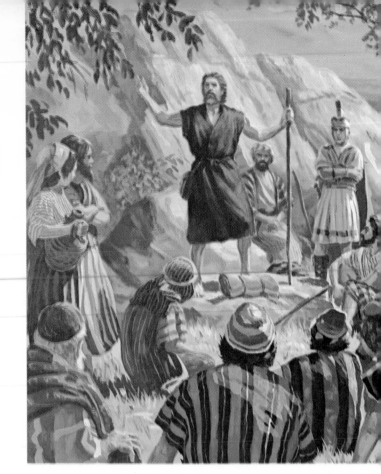

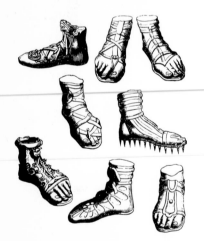

Above: A locust of Bible times. Below it are a number of sandals ("shoes" in some versions). John said he was not worthy to loosen the latchet, or sandal thong, of Jesus' sandals. To the right of the painting of John preaching is a photo of the Judean wilderness, a bleak country.

John Preaches in the Wilderness

MATTHEW 3:1-12; MARK 1:1-8; LUKE 3:1-18

Synopsis

Eighteen years had passed since the boy Jesus amazed the teachers in the temple. Now He and His cousin, John the Baptist, were 30. John had already begun to preach in the wilderness and was attracting crowds from the cities and villages of Judea. John's message was a call for repentance, to turn from sin to a God who could forgive and would forgive. John's message was not the Gospel of Jesus Christ, but was a stepping stone to that Gospel. John told the people that he was not the Messiah, but was there to point to the Messiah, who was coming.

The Rulers over John and Jesus

During the ministry of John and Jesus, the Mediterranean world, that is, the lands surrounding the Mediterranean Sea, were part of the Roman Empire, ruled by Tiberius Caesar, the Roman emperor. The land that had once been part of the nation Israel, under King David, formed several small territories—Idumea, Judea, Samaria, Galilee, Perea, and others. Herod the Great had ruled over all of this, and more, in the years before Christ was born. Then, a year or so after Christ came, Herod died and his kingdom was divided among his sons, Herod Antipas (Galilee and Perea); Herod Philip (lands northeast of the Sea of Galilee); and Archelaus

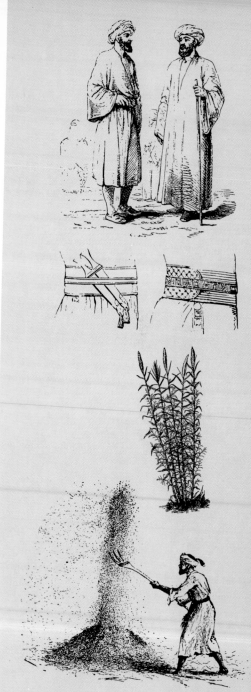

(Judea, Samaria, and Idumea, the largest and most important part of the kingdom, with Jerusalem toward the center).

Archelaus proved to be a poor ruler, so he was deposed and banished. His territory was placed under a series of procurators. Pontius Pilate was the procurator when Jesus was crucified.

The Kingdom of Heaven
John and Jesus each used the term "kingdom of heaven" and "kingdom of God" to mean the same thing—the kingdom over which Jesus, the Messiah, would rule. It was not limited to heaven, or a specific time or place, but to that over which King Jesus rules.

Camel's Hair, Locusts, and Wild Honey
John wore rough hairy clothing, like that of Elijah (2 Kings 1:8). This seemed to be appropriate for prophets with strong messages (see Zechariah 13:4). The "girdle" mentioned in some versions was a wide leather belt. Locusts were acceptable food, eaten by the poor (Lev. 11:21). Wild honey was found in hollowed trees. John could never be accused of living a worldly life!

John appeared with a "girdle" or wide belt. At the top: a garment with, and another without, this belt. Below these two pictures are two examples of these "girdles" or belts. The bottom picture shows a winnowing fork, in some versions translated a "fan," with which farmers threw grain into the air so the chaff could blow away. The picture above it shows some reeds of Bible times. Later, Jesus asked people if they expected to find a reed, shaken in the wind, when they went to hear John.

343

Jesus Is Baptized

MATTHEW 3:13-17; MARK 1:9-11; LUKE 3:21-23

Synopsis

When John and Jesus were about 30, it was time for their public ministry. John preached in the wilderness of Judea, calling on people to repent from their sin and to recognize that the Messiah was coming soon. One day, while John was at the Jordan River, probably baptizing those who believed in his message, Jesus came along and insisted that John baptize Him also.

John the Baptist

He was called "the Baptist" as another way of saying "the baptizer," or "the one who baptizes." Denominations came many centuries later, so the term did not refer to a denomination or people today who are called Baptists. Nor was his given name "the Baptist," but merely John (Luke 1:13, 63).

The Jordan River

Jesus came from Nazareth, in Galilee, to the Jordan River, where John had been baptizing, so that John might baptize Him also. This river was rich in Israelite history. Fourteen centuries earlier, the Israelites who had come from Egypt in the Exodus yearned to cross this river to enter the Promised Land. Because of their disobedience, they died in the wilderness, and the next generation finally crossed to form the new nation Israel.

Four centuries later, David fled across this river to escape his son Absalom, who had seized David's throne, and then returned back across it victorious. Elijah ministered in the Jordan River area some years later.

The Jordan River is no ordinary river. It is a deep valley, or rift, which cuts from north to south through the Sea of Galilee and ends in the Dead Sea at the south.

The waters of the river start in the north near Mount Hermon and collect into Lake Huleh, about 230 feet above sea level. As they flow southward to the Sea of Galilee, they plunge downward to 700 feet below sea level, then empty from the Sea of Galilee and drop another 580 feet to 1290 feet below sea level at the Dead Sea. Compare this with the lowest point in Death Valley, less than 400 feet below sea level. From this one can see that most of the Jordan River is below sea level, and many

hundreds of feet for the most part.

Though the Jordan River runs only 75 miles from north to south, it winds back and forth for a total length of almost 200 miles. It is the longest river in Palestine, the most prominent in Bible history, and certainly the most unusual.

The Voice from Heaven

Time after time throughout the Gospels, God clearly revealed to the people around Jesus that He was God's Son. Thus far in the Gospel narrative, this has happened: (1) when the angel announced to Mary that her Son would be God's Son (Luke 1:32, 35); (2) when Elizabeth, filled with the Holy Spirit, recognized that Mary's baby was the Son of God (Luke 1:43); (3) when the angel announced to Joseph that Mary's baby was the Son of God (Matt. 1:20-23); (4) when the angel of the Lord announced to the shepherds that God's Son had been born in Bethlehem (Luke 2:11); (5) when Simeon took the Child Jesus into his arms in the temple (Luke 2:28-32); (6) when Anna talked of Jesus (Luke 2:38-39); (7) when the Magi visited Jesus (Matt. 2:2, 11) and (8) when Jesus spoke of the temple as His Father's house (Luke 2:49).

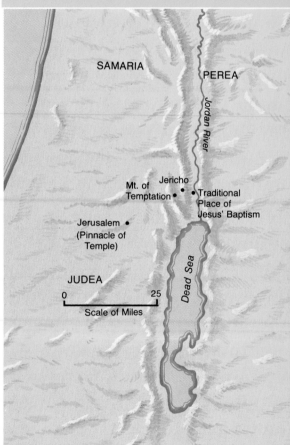

© 1981, SPPI

Far left: Jesus comes from the Jordan River after He is baptized by John. Left: the Jordan River at a place just south of the Sea of Galilee. Top: one type of dove. The Holy Spirit came upon Jesus at His baptism "as a dove." The map above locates Jesus' baptism and temptation.

Jesus Is Tempted

MATTHEW 4:1-11

Synopsis

Jesus and His cousin John were 30 when they began to preach. John preached in the Wilderness of Judea, calling people to repent of their sins, baptizing those who did. Jesus came to him one day and insisted that John baptize Him. When Jesus came up out of the water, the heavens opened and the Spirit of God came upon Him in the form of a dove. Then God proclaimed that this was His beloved Son, in whom He was well pleased. Shortly after that, Jesus was led into the wilderness by the Holy Spirit. There Satan came to tempt Jesus.

Temptation

The Bible records numerous temptations, but two stand out above all others. They also stand in stark contrast to each other. Satan tempted Adam in the paradise called Eden. He also tempted Jesus in the wilderness. He tempted Adam through his helper, Eve, but he tempted Jesus personally and directly. He tempted Adam in a plentiful garden, where he lacked nothing. He tempted Jesus in a barren wilderness, where there was nothing for Him to eat. Adam was well fed. Jesus was almost at the point of starvation. Adam yielded to Satan's temptation and brought sin into the world. Jesus resisted Satan's temptation and conquered sin. Adam's disobedience forced him out of his paradise home, separating him from God. Jesus' obedience brought Him into a closer relationship with God the Father, who sent angels to minister to Him.

Three Desires

At first glance it would seem that Jesus was tempted with three simple desires: food, fame, and power. But a closer look shows that Satan's temptations were not quite that simple. Instead they were food without work, fame without accomplishment, and power without effort. Satan still tempts us today in these three ways. Beware when he offers something for nothing!

Angels

Angels were closely involved with the life of Jesus on earth. An angel: announced that Jesus would be born; assured Joseph that Jesus was God's Son; named Jesus; announced His birth to shepherds; and made plans for Jesus to be taken to Egypt for safety. In His last days, they would minister to Him in Gethsemane.

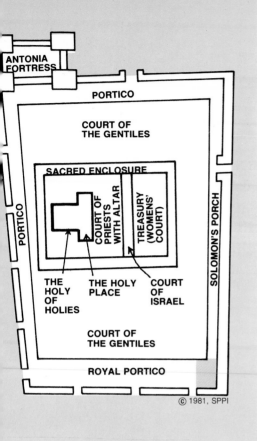

ANTONIA FORTRESS

PORTICO

COURT OF
THE GENTILES

SACRED ENCLOSURE

PORTICO

SOLOMON'S PORCH

COURT OF PRIESTS
WITH ALTAR

TREASURY
(WOMENS'
COURT)

THE
HOLY
OF
HOLIES

THE HOLY
PLACE

COURT
OF
ISRAEL

COURT OF
THE GENTILES

ROYAL PORTICO

© 1981, SPPI

Jesus was tempted in the wilderness near Jericho. Pictured
immediately above is the Mount of Temptation, the traditional
place of that temptation. At the left is the pinnacle of the temple,
as still seen today. A model of the temple of Jesus' time, at the
upper right, shows the royal porch built over the pinnacle. The
pinnacle is located on the diagram of the temple at the upper left.

347

The Wedding at Cana

JOHN 2:1-11

Synopsis

After Jesus was tempted by Satan, He returned to the place where John had baptized Him. John told those around him that Jesus was the "Lamb of God" who would take away the sin of the world. Andrew quickly became a disciple of Jesus, then brought his brother, Simon Peter, and encouraged him to follow Jesus also. The next day Philip became a disciple and immediately brought Nathanael to meet Jesus. Shortly after that, Jesus visited Cana in Galilee and attended a wedding there.

Weddings

In Jesus' time a couple who planned to marry was usually first "betrothed." This was similar to engagement in our times, for two people promised to marry, but as yet did not live together. However, to be betrothed was more binding than our engagement, for the two were considered to belong to one another. Gifts were given and oaths were exchanged.

The wedding came later. Unlike weddings today, these were not religious ceremonies, but a ceremony of taking the bride from the father's house to the bridegroom's house.

The bridegroom dressed in his best, then with groomsmen, left his house for that of the bride, who was waiting for him with her bridesmaids. With shouting and singing, and often musical instruments playing, the bride-

groom escorted the bride back to his home. Wedding guests joined the party along the way.

A feast was prepared at the home of the bridegroom, or his father, and all the friends and neighbors were invited. It was this kind of feast that Jesus attended at Cana. It lasted 7 days, sometimes 14, and was filled with eating, drinking, and festivities. At the end, the bridegroom took his bride to the wedding chamber and their marriage was completed.

Cana
Nobody knows for sure where the Cana of Jesus' time was located. Four places have been thought to be the location of Cana, two of them likely. Kafr Kanna, pictured on these pages, is the traditional site of Cana.

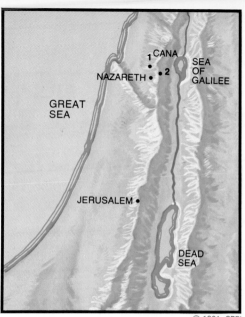

© 1981, SPPI

Number 1 on the map is Khirbet Qana, 10 miles north of Nazareth, one possible site of ancient Cana. Number 2 is Kafr Kanna, the traditional site, pictured on these pages.

Jesus Cleanses the Temple

JOHN 2:13-22

Synopsis
After Jesus turned water to wine at the wedding in Cana, He went to Capernaum with His mother and brothers and disciples. Then when the Passover time came, He went to Jerusalem. While at Jerusalem, Jesus overturned the tables of the money changers in the temple and talked with Nicodemus about being born again.

Time
Probably A.D. 27

Where
The cleansing of the temple took place in the Court of the Gentiles, the large outer courtyard in the temple. Anyone could enter this courtyard, but no Gentile dared go farther, into a more sacred courtyard.

Money Changers
Each Jewish man was expected to attend the Passover, the annual festival being held when

Jesus overturned the money changers' tables. They came from all over the ancient world, for Jews were scattered throughout the lands. Arriving in Israel, they made their way to the temple as soon as possible, for that is why they came, to celebrate the Passover there. With them they brought money from their native lands.

But in the temple this foreign money could not be used to buy animals for sacrifices, for it was considered unclean. So money changers set up little tables in the large outer courtyard, the Court of the Gentiles, where they exchanged acceptable Jewish coins for foreign coins.

There was no standard rate of exchange, so it became a time for bargaining. The money changers usually cheated these visitors as often and as much as they could.

Jesus objected to their cheating. He also objected to His Father's house, a house of prayer, becoming a giant bazaar.

Oxen, Sheep, and Doves
In the Court of the Gentiles of the temple, merchants sold animals for the sacrifices. Three types of animals used in the sacrifices are named here—oxen, sheep, and doves. There were others, such as bulls, goats, and pigeons. Certain offerings called for certain

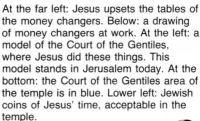

At the far left: Jesus upsets the tables of the money changers. Below: a drawing of money changers at work. At the left: a model of the Court of the Gentiles, where Jesus did these things. This model stands in Jerusalem today. At the bottom: the Court of the Gentiles area of the temple is in blue. Lower left: Jewish coins of Jesus' time, acceptable in the temple.

types of animals. Also, a man's station in life suggested certain types of animals—a bullock for a man on a level with the high priest, a he-goat for a nobleman, a she-goat or sheep for an ordinary person, and a pigeon or dove for a poor person. A very poor person could just offer some fine flour.

Herod's Temple Building

The people with Jesus said that the temple had been under construction for 46 years. Herod the Great, who ruled from 37 B.C. to A.D. 4, was a prolific builder. The temple was one of his most ambitious projects. He began to build it around 20 to 19 B.C. But even though the temple had been under construction for 46 years at this time, it would continue under construction for 30 more, to be finished in A.D. 64. But the sad ending to all this magnificent work came only six years after it was completed, in A.D. 70. The Romans destroyed Jerusalem completely, including this beautiful building. It has never been rebuilt. Over the site of the temple today stands a Moslem mosque, called the Dome of the Rock.

A Scourge of Cords

Jesus wove a whip from rope or cords to punish the merchants. This was quite a mild whip, compared with the scourge which the Romans used against Jesus before His crucifixion. That one had sharp pieces of metal imbedded in the whip to tear the flesh as it beat the victim.

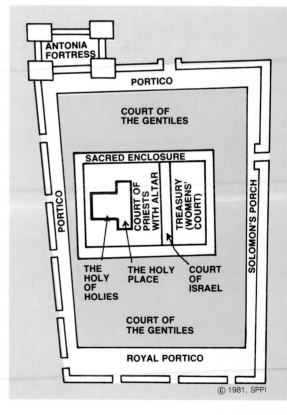

ANTONIA FORTRESS
PORTICO
COURT OF THE GENTILES
SACRED ENCLOSURE
PORTICO
COURT OF PRIESTS WITH ALTAR
TREASURY (WOMENS' COURT)
SOLOMON'S PORCH
THE HOLY OF HOLIES
THE HOLY PLACE
COURT OF ISRAEL
COURT OF THE GENTILES
ROYAL PORTICO

© 1981, SPPI

351

Nicodemus

JOHN 2:23—3:21

Synopsis

After Jesus turned water to wine at Cana He, with His mother and brothers, went to Capernaum, where He stayed awhile. Spring came, and with it, the annual Passover festival. Jesus went to Jerusalem to celebrate, as all Jewish men were expected to do. He visited the temple, where He chased the merchants and money changers from the Court of the Gentiles. During this festival, a high Jewish official named Nicodemus visited Jesus at night, to ask Him more about God.

Nicodemus

He was a "ruler of the Jews," a Pharisee, and a member of the powerful council called the Sanhedrin. As a Pharisee, he was a member of the most strict and one of the most influential groups of Jewish leaders. As a member of the Sanhedrin, he took part in the council of 70 elders who ruled the Jewish people. This council, with the high priest as president, could try a person for a crime. It could pass the death sentence, but under the Romans, could not actually execute that person.

Jesus was tried before the Sanhedrin and was judged guilty and sent to Pilate for His judgment which would lead to execution. This council could even judge a high priest, or the king, so it was similar to a supreme court in today's society.

Nicodemus risked losing this high position when he came to Jesus. As a whole, the council hated Jesus, viewing Him as an imposter and certainly not God's Son, as He claimed. So Nicodemus came at night, when superstition kept most people off the streets.

It seems that Nicodemus became a secret believer. He admitted to Jesus immediately that, despite his position, he believed Jesus had come from God. Later, when the Sanhedrin tried to arrest Jesus, Nicodemus asked if their law permitted them to try a person until he first appeared before them and an attempt had been made to find if he was guilty or innocent (John 7:50-52).

Later, when Jesus was crucified, Nicodemus and Joseph of Arimathea placed expensive spices on His body and buried Him in a new tomb. The Bible is silent about Nicode-

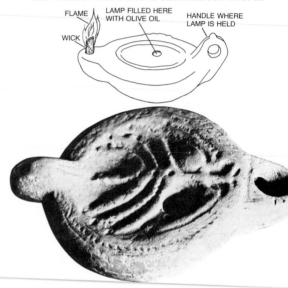

FLAME

LAMP FILLED HERE WITH OLIVE OIL

HANDLE WHERE LAMP IS HELD

WICK

Roman lamps such as the one above were used during the time of Jesus. The picture above it shows how it was used. Oil squeezed from olives was poured into the center hole. A wick inserted in the front hole produced a flame, giving off light. Below: Jerusalem at sunset, reminding us of Nicodemus' night visit.

mus after that, but one tradition says that he was baptized by Peter and John, removed from the Sanhedrin, and was supported by a wealthy relative named Gamaliel.

The Place Where Nicodemus Met Jesus

Most paintings show Nicodemus on a rooftop with Jesus. Although the Bible does not say this, it was probably the only logical place to meet at night. Some say this was a home that the Apostle John owned in Jerusalem, with a guest chamber built on the rooftop, as was often done.

It was a spring evening, with gentle winds blowing through the streets of Jerusalem as Nicodemus made his way up the outside stairway leading to this upper room. The meeting was lighted by oil lamps such as those pictured.

Born Again

Nicodemus had always thought that his religion was the doorway into the kingdom of God. A person received new life after he entered. This thought was used in Nicodemus' time to express what happened to a bridegroom after his wedding, or a king after his coronation.

Jesus told Nicodemus that the new birth, being "born again," was the doorway to God's kingdom. No one could enter heaven without it. The right order was: believe in Jesus as Saviour from sin, turn to God for forgiveness and receive new birth, which leads into His kingdom.

The model of a Bible-time house (below) and the drawings (right) show the flat rooftops of Bible times. The lower drawing shows a guest room built on the roof, reached by an outside stairway.
The upper drawing shows the open area, where people talked and slept on warm evenings.

The Woman at the Well

JOHN 4:1-42

Synopsis

The Passover ended and Jesus left Jerusalem for the open countryside of Judea. With His disciples He went to a quiet place, probably at the Jordan River near the place where He had been baptized. There His disciples began to baptize those who repented from their sins. Some of the disciples of John the Baptist complained to John about this, but John reminded them again that Jesus was from God. Not long after that, Jesus and His disciples headed back toward Galilee, going through Samaria, where most Jewish people refused to travel. At Sychar, He met "the woman at the well."

Samaria and the Samaritans

In 721 B.C. King Sargon of Assyria destroyed Samaria, the capital city of Israel's Northern Kingdom. He took the people away to Assyria and brought foreigners into the land to live. In time these foreigners intermarried with the few Jewish people who were left, producing a mixed race. These people became known as Samaritans. The region in which they lived was called Samaria. The Jewish people hated these "mixed" people and usually tried to avoid traveling through their territory. Some say the Judeans felt this way even more than the Galileans, and that some Galilean people were not as reluctant to travel through Samaria as their Judean kinsmen. Jesus, of course, seemed to have no problem with this, and even chose to go through Samaria. The route was certainly much shorter than going around through Perea.

Top left: Mount Gerizim (left side of picture) and Mount Ebal (right side). Top center: Jacob's well today, inside. Above: for centuries women have carried waterpots on their heads.

354

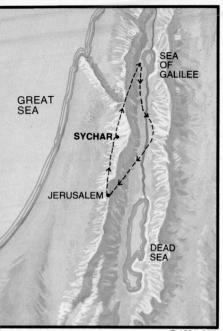

The map at the left shows two routes from Galilee to Jerusalem. The western route went through Samaria. The eastern one went through Perea. Left center: the courtyard of the church covering Jacob's well today. Lower left: two women draw water from an open well, as women did at Jacob's well in Jesus' time. Below: an open well with another device attached to help in drawing the water.

The Well

After Jacob returned from Paddan Aram, where he had lived for 20 years, and where he had married Leah and Rachel, he settled near Mount Gerizim and bought a parcel of land from Hamor, Shechem's father (Gen. 33:18-20). Jacob's son Joseph was later buried at this place (Josh. 24:32). The well where Jesus talked with the Samaritan woman is thought to be the one which Jacob dug at this place. It is four feet wide. In A.D. 670 a visitor wrote that it was 240 feet deep. In 1697 another said it was only 105 feet deep. By 1861 it was only 75 feet deep. The reason for this changing depth is that pilgrims threw pebbles into the well throughout the centuries, gradually filling it in. But water from the well is still pure enough to drink.

Sychar

The village near Jacob's well was on the main road from Jerusalem to Galilee. It was probably on the eastern slope of Mount Ebal, about one-half mile north of Jacob's well. A modern village, Askar, is thought to be the site where Sychar was located.

Mount Ebal and Mount Gerizim

Ebal and Gerizim stand like twins, Ebal slightly more than 3,000 feet, Gerizim slightly less. The Samaritans worshiped in the open at the top of Mount Gerizim.

355

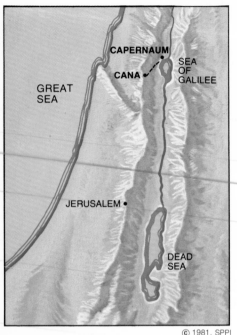

The map at the upper left shows the location of Cana and Capernaum, about 20 to 25 miles apart. At the upper right is Capernaum, situated on the northwest shore of the Sea of Galilee.

The Nobleman's Son Is Healed

JOHN 4:46-54

Synopsis

After leaving the Passover festival in Jerusalem, where He cleansed the temple and talked with Nicodemus, Jesus returned to Galilee, after stopping in Samaria to talk with a woman at a well. Back home in Galilee, Jesus returned to Cana, where He had turned water into wine. There He met a nobleman of Capernaum, who begged Jesus to heal his sick son.

The Nobleman

During the time of Jesus there were a number of types of leaders in the land. The scribes, Pharisees, Sadducees, high priest, and chief priests were religious leaders. Herod was a tetrarch, or Roman civil leader. Pilate was a procurator, another Roman civil leader with somewhat different status, though he had

similar responsibilities.

Centurions were military leaders, over groups of 100 Roman soldiers each. Publicans were tax collectors, appointed by Rome, but many were Jewish men. The nobleman in this story was a courtier, someone appointed to the service of Herod, the tetrarch. He was an official attached to the office of the highest ranking position in the land, and was probably a Jewish man, not a Roman.

A Lesson in Power

The nobleman or courtier brought out a lesson in contrasting power. He, as an officer in the court of Herod, had power over the people of the land, including Jesus. But he had no power over the sickness of his own son. Jesus alone had that, and he begged Jesus to save his son's life. Great and powerful people are,

356

like others, often weak and helpless in certain personal situations.

Capernaum to Cana
Cana was located in the highlands of Galilee, contrasting with Capernaum, which was below sea level, on the northwest shores of the Sea of Galilee. Later, Jesus would make His headquarters at Capernaum. Cana was about 20 to 25 miles from Capernaum. Note their locations on the above map.

The Seventh Hour
Clocks and watches were not developed in Bible times, so people had to tell time in other ways. The sun determined the time during the day, beginning with sunrise and ending with sunset. Between sunrise and sunset were 12 divisions, called hours. When the sun rose at 6:00 in the morning and set at 6:00 in the evening, the hours were exactly 60 minutes each. But when the day shortened, so did the hours.

The seventh hour was 1:00 in the afternoon of a full 12-hour day. The third hour was 9:00 in the morning and the ninth hour was 3:00 in the afternoon.

Sundials were used in some places to measure the progress of the day. But average people could not afford sundials in their yards.

Night was divided into four "watches,"

two before midnight and two after. With sunrise at 6:00 and sunset at 6:00, the first watch began at sunset and ended at 9:00 P.M. The second began at 9:00 and ended at midnight. The third began at midnight and ended at 3:00 A.M. The fourth went from 3:00 to 6:00 A.M. These watches would be longer or shorter, depending on the length of the day.

Miracles of Healing
Thirty-five miracles of Jesus are given in the four Gospels. Of these, 23 are miracles of healing. Three concerned raising someone from the dead.

In His healing miracles, Jesus did many different kinds of work. He drove out demons, stopped a hemorrhage, healed paralysis, cured leprosy, restored a withered hand, removed blindness, caused a dumb person to speak, removed deafness, restored a cut-off ear, and made a lame person walk.

Jesus' miracles showed a power that no mere man possessed. They proved that He had come from God. All who saw them should have realized that He is God's Son. But those who were closest to "religion" seemed to be the most difficult to persuade. They simply refused to believe. Only a few of them ever admitted that this Man who could heal and raise from the dead was more than a mere man!

357

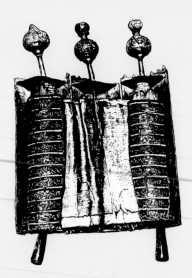

Books of Jesus' Time

Books with separate pages did not come into use until more than a hundred years after the time of Jesus. During His time on earth, books were scrolls.

In Jesus' time scrolls were usually made of animal skins, smoothed so that they could be written on. The skins were rolled on two rods so that the beginning was on the right and the ending on the left.

Writing was done in narrow columns, usually with a reed or metal pen and ink. As these columns were read, the scroll was rolled from the left rod onto the right one.

The scroll was actually not one large skin, but several, sewed together. One found at Qumran was made of 17 skins. One place where they were joined was glued while the other places were sewed.

A scroll might be about a foot high, but when unrolled might be as long as 24 feet. Only the skins of "clean" animals were used.

Jesus at the Synagogue

LUKE 4:16-31

Synopsis
After talking with the woman at the well, Jesus and His disciples returned to Galilee, stopping first at the village of Cana. A nobleman of Capernaum arrived at Cana, asking Jesus to heal his son, who was at home in Capernaum. Jesus spoke, and the child was healed, even though he was 20 or 25 miles away. After that, Jesus returned to His hometown, Nazareth, where He visited the synagogue on the Sabbath.

The Synagogue
As the word "church" refers to both the building and the people who gather there, so also does the word "synagogue." It means "to gather together."

Synagogues began during the time of the Exile, when the temple in Jerusalem was destroyed and the Jewish people were carried away to Babylon. Without home or temple, they gathered together to worship and teach the Scriptures. By the time of Jesus, every Jewish community had a synagogue. Ten or more Jewish men could start one. A city the size of Jerusalem had many.

The synagogue was supposed to be built on the highest hill in town, near water, with the entrance toward the east as was the temple. It was to be built so that the people at prayer faced Jerusalem.

Inside, the synagogue had a Torah shrine, where the scrolls with the Scriptures were kept. Nearby was the bema, an elevated platform of wood or stone, where Scriptures were read and benedictions were given.

Two or three rows of stone benches surrounded the room, with a special row for the elders and rulers of the synagogue. A menorah, a large seven-branched lampstand, as well as other lamps and objects of worship, were placed in the room.

People gathered on the Sabbath to worship at the synagogue. Scriptures were read and prayers offered. A visiting rabbi might preach, though preaching was not a vital part of the service.

The synagogue was also a center of education for the village, for there was no public education at that time.

The Sabbath Call to Worship

As the sun began to set each Friday evening, the Sabbath began. From the roof of the synagogue minister's house, a double blast of a trumpet signaled the time for work to cease. A second time it sounded, and then a third before the horn-blower quickly laid it aside so that he himself would not break the Sabbath by bearing a burden.

The Sabbath had begun and the festive Sabbath lamp was lit. This holy day would last until sunset on Saturday evening.

On Saturday morning, people began to gather early at the synagogue service. Jesus had attended this Nazareth synagogue as a child and young man. He had been known in the last few years as the carpenter.

The people were especially interested when this hometown carpenter stood to read the Scriptures on this particular Sabbath. He had grown up among the people, and was much aware of each person in the room, especially the elders and rulers of the synagogue, who eyed Him suspiciously, wondering at the reports they had heard of His miracles and His activities in the temple in Jerusalem.

Nazareth, Jesus' Hometown

About 30 years earlier, the Angel Gabriel had announced to Mary that she would become the mother of the Messiah, God's Son. Mary and Joseph left Nazareth, where this announcement was made, and moved to Bethlehem, where Jesus was born. After a short time in Egypt, they returned to Nazareth, where Joseph resumed his work as carpenter until he evidently died during Jesus' teen years. Jesus then became the carpenter, supporting Mary, until it was time for His ministry to begin.

Below: the door of the building in Nazareth which is supposedly built over the site of the Nazareth synagogue of Jesus' time.

Right: the Mount of Precipitation, just outside Nazareth, the traditional place where people tried to kill Jesus.

Jesus Moves to Capernaum

MATTHEW 4:13-16

Synopsis
After Jesus began His ministry, He appeared at the Passover in Jerusalem, where He drove out the money changers and merchants, and talked with Nicodemus by night. He returned to His home territory of Galilee, stopping in Samaria to talk with a woman at a well. In Galilee, He healed a nobleman's son and preached at the synagogue in His hometown, Nazareth. But the people of Nazareth tried to kill Him for claiming to be the Messiah, God's Son. Then Jesus moved to Capernaum, and probably lived in Peter's home.

Where Was Capernaum?
Along the northwest shores of the Sea of Galilee, ruins of ancient Capernaum remain today. They are called Tell Hum. In Jesus' time

Capernaum was a thriving village, built at an important checkpoint of two trade routes. Matthew, or Levi, held the post of customs official, collecting taxes on goods that passed along these routes. A Roman garrison was built at Capernaum to keep control over such an important place. It was under the command of a Roman centurion.

Trade along these routes was international, connecting Egypt in the south with important points in the north, such as Damascus. The Roman garrison had the job of patrolling these dirt roads, keeping peace in the village itself, and making sure the caravans which passed that way were kept safe.

From Nazareth to Capernaum was about 20 to 25 miles. Capernaum was below sea level while Nazareth was in the highlands of Gali-

From the southwest, the site of ancient Capernaum may be seen, nestled among a grove of trees. In Jesus' time, this territory was under the control of Herod Antipas. Right: the map shows the location of Nazareth and Capernaum.

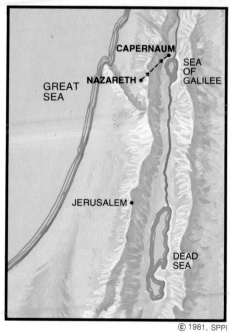

lee. This made a significant difference in the kinds of weather and climate, as well as in the vegetation which grew in those towns.

Peter's House

For hundreds of years, people have identified a place in Capernaum as the site of Peter's house. An octagonal church was built over the site in the fifth century A.D. Its ruins can still be seen there today. Peter was a fisherman while living here, as were many of his neighbors.

The Synagogue

Only a few feet from Peter's house are the remains of a beautiful synagogue, built in the second century A.D. on the ruins of the synagogue of Jesus' time. The entire town is in ruins today, as Jesus prophesied that it would be (Matt. 11:23-24; Luke 10:15).

© 1981, SPPI

361

The Miracle of Fish

LUKE 5:1-11

Synopsis
After the people of Jesus' hometown, Nazareth, tried to kill Him, He moved to Capernaum, a town on the northwest shores of the Sea of Galilee. There He probably lived with His disciple, Simon Peter, a fisherman. One day Jesus was teaching the multitudes by the seaside, but was gradually being crowded toward the water. He stepped into one of the two boats used by Peter, his brother Andrew, and their fishing partners, James and John, also brothers. A short distance from shore, Jesus taught the people. Then He called to Peter to go fishing again, Peter said that he and his partners had fished all night without a catch. But when the fishermen did as Jesus suggested, their nets filled with so many fish that they were almost breaking. Peter bowed before Jesus, who told him that these four would be "fishers of men." These four fishermen later became His most important followers. John and Peter authored books included in the New Testament.

The Fishing Business
Peter and his brother Andrew were apparently involved in a fishing business with James, his brother John, and their father Zebedee. Peter and Andrew lived in Capernaum. James, John, and Zebedee lived a short distance to the east in Bethsaida. Zebedee had hired servants (Mark 1:20), so he must have had a thriving business. It is thought that John may have had a second home in Jerusalem, where Nicodemus visited Jesus by night. John knew the high priest personally, so he was able to go into the courtyard when Jesus was tried. John may have supplied the high priest's household with fish from the Sea of Galilee. If so, he would have become acquainted with the high priest through business dealings.

362

Fish of Galilee

Two fish are pictured above. The smaller one is commonly called the "Pygmy." The larger one is known as "St. Peter's Fish." The Pygmy has a technical name which honors the Jewish historian Flavius Josephus. It is "haplochromis flavii josephi." Josephus was a general of the army before he became a prominent historian. He was wounded in battle and brought to Capernaum for medical treatment.

St. Peter's Fish was the variety from which Peter took his tax money when Jesus told him to throw in a hook and pull out the first fish, which would have a shekel in its mouth. This also points out that fishing with hook and line was common in Jesus' time.

Many of the villages and cities of the land depended on the Sea of Galilee for fish, which were sold fresh to nearby places, but because of the heat had to be dried for distant sales. Josephus, an ancient historian, recorded that there were about 330 fishing boats on the Sea of Galilee during his lifetime, only a few years after Jesus was on earth.

The Sea of Galilee

This "sea" is really a large inland lake about 60 miles north of Jerusalem. As the Jordan River tumbles from north to south toward its final destination in the Dead Sea, it passes through this large hole where the Sea of Galilee has accumulated.

The surface of the water is about 685 feet below sea level. The water in the sea is as much as 150 feet deep.

Since this is a fresh-water body, it provides excellent fishing, the best in the land since Bible times. There were about 30 fishing towns around this sea in Jesus' time, with perhaps 100,000 people in them.

Capernaum was one of the largest of these fishing villages. Bethsaida, home of James and John and Zebedee, actually means "house of fish."

The four fishermen in this story used nets to catch their fish. These were probably drag nets drawn together into a tightening circle between two boats. There were also cast nets, skillfully thrown by one man.

The waters of the Sea of Galilee still splash upon the shore by Capernaum. This scene looks southwest from Capernaum toward the Plain of Gennesaret. In the distance across the lake may be seen the "Horns of Hattin," one of the two traditional places for Jesus' Sermon on the Mount.

363

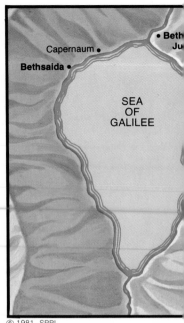

Jesus Calls Four Disciples

MATTHEW 4:18-22; MARK 1:16-20

Synopsis
After Jesus came to live at Capernaum, perhaps at Simon Peter's house, He attracted crowds who came to hear Him teach and preach. One day He taught a crowd while sitting in a boat, speaking to the people on the shore. After He finished, Jesus told Peter, Andrew, James, and John to go fishing again. Even though they had caught nothing all night, they went with Him. As they pulled in their nets, they were so filled with fish that they almost broke. From this miracle, they recognized again that Jesus was more than just a man. Afterward, Jesus would call them to become "fishers of men."

Time
We are not quite sure how much time passed from the fishing miracle to the time when Jesus called the four fishermen to become His full-time followers, "fishers of men." Perhaps it was the same day. Mark and Matthew say that Peter and Andrew were casting nets into the sea, while James and John were sitting in a boat, mending their nets. The picture above shows James and John at work.

The Nets
Peter and Andrew tossed out a type of net called the cast net, or casting net. It was about 10 feet wide, bell-shaped, with lead weights around the edges. A fisherman twirled the net so that it fell flat on the water, with the lead weights causing it to sink over the fish. The fisherman then pulled on a cord attached to the center, drawing the net around the fish.

James and John were probably mending the large drag nets pulled by their boats. Fishermen constantly had the job of washing weeds and other undesirable things from their nets and mending the places where the nets were torn.

The Hired Servants
Zebedee and his family had hired servants, a sign of prosperity (Mark 1:20). Evidently Peter and Andrew's family did not. Some think that Zebedee's real home was in Jerusalem, and that the family fishing business in Bethsaida was "home" only as a convenience. Salome was Zebedee's wife, and mother of James and John. She later followed Jesus and ministered to His need, probably supplying

money for His support and the support of her sons. John's acquaintance with the high priest may have been through his parents, who may have marketed fish from the family business in Jerusalem for years. The parents of Simon Peter and Andrew are not mentioned, only those of James and John. The Bible does mention Peter's mother-in-law, but not his parents. The only reference to Peter's father is that Peter was "Simon, son of John [or Jonah]" (John 21:15).

Leaving the Family Business

A first glance suggests that Jesus walked along the shore of the sea, saw these four men, and told them to follow Him. From this, some have been tempted to think that these were strangers, whom Jesus encountered and abruptly caused them to leave their work to be His followers.

Actually James, John, Peter, and Andrew were seen with Jesus shortly after His baptism and temptation. They began to consider themselves His followers at that time, but not enough to leave their profitable business and follow Him full-time.

James and John may have been Jesus' cousins. Three women were at Jesus' cross and at the tomb on Sunday morning (Mark 15:40; 16:1). Two were named Mary and one was Salome. Two women named Mary were at the cross with the mother of Zebedee's sons, James and John (Matt. 27:56). And two women named Mary were with Jesus' mother and His mother's sister (John 19:25). It seems that Salome, mother of James and John, was also the sister of Mary, mother of Jesus. If so, Jesus was a cousin of James and John.

John the Baptist was also related to Jesus. Mary and Elizabeth were either cousins or Elizabeth was Mary's aunt. John was thus either Jesus' first or second cousin.

Bethsaida

The exact location of Bethsaida is not known for sure. The map shows two possible locations. The name Bethsaida-Julias was a new name Philip the Tetrarch gave it, honoring Augustus' daughter Julia.

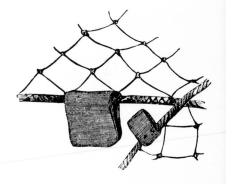

Above: lead weights attached to nets so the edges would sink. Below: one site of Bethsaida. On the map this is at the place marked "Bethsaida Julias."

At the Capernaum Synagogue

MARK 1:21-28; LUKE 4:31-37

Synopsis
After Jesus moved from Nazareth to Capernaum, He performed a miracle for His four fishermen friends. They had fished throughout the night without a catch. After Jesus taught a crowd from one of their boats, He suggested they go out again on the sea. When they did, they caught so many fish that their net almost broke. Later, Jesus called these four fishermen to follow Him, so they left their fishing business to become His full-time disciples. One Sabbath Day, Jesus went into the synagogue at Capernaum, where He healed a man with an evil spirit in him.

Important People at Capernaum
Since Capernaum was at an important checkpoint on two trading routes, a number of important people lived there. Jesus touched the lives of several. He healed the palsied servant of a Centurion, the Roman army officer in charge of the garrison there (Matt. 8:5-13). He healed the son of an official in the court of King Herod Antipas (John 4:46-54), He called the customs officer, Levi or Matthew, to become one of His 12 disciples, and He raised from the dead the daughter of Jairus, the ruler of the synagogue at Capernaum.

Miracles at Capernaum
In addition, Jesus performed other miracles at Capernaum: (1) He caused four disciples to catch fish in a miraculous way (Luke 5:1-11); He drove an evil spirit from a man in the Capernaum synagogue (Mark 1:21-28); He healed Peter's mother-in-law and many others (Mark 1:29-34); He healed a paralyzed man let down through a roof (Mark 2:1-12); He told Peter how to catch a fish that miraculously had a coin in it (Matt. 17:24-27).

The Curse on Capernaum
Jesus predicted Capernaum's ruin because its people refused to fully believe in Him, even though He lived among them (Matt. 11:23-24). Capernaum remains in ruins today, as it has for hundreds of years.

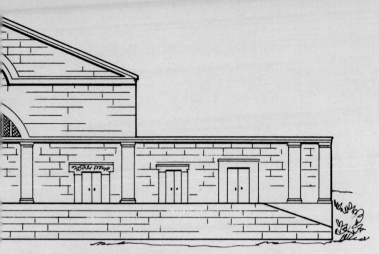

The Capernaum Synagogue

A synagogue must be higher than any other building in town which was used for ordinary use. Any town with roofs higher than the synagogue will end in destruction. So it was understood among the Jewish people of Jesus' time. The synagogue building must be on a high point, if possible, the highest point in town. It should be near water, with the entrance to the east and the seats arranged so that the congregation faced Jerusalem when praying.

Synagogues were places of worship and education. Here the young were trained in Jewish life and language. Worshipers gathered on the Sabbath to pray and read the Scriptures. At Capernaum, the synagogue was one of the best examples of a Galilean synagogue. The ruins seen today are of a synagogue built in the third (some say second, others say fourth) century A.D. on the ruins of the synagogue of Jesus' time.

The drawing above reconstructs what the Capernaum synagogue was probably like.

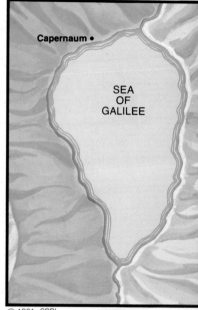

© 1981, SPPI

Upper left: 4 columns and an aisle from the Capernaum synagogue. Lower left: the same area viewed from the right side of the columns. These ruins are from a synagogue built in the third century A.D. upon the ruins of the synagogue of Jesus' time.

Teaching with Authority

Why the difference between Jesus' teaching and that of the scribes, the professional religious leaders? Jesus taught what He had learned firsthand, for He had lived in heaven with His Father, God. He therefore taught what was vital to the lives of His listeners, not merely what had been learned in books. He taught things that would change people's lives and not merely enlighten them. He taught with authority, for He had authority as God's Son, far more authority than the scribes, even though they thought they had more authority than He. He taught what was important for today, and not merely the traditions of the past. He taught truth, God's truth, and not merely man-made rules and principles. And He taught the way to know God, not merely the way to conform to authority.

Evil Spirits and Jesus

Jesus recognized the evil spirit in the man at the Capernaum synagogue. The evil spirit also recognized Him immediately and called him the Holy One of Israel. How strange that the demon knew that He was God's Son, but the religious leaders of the day could not recognize that!

367

Jesus Heals Peter's Mother-in-Law

MATTHEW 8:14-17; MARK 1:29-34; LUKE 4:38-41

Synopsis
When the people of Nazareth rejected Jesus and tried to kill Him, He moved to Capernaum, where He probably lived with Peter in his house. Jesus called Peter, Andrew, James, and John to follow Him full time, leaving their profitable fishing business. One Sabbath after that, Jesus created quite a stir in the nearby synagogue in Capernaum when He commanded an evil spirit to come from a man. After this service in the synagogue was over, Jesus returned home with Peter, Andrew, James, and John and found Peter's mother-in-law sick with a fever. Jesus healed her immediately. By evening, crowds of sick people had gathered to ask Jesus to heal them.

Peter's Home
The synagogue in Capernaum faced southeast, looking toward the Sea of Galilee, only a few hundred feet away. Between the syna-

gogue and the sea were streets lined with private houses. One of these belonged to Peter, where apparently Jesus and Andrew and Peter's mother-in-law also lived. In the fifth century A.D. an octagonal church was built over this site and the ruins of this church may still be seen today among the ruins of ancient Capernaum.

Those who excavated here say that the ruins of a home beneath this church show that it existed between the first century B.C. and the second part of the first century A.D. For many years after Peter's time, the house apparently was used for some Christian purpose, for inscriptions were found with the name of Jesus on them. They call Him the Lord, the Most High God. These inscriptions are in four languages including Greek and Aramaic, languages common in Jesus' time and later in Galilee.

This house, which many believe was

Peter's house, where his mother-in-law was healed by Jesus, was southeast of the synagogue, toward the Sea of Galilee. It was only about 200 to 300 feet from the synagogue.

Houses of Capernaum were made of basalt stones with doorways leading into the street. Doorjambs found on these houses show that they had doors which opened and closed. Doorways inside the houses were open, without doors that opened or closed. They were single-story homes, with roofs of mud mixed with straw. Nothing was found to indicate drainage or private toilets within the houses.

Homes were very modest, with no touches of luxury. But Peter was a town dweller, not a bedouin who lived in a tent, so he probably enjoyed a private stone house with enough room to include Jesus, Andrew, and his mother-in-law also. This seems to show that Peter was certainly not a wealthy man, but he was prosperous enough to have his own home in a neighborhood close to the most important building in town, the synagogue, which was also the highest point in town.

Peter and Jesus

- Peter was a fisherman; Jesus was a carpenter by trade.
- Peter owned a house; Jesus never owned a house, as far as we know.
- Peter was married, for he had a mother-in-law; Jesus was not.
- Peter recognized that Jesus was the Messiah, God's Son, but perhaps not at first.
- Peter followed Jesus and became a dynamic apostle, one of the truly great figures in our Christian heritage.
- Peter wrote two books in the New Testament; he dedicated his life to tell others about Jesus, his Saviour and Lord.

The ruins below show part of the foundation of the octagonal church built over Peter's house.

A Healing Tour of Galilee

MATTHEW 4:23-25; MARK 1:35-39; LUKE 4:42-44

Synopsis

While Jesus lived in Capernaum, He called Peter, Andrew, James, and John to become His full-time disciples. Shortly after that, Jesus created a stir in the synagogue at Capernaum by commanding an evil spirit to leave a man. That same day, Jesus healed Peter's mother-in-law at Peter's house. By evening crowds of sick people had gathered for His healing. The next morning Jesus went to a lonely place, but the crowds followed Him there. Then He went with Peter, Andrew, James, and John on a tour of Galilee, preaching and teaching in the synagogues and healing many.

Disease and Sickness

During New Testament times there were many who were burdened with disease, injury, and other health problems. Sanitation was poor with almost no strict controls over garbage, waste water, or toilets. Flies were abundant and through them and open garbage, disease was easily spread from one person to another. Detection of disease was primitive. Medicine was crude, with little recognition of the causes of sicknesses, and very little knowledge of diseases themselves. Remedies were crude, like home-made medicines. Compared with medicine today, and the advances in diagnosis and surgery and drugs for healing, little was known. Doctors were almost powerless to help the sick.

370

The map at the right shows Galilee in relationship to the other regions.

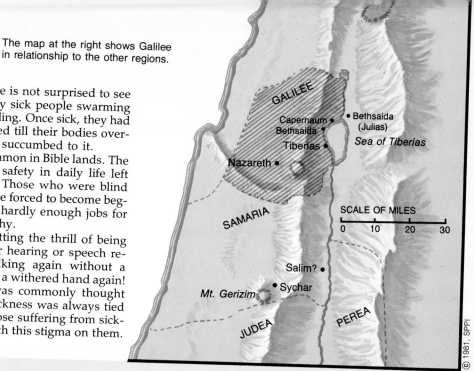

GALILEE

Capernaum •
Bethsaida •
Tiberias •
Nazareth •

• Bethsaida (Julias)

Sea of Tiberias

SAMARIA

SCALE OF MILES
0   10   20   30

Salim? •
• Sychar
Mt. Gerizim •

JUDEA   PEREA

© 1981, SPPI

In this setting, one is not surprised to see crowds of hopelessly sick people swarming around Jesus for healing. Once sick, they had little hope and waited till their bodies overcame the disease or succumbed to it.

Blindness was common in Bible lands. The failure to recognize safety in daily life left many with injuries. Those who were blind or lame or dumb were forced to become beggars, for there were hardly enough jobs for the strong and healthy.

Imagine in this setting the thrill of being healed, with sight or hearing or speech restored! Imagine walking again without a crude crutch or using a withered hand again!

Unfortunately it was commonly thought in Jesus' time that sickness was always tied to some sin. Thus those suffering from sickness also suffered with this stigma on them.

Healing from His Hands

Jesus healed many different types of diseases and injuries. Though the names of some diseases differ, it is thought that these were not different from diseases which still trouble people today. Here are some of the sicknesses and health problems which He healed:

- *He drove out demons and evil spirits.*
- *He gave sight to the blind.*
- *He gave hearing to the deaf.*
- *He gave speech to those who could not talk.*
- *He cured leprosy.*
- *He helped lame people walk.*
- *He stopped hemorrhage.*
- *He removed paralysis.*
- *He restored a withered hand.*
- *He restored an ear that was cut off.*
- *He took away a fever.*
- *He raised people from the dead.*

Left: Jesus heals a paralyzed man, forgiving his sins. Below: a model of a Bible-time house in Jerusalem. Below right: a drawing of another Bible-time house. Both pictures show the flat roofs of houses, the stairways to the roofs, and the stone construction. Stone was plentiful.

Through the Roof to Jesus

MATTHEW 9:1-8; MARK 2:1-12; LUKE 5:17-26

Synopsis
When Jesus arrived home in Capernaum, where He may have been living with Peter, He found Peter's mother-in-law sick with a fever, after a synagogue service. He healed her, and the word of His healing power spread. By evening crowds of sick people were surrounding Him for healing. The next morning He went to a lonely place, but the crowd followed. Jesus then began a tour of Galilee with Peter, Andrew, James, and John, preaching and teaching in the synagogues and healing many. When He returned to Capernaum, crowds surrounded the house so that some men could not bring a paralyzed friend inside for Jesus to heal him. So they lowered the man through the roof and Jesus healed him.

A Hole in the Roof
Most people are confused by this incident, for they immediately think of a modern home with a very sturdy wood roof covered by composition shingles or tar and gravel. But the rooftops of Bible-time homes were usually flat, not with a peak as is true of many homes today. There were a number of designs, a few pictured on these pages. Houses of Capernaum, where this story took place, have been excavated. Archeologists have found that these homes were simple, with walls made of stone and the flat roofs probably made of mud mixed with straw. It would have been a simple matter to pull apart a section of

372

this sun-baked mud and straw mixture and let the lame friend down through the opening. Most houses in Capernaum, at least those near the synagogue where Peter's home was probably located, had courtyards with outside stairways leading to the roof. Thus the men found it easy to carry their paralyzed friend to the rooftop by way of this stairway.

People often sat on the rooftops of their homes on warm nights. Sometimes they slept on these flat roofs to escape the heat and lack of ventilation in the houses themselves.

Some houses which were strong enough to support the weight had guest rooms on the roof. But the archeologists who excavated Capernaum tell us the rooftops in Peter's neighborhood were not that strong.

Size of Houses

The Mishnah, important Jewish writings before the third century A.D., contains much information about life in ancient times. It says Bible-time houses were quite small. It says smaller homes were about 9 by 12 feet and larger homes 12 by 15 feet. However, some think this referred only to the main room. Otherwise it would have been most difficult for a family to live within such a space. The photo below shows a model of a Bible-time house in Jerusalem, larger than the size mentioned. However, this was probably the home of a more wealthy person. People in Bible times were much poorer than people today. Thus a middle-class person then was much poorer than a poor person today.

Forgiveness of Sins or Healing?

Jesus could have told the man that he was healed. Instead He told him that his sins were forgiven. First, Jewish people of Jesus' time thought that sickness was usually the result of sin. Second, in this man's situation, this may well have been true, for as soon as Jesus forgave his sins, the man was healed.

Probably the most important reason for Jesus' statement was to inform the religious leaders there that He could forgive sins, which He proved by healing the man. They were angry at His statement, for it showed that Jesus was from God, for only God could forgive sins. The man and his friends had shown faith by coming to Jesus. Their faith brought healing and forgiveness to the man.

The religious leaders called Jesus' statement "blasphemy" for they did not accept Him as God's Son. If they had accepted Him as God's Son, they would have accepted His statement as truth from God.

Jesus Calls Matthew

Sitting at his customs booth near the sea, Levi hears Jesus call him to be His full-time disciple.

MATTHEW 9:9; MARK 2:13-14; LUKE 5:27-28

Synopsis

After Jesus drove out a demon from a man in the Capernaum synagogue, and healed Peter's mother-in-law, crowds began to gather, coming to be healed and bringing others to be healed. Jesus toured Galilee, healing and teaching, returning at last to His home in Capernaum. A paralyzed man was healed when he was lowered through a roof where Jesus was speaking. While Jesus was still in Capernaum, He walked to the customs booth, located on the main road that stretched from Egypt to Syria. The customs officer, or tax collector, was at work. Jesus called him to leave his work and become His full-time disciple. Levi, also called Matthew, obeyed and became one of the 12 disciples, later known as the 12 apostles.

Matthew

Levi was a Jewish tax collector in Capernaum. His work was to collect customs taxes on the main road that passed through Capernaum from Egypt to Syria. Levi, who took the name Matthew when he became Jesus' follower, was an officer in the service of Herod Antipas, and was thus a nobleman or courtier.

Matthew may have been in touch with Jesus before. It is possible, though there is no way to know for sure, that he was the nobleman who rushed to Jesus at Cana a short while earlier, begging Jesus to heal his son (John 4:46-54). If so, he certainly had experienced the miracle-working power of Jesus, and was prepared to follow Him if called.

After he decided to follow Jesus as a full-time disciple, Matthew gave a dinner reception at his home for Jesus, inviting other tax collectors. He undoubtedly was trying to win them to Jesus also.

The hatred for tax collectors comes out at this time. Pharisees and their scribes bitterly denounced Jesus for eating with these publicans (tax collectors) and sinners.

Matthew is not mentioned again in the Gospels, except in the lists of the 12 apostles.

People Paid Taxes In Jesus' Time Too

Taxes are as old as government, for government is usually supported by the working people who are governed. In Jesus' time, the land where He lived was under the control of the Roman Empire. Under the Roman Emperor were officials in charge of specific lands. Galilee was under the direct control of Herod Antipas, whereas that part of the land where Jerusalem was located was under the control of Pontius Pilate.

These rulers were given various names, such as governor, tetrarch, king, and others. The title usually referred to the amount of power or authority given by the emperor and the amount of land governed.

These rulers collected taxes to support their local governments and to support a part of the Roman government as a whole. Taxes were also levied to support the temple and the religious leaders. Matthew, or Levi, was part of that hated group in charge of collecting these taxes.

Taxes and Tax Collectors

The Romans gathered many different kinds of taxes from their conquered nations. Every five years they put up the job of tax collector at auction. The highest bidder received the job and went about the work of collecting the taxes for which he was responsible. No one could tell him how much to collect, so he often collected far more than he should, as Zaccheus evidently did, cheating the people and often the Roman government.

In Jesus' time, there were taxes on real estate, customs taxes at seaports and city gates for goods shipped through them (which was Matthew's work), a tax on the produce of the land, usually 10 percent, or even 20 percent in some instances, income taxes, road taxes, taxes on animals and vehicles, sales taxes, and even taxes on the sale of slaves and other property. In addition to all of these taxes which the Romans gathered, the religious leaders collected a tax for their own support and the support of the temple.

Chief tax collectors were often Romans, but not always. Zacchaeus was a chief tax collec-

tor and apparently he was Jewish. These officials were in overall charge of collecting taxes. People such as Matthew may have been a step lower, doing the actual work.

A census was taken from time to time to make sure all the people were on the tax rolls. It was such a census that took Mary and Joseph from Nazareth to Bethlehem, where Jesus was born.

Tax collecting was often a family profession, passed from father to son, as was the work of carpenter or farmer. The Jewish people hated the tax collectors, for they gathered money from their own people to support the Gentiles, the Romans, and collected enough so that the people of Rome did not have to work, but spent their days at the games and easy living. Also many of the tax collectors made themselves rich at the expense of the poor.

The Jewish leaders tried to trick Jesus by asking if it was right to pay taxes to Caesar. If He answered yes, the people would hate Him. If He answered no, then Rome would hate Him.

A Dinner at Matthew's House

MATTHEW 9:10-13; MARK 2:15-17; LUKE 5:29-32

Synopsis

After a tour of Galilee, healing and teaching, Jesus returned to Capernaum, where He was probably living with Peter. After healing a paralytic who had been let down through a roof, He went out to the customs booth along the trade route through Capernaum. Matthew, or Levi, was collecting tolls, or customs taxes from merchants who passed that way. Jesus told him to follow Him as a full-time disciple. Matthew gave up his business and followed Jesus. His first act was to give a dinner at his home, where he invited other tax collectors to meet Jesus. But this angered the religious leaders, who rebuked Jesus for eating with tax collectors and sinners.

Two Views of Sinners

This story points out the conflict between two views of sinners. The Pharisees looked on sinful people as tainted, to be avoided. They did not approve of a rabbi or any other important religious person mingling or eating with sinful people, especially with sinners such as tax collectors who were hated by the people.

Jesus took the other view. He did not hate sinners, but their sins. He did not want to separate Himself from them, but mingled with them and taught and preached the Word to them so that they might be sorry about their sins and come to God.

The distinction is important today for those of us who follow Jesus. None of us is perfect. We are not to hate any sinner, but

his sin. We are not to isolate ourselves from sinners, but mingle with them (not with their sin!), so that we might help them come to God through Jesus.

Jesus summed it up by telling the Pharisees that sick people (sinners) needed a physician (Himself). People who were well (without sin) did not. Of course, since there are no people without sin, even the self-righteous Pharisees needed Him more than they realized.

The Pharisees

The Pharisees were the "separated ones" or separatists, for they set themselves apart from others by the way they dressed and believed. Like other Jewish religious groups, they believed in the Old Testament Law. But the Pharisees thought that the oral law, the rules made up by the religious leaders, was equally inspired and was thus to be followed as much as God's Law.

The Pharisees and Jesus often opposed each other on this. Jesus taught that the Scriptures were the Law and were to be followed. But the man-made rules were not.

The Pharisees were middle-class people, not the wealthy aristocrats, as were the Sadducees. Many Pharisees were businessmen, merchants, and tradesmen. But even though they were part of these daily trades, they separated themselves from others by the strict way they adhered to both the Law and to man-made rules.

Because they were separatists, and thus separated themselves from others, they also gathered together into a close-knit group. There were about 6,000 during the time of Jesus. The Pharisees believed that they were being so righteous that they were helping to bring the Messiah.

Pharisees and Phylacteries

Jesus denounced the Pharisees and other religious leaders for a number of things, including the way they pretended to be holy by wearing phylacteries (Matt. 23:5). These little boxes came from a very literal interpretation of Exodus 13:9, 16, where Jews were commanded to keep the Scriptures close to their hearts and minds. Instead of memorizing Scripture and taking it to heart, many men of Jesus' day wore it in little boxes called phylacteries.

One box was worn on the head, another on the arm in such a way that it would be brought near the heart. A typical box was about a 1½-inch cube. Leather straps fastened it on the head and arm as shown in the pictures.

Inside the phylacteries were strips of parchment, on which were written the following four passages of Scripture— Deuteronomy 11:13-21; Deuteronomy 6:4-9; Exodus 13:1-10; Exodus 13:11-16, in that order. Men wore the boxes during prayer times.

As a man put on each box, he recited a benediction. Some men made "broad their phylacteries" by enlarging both straps and boxes, trying to be even more devout by doing this. In a very real sense, these boxes became like charms or amulets.

Wineskins and Patched Garments

MATTHEW 9:14-17; MARK 2:18-22; LUKE 5:33-39

Synopsis
After Jesus called Levi, or Matthew, the tax collector, to follow Him full time, Matthew invited Jesus to a reception at his house, where a number of other tax collectors were guests. This angered the Pharisees and other religious leaders. They openly criticized Jesus for eating with tax collectors and others of bad reputation. Jesus was also criticized by the disciples of John the Baptist for permitting His disciples to feast while they were fasting. Jesus responded with three parables—a parable about a bridegroom, one about patched cloth, and a third about wineskins.

Meanings
The first parable about the bridegroom meant that Jesus' disciples had no reason to fast while they were with Him, the Bridegroom. But after He was gone from them, they might wish to mourn by fasting. The second parable meant that His teaching was not merely a patch on the old religion of the day. It was a new garment to clothe His people. The third parable meant about the same. It was a new "bottle" or wineskin, not a new infilling of an old container, the religion of the day. To patch the dynamic new Gospel to the old religion would not work.

John and His Disciples
Andrew was one of John the Baptist's disciples before he began to follow Jesus. When Andrew recognized Jesus as the Messiah, he found his brother, Simon Peter, and brought him to Jesus also. Some of John's disciples began to follow Jesus instead of John. Others remained with John, and in this incident, even criticized Jesus and His disciples. John himself had said that he must become less important and Jesus become more important. Apparently John never complained when a disciple stopped following him so that he might follow Jesus. John saw his work as God saw it—to point others to Jesus, the Son of God.

Wineskins, or "bottles" as some versions call them, held water or wine. At the right, a water vendor pours from his wineskin. Another wineskin hangs on the wall.

378

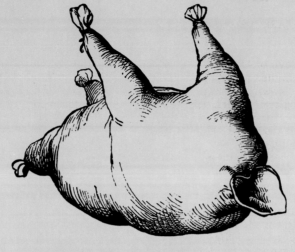

Bottles Made of Skins

In Bible times, glass bottles were expensive and therefore not in common use. Most people carried water or wine in goat-skins, sewed around the edges to make them watertight. The hair was on the outside.

These bottles, or wineskins, were often used for wine. As wine ferments, it expands, and the wineskin would stretch. A new skin would be flexible, so it would stretch without being harmed. But once a skin was stretched, it was considered an "old" wineskin. To put new wine into that old wineskin, already stretched once, was asking for that skin to burst, for it could not stretch again.

The pictures show, counterclockwise from the top: (1) a wineskin; (2) an Assyrian woman giving a child a drink of water from a skin bottle; (3) a woman and a man with skins fastened on their backs with straps, probably water-carriers who sold water in the streets; (4) drawings of Roman figures, found on the walls of Pompeii and Herculaneum, with skins draped over their shoulders, and drawings of Roman skins below them; and (5) a yoke with a skin balanced with a jug in a basket, as well as two nomads with skins on their backs.

379

At the Pool of Bethesda

JOHN 5:1-47

Synopsis
After Jesus called Levi, or Matthew, to become His full-time disciple, Matthew gave a reception for Jesus and invited many tax collectors. The Pharisees criticized Jesus for eating with such sinful people. Not long after that the disciples of John the Baptist criticized Jesus for letting His disciples feast while John's disciples and the Pharisees were fasting. Later, Jesus left Galilee, and went to a great festival in Jerusalem, probably the Passover, where He healed a man at the Pool of Bethesda.

Water for the City
Jerusalem in Bible times required enormous amounts of water, especially for the sacrifices at the temple. Water from rainfall was never enough. To bring water into the city, conduits were laid from large pools near Bethlehem, called Solomon's Pools. Inside the city, pools and cisterns held water until needed. One pool, called the Towers Pool, was just north of Herod's palace. A second was the Siloam Pool, south of the temple. A

third was Israel Pool, joining the wall of the temple enclosure along the north. A fourth was the Sheep Pool, where the sheep were washed before being sacrificed in the temple. It was north of the Israel Pool. Farther north was another pool, the Pool of Bethesda.

The temple mount itself was filled with cisterns, many quite large. These served the water needs of the temple.

The Pool of Bethesda
This pool was located near the sheep gate of Jerusalem, the gate farthest east on the northern wall. It had five porches, and its water was traditionally thought to cure people when an angel stirred it.

Bethesda was also called Bethzetha or Beth-zatha. It is mentioned only once in the Bible, in connection with this story. The name means "house of the olive." The two photos on these pages show its remains, located at the place shown on the map at the upper right. The Pool of Bethesda was actually twin pools, separated by a 20-foot rock partition.

380

The arches at the left and below are ruins from a 5th century A.D. church built over the Pool of Bethesda, and destroyed by the Persians in 614.

The map at the right shows the location of the Pool of Bethesda. One tradition says the sheep to be sacrificed were washed in one of the twin pools. Another tradition speaks of treasure buried in one of the pools.

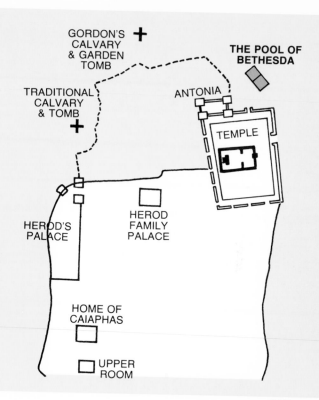

GORDON'S CALVARY & GARDEN TOMB

THE POOL OF BETHESDA

TRADITIONAL CALVARY & TOMB

ANTONIA

TEMPLE

HEROD'S PALACE

HEROD FAMILY PALACE

HOME OF CAIAPHAS

UPPER ROOM

Sabbath in a Wheat Field

MATTHEW 12:1-8; MARK 2:23-28; LUKE 6:1-5

Synopsis
After Jesus visited Jerusalem, attending a great festival where He healed a man at the Pool of Bethesda, He returned to Galilee. Along the way, His disciples gathered a little wheat in a field and began to eat it. This angered the Pharisees, who accused the disciples of harvesting, or working, on the Sabbath.

Sabbath Rules
The Law of Moses set apart the Sabbath as a day unto the Lord (Ex. 20:10; Deut. 5:14). It was to be a day of rest. But the Pharisees and others added to the Law, spelling out far more specifically than it did, what this meant. Harvesting was work, they said, so it should not be done on the Sabbath. Any form of plucking grain was harvesting. Therefore, even taking a few heads of wheat into one's hands and removing the grain

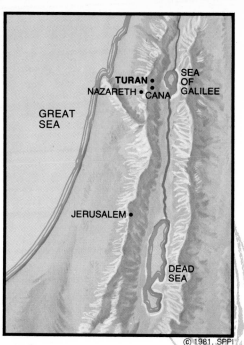

At the left, wheat is ripe for harvest in the traditional meadow where Jesus' disciples plucked the grains to eat. Above: this place, called Turan, is about 10 miles north of Cana.

© 1981, SPPI

was harvesting, which was breaking the Sabbath.

Jesus knew this was adding too much to the Law. When the Pharisees criticized His disciples for "breaking the Sabbath," Jesus told them that He was Lord of the Sabbath.

Were the Disciples Stealing?

The disciples were hungry, so they walked into a field and gathered some wheat to eat. Was this stealing? Today it would be thought to be stealing, for our laws do not arrange for hungry people to eat their neighbors' crops.

But the Law of Moses, which guided the people of Israel, did provide for such things. A hungry person could go into a neighbor's field or vineyard and eat his fill (Deut. 23:24-25). But he could not carry grapes away in a vessel or harvest his neighbor's wheat with a sickle.

The disciples were doing exactly what was right. They were taking food that the Law provided and they were not "harvesting" on the Sabbath, but merely gathering some food to eat.

Turan

One tradition locates the wheat field where the disciples plucked the grain near a small village called Turan. It is about 10 kilometers, or 6 miles, north of Kefar-Kana, the traditional location of Cana. In Arabic it is called Merj es-Sunbul—meadow of the ears of corn. The map at the top locates this lovely meadow immediately south of the little village of Turan. The photo at the upper left is of this meadow, or field.

Sabbath Day's Journey

Some people think Jesus was on the way to the synagogue referred to in the next story, for that healing took place on the Sabbath. There is nothing to confirm this, of course. But wherever He was traveling, it was within approximately three fourths of a mile (2,000 cubits), for that was the limit a Jew was to travel on the Sabbath.

Time

Wheat harvest was in June. Barley harvest was in May. The word "corn" should be translated "grain."

383

The Withered Hand

MATTHEW 12:9-14; MARK 3:1-6; LUKE 6:6-11

Synopsis

While returning to Galilee, after attending a great festival in Jerusalem, Jesus and His disciples stopped in a grainfield to eat. The Pharisees criticized Jesus for letting His disciples gather some grain to eat on the Sabbath. They criticized Him again when He reached a synagogue, possibly the one in Capernaum, and healed a man with a withered hand. The Pharisees then plotted with the Herodians to kill Jesus.

The Herodians

Who were they? Nobody is quite sure. Some say they were Herod's soldiers, or courtiers, or some other group related to the rule of the Herod family. They were political, not religious. Undoubtedly in some way they supported the rule of the Herods over the land.

The rule of the Herods began with Antipater, father of Herod the Great. When the Roman general, Pompey, captured Jerusalem and Roman rule began, Antipater rose in power. This was in 67 B.C. Later, in 48 B.C., he risked his life for Julius Caesar in Caesar's struggle with Pompey. For this, Caesar rewarded him with Roman citizenship and appointed him procurator of Judea.

Antipater appointed his son, Phasael, as governor of Jerusalem and his son, Herod, as governor of Galilee. At this time, Herod was only 25 years old. In the numerous struggles that took place, Herod's power increased until in 40 B.C. Caesar and the Roman senate made him king of Judea.

Herod the Great, as he was called later, ruled until A.D. 4. During his rule, Jesus was born and the babies of Bethlehem were massacred in an attempt to kill Jesus. When he died, his son, Archelaus, ruled Judea, Idumea, and Samaria until A.D. 6, when he was deposed because of his brutality. His brother, Herod Antipas, ruled Galilee and Perea; and his brother, Herod Philip, ruled a kingdom east of the Sea of Galilee. Antipas still ruled Galilee during Jesus' ministry.

During Jesus' time, Herodians were a group that wanted to keep the Herod family in power. Normally the Pharisees would have been their enemies, for loyal Jewish leaders hoped the Jews would regain their independence. But a common hatred for Jesus, plus fear that Rome would remove their power, caused the Pharisees and Herodians to join forces against Jesus.

The ruins of the Capernaum synagogue at the right show elements of the exterior of a Galilean synagogue. The drawing below shows the interior. Jesus visited many of these Galilean synagogues, perhaps all that stood in His time. He taught and spoke in them, and healed people who came with needs.

Synagogues—Inside

When Jesus went inside a synagogue, as in this story, what would He find? The most important piece of "furniture" was the shrine which held the Torah, the sacred roll or scroll on which the Scriptures were written. This roll, of course, contained nothing of what we know today as the New Testament, and only parts of what we know as the Old Testament. This Torah shrine was often carved wood, sometimes ornamented with beautiful hangings. It might hold one or more scrolls.

The bema, made of stone or wood, was an elevated platform next to the Torah shrine. Lessons and benedictions were given from this platform.

Rows of stone benches surrounded the walls and provided seating for the people. The elders and rulers sat in an isolated section.

Teaching by the Sea

MATTHEW 12:15-21; MARK 3:7-12

Synopsis
While returning from a great festival in Jerusalem, Jesus and His disciples stopped in a grainfield to eat. The Pharisees criticized Him for letting the disciples pluck grain on the Sabbath. They said it was work and should not be done on the Sabbath. They criticized Him again when He healed a man with a withered hand on the Sabbath. After that, Jesus taught a great crowd by the shore of the Sea of Galilee.

The Region around the Sea of Galilee
Most of Jesus' ministry was focused on the small band of land surrounding the Sea of Galilee. Names such as Capernaum, Bethsaida, Chorazin, Gergesa, Magdala, Gennesaret, and Tiberias bring to mind a number of important events in His ministry. One is reminded also of a miraculous catch of fish, Jesus walking on the water, and Jesus stilling a storm on the sea itself.

The home of Mary Magdalene was thought to be at Magadan, or Magdala. This is also mentioned as a place where Jesus landed on one of His journeys around the sea.

Tiberias was the capital of Herod Antipas, whom Jesus called "that fox." Herod ruled the region of Galilee and Perea and would later question Jesus when He was being judged for crucifixion. There is no mention

From the area near Capernaum, one looks across the Sea of Galilee toward Tiberias. The hills, or mountains, which surround the sea may also be seen on the other side.

that Jesus ever visited Tiberias, even though it was only a few miles across the sea from His home in Capernaum.

Near Gergesa, Jesus healed a man possessed with many demons, causing the demons to enter some pigs who rushed into the sea. Somewhere, not far from the sea, Jesus multiplied loaves and fish so that He could feed 5,000 men, plus women and children.

The Jordan River enters the sea at the north and leaves it at the south, pausing to fill this deep basin with water. Surrounding the sea are gently rolling hills, sometimes called "mountains," with an occasional plain along the shore. The Plain of Gennesaret is a rather large, fertile plain along the western side of the sea, one of the few rich agricultural areas adjoining it.

Names of the Sea of Galilee

This sea, which is actually a large inland fresh-water lake, has had four names. Often in the Gospels it is called the Sea of Galilee, named for the region in which it was located. It is also called the Lake of Gennesaret (Luke 5:1), the Sea of Tiberias (John 6:1; 21:1), and the Sea of Kinnereth, or Chinnereth in some versions of the Bible (Num. 34:11). Gennesaret and Kinnereth, or Chinnereth, were areas near the sea. Tiberias was a town near it. Today it is called Lake Kinneret, but the name Sea of Galilee often appears as a second name.

387

Choosing the Twelve

MARK 3:13-19; LUKE 6:12-16

Synopsis
On one occasion, Jesus spent all night in prayer. In the morning He chose the 12 men who became known later as the 12 Apostles. These 12 would be His closest followers.

Simon Peter
With his brother Andrew, Peter was active in a fishing business, probably in partnership with James, John, and their father Zebedee. Originally Peter was from Bethsaida, but moved to Capernaum, where Jesus probably lived in his home. Peter was a strong leader among the Twelve, though impetuous at times. His name originally was Simon, but Jesus changed it to Peter. He authored 1 and 2 Peter, two epistles of the New Testament.

Andrew
Simon Peter's brother, Andrew, was at first a disciple of John the Baptist. When he came to believe in Jesus as Messiah, he quickly became Jesus' disciple and led Peter to Jesus also. Andrew and Peter were both sons of a fisherman named John, or Jonah, also probably of Bethsaida. At the feeding of the 5,000, Andrew told Jesus about the boy with the loaves and fish.

James, Zebedee's Son
Like his brother John, James was in the fishing business. He was probably in partnership with Peter and Andrew, and with his father Zebedee. The family was probably wealthy, for Zebedee had hired servants. James was the first of the Twelve to be martyred.

John
Author of the Gospel according to John, and the three Epistles of John, this apostle was among the "inner circle," those closest to Jesus. With his brother James, he was called a son of thunder, perhaps because of an emotional nature. He, with Peter and James, was with Jesus when He went apart from the others to pray in Gethsemane. After Jesus' crucifixion, John took care of Jesus' mother.

Philip
Like Peter and Andrew, Philip came from Bethsaida. When Philip believed in Jesus, he also brought Nathanael. He was present at the feeding of the 5,000, and Jesus asked him how they might buy bread for all of the people who were present.

Bartholomew (Nathanael)
Little is known about Bartholomew. It seems likely that he was also known as Nathanael. If so, Philip found him and brought him to Jesus not long after Philip had believed in Him. Nathanael was the one who asked if any good thing came from Nazareth; but when Jesus told about him sitting under a fig tree, he believed on Him.

Thomas
Thomas was also called Didymus in some Bible versions, which meant "twin." Nobody is quite sure why he was called "twin." Thomas is often remembered as the doubter, the one who could not believe in Jesus' resurrection unless he felt Jesus' wounds.

Matthew
Levi was a tax collector, manning a booth along the busy trade route that led through Capernaum. Jesus called him to follow Him full time. After that, it seems that his name changed to Matthew, which meant "true." Matthew is the author of the first Gospel.

James, Son of Alphaeus
James was also known as James the Less or James the younger. He may have been shorter or younger than James, brother of John.

Simon the Zealot
He was also called a Cananean (Matt. 10:4 in some Bible versions). Zealots belonged to a political party which wanted to overthrow Roman rule.

Thaddaeus
Two lists in the Gospels of the Twelve name Thaddaeus. The other two lists name Judas (not Iscariot). He has also been called Lebbaeus.

Judas Iscariot
For 30 pieces of silver, Judas betrayed Jesus into the hands of His enemies. Later, he threw the money back at them and hanged himself.

At the far right, sheep graze on the slopes of the Horns of Hattin. Below: the Horns of Hattin as seen from the east. Upper right: the graceful church on the Mount of Beatitudes, built in 1937 to commemorate the Sermon on the Mount. From its porch (left) is a beautiful view of the Sea of Galilee toward the south, and across the sea, the Horns of Hattin in the distance.

The Sermon on the Mount

MATTHEW 5:1—8:1; LUKE 6:17-49

Synopsis
After Jesus returned from a great festival in Jerusalem, He was criticized by the Pharisees when His disciples gathered some grain to eat on the Sabbath. He was criticized again when He healed a man with a withered hand on the Sabbath. But Jesus continued to teach great crowds of people. After one night of prayer, He chose the Twelve, who would be His closest followers. Then his disciples followed as He led them into a high mountain not far from Capernaum, where He presented what we know as the Sermon on the Mount.

The Place

No one is sure about the exact location for the Sermon on the Mount. However, two locations are traditionally accepted—the Horns of Hattin, a short distance south of the Sea of Galilee, and a hilly region not far from Capernaum, toward the west. This second location is now called the Mount of Beatitudes, and a graceful church is erected on the highest "mountain" or hill in the region to commemorate the Sermon on the Mount, and especially the Beatitudes.

Since the thirteenth century A.D. the mountain known as the Horns of Hattin has been accepted by some as the location for the Sermon on the Mount. This mountain has twin peaks, separated by a crater-like formation.

The Mount of Beatitudes is much nearer to Capernaum. But there is as much reason to think that Jesus wanted to go to a lonelier mountain a few miles away. So the mystery remains as to where the Sermon on the Mount was given.

Beatitudes

As God gave the Law to Moses on Mount Sinai to guide His people's conduct and service, so Jesus gave His disciples the Sermon on the Mount to guide their conduct and service to Him and His Father.

The Beatitudes state simply some guidelines to happiness. "Blessed" in some Bible versions could as easily be translated "happy." Both the Ten Commandments and the Beatitudes say, "Accept the Lord as King and obey Him, for that is the way to happiness."

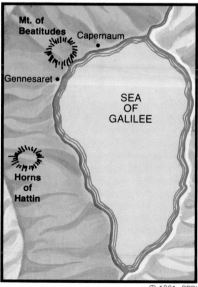

© 1981, SPPI

391

A Centurion's Servant

MATTHEW 8:5-13; LUKE 7:1-10

Synopsis
After a night of prayer, Jesus chose the 12 men who would be His apostles. Then, in a mountain of Galilee, He gave a beautiful discourse which we have come to know as "The Sermon on the Mount." Jesus returned to Capernaum and was met by a centurion who pleaded with Jesus to heal his servant.

Centurions in the New Testament
(1) *The centurion in charge of Jesus' crucifixion.* When Jesus was sentenced to death, it was the job of this centurion and his men to nail Jesus to the cross. Later, Pilate called the same centurion in to confirm Jesus' death (Mark 15:39, 43-45). (2) *Cornelius.* This centurion was a devout Gentile who respected God and prayed often. He and his family were baptized by Peter (Acts 10). (3) *Centurions who saved Paul from being beaten to death.* Some Jews who hated Paul formed a mob and began to beat him. The Roman commander immediately sent centurions to restore order (Acts 21:27-40). Later, Paul was about to be whipped, but when he told a centurion that he was a Roman citizen he was quickly released (Acts 22:24-29). (4) *Centurions who looked after Paul's safety.* A plot against Paul's life was uncovered by his nephew. Escorted by two centurions, Paul slipped out of the city to a safer place (Acts 23:11-24). (5) *Julius.* This centurion guarded Paul on his voyage to Rome (Acts 27).

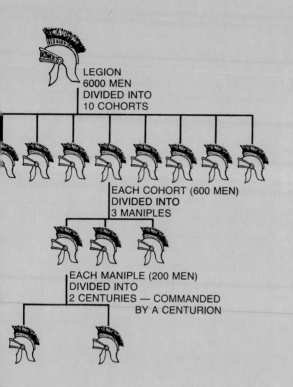

LEGION
6000 MEN
DIVIDED INTO
10 COHORTS

EACH COHORT (600 MEN)
DIVIDED INTO
3 MANIPLES

EACH MANIPLE (200 MEN)
DIVIDED INTO
2 CENTURIES — COMMANDED
BY A CENTURION

Centurions and Rome's Army

The chart at the left shows a simplified structure of a Roman legion, with about 6,000 soldiers. A legion was divided into 10 cohorts of 600 soldiers each. A cohort was divided into three maniples of 200 soldiers each. A maniple had two centuries of 100 soldiers each. Some historians use slightly different numbers for each of these divisions.

One Roman historian wrote that centurions were chosen for their ability to keep cool in a crisis. The Roman army did not want daredevils in this office. In battle, their strategy was to show caution, not foolishness, but caution coupled with courage.

Centurions were chosen from among the ranks, and worked their way up to the job. But once a centurion, often always a centurion. They were seldom promoted to a higher office. Their promotions were to more desirable positions as centurions, whether to better geographical locations, or to better grades within the rank.

The centurions of the Bible appear to be men of high character. Some of them became Jesus' disciples, openly acknowledging Him as God's Son, showing faith beyond that of Israel's religious leaders.

Right: Roman standards. Second from the left is the Roman silver Eagle, with its claws resting on a thunderbolt. This was carried by a soldier known as Eagle-bearer, and came next to the centurions in rank. When the legion was camped, the Eagle was placed on a low pole in the middle of the camp.

The Widow of Nain

LUKE 7:11-17

Synopsis
After Jesus' famous discourse, now known as "The Sermon on the Mount," He returned to Capernaum. A centurion came to Jesus, pleading for Him to heal a servant. Jesus spoke the word, and the servant was healed. Soon after this, Jesus entered Nain as a funeral procession was leaving, preparing to bury a widow's only son. Jesus spoke, and the son was raised to life again.

Nain
The small town where Jesus raised the widow's son is reached from the west by traveling up a steep road with rock tombs on either side. Many believe that it was in one of these tombs that the widow's son was about to be buried. The road leading from Capernaum to Nain, which Jesus would have traveled, enters the town from the northeast. Along this road, only a short distance from Nain, is a small burial ground where others believe the funeral procession was heading.

Funerals in Jesus' Day
Failing to honor the dead was perhaps the greatest lack of respect a Jew could display. Bystanders were obligated to follow a funeral procession, with hired mourners adding to the wails of friends. The body was wrapped in cloth and carried on a bier. After the funeral, mourning continued for 30 days.

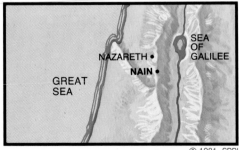

© 1981, SPPI

At the top, a funeral procession marches solemnly to the shallow grave or rock-cut tomb. Funerals were often the same day as the death, because of the heat and lack of embalming. The photo above is Nain today, from the northeast.

A Curse on Three Towns

MATTHEW 11:20-30

Synopsis
Jesus had performed many miracles in His native Galilee. He had raised a widow's son from the dead, healed a centurion's servant without even going to his home, and healed a withered hand in His hometown synagogue at Capernaum. Still, many refused to believe in Him as God's Son, the Messiah. Then Jesus told of the future destruction and desolation of three unbelieving towns—Capernaum, Chorazin, and Bethsaida.

Bethsaida
Called the "House of Fisher," Bethsaida was probably located on the northern side of the Sea of Galilee. Despite being the home of Peter, Andrew, and Philip, and near the feeding of the 5,000, the people would not accept Jesus' ministry.

Chorazin
Jesus performed most of His miracles in Chorazin, Bethsaida, and Capernaum (Matt. 11:20). Yet, it was the people in these three towns who rejected Jesus more than any of the other places He visited. Angered by this, Jesus compared Chorazin and Bethsaida to Tyre and Sidon, saying that had He gone there instead, those cities would have repented.

Capernaum
Though Jesus made His home in this village for a long period of time, these people rejected His teachings as well. Jesus compared Capernaum to the wicked city of Sodom, saying that even that city would have turned to God had it been exposed to His ministry. Capernaum, like Chorazin and Bethsaida, lies in ruins and has never been rebuilt.

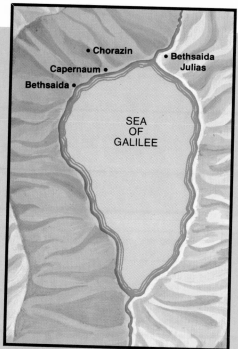

The map at the left shows the location of Capernaum, Chorazin, and the two possible locations of Bethsaida. At the far left is a view of the location shown as Bethsaida Julias. Below: the ruins of Chorazin. At the bottom, the Capernaum area is seen across one part of the Sea of Galilee.

Jesus' Family

MATTHEW 12:46-50; MARK 3:31-35; LUKE 8:19-21

Synopsis
Throughout Galilee, Jesus taught and healed. Many believed on Him as God's Son, the Messiah. Many did not. Among the unbelieving people were a number of the religious leaders, including the Pharisees. As Jesus' popularity increased, so did their hatred for Him. At one point, Jesus' mother and brothers came to take Him back to His childhood home in Nazareth.

Ancestors of Jesus
The lineage of Jesus runs through a great variety of people. Some were important men and women who followed God wholeheartedly, and were highly respected. Others earned reputations that were not so good. Some held positions of great importance; some were even kings, while others were poor or rejected.

Among the ancestors of Jesus were King David, Israel's greatest king of battle, and King Solomon, Israel's richest king. Abraham and Jacob were shepherds who feared God and led their people wisely. Ruth was a Moabite and a woman highly respected.

Also included in Jesus' family tree was Judah, Jacob's son who sold his own brother Joseph into slavery, and Leah, who was forced upon Jacob as a wife and was never really loved.

The family genealogy of Jesus appears in two places in the Bible. The first place is Matthew 1:1-17, which moves forward in time from Abraham to Mary's husband, Joseph. The second place is Luke 3:23-38, which traces Jesus' lineage backward through time from Joseph to Adam. While both Gospels mention Joseph, they are quick to point out that Jesus is God's Son and that Joseph was chosen to care for Him. Mary's family tree included people like Abraham and David as well.

Mary, Jesus' Mother
Mary had the highest honor a woman could have—to be the mother of the Messiah, God's Son.

James
Probably the oldest brother. Became a leader of the church in Jerusalem and author of the Epistle of James.

Joseph
Listed as a brother of Jesus. All Jesus' brothers seem to have rejected Jesus as Messiah until after the Resurrection.

Joseph, Mary's Husband
Joseph knew that this Child was not his son, but was born of the Holy Spirit. But he willingly cared for Jesus.

mon
ke Joseph, he is listed as sus' brother without fur-er information. Jesus' others apparently later came active Christian aders (see Acts 1:14 and Cor. 9:5).

Judas
An unbeliever until Jesus' resurrection, he probably became a Christian leader afterward. The Book of Jude may have been written by this brother.

Jesus' Family on Earth

Some information is available about Jesus' family, but not nearly enough to satisfy our curiosity. We do know that Joseph was a carpenter, who had his shop in Nazareth before Jesus' birth and after the return from Egypt. Joseph must have died after Jesus was 12 and Jesus probably took over the work of the shop.

One tradition says that Joseph was an older man when he married Mary, who was perhaps only 12 or 13. This tradition says that Joseph already had the "brothers and sisters" of Jesus mentioned in Matthew 13:55 and Mark 6:3, children of a previous wife who had died. Another tradition says that these were children born to Joseph and Mary after Jesus' birth.

It was not unusual in Bible times for an older man to marry a much younger woman. It would appear that Jacob was 80 when he first married. Rachel and Leah were young women. The facts concerning Jesus' brothers and sisters are not clear, and traditions are certainly not often reliable. But we do know He had brothers and sisters, which were actually half-brothers and half-sisters, for they are mentioned in the passages given above.

The Bible is clear that Jesus was born of Mary, conceived by the Holy Spirit, and that Joseph married Mary and helped raise the boy Jesus. It is clear, then, that He was both Mary's son and God's Son.

The Sower and Other Parables

MATTHEW 13:1-52; MARK 4:1-34; LUKE 8:4-18

Synopsis

Jesus taught and healed in Galilee, giving a long discourse known as The Sermon on the Mount, healing a centurion's servant, and raising a widow's son from the dead at Nain. Jesus also warned of the coming destruction and desolation of three unbelieving towns—Capernaum, Chorazin, and Bethsaida. One day His mother and brothers came to take Him back to Nazareth, but He refused to go. Then He taught using parables, including a parable about a sower.

Teaching in Parables

For centuries, people have told stories, or parables. A parable is a special type of story that teaches people something they do not know, by comparing it to something they do know. Jesus was a master storyteller. He used parables to help people understand things they did not know about God, by comparing them to things they did know on earth. For example, Jesus compared the kingdom of God to a mustard seed. God's kingdom was not easy to understand, but most knew about the tiny mustard seed. Jesus showed how the Gospel is like a little seed. When planted in someone's life, it grows and matures until it becomes great and useful.

The Sower

After the soil had been plowed with a crude wooden plow, pulled by oxen or other animals, the farmer "sowed" the seed on the ground and then used some method to get it under the soil. One easy method was to have animals walk over the planted soil until they had trampled the seed beneath.

Sowing followed one of two widely used methods. The first was to toss the seed by hand, as seen in these drawings taken from Egyptian tomb paintings. The drawing above also shows a crude plow pulled by oxen, and the bags which held the seed while sowing. The lower picture shows Egyptian farmers with crude wooden hoes, turning seeds under, hoeing weeds, and breaking up the hard soil. Though these pictures from Egypt are from an earlier time, the methods remained much the same throughout Bible times.

The second method of sowing was to attach the bags of seed to animals, with holes in the bags large enough for the seeds to trickle out. As the animal walked over the plowed ground, the seeds were distributed.

Jesus' parable seemed to suggest the first method, with the seeds distributed by hand, as in these pictures. Thorns and stones were common problems for Bible-time farmers, familiar to those who heard Jesus.

The mustard plant (far left) was mentioned by Jesus as a plant which grew from a tiny seed. It grew large enough for birds to perch in its branches. The tares mentioned by Jesus (above) were weeds called darnel. In the early stages, tares looked exactly like wheat, but produced small seeds which carried a poisonous fungus.

401

Jesus Stills a Storm

MATTHEW 8:18, 23-27; MARK 4:35-41; LUKE 8:22-25

Synopsis
One day in Galilee Pharisees and their scribes came to Jesus, demanding a sign which would prove who He was. He refused. That same day, Jesus' mother and brothers came to take Him home to Nazareth. Again He refused. Then He taught His disciples by the Sea of Galilee, using parables to communicate His message. Also on that same important day, Jesus and His disciples crossed the Sea of Galilee. When a storm arose, Jesus stilled the storm, showing His disciples, and all others, that He is truly the Messiah, God's Son.

Storms on the Sea of Galilee
Like a giant bowl of water among the hills of Galilee, lies the Sea of Galilee. Three and one-half miles long and two and one-half miles wide, this is no ordinary lake, but an inland sea capable of quick and violent storms. At the surface, the Sea of Galilee is 680 feet below sea level. This makes it easy for the winds blowing across the land of Galilee to come rushing down the hillsides and stir up the sea, as if someone was stirring a large bowl of water with a spoon. Within a very short time a storm can arise. These storms do not always have rain and dark clouds, but can occur simply from the violent winds. Some waves have been reported as high as 20 feet in recent years. These storms have caught fishermen off guard and can become very dangerous.

Boats on the Sea of Galilee
In Jesus' day, the Galilean fishing boat was probably the most common. It had to be sturdy, built to stand up to the sudden storms that rushed down on the sea. The historian, Josephus, thought there might have been as many as 330 fishing boats on the Sea of Galilee in his day.

he right, dark clouds
er over the Sea of
lee, reminding us of
storm that Jesus stilled.
ve: a Judean mer-
t ship, similar but
ewhat larger than
e used on the Sea of
ee in Jesus' time.

403

Jesus Heals a Man with Demons

MATTHEW 8:28-34; MARK 5:1-20; LUKE 8:26-39

Synopsis

One day in Galilee was especially busy for Jesus. He had just returned from a teaching and healing tour when some religious leaders accused Him of working for Satan. Some of them demanded that He show them a miracle to prove that He was God's Son. Jesus refused, for He knew that even a miracle would not convince them. That same day, Jesus' mother and brothers came from Nazareth to take Him home. But He refused to go with them. Instead, He taught the people with parables. As soon as He finished, Jesus and His disciples crossed the Sea of Galilee in a boat. A storm arose, and Jesus showed His miracle-working power by stilling the storm. When He arrived on the other side of the sea, or lake, he healed a man who was possessed with demons.

Demons

Was the man Jesus healed insane? If not, why would he hide in tombs and rush out at people? At first glance, it would seem to people today that this must have been insanity. It was clearly not that, but that the man was inhabited by demons, evil personalities which controlled him.

Demons were (and still are) spiritual beings with intelligence and personality. Jesus spoke to demons which inhabited people, and they spoke to Jesus through the inhabited persons. Demons often left the persons they inhabited deranged mentally or sick in other ways and robbed them of their own personalities. Demons are on Satan's side in the great struggle between good and evil, God and Satan.

Demons apparently had unusual strength and caused that strength to pass on to the persons they inhabited. They often caused blindness (Matt. 12:22), dumbness (Matt. 9:32-33), defects and deformities (Luke 13:11-13), and suicidal tendencies (Mark 9:22).

Demons are thought to be fallen angels, once like other angels, but who willfully cast their lot with Satan instead of God. They are still at work in the world today, though in the time of Jesus they seemed to be more evident as personalities, perhaps because God's Son was there, and Satan sent his powerful forces to fight Him. Jesus had complete power over demons. When He spoke they had to obey Him.

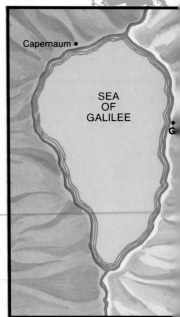

Legion

When Jesus asked the evil spirit his name, he replied that it was Legion for there were many demons present in the man. A Roman legion had 6,000 men in it, so the word legion meant "many," probably a large undetermined number in this case. When the demons went into the herd of pigs, however, they did inhabit 2,000 of them. This suggests that many demons were present.

404

The map shows the relationship between Capernaum and present-day Ein Gev, approximately at the location where Jesus healed the demon-possessed man. At the right of the map is a photo of the Ein Gev area today, with a sloping hill toward the sea. The cave at the bottom right is typical of large caves in the land. People often lived in such caves or buried their dead in them.

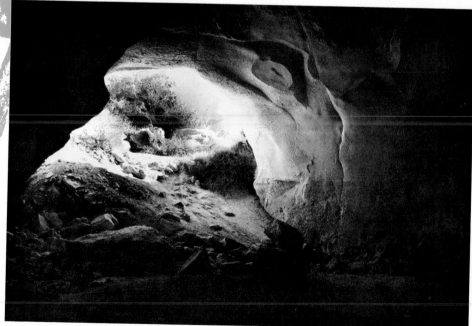

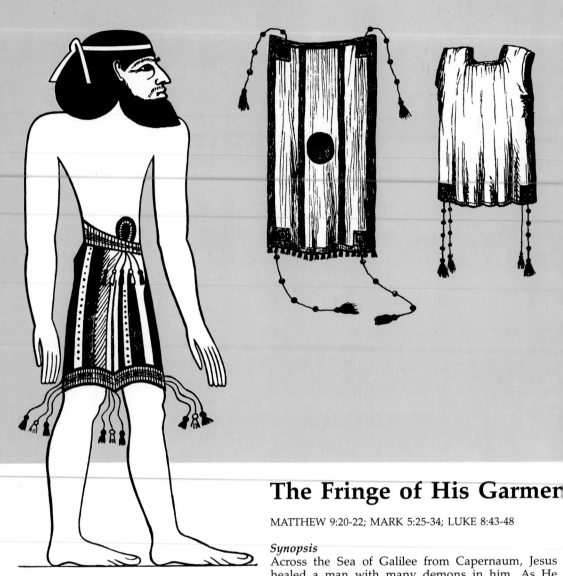

The Fringe of His Garment

MATTHEW 9:20-22; MARK 5:25-34; LUKE 8:43-48

Synopsis
Across the Sea of Galilee from Capernaum, Jesus healed a man with many demons in him. As He returned home, Jairus, ruler of the synagogue, sent for Him to heal his daughter. On the way to Jairus' house a woman touched Jesus' cloak and was healed.

The Issue of Blood
The woman had a chronic hemorrhage. She was not only physically sick, but ceremonially unclean according to the Law of Moses (Lev. 15:25-27). Luke, a physician, says she spent all her money on physicians, but none could heal her. The Talmud says physicians had at least 11 remedies for chronic hemorrhage, and she had evidently tried them all, but not one worked. The

Fringes on Garments

According to the Law of Moses, every Jewish man was supposed to wear a fringe or tassel at each of the four corners of his tallith, the rectangular or square outer garment worn over the upper part of the body. Two fringes hung at the bottom of the cloak, and two hung over the shoulders where the cloak folded over him.

The woman probably touched one of these fringes of Jesus' cloak as He passed through the crowd. The pictures at the left show three types of fringed garments worn in the Middle East. At the far left the man is wearing a lower garment with fringes hanging down. This is a drawing from early Jewish history, showing a captive Jewish man stripped of his upper garments. Styles in Jesus' time were somewhat different, as described below. The garment in the middle is the tallith, which Jesus probably wore on the upper part of His body. Another upper garment is shown at the right side. Each of these had fringes or tassels on them.

The Law of Moses requiring these fringes is recorded in Numbers 15:37-40 and Deuteronomy 22:12.

woman tried to be healed secretly by touching Jesus' cloak, but He wanted her to tell her story publicly.

Men's Clothing in Jesus' Time

How did Jesus and the other men of His time dress? Jesus had to be more careful than His neighbors for He was accepted as a rabbi, and rabbis were expected to dress well, even above their means. A man was expected to cover his head as a sign of respect to those he met. A man also wore an inner garment close to the skin, called a coat or tunic. The outer garment, his cloak, was wrapped at the waist with a wide cloth or leather belt called a girdle.

An upper garment, a goltha or tallith, was worn, with fringes or tassels at each corner. On the feet, he wore sandals.

Thus, Jesus was probably clothed with the close-fitting undergarments which went down to His feet, as teachers were supposed to do, plus the tallith with the four fringes as an upper and outer cloak or covering. On His feet were sandals. A cloth belt secured the clothing at His waist. His head was covered with the outer cloak, brought up over His head, or by a separate cloth wound around His head.

Jairus' Daughter

MATTHEW 9:18-19, 23-26; MARK 5:21-24, 35-43;
LUKE 8:40-42, 49-56

Synopsis
One day in Galilee, some of the religious leaders demanded a miracle from Jesus. He refused. Later that day, Jesus stilled a great storm on the Sea of Galilee, healed a man possessed with demons, and healed a woman at Capernaum who merely touched His cloak. Then He went to the home of the synagogue ruler, Jairus, and raised his daughter from the dead.

The Synagogue Ruler
Jairus was one of three synagogue rulers mentioned in the New Testament. The other two were Crispus (Acts 18:8) and Sosthenes (Acts 18:17).

The synagogue ruler was also called president of the synagogue. He was in charge of the service, including the reading of the Torah, the Scriptures, and the people who led the service. He also was responsible for the synagogue building, including maintenance and repair, and even the cleaning chores. As an official, he kept order during the service and made sure that people did not become unruly or do anything they should not do in a synagogue.

The synagogue was one of the most important places in town, the center of Jewish religious life in that community. This placed the synagogue ruler in a place of prominence, a civic leader as well as a religious leader. He was also an elder of the synagogue, so he sat in one of the seats reserved for important people at the services.

Paid Mourners
By the time Jesus reached Jairus' house, the paid mourners were there with the mournful cries of their profession. Paid mourners developed as a profession in Old Testament times, but continued into the time of Jesus. They did this as a career which usually passed from mother to daughter. They were almost always women. Their mourning was with dirges and eulogies, sometimes accompanied by flutes. (See Jer. 9:17-20; Amos 5:16; 2 Chron. 35:25.)

1. The Blind See
Jesus gave sight to blind people on four occasions (Matt. 9:27-31; 12:22; 20:29-34; Mark 8:22-26; John 9:1-8).

2. The Deaf Hear
Jesus healed a deaf mute (Mark 7:31-37).

3. The Speechless Speak
Twice He caused those without speech to speak again (Matt. 9:32-33; Mark 7:31-37).

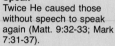

4. The Lame Walk
Jesus raised a paralyzed invalid at Bethesda (John 5:1-16).

5. The Maimed Are Whole Again
Jesus restored Malchus' ear which Peter had cut off (Luke 22:49-51); restored a withered hand (Matt. 12:9-13); and stopped chronic hemorrhage (Mark 5:25-34).

6. Lepers Are Cleansed
Lepers had no hope until Jesus came (Matt. 8:1-4; Luke 17:11-19).

7. The Dead Are Raised to New Life
Jesus raised Jairus' daughter (Matt. 9:18-19, 23-26); the widow's son at Nain (Luke 7:11-16); and Lazarus (John 11:1-46). He also cast out demons and did many other things that only God's Son could do.

Jesus' Miracles

Through His miracles, Jesus showed that He had power beyond that of an ordinary man. The laws of the natural world, which He had helped His Father create, were not boundaries for Him, only for mortal men.

Jesus' miracles prove that He is the Messiah, God's Son. Who else could raise the dead, cause instant healing of leprosy and injury, still a storm, and give sight to the blind?

It is strange that the very people who should have recognized that these miracles proved He is the Messiah failed to do so. Those closest to Him, even His own family in the early years, could not bring themselves to see these things. His hometown, Nazareth, rejected Him as Messiah, as did most of the religious leaders of His time.

Even when many of these people saw Him raise Lazarus from the dead after four days in the grave, they refused to see Him as God's Son. It seems that they never stopped to ask how He did these things. They only worried that by doing them, He put them and their jobs in danger with the Romans.

409

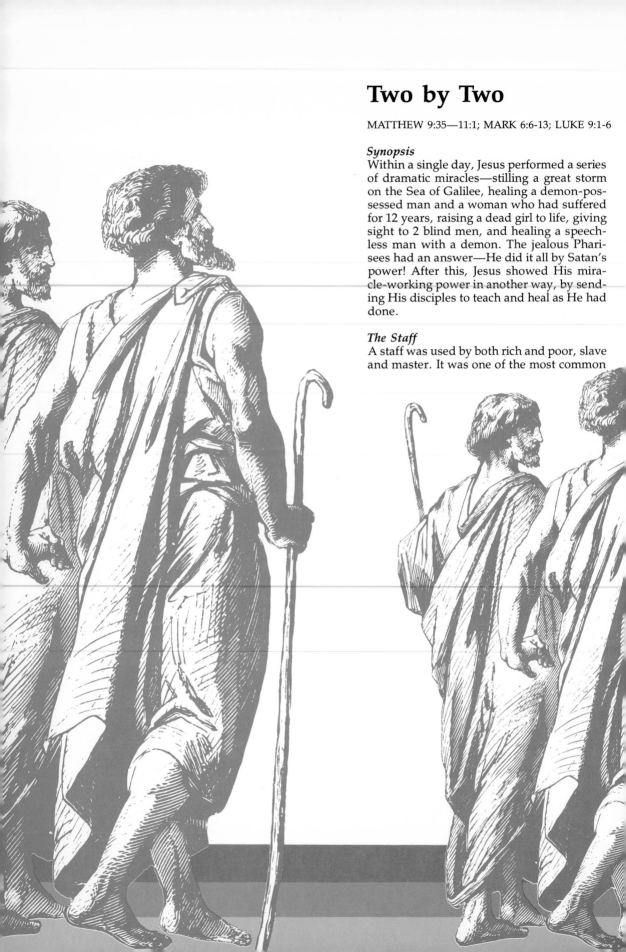

Two by Two

MATTHEW 9:35—11:1; MARK 6:6-13; LUKE 9:1-6

Synopsis
Within a single day, Jesus performed a series of dramatic miracles—stilling a great storm on the Sea of Galilee, healing a demon-possessed man and a woman who had suffered for 12 years, raising a dead girl to life, giving sight to 2 blind men, and healing a speechless man with a demon. The jealous Pharisees had an answer—He did it all by Satan's power! After this, Jesus showed His miracle-working power in another way, by sending His disciples to teach and heal as He had done.

The Staff
A staff was used by both rich and poor, slave and master. It was one of the most common

instruments in Bible times. It supported the poorest beggar, yet in the hands of a shepherd or a king, it represented the power over life and death.

Moses' staff, for example, was probably a crude shepherd's rod cut from the branch of a tree. But as shepherd of the people of Israel, Moses represented the power and authority of God, and his staff was his scepter, more powerful than Pharaoh's scepter.

A shepherd always carried a staff. He used it not only as a walking stick, but also as a rod to beat down the bushes where the flocks strayed, checking for snakes and lizards. When wild animals attacked, his staff became a weapon to protect the sheep.

Traveling in Bible times involved walking long distances on difficult roads. Most travelers carried a staff. It supported and protected them while they walked or rested.

Shaking the Dust Off One's Feet

When the Jews returned to Palestine from despised Gentile lands, they shook the dust from their feet. This symbolized breaking off all ties with the Gentiles they had been in contact with. Jesus' disciples shook the dust from their feet whenever a Jewish or Gentile city rejected them.

The Scrip

When the disciples went out two by two, Jesus told them not to take a "scrip," as some versions call it, or "bag," as others call it.

This little leather bag was simply a small travel bag for personal effects. Farmers, shepherds, pilgrims, and even beggars carried one, almost as a lady would carry a purse today. They kept small personal effects in it.

When David fought Goliath, he carried his five stones in one of these little bags. It was made from the skin of an animal, such as a goat, tanned by a simple process.

Jesus was simply telling His disciples that they were to carry nothing with them, to depend on others for their needs.

The drawing below, taken from an ancient monument, shows a scrip. The material is unknown, possibly woven strips of leather, papyrus or other fiber.

John Is Beheaded

MATTHEW 14:1-12; MARK 6:14-29;
LUKE 3:19-20; 9:7-9

Synopsis
Herod Antipas, ruler of Galilee, soon heard the news of Jesus' miracles. His first thought was that John the Baptist, whom he had beheaded, had risen from the dead!

Machaerus
The ruins of the fortress of Machaerus may still be seen on a high mountain east of the Dead Sea. Many believe this is the place where John the Baptist was imprisoned and beheaded by Herod Antipas. Herod probably placed John at Machaerus because it was far from Herod's capital at Tiberias and therefore far from Herod's wife, Herodias. She hated John and wanted him killed because John had criticized her for divorcing her husband, Herod Philip, and marrying her husband's brother, Herod Antipas. Because of John's popularity, Antipas did not want to kill him, and feared a riot if John was executed. But because of Antipas' foolish oath, no distance was far enough to save John's life.

Intermarriage of the Herods
The family of Herod the Great certainly did not follow the teachings of Jesus. Marriages took place within the family and brother fought against brother. Herod the Great had many wives. One of his sons, Herod Philip, married his own niece, Herodias. Herodias then left Philip and married his brother, Herod Antipas. Herod Philip II, another brother of Herod Philip, married his great-niece, Salome, who was the daughter of Herodias. It was Herodias and Salome who tricked Herod Antipas and forced the execution of John the Baptist. Bernice, daughter of Herod Agrippa I, married her uncle, Herod Chalcis. These intermarriages caused nothing but grief and strife to a family already riddled with greed and selfish pride.

Herod Antipas
As a son of Herod the Great, Herod Antipas played an important role in New Testament events. He inherited a portion of his father's kingdom and became tetrarch, ruler of Galilee and Perea. It was Herod Antipas who imprisoned and beheaded John the Baptist, and judged Jesus before He was

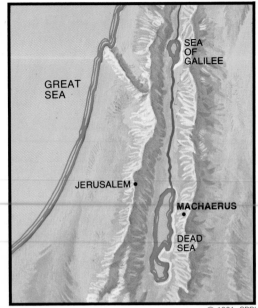

Coin of Herod Philip II, brother of Herod Antipas and son of Herod the Great. Philip's coins were struck at Caesarea and carried the portraits of the Roman emperors Augustus and Tiberius. Philip is mentioned in Luke 3:1. Machaerus, where John was beheaded, is shown on the above map.

crucified. And it was because of Jesus' trial that Antipas and Pilate, previously enemies, became fast friends.

In A.D. 6, Rome gave Antipas the distinguished title of Herod, impressive in the political and social society of the Roman world. He then married the daughter of Aretas, king of Arabia, probably for political reasons. But he soon left her for Herodias, the wife of his brother Herod Philip. Herodias had a brother, Herod Agrippa I, who had earned the title of king.

Herodias persuaded Antipas to go to Rome and ask for the title of king as well. Agrippa quickly brought charges against

Grandfather: Herod the Great
Murdered the babies of Bethlehem, hoping to kill the child Jesus (Matt. 2:1-18).

Uncle and second husband: Herod Antipas
Ruled Galilee during Jesus' lifetime. Judged Jesus before His crucifixion (Luke 23:7-12).

Father: Herod Aristobulus
Also father of Agrippa I and grandfather of "King Agrippa," Herod Agrippa II, before whom Paul went (Acts 25:13—26:32).

Uncle and son-in-law: Herod Philip II
Married Salome, even though he was her great-uncle.

Uncle and first husband: Herod Philip I
Father of Salome, whose dance brought about the death of John the Baptist (Mark 6:14-29).

Herodias and Her Family

Herodias was one of the Bible's evil women. Like Jezebel, in the time of the kings of Israel, she was an influential wife of a powerful and ruthless ruler.

Herodias came from a long line of evil relatives. The chart here shows her relationships to the various members of the Herod family.

Various members of Herodias' family were involved with people of the New Testament. They were the rulers of the land in which Jesus lived, and kept that rule from the time of Herod the Great's father, Antipater, in 48 B.C. until the death of Herod Agrippa II, who died around A.D. 100.

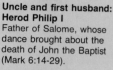

Brother: Herod Chalcis
Married Bernice, his niece.

Herodias

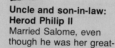

Brother: Herod Agrippa I
Father of "King Agrippa," Bernice, and Drusilla. Murdered the Apostle James (Acts 12:1-2), imprisoned Peter (Acts 12:3-11).

Nieces: Bernice and Drusilla
Bernice married Herod Chalcis, but was with Agrippa II when Paul appeared before him (Acts 25:13); Drusilla married Felix (Acts 24:24).

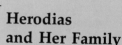

Daughter: Salome
The girl who danced before Antipas. Married her great-uncle, Herod Philip II.

Nephew: Herod Agrippa II
Paul appeared before "King" Agrippa (Acts 25:13—26:32).

Antipas and Antipas was exiled to what is France today. Agrippa, a friend of the emperor Caligula, was then given all the territories of Antipas.

Salome's Dance
After Moses led the Israelites out of Egypt, the people celebrated with a dance of joy and thanksgiving to the Lord. Salome's dance was completely opposite to a dance of worship. Prompted by her mother, Herodias, Salome's purpose was to entice Herod Antipas. An evil dance for evil reasons ended with his foolish vow that could not be broken. Herod Antipas was deceived by Salome's dance, a dance of death.

Top: Bible-time loaves of bread. They were round and flat. Barley bread was eaten by the poor, for barley was less expensive than wheat. Above, lower picture: baskets, drawn from Egyptian tomb paintings, perhaps similar to those in this incident.

Jesus Feeds 5,000

MATTHEW 14:13-21; MARK 6:30-44;
LUKE 9:10-17; JOHN 6:1-13

Synopsis
After Jesus performed a number of miracles in Galilee—stilling a storm, driving demons from a man, and even raising a girl from the dead—His fame spread everywhere. Even Herod Antipas, ruler of Galilee, was startled. He felt certain that Jesus was John the Baptist, risen from the dead. Now Jesus was about to perform a different sort of miracle—feeding a multitude with one boy's small lunch.

The 5,000
The crowd was really many more than 5,000. Only the men were numbered (Matt. 14:21). The total number may have been more than double that number, if there were more women and children than men. Thus the feeding of the 5,000 may actually have been the feeding of more than 10,000.

Bethsaida
Where was Bethsaida? Nobody knows for sure. Some point to a place just east of the Jordan River, and others point to a place a few miles west of Capernaum. The eastern location was in the territory ruled by Herod Philip. The western location was in the territory ruled by Herod Antipas, in Galilee.

We read in Luke 9:10 that the feeding of the 5,000 took place near Bethsaida. It was in a desert (lonely) place (Matt. 14:13). Then we read that Jesus and His disciples left this place and sailed across the Sea of Galilee to Capernaum (John 6:17).

It would seem that there were in Jesus' time two towns named Bethsaida. The one west of Capernaum, in Galilee, was located at the place shown on the map. The other, just east of the place where the Jordan River enters the Sea of Galilee, also went by the name Bethsaida Julias.

One tradition locates the feeding of the 5,000 at a place known today as Tabgha, the western Bethsaida. However, some scholars believe it happened at the eastern location. As was said earlier, nobody knows for sure.

When
From John 6:4 we learn that this was just before the time of the Passover, almost exactly one year before Jesus was crucified.

414

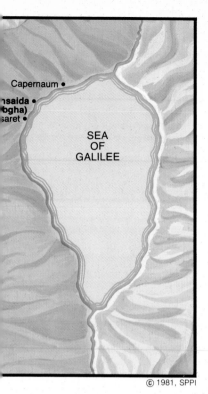

Capernaum •

nsaida
bgha)
saret •

SEA
OF
GALILEE

The map at the left shows the location of Bethsaida
west of Capernaum, one possible site of the miracle.
The picture below shows Tabgha, located at this
site, a traditional place for the feeding of the 5,000.
The fish mosaic above is part of an ancient church
at Tabgha.

Jesus Walks on the Sea

MATTHEW 14:24-33; MARK 6:47-52; JOHN 6:16-21

Synopsis
Only recently Jesus had healed a demon-possessed man, raised a girl from the dead, and fed more than 5,000 with one boy's small lunch. All Galilee was astir because of these miracles. What would He do next? The people did not have long to wait. On the same day that He fed the multitude, He walked on the waters of the sea. No one had ever done that before!

How Far?
From the place where the more than 5,000 were fed, the disciples rowed toward Capernaum, about six miles away. Some Bible versions say the disciples had rowed only 25-30 furlongs by early morning, probably rowing since sunset (John 6:19). A furlong was about 607 feet, so they had rowed only a little over 3 miles, slightly more than half of the way back home to Capernaum. Their progress was slow because they were going against the wind and waves.

The Fourth Watch

It seems likely that the disciples started across the sea, or lake, about sunset. They rowed until the fourth watch of the night (Matt. 14:25; Mark 6:48). The Romans, who ruled the land where Jesus lived at that time, divided the night into four "watches" of three hours each. Starting with 6 o'clock in the evening, the end of the first watch would have been 9 o'clock. The end of the second watch would have been midnight, the end of the third watch 3 o'clock in the morning, and the end of the fourth watch 6 o'clock in the morning. Using this system, one realizes that the disciples were still trying to row back to Capernaum sometime between 3 and 6 o'clock in the morning. Still they were only a little more than halfway home.

The Ship

A better translation is "boat." The Galilean fishing boats had both oars and sails. The wind on this particular night was too strong to use sails, or perhaps too uncertain. The Bible says "the wind was contrary" (Matt. 14:24, KJV). The boat was apparently large enough for at least 13 people, for it seems that all 12 disciples were in this boat (Matt. 14:22) and there was still room for Jesus to board (Mark 6:51).

Matthew and John

The story of Jesus walking on the water appears in three Gospels—Matthew, Mark, and John. Matthew and John were in the boat that night and saw it happen. Matthew had been a tax collector for the Romans while John had spent his life fishing on the sea. Mark would hear the story from others later and record it, primarily for Gentile readers.

This sunrise over the Sea of Galilee (below) reminds us of the early morning when Jesus returned to Capernaum with His disciples. They were awed by seeing Him walk on the water and seeing the high winds die down as He stepped into their boat. The view in this picture is from Tiberias.

The map at the far right shows the relationship of Capernaum and the plain of Gennesaret. This plain is pictured at the upper right, looking toward the south. Note the fertile crops there today.

Healing at Gennesaret

MATTHEW 14:34-36; MARK 6:53-56

Synopsis
Crowds followed Jesus everywhere, hoping that He would heal, feed, teach, or give them something He had given others. When He walked along the road, they followed. When He climbed into the hills, they went with Him. And even when He crossed the sea to Gennesaret, they would not let Him go alone.

Gennesaret
In Jesus' time Gennesaret was the name of the fertile plain on the west side of the Sea of Galilee, as well as the name of a village in that region. The sea itself was sometimes called the Sea of Gennesaret or the Lake of Gennesaret (Luke 5:1).

The plain lies between Capernaum and Magdala, running north and south along the western coast of the Sea of Galilee. It is about four miles long and two miles wide.

In Jesus' time this plain was the garden spot of the land. Streams from the surrounding hills watered the rich land. With the warm climate, it was an ideal agricultural area, where trees and flowers added beauty to the grapes, olives, wheat, melons, figs, rice, and vegetables. Some called the area a paradise, the Garden of God.

Jesus' Reputation
When Jesus landed in Gennesaret, the people who saw Him knew that He had the power to heal. His reputation as a miracle healer had gone before Him to this place. It is interesting to notice that the people did not run to Jesus themselves, but sent word immediately to the sick people of the area, so that all of the sick might come for healing. This was an unselfish act on their part.

The Border of His Garment

These people must have heard about the woman who was healed by touching the fringe of Jesus' cloak (Matt. 9:20-21). Somehow they knew that they would be healed if only they touched this fringe, instead of touching Jesus Himself.

Beds

The people carried their sick to Jesus on their "beds." When we think of modern beds with innersprings and mattresses, as well as headboards and footboards, this seems strange. But the beds of Jesus' time were not like ours at all.

The beds on which these people carried their sick were more like mats of woven fabric or other type of cloth. It was easier to carry a person on this mat than without it.

Marketplaces

The people of Gennesaret laid their sick in the marketplaces, the bazaars of that time where people brought their goods to sell, came to hire laborers, and to talk together.

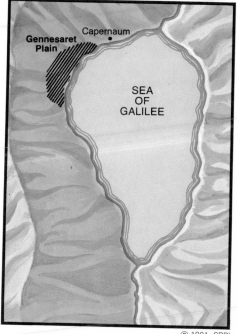

419

The Syrophoenician Woman

MATTHEW 15:21-28; MARK 7:24-30

Synopsis

The crowds had seen Jesus perform miracles that no mere man could perform. He had healed the sick, given sight to the blind, and even raised the dead. They had heard of other miracles from His disciples—stilling a storm and walking on water. Of all the miracles, feeding over 5,000 with a small lunch caught their attention the most. Food was scarce, and here was a man who could feed them with almost nothing. He must become their king, not because He was the Messiah, but because He supplied food. Jesus would have none of this. He left Galilee and traveled north to the region of Tyre and Sidon.

At the right are three silver Phoenician coins showing Astarte, a goddess commonly worshiped by the people of Tyre and Sidon. The upper right coin shows the head of Astarte. The upper left coin shows Astarte in a vehicle. The coin in the center is Astarte at Tyre.

420

The Region of Tyre and Sidon

In Jesus' time, the territory surrounding the cities of Tyre and Sidon was inhabited mostly by Phoenician people, though a number of Jewish communities were scattered throughout. The home where Jesus stayed was probably Jewish (Mark 7:24). But the woman who came for Jesus' help was a Gentile.

Galilee in Jesus' time was ruled by Herod Antipas, under the control of the Roman emperor. Herod at this time was involved in the execution of John the Baptist and the problems that surrounded that execution. The territory around Tyre and Sidon was under the rule of the proconsul of Syria, who was governed by the Roman emperor.

Jesus left Galilee at this time for several reasons. His public miracles had created quite a stir, so much that the people wanted to make Him king, not because of the miracles, but because He had fed them. Crowds were swarming around Jesus daily. He needed to take His disciples away to a lonely place, where He could train them. Also, it was important to show them that He reached out to include Gentiles in His love and help too.

The Syrophoenician Woman

The woman who came to Jesus for help was called Syrophoenician (Mark 7:26), Greek (Mark 7:26), and Canaanite (Matt. 15:22, TEV). "Greek" was a way of saying she was a Gentile, not a Jew. "Syrophoenician" meant she was Phoenician by race, living in the region of Syria. "Canaanite" was an Old Testament term for the people who lived here.

Below: a map shows the possible route Jesus followed through the regions of Tyre and Sidon and then to the north and east of the Sea of Galilee. At the left is a silver coin which boasts that Tyre is the "mother of the Sidonians." Jesus may not have actually visited the cities of Tyre and Sidon, but the countryside nearby.

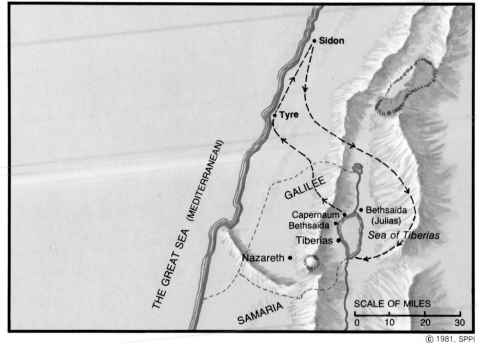

421

Jesus Heals a Deaf and Dumb Man

MATTHEW 15:29-31; MARK 7:31-37

Synopsis
With a small lunch Jesus fed a great multitude in Galilee. They wanted to make Him king, not because of the miracle, but because of the food! But Jesus left Galilee and went to the region of Tyre and Sidon, where He healed the daughter of a Gentile woman, then on to the north and east of the Sea of Galilee, where He healed a man who was deaf and dumb.

The Lands Where Jesus Walked
Throughout the life of Jesus, a number of geographical names appear—territories through which He walked. His hometowns, Nazareth and Capernaum, were in Galilee. The regions of Tyre and Sidon are mentioned in the preceding story. This one speaks of the Decapolis. In other places in the life of Jesus, Judea, Perea, Samaria, and Idumea are mentioned. The following tells briefly how these regions appeared politically and what they were.

The Kingdom of Herod the Great
When Jesus was born, Herod the Great ruled the land. His kingdom included territories such as Judea, Idumea, Samaria, Perea, Galilee, and the region east of the Sea of Galilee. But when Herod the Great died, his kingdom was divided.

Herod Antipas ruled Galilee and Perea. Herod Philip ruled a territory east of the Sea of Galilee. Archelaus ruled Judea and Idumea. These three sons quarreled and Archelaus was sent into exile. His territory, Judea and Idumea, was placed under the control of a procurator. When Jesus died, Pontius Pilate was procurator of these territories.

Galilee
Most of Jesus' early ministry was in Galilee. It included such towns as Cana, Nazareth, Capernaum, Magdala, Korazin, and Herod's capital, Tiberias. Galilee was part of the territory ruled by Herod Antipas, whom Jesus called "that fox." He was the son of Herod the Great. Herod Antipas beheaded John the Baptist and later took part in judging Jesus.

Galilee is a region of rolling hills, plus some large plains. The Sea of Galilee is the focal point of the region.

Joseph and Mary lived in Galilee before Jesus was born. Then they went to Bethlehem, in Judea, to enroll in Caesar's census. Next they moved to Egypt, then back to their hometown Nazareth, in Galilee. Here Jesus lived till He was rejected. Then He moved to Capernaum, also in Galilee.

Judea
Jerusalem and Bethlehem were in Judea, a region of hills high enough to be called "mountains." Jerusalem, for example, is in mountains about 3,000 feet above sea level, compared with Jesus' home in Capernaum, below sea level. When Jesus was born, Judea was ruled by Herod the Great, who killed the babies of Bethlehem in an effort to kill the baby Jesus. After this Herod died, his son Archelaus ruled a while; then came a line of procurators, including Pontius Pilate.

Perea
Perea was the territory east of the Jordan River, across from Samaria and Judea. It was also ruled by Herod Antipas. Jesus worked here before His last week in Jerusalem.

Samaria
Between Galilee and Judea was a region with "mixed people," part Jewish and part foreigners, brought in during the Exile. It was also ruled by procurators during Jesus' life on earth. Most Jews did not travel through Samaria, for they hated these "foreigners."

A Visit to Magdala

MATTHEW 15:39—16:4; MARK 8:10-12

Synopsis

The people of Galilee wanted to make Jesus king, not because He could lead them to God, but because He gave them food when He fed over 5,000. Jesus left Galilee for a while, ministering to those in other places. When He returned, He visited Magdala.

Magdala

Magdala is remembered most as the home of Mary Magdalene, who followed Jesus faithfully. The town's location is not completely certain, but it is thought to be a small village named Mejdel, on the western shore of the Sea of Galilee.

Magdala apparently was known by two other names—Magadan and Dalmanutha (Matt. 15:39; Mark 8:10). It was about three miles north of Tiberias, where Herod Antipas, ruler of Galilee, had his capital.

The name Magdala is associated with the word "migdol," which meant "a tower."

Weather Signs, Signs from Heaven

Rabbis of Jesus' time believed that certain miracles could be performed by demons and false gods. These were miracles of an earthly nature that did not come down from the heavens. They believed that miracles which came down out of the heavens were certainly from God.

Examples of miracles from the heavens were: (1) when the sun and moon stood still for Joshua; (2) when thunder came to Samuel's rescue; (3) manna which came from heaven to feed Moses and his people.

Jesus' miracles did not call down such things from heaven. They were of a person-to-person nature—healing the sick, giving sight to the blind, even raising dead persons.

Thus the religious leaders were asking Jesus to "prove" His miracles were from God by calling down something from the heavens.

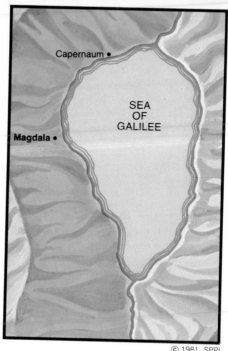

At the upper left: a view of the shore of the Sea of Galilee, looking north from Magdala. Above: the scene is from about the same location, but looking toward the southeast. The map at the right shows the approximate location of the Magdala of Jesus' time.

425

Jesus Heals
at Bethsaida

MATTHEW 16:5-12; MARK 8:13-26

Synopsis
Who can heal the sick, raise the dead, still a storm, walk on water, and perform amazing miracles of many sorts? Who else but God and His Son! But the Pharisees and Sadducees could not accept Jesus as God's Son. They had seen and heard of His miracles, but still they would not believe. It seemed that no miracle could be great enough to convince them that He was God's Son, not even healing a blind man at Bethsaida.

Bethsaida
This seems to be Bethsaida Julias, on the eastern side of the Jordan River as it enters the Sea of Galilee, not the Bethsaida west of Capernaum.

Bread
Loaves of bread were flat, like extra-thick pancakes. They were also of a thicker consistency than modern bread, more like that of pancakes.

Leaven
Whenever bread was made, a piece of the sour or fermented dough was kept apart. This leaven, as it was called, was placed in the next batch of dough to cause it to ferment and rise. Leaven served the same purpose as yeast does today.

The Bible also uses the word leaven to mean an influence which something has on people. For example, in this incident, Jesus warned the disciples to beware of the leaven of the Pharisees and Sadducees. By this, He meant to beware of their teachings, which may have seemed religious, but did not honor God.

The Blind
In Jesus' time blind people lived hopeless lives. Not only were they handicapped by

Bethsaida Julias was located in this area above, where the Jordan River enters the Sea of Galilee. In Jesus' time, this area east of the Jordan was ruled by Herod Philip. Right: leading the blind, common then and now.

their blindness, but were unable to find work to support themselves. A blind person was forced to become a beggar, depending on donations to feed himself and his family.

Blindness was common in Jesus' time, from many causes, including unsanitary conditions, bright sunlight, fly-carried disease from person to person and from waste to people, blowing sand, venereal diseases, accidents, and war injuries.

Jobs were scarce for strong, healthy men, and almost completely unavailable to the blind. Blindness was also viewed as a result of sin, either by the blind person or by his parents. Sometimes this was true, as in the case of blindness from venereal diseases.

Many people had more than one handicap, such as being both blind and deaf, or deaf and speechless, or blind and crippled.

427

Above: one of the numerous waterfalls at Caesarea Philippi; some are much higher. One source of the Jordan River is here, adding a refreshing touch to the cool mountain air.

A Visit to Caesarea Philippi

MATTHEW 16:13-20; MARK 8:27-30; LUKE 9:18-21

Synopsis
For some time Jesus had performed numerous miracles in Galilee, His home territory. But now He was traveling to other places—the regions of Tyre and Sidon, into the cities of the Decapolis, including Caesarea Philippi.

Caesarea Philippi–Location
The map at the upper right shows the location and approximate distance from Capernaum, where Jesus lived, to Caesarea Philippi, northeast of Capernaum. The distance was about 30-40 miles, depending on the route traveled, but it lay in much different land than Capernaum.

Capernaum, on the shore of the Sea of Galilee, was about 680 feet below sea level. Caesarea Philippi was built in the high foothills of Mount Hermon, at a height of about 1,150 feet above sea level. Rising to the north and east, Mount Hermon reached an elevation of about 9,100 feet. When the heat of summer baked Capernaum, Caesarea Philippi enjoyed a much lower temperature, plus mountain breezes which came down from snow-capped Mount Hermon. It must have been a lovely retreat for Jesus and His disciples as He went apart from the crowds for a time of training, something like an original summer Bible conference, with Jesus as the teacher!

Caesarea Philippi–The Place
After the death of Herod the Great, who killed all male babies of Bethlehem in an effort to kill the baby Jesus, Herod's son Philip was made "tetrarch," and placed over the territory in which Caesarea Philippi was located. Philip named the city Caesarea to honor his emperor, Caesar, but added the name Philippi to distinguish the city from the Caesarea on the western coast.

Caesarea Philippi was one of the 10 towns known as the Decapolis.

The Decapolis
The 10 towns of the Decapolis formed an alliance, probably for mutual protection, for they were quite scattered in a territory which bordered on hostile country to the east. Under Alexander the Great, Greek influence moved into the area, and with it, political independence for cities such as these. Thus, the cities and their surrounding territories

428

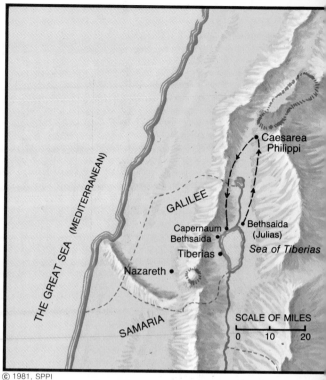

© 1981, SPPI

At the left is a view of the foothills of Mount Hermon, where Caesarea Philippi was located. The ancient city of Dan, founded during the time of the Judges, was only a short distance to the west.

were like small kingdoms, but allied for their protection.

In the time of Jesus, the Decapolis was flourishing, with temples and amphitheaters, art, literature, and games. It was a Gentile world on the doorstep of Galilee. The prodigal son may have gone into such a Gentile world for his taste of loose living, breaking with his Jewish heritage. This is seen in the fact that he took care of pigs, which were eaten only by Gentiles.

Time
Jesus' visit to Caesarea may have been in the heat of summer. The training of the 12 disciples began before Passover (John 6:4), in the spring, and continued till the feast of Taber-nacles (John 7:2) in the autumn. This incident took place somewhere in the center of that training period.

Son of Man
Jesus spoke often of Himself as the "Son of man." What did He mean? No one is completely certain, but it seems that He meant: (1) the Son of God in human form, not merely anyone descended from man; (2) thus, He was unique, the only One who was both God and man, God in heaven and man on earth; (3) as God and man both, He was the bridge between the two, God redeeming man through His Son; and (4) He is Lord over mankind, who must ultimately bow before Him and confess Him as Lord.

429

Booths such as those above were built of tree branches, usually from palm, myrtle, willow, or olive. They were temporary shelters from the scorching sun for those who camped for a few days. People built them on their houses for the feast of Booths or Tabernacles. Mount Tabor is in the top photo below; Mount Hermon is in the bottom photo.

The Transfiguration

MATTHEW 17:1-8; MARK 9:2-8; LUKE 9:28-36

Synopsis

After performing many miracles in Galilee, Jesus went into the surrounding territories—the region of Tyre and Sidon, the territory where the 10 cities known as the Decapolis were located, and specifically into the area of Caesarea Philippi. On a high mountain one day, He was transfigured, changed in appearance, as the glory of God shone through Him.

Transfiguration—Meaning

What happened when Jesus was transfigured? What did this term mean? Three things happened as part of the transfiguration of Jesus: (1) Jesus' appearance changed, so that for a short time He looked different; (2) Moses and Elijah talked with Jesus, as God brought personalities back from the dead to communicate with someone on

430

earth; and (3) God's voice spoke from heaven, stating that Jesus is His Son. All three of these signs indicated that Jesus is the Messiah, God's Son. God used many ways to show us that Jesus is His Son—His spoken word at Jesus' baptism and transfiguration; His written Word, the Bible; Jesus' own words; the testimony of those who walked with Him for three years; His miracles; His resurrection.

Where?

Where was Jesus transfigured? Some say on Mount Tabor; others say on Mount Hermon. He was near Mount Hermon when Peter gave his "great confession" that Jesus is the Messiah. But as early as the fourth century A.D., a tradition pointed to Mount Tabor, and within the next 200 years, three churches were built on its summit to commemorate the Transfiguration.

However, it has since been learned that a fortified city occupied the top of Mount Tabor in Jesus' time, so this would not have been a likely place for this event. Scholars think Mount Hermon, near Caesarea Philippi, was where this event took place.

When?

Jesus' transfiguration was about six days after the incident at Caesarea Philippi. Thus it was still summer or early autumn.

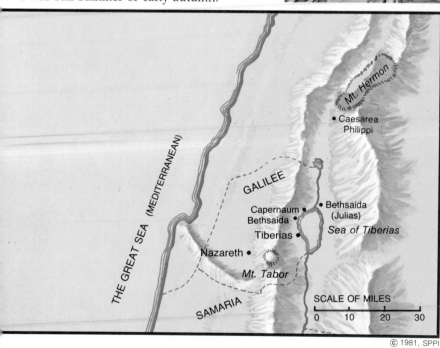

© 1981, SPPI

431

Silver Shekel of the First Revolt

Silver Half-Shekel of the First Revolt

A Fish with Tax Money

MATTHEW 17:24-27

Synopsis
Jesus had returned to Capernaum at last after traveling through a number of regions surrounding Galilee. It must have been time to pay taxes, for Jesus sent Peter on an unusual mission to get the money.

Taxes in Bible Times
Taxes are not new. They are as old as governments, for kings and their officials have long used a system of taxes to gather the money for their support while they run the affairs of the land. In Bible times there were many kinds of taxes. Here are a few: (1) taxes on land, (2) customs taxes on goods which went through a country on a trade route, (3) export and import taxes at seaports, (4) taxes on crops grown in fields, (5) income taxes, (6) road taxes, (7) taxes on vehicles, (8) taxes on animals, (9) salt tax, (10) taxes on the sale or transfer of property. Many of these sound quite modern!

In addition, Jewish people were taxed to keep up the temple. This was the tax to which Jesus referred. The temple tax, which every Jewish male in the world was supposed to pay, was one-half shekel per year.

The silver coins pictured above were shekels and half-shekels, coined during the time when the Jewish people revolted against Rome in A.D. 66-70, several years after the crucifixion, and a short time after Paul's final journey to Rome. These Jewish coins were not

available for temple taxes in Jesus' time. The coins which were probably used during the time of Jesus were the tetradrachms of Tyre, or of other places, the coins which Judas received when he betrayed Jesus.

Fishing in Jesus' Time

Jesus told Peter to fish with a hook (Matt. 17:27). The pictures above show scenes from a much earlier time in Egypt, when men were fishing with hooks and poles. The man at the top has caught one. In addition to fishing with hook, line, and pole, fishermen in Jesus' time also used three types of nets, including these two:

The cast net was a circular one which a fisherman skillfully threw on the water. Around the edges were weights which quickly sank into the water, taking the net over the fish below. A line, attached to the center of the net, was drawn by the fisherman, so that the net closed tightly around the fish. With that, he could draw the netted fish to him.

The draw net was a long rectangular net, with weights along the bottom. It was pulled between two boats, with the bottom of the net below the water and the top floating on top of the water. As the two ends of the net were drawn together the fish were trapped in the closing circle made by the net. At last the net closed in on the fish, trapping them for the catch.

Where?

Jesus told Peter to fish in the sea. This was obviously the Sea of Galilee, for they were at Capernaum. Actually this "sea" is, and was, a large lake fed by the Jordan River.

For some time, people thought the silver shekel and half-shekel pictured at the upper left were coined by Simon Maccabeus. Lately, however, scholars think they were coined about A.D. 66-70, when the Jewish people revolted against the Romans, who in turn destroyed Jerusalem. The center drawing shows a fisherman casting a cast net. At the right are two Egyptian scenes, taken from paintings much earlier than the time of Jesus. They show Egyptian fishermen using hook, line, and pole to fish. The water in the bottom picture is symbolic, perhaps representing a formal pool.

433

Who Is Greatest?

MATTHEW 18:1-6; MARK 9:33-37; LUKE 9:46-48

Synopsis

Jesus had performed miracles that no one had ever done before—stilling a storm, healing blind people, driving out demons, feeding a multitude with a small lunch, and walking on water. He had taken the Gospel to regions surrounding Galilee. The disciples had seen all these things. But suddenly miracles were not uppermost in their minds. This day they were more concerned about who would be first in Jesus' new kingdom.

The Kingdom

Jesus' kingdom is more than heaven. It is wherever He is. Thus His kingdom reaches into earth, and even into our hearts, minds, and souls. Many who followed Jesus thought His kingdom would be Israel, and He would be the new king who would free the people from the Romans.

The Romans

Many years before, the people of Israel were free, ruling their own land. Under King David and King Solomon, almost a thousand years before the time of Jesus, Israel was at its peak, one of the most powerful nations of the Middle East.

But during the latter part of Solomon's reign, he let his foreign wives build altars to pagan gods. Israel's people began to worship these gods, turning from the true God who had freed them from slavery in Egypt and had given them this Promised Land.

The centuries passed, with Israel growing weaker with each evil king who ruled. The nation divided shortly after Solomon's death and never united again before it was carried at last into exile in Assyria and Babylon. This happened between 722-586 B.C.

During this time the Assyrians grew weaker and the Babylonians took over as the world power. During the time of Daniel they were conquered by the Persians, so the land became part of the Persian Empire. In 334-331 B.C. it became part of the Greek (Macedonian) Empire. (Greek kings called Ptolemies ruled the land then from about 323-198 B.C., and another group of Greeks, called Seleucids, ruled from 198-165 B.C.) Then the Jews ruled their land again, from 165-63 B.C., when it became part of the Roman Empire, as it was in Jesus' time.

Millstones

Jesus said that whoever would offend a little child (cause him to be led astray) would be better off if he had a millstone tied about his neck and was thrown into the deep sea. Millstones were commonly used in Jesus' time, and were very heavy.

Four types are pictured at the left. The one at the top was powered by two people, one pushing against each side of the pole, moving the millstone around the center pole, grinding as it moved.

The type in the center was a small hand mill. One or two people, usually women, turned the handle around. The one whose right hand was free put in the grain.

Another hand mill is at the lower left. The bottom half is seen, then the top with it. Grain was ground between the two parts.

The fourth type was large, powered by an animal, such as an ox (lower right).

The Two Debtors

MATTHEW 18:15-35

Synopsis

Jesus' ministry in Galilee had proved beyond a doubt that He is God's Son. He had healed the sick, given sight to the blind, and even raised the dead. Transfigured before His three closest disciples, Jesus was proclaimed God's Son by a voice from heaven. Now that the disciples knew that He would someday set up a kingdom, they quarreled about who would be the greatest in that kingdom. Not only that, Jesus' disciples had forbidden another man from casting out demons in Jesus' name because he was not part of their group. Jesus responded to the disciples with some parables, including one about two debtors. This parable told of forgiving both great and small things.

Debts and Debtors

In Bible times, a person was in serious trouble if he could not pay back money that he owed. The creditor, the person lending the money, was allowed to seize the debtor and force him to work until the debt was paid off. He could keep the debtor in chains, and even throw him into prison. The creditor also had the option of selling the debtor as a slave, taking away his house and personal belongings, or selling his wife and children into slavery.

A debtor was thrown into prison with the hope that he might have some secret property he would sell to pay off the debt. If he did not, the creditor hoped that friends or relatives would quickly pay off the debt. If they could not, the debtor might have to spend the rest of his life in prison.

Talents . . .

and Other Money in Jesus' Time

Gold and silver, and to a lesser degree other metals such as copper, have always been a measure of wealth. People far back into early history have used precious metals as an exchange of value. However, it was not until the seventh century B.C. that this metal was molded into the shape of coins. Rulers began to like the idea of stamping their own images on the coins, often with some symbol of their power on the back.

The Lydians were the first to make coins, about the seventh century B.C. They were conquered by the Persians, who made their own coins. The Greeks came into power and they followed with silver tetradrachms with owls on the back.

However, the Jewish people had no coins until the time of their captivity in 587 B.C. Thus Bible references to money referred to weights of metal, in ingots or jewelry. But by the time of Jesus, there were numerous coins used by the Jews, including some which they minted before the Romans conquered them.

LEPTON
Jewish coin "mite" in Mark 12:42; Luke 21:2, KJV = 1/8¢.

FARTHING
or assarion Roman copper coin (Matt. 10:29; Luke 12:6, KJV) = 8 leptons or 1¢.

DENARIUS
Roman silver coin—"penny" in Matthew 22:19, KJV— a day's wages = 16 farthings or 16¢.

TALENT
Not an actual coin, but a value of money (Matt. 18:24) = 60 minas or 6,000 denarii or $960.

SHEKEL
Jewish coin, temple taxes paid with shekels = 4 denarii or 64¢.

MINA
"Pound" in Luke 19:12-26, KJV = 100 denarii or 100 drachma or $16.

Note: it is impossible to fix an actual value on a Bible-time coin. The values expressed above are for comparison with each other only. Values of gold and silver change constantly and dramatically.

The above is a copper coin ("mite" in the KJV Bible, but often called a lepton) of Archelaus.

An assarion of Chios, a Greek isle. Note "farthing" at the left, for value.

A denarius of Tiberius, with the head of the emperor on the front and a seated female figure on the back.

The copper shekel of Simon Maccabeus, a Jewish coin. On the front is a vase with Hebrew which says "for the liberation of Zion." On the back is a palm tree or sheaf with "year four."

437

The Pool of Siloam

JOHN 9:1-41

Above: a model of the Pool of Siloam in Jesus' time. Above left the Pool of Siloam today. The map at the right shows the Pool of Siloam in relationship to the temple and other important sites in the Jerusalem of Jesus' time.

Synopsis

In Galilee, where He had lived since a child, Jesus performed many miracles to show that He is truly God's Son. He healed the sick, gave sight to the blind, drove out demons, fed over 5,000 with a small lunch, walked on water, and stilled a storm. He had been transfigured before three of His disciples, with God's voice confirming that He is indeed the Messiah, His Son. Now Jesus was leaving Galilee. From this time on, His ministry would focus in Jerusalem and in the surrounding regions of Judea and Perea. Before long, He would face the Cross. In the meantime, people from Jerusalem, Judea, and Perea would see His miracles, such as the one near the Pool of Siloam.

The Pool of Siloam

Just south of Jerusalem lies the Gihon Spring. Seven hundred years before the time of Christ, King Hezekiah was being threatened by the invasion of King Sennacherib and the Assyrians. To prepare for the attack, Hezekiah built a water tunnel which traveled from the Gihon Spring, beneath the city walls, and into Jerusalem. In this way, the city would have plenty of water even if Sennacherib sur-

438

rounded the city for months. The place where the water tunnel emptied into the city was called the Pool of Siloam. Here, within the safety of the city walls, the people came to draw water with their pots and animal skins. In Jesus' time, the pool must have been a bathing place as well, for Jesus told a blind man to wash there in order to receive his sight.

Other Pools of Jerusalem

Before the age of modern plumbing, the city of Jerusalem had a big water problem. There was little rainfall, and the city was many miles from the salty Mediterranean Sea to the west and the Jordan River to the east. However, there were springs in the area, and the Israelites solved their problem by building tunnels or aqueducts to channel this water into Jerusalem, where large pools were built to collect the water.

One of these pools is known as the Towers' Pool, because it is located just outside the towers of Herod's citadel. Built by Herod the Great, it is fed by a spring located just south of Bethlehem. The aqueduct first carried the water through Herod's palace, and then emptied into the pool.

The Pool of Israel was also constructed by Herod the Great, when he built the temple. The walls of the temple platform served as a dam, blocking the path of the Bezetha Brook. As a result, a pool of water collected just outside of the temple. It was still used into the 20th century when it was found to be contaminated and had to be filled.

The Pool of Bethesda is said to have been near the Jerusalem sheep market. It was used to wash the sheep that were to be sacrificed at the temple. It was also the place where Jesus healed a man who had been sick for 38 years (John 5:1-10).

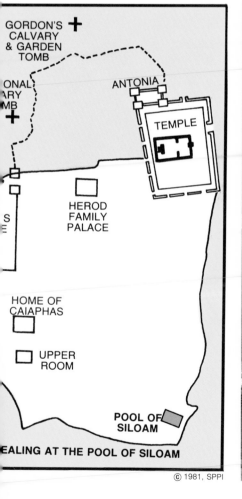

GORDON'S CALVARY & GARDEN TOMB

ONAL ARY MB

ANTONIA

TEMPLE

HEROD FAMILY PALACE

S E

HOME OF CAIAPHAS

UPPER ROOM

POOL OF SILOAM

EALING AT THE POOL OF SILOAM

© 1981, SPPI

The Good Shepherd

JOHN 10:1-21

Synopsis

For about two years, Jesus had ministered in Galilee, healing and performing other miracles which no mere man could do. Now He moved on to Judea and Perea, regions surrounding Jerusalem, where other people would see His miracles. A man who was born blind was healed at the Pool of Siloam. The religious leaders were angered by this, for it was another reason for people to recognize Jesus as the Messiah, God's Son. With their anger and hostility toward Him as a backdrop, Jesus told how He, the Good Shepherd, would die for His sheep.

Qualities of a Good Shepherd

A good shepherd is familiar with each one of his sheep. He knows which ones may wander and which ones need special care. Day and night the shepherd watches over his flock and will risk his own life to protect them. If a single sheep gets lost, the shepherd will ask someone else to watch over the flock while he searches for it.

A good shepherd always leads his sheep and never drives them. Every day he finds food and water and every night he leads them back to the safety of the sheepfold. Knowing this, it is easy to see why Jesus is called the Good Shepherd.

The Sheepfold

Sheep are helpless animals. They may wander aimlessly about the countryside, unable to defend themselves. For this reason, shepherds built sheepfolds.

A sheepfold was a place of shelter for the sheep. A simple sheepfold was built of four walls made of stones gathered from the fields. The walls were just high enough to keep wild animals out. Some walls had thorns laid along the top, to discourage thieves.

A single entrance led into the fold, and a shepherd could be found there guarding his sheep. Often many shepherds used the same sheepfold and took turns guarding the entrance. The shepherds did not worry about mixing their sheep together, because each sheep knew its own shepherd's call, usually a loud piercing cry.

440

Above: a present-day shepherd leads his sheep across the fields near Beersheba. Note how the sheep follow him in single file. Right: a shepherd with his sheep. Below: a shepherd leads his sheep toward the door of the sheepfold.

441

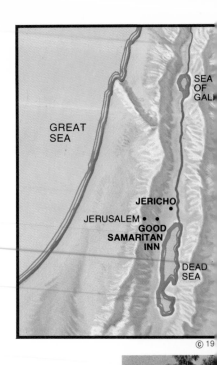

© 19

The Good Samaritan

LUKE 10:25-37

Synopsis
After about two years of ministry in Galilee, Jesus began to teach and work miracles in Judea and Perea, territories near Jerusalem. After healing a blind man near the Pool of Siloam, Jesus taught how He, the Good Shepherd, would be killed for His sheep. An expert on the Law of Moses asked Jesus about eternal life, and He answered with a parable about a Samaritan who helped an injured traveler.

Samaria and the Samaritans
Who were the Samaritans? Little is known about their origin and there is much confusion about their history. Most, including the Israelites, believe that the Samaritans began when King Sargon and the Assyrians captured the city of Samaria in 721 B.C. and deported the inhabitants, including thousands of Israelites. Assyria then repopulated the region of Samaria with captured foreigners from other lands. These foreigners intermarried with the Israelites who were left in Samaria. Years later, when the exiled Israelites returned to Samaria, they could not accept this mixed race as true Israelites. They called them *Cuthim* or *Samaritans*. As a result, an intense hatred developed between the Samaritans and the Jews.

442

But the Samaritans claimed that their race had never intermarried with foreigners. They insisted that they began when Joshua gathered the 12 tribes together at Mount Gerizim and Mount Ebal, and that Moses hoped the tabernacle would be built on Mount Gerizim. The Jews, of course, considered this remark as heresy because they believed the temple at Jerusalem was the sanctuary of God. These opposing beliefs served only to deepen their hatred for each other.

Bible-time Inns

The inn where the Good Samaritan stopped with the wounded man was by no means luxurious. The only thing it offered was protection from the dangers of traveling by night. In most cases, travelers had to supply their own food and sleeping pads. Some inns did not even have innkeepers, but were simply empty buildings surrounded by high walls with a well in the courtyard. The inn where the Good Samaritan stopped may have been a Greek type of inn. Here a traveler felt a bit closer to home, for the innkeeper acted more as a host, offering both food and entertainment.

The Jericho Road

Known as "The Way of Blood," the Jericho Road winds its way down from Jerusalem to Jericho. The steep descent is a rugged and rocky pass, well suited to the wiles of criminals and thieves. The road was a busy one, especially in the winter when travelers came from the cold hills of Jerusalem (2,500 feet above sea level), to the warm climate and beautiful springs of Jericho (800 feet below sea level). Why did Jesus mention a priest and a Levite in His parable of the Good Samaritan? A large number of them lived in Jericho and traveled to Jerusalem for their service in the temple.

The map at the upper left shows the relationship between Jerusalem, Jericho, and the traditional site of the Inn of the Good Samaritan, in between the two cities. Top center: a scene on the old Roman road from Jerusalem to Jericho. Center: an "inn" traditionally called the Inn of the Good Samaritan, on the road from Jerusalem to Jericho. Bottom: courtyard of a Bible-time inn.

443

Mary and Martha

LUKE 10:38-42

Synopsis

After two years of ministering in Galilee, Jesus returned to Judea and Perea, territories near Jerusalem, to minister there. In Jerusalem, He healed a man by the Pool of Siloam and told a parable about Himself as the Good Shepherd who would give His life for His sheep. Somewhere in Judea, He answered the question, "Who is my neighbor?" with a parable about a good-hearted Samaritan who helped a fellow traveler. After that, He went to Bethany, to visit Mary and Martha's home.

Bethany

The small town of Bethany was the home of Mary, Martha, and Lazarus, close friends of Jesus. It still exists today, about two miles east of Jerusalem on the Jericho Road.

When in the area, Jesus often stayed in the home of these friends. In Bethany, He raised Lazarus from the dead (John 11), ate dinner with Simon the Leper, and was anointed by Mary (Matt. 26:6-13; Mark 14:3-9; John 12:2-8).

On this occasion, Jesus probably visited Mary and Martha because the Feast of Taberna-cles was being held at Jerusalem. But it is likely that Jesus did not stay in the house itself, for it was during this feast that Jewish people lived in booths made of the branches of living trees. According to Jewish law, it was their duty to eat, sleep, and live in these booths during the festive week.

The Family of Mary, Martha, and Lazarus

Mary, Martha, and Lazarus were sisters and brother. Martha was the older sister and mistress of the house. This put her in charge of the household duties which included going to the market and preparing meals. During the Feast of Tabernacles, Martha was especially busy making sure that everything was just right for her special Guest. Martha showed her love for Jesus through hospitality.

Mary showed her love for Jesus in a different way. She chose to sit and listen to Jesus. When Jesus visited Bethany for the last time, Mary anointed Jesus' feet with a most expensive perfume. Some of His disciples were irritated, but Jesus recognized this was a token of her love.

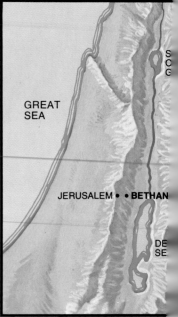

GREAT SEA

JERUSALEM • • BETHAN

S
C
G

DE
SE

© 1981, SPPI

Lazarus was probably celebrating the Feast of Tabernacles in Jerusalem when Jesus came to visit Mary and Martha. Later, after Lazarus died, Jesus wept with Mary and Martha, but knew that Lazarus' death would reveal the glory of God. When Jesus raised Lazarus from the dead, many of Jesus' skeptics believed in Him.

Hospitality and Entertaining Guests

Hospitality to guests was one of the most important social functions of the ancient East. A guest was highly honored even if he was a stranger passing by.

Though there were inns in Jesus' day, most travelers looked for a home where they could spend the night. When a stranger knocked on someone's door or passed by close to evening, the head of the household almost always let him in and asked him to spend the night. If he refused to be hospitable, he could be snubbed by friends and neighbors. A host always kept in mind that someday he too might be a weary traveler looking for shelter and company.

Once inside, the host brought water to wash the guest's feet. If he had no servant, the host would do the washing himself. Since the roads were always dusty and most people walked, washing was an important step in making one's guest feel at home.

When a guest was in the home, a large meal was prepared. Often the guest would be served first and the host waited until he was finished. Other customs included anointing the guest with oil, which they used as soap, or even providing clothing for the mealtime.

According to custom, a guest should stay no longer than three days in his host's home. While there, he was protected by his host. On leaving, the host was to escort his guest a short distance, sending him on his way.

Far left: Bethany today. The map next to the picture shows Bethany in relationship to Jerusalem. The scene at the immediate left is from Bethany, looking northwest toward Jerusalem. Below: Jesus visits with Mary and Martha.

Fig Trees
and Locked Gates

LUKE 12:1—13:30

Synopsis
From Galilee, Jesus had come to Judea to minister to the people of Jerusalem and its surrounding countryside. He had healed a blind man in Jerusalem, taught there about His coming death as the Good Shepherd, and given a parable about a Samaritan who had helped an injured fellow traveler. After visiting with Mary and Martha in Bethany, He traveled again in Judea, giving His disciples the Lord's Prayer, answering the bitter charges of the Pharisees, and telling parables, including those about a rich fool, watchful servants, a wise steward, a barren fig tree, and a locked gate.

Fig Trees
The Bible says much about fig trees. They are not only a source of food, but a symbol of Israel's wealth and abundance, as well as a symbol of that nation's sin and destruction.

Figs were a popular fruit in Bible times. They could be eaten straight from the tree, or dried in the sun and pressed into cakes which could be eaten any time. The Law of Moses permitted travelers to eat figs from the trees that grew along the roads.

A fig tree takes three years from the time it is planted until it is able to bear fruit. Figs grow in large clusters on the trees, which bear fruit twice each year. The harvests come in May or June, and again in August or September.

Fig trees make excellent shade trees, grow-

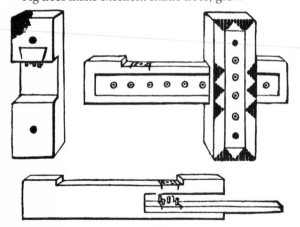

Left: one type of Bible-time lock and key, used in ancient Egypt. The upper-right view is of the front view of the lock, with bolt drawn back. The view at the left is a side view of the lock. The lower view shows the key, the strip protruding from the center, as it fits into the lock. The picture in the center is of a fig tree. At the far upper right is a drawing of mature figs.

446

ing as tall as 30 feet, with thick, large leaves. Their cool shade is welcome in the hot climate of Palestine. The trees are also planted next to wells, to help keep the water cool.

Jesus mentioned the fig tree as a symbol of Israel. In His parable, He likened a barren fig tree to the barrenness of Israel for refusing God's Son. That fig tree would be cut down for failing to yield fruit, and Israel would be cut off from God for refusing His message.

Gates and Locks

Two common types of gates existed in Bible times; the city gate and the gate which protected a building or a home. The city gate was the only entrance through large walls that surrounded many ancient cities. The walls were built for protection and the gates were most vulnerable to an enemy attack. City gates were usually double doors that were opened only after sunrise and closed well before dark. The gate doors were made of iron, or wood covered with bronze, and swung open or closed on large stone sockets. City gates swung into the city when opened. After dark, they were locked on the inside by heavy bars that swung across them.

Most cities had one main gate and only a few smaller ones. The main gate was the center of commerce for the city. There merchants bought and sold their wares, elders gathered to discuss city business, and trials of justice took place. Convicted criminals and captured soldiers were slain outside the city gate.

Many Bible-time houses were surrounded by a walled courtyard, with a heavy door, or gate, which served as the entrance. This was much smaller than a city gate, and in the daytime was left open as a sign of hospitality. Before dark it was closed and locked. Most locks were long, hollow pieces of wood fixed inside the door. A key was placed in the door and turned to slide the piece of wood part of the way into a hole drilled in the doorpost. Keys were usually made of wood, some as long as two feet.

447

Above and right: four coins of the Roman emperor Vespasian, commemorating his victory over Judea. Note the words Judea Capta on the back of the coins. Above right: a Roman military tower used in warfare against city walls. Center: Coin of Titus showing front and back.

Tears for Jerusalem

LUKE 13:31-35

Synopsis

Herod was a fox! Jesus said so Himself. Herod was a member of the crafty family who had ruled the land since before Jesus was born. But Jesus would certainly not run away from Herod. He taught openly throughout Jerusalem, Judea, and Perea, giving parables and working miracles which must have startled Herod. Herod was in charge of Jesus' home territory of Galilee, but not over Judea and Jerusalem. That was under the rule of Pilate, who represented the Romans. In a few years the Romans would completely destroy Jerusalem. Jesus wept for the city, which would reject its Messiah and fall to its enemies.

Destruction of Jerusalem in A.D. 70

Jerusalem continued to be a thriving city after Jesus left the earth. Herod Agrippa I initiated many building projects, indicating more growth and activity in this city that had already become important in the eyes of the world. Christianity had spread rapidly as well, despite rising persecution (Acts 21:20).

But in A.D. 66, the Jews began to revolt against Roman control. This revolt began nearly 30 years after Jesus was crucified. Jesus' prediction about Jerusalem's destruction was about to unfold (Mark 13:2).

For three years the Romans tried unsuccessfully to put down the Jewish rebellion in Jerusalem. The Roman emperor, Vespasian, finally became angry and sent his son Titus, a

In the center is a photo of the Arch of Titus in Rome, commemorating Titus' victory over Jerusalem. It still stands. Above: a statue of Titus and an image of Titus in metal. Titus was son of the emperor Vespasian, and general of the army that conquered Judea.

Roman general, to crush the rebellion.

Jerusalem was a difficult city to attack, with its strong walls and strategic hilltop location. Titus and his Roman legions first attacked the city walls from the north. The Jews were ready and threw large rocks from the battlements. Fierce fighting lasted for two weeks until the Romans finally broke through the northern wall. But Titus' 80,000 Roman soldiers could not enter the city and were driven back.

Titus now realized that Jerusalem would not be taken by force. But he had another plan. He ordered his soldiers to allow no one in or out of Jerusalem. Any Jews caught trying to escape would be crucified.

After a year of starvation, the Jews could no longer withstand the Roman siege. In A.D. 70, Titus attacked the city walls once again. The Jews' strength was gone. They could no longer defend themselves and the Romans stormed through the city. The Antonia fortress was the first to fall. Many of the Jews fled to the temple but could not hold it. Titus had wanted the building spared, but during the fighting a soldier threw a flaming torch into the sanctuary. The temple was soon in flames and the fire spread across the city.

The entire city of Jerusalem was destroyed. Only the towers of Herod's palace and a part of the western wall of the temple platform were left standing among the smoldering ruins. Six hundred thousand Jews had been killed. Survivors were taken to Rome to become slaves or be thrown to beasts.

The Lost Sheep

LUKE 15:1-7

Synopsis
In Judea and Perea, Jesus spoke to people in parables, short stories which taught spiritual truths. To those who understood His teaching, the parable would be clear. To others, it would be only a story. This way, He could keep on teaching His followers while His enemies would not know His message.

Shepherds and Sheep
A shepherd's work has seen little change over the centuries. In Israel, shepherding was a respected occupation. Such men as Jacob, Moses, and David were shepherds.

Shepherding was an important occupation because sheep were such important animals. As a source of food, sheep provided both meat and cheese. Their thick wool and tanned skins were used to make clothing and tent materials. Sheep were also offered as sacrifices to God till the Romans destroyed the temple.

But sheep are helpless animals, unable to find their own food and water, while wandering aimlessly about the countryside. A shepherd is essential for the care and protection of the flock.

Each day a shepherd must look for a pasture where his sheep may graze. There is no need to drive them, for the sheep willingly follow wherever he leads. At noon, the sheep are led to the nearest stream, which may be miles away. In the evening, the sheep are taken into the sheepfold, a fenced pen which keeps them from wandering. Only one door leads into the sheepfold, and the shepherd sleeps

450

The three pictures, below and right, show the fat-tailed variety of sheep common in Jesus' time and still most frequently seen in Israel today. The one at the upper right is a young lamb.

in front of it. If there is no sheepfold, a shepherd might have to stay up all night watching his sheep.

The shepherd always carried a staff and a sling. Both were used to protect his flock from snakes and wild animals. Many times he was forced to fight jackals, wolves, and even bears. Each day the shepherd lived with his flock, cared for them, and protected them. Out of this grew a tremendous bond of affection. If a single sheep wandered, the shepherd risked his life to bring it back safely.

The shepherd was careful to make sure that each member of his flock was well cared for. An injured sheep was carried on his shoulders until it was able to walk again. And a newborn lamb was sometimes carried in the shepherd's cloak, till it was strong enough to move along with the rest of the flock.

Two kinds of shepherds were found in Bible lands. One is the settled type, who led his sheep out to pasture each day and brought them home at night. The other was the nomad, who traveled the countryside looking for good pasture, while living in a tent.

Why Jesus Taught in Parables

Jesus taught much about Himself, His home in heaven, and His heavenly Father in parables, short stories from everyday life. Why? Why not just tell these truths in plain language instead of hidden in stories?

Jesus' enemies heard the parables as stories, little more. But those who earnestly sought Him and believed in Him saw the hidden meanings. So it also is today.

The Lost Coin

LUKE 15:8-10

Synopsis
In Jerusalem, Jesus had taught that He was the Good Shepherd, who would die for His sheep. In the countryside east of Jerusalem, in Perea, He taught about this Good Shepherd searching for lost sheep—like us!

Coins of Jesus' Time
When Jesus was on earth, there were numerous coins available. People came to the temple from all parts of the known world. There they exchanged their foreign coins with the money changers so they could buy birds or animals to sacrifice. Foreign coins were not accepted, so visitors had to exchange their money for the specific coins accepted in the temple.

Several events in Jesus' life are also associated with the coins of His time. In some cases these were coins He mentioned, or which were mentioned as part of the background of the story in which He was involved. Some of these coins bore images of people associated with the life of Jesus.

During Old Testament times, coins were not widely used. Gold and silver were the medium of exchange, but these metals were in the form of jewelry or broken pieces which were weighed. Numerous references throughout the Old Testament refer to men or women of wealth as those who possessed large amounts of gold, silver, or bronze. Animals were also a measure of a person's wealth, especially among the Bedouin.

Coinage began with the Lydians during the seventh century B.C. They were captured by the Persians in the fifth century B.C. and coinage spread. Athenians issued silver coins known as tetradrachms. This same term later was used among other nations to represent their silver coins. The tetradrachms of Tyre were probably the "30 pieces of silver" Judas got for betraying Jesus. Antioch, Rhodes, and other places minted silver tetradrachms.

No gold coin is mentioned by name in the New Testament. The Jewish people did not mint a gold coin. The reference in Matthew 10:9 may be to gold and silver coins. So also may other references to silver and gold (Acts 3:6; 1 Cor. 3:12; James 5:3; 1 Peter 1:18).

It is hard to assign present-day values to these coins except by comparing the values of their metal. Purchasing power of silver and gold has varied greatly since Bible times.

452

His birth: the denarius of Augustus Caesar, Roman emperor at that time.

Flight to Egypt: copper coin of Herod the Great, who tried to kill Jesus.

Return to Nazareth: coin of Herod Archelaus, ruler of Judea then.

Teaching in temple: lepton or mite of Coponius, procurator of Judea at this time.

John the Baptist: coin of Herod Philip, father of Salome, whose dance led to John's death.

n Coins He Saw

Render to Caesar: denarius of Tiberius Caesar to which Jesus referred.

The widow's mite: a mite or lepton to which Jesus referred.

Judas betrays Jesus: a silver tetra-drachm of Tyre. Judas received 30 of them.

Pilate judges Jesus: coin struck by Pontius Pilate.

Jesus is crucified: a coin of Herod Antipas who, with Pilate, judged Jesus.

A crude homemade broom from Bible times is shown above. This one comes from Egypt, quite some time before Jesus was on earth.

453

The Prodigal Son

LUKE 15:11-32

Synopsis

Traveling throughout Judea and Perea, Jesus taught that He was the Good Shepherd, searching for lost sheep. He taught with many parables, making truths clear to those who wanted to learn and confusing to those who did not. The disciples would understand much more later, after the Holy Spirit came. They would recognize that God was like a loving father, welcoming home a wandering son.

Carob Pods

The prodigal son became so hungry that he was forced to eat the "pods" or "husks" that were the pigs' food. These were probably carob pods which come from the carob or locust tree. This tree is an evergreen and can grow as tall as 50 feet. The pods which grow on the tree are usually 6 to 10 inches long, and very bitter when still green. But as they ripen, they take on a darker color and a sweet syrup forms inside. Today this syrup is extracted as a gum and is used in the food, textile, and cosmetic industries.

In Jesus' time, these pods were used as food for pigs and cattle. Poor people also ate them because they were cheap. A few scholars think that these pods may have been the "locusts" John the Baptist ate, since they came from carob or locust trees.

454

Upper left: the father welcomes home the prodigal son. Upper center: carob pods, perhaps the food which the prodigal son ate. Above: pods grow on a carob tree while a bird nests among the branches. Left: a pig farmer in Bible-time Egypt. The faraway country where the prodigal went must have been outside Israel, for Israelites were not pig farmers.

Swine

Swine, or pigs, were forbidden food in Israel, considered the most unclean and sinful of animals. As a Jew, the prodigal son must have detested these swine. But now in a foreign country and at the brink of starvation, the only available job was feeding and tending these animals. To make matters worse, he was forced to eat the swine's food in order to survive. In the eyes of any Jew, including himself, he could stoop no lower.

The Fattened Calf

The Israelites were always ready for hospitality, so many homes kept a fattened calf on hand for special events. Meat was often hard to come by and killing the fattened calf was a sign of honor and respect. The arrival of a special guest meant that a great feast was on hand.

455

The Rich Man and Lazarus

LUKE 16:19-31

Synopsis

Jesus taught hidden lessons in one parable after another. With a story about a lost sheep, He told how He, the Good Shepherd, searched for His own. In another story, about a lost son, He told how His Father in heaven welcomed a lost but repentant sinner home. In this parable He told of a poor man who loved God and a rich man who did not. The poor man was rich and the rich man was poor.

Rich People

Middle-class society was rare in Israel during New Testament times. A few families lived with great wealth; most had almost nothing. A tremendous gap existed between rich and poor, and as a result the poor were exploited.

A man usually acquired wealth because he was born into the right family. Most wealthy men rode in chariots drawn by their own horses, and owned much land and many slaves. Their houses were filled with expensive furniture and beautiful oriental rugs in a variety of colors. They wore white wool or silk robes and their wives wore embroidered linen and bracelets, necklaces, and armbands of gold and silver.

Poor People

A poor man struggled to make ends meet, but he was not necessarily a beggar. He hoped to earn a denarius each day (a day's wages). This was just enough to buy food and keep up with the oppressive Roman taxes. For some, slavery was preferred to poverty. A man might sell himself or his children into slavery, giving him some security when it came to food and shelter.

The pictures of dogs on these pages have been taken from actual Bible-time drawings, paintings, or carvings on tombs or other remains. They give an accurate image of the dogs of Bible times.

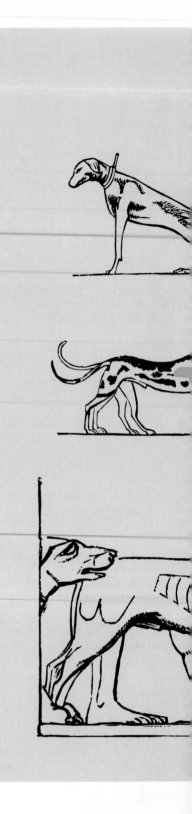

456

Dogs of Bible Times

In Bible times dogs had a different role than they do today. Modern people think of dogs most often as "man's best friend," warm spirited pets, or household animals. Bible-time people did not usually keep dogs as pets, especially as affectionate animals. Israelites thought of dogs as unclean, for they were scavengers, living off refuse and dead animals. So dogs were one source of diseases.

Wild dogs that roamed the streets ate the flesh of Jezebel almost as soon as she had died. Dead bodies were often thrown to dogs to eat, so Jezebel's case was not so unusual (see 2 Kings 9).

But in Egypt, the dog was esteemed and often associated with a god, such as Anubis. In Mesopotamia also dogs were valued, and many were used for hunting and guarding a person's property. Assyrians, for example, had hunting dogs, pictured at the bottom center. The dogs in the center and upper center were Egyptian, carved or painted on sculptures of ancient Egypt and redrawn in these pictures.

The dog above is from an ancient Persian carving. The ones at the far left depict street dogs, which roamed the streets, eating refuse and dead animals.

When Jesus spoke to the Syrophoenician woman about "dogs," He was undoubtedly referring to those so common in Israel, the scavenger dogs. The dogs which licked the sores of poor Lazarus were held in contempt, as Lazarus was. They were mentioned to show the low estate to which Lazarus had sunk.

457

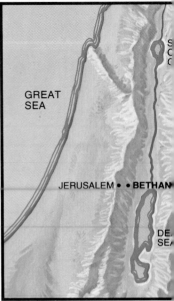

GREAT
SEA

JERUSALEM • •BETHAN

DE
SEA

Upper left: the joy of the resurrection as friends welcome Lazarus back to life. Above: the map shows the relationship of Bethany and Jerusalem. Upper right: Bethany today. Lower right: the so-called "St. Lazarus' Tomb," from which traditionally Lazarus was raised.

Jesus Raises Lazarus

JOHN 11:1-44

Synopsis

In His travels around Judea and Perea, Jesus had visited the home of Mary, Martha, and Lazarus before, probably many times. These people were like a family to Him, with a bond of affection. But Jesus deliberately let Lazarus die, so that he might live again.

When

Jesus raised Lazarus from the dead sometime between the Feast of Dedication, which took place in December, and the Passover, when He was crucified. It was probably on a brisk winter day in January or February when Jesus arrived in Bethany. The town is just two miles from Jerusalem, and only slightly higher in elevation. Both experience much the same weather, and in Jerusalem at that time of year, the average temperature is 49°F., with mild afternoons but very cool nights.

Lazarus

As brother of Mary and Martha, Lazarus must have known Jesus quite well. In fact, Jesus had a deep love for Lazarus and his sisters (John 11:5, 36). But little is known about the personality of Lazarus. In the Bible he does not speak a word. When he was raised, it caused many Jews to believe in Jesus (11:45),

but it also prompted the Sanhedrin to lay plans for Jesus' death (11:47-53). And because Lazarus was a key witness to the authority of Christ, the chief priests and elders plotted his death as well (12:10).

A Tomb in a Cave

The Bible tells us that Lazarus was buried in a cave. This could have been a natural cave or a tomb or vault cut into the rock. A large round stone was often rolled across the entrance of such a tomb after burial. Some of these tombs had a "court" cut into the rock just in front of the tomb entrance. It was only large enough for the bier and its bearers.

Upon death, the body was sealed inside the tomb. After the flesh had decayed and only the skeleton remained, the bones were placed in a box called an ossuary. This small box was then placed on a shelf which had been carved out of the tomb wall. In this way, a whole family could be buried in the same tomb.

458

Some wealthy people preferred to be buried in large stone coffins called sarcophaguses. Special niches were carved in the tomb wall for these coffins. Such tombs had to be much bigger to accommodate the large-size sarcophaguses. Soon catacombs developed, which were large underground mazes of tombs.

Preparing the Body for Burial

Because of the warm climate in Palestine, burial usually took place the same day as death. But before the funeral, the body was prepared for burial.

Rarely did the immediate family become involved in preparing the body for burial. Friends and other family members took the body and washed it, and clipped the hair and nails. Strips of linen were then wrapped around the body. Spices, such as hyssop, rose oil, and rose water were placed in between these strips. Finally, a linen napkin was placed over the face, and the body laid on an open bier.

459

Ten Lepers

LUKE 17:11-19

Synopsis
The time was approaching when Jesus would enter
Jerusalem for His last week before the crucifixion. He
was traveling throughout Judea and Perea, teaching
through many parables about His Father and His heavenly home. In certain places He paused to perform
miracles on some needy persons, such as healing the
10 lepers.

The Border between Samaria and Galilee
Shortly after the raising of Lazarus, Jesus went from
Ephraim (John 11:54) north into southern Galilee to
join the pilgrims to Jerusalem. The border between
Samaria and Galilee ran roughly from Mount Carmel
southeast through the Plain of Esdraelon and the inter-

460

vening hills to Mount Gilboa and the Jordan River. There were two main roads through Samaria, one along the coast, the other along the high ridge. On their way to Jerusalem for the Passover, Jesus and the pilgrims took the high road.

A Village

It is impossible to determine exactly which village is intended. Luke may not have known. But possible villages include Capercotnei, Agrippina, and Scythopolis.

"Show Yourselves to the Priests"

The Old Testament gives detailed regulations for the ceremonial cleansing of those cured of infectious skin diseases such as leprosy. Moses, for example, mentions the offerings and rites involved (Lev. 14). The offerings included live clean birds, one to be killed over fresh water in a clay pot, the other dipped in its blood. On the eighth day two male lambs and a ewe, flour, and oil were taken to the temple, with the individual cured from the disease. If the person was too poor, a substitute offering was possible. The ceremonies could be performed by any local priest, not just those in Jerusalem.

Note that Luke, in his concern for "minorities," focuses on a grateful Samaritan.

Leprosy

One of the most feared diseases of the ancient world was leprosy, especially among the Israelites. The disease itself was frightening, but the Israelites added an even more terrifying note—complete isolation. A leper could not live among family and friends, but had to go away to live by himself or with other lepers.

Leprosy came in two types. The tuberculoid type started with a change in skin color, to a white or pink spot. Sometimes it went away by itself. In any case it did not cause the severe problems caused by the other type.

Lepromatous leprosy also started with a change in skin color, such as a white or pink spot. But this type spread rapidly, with swellings appearing. In time the hands and feet became deformed, bones deteriorated, and nerves were destroyed.

The leper in Bible times faced a tragic future, for there was no known cure. He was condemned to be an outcast and suffer alone.

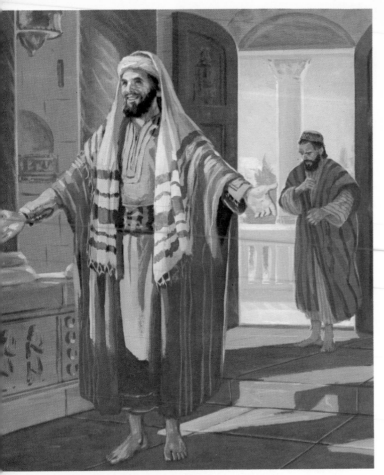

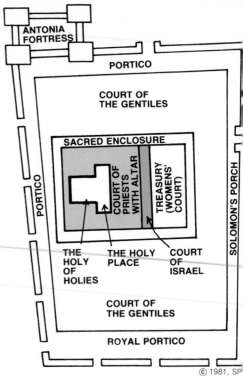

© 1981, SP

As seen in the picture at the left, the Pharisee proudly entered the temple to pray, telling God how good he was. The publican, ashamed of his sin, just humbly asked for God's help. Above: the court of Israel, where this scene probably took place.

A Pharisee and a Publican

LUKE 18:9-14

Synopsis

As Jesus traveled through Judea and Perea, territories near Jerusalem, He often faced the proud Pharisees. These people separated themselves from many ordinary things of life, pretending to be holier than others. But in their pretended holiness, they were blind to their one hope for heaven—the Messiah, God's Son, who had come to show them the way to His home. One day Jesus told a story about a Pharisee, who thought he was holy, and a publican, who did not.

Pharisees

Josephus, famous Jewish historian, knew that three Jewish parties (Pharisees, Sadducees, and Essenes) existed as early as 145 B.C.

As Judaism's legalistic branch, Pharisees separated themselves from those who neglected the Law. Their piety made them popular. Jesus condemned their self-righteousness and hypocrisy, not their basic beliefs.

Tax Collectors

There were two kinds of "publicans" or tax collectors in Jesus' day: (1) the taxgatherer who collected land, income, and poll taxes; (2) the more hated customs men, who collected tolls on everything from bridges to food.

Fasting and Tithing

Fasting means not eating, and sometimes also not drinking, from sunrise to sunset. Jews were expected to fast on the Day of Atonement and in times of crisis. A second-century document called the *Didache* notes that while Jews fasted on Monday and Thursday, the Christians fasted on Wednesday and Friday.

Tithing is giving one-tenth of one's income. Egyptians gave even more to their Pharaohs.

Postures for Prayer, Petition, and Penitence

People often kneel in prayer, as a sign of respect or worship to the Lord. Kneeling was only one of the postures used in ancient times, when a person came before a man of great power with a request.

The pictures on this page show different drawings, taken from Bible-time art of various kinds, and from customs of Bible lands in later times. At the top, a man begins upright with arms uplifted, then bows with hands to his legs and up again. A second man kneels with his face to the ground, then sits back on his legs, then puts his face to the ground again and then rises or sits.

The picture below the top series of drawings, at the right, shows a slightly different version of a man bowing with his face to the ground, arms outstretched.

Along the left side, from top to bottom: two people bow from the waist up as they kiss a man's hand; the Egyptian drawing shows two forms of bowing before a great man–knees bent and hands uplifted, and kneeling with hands outstretched. In the picture below that, a man lies almost prostrate before the great person; the Egyptian picture below that shows four people with various positions of uplifted hands. At the bottom: an Egyptian (far left) is on hands and knees before a god, a man bows on his legs (top center), three men kneel with one arm lifted and another to the chest (bottom center), while the two men at the bottom-right each outstretch a hand.

463

Jesus and the Children

MATTHEW 19:13-15; MARK 10:13-16; LUKE 18:15-17

Synopsis
When Jesus raised His friend Lazarus from the dead, He startled the people of that part of the land. Some believed on Him as God's Son. Others wanted all the more to kill Him. For a time, Jesus returned to Galilee, then made His way to Perea, east of the Jordan River. One day some parents brought their young children to Jesus, so that He might bless them. The disciples rebuked the parents. Why did these people think that Jesus had time for children?

Perea
Perea is the region on the east side of the Jordan River (Matt. 19:1). Luke's account follows the story of the healing of the 10 lepers on the west side of the Jordan, so all 3 accounts harmonize. If Perea is used in a general geographical sense, this moving narrative may

have taken place in or near Pella; if it is used in the stricter, more political sense, the site may have been Gedor or Philadelphia. If it took place in the same house in which Jesus so strongly supported the marriage bonds, no wonder the mothers brought their children to Jesus to bless them!

Little Children
There are several words in Greek that refer to children. The word used by Matthew and Mark refers to very small children. Luke reveals that they were babies in the arms of their mothers. That this is the age of the little children to which Matthew and Mark refer is confirmed by Mark's reference to the fact that Jesus took them in His arms (Mark 10:16).

As was so often true, Jesus once again upset traditional values, as the reaction of the disciples suggested. Rabbis did not lower their dignity by associating with little children. Jesus, on the contrary, used children to illustrate some of His most basic teachings.

The Laying on of Hands
The act of laying one's hands on another per-

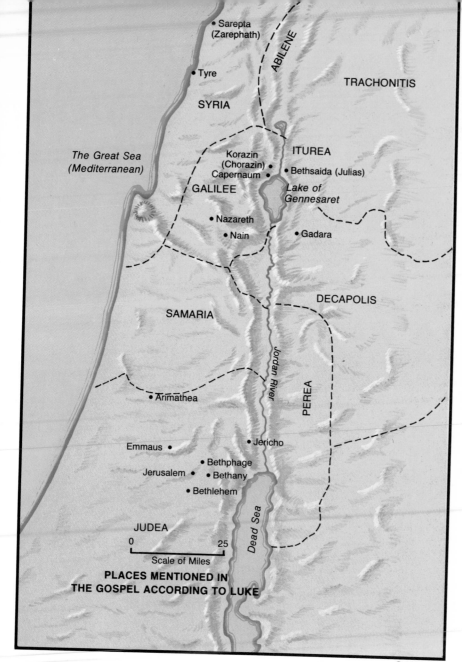

Sarepta
(Zarephath)

ABILENE

Tyre

TRACHONITIS

SYRIA

*The Great Sea
(Mediterranean)*

Korazin
(Chorazin)
Capernaum

ITUREA

Bethsaida (Julias)

GALILEE

*Lake of
Gennesaret*

Nazareth

Nain

Gadara

DECAPOLIS

SAMARIA

Jordan River

PEREA

Arimathea

Emmaus

Jericho

Bethphage

Jerusalem

Bethany

Bethlehem

Dead Sea

JUDEA

0   25

Scale of Miles

**PLACES MENTIONED IN
THE GOSPEL ACCORDING TO LUKE**

The map at the left shows many of the familiar territories mentioned in the four Gospels, especially Luke's Gospel. Galilee was Jesus' home territory, and the place where He ministered most during the early time of His stay on earth. It included such places as Nazareth, Nain, and Capernaum. Jesus also visited Syria, the region of Tyre and Sidon. He must have been in Bethsaida Julias many times. In Samaria, He talked with a woman at a well. He was born in Bethlehem of Judea, and ministered during His last days in Jerusalem in Judea. At the time described in our text He ministered in the region called Perea. Pontius Pilate ruled Judea, Samaria, and Idumea (south of Judea, not shown on this map). Herod Antipas ruled Galilee and Perea. Herod Philip ruled most of the regions of Iturea, Trachonitis, and Abilene on this map.

son is an ancient tradition with many meanings. The mothers who brought their children to Jesus undoubtedly were seeking His blessing, much as Jacob blessed Joseph's children (Gen. 48:14). The words used in a blessing were considered full of power, so the mothers of the children clearly recognized that Jesus' blessing and touch had special significance.

Children and God's Kingdom
What did Jesus mean when He said the kingdom of God belongs to those who are like children, and that anyone who does not re-

ceive the kingdom like a little child will never enter it? Some have suggested such qualities as humility, receptiveness, meekness, simple trust, innocence, simplicity, and directness. Probably the best answer is that Jesus was not thinking of any such qualities, since the children were just babies. He probably referred to their absolute dependence on their parents. Christians too depend totally on God for salvation and life.

What a beautiful picture of Jesus this story contains! Though busy and important, Jesus still had time for the tiniest baby.

465

The Rich Young Ruler

MATTHEW 19:16-30; MARK 10:17-31; LUKE 18:18-30

Synopsis
After He had raised Lazarus from the dead, Jesus returned for a while to Galilee. Later He went to Perea, east of the Jordan River, to minister. Some mothers brought their young children to Jesus and He blessed them. Then a rich young man came to see Jesus, asking what good thing he had to do to get eternal life.

The Rich Young Ruler
Who was this man? The word "young" means that he would have been between 24 and 40 years old. To say that he was a ruler probably meant that he was a member of the Sanhedrin. The Sanhedrin, which literally means "sitting together," was the highest Jewish authority in all of Palestine. The man must have been unusually devout in his faith if he was a member of this important council at such a young age. The genuineness of his zeal for God may be shown by the fact that Jesus loved him (Mark 10:21).

The Eye of the Needle

What did Jesus mean when He said it was easier for a camel to go through a needle's eye than for a rich man to enter the kingdom of God? It is impossible for a camel to go through the eye of a sewing needle. Does this mean that it is impossible for a rich man to enter the kingdom of God?

That certainly cannot be true, for many rich men have been devout Christians, using their wealth to serve God. What then did Jesus mean?

There were two types of needle's eyes in Jesus' time. One was a sewing needle, almost like those we use today, except larger and made of bronze or iron. It had an eye through which thread was passed as with modern needles. Some people believe Jesus spoke literally about this kind of nee-

dle. Perhaps, but it seems more likely that He spoke about the other type.

This second type of needle's eye was a small door within a larger door, usually in the large wooden door that was a city gate. Humans could walk through these small gates, but large animals such as camels could not.

When the large door was closed, such as late in the evening, people could still go through the "needle's eye," the smaller door. But if a camel came, burdened with a heavy load on its back, it became necessary for the load to be removed and for the camel to almost crawl through the "needle's eye" on its knees. It suggests that Jesus was saying a rich man must lay aside his burdensome "things" and kneel to enter God's kingdom.

The Ten Commandments

There are two interesting things about the list of commandments Jesus gave. First, the Ten Commandments were traditionally broken into two parts, with the first four commands on the first tablet and the last six on the second tablet. Every commandment Jesus mentioned came from the second tablet, the one that has to do with social responsibilities.

Second, there is no reference to the commandment not to covet. It is almost as if Jesus knew this was the rich young ruler's real problem.

If You Want to Be Perfect

Nobody is perfect. For a perfect person would never do anything wrong.

In Bible times the word meant something a bit different. When Jesus said to the young man, "If you want to be perfect," He meant, "If you want to be fully developed in a moral sense." The word was a synonym for "complete" or "mature." It sometimes meant "adult" or "full-grown." The word was also used of a person who had been fully initiated into one of the "mystery" religions of New Testament times.

Sell Your Possessions

Some people have wondered if all Christians are supposed to sell everything they own and give the proceeds to the poor. Most of us probably need to give more to help others than we do. But Jesus' command was given specifically to a rich young ruler because he had a problem with covetousness. For some people, like St. Francis of Assisi, following Christ does mean selling everything. But for other wealthy men, such as Philemon, wealth should be used in a Christian way. The danger is that our concern for keeping too much for ourselves can keep us from following Christ.

The Rich and the Poor

Why were the disciples "greatly astonished" at Jesus' words about the difficulty of rich people getting into heaven? Because it was the popular view that riches were God's reward for a good life. Sometimes that is true. A good life makes a man richer than a wasteful life.

But the New Testament is full of reminders that riches can distort life too.

The drawing below shows laborers in a Bible-time vineyard, much like the vineyard described in this incident. Note the watchtower in the background. At the right is a vineyard near Hebron today. A watchtower north of Jerusalem is pictured at the bottom center.

The Laborers in the Vineyard

MATTHEW 20:1-16

Synopsis
After raising Lazarus from the dead, Jesus returned to Galilee for a while. Then He went to Perea, east of the Jordan River, where He blessed some young children who were brought to Him and talked with a rich young man about eternal life. Then Jesus told a parable about some laborers in a vineyard.

Vineyards
The vineyards the landowner hired laborers to work in would have been quite different from today's vineyards. The vines would most likely have been trailing along the ground, though in some cases Jews allowed them to grow up trees or on trellises. Most vineyards were

Augustus Caesar, the Caesar who was Roman emperor when Jesus was born, is pictured on the denarius above. At the left is a winepress, with men trampling the grapes with their feet, while hanging onto ropes above them. The juice of the grapes ran into containers sitting beside the large basin in which the men stood.

on the south side of hills so the vines would mature in the sun. They were surrounded by walls to keep out wild animals, such as foxes and boars, with a watchtower from which thieves could be seen.

Raising grapes is one of the hardest forms of farming because the grapes require constant attention.

The Marketplace

Greek and Jewish marketplaces differed. Greek marketplaces were for trials and disputes; they were surrounded by statues and temples. Jewish marketplaces were more like bazaars, busy with buying and selling, children playing, and men hiring workers.

Time

In ancient times people did not divide time the way we do. The Old Testament speaks only of morning, afternoon, evening, and night. The Babylonians were the first to divide daylight into 12 equal parts, and everyone else followed them. The day began at 6:00 in the morning. So the third hour was 9 A.M.; the sixth, noon; and so on.

Denarius

A denarius or "penny" was a full day's pay. About the size of our dime, it had Caesar's head on the front and another image on the back.

469

Blind Bartimaeus

MATTHEW 20:29-34; MARK 10:46-52; LUKE 18:35-43

Synopsis
Jesus had left Galilee to minister in Judea and Perea. In Judea, at the village of Bethany, He had raised Lazarus from the dead. In Perea, He had welcomed little children and blessed them. Now He was on His way to Jerusalem, where He would be crucified. The way to Jerusalem led through Jericho.

Jericho
The pilgrims on their way to Jerusalem from Galilee crossed over the Jordan from Perea, into Jericho, the last major stop on their journey. The town of Jericho is tied in the minds of Bible-readers with Joshua, Zaccheus, and the Good Samaritan. It may have received its name from Yarih, an ancient Semitic moon goddess. The town is located near a spring, which makes it an attractive place to dwell. Built by Herod the Great as his winter capital because it was much warmer and drier than Jerusalem, the Jericho of New Testament times was built partly of cut stone and partly of a distinctive construction of small rectangular stones set in mortar. Herod probably saw a building in this style when he was on a trip to Rome. The modern city of Jericho is about a mile east of the New Testament town.

Beggars
One writer has said that beggars existed in the Middle East wherever wealth was found.

People became beggars for many reasons. Sometimes, as in the case of Bartimaeus, blindness or some other illness made them incapable of working. Sometimes robbers, heavy taxes, or even laziness left people so poor they became beggars.

Cloak
Mark alone tells us that Bartimaeus threw his cloak aside when Jesus called him. This might have been the outer of three garments he was wearing. But a poor begger would probably have only one, a garment like a nightgown with openings only at the neck, arms, and hemmed bottom. Jesus' seamless robe would have been this garment.

At the right, blind Bartimaeus pleads for Jesus to help him. The map shows the location of Jericho, especially as it relates to Jerusalem and the Jordan River. The picture at the upper right is of the ruins of New Testament Jericho, with the old road that stretched from Jerusalem to Jericho in the left center. Bartimaeus was healed along this road.

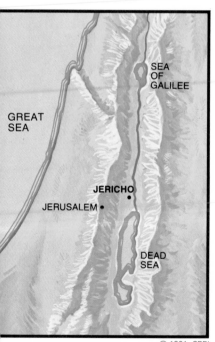

The garment most people wore over this undergarment would be the *tallith,* a shirt almost as long as the undergarment, but made of wool, flax, or even leather. It was a close-fitting, sleeved garment that was fastened around the waist by a belt.

The outer garment Bartimaeus threw aside would have been a light coat or jacket of a coarser material, which came in various shapes. This long jacket had white knots (fringes) attached with a blue cord at each of its corners.

In addition to these three pieces of clothing, the Jew would wear a turban or some other type of headgear on his head and sandals on his feet.

The outer garment was the garment people in mourning would tear; it was also the garment that was removed before a person was flogged.

Blindness

Blindness was common in Egypt, Israel, and the other countries of the neighboring Near East. It had numerous causes, including poverty and inadequate food, unsanitary conditions at home, overexposure to the sun, excessive heat, blowing sand, accidents, and war injuries. Blindness is mentioned no less than 34 times in the Gospels alone.

Zaccheus and the
Parable of the Three Servants

LUKE 19:1-27

Synopsis
Throughout the early part of His ministry, Jesus spent most of His time around the Sea of Galilee, ministering in villages such as Capernaum and Bethsaida. Now He had left that region and was heading toward Jerusalem, ministering in both Judea and Perea. On the way to Jerusalem, He stopped in Jericho where He healed a blind man and met a tax collector named Zaccheus.

Chief Tax Collector
Zaccheus was the chief tax collector, the head of the regional taxation division of the Roman government. Usually such men were Romans. But Zaccheus probably represented the Jews in Jericho, which was the central station for collecting taxes for the whole region. He would have been the equivalent of the Roman *censor*, the one who sold the privilege of collecting taxes to the highest bidder. This man, the *publicanus*, could then add as much of a commission as he could collect. One's right to collect taxes usually lasted for five years. Tax collectors were notorious for cheating both the government and the people. Sons of tax collectors often continued their fathers' work. In Jesus' day taxes were levied on everything the Romans could think of, so tax rebellions were common and people were often reduced to poverty by the numerous taxes. A drawing on an Egyptian tomb shows a man being beaten because he failed to pay his taxes. It is little wonder the common people hated tax collectors. That Jesus could love them is one more example of His love for the unlovely.

Lower left: Jesus calls Zaccheus to come down from the sycamore tree. Lower center: a large sycamore tree. The sycamore-figs are pictured at the far right on a leafy branch. At the right are Jericho ruins from New Testament times, south of the Jericho ruins from Old Testament times.

The Sycamore Tree

A sycamore tree was a type of fig tree, often called the fig-mulberry. It had many strong, wide-spreading branches, so it was easy for a person to climb. The sycamore-fig bore fruit several times a year, in clusters. People did not often eat it, however, because it was not as tasty as ordinary figs. To make them ripen properly, workers would puncture the fruit with the point of a knife.

The sycamore-fig was just one of many trees that grew in the warm climate of Jericho. So many palm trees grew there that Jericho was known as "The City of Palms." The perfume of the sweet-scented balsam, carried for miles by the wind, may even have given the city its name, which may mean "The Perfumed."

Mina

To the crowds who welcomed Him in Jericho, Jesus told the Parable of the Pounds. The pound was a mina, a Greek rather than a Roman coin. Coins were first introduced by the Lydians in the seventh century B.C. The mina was 100 drachmas. Since a drachma was the equivalent of a day's wages, similar to the value of a Roman denarius, a mina might be roughly equivalent to $2,500 in today's money. Ten "pounds" might therefore be about $25,000.

It is extremely difficult to fix values on Bible-time money for even in our times the value of gold and silver has increased more than 20 times, then decreased, then increased again until within a few years values become difficult to fix.

473

Left: Jesus rides into Jerusalem in triumph. Right: the route from Bethany and Bethphage, across the Kidron Valley, and into Jerusalem. Note also on this map the relationship to other places involved in Jesus' last week.

Above: a lulab, made of palm or willow branches and waved at feasts.

Jesus' Triumphal Entry into Jerusalem

MATTHEW 21:1-9; MARK 11:1-10; LUKE 19:29-44; JOHN 12:12-19

Synopsis
Jesus had left His native region, Galilee, to minister in Judea and Perea on His way to Jerusalem. On this visit to Jerusalem, He would be crucified, and would rise from the dead. As He entered the city triumphantly, He fulfilled an old prophecy, which pointed to Him as the Messiah, God's Son. But many failed to recognize Him.

Bethphage and Bethany
Both of these villages are on the Mount of Olives. Bethphage, meaning "the place of unripened figs," is nearer the top of the mount. Since it is only about two miles from Jerusalem, it is not surprising that it is often mentioned in Jewish literature as part of the capital. Scholars differ as to whether ancient Bethphage was on the site of present-day Abu-Dis, near the top of the Mount of Olives, or Kefr et Tûr, on the very top.

Bethany, meaning "house of dates" or "house of figs," is farther down the slope of the Mount of Olives. Identified today with the Arab village of el-Azariyeh, it now has about 1,000 inhabitants. Over the ruins of the traditional site of the home of Mary, Martha, and Lazarus is the modern Church of St. Lazarus, Mary, and Martha.

474

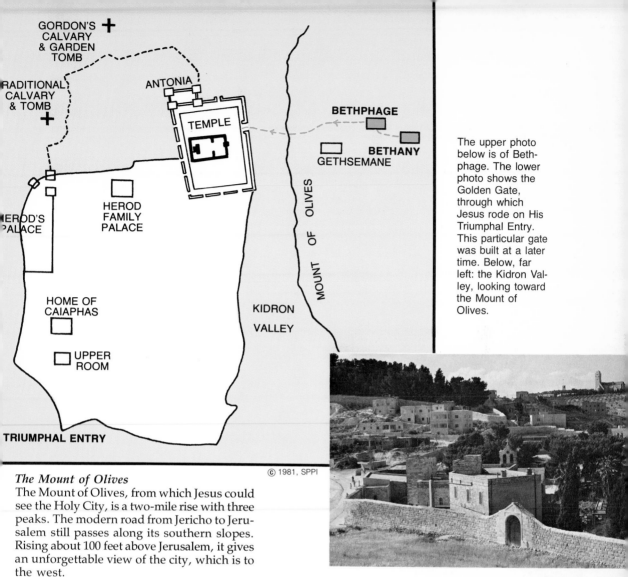

GORDON'S CALVARY & GARDEN TOMB

TRADITIONAL CALVARY & TOMB

ANTONIA

TEMPLE

BETHPHAGE

GETHSEMANE

BETHANY

HEROD'S PALACE

HEROD FAMILY PALACE

MOUNT OF OLIVES

HOME OF CAIAPHAS

KIDRON VALLEY

UPPER ROOM

TRIUMPHAL ENTRY

© 1981, SPPI

The upper photo below is of Bethphage. The lower photo shows the Golden Gate, through which Jesus rode on His Triumphal Entry. This particular gate was built at a later time. Below, far left: the Kidron Valley, looking toward the Mount of Olives.

The Mount of Olives

The Mount of Olives, from which Jesus could see the Holy City, is a two-mile rise with three peaks. The modern road from Jericho to Jerusalem still passes along its southern slopes. Rising about 100 feet above Jerusalem, it gives an unforgettable view of the city, which is to the west.

Colt and Donkey

The donkey was the usual animal for traveling in Palestine because it could travel the steep, narrow, rocky roads. Kings usually rode in wheeled vehicles. But according to Zechariah 9:9, the Messiah, the King of kings, would arrive on a lowly donkey.

Temple and Eastern Gate

Jesus would have had a magnificent view of the gleaming white marble and golden dome of the temple as He rode into Jerusalem. Herod's temple, completed later, just six years before Jerusalem was destroyed (A.D. 70), was almost an exact replica of Solomon's temple, built a thousand years before. Jesus would have crossed the Xystus bridge, 450 feet above the Kidron Valley, and entered the Susa Gate (now the Golden Gate).

475

Throughout the years, artists have tried to picture how the temples, both Herod's and Solomon's, must have looked. Two of these reconstructions are shown below. Nobody knows exactly how they looked, even though a number of details are given in the Bible.

Jesus at the Temple

MATTHEW 21:10-17; MARK 11:11-19;
LUKE 19:45-48

Synopsis

As He came to Jerusalem from Perea, Jesus stopped in Jericho, where He healed a blind man and brought new life to the tax collector, Zaccheus. From there, Jesus came to the village of Bethany, east of Jerusalem, where He frequently stayed at the home of Mary, Martha, and Lazarus. As the Passover drew near,

Jesus rode triumphantly into Jerusalem as the prophets of old had said the Messiah would do. There He taught in the temple.

The Greeks

To us today the word "Greek" means someone from Greece. The Greeks who came to Jerusalem to worship, however, were a special type of Greek. They were proselytes. That means they accepted the beliefs and practices of the Jewish religion. Some proselytes were called "God-fearers"; they accepted the Jewish faith but rejected circumcision, a practice not popular outside Judaism.

476

Solomon's Porch and the Royal Portico

All around the outer courts of the temple were covered walkways, called "porches" or "porticoes." The walkway on the east side was called "Solomon's Porch," perhaps because a tradition said Solomon had built a similar wall. It was 1,562 feet long and was built over a retaining wall above the Kidron Valley. People were free to meet, talk, and even teach in this area. Jesus loved to walk and talk here, and so did His disciples after His death and resurrection.

The Royal Portico was the walkway that went along the south wall of the temple courts. It was a magnificent structure with 160 ornate columns gracing its 921 feet. This is the area in which the money changers and other businessmen conducted their business. Close to the center were the two Huldah Gates through which pilgrims entered the temple. This area has been the site of many excavations since 1968. As a result many no longer believe Robinson's Arch led to a bridge over the Tyropoean Valley that led to the upper city. There was probably a stairway, which led down to a street 32 feet wide, that went along the west wall.

The Money Changers

Money changers were in the Royal Portico to change unacceptable foreign currency into acceptable half-shekels (didrachms), shekels (tetradrachms), and other forms of offering. How surprising that the shekel, a coin from Tyre that had the picture of Tyre's god, Baal Melcarth, on it, was acceptable!

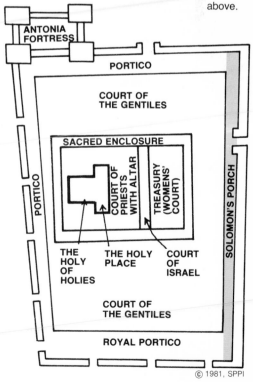

ANTONIA FORTRESS

PORTICO

COURT OF THE GENTILES

SACRED ENCLOSURE

PORTICO

COURT OF PRIESTS WITH ALTAR

TREASURY (WOMENS' COURT)

SOLOMON'S PORCH

THE HOLY OF HOLIES

THE HOLY PLACE

COURT OF ISRAEL

COURT OF THE GENTILES

ROYAL PORTICO

Jesus Teaches in Parables

MATTHEW 21:23—22:14; MARK 11:27—12:12;
LUKE 20:1-19

Synopsis
After Jesus rode triumphantly into Jerusalem,
He went to the temple to teach. First He threw
out the merchants and money changers, as
He had done one time earlier in His ministry.
While the religious leaders of His own people
sought ways to kill Him, some Gentiles came
to seek Him. Jesus taught several important
lessons to all who listened, presenting His
messages at times in parables.

The Courts of the Temple
Where did Jesus teach these parables? Perhaps He was out on Solomon's Porch again.
But He may also have gone into the temple
courts. The temple had several courts: (1) The

outer court, or Court of the Gentiles. This
court went from the inner side of the porticoes
to a wall on the inside that said: "No Gentile
may enter within the railing around the sanctuary and within the enclosure. Whoever
should be caught will render himself liable
to the death penalty which will inevitably follow." (2) The Women's Court. This court was
to the east of the temple proper and connected
to it by the Great Gate. It was 15 steps lower
down a stairway of curved steps. In its four
corners were four Corner Courts, each with
its own name. (3) The Priests' Court and the
Court of Israel. The latter surrounded the
former on three sides and was separated from
it either by a one-and-one-half-foot wall or
by a flat marker. The Court of Israel was reserved for Jewish adult males. Jesus may have
been teaching in the Court of the Gentiles.

*Chief Priests, Scribes, and Elders
of the People*
All three were religious leaders of the Jews.
The chief priests included all the temple offi-

The photo at the upper left shows a vineyard near Hebron today. Grapes in these rich vineyards grow into large bunches, like those at the left. Among the many duties of vineyard workers was treading the grapes, extracting the juice by treading with bare feet in a large vat filled with grapes.

cers, including the high priest and the captain of the temple. All sat on the Sanhedrin. The scribes were scholars who knew the Jewish law. They could be either Pharisees or Sadducees. Some of them later became rabbis. The elders may have been laymen. The Sanhedrin consisted of 71 elders. They were elected, then ordained by the laying on of hands. Their responsibilities included governing the Jewish community.

Husbandmen
Though husbandmen were farmers, plowmen, tillers of the soil, or laborers, in the parable in this section they are clearly tenant vinedressers. That means they rented the vineyard from the landowner and paid him from each year's grape crop. The Gezer Calendar suggests they may have worked all 12 months of the year.

Vineyards, Walls, Winepresses, and Watchtowers
Most Jewish vineyards were on the slopes of hills where they got the most sun. The vines usually grew along the ground. Around them were stone walls (hedges) which had watchtowers, both of which helped keep out animals, thieves, and other intruders. Winepresses were cut out of solid rock.

Clothes for Wedding Banquets
People wore special clothes for wedding feasts (Isa. 61:10). These feasts could last seven or more days.

479

AUGUSTUS
31 B.C.-A.D. 14
When Gaius Octavius, who became Augustus Caesar, heard that his great-uncle Julius Caesar had been murdered, he rushed to Rome where he learned that he was Caesar's heir. In 31 B.C. he became the new Caesar, or Roman emperor, and ruled until A.D. 14. He ordered the census which took Mary and Joseph to Bethlehem, where Jesus was born.

TIBERIUS
A.D. 14-37
When Augustus died in A.D. 14, Tiberius became the second Roman emperor. He was the son of Augustus' wife, the Empress Livia, but by her first husband. He was the Roman emperor at the time Jesus was crucified and during the early years of the church. Tiberius died on March 16, A.D. 37.

CALIGULA
A.D. 37-41
When Tiberius died, his grandnephew became the third Roman emperor in A.D. 37. When he shortly became insane, he began a reign of terror, torturing people at his meals and sending his army on wild and foolish campaigns. At last, in A.D. 41, he was assassinated by a conspiracy of officers.

CLAUDIUS
A.D. 41-54
Claudius, Tiberius' nephew, was a weak ruler, dominated by his wife and friends. During his reign, he forced all Jews to leave Rome, including Priscilla and Aquila (Acts 18:2). He put Herod Agrippa I over all Palestine. Herod murdered James the apostle and tried to murder Peter (Acts 12:1-11).

Give to Caesar

MATTHEW 22:15-22; MARK 12:13-17; LUKE 20:20-26

Synopsis
After Jesus rode triumphantly into Jerusalem, He taught in the temple. The religious leaders tried to trap Him, for they wanted Him out of the way. He was a threat to them. In one of their efforts, they tried to get Jesus to take sides—the Roman emperor Caesar, or the people.

Pharisees and Herodians
It is surprising to find these two groups linked together. The Pharisees originally stood against evil in society and in personal lives, though by Jesus' day many had often become narrow and petty, more concerned with rules than with God. Pharisees were middle class and more religious than the Sadducees, who often were willing to compromise with the political leaders of the country and tended to be more upper class. It has been estimated that in Jerusalem alone there were more than 20,000 associated with the Sadducees.

The Herodians, on the other hand, were probably more political than religious. While they in some sense supported the dynasty of Herod the Great, opinion differs widely as to whether they were soldiers, courtiers, Jews from regions ruled by Herod's sons, or those who favored direct rule by Herod rather than by Rome. The most widely held view is that they were supporters of Herod Antipas.

Both of these groups, religious and political, united in an effort to trap Jesus.

Caesar
Originally "Caesar" was the last name of the family of Julius Caesar. His successors adopted it as a title, so that it came to mean something like "king."

The Caesar who ruled the Roman Empire when Jesus was born was Julius Caesar's grandnephew, but Julius Caesar adopted him. He took the name Caesar Augustus. "Augustus" means "revered." He was the emperor who defeated Antony and Cleopatra

NERO
A.D. 54-68

first Nero seemed [to] be a good ruler, but [lat]er he married Pop[pa]ea, he began a reign [of] terror. Paul was [app]arently freed dur[ing] Nero's early reign, [aft]er he appealed to [Ca]esar (Acts 25:10-[11]. But Paul died a [ma]rtyr during Nero's [lat]er rule. Nero perse[cut]ed the Christians, [kill]ing many of them.

GALBA, OTHO, AND VITELLIUS
A.D. 68-69

Servius Sulpicius Galba, a wealthy nobleman, was made emperor when Nero died, but less than a year later he was murdered and Marcus Salvius Otho became emperor. He committed suicide only a few months later, after he was defeated by Aulus Vitellius, who was also murdered within a few months. During this time, which was after Paul's death, the Jewish people had begun to rebel against Rome.

VESPASIAN
A.D. 70-79

Jewish rebellion in Palestine came to a head during his rule as emperor. In the year A.D. 70, when he became emperor, Vespasian put his son Titus in charge of fighting the rebellious Jews. Titus defeated them, burned Jerusalem, and carried many temple treasures back to Rome. This was the destruction which Jesus foretold (Luke 19:41-44).

TITUS
A.D. 79-81

When his father Vespasian died, Titus became the new emperor. He had been successful in defeating the Jewish rebels and in burning Jerusalem. An arch still stands in Rome today, commemorating this victory. Titus, however, ruled only two years before he died an untimely death.

DOMITIAN
A.D. 81-96

The last living apostle, John, was exiled to Patmos during the reign of Domitian. During his reign, John wrote the Book of Revelation. Like Titus, Domitian was a son of Vespasian. Thus, with him, the New Testament era drew to a close, and with it, the first century.

at the Battle of Actium in 31 B.C. and made Egypt a Roman province.

The Caesar mentioned most often in the New Testament, however, is Tiberius, who was emperor from A.D. 14 to A.D. 37. Tiberius was the stepson of Augustus and also, by marrying his daughter, his son-in-law! The denarius mentioned in Jesus' comments about paying taxes to Caesar probably had the head of Tiberius on it.

Tribute to Caesar

The tribute was a tax that was required to support the Roman government. Jews hated it because it went directly to the emperor's treasury. This proved that the Jews were subject to Rome. Note that neither Jesus nor His questioners had the required silver money in their possession. They had to ask someone for it. The coin would have been a denarius, not the shekel that was used to pay the temple tax. The wording on the coin probably said that the emperor, Tiberius, was the divine son of Caesar Augustus. No wonder Jews didn't like it!

The coin which was shown to Jesus was probably a denarius with the image of Tiberius on it, as shown at the upper right. An enlarged drawing of Tiberius, taken from a coin, is at the right.

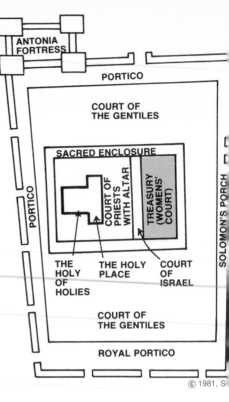

© 1981, S

The Widow's Mite

MARK 12:41-44; LUKE 21:1-4

Synopsis
Jesus rode triumphantly into Jerusalem on Sunday, with crowds cheering Him. That night He stayed in Bethany, probably at the home of Mary, Martha, and Lazarus. On Monday morning, He pronounced a curse on a barren fig tree as He returned to Jerusalem, where at the temple, He drove out the money changers and merchants. On that same day, while the religious leaders tried to trap Him, Gentiles came to seek Him. On Tuesday, as Jesus made His way back to Jerusalem from Bethany, He and His disciples noted that the fig tree He had cursed was now withered. In Jerusalem, while Jesus was in the temple, the religious leaders tried to question Jesus' authority as a teacher (rabbi), but through parables He showed how His authority came from God. They tried to trick Him again by asking if the people should pay taxes to Caesar, the Roman emperor. Jesus answered simply that they should give Caesar what was his, and God what was His. That same Tuesday afternoon, while Jesus and His disciples were in the treasury, or Women's Court of the temple, Jesus pointed out the great value of a gift which a widow was giving.

Mite and Farthing
What was the gift the widow was giving? The words "mite" and "farthing" do not help us much because they are 17th-century English

Upper left: the poor widow gives her all—two mites, while wealthy men wait to give only a small part of what they own. The coin above is a "mite," actually called a lepton. It was minted by Coponius, the first procurator (Pilate was procurator during Jesus' time). It is a small brass coin with a legend "Of Caesar" on the front.

482

The "farthing" above was actually a Roman quadrans, described below. The widow gave her two mites in the temple treasury, pictured at the right in the model of the temple. It is shown on the map at the left, assuming it was in the Court of the Women.

words used to translate the Greek word *lepton* and the Roman word *quadrans*. The tiny lepton (mite) was the smallest bronze or copper coin made. There were many different lepta. On the front and back they may have had pictures of open flowers, anchors, grape clusters, helmets, fringed umbrellas, ears of corn, a wine jug, or a palm tree with two date clusters. Most had inscriptions referring to the emperor or some other ruler.

The quadrans (farthing) was a large bronze or copper Roman coin. At the time of this story the quadrans probably had the head of Tiberius Caesar on one side and a wreath enclosing the letters "S.C." on the other. The letters were short for *Senatus consulto*, meaning "by decree of the senate." A quadrans would buy two sparrows, the only meat the poor could afford.

The Temple Treasury
Where was the temple treasury? The answer is that we don't exactly know! Since the widow was able to put her small copper coins into the treasury, it was probably in the part of the temple called The Court of the Women, but where in that room we do not know. It was the room most used for worship and meetings, so the treasury may have been located in a columned walkway around the outside

of the Court of Women.

In this area there were 13 boxes or urns with trumpet-shaped tubes called "trumpets" on the top to receive money offerings. Seven of these trumpets were for men to deposit their half-shekel temple tax; the other six were for free-will offerings such as the one the widow gave.

In the Old Testament the "tithe" or a tenth of one's goods was to be given to God. Jesus used the widow to teach that Christians should give more than they can easily afford. The purpose of giving is to support God's work and help those who are physically and spiritually needy.

Widows
It was not easy to be a widow in New Testament times. People grouped widows with orphans and foreigners as the most to be pitied. Though she might live with her children or her deceased husband's parents, she really belonged nowhere until she remarried. To make a widow's life more tolerable, a custom called "levirate marriage" required the husband's brother or other member of the family to marry her, if she was childless, and have children so the dead man would not be forgotten. The church made special provision for widows (see 1 Tim. 5:3-16).

483

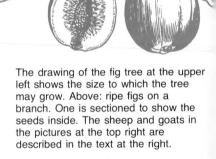

Figs, Lamps,
and Sheep—Some Parables

MATTHEW 24:32—25:46; MARK 13:28-37; LUKE 21:29-36

Synopsis
As Jesus left Jerusalem on Tuesday afternoon to return to Bethany for the night, He and His disciples stopped on the Mount of Olives. He taught them many things, among which were important truths presented in parables. Some parables were about simple, everyday things such as figs, lamps, and sheep. But they taught eternal truths.

Figs
The fig tree exists in both wild and cultivated forms. It can, under proper conditions, grow to a height of 30 feet or more. It bears its fruit twice a year, a winter crop in May or June and a summer crop in late August or September. The fruit buds appear in February, some two months before the leaves appear. A tree can live for as long as 400 years. Figs often grow in the corners of vineyards in Palestine.

The fruit has some interesting characteristics. The flower grows inside what we think of as the fruit of the tree. At the tip there is an opening through which a fig wasp crawls to pollinate the plant. The pear-shaped, hollow fruit is, strictly speaking, not the fruit at all. The real fruit is the tiny little seeds inside.

The fig has many uses. Ancient peoples made it into cakes (1 Sam. 25:18). A poultice to cure boils

The drawing of the fig tree at the upper left shows the size to which the tree may grow. Above: ripe figs on a branch. One is sectioned to show the seeds inside. The sheep and goats in the pictures at the top right are described in the text at the right.

484

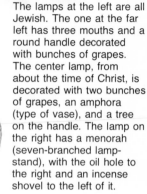

The lamps at the left are all Jewish. The one at the far left has three mouths and a round handle decorated with bunches of grapes. The center lamp, from about the time of Christ, is decorated with two bunches of grapes, an amphora (type of vase), and a tree on the handle. The lamp on the right has a menorah (seven-branched lamp-stand), with the oil hole to the right and an incense shovel to the left of it.

was made from pressed figs (2 Kings 20:7). And the large, hand-shaped leaves were used by Adam and Eve as clothing (Gen. 3:7).

Lamps

It is strange that the Bible nowhere describes the ordinary, domestic lamp. It does mention, however, the twisted flax-thread wick and the jar of olive oil that was stored as lamp fuel.

Archeologists have discovered lamps from all periods of ancient history and can trace the changes in lamps through the centuries. The earliest Palestinian lamps were made of clay pottery, though they may have been copied from the metal lamps of other cultures. Early lamps had four, or even seven, spouts for wicks. Later lamps in Canaan had a single spout. But these lamps tipped easily and caused fires, so a base was added and under Greek influence Jews learned how to close in their lamps and fill them through a nozzle or filling hole. Because lamps were fed by oil, women got up a couple of times each night

to "trim their lamps," i.e. raise the wick so the fire wouldn't go out.

Sheep and Goats

Sheep and goats are among the earliest of man's domesticated animals, as early as 6000 or 7000 B.C. The earliest evidence suggests that they may have been domesticated that early in northern Iran. Dogs have been used to herd sheep from 5000 B.C. on. These sheep were probably brown and reddish in color, not the white color we expect. They were first valued for their meat, then later for their wool, milk and cheese, skins, and manure. The broad-tailed sheep is most common, its 10-15-pound tail being considered a delicacy.

Though the skeleton of a goat is almost indistinguishable from that of a sheep, it has quite distinct habits. It was first valued for its milk, but with the development of the cow it declined in popularity. The goat can strip land rapidly in quest of food. Ancient peoples normally ate only kid meat. Goats' skin was used to make water bottles and its hair was valued for making cloth.

Sheep are gentle, dependent; goats are not.

Mary Anoints Jesus' Feet

MATTHEW 26:6-13; MARK 14:3-9; JOHN 12:2-11

Synopsis
The last week before Jesus' crucifixion had come. On Sunday, Jesus had entered Jerusalem triumphantly, riding on a donkey. On Monday, He pronounced a curse on a barren fig tree and drove out the merchants and money changers from the temple. On Tuesday, He answered a question about paying taxes to Caesar and pointed out a widow giving her small coins in the temple. That evening, He taught His disciples on the Mount of Olives. Tuesday evening, Jesus was a guest at the home of Simon the Leper. While there, Mary of Bethany anointed His feet.

The Alabaster Box
There is only one word for this in Greek; it should probably be translated "an alabaster jar." Alabaster is a soft marble common in the area of Alabastron in Egypt, from which the word may come. It is very fine-grained and pure white or translucent when no impurities are present, but the presence of iron oxide and other impurities produces beautiful combinations of yellow, pale and dark brown, and red. This soft marble was so often used for ointment containers that the word came to mean an ointment jar. Alabaster is formed by water dripping in limestone caves to form stalactites and stalagmites.

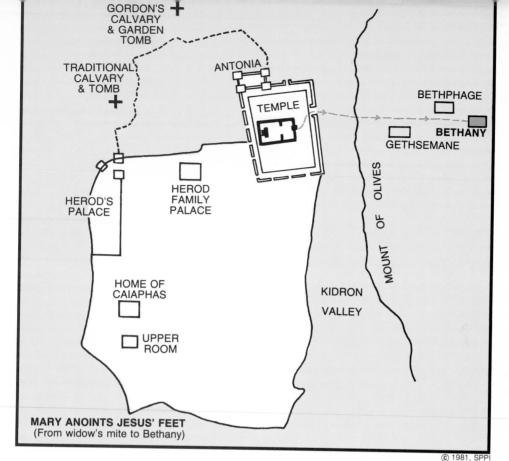

GORDON'S CALVARY & GARDEN TOMB

TRADITIONAL CALVARY & TOMB

ANTONIA

TEMPLE

BETHPHAGE

BETHANY
GETHSEMANE

HEROD'S PALACE

HEROD FAMILY PALACE

MOUNT OF OLIVES

HOME OF CAIAPHAS

KIDRON

VALLEY

UPPER ROOM

MARY ANOINTS JESUS' FEET
(From widow's mite to Bethany)

Lower left: the plant from which nard, probably spike-nard, comes. It grows in the Himalayan Mountains and other high regions in that part of the world. The ala-baster jar at the left, from ancient times, held oint-ments such as nard. The map above shows the possible route Jesus took through the temple to Bethany.

Today's alabaster is a form of gypsum used to decorate houses.

Spikenard
What an interesting history this word has! The word resulted from the fact that the Greek adjective describing the nard is very rare and very difficult to translate. Wycliffe seems to be the first to coin the word; he speaks of "spikanard." Today we believe the word means "pure," though a good case can be made for the conclusion that the adjective is a technical word for a specific kind of nard, or even that the phrase should be translated "Indian nard."

Nard comes from the Himalayan Mountains and other high altitude places in northern India. Cheaper varieties come from other countries. It is a fragrant ointment made from the shaggy roots and lower stems of an Indian plant. It is used to anoint royalty. John may have seen Mary's act as a symbol of the anointing of Jesus as king of the Holy City. One historian tells us nard was very expensive.

The Bag
Mark says simply that some complained about the waste of the oint-ment. Matthew adds that they were disciples. John singles out Judas Iscariot and mentions that he had the bag. What was this bag? The word John uses refers to a money box or chest made of wood or some other hard material such as tortoiseshell. Originally it referred to the small case in which reeds and mouthpieces for woodwind instruments were kept. Then it came to mean the money box in which some people kept money to help the poor.

487

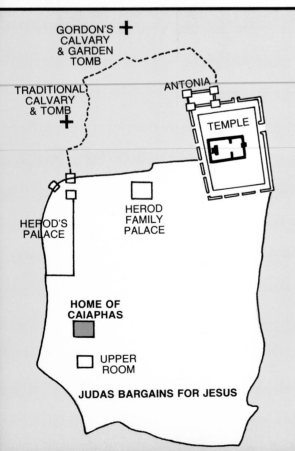

JUDAS BARGAINS FOR JESUS

Thirty Pieces of Silver

MATTHEW 26:14-16; MARK 14:10-11; LUKE 22:3-6

Synopsis

Tuesday had been a busy day for Jesus. He had taught in the temple and answered questions about paying taxes to Caesar. He also pointed out a widow who had given her all—two small coins. He entered into discussions with the religious leaders, who questioned His role as a teacher. That evening, on the way back to Bethany, He stopped at the Mount of Olives to teach His disciples there. In Bethany, while eating dinner at the home of Simon the Leper, Mary of Bethany anointed His feet with expensive ointment. After this happened, Judas Iscariot went into Jerusalem, and sold his loyalty to Jesus for 30 pieces of silver.

Judas Iscariot

Iscariot seems to be a surname, since his father Simon also had it (John 6:71). The name may mean "from Kerioth," a small town in southern Judea. But it may also refer to the Sicarii, or "dagger men," who were the most radical of the Jewish nationalistic groups. Jewish historian Josephus said that they did not hesi-

tate to put their opponents to death with Roman *sicas*, or daggers.

Matthew and Mark both tell us that immediately after Judas complained about Mary's "extravagance" in anointing Jesus' feet with nard, he went to the chief priests to betray Him. Why did he choose this moment? Perhaps he finally decided Jesus wasn't going to overthrow Rome. Perhaps he could not appreciate the lavish attention Mary paid to Jesus. But the best answer is perhaps that Jesus' rebuke (John 12:7-8) made Judas so furious he finally decided to do what he had been thinking about for some time. Or he may have felt he would get more money by betraying Jesus than by being His treasurer.

The Chief Priests

The chief priests would have been the current high priest, all former high priests, members of a few select families from whom the high priests were selected, and the treasurer and captain of police. The office of high priest was no longer hereditary or for life. It had become a political plum. Members were always Sadducees. Though they are always men-

The map at the far left locates the house of Caiaphas, high priest at this time. The 30 pieces of silver, pictured above, are described below (silver shekel or tetradrachm of Tyre).

tioned in the New Testament before scribes and Pharisees, they no longer were respected by the common people.

Thirty Pieces of Silver

The same Greek word is translated "silver" in Matthew and "money" in Mark and Luke. In all cases the reference is probably to the silver shekel pictured above. About the size of an American half dollar, the usual shekel used in Palestine to pay the temple tax was from Tyre in Syria. It was the equivalent of the Greek tetradrachm.

The head on the front was the Tyrian god, Baal Melcarth, with a wreath of laurel in the style of Heracles. On the reverse was the Seleucid eagle with the palm of victory over his shoulder. The inscription means "From Tyre, Sanctuary and Asylum."

The Last Supper
—Preparations

MATTHEW 26:17-20; MARK 14:12-17;
LUKE 22:7-18, 24-30; JOHN 13:1-20

Synopsis
The week prior to the crucifixion was quickly
drawing to a close. Events moved toward the
cross, where Jesus would be crucified. On
Thursday afternoon, preparations were
made for the Passover meal to be eaten. Jesus
and His disciples would eat together in an
upper room.

The Passover Meal
According to the Talmud, a commentary on
the laws of Moses by the rabbis, four or five
cups of red wine were drunk at various times
during the paschal supper. The wine was
mixed with water, one part to three of the
wine. The first cup (see Luke 22:17) introduced a blessing on the day and the wine.
This was followed by ritual washings. Bitter

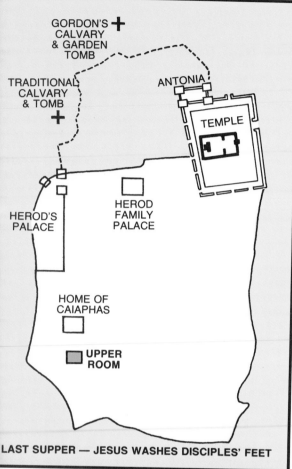

GORDON'S ✝
CALVARY
& GARDEN
TOMB

TRADITIONAL
CALVARY
& TOMB
✝

ANTONIA

TEMPLE

HEROD'S
PALACE

HEROD
FAMILY
PALACE

HOME OF
CAIAPHAS

UPPER
ROOM

LAST SUPPER — JESUS WASHES DISCIPLES' FEET

© 1981, SPPI

The location of the traditional Upper Room is shown above, top. Note its nearness to Caiaphas' house. Left: upper rooms of Jerusalem in recent times. Above, bottom: the Cenacle, traditional Upper Room.

herbs, unleavened bread, roast lamb, a special feast called "the Chagigah of the 14th day," and a spicy sauce were then brought in. The ritual in which the son was instructed in the meaning of the Passover was followed by the singing of Psalms 113—114 (the Hallel). After the second cup of wine, a blessing was made on each item of food. Guests ate in a reclining position, with the lamb eaten last. The ceremony was completed with thanks, a third cup of wine called "the cup of thanksgiving" (see 1 Cor. 10:16), Psalms 115—118 (the remainder of the Hallel), and a final cup of wine. Sometimes the Great Hallel (Pss. 120—136) and a fifth wine cup were added.

Jesus probably introduced the "Lord's Supper" after the meal and before the cup.

The Upper Room

An upstairs room is mentioned in connection with the Last Supper, the post-Resurrection meetings of the apostles, and Pentecost. Luke, however, uses two different words, so two different places may have been meant.

Large upstairs rooms with both inside and outside stairs are known in Old Testament times (see 2 Kings 1:2 for an example). The room in which the Last Supper took place could have been such an enclosed room; it could also have been an open room, or *medhafeh*, above a clay-covered roof, on which Arab families in the main house of the village still spend a lot of time.

It is probably impossible to locate the site exactly today. Some identify it with the house of Mary, John Mark's mother. Epiphanius tells us the Emperor Hadrian visited it in A.D. 135. What is now called the "Cenacle," a traditional Upper Room, is located in a church that was until recently the En Neby Daud Mosque.

Benefactor

Gods, kings, and outstanding citizens were called benefactors for some special act they had performed. They received a title and their names were recorded in a register. Even cruel despots, as Ptolemy VII of Egypt (147-117 B.C.), nicknamed "Big Belly" and "Malefactor," were given the title of Benefactor.

Footwashing

Moses wrote of a ritual washing for priests (Ex. 30:17-21). The wife or a servant usually washed the feet of houseguests, though the host might do it for a special guest.

491

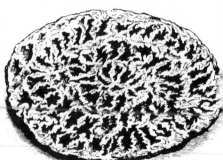

Far left: Jesus serves His disciples at the Last Supper. Above: Passover bread. Note that it is flat and round, like a pizza crust.

The Last Supper—Eating Together

MATTHEW 26:26-29; MARK 14:22-25; LUKE 22:19-20

Synopsis
Wednesday of that last week before the crucifixion was a day of silence. The Bible says nothing about it. Jesus probably rested in Bethany with His disciples. But on Thursday, preparations were made for the Passover, which we remember as the Last Supper. In an Upper Room in Jerusalem, Jesus ate with His disciples.

The Cup
Cups were made of pottery or metal in ancient times. There were two basic types. Some had handles. The more common cup was a shallow bowl without handles, which came in a variety of shapes and sizes. Many materials were used to make cups. Gold, silver, bronze, pottery, wood, horn, and, somewhat later, lead and pewter were used. Zephyrinus of Rome, a contemporary of Tertullian, and Jerome both spoke of glass cups for communion

(Jerome also spoke of baskets for bread).

Numerous rituals and ceremonies came to be associated with cups. The Jewish Talmud, for example, prescribes ritual cleansing for seven types of containers, including earthenware, metal, bone, and wooden vessels. Strict Jews, as the Pharisees, washed all cups that had in any way come into contact with sinners and the "people of the land," the average citizen. This special washing ceremony did not only include cups, but also pitchers and kettles (Mark 7:4). Its purpose was to distinguish Jews from their Gentile counterparts.

Much symbolism is also connected with cups. In the Old Testament a cup is a symbol of blessing for a good man; for an evil man it symbolizes punishment. In the New Testament a cup is always a symbol of suffering or trouble. Yet it also symbolizes fellowship with the Lord Himself.

492

Right: couches on which people in Roman times reclined to eat. The Last Supper may have been eaten on couches much like these. Above: Mount Zion. In this general area were Caiaphas' house, the Upper Room, and also King David's tomb.

Luke mentions two cups at the Last Supper. This may reflect the influence of the paschal meal or a local tradition in the church.

Bread

Along with water, bread has long been considered the staff of life. If someone ate bread and drank wine with another it was a sign of intimate friendship.

In biblical times bread could be made from wheat, barley, bean, lentil, millet, or spelt meal or flour (see Ezek. 4:9), though the first two were the most common. The grain would be ground with a mortar and pestle or taken to a mill. The ground meal or flour was then mixed with water. In 1941 at ez-Zeb the clay figure of a woman kneading bread was discovered in a cemetery; it dated back prior to 600 B.C. After kneading, the bread was baked in one of four ways: (1) on heated flat rocks, (2) on a flat clay griddle or saucepan, (3) around a heated earthenware cylinder, or (4) in a portable firepot or cooking jar. The fuel consisted of twigs, sticks, stubble, or grass. The bread was round, flat, spherical, or heart-shaped. It was usually about 18 inches in diameter and was sometimes punctured with holes.

The New Testament

A testament can be either a will or a covenant. When after the supper Jesus took the third cup of the paschal meal and spoke of the New Covenant in His blood (Luke 22:20), He combined the truths in Exodus 24:8 and Jeremiah 31:31. A covenant is God's declaration of His will. Jesus was perhaps talking about His will, since He was about to die. Both meanings are possible.

493

This large outcropping of rock on the Mount of Olives is thought to be the place where Jesus prayed. A portion of the rock is included in the Franciscan Basilica of the Agony, mentioned on the next page. Right: approximately the route which Jesus followed on the way to Gethsemane, and back again. This route may actually have gone through the temple.

Gethsemane

MATTHEW 26:36-46; MARK 14:32-42; LUKE 22:39-46

Synopsis
Early that Thursday before the crucifixion, the disciples prepared the Passover meal in an Upper Room in Jerusalem. After sunset, when the time of the Passover began, they ate with Jesus, celebrating what we have come to know as the Last Supper. As the supper ended, they made their way to a lonely garden on the Mount of Olives, a place known as the Garden of Gethsemane.

From the Upper Room to Gethsemane
The Upper Room is, according to tradition, close to David's tomb, south of the house of Caiaphas and Herod's palace in what was then the wealthy Upper City in Old Jerusalem. Today it is easy to go from this spot directly to Gethsemane on the Ophel Road just south of the Zion and Dung Gates. But the western portion of the Ophel Road was built less than 10 years ago. And in New Testament times the wall went south of the Cenacle, the traditional site of the Upper Room, and enclosed it, whereas today the wall is on the north and excludes half of Mount Zion. The Bible says simply that Jesus and His disciples went out into the Mount of Olives as was their custom. John tells us they crossed the Kidron Valley, through which a winter stream flows (St. Mary's Spring). Thus, the exact route Jesus followed is not known today.

494

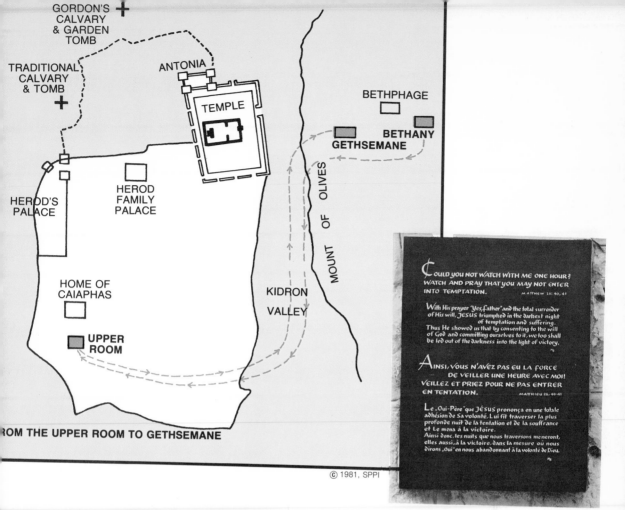

GORDON'S CALVARY & GARDEN TOMB

TRADITIONAL CALVARY & TOMB

ANTONIA

TEMPLE

BETHPHAGE

BETHANY
GETHSEMANE

HEROD'S PALACE

HEROD FAMILY PALACE

MOUNT OF OLIVES

HOME OF CAIAPHAS

KIDRON VALLEY

UPPER ROOM

ROM THE UPPER ROOM TO GETHSEMANE

© 1981, SPPI

Could you not watch with me one hour? Watch and pray that you may not enter into temptation.
MATTHEW 16: 40, 41

With His prayer "Yes, Father" and the total surrender of His will, JESUS triumphed in the darkest night of temptation and suffering.
Thus He showed us that by consenting to the will of God and committing ourselves to it, we too shall be led out of the darkness into the light of victory.

Ainsi, vous n'avez pas eu la force de veiller une heure avec moi! Veillez et priez pour ne pas entrer en tentation.
MATTHIEU 26, 40-41

Le "Oui-Père" que JÉSUS prononça en une totale adhésion de Sa volonté, Lui fit traverser la plus profonde nuit de la tentation et de la souffrance et Le mena à la victoire.
Ainsi donc, les nuits que nous traversons meneront, elles aussi, à la victoire, dans la mesure où nous dirons "Oui" en nous abandonnant à la volonté de Dieu.

Lower left: the Basilica of the Agony, built over a portion of the rock where Jesus is thought to have prayed. The largest part of the rock protrudes behind the church. Outside, the sign (above) reminds visitors of that event.

Gethsemane

Gethsemane was a garden, field, or enclosure in an olive grove on the southwestern slopes of the Mount of Olives. The word "Gethsemane" means "olive vat" or "olive press," so there probably was a stone structure of that type there, as there still are in many places in Israel today. Matthew and Mark both suggest that Gethsemane was some distance inside the area called the Mount of Olives.

Two of the sites in present-day Jerusalem identified with Gethsemane are: (1) east of the modern road from Jerusalem to Bethany, where the Church of the Tomb of the Virgin and the Franciscan Basilica of the Agony are located; (2) higher up the Mount of Olives where the Russian Church of Magdalene and the Franciscan Basilica are located.

495

Judas Betrays Jesus

MATTHEW 26:47-56; MARK 14:43-52; LUKE 22:47-53; JOHN 18:2-12

Synopsis
After the Passover meal, the Last Supper, had ended on that Thursday night, Jesus went with His disciples to a lonely garden on the Mount of Olives. There, in Gethsemane, He prayed. But as Thursday night wore on into the very early hours before dawn on Friday, Judas came to betray Jesus.

Torches, Lanterns, and Weapons
The detachment of soldiers and officials from the chief priests and Pharisees came to arrest Jesus with torches, lanterns, and weapons. What did these lights look like?

Lanterns and torches are so much alike it is difficult to distinguish them in Hebrew and Greek. When the lamps used in houses were inadequate, as they would be outdoors at night, torches were often used, but the Romans also had lanterns made of various kinds of translucent material.

Weapons were basically of two kinds, offensive and defensive. Some of the common offensive weapons were: swords and shorter daggers (double-edged and worn in a leather sheath at the side, the sword on the right, the dagger on the left), spears (long wooden shafts tipped with stone or metal heads), javelins (spears used for hurling; all Roman legionnaires had them), lances (spears with longer shafts used for thrusting in the front lines of battle), and mauls (war clubs made

496

with stones, balls of metal, or wood).

Defensive weapons included shields and armor. Archeologists have never discovered a shield in Israel. This is because, contrary to what we might think, they were made of perishable materials such as skins, wood, leather, and wickerwork—usually not metal. Two exceptions are King Solomon's gold-plated and King Rehoboam's bronze shields. Two shapes were common: those round at the top and square on the bottom, and smaller, round ones. The ordinary soldier had a leather shield over a wooden frame, reinforced with a metal stud in the center. It had a handle on the inside.

The ordinary soldier did not have the coat of mail the medieval knight wore. His armor was made of leather cut in strips, wrapped with metal, and wired together. To this body armor a heart guard of bronze and shoulder pieces were added. The whole suit was tied in the back. To this body armor were added a helmet (usually a leather cap, then metal lined with felt or sponge) and greaves (leg armor made of bronze molded to the shape of the leg; Greek greaves wrapped their legs, but Roman greaves covered only the fronts of their legs).

Olive Trees

Olive trees are so important in the life of Israel they have been called the tree of life! This small, gray, twisted evergreen with its pale olive undersides will grow where no other tree will grow. Its oil has many uses: cooking, lighting lamps, treating wounds, anointing kings. Its wood was used for furniture. Olives were eaten as a relish, much as they are today. One tree can produce as much as 20 gallons of olive oil in a year. To get the fruit from the trees, the trees are shaken. So many blossoms are produced in the spring they thickly blanket the ground. They are so hardy only locusts can destroy them. Gethsemane probably had an olive vat. This was an upright stone with a wooden handle, which was rolled over olives on a flat round stone with grooves, which let the oil flow out.

Judas' Kiss

In the Near East kissing is more of a ceremony than it is for us. Children in Jewish families would normally kiss older people on the hand or beard. Fathers and husbands would kiss their children and wives on the forehead. Disciples would not normally kiss their masters on the face first, as Judas did to Jesus.

Upper left: from the temple area, one may look east toward the Mount of Olives, where Judas betrayed Jesus. Below that photo are drawings of Roman torches, as they appear on various sculptures, plus a Roman lantern (center), as it appears on Trajan's column. Bottom center: the great olive trees in Gethsemane. Though some say these date from the time of Christ, this is not likely, for all trees were destroyed in A.D. 70. A branch of the olive tree appears at the right. Below: the Golden Gate and the temple area as seen from Gethsemane, from the traditional place of Jesus' agony.

497

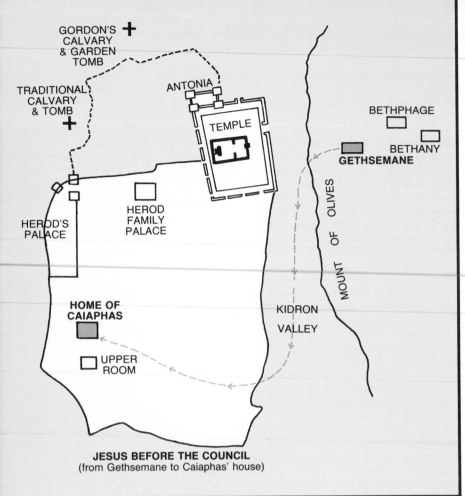

JESUS BEFORE THE COUNCIL
(from Gethsemane to Caiaphas' house)

© 1981, SPPI

The map at the left shows one possible route from Gethsemane to the house of Caiaphas. Another possible route lay through the temple.

Jesus on Trial—Annas, Caiaphas, and the Council

MATTHEW 26:57-68; MARK 14:53-65;
LUKE 22:54, 63-65; JOHN 18:12-14, 19-24

Synopsis

The Passover meal, which we remember as the Last Supper, began after sunset on Thursday evening. When it ended, Jesus went with His disciples to Gethsemane, a garden in an olive grove on the Mount of Olives. There He prayed and waited until Judas led a band of men to capture Him. As night wore on into early morning, Jesus was led to Annas, then Caiaphas, and the council for trial.

Annas the High Priest

Annas, or Ananos, was high priest from A.D. 6 to 15. So powerful and influential was he, however, that even after he was deposed by Valerius Gratus he was able to control the selection of his successors. Five of his sons, his son-in-law Caiaphas, and his grandson Matthias became high priests after him! Appointed by the Quirinius who is mentioned in Luke 2 as governor of Syria, he seems to have controlled the priestly party in Jerusalem for the rest of his life. This conclusion is supported by John's insistence that Jesus appeared before Annas before He went to Caiaphas (John 18:13).

Visitors to Jerusalem today may see the house of Annas, just outside the present wall. An olive tree at the northeast corner of the chapel of the Convent of the Olive Tree is said to be the tree to which Jesus was chained while awaiting Annas' examination, but this is very unlikely.

Above: a coin issued by Valerius Gratus, fourth procurator of Judea (Pontius Pilate was fifth). The coin was struck in A.D. 16. Valerius Gratus appointed Caiaphas, son-in-law of Annas, as high priest after he deposed Annas. Below: from the south wall of Old Jerusalem today one may see the area where the house of Caiaphas was thought to have been, in the place where construction is in progress. This house is pictured as it might have been, reconstructed in a model city in Jerusalem today (left).

Caiaphas the High Priest

Joseph Caiaphas (or Caiaphas) was made high priest by Valerius Gratus in A.D. 18 and was deposed by the Roman Procurator Vitelius in A.D. 36. He was succeeded, however, by Annas' son Jonathan. The Roman government controlled its Jewish citizens by appointing both civil and religious leaders. The fact that Caiaphas held office for so long while all the others had such short tenures suggests that he was shrewd and flexible. A Sadducee, Caiaphas first suggested the idea of Jesus' death to save the nation. He continued to persecute the church after Jesus' death.

In Jerusalem today a ruined Armenian shrine that is being rebuilt is claimed to be the house of Caiaphas. That claim goes back to the fourth century. The shrine contains the prison in which Jesus is supposed to have been imprisoned and has an excellent view overlooking the temple.

The Christ and the Son of Man

When the high priest asked Jesus if He was "the Christ," he was asking if Jesus was the Messiah. The first word is Greek, the second Hebrew. The word, meaning "the anointed one," has a very special meaning in Jewish history. Kings were anointed to indicate the special role God wanted them to play. Jesus preferred to be called "Son of man," however (Dan. 7:13).

499

Peter Denies Jesus

MATTHEW 26:58, 69-75; MARK 14:54, 66-72; LUKE 22:54-62; JOHN 18:15-18, 25-27

Synopsis

After the Last Supper, the Thursday evening Passover meal, Jesus left Jerusalem with His disciples and went to a quiet grove of olive trees called Gethsemane, on the Mount of Olives. There He prayed and waited. In the early morning hours, Judas came with a band of men to betray Jesus and take Him prisoner. Jesus was taken for trial first to Annas, then to Caiaphas and the high council. During these trials, Peter waited in the courtyard of the high priest. But when Peter was recognized as a disciple, he cursed and denied that he knew Jesus.

Inside the High Priest's Palace

To understand the scene of Peter's denial, the reader of the New Testament needs to have a general idea of what the high priest's palace or house looked like. Otherwise it is hard to understand why someone would build a fire in the midst of "the hall."

Below left: Peter warms himself by the fire, and denies his Lord. Below center: stone steps from Jesus' time, southeast of Caiaphas' house, with the Mount of Olives in the background. Jesus may have walked on these steps. Right: St. Peter in Gallicantu Church, which is described at the right.

500

First of all, "hall" (Luke 22:55) is better translated "courtyard" NIV, what we sometimes call a "quadrangle." This is a space surrounded on four sides, usually by buildings. Today it may be covered with grass, but most often in the Near East a courtyard would be paved or covered with flagstones. To enter this "hall" a person first opened either a heavy folding gate or, in the case of one or two individuals arriving on foot, a small door. That gate or door opened onto a passageway that led to the courtyard, which was open to the sky and in which a fire could be built on colder nights.

The passageway, called a "porch" in the King James Version (Matt. 26:71), that led from the street to the courtyard was probably selected by Peter for an easy escape, should his identification as Jesus' disciple become so dangerous it might lead to arrest.

While Peter was out in the courtyard with the temple guards and the high priest's servants and maids, Jesus was probably in one of the open rooms that faced the courtyard, since He could both see and hear Peter. Mark suggests that the rooms were raised somewhat above the level of the courtyard (Mark 14:66). Rooms that were open on the courtyard side were common in houses of this type.

It is possible that Peter made more than three denials of his close association with Jesus. At least the four Gospel writers list more than three people who asked Peter about his association with Jesus. Mark mentions that the servant girl, probably a female porter, questioned him twice, followed by those who were standing near Peter. Matthew mentions this "damsel" only once; then another servant girl and those standing near Peter question him. Luke tells of a servant girl, someone else (a man), and another man. John mentions the girl at the door, an unspecified person, and Malchus, the high priest's servant who was a relative of Annas, and whose ear Peter had cut off.

St. Peter in Gallicantu Church

Just 50 years ago the Church of St. Peter in Gallicantu (cockcrow) was built to memorialize Peter's triple denial of Christ and his bitter weeping after the cock crowed. It is built over the ruins of an old Byzantine monastery that tradition identifies as the spot where Peter wept.

About a century ago archeologists excavated an area near the church and discovered an ancient stone pathway Jesus may have used on His trips to and from Bethany.

The priests at the church also argue that the church is on the site of the house of Caiaphas. The church is some distance to the east of the more traditional location for that house, however. But when you visit, they will show you not only an ancient Jewish stone mill and a set of Hebrew measures, but also another dungeon in which Caiaphas supposedly imprisoned Jesus.

Judas Hangs Himself

MATTHEW 27:3-10; ACTS 1:18-19

Synopsis
After the Passover meal, the Last Supper, ended, Jesus went with His disciples to Gethsemane, a garden among olive trees on the Mount of Olives. While He prayed until the early morning hours, Judas came with a band of men to capture Him. Jesus was taken before the high priests Annas and Caiaphas, and the council, for trial. During the trial Peter, waiting in the courtyard of the high priest's home, denied that he knew Jesus. By dawn the council had condemned Jesus to death. When Judas learned this, he was suddenly filled with remorse, tossed the 30 pieces of silver at the chief priests, and hanged himself.

The Potter's Field
Today the phrase "potter's field" means a cemetery, usually in a large city, in which the poor, criminals, and the unknown are buried. But how did it get such an unusual name? The answer is found in Matthew 27:8. The chief priests apparently needed a burial place for "strangers," people from other towns and cities. When Judas threw at them the 30 Tyrian shekels they had given him to betray Jesus, they agreed to buy the much-needed field from a potter who had offered to sell it to them. It is interesting that they had had enough money to pay Judas

502

to betray Christ, but not enough to provide a place to bury foreigners. Sin distorts priorities in unbelievable ways!

Akeldama, the Field of Blood

Two traditions tell us that what Matthew calls the "potter's field" came to be known as the Field of Blood. Matthew tells us that the name was based on the fact that Judas said he had betrayed innocent blood, namely that of Jesus.

Acts, however, gives a slightly different tradition: It says that Judas bought a field with "the reward for his wickedness" (Acts 1:18) and poured out *his* life's blood as a result of a fall in the field.

Some argue that Matthew's account may in some way reflect the influence of Zechariah 11:12-13. But an easier answer is that Luke, in Acts, is reporting a local tradition that differs from the tradition Matthew heard.

Akeldama (Haceldama or Hakeldema), "the Field of Blood," has traditionally, and perhaps correctly, been identified with Hakk ed-Dumm, near the Greek Orthodox Church and Convent of St. Oniprius, at the point where the Valley of Hinnom joins the Kidron Valley, south of Gethsemane. Another tradition says the apostles hid here when Jesus was on trial.

Left: a view of the Hinnom Valley from the Mount of Olives. In the lower center is a large monastery among tombs of New Testament times, thought to be at Akeldama. The lower right part of the picture shows Ophel, the Jerusalem of King David's time. Lower left: tombs at Akeldama. Below: location of Akeldama on map.

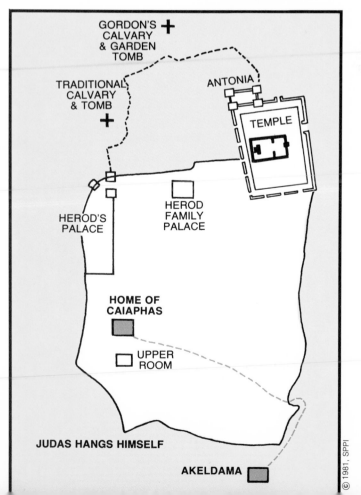

503

Jesus Is Sent to Pilate

MATTHEW 27:2, 11-14; MARK 15:1-5;
LUKE 23:1-5; JOHN 18:28-38

Synopsis

The week before Jesus' crucifixion was filled with activity in and around Jerusalem. Jesus rode triumphantly into Jerusalem on Sunday. On Monday He drove out the merchants and money changers from the temple. On Tuesday He taught in the temple, answered questions about paying taxes to Caesar, and pointed out a widow giving her two small coins in the temple treasury. Wednesday appears to have been a day of rest. On Thursday the disciples prepared the Upper Room for the Passover supper, the Last Supper, which they ate with Jesus Thursday evening after sunset. That night, after the supper was ended, they went to Gethsemane, where Jesus prayed until the early morning hours, when Judas came with a band of men to capture Him. Jesus was then taken to the high priests Annas and Caiaphas, and before the council, for trial. When the council condemned Jesus to death, Judas was filled with remorse and hanged himself. Jesus was then taken before Pilate, procurator of Judea, to be sentenced.

The Praetorium or Hall of Judgment

Where was Pilate when Caiaphas sent Jesus to him? Scholars suggest two possible places: (1) the palace of Herod, a magnificent building with three towers straight north of Caiaphas' palace. One of these three towers is still standing. It is known as "The Tower of David." Jesus could have appeared before Pilate in the "barracks," which was part of Herod's palace; (2) the Tower of Antonia, on the northwest corner of the temple and connected to it by both stairs and underground passages. Herod the Great had used this fortress as his praetorium before his palace was built.

The word "praetorium," which the Bible uses for the place where Pilate was, originally meant the place where the military general's headquarters were during a military cam-

Below: the Antonia Fortress, sometimes called the Tower of Antonia, is attached at the upper left part of the temple diagram.

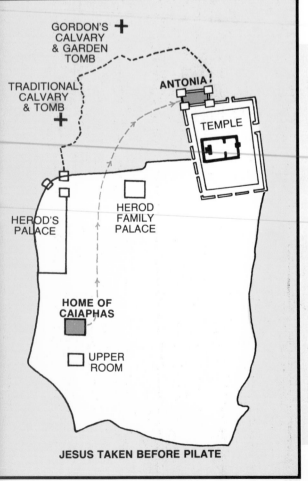

JESUS TAKEN BEFORE PILATE

© 1981, SPPI

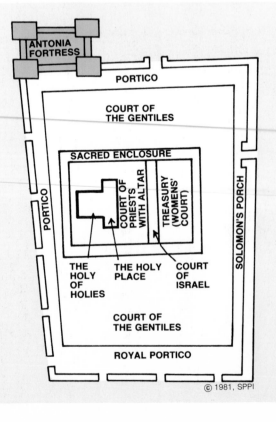

© 1981, SPPI

paign. Then it came to refer to the governor's official residence. In its atrium or open court was the *bema* or judgment seat, where Pilate would have condemned Jesus to death.

Pontius Pilate, Governor of Judea and Samaria

We don't know much about Pontius Pilate. We don't know anything about where or when he was born (perhaps Italy before A.D. 1). We know nothing about his family, beyond the fact that he was married. He must have been an *equestrian*, a member of the second-highest class in Rome, to have become a procurator or governor. We do know he was appointed by the emperor Tiberius in A.D. 26 to succeed Valerius Gratus and that he held this post until A.D. 36.

At least three times Pilate handled the Jews badly. The third time led Vitellius, governor of Syria, to depose him and send him to Rome, where he may have committed suicide.

Lower left: from the house of Caiaphas, where Jesus was judged by the high priest, to Antonia, where He was judged by Pilate.

Above and left: two coins issued by Pontius Pilate, showing both front and back. A Roman judgment seat is pictured between them. Left: an inscription mentioning Pilate, found at Caesarea.

Jesus Is Taken to Herod Antipas

LUKE 23:6-12

Synopsis

After Jesus was taken prisoner in the Garden of Gethsemane, He was brought to trial before the high priests Annas and Caiaphas, and the council. This council, the Sanhedrin, condemned Jesus to death. But the council did not have the authority to sentence Jesus, so they sent Him to Pilate, procurator of Judea, who in turn sent Him to Herod, ruler of Jesus' home territory, Galilee. Pilate was visiting in Jerusalem at that time.

Herod's Palace

Just as Pilate could have been at one of two different places, so could Herod have been at either the old Maccabean or Hasmonean palace, about halfway between the temple and what is now the Citadel, or at the Citadel itself, formerly Herod's palace.

If Pilate were at Herod's palace, Herod Antipas must have been at the old Maccabean palace (see the Herod family palace on the map). Built by an unknown Hasmonean ruler, this palace is higher up the hill of Zion than Caiaphas' house and not far from the temple. Herod would have been in Jerusalem on a visit for the Passover feast. His normal residence was in Tiberias in Galilee.

If Pilate were at the Tower of Antonia (named after Mark Antony), however, Herod could have been at his luxurious palace just inside the Jaffa Gate. Built by his father, Herod the Great, in 24 B.C. on the site of a Hasmonean

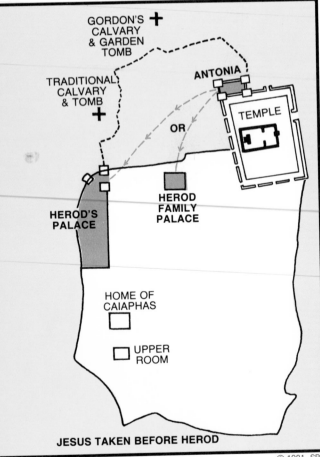

506

Left: two possible places where Jesus met Herod Antipas, and the route from Antonia. The upper photo is of so-called "David's Tower" built on the ruins of Herod's Phasael Tower. The lower photo shows the Citadel, nearby, also part of Herod's palace. A coin issued by Herod Antipas is above. The two photos at the right show a model of Herod's palace in Jesus' time. The lower photo is of the three towers. The Phasael Tower is at the far left of the picture.

city wall, this palace was surrounded by walls that were protected even further on the north by three enormous towers. One was called Phasael (his brother), another Mariamne (the wife he murdered), and the third Hippicus (a friend). Today all that stands is the Phasael Tower. Now called the Tower of David (tradition says David first saw Bathsheba here), and the Citadel, it contains what was a Moslem prayer room. The Citadel has four other towers, besides the ruins of the Phasael Tower, and is now an art center for the Civic Museum.

Herod Antipas
The son of Herod the Great by one of his several wives, Herod Antipas became tetrarch of Galilee and Perea. He is the Herod mentioned most often in the New Testament. His capital, Sepphoris, was only four miles from Nazareth, so Joseph may have worked on it. Around A.D. 25 he built a new capital, Tiberias, on the Sea of Galilee. His half nephew Herod Agrippa denounced him to Caligula, the Roman emperor, and he was banished to Gaul in A.D. 39.

507

Pilate Sentences Jesus

MATTHEW 27:15-26; MARK 15:6-15; LUKE 23:13-25; JOHN 18:39-40; 19:6-16

Synopsis

After Judas betrayed Jesus in the Garden of Gethsemane, Jesus was taken into Jerusalem for an early morning trial. First, He was taken to the house of Annas, a retired high priest. Then he was taken before Caiaphas, acting high priest, and then before the Sanhedrin, the council of religious leaders. Jesus was condemned to die, but because the council did not have the authority to sentence Him, they sent him to the Roman procurator, Pontius Pilate. Pilate was nervous about sentencing this Man, so he sent Him to Herod Antipas, who ruled Jesus' home territory, Galilee. Herod returned Jesus to Pilate who, after much struggle, sentenced Jesus to death by crucifixion.

The Tower of Antonia

The Tower of Antonia, called the "barracks" or "castle" in the New Testament, was a great square fortress built by Herod the Great to protect the temple. The Roman procurators who succeeded him used it more as part of their surveillance system against the Jews.

Named in honor of Mark Antony, Herod's friend and patron from army days, the spot has a long and interesting history. It may have been David's "Millo." Solomon made it part of his wall around the

Temple Mount. Nehemiah built a fortress on the spot after he returned to Jerusalem. John Hyrcanus built a fortress on the site in the days of the Maccabees, but it was destroyed by Pompey in 63 B.C.

Built on Zion, the highest hill in the area, the Tower of Antonia was located on a cliff that towers 75 feet above the valley below. Its walls rose 60 feet above the cliff. And three of its four towers rose 75 feet above the cliff. The fourth tower looked over the temple and rose a spectacular 100 feet. The west wall was built above the Tyropoeon Valley, the north wall was separated from the hill Bezetha by a deep moat, and the south wall adjoined the temple. Nothing is known about the east wall. The building was 490 feet by 260 feet and served both as a royal residence and as a military barracks. It probably had a large courtyard in the center, where the judgment seat *(bema)*, from which Pilate may have delivered his verdict, was located. The original courtyard and some of the massive stones can still be seen in the Church of the Sisters of Zion. Titus destroyed the structure in A.D. 70 by setting fire to it. As many as 500-600 soldiers (a cohort) were stationed in the castle.

Barabbas

Not much is known of Barabbas. Mark and Luke tell us he was in prison with a group of revolutionaries who had murdered people during an uprising. Matthew says only that he was a notorious prisoner, and John says he had taken part in a rebellion. His father may have been a rabbi.

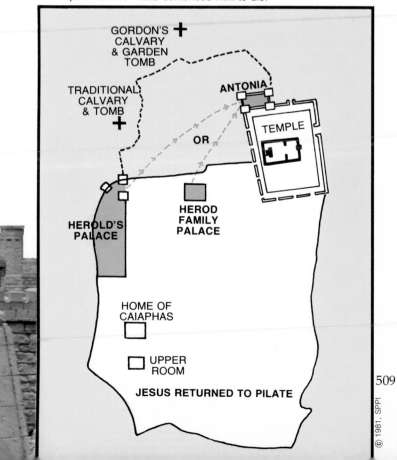

Lower left: a model of the Tower of Antonia, or Antonia Fortress, as it may have appeared in Jesus' time. The area where it stood is shown partly in the far-left photo. The map below shows the routes from the two possible sites where Herod talked with Jesus, to Antonia, probably the place where Pilate sentenced Him to die.

GORDON'S CALVARY & GARDEN TOMB

TRADITIONAL CALVARY & TOMB

ANTONIA

TEMPLE

OR

HEROLD'S PALACE

HEROD FAMILY PALACE

HOME OF CAIAPHAS

UPPER ROOM

JESUS RETURNED TO PILATE

509

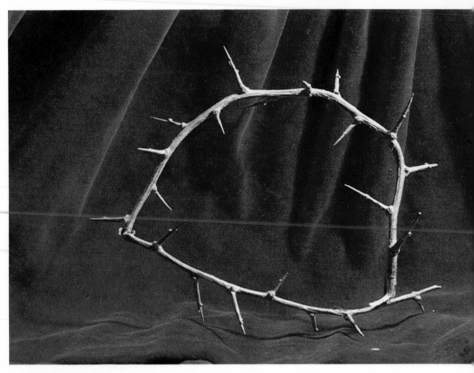

Jesus Is Scourged

MATTHEW 27:27-30; MARK 15:16-19; JOHN 19:1-5

Synopsis

While Jesus prayed in the Garden of Gethsemane on Thursday night, and into the early hours of Friday morning, Judas led a band of men to capture Him. They led Him back into Jerusalem before dawn, where He was tried—first by the retired high priest Annas, then by the acting high priest Caiaphas, then by the council, and after that by Pontius Pilate, the Roman procurator. Pilate was frightened, so he sent Jesus to Herod Antipas, who was visiting Jerusalem from Galilee. Herod sent Jesus back to Pilate, where the leaders of the people pressured Pilate into sentencing Jesus to die by crucifixion. In one last effort to free Jesus, Pilate had Him scourged, hoping the religious leaders would pity Him.

Scourges

The ancients used many kinds of scourges to punish those convicted of criminal or religious offenses. The Law of Moses allowed a convicted person to be placed in a bent-over position in front of the judge and whipped. The number of lashes was determined by the severity of the crime, up to a total of 40. More than that was considered "degrading." Later, synagogue and Sanhedrin officials used a three-pronged whip. The Mishna tells us that an offender was first examined to see if he was physically fit. Then his hands were tied to a pillar and the upper half of his body bared. His chest and each of his shoulders were then given 13 strokes. If the individual died as a result, his punishers were thought to be guiltless.

510

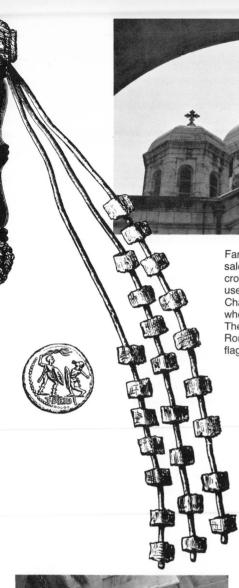

Far left: two thorn plants which grow near Jerusalem, and which may have been used for the crown of thorns. The Roman scourge at the left used metal or bone to tear the skin. Above: the Chapel of the Flagellation, built over the place where it is thought that Jesus was scourged. The courtyard of this chapel is seen below. The Roman coin at the left shows scourging or flagellation.

Roman citizens could not be scourged, but freemen, slaves, and foreigners could be beaten with elm or birch rods, or whipped. The cruelest form of scourging, called flagellation, consisted of beating with whips into which had been tied knots and pieces of metal or bone. Given on the back, this was often fatal. A whip could have as many as 12 separate lashes and consisted of a club to which a knotted cord with metal beads was attached.

More severe than rods, but less severe than weighted whips were whips made of hide (the so-called "scorpion," for example) or of calfskin folded over twice and interlaced with two donkey-hide strips.

The Crown of Thorns
The shrub from which the crown of thorns was made could have been one of two plants. The Christ-thorn grows to a height of 12 feet with sharp thorns at the bottom of its leaves. It is common around Golgotha. A smaller shrub of a similar name grows to a height of eight feet and has branches that can far more easily be woven into a crown of the kind mentioned in the Bible. It is definitely not the plant that is called a crown of thorns today.

Note that Luke, ever sensitive to cruelty to Jesus, omits any reference to scourging and the crown of thorns.

The Reed
Matthew mentions that the mocking soldiers put a reed into Jesus' hand as a royal staff. This reed could have been one of many plants: (1) the giant Persian, or bulrush reed, (2) Jerusalem corn, related to Egyptian rice corn, (3) the common reed of Palestine, or (4) the papyrus reed that grew in the shallow parts of the Nile River.

511

The Way of the Cross

MATTHEW 27:31-34; MARK 15:20-23;
LUKE 23:26-33; JOHN 19:16-17

Synopsis
After Jesus was taken prisoner by the mob
which Judas brought to Gethsemane, He was
brought before the high priests Annas and
Caiaphas for trial, and then was condemned
by the Sanhedrin, the high council. But this
group had no authority to sentence Jesus to
death, so they sent Him to the Roman procurator, Pontius Pilate. Pilate didn't want to sentence Jesus, so he sent Him to Herod, who
in turn sent Jesus back to Pilate. Pressured
by the religious leaders, Pilate at last condemned Jesus and had Him scourged, beaten
with whips. Then Jesus was forced to carry
His cross on the way to Golgotha, a path
which has become known as Via Dolorosa,
the Way of the Cross.

The Fourteen Stations of the Via Dolorosa
The Via Dolorosa is the traditional route by
which Jesus went from Pilate's hall of judgment to Calvary. The words are Latin for "Way
of Sorrows." Every Friday some Christians
in Jerusalem walk along the 14 "stations" associated with Jesus' sad final journey. These 14
stations are listed here in an effort to make
you feel part of those taking that walk. Remember, these are only traditions, not known
facts.

1. *The place where Jesus was condemned.* As you stand on St. Mary's Street looking west you can see an arch, the first of three. On the left side of the street is the Al Omariya School. Some say the part of the Antonia Tower courtyard where Pilate sentenced Jesus was under the present yard of this school.

2. *The place where Jesus took the cross.* Across the street on the wall of a building owned by Franciscan monks is a Roman "II" that marks this site. The wall is part of the Condemnation Chapel.

3. *The place where Jesus fell.* A pillar in the wall of a small Polish chapel marks this spot, not part of the biblical story.

4. *The place where Mary met Jesus.* In the crypt of a small chapel of an Armenian church, "Our Lady of the Spasm," are mosaic footprints to mark the spot where Mary supposedly stood.

5. *The place where Simon the Cyrenian took the cross.* At the intersection of El Wad Road and El Khanqa Street, just south of the last two sites, is a Franciscan chapel that marks this spot.

6. *The place where Veronica wiped Jesus' face.* Also on the left as you go west along El Khanqa is the Church of St. Veronica. Tradition says she wiped the blood, sweat, and dust off Jesus' face at this spot.

7. *The place where Jesus fell again.* The spot is at the corner of El Khanqa and Suq Khan Ez-Zeit, marked on the doorway in the Khan Ez-Zeit Market.

8. *The place where Jesus spoke to the women of Jerusalem.* A cross in the wall of the Greek Orthodox monastery of Charalambos, across the street from the market, marks the spot where Jesus foretold Jerusalem's destruction.

9. *The place of Jesus' third fall.* Going south on Suq Khan Ez-Zeit you come to a column built into the door of the Abyssinian Coptic Church that marks this spot.

10-14. *The place where Jesus was stripped of his clothes, nailed to the cross, died, was removed from the cross, and was buried.* Touching the Abyssinian Coptic monastery is the Church of the Holy Sepulchre, the traditional site of Jesus' death at Calvary. As you enter the church from the south, Calvary is on the right up a steep flight of stairs over the Rock of Golgotha. The church was built by the emperor Constantine in A.D. 336. This traditional place of Jesus' death is marked by a silver disk on an altar.

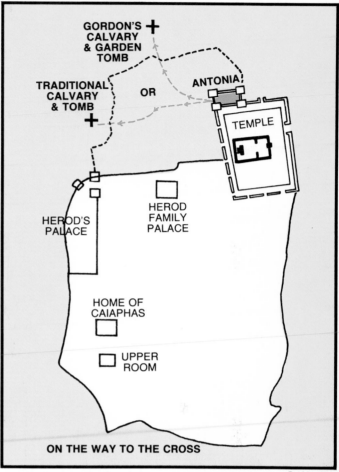

ON THE WAY TO THE CROSS

© 1981, SPPI

Each year, thousands of pilgrims walk the Via Dolorosa, seen at the far left in two photos. The streets are thought to follow the route which Jesus walked on the way to the cross, though not the exact streets of that time. The two possible routes may be seen in the map above, one to "Gordon's Calvary" and the other to what is now the Church of the Holy Sepulchre. The coin above is from Cyrene, from which Simon of Cyrene came.

The Day Jesus Died

MATTHEW 27:27-56; MARK 15:16-41;
LUKE 23:26-49; JOHN 19:14-30

Synopsis
After the Lord's Supper ended, Jesus went with His disciples to Gethsemane, where He prayed. But while Jesus prayed, Judas led a band of soldiers and a mob to arrest Jesus. In the darkness they led Him back to Jerusalem to the high priest and Sanhedrin, the Jewish high court, for trial. The council then sent Him to Pilate, who was afraid to try Him and sent Him to Herod. But Herod would not condemn Jesus either and sent Him back to Pilate. While Jesus was with Pilate, the crowd and religious leaders forced Pilate to condemn Jesus to death. When Jesus had been "scourged" or beaten, He was forced to carry His cross toward Golgotha.

Golgotha—Where Was It?
Two places have been suggested for Golgotha. The traditional place is The Church of the Holy Sepulchre shown in the picture at the upper left. The other place, sometimes known as Gordon's Calvary, is shown in the picture at the upper right.

Gordon's Calvary looks like a human skull and is just outside the Damascus Gate, north of the city. It is also a short distance from The Garden Tomb, thought by many to be the burial place for Jesus. Golgotha was called "The Place of a Skull" (John 19:17).

In the time of Jesus, the wall went westward for a short distance from the Damascus Gate, then south, then west again. It was north of this last section that the place on which The Church of the Holy Sepulchre is located. There is no hill on the site today. Some say it was cut down in the years that followed the crucifixion.

Both places were "outside the gate" (Heb. 13:12) and "near the city" (John 19:20). The two places are only a few hundred feet apart.

The name Golgotha is Hebrew and means a skull-like mound or hill which is barren. The name Calvary is Latin and means about the same thing.

Golgotha was a place where criminals were executed and was located near the public highway so that all could see the criminal put to death.

There were three crosses on Golgotha when Jesus was crucified. On one was the Saviour, on another a repentant sinner, and on the third an unrepentant sinner.

514

Pilate, the Roman Governor

Pilate had no reason to kill Jesus except that he was afraid that he might get into trouble if he did not kill Him. Pilate had made two political mistakes already. A third mistake would have caused Caesar to bring him back to Rome and account for the problems. Pilate was afraid that a riot might break out if he did not crucify Jesus and that would be his third mistake.

The Roman Soldiers

The Roman soldiers were acting on orders from Pilate. They were forced to crucify Jesus. But they were not forced to show as much cruelty to Him as they did, forcing Him to carry His own cross, mocking Him, forcing a crown of thorns over His head, and insulting Him. However, when Jesus died, the Roman centurion and "those with him" confessed that He was the Son of God (Matt. 27:54). The religious leaders did not.

The Religious Leaders

The Pharisees and other religious leaders of the Jews were afraid that Jesus would gather a large following who would depart from their control. They were angered that He was accepted by many as the Messiah, God's Son. Unable to cope with His growing popularity among the people, the only way out seemed to be to have Him killed.

The Other Two

The other men died the same day in the same way that Jesus died. They, like Jesus, were crucified and died on a cross for that was the Roman method of capital punishment. Stoning was the Jewish method. These two were criminals and were being punished for their crimes. Jesus was God's Son, being sacrificed for the sins of the world.

Daughters of Jerusalem

Among the women of Jerusalem whom Jesus addressed as "daughters of Jerusalem," there was a group who provided strong wine mixed with myrrh at crucifixions. It was a mixture which deadened pain and consciousness. Jesus refused this mixture when it was offered to Him, choosing to die fully alert.

Sunrise to Sunset The Day Jesus Died

The events of Jesus' crucifixion are divided into three-hour periods of time: 6-9 A.M.: Jesus before Pilate, then Herod, then Pilate, where He is condemned. He is taken to Golgotha to be crucified. 9 A.M.-Noon: Jesus is crucified. He is nailed to the cross, where He speaks His first three sayings. The Roman soldiers gamble for His clothing.

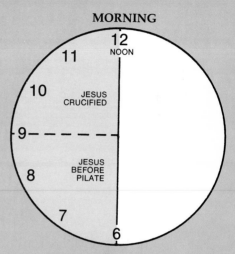

MORNING

Noon-3 P.M.: As Jesus dies, darkness comes over the land. Jesus gives His fourth through seventh sayings on the cross. 3-6 P.M.: After Jesus dies at 3:00 in the afternoon, Joseph of Arimathea and Nicodemus wrap His body, putting spices with it, and lay it in a tomb.

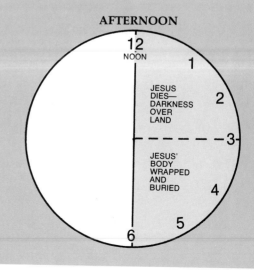

AFTERNOON

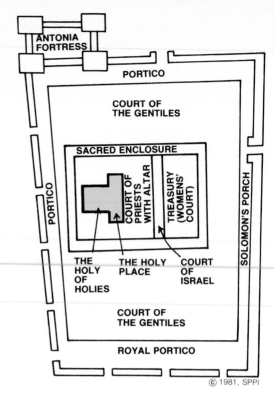

© 1981, SPPI

Roman Soldiers Beneath the Cross

MATTHEW 27:35-36; MARK 15:24; LUKE 23:33-34; JOHN 19:18, 23-24

Synopsis
After Jesus was condemned to die by Pilate, He was forced to carry His cross through Jerusalem's streets. On a hill just outside the gate, He was crucified. Beneath the cross, while friends and enemies alike watched Him, the Roman soldiers divided His clothing, but cast lots for His seamless robe.

The Roman Army
The Roman military unit that occupied Palestine in the days of Jesus was the 10th legion. Each legion had its own name; the 10th legion was called Frentensis, a name of honor it bore for centuries.

What was a legion? In the third century B.C., the Republican Citizen's Army consisted of several legions, each having about 3,000 soldiers organized into 3 lines. Each line was composed of 10 maniples, units of 100 to 120 men. The first line was the one that engaged in the first hand-to-hand combat that began a battle. It was made up of young foot soldiers, each armed with two javelins, a thrusting sword, a four-foot-long semi-cylindrical shield, a helmet, breastplate, and greaves for the legs. Behind them was the second line, made up of veteran infantrymen. Behind them were other veterans in the third line, primarily reserves.

In addition to the legion were the light infantry and the cavalry. The light infantry consisted of about 1,000 men equipped with javelins, swords, and round shields to hurl missiles and occasionally enter into light combat. A cavalry unit in each legion would consist of only about 300 mounted men. Its purpose was to attack the enemy's cavalry

Top: a column of the 10th Roman Legion lies in a courtyard across from the Citadel. This legion took part in Jesus' crucifixion. A centurion's costume, drawn from a Roman monument, may be seen above. The veil that was rent was between the Holy Place and Holy of Holies (see above).

516

Top: the so-called Passion Flower, a reminder of the crucifixion. Below it are dice from Roman times. The soldiers may have used such dice to gamble for Jesus' cloak. At the left and right are drawings of Roman soldiers' costumes and armor. The drawing at the right is from Trajan's column.

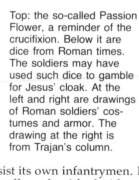

and assist its own infantrymen. It was not highly regarded; its non-Italian staff was furnished with small shields, swords, lances, helmets, and breastplates or cuirasses.

In 100 B.C. Marius the consul reorganized this army. In place of a legion of 30 maniples he put 1 of 10 cohorts. He preserved the practice of dividing these units into "centuries," however. A century consisted of from less than 50 to more than 100 men under the leadership of a centurion, a sharp soldier who had risen through the ranks of the democratically organized army. Marius had the light infantry go into battle first, with the cavalry flanking the three lines on the left and right.

The symbol of the army's pride was its eagle. When a legion was defeated it was dissolved in shame. Soldiers came from the provinces.

Casting Lots

Jewish "lots" were stones of different colors or symbols, placed in a container and shaken onto the ground or into the lap to make decisions. Romans had dice, as seen in the above picture.

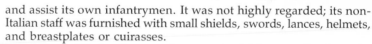

517

The two drawings above show the aloe plant. Myrrh mixed with aloes was used to embalm Jesus' body.

Jesus' Body Is Buried

MATTHEW 27:57-60; MARK 15:42-46; LUKE 23:50-54; JOHN 19:31-42

Synopsis

After Jesus was taken prisoner in the Garden of Gethsemane, He was tried before Annas and Caiaphas, the high priests; the Sanhedrin, Jewish high council; Pilate, the Roman procurator; Herod Antipas, ruler of Galilee; and was finally condemned to die by Pilate. Through the streets of Jerusalem, He carried His cross to Golgotha, where He was crucified. The soldiers divided His clothing, but cast lots for His seamless robe. After Jesus died, Joseph of Arimathea asked Pilate for His body and with the help of Nicodemus, embalmed it with spices and buried it in his own new tomb.

Joseph of Arimathea

Who was Joseph of Arimathea? The New Testament tells us he was a member of the Jewish council or Sanhedrin who had not agreed with the decision to condemn Jesus to death and that he went to Pilate to get Jesus' body so he could put it in his new, rock-hewn tomb.

Some believe that the town of Arimathea is today called Ramla, about 20 miles northwest of Jerusalem. It was one of three prefectures in Samaria that Demetrius II Nicanor of Syria gave to Jonathan the Maccabee in 145 B.C., when it was called Ramatha. Samuel the prophet is buried here (1 Sam. 25:1). Today it is a large village that sits on two hills at the edge of the Ephraim Mountains. To the west there is a beautiful panoramic view of the Mediterranean Sea. The remains of a Crusader Abbey of St. Joseph of Arimathea can still be seen.

Despite his humble origins, Joseph had reached the peak both

518

At the left is the plant from which myrrh was taken. The two photos are of Ramla, thought to be ancient Arimathea, from which Joseph of Arimathea came. The tower is the White Mosque or White Tower, built in A.D. 1318. The Church of St. Joseph of Arimathea may be seen in the center of the top photo.

socially and financially. Only the very wealthy could afford to have a rock tomb, and if as has been suggested this was an extra tomb because executed criminals could not be buried in family tombs, he was especially wealthy.

Why would he ask for Jesus' body? Two factors might be involved. First, it is not too surprising that one or two religious leaders might be attracted to Jesus' teaching about the kingdom. But more important is the fact that Joseph seems to have taken the rabbinic tradition about bodies being buried on the day of death more seriously than the others (see Deut. 21:22-23).

Myrrh and Aloes

Myrrh is the fragrant resinous gum of certain trees in Arabia. It was used to anoint kings. When branches are cut they produce abundant quantities of an oily substance that quickly solidifies.

Myrrh is mixed with aloes and sprinkled over the embalming cloths of the dead. The aloe is the pure aloe plant, not the tree mentioned elsewhere in the Bible. It is bitter.

519

Women Visit Jesus' Tomb

MATTHEW 27:61—28:4; MARK 15:47—16:8; LUKE 23:55—24:8; JOHN 20:1-8

Synopsis
When Jesus was crucified, the Roman soldiers gambled for His seam-less cloak and divided His other clothing. After He died, Joseph of Arimathea asked Pilate for His body, and with Nicodemus' help, embalmed it with spices and buried it in his own new tomb. On Sunday morning after the crucifixion, some of the women who had followed Him came to the tomb.

Ancient Burial Practices
People have buried their dead through the years in everything from a hole in the ground to elaborate burial caves, mausoleums, and pyramids. One practice that has greatly aided our understanding of ancient times, including biblical times, was the burial of cherished objects with a deceased person.

The earliest graves discovered date about 8000 B.C. At Mount Car-mel, for example, a communal grave for about 60 people in Natufian times has been excavated. But as late as 5000 B.C. in Jericho dead bodies seem to have been buried with no ceremony at all.

The next stage included stone pit tombs, called "cists," and dolmens, house-shaped tombs constructed of two upright stone slabs topped by a flat stone slab. A dolmen, for example, has been found across the Jordan from Jericho.

Caves, both natural and man-made, became popular sites for tombs. The limestone hills of Israel today are still honeycombed with these ancient tombs. Sometimes hundreds of bodies in containers have been discovered in a cave sealed with a large stone. The cave at Machpelah that Abraham purchased for Sarah may be an example. Man-made caves were dug from the top down 3-15 feet by a shaft 3-10 feet in diameter. To prevent thieves from entering, the shaft would be filled with debris after burial. Several such shafts mark family tombs. When bones accumulated, they were gathered into a common pit or thrown out to make room for new bodies. Skulls, however, were respected and retained.

No tombs, however, match the Egyptian flat-topped mastabas and their even more elaborate pyramids. Mummification involved drying a body, placing internal organs in alabaster and marble jars, and wrapping the body in linen sheets as long as 24 yards.

In Jesus' day Jews washed the body, dressed it in linen sheets sprinkled with a mixture of aromatic spices (calamus, myrrh, cassia, aloes, cinnamon) and pure olive oil that made an ointment, and laid it on a bier or pallet for burial. From Roman times, every kind of tomb has been found in excavations. Pliny, Roman first-century historian, criticized the extravagant cost of the embalming spices.

Below: the Garden Tomb, near Gordon's Calvary, is visited annually by thousands of pilgrims who think of this as Jesus' tomb. Others believe His tomb, and Calvary, are now covered by the Church of the Holy Sepulchre. Above: the Herod family tomb, with a fine example of the rolling stone which covered a tomb's entrance.

Peter and John Visit Jesus' Tomb

LUKE 24:11-12; JOHN 20:2-10

Synopsis

After Jesus was crucified, Joseph of Arimathea asked Pilate for Jesus' body, and with the help of Nicodemus, embalmed it with spices and buried it in Joseph's new tomb. This was Friday afternoon, shortly before sundown, and the beginning of the Sabbath. When the Sabbath ended at dawn on Sunday morning, some of the women who had followed Jesus came to visit this tomb. But they found the stone rolled from the entrance and Jesus' body gone. They quickly reported this to the disciples and Peter and John rushed to see for themselves.

Jesus' Garden Tomb through the Centuries

What happened to Jesus' tomb in the years that followed His death? Some say His tomb is near Gordon's Calvary. Others say its location is where the Church of the Holy Sepulchre now stands. The following tells what happened to that location.

1. *Hadrian's Aelia Capitolina.* In A.D. 135 the Roman Emperor Hadrian, seeing Christianity as nothing more than a sect of Judaism, destroyed all its holy places along with those of the Jews and erected a Roman city, the Aelia Capitolina, in place of Jerusalem. Over this traditional site of Jesus' tomb he built a Temple of Venus.

2. *The Visit of Queen Helena, Constantine's Mother.* The godly Queen Helena visited the Holy Land in A.D. 326 to locate all the sites connected with Jesus' life. Because she knew that Hadrian had built the Temple of Venus over what was thought to be Calvary, she was able to locate the place. In an unused cistern she found many objects that today

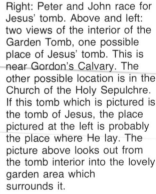

Right: Peter and John race for Jesus' tomb. Above and left: two views of the interior of the Garden Tomb, one possible place of Jesus' tomb. This is near Gordon's Calvary. The other possible location is in the Church of the Holy Sepulchre. If this tomb which is pictured is the tomb of Jesus, the place pictured at the left is probably the place where He lay. The picture above looks out from the tomb interior into the lovely garden area which surrounds it.

are associated with the death of Jesus. She did what she could to restore this and other places connected with the Christian faith.

3. *Constantine's Church of the Holy Sepulchre.* Constantine removed Hadrian's temple and erected in its place a huge, magnificent basilica. He cut away the rock from three sides of the cavern and leveled and paved the area so he could erect columns and a cupola to form a rotunda called the Anastasis (Resurrection). He made lavish use of gold, silver, precious stones, marble, mosaics, and stone carvings.

4. *Subsequent History.* In A.D. 614 the Persians destroyed this magnificent structure. But two years later the patriarch of the Greek Orthodox Church, Abbot Modestus, rebuilt it on a modest scale. The mad Egyptian caliph, El Hakim, destroyed that, and it was hastily rebuilt in A.D. 1037. The church built by the Crusaders in the 12th century was partially destroyed in A.D. 1240 by Tartan invaders. Only recently have six Christian groups agreed to reconstruct the church. Today the sepulchre is located behind the Chapel of the Angel and is marked by a white marble slab.

Mary Magdalene's early home was at Magdala, on the northwestern shore of the Sea of Galilee. The picture at the right shows the shore near some ruins which are thought to be Magdala. This scene looks toward the north.

Mary Magdalene

MARK 16:9-11; JOHN 20:11-18

Synopsis

Joseph of Arimathea and Nicodemus prepared Jesus' body for burial and laid it in Joseph's new tomb not far from Golgotha. The Sabbath passed and some women who had followed Jesus came to visit the tomb. But they found the stone rolled from the entrance and the body of Jesus gone. Quickly they returned to Jerusalem and told the disciples. Peter and John came to see for themselves. Later, alone, Mary Magdalene was startled when Jesus appeared to her.

Mary Magdalene

Mary Magdalene was as prominent among the women as Peter was among the apostles. She came from the city of Magdala. She should not be confused with Mary of Bethany or the woman who anointed Jesus' feet. The expulsion of seven demons from her suggests that she had been "mentally ill," not morally dissolute. She appears to have been a person of some means and to have possessed leadership abilities, for she is always listed first when grouped with others. Some say she had aroused public indignation by divorcing her Jewish husband, Pappus ben Juda, to marry Panther, an officer of Herod Antipas' entourage, but this is probably not historically cor-

524

Left: Mary Magdalene meets Jesus outside the tomb, the first to see Him alive after the Resurrection. Mary Magdalene Church, lower left, was built by Czar Alexander III in memory of his mother and Mary Magdalene. Behind it is the Kidron Valley, the city of Jerusalem, and its wall.

rect. When she first met Jesus we do not know, but it was probably on one of His visits to Gennesaret, near Magdala. Present at Jesus' crucifixion, she was the first to see the risen Lord, whom she thought was the gardener.

Today the Mary Magdalene Church, named in her honor, stands halfway up the Mount of Olives.

Magdala

Some ruins of Magdala may be found along the shores of the Sea of Galilee today. Located just three miles north of Herod Antipas' capital of Tiberias, it was called Tarichea by the Greeks who caught a small fish of that name, still used as a relish, in its lakes. Once famous for its fine woolens and dyed products (the dye came from shellfish caught in its waters), the area is today near the village of Mejdel or Majgal, a modern name which preserves both its ancient name and its locality. Josephus, who once lived here, said it had 4,000 inhabitants and 230 boats. The Talmud tells us it had 80 weavers' shops and 300 shops that sold pigeons for sacrifices. The word "Magdala" is Hebrew for "watchtower." In Jesus' day it was primarily a Gentile city, as its horse and chariot race track indicates. A human skull from early history was found not far from Magdala, in 1925.

The Road to Emmaus

MARK 16:12-13; LUKE 24:13-35

Synopsis
After Jesus was crucified, Joseph of Arimathea and Nicodemus prepared His body for burial and laid it in Joseph's new tomb. On Sunday morning, when some women visited the tomb, they discovered the stone rolled from the entrance and His body missing. They reported this to the disciples and Peter and John came to see. Then Jesus appeared personally to Mary Magdalene. Later that day, He appeared to two people walking on the Road to Emmaus.

Cleopas and His Companion
Who were these two disciples? No one knows for sure. Cleopas may be a variant of the name Cleopatros or Alphaeus. There is no evidence either for or against the identification of Cleopas with the Clopas of John 19:25.

Because the other disciple is not named, he has fascinated biblical scholars. Traditionally, he is called Simon. Several modern interpreters have been fascinated by the idea that he may be Luke himself, since the account has all the reality of personal experience.

The two disciples may have belonged to the 70 (Luke 10:1-24).

Emmaus
Where is Emmaus? Once again, we do not know exactly. But at least we have some clues. First, the name means "hot springs," and Bible students have tried to locate the village by locating wells, springs, or baths near Jerusalem. Second, Luke says it was 60 stadia, or 7½ miles, from Jerusalem, though he does not indicate in which direction. The two most likely sites are:

1. *El Kubeibeh (Qubeibeh)*. This village, seven miles northwest of Jerusalem, has a number of things to suggest it was Emmaus. Crusaders in 1099 discovered an ancient Roman fort called Castellum Emmaus near here. In 1878 the Franciscans built the Church of St. Cleophas here and discovered the remains of a basilica that dates from either Crusader or Byzantine times.

2. *Imwas or Amwas*. This city preserves the name and has two hot springs. It also has the earliest support, since two pilgrims in about A.D. 333 accepted Imwas as Emmaus, and Jerome, the great biblical scholar, agreed. But it was a city, not a village, and it is 20 miles, not 7½ miles, from Jerusalem.

The two possible locations for Emmaus, as described above, are pictured at the right. The first, El Kubeibeh (Qubeibeh), is in the center. The scene is looking toward the east. At the near right is Imwas, looking toward the south.

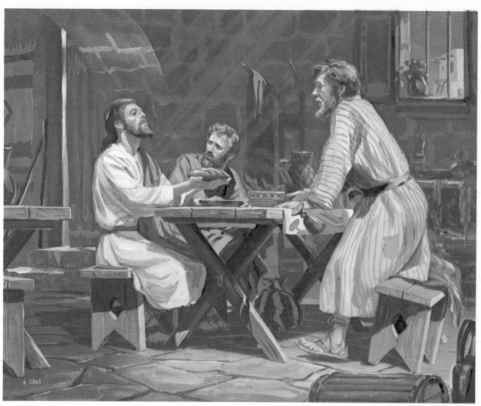

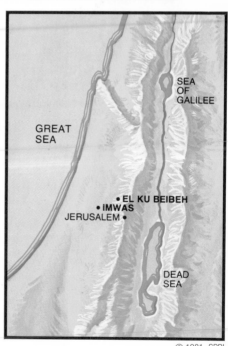

At the top, Jesus broke bread at Emmaus for the two men who had walked with Him on the way. Suddenly they realized who He was. The map above shows the location of Imwas and El Kubeibeh, two possible sites for Emmaus.

527

40 DAYS—from Resurrection to Ascension

SUNDAY MORNING

1. *An Angel Rolls Away the Stone from Jesus' Tomb*
(Matt. 28:2-4)
Early on Sunday morning, before sunrise, an angel of the Lord rolls away the stone from the tomb.

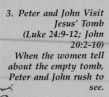

2. *Women Visit Jesus' Tomb*
(Matt. 28:5-8; Mark 16:2-8; Luke 24:1-8; John 20:1)
Women who followed Jesus visit His tomb and discover Him missing.

3. *Peter and John Visit Jesus' Tomb* (Luke 24:9-12; John 20:2-10)
When the women tell about the empty tomb, Peter and John rush to see.

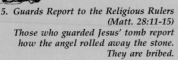

4. *Jesus Appears to Mary Magdalene*
(Mark 16:9-11; John 20:11-18)
While Mary is alone in the garden by His tomb, Jesus appears to her. He then appears to other women.

5. *Guards Report to the Religious Rulers*
(Matt. 28:11-15)
Those who guarded Jesus' tomb report how the angel rolled away the stone. They are bribed.

SUNDAY AFTERNOON

6. *Jesus Appears to Two Men on the Road to Emmaus*
(Mark 16:12-13; Luke 24:13-32)
While two men walk to Emmaus, Jesus appears to them.

SUNDAY EVENING

7. *The Two Disciples from Emmaus Report to Others*
(Luke 24:33-35)
The two disciples from Emmaus tell the others they have seen Jesus.

8. *Jesus Appears to 10 Disciples; Thomas Absent*
(Mark 16:14; Luke 24:36-43; John 20:19-25)
Jesus appears to 10 disciples, with Thomas absent, in Upper Room.

Doubting Thomas

MARK 16:14; LUKE 24:36-43; JOHN 20:19-31

Synopsis

On the Sunday after Jesus' crucifixion, some women visited His tomb, only to find the stone rolled from the entrance and His body missing. Then Peter and John rushed to the tomb to see for themselves. Later, Jesus appeared alive to Mary Magdalene, to some other women, and that afternoon to two people walking on the Road to Emmaus. That night Jesus appeared to His disciples in a closed room, but Thomas was not there. When Thomas heard about this, he doubted. He would not be satisfied until he had touched the wounds of the risen Christ. A week later, again on Sunday night, Jesus appeared to the disciples again. As Jesus invited Thomas to check out His wounds, Thomas believed!

The Fact of the Resurrection

Many believe that Jesus never rose from the dead. In fact, ever since the Resurrection, some have claimed that Jesus' resurrection was a lie and a conspiracy. But the real conspiracy involved the chief priests.

When the Roman guards noticed the empty tomb on Sunday morning, they reported it to the chief priests. Matthew says that the guards were given a large amount of money by the chief priests as a bribe. They were then told to spread the news that the disciples had stolen Jesus' body (Matt. 28:11-15).

This might be a believable story had the disciples never been heard from again. But why would these disciples spend the rest of their lives risking death and preaching about something that wasn't true? And if Jesus' enemies had stolen His body, they would have produced it as proof that Jesus did not rise from the dead. So the facts are clear. Jesus Christ and His followers are very much alive

THE FOLLOWING SUNDAY

*9. Jesus Appears to His Disciples,
Including Thomas
(John 20:26-31)
When Jesus asks Thomas to touch
Him, Thomas believes.*

THE FOLLOWING 32 DAYS

*10. Jesus Appears to Seven Disci-
ples by the Sea of Galilee
(John 21)
He also performs a miracle of
fish.*

*11. Jesus Appears to 500
(Matt. 28:16-20; Mark 16:15-18; 1 Cor. 15:6)
At a mountain in Galilee, Jesus appears to
500.*

*12. Jesus Appears to James
(1 Cor. 15:7)
Sometime during these days, Jesus appears to His
half brother James.*

*13. Jesus Appears Again to His Disciples
(Luke 24:44-49; Acts 1:3-8)
At Jerusalem, Jesus appears to the disciples.*

*14. Jesus Ascends into Heaven
(Mark 16:19-20; Luke 24:50-53; Acts
1:9-12)
On the Mount of Olives, Jesus
ascends while the disciples watch.*

in the world today!

Thomas

Thomas was one of Jesus' 12 Apostles. He is always listed in the second of the three groups of four apostles when the Gospel lists the Twelve. This may suggest that he was neither the most important nor the least important of the Twelve.

Pessimistic, loyal, honest, dull, disillusioned, skeptical—all these characteristics spring from the New Testament and give us one of the most precise portraits of an apostle available.

But this same man utters a climactic confession of faith in Jesus in John's Gospel, a confession unequaled in all literature—"My Lord and My God!" This confession may have come after Thomas touched Jesus' wounds. Whether Thomas did or not, he was in awe over the fact that Jesus had truly risen from the dead, and is therefore God's Son.

Greetings and Salutations

As the apostles gathered in the Upper Room Jesus appeared in their midst and greeted them by saying "Peace be unto you." This was one of the common greetings of the day, as ordinary as if we said "Good morning" today.

The Upper Room

The traditional site of the Upper Room can be seen in Jerusalem today. But if this was the room where Jesus gathered with His disciples, no one knows just how it looked in their day.

Some think the Upper Room was simply a room built on the top of a roof, quite common in Bible times. Others believe this was a most important room. In many expensive homes, a special room was built facing the courtyard. This room was expensively decorated and used for special occasions or for business.

The Miracle of Fish

JOHN 21

Synopsis

After Jesus arose from the dead, He appeared to many people. On the Sunday after His crucifixion, He appeared to Mary Magdalene, some other women, and then to two disciples walking on the Road to Emmaus. That night He appeared to the disciples in a closed room, but Thomas was not present. A week later, on the following Sunday night, He appeared to the disciples again, with Thomas there. When Jesus asked him to touch His wounds, Thomas believed that He had truly risen from the dead.

The Sea of Tiberias

The Sea of Tiberias is the same as the Sea of Galilee. Strictly speaking it is not a sea at all, but a freshwater inland lake.

Various names have been given to the lake through the years. The earliest name, the Sea of Chinnereth, possibly comes from the Hebrew word for "harp," the shape of the lake.

The Gospels, however, usually speak of the Sea of Galilee, so named because of the region to the northwest and west. The word means "ring" or "circle," probably because the region was known as the "district" of the Gentiles. The Gospels also occasionally speak of the Sea of Gennesaret (Gennesar), so named for the fertile, thickly populated plain southwest of the city of Capernaum. Following New Testament times it came to be known as the Sea of Tiberias, after the capital city of Galilee, and today's Arabic name, Tabariyeh, preserves that designation.

Located about 60 miles north of Jerusalem, the limestone formations that underlie the mountains, valleys, and lake resulted from volcanic eruptions. The mountains of Galilee on the north side of the lake rise some 4,000 feet above sea level. The hills to the east and west rise only about 2,000 feet, but because they drop so sharply and the lake is 685 feet below sea level, abrupt drops of as much as 2,650 feet occur. Standing on the southern shores of the lake, one can see Mount Hermon in the north. The Sea of Galilee is 13 miles at its longest point and 7½ miles at its widest

At the left, Peter jumps into the water and rushes to Jesus. This is Jesus' first appearance in Galilee after He arose from the dead.

Fishing on the Sea of Galilee

In addition to the use of nets, as described below, a Galilean fisherman also sometimes used a simple hook and line. Jesus told Peter to use this method (Matt. 17:27).

Peter, Andrew, James, and John, as well as Zebedee, father of James and John, were fishermen on the Sea of Galilee, operating a fishing business.

It appears that they sold their fish as far away as Jerusalem, and that the high priest may have been a customer (John 18:15).

Fish were sold fresh or dried and were an important source of meat at this time. In Jesus' time a large fleet of fishing boats operated on the Sea of Galilee.

About two miles southwest of Capernaum is a small chapel built on the shore of the Sea of Galilee (left), Saint Peter's Church, or Chapel of the Primacy. One tradition says that this was the place where Jesus met the disciples and told Peter to feed His sheep.

point. It is 32 miles around and 160 feet deep in some spots. Though the shore is made up of pebbles and small shells, the fertile plains surrounding the lake produce an abundance of wheat, barley, figs, grapes, and other fruits and vegetables. In biblical times 9 cities with populations over 15,000 surrounded the lake and as many as 22 varieties of fish have been caught in its waters. At one time the whole Jordan Valley may have been one big lake.

Fishing Nets
Three different types of fishing nets were known in Bible times:

1. *The casting net.* Standing on shore a fisherman could throw this cone-shaped net weighted with lead on the outside over a school of fish. This type of net was not used commercially.

2. *The gill net.* Used for catching medium-sized fish, this was a long net fitted with floats that would stay in the water all night and be hauled in by boat the next day. Its openings were large enough for small fish to escape but small enough to trap the big fish! The seven apostles were probably using this type of net.

3. *The drag net.* Boats would lower this long net in a semicircle and pull the ends to shore together with everything they caught.

Left: Jesus ascends into heaven bodily, so that His disciples may see and report this to us, and others. Above: the Chapel of the Ascension, described below. Below: from the temple area, one looks to the east toward the Mount of Olives. The tall structure in the center is the Russian Bell Tower, another traditional site of the Ascension. The map shows the possible route between the Upper Room and the place of the Ascension.

Jesus Ascends into Heaven

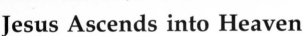

MARK 16:19-20; LUKE 24:50-53; ACTS 1:9-12

Synopsis

Jesus appeared to many after He arose from the dead. On Sunday morning, He talked personally with Mary Magdalene and appeared to other women. On Sunday afternoon, He talked with two disciples on the Road to Emmaus. That night, He appeared to the disciples in a closed room. On the following Sunday night, He appeared to them again and Thomas saw His wounds and believed. In Galilee, Jesus appeared to His disciples by the Sea of Galilee, and then to 500 on a mountain in Galilee. He appeared to James, and again to His disciples. Then on the Mount of Olives, His disciples clearly saw Him go up into heaven.

The Chapel of the Ascension

Jesus ascended into heaven from a place somewhere on the Mount of Olives. Today there are two places on the Mount of Olives marked with shrines, each claiming to mark the spot where Jesus ascended.

Of course, no one knows for sure where the exact

532

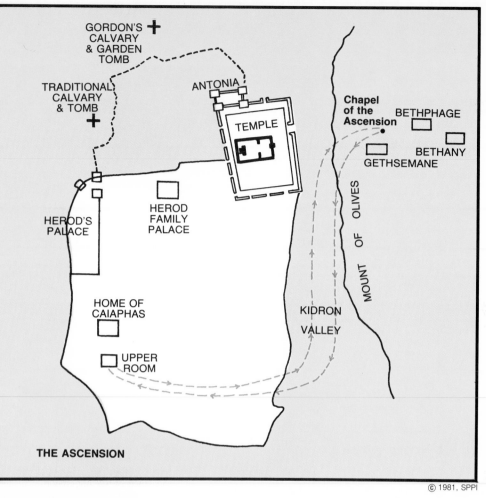

THE ASCENSION

© 1981, SPPI

spot was located. Shrines such as these usually mark a traditional place claimed by people through several centuries.

The Russian Orthodox Church and Bell Tower of the Ascension is one of the two shrines, chosen by Russian Christians. The Chapel of the Ascension, pictured above, is the other. It stands at the top of the Mount of Olives. This shrine was first built by Queen Helena, mother of the Roman Emperor Constantine. She lived from A.D. 248 to 327. Her shrine was destroyed and rebuilt at least twice through the centuries. The present structure was built some 900 years ago, during the time of the Crusaders. It covers a rock from which some say Jesus ascended into heaven. Of course, no one knows this for sure.

Jesus' Ascension

Jesus' ascension was the time when He bodily left this earth to return to heaven. As He came in Bethlehem, in the form of a baby, so He ascended as a full-grown man. Jesus ascended visibly so there would be no doubt. A large number of disciples saw Him go and recorded this as eyewitnesses.

When

Jesus' ascension was 40 days after His resurrection. During these 40 days, He showed Himself alive to many of His disciples, who recorded these appearances as eyewitnesses.

533

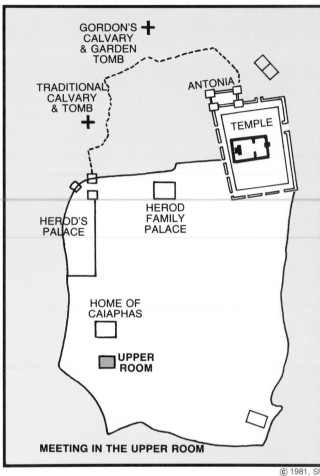

GORDON'S CALVARY & GARDEN TOMB

TRADITIONAL CALVARY & TOMB

ANTONIA

TEMPLE

HEROD'S PALACE

HEROD FAMILY PALACE

HOME OF CAIAPHAS

UPPER ROOM

MEETING IN THE UPPER ROOM

Pentecost

ACTS 2

Synopsis

After Jesus was crucified, many of His disciples saw Him, the risen Christ, alive again. He walked among them and touched them, both in Jerusalem and in Galilee. One day Jesus ascended into heaven while the disciples watched. Then they returned to Jerusalem to wait, as He had told them to do. While waiting in the Upper Room, they chose Matthias to take the place of Judas as one of the Twelve. When the Day of Pentecost came, while they were waiting in the Upper Room, the Holy Spirit came on them as tongues of fire and gave them power. He appeared as had been prophesied in the Old Testament, yet was a surprise to all who were there.

Pentecost

Pentecost is the Greek word for "50." To Christians it means 50 days after the Resurrection, but to Jews it speaks of the 50 days of harvest that follow the offering of the barley sheaf at the Passover. Together with Passover and the feast of Tabernacles or Booths, it was one of the three great pilgrim festivals of Judaism. Since A.D. 70 it has commemorated the giving of the Law at Mt. Sinai, though originally it began the seven-week period called "firstfruits." It appears to have played a far less important role in Judaism than the other two festivals, since it is not mentioned nearly as often in the literature of the Jews.

The same Greek word was used to refer to a harbor tax in ancient Greece, the pentecost tax.

Originally Pentecost (Shavuot) fell on a Sunday 50 days after the barley sheaf Sabbath. But after A.D. 70 the practice of the Pharisees

The building now housing David's Tomb and the Upper Room is seen at the far left. It is located on the map of Jerusalem at the left. During Jesus' time, the house with the Upper Room would have been next to David's Tomb, a separate structure. Today one building covers both pieces of ground.

prevailed: 50 days after the first day of Passover.

To Christians it celebrates the beginning of the church. Some early Christians stood to pray instead of kneeling, and candidates for baptism were baptized on this day.

The "Nations" of Pentecost

In general the "nations" are listed in a circle from east to west. These "nations" were Jews of the diaspora, living in nations other than Israel. Parthians, Medes, and Elamites came from present-day Iran; the Mesopotamians from Iraq; the Cappadocians, residents of Pontus, Asians, Phrygians, and Pamphylians from Turkey; the Egyptians from Egypt; the Libyans from Cyrenaica west of Egypt on the African coast; the Romans from Italy; and the Cretans from Crete. "Judeans" may perhaps refer to Armenians and "Arabs" to Cilicians. Pentecost temporarily ended the confusion of Babel.

David's Tomb

David's Tomb is below the traditional Upper Room. Peter referred to it (Acts 2:29). In 1948 it became a synagogue; Jews still flock to it on Pentecost, David's traditional death date.

Two shrines occupy the same building today. On the ground floor is David's Tomb. On the second floor, the traditional Upper Room. Outside stairs lead up to this room (left). The coins above are from Cappadocia, pictured above. Some of the visitors in Jerusalem on that Pentecost of long ago were from Cappadocia, now in the heart of present-day Turkey.

535

Peter and John Heal a Lame Man

ACTS 3

Synopsis

After Jesus ascended into heaven, the disciples returned to Jerusalem, where they waited in the Upper Room. On the day of Pentecost, the Holy Spirit came on them and they were filled with power. Peter preached a great sermon and thousands turned to Christ. Believers united, shared their possessions, and provided for the needs of others. One day, at the hour of prayer, Peter and John went to the temple. As they entered, a lame man begged them for coins.

The Gate Called Beautiful

There is no reference to this gate in Jewish writings. Josephus, however, refers to a gate that was made of solid Corinthian bronze and greatly excelled the other nine gates that were merely covered with silver and gold, without bronze. The gate could be the Nicanor Gate, named after the man who contributed its cost, that led from the Court of the Gentiles to the Court of the Women. Josephus also tells us that whereas the other gates had two doors 30 cubits high and 15 cubits wide, this gate was 50 feet high and each of its two doors was 40 feet wide. The gold and silver on this gate, contributed by Alexander, the father of Tiberius, was much thicker than on the others.

Christian tradition identifies it with the Susa or Golden Gate, however.

Left: Peter and John heal the lame man at the Beautiful Gate. Above: one possible Beautiful Gate—the Nicanor Gate, between the Court of the Gentiles and the Court of the Women, as seen in a model of the temple.

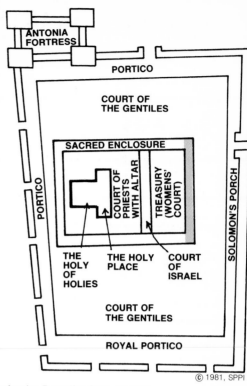

© 1981, SPPI

Above left: a second possibility for the Beautiful Gate, traditionally accepted by many Christians. This is called the Golden
Gate, and faces the Mount of Olives. It is now closed. The
diagram above shows the floor plan of the temple, and thus
locates the Nicanor Gate. The Golden Gate would have been
located in the wall to the right of the Nicanor Gate.

Solomon's Porch or Colonnade

The temple built by Herod the Great was surrounded on all four sides
by a roofed colonnade or walkway. The colonnade on the east side,
leading into the Court of the Women, was called Solomon's Colonnade
because of a tradition that Solomon had a similar portico in about the
same area. Zerubbabel may also have had a similar walkway around
the second temple.

Built on a platform or high retaining wall, Solomon's Colonnade
was a place for people to walk and talk, and for teachers to share
their learning. It was about 50 feet wide and had 3 separate rows of
columns made of white marble. The columns were about 40 feet high.
Carved cedar beams formed the roof, and on the floors were mosaic
stones, all in the latest Hellenistic architectural style.

Prayer Times

Though people also prayed when they needed to, certain times came
to be traditional. At first morning and evening prayer were customary,
but then three different times became common. The most commonly
observed were those at "the sixth hour" and "the ninth hour" (see
Acts 10:9, 30; 3:1). Since the day began officially at 6 A.M., the sixth
hour was noon and the ninth hour was 3 P.M.

Based on Psalm 119:164, monks said prayers seven times a day.

537

Peter and John before the Council

ACTS 4:1-31

Synopsis

After Jesus ascended into heaven, the believers returned to the Upper Room where they waited. On the day of Pentecost, the Holy Spirit came and gave them power. They shared their possessions, helped one another, and witnessed about Jesus. Peter preached a great sermon which convinced thousands to accept Jesus as Saviour. At the temple, Peter and John healed a lame man, which brought much excitement and caused Peter to preach again to the people who gathered. The religious leaders were angry about this and arrested the two men and took them before the Sanhedrin, the high council.

The Temple Guard

The ones who actually arrested Peter and John were probably members of the temple guard. Much as Potiphar guarded the Egyptian pharaoh, Herod used a member of his guard to decapitate John the Baptist, and Pilate stationed guards at Jesus' tomb, so too the temple had its corps of soldiers. We know little of this body beyond the fact that its head was called a "captain." Jeremiah (20:1-2) mentions a priest named Pashhur the son of Immer who had the power to arrest prophets who did not conform and put them in the stocks at the Upper Gate of Benjamin in the temple. Other references reinforce the fact that priests had police powers.

Though the highest officials in the Roman colony at Philippi were also called "captains," the captain of the temple guard seems rather to be related to the "sagan," a priestly official who ranked next to the high priest and was responsible for guarding some 24 posts in and around the temple. This included 3 chambers in the temple, and 21 other sites, including the temple gates, guarded by Levites.

The Sadducees

The Sadducees were not a distinct group like the priests. Rather they were a party, like the Pharisees and Essenes. They consisted of both priests and laymen, especially wealthy, aristocratic rural landlords. They had a reputation for being far less polished and refined than the more cultured urban Pharisees.

The origin of the three parties is shrouded in the unrecorded pages of history. Some suggest that the Sadducees owe their origin to

Right: Peter and John are brought before the council, the Sanhedrin. This was the highest authority among the Jewish people, with 71 members, including the high priest. This council tried to stop Peter's and John's preaching, but the apostles told them they must obey a higher power, the Lord Himself.

538

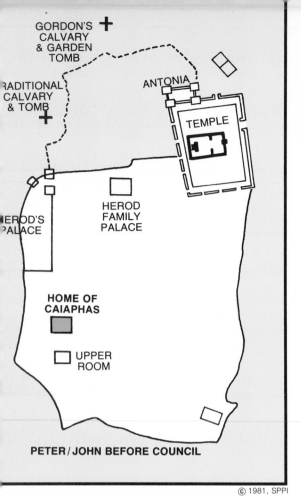

GORDON'S CALVARY & GARDEN TOMB

ANTONIA

TEMPLE

TRADITIONAL CALVARY & TOMB

HEROD'S PALACE

HEROD FAMILY PALACE

HOME OF CAIAPHAS

UPPER ROOM

PETER/JOHN BEFORE COUNCIL

© 1981, SPPI

Zadok, a leading priest during the reigns of David and Solomon. The problem with this theory is that not all Sadducees were priests.

Another theory is that the Sadducees originated with the "syndics" or judges in the days of the Maccabees, with whom they were close until 76 B.C.

The common people tended to hate the Sadducees because as politicians they compromised with Rome and adopted some of the influences of Hellenization (Greek customs). They were, nevertheless, conservative Jews who did their best to avoid any disturbance of the delicate peace they had worked out and were ready to stamp out popular movements like the one Peter and John represented. They rejected the oral traditions of the Pharisees and accepted only the Torah.

The Sanhedrin

The Sanhedrin, the supreme administrative and legal body of the Jews, consisted of 71 members. Jerusalem also had two lower tribunals, each with 23 members, to whom the name was given. Tradition traced its origin back to the 70 elders who assisted Moses. Most of its members, including the high priest, were Sadducees; hence the Sanhedrin was an aristocratic body. It could not meet at night, so Peter and John were questioned the morning after their arrest.

The high priest, who was president of the Sanhedrin, was at this time Caiaphas. His house is marked on the above map. The Sanhedrin, or council, probably met in the temple, in the large outer courtyard called the Court of the Gentiles. The house of Caiaphas, the high priest, is pictured at the left, in a model of Jerusalem.

Annas and His Family

Though at this time priests were appointed or deposed easily by the Roman government, Annas remained a powerful figure even after he ceased to be high priest. Five of his sons, his son-in-law Caiaphas, and his grandson Matthias all followed him as high priests.

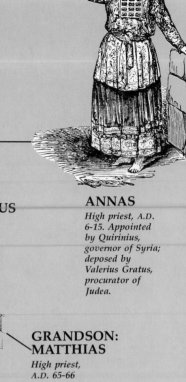

SON: ELEAZAR
High priest, A.D. 16-17

SON: JONATHAN
(possibly "John" in Acts 4:6)
High priest, A.D. 36-37

SON: THEOPHILUS
High priest, A.D. 37-41

ANNAS
High priest, A.D. 6-15. Appointed by Quirinius, governor of Syria; deposed by Valerius Gratus, procurator of Judea.

GRANDSON: MATTHIAS
High priest, A.D. 65-66

The Believers

ACTS 4:32—5:16

Synopsis
Exciting things happened in Jerusalem after the Holy Spirit came on the disciples. People shared what they had with other believers and told what Jesus had done for them. Peter preached a sermon which brought thousands to Christ for forgiveness. At the temple Peter and John healed a lame man, but this and their teaching angered the religious leaders, who brought them before the council. Meanwhile, more people believed in Jesus and the mighty works continued.

When
About A.D. 61: Some 30 years earlier, Jesus had planted the seed of the Gospel. The disciples watered that seed, first preaching the Gospel in Jerusalem, and eventually throughout all the Bible world. At the time of this story, the church was growing almost overnight. Men, women, and children were believing in Jesus as Christianity spread.

Time Frame
The Old Testament, from beginning to end, covers a period of thousands of years. But the events of the New Testament scarcely take up 100 years.

In the Old Testament we read about the lives of Noah, Abraham, Samson, Ruth, David, Isaiah, Daniel, Esther, and many, many more. But the New Testament focuses in only on Jesus, the apostles, and Paul.

Because the events of the Old Testament lasted many more years than the New, archeologists have found a greater number of artifacts, or ancient objects, from the time of the Old Testament.

Barnabas
This is the first time we meet Barnabas. Later he comes to play an important role in the history of the early church by singling out Paul and encouraging his leadership abilities. In fact, Barnabas' name means, "son of encouragement."

We do not know how Barnabas came to believe in Jesus, but it is interesting to note

540

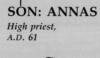

SON: MATTHIAS
High priest,
A.D. 42

SON: ANNAS
High priest,
A.D. 61

SON-IN-LAW: CAIAPHAS
High priest,
A.D. 18-36. Also
called Joseph,
his personal name.
Appointed by
Valerius Gratus.
Deposed by
procurator
Vitellius. A
Sadducee.

that more than one member of his family became a member of the early Christian community. John Mark, his cousin, wrote the Gospel of Mark and joined Paul and Barnabas on their first missionary journey (see Col. 4:10).

Barnabas seems to have been trained in the Christian community as a Levite. Levites were assistants to priests in the temple and performed more minor priestly functions than priests did. But Barnabas does not seem to have had the gifts needed to become a great leader. After he became a Christian, it appears that his talent was not one of preaching, but rather of discovering and encouraging someone as talented as Paul.

A Resident of Cyprus
Barnabas came from the island of Cyprus. This is a large island, the nearest island of any size to Antioch and Jerusalem (about 60 miles west). When Barnabas became one of the leaders of the Christian community at Antioch, he returned to Cyprus on a missionary journey, with Paul and John Mark. This might reveal that he had many relatives and acquaintances on the island.

Cyprus is 160 miles wide and 60 miles from

north to south. This island was probably evangelized from Antioch, but Barnabas probably became a Christian through contact with Christians while he lived in Jerusalem.

Christianity did not become a major force on the island until the days of Constantine. Though Barnabas and John Mark returned to Cyprus on a second missionary tour, Paul probably did not return to the island, though he did pass near it on two occasions.

It is interesting that though Barnabas was a Levite he owned land. Perhaps the Old Testament rule against Levites owning property was no longer observed, or perhaps it did not apply outside Israel.

Ananias and Sapphira
We know nothing about this Christian couple other than what is recorded in Acts. The name "Ananias" means "God is gracious." "Sapphira" means "beautiful." Yet Ananias did not appreciate God's graciousness, and Sapphira's moral integrity was certainly not beautiful. The two of them were apparently impressed by the high regard their fellow Christians held for those who sold their land and gave the money to the church.

541

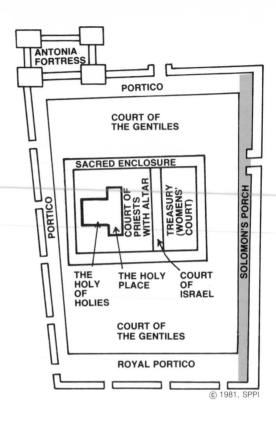

Diagram labels:
ANTONIA FORTRESS
PORTICO
COURT OF THE GENTILES
SACRED ENCLOSURE
PORTICO
COURT OF PRIESTS WITH ALTAR
TREASURY (WOMENS' COURT)
SOLOMON'S PORCH
THE HOLY OF HOLIES
THE HOLY PLACE
COURT OF ISRAEL
COURT OF THE GENTILES
ROYAL PORTICO
© 1981, SPPI

The Apostles Are Taken before the Council

ACTS 5:17-42

Synopsis

Thousands of people in Jerusalem were becoming believers, for when they heard the apostles teach and preach, they realized their need for forgiveness. When Peter and John healed a lame man at the temple, they were taken before the Sanhedrin, the high council. But the council freed them after a few threats. The apostles continued to preach and the ranks of the believers grew. Though the believers were shaken when Ananias and Sapphira died for trying to deceive the Lord, that did not diminish their rapid growth. Many began coming from the surrounding areas, bringing the sick for healing. At last the high priest decided to take action, so he threw the apostles into prison. But the angel of the Lord released them. Then the officers of the high priest arrested them again and took them before the council. But though the council wanted to kill the apostles, one of their members, a man named Gamaliel, cautioned them to be careful. After beating the apostles, the council freed them. The apostles returned to their work, preaching and teaching about Jesus Christ as Saviour.

Luke tells us that the believers met at Solomon's Colonnade (porch) to hear the apostles teach (Acts 5:12). This area is shown on the diagram of the temple above. At the above left are two photos of the Sanhedrin Tombs. The photo at the top shows the exterior and the other the interior of the tombs, with the burial places visible at the back.

542

The Sanhedrin Tombs or Tombs of the Judges

According to an ancient tradition, the 71 members of the Sanhedrin, the supreme court of Israel in New Testament times, were buried in the *Qoubour el Qoda,* which the Jews call the Sanhedrin Tombs and Christians call the Tombs of the Judges. These tombs date from the first or second century, but surprisingly little is said about them until A.D. 1253.

Today if you go north out of the Damascus Gate and up *Rehov Shemuel Hanavi,* the Street of Samuel the Prophet, toward the towers of the tomb where Samuel is said to be buried and toward Mea Shearim, the picturesque stronghold of Jewish orthodoxy where according to tradition there were once 100 gates, you will come to a garden near which the Sanhedrin Tombs are located.

The entrance to the tombs is a doorway over which ornate carvings of pomegranates, lemons, and acanthus leaves have been placed. The inside, on three levels, one underground, has been hewn out of solid rock. On the floor in front of the entrance a basin, hollowed out of the floor, was once used for ritual purification of the dead. The actual burial chambers have 71 burial niches into which the stone coffins were placed.

Gamaliel

Gamaliel belonged to a distinguished line of Jewish leaders. His grandfather is said to have been the famous Hillel. Gamaliel is usually referred to as Gamaliel the Elder because his grandson named Gamaliel also became a leader in the Sanhedrin. So distinguished was the career of Gamaliel the Elder that he was awarded the title of Rabban, meaning "Our Master." A moderate Pharisee known in both the New Testament and the Talmud for his knowledge of the Law, he was described at his death in A.D. 70 as follows: "When Rabban Gamaliel the Elder died, the glory of the Law ceased and purity and abstinence died."

At the bottom, one artist's concept of the council chambers of the Sanhedrin. The Sanhedrin met in the temple, perhaps by the Court of the Gentiles. Below: two sets of coins of "Simon, son of Gamaliel," who at the time may have been head of the Sanhedrin (coins of this type were likely those of the Nasi, or president, of the Sanhedrin).

543

The Seven Deacons

ACTS 6:1-7

Synopsis

After healing a lame man in the temple, Peter and John were taken before the high council, warned, and released. But they continued to preach, heal, and teach, which angered the high priest. He brought them before the council again and would have killed them had not Gamaliel, a member of the council, cautioned his fellow members to be careful. The numbers of believers grew, until some tension arose because there were not enough apostles to take care of the distribution of food. To solve the problem, seven deacons were chosen to do this work, so that the apostles could have time to teach and preach.

The Seven

Who were the seven men selected to "serve tables"? They have traditionally been called deacons. This is because the Greek word for "serve" and the Greek word for "deacon" have the same root. The seven men mentioned in Acts 6 should not be seen as deacons in the later sense of church officers, though there are some similarities. The deacons were assistants of the elders in local leadership in the churches. Similarly, the seven were assistants of the apostles in the sense that they freed them for preaching the Word of God. Yet the seven probably only *supervised* the serving of food to the widows, since it is not likely that men would actually wait on the tables when the widows could do that for themselves. The fact that Stephen and Philip are better known for their preaching and evangelism also indicates that in no sense were they or their colleagues limited to the supervision of food distribution and other charitable activities in the local Christian community.

All seven have Greek names. This indicates that they may have been Gentile converts to Christianity. Though the complaint is made by Greek-speaking Jews against Aramaic-speaking Jews, nothing in the text suggests that the seven were Jewish—though they could have been.

What do we know about the seven men who were selected to be in charge of food distribution? From the New Testament we know that Stephen was martyred. Eusebius the historian tells us that Philip and his prophesying daughters later settled in Hierapolis in Asia Minor. According to tradition Procorus

THE NUMBER 7

Some have gone to great lengths to find a mystical or symbolic meaning behind numbers in the Bible. This has led to abuse, for it can be carried to ridiculous conclusions. But it is worthwhile to note the similarity between certain uses of a certain number, such as the number 7. Other numbers used in many circumstances are: 3, 12, and 40.

1. THE FLOOD—7 PAIRS OF ANIMALS AND BIRDS (Gen. 7:1-2)

God told Noah to take on the ark 7 pairs of birds and 7 pairs of clean animals. The Flood would come 7 days after these commands.

2. THE BATTLE FOR JERICHO (Josh. 6:6-16)

In the battle for Jericho, the Israelites were to circle the city on each of 7 days, and 7 times on the 7th day. In addition, 7 priests were to blow on 7 trumpets on the 7th time around the city.

was John's secretary when he wrote the fourth Gospel. Clement of Alexandria, an early church father, tells us that Nicolas from Antioch, a convert to Judaism before he became a Christian, was very jealous of his beautiful wife. Other church fathers identify him as the founder of an unorthodox Christian sect called the Nicolaitans. This sect is mentioned by John (Rev. 2:6, 15). Tradition tells us that Parmenas was at one time bishop of Soli, a town west of Tarsus in Cilicia, and that he suffered martyrdom at Philippi under Emperor Trajan. Procorus is said to have been consecrated bishop of Nicomedia, a city east of present-day Istanbul in Turkey now called Izmit, by Peter. Dorotheus of Tyre tells us that Timon was one of the 70 disciples and that he later became bishop of Bostia, a town east of Samaria, where he was later burned as a martyr.

It has been suggested that just as 12 represents the 12 tribes of Israel to Luke, so too the numbers 7 and 70 represent the world. Hebrew tradition does say there were 70 na-

3. JACOB, 7 YEARS FOR RACHEL
(Gen. 29:16-30)

Jacob worked 7 years to marry Rachel, but was tricked to marry Leah, then worked another 7 years for Rachel.

4. SAMSON—7 LOCKS OF HAIR
(Jud. 16:19)

Samson's strength was related to 7 locks (or braids) of hair. Note how Samson also chose 7 for the number of leather thongs (Jud. 16:7).

5. NAAMAN DIPPED 7 TIMES IN THE JORDAN RIVER
(2 Kings 5:10-14)

The Syrian commander Naaman had leprosy. To cleanse himself from it, he was ordered by Elisha to dip in the Jordan River 7 times.

6. JESUS FED 4,000 WITH 7 LOAVES AND HAD 7 BASKETS OF SCRAPS LEFT
(Mark 8:6-9)

With 7 loaves of bread, Jesus fed 4,000. There were 7 baskets of broken pieces left.

7. JOHN WROTE TO 7 CHURCHES IN ASIA MINOR
(Rev. 1:4)

John addressed the Book of Revelation to the 7 churches of Asia Minor. He used the number 7 a total of 44 times in this letter.

tions in the world. Luke is saying that just as the 12 apostles represent the 12 tribes of Israel, so the 7 in a sense represent the rest of the world.

It has also been suggested that the underlying reason for the complaint that resulted in the appointment of the seven men was that some of the Aramaic-speaking widows still had difficulty eating with those who did not observe their strict *kosher* eating habits. Later the Jews accused Stephen of laxity in keeping the Law and temple attendance, so the suggestion may have some truth to it.

The Aramaic Language

Who were the "Hebrews" who were apparently overlooking the "Grecian" widows in the daily distribution of food?

The Christian community was growing so quickly that, Luke tells us, Greek-speaking Jewish Christians and those who spoke "Hebrew," i.e. a Palestinian version of Aramaic, were forming distinct subgroups.

The Aramaic language has a very interesting history. Originally the language spoken by the people of Syria, a land once known as Aram and called that sometimes in the Old Testament though it is generally translated Syria or Mesopotamia, Aramaic was based on an alphabet rather than on cuneiform syllables. When the Persians looked for a language that could be used throughout their vast empire, they liked the alphabetical foundation and adopted Aramaic for use from India to Egypt. It thus completely superceded the earlier Akkadian cuneiform language.

After their exile in Babylonia and Persia, Jews who spoke Aramaic had such difficulty with the Hebrew Bible that it was regularly translated orally into Aramaic. Those translations have been preserved in the Mishnah portions of the Talmud. The New Testament indicates that Jesus knew Aramaic. Among the many Aramaic works that have been discovered are the Elephantine Papyri, the Dead Sea Genesis Apocryphon, the Targum of Onkelos on the Pentateuch, and that portion of the Talmud called the Gemara.

Stephen Is Killed

ACTS 6:8—7:60

Synopsis
The apostles taught and preached about the risen Christ. As they did, thousands of new believers were added to their already large number. Peter and John were taken before the council and warned not to preach about Jesus, but they continued. The high priest got angry and took the apostles before the council. But Gamaliel, a member of the council, warned against killing them. So the apostles were beaten and released. The number of believers continued to grow. Seven deacons were chosen to minister to those who needed food. One of these seven, a man named Stephen, was accused of wrongdoing and stoned to death.

The Place Where Stephen Was Stoned
Two churches stand as memorials to Stephen today. The first, the Church of St. Stephen, is a modern Greek Orthodox church. It is said to stand on the spot where Stephen met his death. Located at the foot of the southern tip of the western slope of the Mount of Olives, it lies north of Gethsemane on the Jericho Road. In A.D. 415 a priest named Lucian discovered what he believed to be Stephen's skeleton at a place he called Caphar Gamala. In 1916 at Beit Jimal, about 20 miles south of Jerusalem on the way to Beersheba, a small church with mosaics dating back to the fifth or sixth century was discovered.

Below: Stephen stands before the council. False charges were brought aga him and he was killed. Above: Stephen's Gate, n the traditional place where Stephen was stoned to death.

546

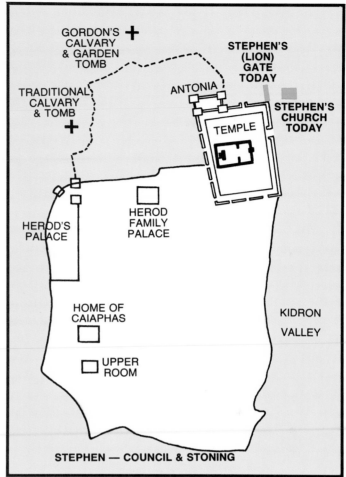

STEPHEN — COUNCIL & STONING

© 1981, SPPI

GORDON'S CALVARY & GARDEN TOMB

TRADITIONAL CALVARY & TOMB

STEPHEN'S (LION) GATE TODAY

ANTONIA

STEPHEN'S CHURCH TODAY

TEMPLE

HEROD'S PALACE

HEROD FAMILY PALACE

HOME OF CAIAPHAS

UPPER ROOM

KIDRON VALLEY

Above: the Church of St. Stephen, just east of Stephen's Gate. The map above locates this church and Stephen's Gate.

Under it was a tomb believed to be the spot of which Lucian wrote. (A new church, built according to the plan of the original one, has been built here in Stephen's honor.)

In A.D. 460 the Empress Eudoxia built the second memorial to Stephen, the Basilica or Cathedral of St. Stephen, her patron saint. It was built to house the relics of the martyred saint. Today one of the most important biblical and archeological schools in the world is located near this cathedral, just north of the city.

Stephen's Gate (The Lion's Gate)

Christians have called this gate, the first one north of the Golden Gate and the Temple Mount, St. Stephen's Gate because it is located near the traditional site of Stephen's martyrdom. It is located a few blocks east of the Via Dolorosa and just north of the temple. The Pool of Bethesda, to the right of the gate, was once used to wash the sheep to be sacrificed in the temple.

547

Philip in Samaria

ACTS 8:1-25

Synopsis

Since the coming of the Holy Spirit at Pentecost, the numbers of believers in Jerusalem grew daily. Not only that, but the believers shared their possessions and helped others in need. With the increased numbers of believers came increased needs. Seven deacons were appointed to distribute food to the needy. But one of these seven, accused of wrongdoing, was stoned to death. The increasing persecution drove the other believers from Jerusalem. As they went to other parts of the land, they took their Gospel with them, so the Good News about Jesus spread rapidly, even into Samaria.

Samaria

Should Acts 8:5 be translated "the city of Samaria" or "a city of Samaria"? Those who have studied the topic seem to split evenly on the question. Those who think it refers to the city named Samaria refer to the magnificent structure built by Herod the Great and renamed Sebaste (the Greek form of Augustus) in honor of Caesar Augustus. Herod, who was even more of a builder than Solomon, loved Sebaste more than all the other cities he had built and spent 10 years in its

548

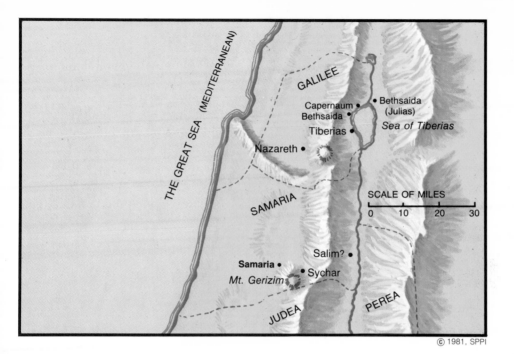

© 1981, SPPI

The three photos above and at the left show different scenes of the city of Samaria today. At the left are Roman pillars from New Testament times. The photo above shows the village of Sebastiye, adjoining the ruins of the ancient city of Samaria. The map above locates the city of Samaria within the region also known as Samaria.

construction. In the city he built an impressive temple on the site of Israeli King Omri's palace—for the worship of Caesar Augustus as a god! The only part of the two-mile-long wall Herod built around the city that has been excavated is a cluster of circular towers that formed the western section. Because the workmanship is not as refined as that of the temple in Jerusalem, it has been suggested that local artisans were used. A large fragment believed to be part of a statue to Caesar Augustus was found in the debris east of the altar at the foot of a staircase 90 feet wide.

Sebaste was captured and sacked by the Jews in A.D. 66, as part of their revolt against Rome.

Some ancient manuscripts read "a city of Samaria," however. Justin Martyr, A Christian theologian of the second century who was born in Samaria, says Simon Magus came from Gitta; this too has been suggested as the city intended in Acts.

Simon Magus

The Simon in Acts 8 may have been the famous leader of the Gnostic heresy that so plagued the early church. But no one knows for certain.

549

Philip and the Ethiopian

ACTS 8:26-40

Synopsis

After Stephen was stoned to death, Saul began to persecute the Christians in Jerusalem. Though it may have seemed as if the Christians were being punished, it was God's way of sending the Christians into surrounding areas with the Gospel. Philip took the Good News of Jesus to Samaria, where many believed.

In the midst of Philip's successful work at Samaria, an angel of the Lord ordered him to leave and go to a lonely place on the road that led from Jerusalem to Gaza.

It must have been difficult for Philip to leave a place where dozens or perhaps hundreds were coming to Christ. But his faithfulness in going opened the way for Ethiopia to hear the Gospel through one of the nation's own people, a high-ranking government official.

Below: Philip's Springs still provides water for neighbor who bring their pails and animals. Today the spring is enclosed in concrete and stone.

Philip's Springs—On the Gaza Road

Between Bethlehem and Hebron there is a spring of water known as Ain ed Dirweh, or Fountain of St. Philip. According to tradition, this is the place where Philip stopped to baptize the Ethiopian. Philip's Springs is only a short distance north of Mamre, where Abraham lived for some time. If this was the place, it was certainly not a desert area, as we often think, but rather a deserted area. The land in this region is very fertile, not far from the Valley of Eshcol, from which the Hebrew spies brought enormous bunches of grapes when they reported to Moses and the people at Kadesh Barnea. The road led on to Gaza, which was sandy desert.

The Chariot

A two-wheeled cart drawn by horses, the chariot was used both as transportation for officials and as an instrument of war. Chariots are mentioned many times in the Bible (Joseph, Gen. 41:43; Jacob's

550

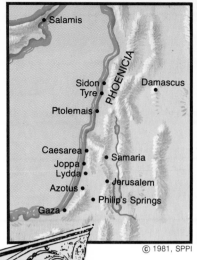
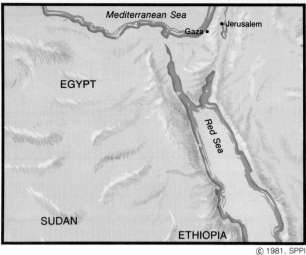

© 1981, SPPI

© 1981, SPPI

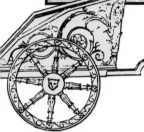

Upper left: On the road to Gaza, which led from Jerusalem, Philip met the Ethiopian treasurer. The map at the left shows how Philip's Springs is nearer to Jerusalem than Gaza, while the map at the right shows how the Ethiopian was many miles from home when he met Philip.

The three pictures at left show Roman chariots. Two pictures are ancient Roman coins. Notice in those pictures how the chariots were drawn by four horses, hitched side by side.

funeral, Gen. 50:9; Philistines, 1 Sam. 13:5; Solomon, 1 Kings 9:19). But they are seldom mentioned in the New Testament.

Philip

There were two Philips who lived at this time and who were prominent in the Book of Acts. One was Philip, the apostle. The other was Philip, the evangelist or deacon, who is the Philip of this story. Paul stayed later at his home (Acts 21:8-9). Philip preached to the Gentiles long before Peter or Paul did. Luke also tells us that Philip had four unmarried daughters who were prophets (Acts 21). Of course this was much later than this story.

The Ethiopian

He was an African, Treasurer of Ethiopia under Queen Candace. He was a nobleman, a man of great importance who would have much influence for Christ when he returned to his own country. He was already a devout man, for he was reading from the Scriptures when Philip met him and wanted to know more about what he was reading. The Scripture from which he was reading was Isaiah 53, which told about Christ.

551

© 1981, SPPI

Saul Becomes Paul

ACTS 9:1-22

Synopsis

As more people became believers in Jesus, the council and other religious leaders became more angry. Persecution of the believers began, causing many to leave Jerusalem for other places, not only in Israel, but in Samaria, and even beyond. Saul hated these believers and persecuted them bitterly. In one great effort to track them down, he headed toward Damascus to persecute the believers there. But on the way, he fell to the ground and Jesus spoke to him. Saul became a new person—a believer, like those he had persecuted.

Damascus

The city of Damascus was situated on an oasis about 175 miles northeast of Jerusalem in the Roman province of Syria. The Amana River flows north of its north wall. The walls of the city form a rectangle, with two parallel streets going from the west to the east wall. Politically it was often considered part of the Decapolis, and it is close enough to Palestine that Mt. Hermon can be seen from there on the western horizon. At the time of Paul's conversion it appears that Tiberius may

Above left: an early drawing from the 1800s, showing Straight Street, in Damascus, as it looked then. The coin above is from Damascus.

552

have allowed King Aretas of the Nabateans to have a representative ("ethnarch" or "governor") in Damascus to protect the interests of its many Nabatean residents.

Straight Street

One of the two parallel streets that ran from the western to the eastern wall was called Straight Street (sometimes known as the Via Recta, its Latin name). Today the street goes only from the eastern gate to the middle of the city. It is really more of an alley than a street, since it is very narrow and so covered over with archways that even in the daytime parts of it are dark. In Paul's day the theater was at its western extremity and the king's palace was near its center. Today tourists are shown what is reputed to be the same window in the wall where Paul was lowered in a basket, the spot where Paul received his vision, and even the house of Ananias.

Tarsus

Paul's original name was Saul. He came from Tarsus, a city on the southern coast of present-day Turkey. In Paul's time it was in the Roman province of Cilicia. Ten miles inland from the Mediterranean coast, it was proud of its reputation as a port. The Cyndus River, up which Cleopatra once sailed to meet Mark Antony, was a major highway through the Taurus Mountains. It helped make Tarsus a cultural crossroads, an ideal background for Paul's future role.

Below: the Damascus Gate, in Jerusalem, the start of the road to Damascus. Lower left: Saul is struck down on the road to Damascus as Jesus speaks to him. The map at the left shows the location of Tarsus as it relates to Jerusalem and Damascus.

In the above coin, King Aretas of Damascus kneels beside his camel in submission to the Romans. The chariot on the other side is drawn by four horses. At the right: a 19th-century woodcut, showing the ancient wall of Damascus. A drawing from about the same time shows Paul's escape from this wall (lower right).

Saul Escapes

ACTS 9:23-31

Synopsis

Believers multiplied rapidly in Jerusalem, and as they did, the high priest and the council began to persecute them for their beliefs. Many moved out of Jerusalem and took the Gospel with them. But Saul, a Jewish religious leader, headed for Damascus to persecute believers there. On the way, Jesus spoke to him and he became a believer. Now others who persecuted the believers wanted to kill Saul, but some fellow believers helped him escape from Damascus in a basket.

Caesarea

After Saul left Damascus, he returned to Jerusalem and was introduced to the Christian community there by Barnabas. But Grecian Jews tried to kill him when he boldly wit-

nessed to his newfound faith in Christ. So members of the church took him down to Caesarea and put him on a boat.

Caesarea was a very important city at the time. It had, under the Roman procurators of Palestine, become the capital of the country. Though first called Straton or Strato's Tower after the Phoenician king who first occupied it, the city as Saul saw it was the result of a major building project of the master builder Herod the Great, started in 22 B.C. A gift from Caesar Augustus, it was pounded by the gale-swept waves of the Mediterranean, so Herod's first task was to fill the harbor with enormous blocks of limestone, some 50 feet by 10 feet by 9 feet thick. After 12 years the city was a model of Hellenistic culture with its own hippodrome, theater, temple to Caesar (after whom Herod named it), and exposed brick aqueduct. A small garrison of 3,000 soldiers was stationed there. When fighting broke out between Jews and Gentiles, at

554

the start of the Jewish uprising against Rome in A.D. 66, the soldiers wiped out Caesarea's substantial Jewish population. Though Caesarea later became one of the seven major centers of the Christian church with its own very influential bishop, it otherwise fell into relative oblivion and was captured by Muslim invaders near the end of the Roman Empire. The Crusaders did some restoration, and Israeli archeologists are currently excavating in that area.

Tarsus

With over 6,000 years of continuous existence, Tarsus may well be the oldest city in the world still in existence, even older than Damascus, its chief rival for the title. A walled town as early as the third millennium B.C., its name is at least as old as the Hittite empire that made it the capital of an area called Kizzuwatna. It was destroyed around 2000 B.C., but then after the Trojan War it was resettled by Greeks. The city began minting its own coins in the fifth century B.C. Alexander the Great in 333 B.C. replaced images of Persian satraps with those of Baal Tars, the god of the city. During his stay in Tarsus, Alexander took a bath in the chilly waters of the Cyndus River and became seriously ill. The notorious Seleucid (Syrian) king Antiochus IV Epiphanes changed the city's name to Antioch on the Cyndus, but the change did not last. The Romans made Tarsus the capital of the Roman province of Cilicia in 67 B.C. Shortly afterward Cicero, the famous Roman orator, became its governor. After the murder of Julius Caesar, Cassius levied a gargantuan fine against the city for opposing him, but Mark Antony redressed the fine by exempting the city from taxes. Dressed as Aphrodite, Cleopatra sailed up the Cyndus to meet him during his stay in Tarsus. Tarsus became an intellectual center of some half million people, with its schools rivaling those of Alexandria. It was indeed "no mean city," an ideal place of preparation for the one who transformed Christianity from a Jewish sect into a world faith.

© 1981, SPPI

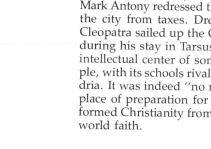

Above: to reach Jerusalem from Damascus, Paul traveled south about 175 miles. To go on to Tarsus, he first had to go to the seaport of Caesarea, then sail northward to his hometown Tarsus, near the coast of Cilicia.

555

Aeneas

ACTS 9:32-35

Synopsis
While Saul tried to track down some believers in Damascus to persecute them, Peter went to Lydda to visit. There he found a sick man named Aeneas and healed him.

How the Church Started Spreading
After Stephen was killed because of his faith, the church in Jerusalem was under great pressure, and persecution started to increase. This pressure caused Christians in Jerusalem to look for a new base of operations where their work might continue unhindered. Jerusalem was now a dangerous place for those involved in missionary work.

Christians soon began looking away from Jerusalem, hoping to find a new place to keep preaching the Gospel. This seemed to fulfill Jesus' words, "Go and make disciples of all nations" (Matt. 28:19). This is certainly one of the reasons we find Peter at Lydda.

556

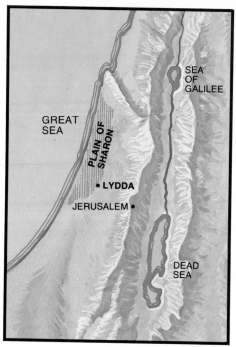

© 1981, SPPI

Lydda and the Plains of Sharon are located on the above map. In the village of Lydda, now called Lod, today one may see the Greek Orthodox Church of St. George (left) and a bridge built in Crusader times, the 13th century A.D. (above). Between two lions is an inscription in Arabic which says, among other things, that the sultan of that time ordered the bridge to be built. It is dated A.D. 1278. At the upper left, a photo of the Plains of Sharon, where Aeneas went with his good news of healing.

Lydda

The last we had heard of Peter before he arrived in Lydda was that he and John had traveled to Samaria to see for themselves the great success of Philip's missionary work. Peter and John stayed in Samaria for a while preaching the Gospel, and then returned to Jerusalem.

Lydda, or Lod as it is now called, was about 10 miles southeast of the seacoast city of Joppa. It was strategically located at the intersection of the highways from Jerusalem to Joppa, and from Egypt to ancient Babylon. This helped make it an important commercial center. The "merchants of Lydda" were famed as businessmen in Jewish literature. Today Israel's international airport, largest in the land, is located just north of the city; it is the modern gateway to and from Israel.

The city's name goes back so far in history its origin is unknown. Its name is found inscribed into the walls of the Egyptian temple to Amon at Karnak. There it is mentioned as belonging to Pharaoh Thutmose III, perhaps as early as 1500 B.C. By the time Peter visited the city it had grown much larger. But it is mentioned only here in the New Testament.

Aeneas

Little is known of this man other than what is said in the Book of Acts. He had a classical Greek name, which appeared as early as the writings of Homer, author of the *Iliad* and the *Odyssey*. It means "praise."

Aeneas was a Jew who spoke Greek (these people were called Hellenists). After eight years of being paralyzed and confined to a bed, he was healed at Lydda by Peter who was traveling through the area. Whether he was a Christian before he was healed we do not know.

The Spread of Christianity

Why did Christianity spread so quickly during this time? There are a number of important reasons. First of all, almost the entire world was speaking Greek, or was familiar with the Greek language at this time. This made it easier for missionaries to communicate with almost everyone.

Secondly, Christianity was spreading behind the borders of Rome. Nearly all of the world was under the Roman Empire. Passports or visas were not needed to travel from country to country. God was actually using the aggressive Roman army to help spread His great message!

Dorcas

ACTS 9:36-42

Synopsis
As the believers scattered from Jerusalem because of
the persecution, Peter went to Lydda to visit. There
he healed a sick man named Aeneas. At Joppa, he
raised Dorcas from the dead. This brought much excitement in those parts and many believed in Jesus because
of it.

Sharon
Peter's fame traveled from Lydda to Joppa, apparently
because Aeneas traveled to Joppa and "Sharon."
"Sharon" is the Hebrew word for "plain." It refers to
the great plain that stretches from Joppa all the way
to Haifa and Mt. Carmel to the north, some 50 miles
away. The largest of the coastal plains of Israel, it is
about 10 miles wide. Its swampy dunes have a reddish
hue, especially in the north. Once densely covered
with oaks and other vegetation, and then denuded, it
is once again, thanks to irrigation, covered with lemon
groves and even banana fields. Five streams and countless underground springs water its surface. Near its
midsection, around Caesarea, the red sand rises as
much as 180 feet above sea level. It was not heavily

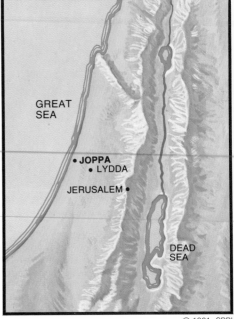

Upper left: Dorcas, or Tabitha, was
loved for her generosity, for she
gave many lovely gifts to her neighbors. Top center: the Russian
monastery which is claimed to be
the burial place of Tabitha.

558

Top: from Joppa, one looks across the bay to Tel Aviv. Joppa today is called Jaffa. Some of Israel's finest oranges are named for the city, Jaffa Oranges. Tel Aviv is a modern city. Jaffa has a charming reconstruction along the waterfront.
The name Dorcas meant "gazelle," which may have been a nickname for Tabitha. A gazelle is pictured above. She may have often run like a gazelle, doing good things for others.
The map at the left shows the location of Joppa.

populated in Old Testament times. David's shepherd chief, Shitrai, pastured his flocks in the area when the hill regions were dry.

Joppa

The city of Joppa is today Jaffa, a suburb of Tel Aviv. With about 800,000 inhabitants the greater Tel Aviv area today has roughly one third of Israel's population. Jaffa itself has about 75,000 Jews and 7,000 Muslims and Christians. (Haifa, some 50 miles to the north, is Israel's major seaport.) Set on a rock that rises about 125 feet above sea level and juts out into the Mediterranean, Jaffa has an excellent location for defense. Its sandy beaches hide treacherous reefs 300 to 400 feet offshore, but ships can enter from the north. In ancient times it was the only natural harbor from Egypt to Ptolemais, north of Mt. Carmel.

First mentioned in the list of cities captured by Thutmose III in the 15th century B.C., it long remained a key Egyptian governmental center. Under the Philistines it became the nation's northern seaport. David recaptured it and Solomon used it to receive the cedar logs he floated down from Lebanon and transported overland to Jerusalem to be used in his temple. Jonah fled from Joppa by ship to avoid going to Nineveh. In 701 B.C. Sennacherib destroyed the city but by Ezra's time it was once again available to Zerubbabel for transporting cedar logs to his temple in Jerusalem. Alexander the Great changed its name from Yapho to Joppa in honor of Jope, the daughter of Aeolus, god of the winds. Under Rome it became part of Herod the Great's territory. Because the people of Joppa hated Herod, he built Caesarea some 40 miles to the north and Joppa declined in importance.

Tabitha—Burial Place

Near the Russian monastery in Tel Aviv is a tomb said to be that of Tabitha (Dorcas). The monastery's tall, pointed tower is surrounded by palms.

Cornelius

ACTS 9:43—10:48

Synopsis

Peter visited Lydda, where he healed a man named Aeneas. Then he went on to Joppa, where he raised Dorcas from the dead. While staying at Joppa, he saw a vision from the Lord, a sheet filled with unclean animals. This was followed by a visit by some men from Caesarea, who took him to Cornelius' home. There Peter told this Roman centurion about Jesus and he too became a believer.

Caesarea

Caesarea is sometimes known as Palestinian Caesarea to distinguish it from the Caesarea Philippi in the Decapolis. From Joppa to Caesarea, Peter and Cornelius' three messengers traveled 32 miles up the coast, a long journey by foot. Caesarea is 25 miles south of Mt. Carmel and 75 miles northwest of Jerusalem. The city is important in the history of Christianity as the first city ever to have Gentile Christians and a non-Jewish church.

In New Testament times Caesarea was capital of the Roman province of Judea, the place

The Roman columns below were once part of the beautiful city of Caesarea, which stood as a tribute to Augustus Caesar. Now they are a heap of ruins. The building at the lower left, at Joppa, stands over the traditional site of the tannery which Simon operated.

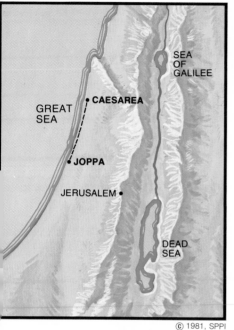

© 1981, SPPI

from which the Roman procurators governed the nation. Though the city was built in the typical Hellenistic Greek fashion with amphitheaters, temples, and palaces, its population was a mixture of Greeks and Jews. An aqueduct on the north brought water from Mt. Carmel and the Crocodile River. In the third century A.D. the great theologian Origen taught here. When Arabians conquered the area, however, Caesarea lost its prestige. Most of the stones of the old city were transported north to Acre, just north of Mt. Carmel and present-day Haifa.

Simon the Tanner
Simon lived by the seashore outside the walls of Joppa because tanning, which required contact with dead bodies, was regarded as unclean in Jewish eyes (see Lev. 11:40). Christians, however, readily accepted tanners. That Peter would stay with someone like Simon suggests that already he did not share the strict attitudes of more traditional Jews.

What was probably the only tannery in Joppa has been unearthed. It has three oval-shaped tanners' vats hewn out of rock and lined with Roman cement.

Cornelius, the Roman Centurion in the Italian Cohort
Cornelius was probably a descendant of the slaves who took the name of Cornelius Sulla when he freed them.

Centurions, in command of a "century," technically 100 men, were the backbone of the Roman army. Six centuries formed a cohort. Centurions carried vine staffs.

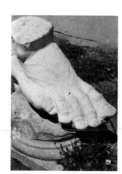

Top center: the map shows the location of Joppa and Caesarea. At the far left, Peter presents the Gospel to Cornelius, a Roman centurion. The drawing of a centurion at the left is taken from an ancient piece of Roman artwork. The foot at the left is from a Roman statue at Caesarea. It reminds us of the extensive walking which Peter and the other apostles did to take the Good News to the Gentiles, including the Romans.

561

Christians at Antioch

ACTS 11

Synopsis
Something new was happening in the circle of believers. When Peter was in Joppa, he saw a vision of unclean animals. Soon some men took him to the home of Cornelius, a Roman centurion, who with his household became believers. Now Gentiles were added to the growing number of believers. Barnabas went to Antioch, saw a need, and traveled to Tarsus to bring Saul back to help him. There in Antioch, in a growing church, believers were first called Christians.

Antioch
Often called Syrian Antioch to distinguish it from the Antioch in Pisidia in Asia Minor, this city became part of Turkey in 1939 after centuries of existence as part of Syria. It is now called Antakya, a name that suggests its ancient name, and is a town of about 30,000 people.

In ancient times, Antioch had periods of great splendor and at the time of Herod the Great may have been a city of half a million people. Located 15 miles inland from the Mediterranean Sea on the Orontes River and vulnerable to earthquakes, flooding, and enemy attack from the east, it was nevertheless happily situated on major land routes and became a major trade center.

562

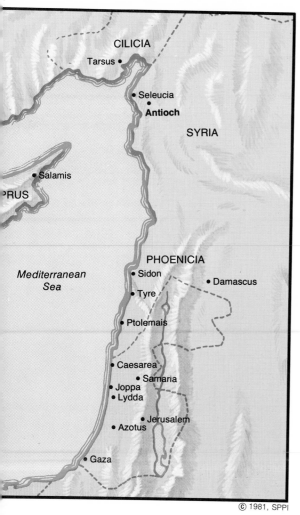

Antioch was founded in 300 B.C., shortly after the death of Alexander the Great. Seleucus, head of the Seleucid (Syrian) empire, named it after his father, Antiochus, and modeled it after Alexandria in Egypt. Located at the foot of Mt. Sulpius and Mt. Staurin, it depended for its water supply on an aqueduct from Daphne, a hillside resort four miles to the west known for its temple to Apollo and the lax morals that also tarnished Antioch the Golden. Under Antiochus IV Epiphanes (175-163 B.C.) the city flourished as the capital of a great empire. After Pompey's conquest in 64 B.C. Antioch was settled by Roman businessmen and once again became a major trade center. Various emperors contributed a temple, theater, circus, bath, and aqueduct and expanded its walls to make it more secure. Herod the Great added its still-famous 2-mile-long, 90-foot-wide boulevard. Under Tiberius Caesar magnificent columns, gates, and statues were added. Then at the height of its glory, it became the eastern hub of the Roman Empire.

Relations between its heavy Greek population and its Jewish population were never particularly good. The coming of Christianity only aggravated the problem. We know from Acts 6 that one of the seven deacons, Nicolaus, a convert from Judaism, came from Antioch. Whether he returned and founded the Christian community there or not, Antioch became a strong Christian center. The word "Christian" was first used here. Only after a great deal of conflict between Jewish and Greek Christians did Paul's Gospel finally triumph, free from the burdens of the Law. When Jerusalem fell in A.D. 70, Antioch became the center of Christianity. The names of great men, such as Peter and Ignatius, are listed as bishops of Antioch. But Simon Magus' descendants also made it a strong center of the Gnostic heresy.

The Emperor Claudius

Claudius was emperor of Rome from A.D. 41 to 54. Affected as a young man by both physical and mental problems, his position as Tiberius' nephew did not prevent him from being regarded as stupid and inconsequential. Caligula was amused by his handicaps and, perhaps in jest, gave him important leadership posts. As a result the Roman guard made him emperor at Caligula's death. His early reign was efficient, quite the contrast to his later reign, and to the reigns of his predecessor and successor, which were marred by suspicion and intrigue.

© 1981, SPPI

The map above shows a number of the cities associated with Bible events in the early life of Paul, including Antioch of Syria. Antioch today is pictured at the upper left, looking toward the northwest. The coin at the upper left (front and back) was a tetradrachm of Antioch, otherwise called a stater (standard piece), equal to two half-shekels, a temple tax for two. The lower coin at the left (front and back) was minted by Seleucus I, founder of Antioch, 312-280 B.C.

The prison keys above are thought to be from antiquity, though their date is not known. At the right, Peter is led from prison by an angel.

Peter in Prison

ACTS 12:1-5

Synopsis

Peter had left Jerusalem to visit Lydda, where he healed Aeneas, then Joppa, where he raised Dorcas from the dead. While at Joppa, Peter saw a vision of unclean animals and received visitors who took him to see Cornelius, a Gentile Roman centurion. Cornelius became a believer in Jesus. The door was open for the Gentiles to receive the Gospel also and before long a strong church appeared at Antioch, with many of its members Gentiles. Barnabas went to Tarsus to find Saul and bring him back to work with him there. But about that time, Herod Antipas began persecuting the believers, killing James, John's brother, and putting Peter into prison.

Herod Agrippa I

The Herod referred to in Acts 12 is Herod Agrippa I, one of many people to bear the name "Herod," which had come to be synonymous with "king." Agrippa was the grandson of Herod the Great; the half nephew of Herod Agrippa I, Archelaus, and Philip; the brother of Herodias; and the father of Bernice, Drusilla, and Herod Agrippa II, all mentioned later in Acts.

Born in 10 B.C., this Herod was one of the worst. His mother took

The two photos above show Caesarea today. The one a the top shows the theater built in Roman times. The lower photo shows a massi

him to Rome when he was six, but he neglected his studies to lead a spendthrift existence that made him run out of money and into debt. When the Emperor Tiberius' only son Drusus was poisoned in A.D. 23, Agrippa fell out of imperial favor and sometime later retired to a small fortress town in Idumea called Maltha. He left Rome without paying his debts. Depressed at his humiliation, he contemplated suicide, but his sister Herodias got her husband and half uncle, Herod Antipas, to make him a civil servant in Tiberias. He quarreled with Antipas and with his friend Flaccus, the Roman governor of Syria. Back in Rome he became the friend of Caligula, and on Tiberius' death Caligula made him a king over two Palestinian tetrarchies and, later, Antipas' territories as well. He also was rewarded for helping make Claudius emperor. He died in Caesarea in A.D. 44.

Four Squads of Soldiers
Greeks and Hebrews divided the night into three watches. Romans, however, broke the night into four three-hour periods from 6 P.M. to 6 A.M., the evening, midnight, cockcrowing, and dawn watches. Each detachment or squad of soldiers would have had one watch.

The Feast of Unleavened Bread
The seven days following the Passover meal were observed by eating unleavened bread, baked without yeast, to remind Jews that their ancestors left Egypt so quickly they took dough and baked it on the way.

565

Peter Released from Prison

ACTS 12:6-23

Synopsis

While Peter was visiting in Joppa, he saw a vision of a sheet filled with unclean animals. The Lord commanded him to kill and eat, but he would not. This was a prelude to Peter helping a Gentile become a believer, for as he had not eaten "unclean" meat, so he also had not wanted an "unclean" Gentile to join the believers. But the Lord showed that what He cleansed was not unclean. About that time, Agrippa I began persecuting the believers, killed James the brother of John, and threw Peter into prison. But an angel of the Lord set Peter free.

The House of John Mark's Mother, Mary

In the south-central section of Old Jerusalem, only a short distance south of the Church of the Holy Sepulchre on St. Mark's Road, is a Syrian Orthodox monastery called St. Mark's House. It is said to be the site of the house of Mary, the mother of John Mark, to which Peter headed when he was released from the prison in Herod's palace. The monks, who speak and pray in Syriac or Aramaic, the language most people in Jerusalem spoke in Jesus' day, claim that the Last Supper was celebrated in the upper room of the house, that Peter founded the first church here, and that Mary, the mother of Jesus, was baptized in the church's little baptistry.

Under the lectern of the church are the tombs of the Armenian patriarchs and archbishops, buried seated on their elaborate thrones according to Syrian custom. An ancient painting of the Virgin and Child is said to have been painted by Luke.

The Death of Herod Agrippa I

Josephus, the Jewish historian, gives an interpretation of Agrippa's death that differs from that given by Luke in Acts 12. He relates that on the second day of a festival in honor of Caesar in Caesarea, Agrippa dressed in spectacular robes made wholly of silver. They reflected the sun's rays and led certain people to call him a god. Agrippa did not rebuke them, but he immediately saw an owl sitting on a rope on the awning of a theater, an omen that his death was imminent. Seized with violent abdominal pains, he was carried to his palace where he died five days later. Though he received 12 million drachmas a

While Peter's friends prayed inside he, the answer to their prayers, waited at the courtyard gate (left). Rhoda tries to tell the believers that he is there.

year, he nevertheless still owed others huge sums because his expenses were even greater.

Luke says Agrippa was addressing ambassadors from Tyre and Sidon when he was smitten by the Lord's angel and died of worms.

Some interpreters have rejected the biblical account as legendary. It seems, however, that we have several accounts of the same event because each historian looked at the event from a different perspective.

Tyre and Sidon

Tyre and Sidon were two port cities in Phoenicia, north of Israel. They were located about 30 miles apart on the Mediterranean coast.

Tyre, located on a 140-acre island rock, was forced to build "up," and constructed buildings with more stories than even Rome had. In 333 B.C. Alexander the Great connected the island to the mainland by means of a "mole" half a mile long. Today shifting sand has shortened that distance to one-third of a mile. Tyre was a commercial city but insignificant politically.

Sidon to the north is situated on a hill that juts into the Mediterranean. Millions of murex shells produced the dye for which Sidon was famous. Its eastern wall protected it from enemy attack.

Above: a Roman seat of state (left), and a Roman chair of state (right). Roman officials used these for official business. Top: traditional house of Mark's mother. Right: a courtyard.

Paul's First Missionary Journey

ACTS 13:1-3

Synopsis

Saul had been one of the most violent men who persecuted the believers, pursuing them to Damascus to kill or imprison them. But Jesus talked to him on the Damascus Road, and Saul became a believer himself. Later, he returned to Jerusalem with Barnabas to work with believers there, and in time was back at his hometown Tarsus. There Barnabas found him and brought him back to Antioch, to work in the church. This church set Saul and Barnabas apart and sent them on their first missionary journey.

The Cities Paul Visited

Between A.D. 46 and 48 Paul and Barnabas visited the following nine cities mentioned in the New Testament:

1. *Antioch.* A splendidly "modern" city of half a million people with a spectacular boulevard constructed by Herod the Great, Antioch in Syria lay about 15 miles inland from the Mediterranean Sea. Located on a major trade route, its colonnaded 90-foot-wide main street was busy with commerce. After the fall of Jerusalem in A.D. 70, Antioch became the center of Christianity, and by A.D. 400 as many as 100,000 Christians lived here.

2. *Seleucia.* Fifteen miles west of Antioch, Seleucia was for a brief time capital of Syria after the death of Alexander the Great. Founded by Seleucus I in 300 B.C. and busy with naval activity during Roman times, the city declined when the harbor filled with silt. After a day's journey from Antioch, Paul and Barnabas sailed for Cyprus from here.

3. *Salamis (on Cyprus).* Tradition tells us that the city was named after the island in Greece from which Teucer, its founder, came. In Greek and Roman times Salamis was prosperous as a result of an excellent harbor. The New Testament reveals that many Jews lived here and that Salamis had its own synagogue. How long Paul and Barnabas stayed here we do not know, but Barnabas made a second visit with John Mark and, according to tradition, was martyred here under Nero.

4. *Paphos (on Cyprus).* Located across the island on the west, Paphos was the capital of Cyprus. Barnabas and Paul visited New

Paphos, a Roman city which had only recently been rebuilt by Caesar Augustus. The old city with its temple to Aphrodite lay about 10 miles southeast.

5. *Perga.* Located in the Roman province of Pamphylia, Perga was northwest of Cyprus in Asia Minor. Twelve miles east of Attalia (the important modern port of Antalya) on the River Cestris and inland some eight miles to avoid Cilician pirates, it had a famous temple dedicated to Artemis (Diana). The ruins of a theater that could have held 13,000 people and dates back to the first century can still be seen.

6. *Antioch in Pisidia.* Seleucus, founder

of the Syrian dynasty that took his name, founded this Antioch too. Strictly speaking not part of Pisidia, Antioch became part of the Roman province of Galatia in 25 B.C. and could therefore justifiably be called Galatian Antioch. A fortified Roman colony and capital of southern Galatia, it controlled the area's barbarian tribes.

7. *Iconium.* A two- or three-day trip from Antioch along the Via Sebaste, Iconium was an oasis entrance to an enormous plain after crossing through a mountain pass. On the trade route leading west to Ephesus and Rome, it became a Roman colony under Hadrian.

8. *Lystra.* Twenty miles southwest of Iconium through the cool Galatian plateau, Lystra was founded by Caesar Augustus. A statue to Zeus and Hermes (Jupiter and Mercury to the Romans) has been discovered here. Ovid tells us that Philemon and Baucis entertained the two gods when other Lystrans ignored them.

9. *Derbe.* Today an uninhabited sheep land, Derbe was about 25 miles southeast of Lystra. On the borders of the Roman province of Galatia, it was a frontier town of no special significance. To have gone further east would have taken Paul and Barnabas into Cappadocia.

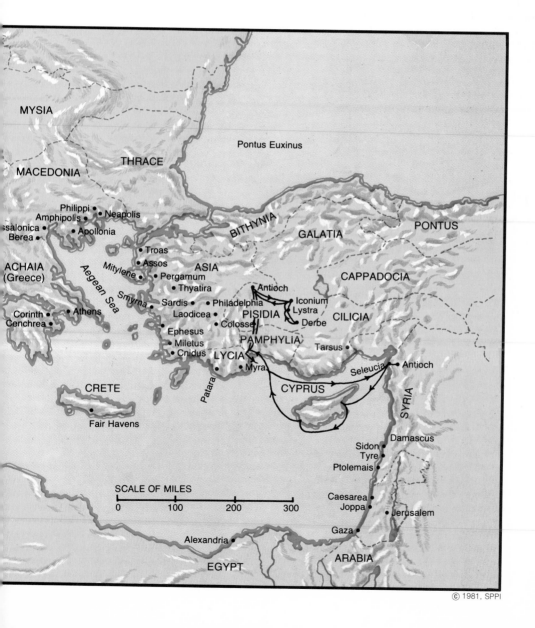

The three drawings of Roman ships on these pages have been taken from monuments of Roman times. They show some different types of sailing ships of the time. Paul traveled extensively on ships that carried cargo from place to place on the Mediterranean Sea.

Paul's Journey Begins

ACTS 13:4-52

Synopsis
Saul, who became known as Paul, was commissioned with Barnabas by the church at Antioch, and sent forth on a missionary journey. The journey took them first to Cyprus, then to the mainland where John Mark deserted them and went home. Paul and Barnabas went inland to Antioch of Pisidia, where many believed because of Paul's preaching.

Ships and Sailing
Ships were nothing new to the people of Paul's day. The vessels were used mainly for trade, travel, and war. Due to the great number of shipping routes on the Mediterranean Sea, pirate ships grew common, attacking unarmed vessels and stealing their goods. But the Romans built a large fleet of navy ships which put an end to this piracy.

Paul frequently sailed on ships during his missionary journeys (Acts 13:4, 13; 14:26; 16:11; 18:21; 27; 28:11-13). There were no ocean liners or cruise ships in that day, so those who wanted to travel by sea rode on merchant or trade ships. Paul began his voyage to Rome on a ship carrying wheat (27:38).

The shipping season lasted from April to October. During the winter months, the weather was rough and unpredictable. Since this was also the rainy time of the year, the sky was usually cloudy, and the stars, the compass of ancient times, could not be seen.

Jealous Jews
Many Jews did not accept Jesus as the Messiah so they continued to follow the Old Testament laws as well as their own laws very carefully, believing this would bring them salvation.

Paul, however, entered the Jewish synagogues and claimed that Jesus' death had given people freedom from these strict laws.

570

Ruins of an ancient Roman aqueduct may still be seen where Pisidian Antioch once stood (top photo above). The lower picture above shows a scene from Konya, in modern Turkey, where Iconium was located. The various places associated with Paul's early travels may be seen on the map at the left.

© 1981, SPPI

Naturally many people were very interested and wanted to hear more. This left many important Jews, usually prominent speakers on the Sabbath Day, no longer the center of attention. Of course this made these Jews jealous of Paul, who was becoming quite popular. Jealousy often buds into hatred, and soon these leaders began plotting Paul's death, much as they had plotted Jesus' death.

Preaching to Jews or Gentiles?
Most Jews were familiar with the laws, lessons, and prophecies of the Old Testament. But the Gentiles were not Jews, and often were called "pagans." They were men and women who usually had no knowledge of the Scriptures. In preaching the Gospel to these two diverse groups of people, the message was always the same, but the method of telling it was different, so that each group could understand.

Both Jews and Gentiles needed to know that Jesus' death meant a new life for all, and that accepting this new life meant rejecting sin. To the Jews, Paul showed Jesus as the Messiah, the fulfillment of Old Testament prophecy. Jesus rescued people from the old laws which they could not keep.

But to the Gentiles, Jesus is portrayed as the conquerer of all evil. He is still the same Lord, but He is shown as One who can bring sense and meaning into an evil world because He knows sin will someday be destroyed.

A Notable Convert
To Paul, no person was too great or too small to hear the message of Christ. On the island of Cyprus lived a most important man named Sergius Paulus, the Roman proconsul. He was in charge of the entire island, for though Cyprus was far from Rome, it was under the control of the Roman government. As Paul spoke, this man became a Christian believer (Acts 13:4-12).

571

Mistaken for Gods

ACTS 14

Synopsis

Paul and Barnabas worked together in the church at Antioch, which in time sent them out on a missionary journey. Their first stop was the island of Cyprus, and then on to the mainland, where John Mark deserted them and returned home. Paul and Barnabas continued on to Antioch of Pisidia, where many believed because of Paul's preaching. From there they traveled to Iconium, where, as at Antioch of Pisidia, local Jewish people stirred others against them. Moving on, the two went to Lystra and Derbe. At Lystra, after Paul healed a lame man, the people thought that he and Barnabas were gods. Shortly after this, some people came from Antioch of Pisidia and Iconium and accused Paul of certain things. Paul was stoned and left for dead. Then, after recovering, Paul and Barnabas retraced their steps to the home church at Antioch. This ended their first missionary journey.

Iconium

Though the other towns of Paul's first missionary journey have all but disappeared, Iconium, the modern Konya, is today a Turkish provincial capital, on the major crossroads south of Ankara.

In Greek and Roman times it was the leading city and capital of a region known as Lycaonia, though it still identified itself with

572

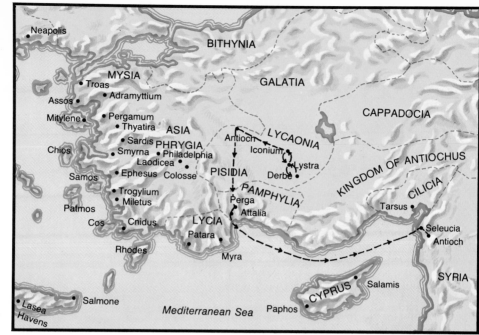

The four coins at the far left show figures of Jupiter (Zeus). The bust is also of Jupiter and the running figure is Mercury (Hermes). At the bottom center, ruins of an aqueduct at Pisidian Antioch. Paul's travels at this time are shown on the above map. At the far left: Paul and Barnabas watch the lame man who has just been healed. This event stirred the people of Lystra to think they were gods.

Phrygia. About 80 miles from Pisidian Antioch (Antiochea on today's maps) along the Via Sebaste, the great Roman road leading from Ephesus to the Euphrates, it is still today a city of beautiful scenery, fertile land, comfortable climate, and 50,000 people. The name may have come from the images Prometheus and Athena, who were made after a great flood destroyed many people.

Lystra
Lystra has been identified with an unexcavated mound near Hatunsaray in modern Turkey, 20 miles southwest of Iconium (Konya). It has been a relatively insignificant rural settlement throughout its long existence. Little is known about it. In 6 B.C. Caesar Augustus made it a Roman colony and renamed it Julia Felix Gemina Lustra. Perhaps he chose it because he needed an eastern frontier fortress. He built a branch of the Via Sebaste to it.

Zeus and Hermes (Jupiter and Mercury)
There was at this time a myth that Zeus and Hermes had once come to the area disguised as human beings seeking lodging. After a thousand people rejected them, a poor, elderly man named Philemon and his wife Baucis fed them lavishly and housed them. They destroyed the inhospitable people but made Philemon and Baucis priest and priestess of their straw-roofed reed cottage, which they transformed into a gold and marble temple. No wonder Lystrans welcomed Paul and Barnabas so enthusiastically!

Zeus (Jupiter) was the chief of the Greek gods. Hermes, son of Zeus and spokesman of the gods, was called Mercury by Romans.

573

Paul's Second Missionary Journey

ACTS 15:36-41

Synopsis
After Paul and Barnabas returned from their first missionary journey, they reported to the people at Antioch, remaining there for some time. A controversy arose concerning circumcision, for some said a man could not be saved without it. The church at Antioch sent Paul and Barnabas to Jerusalem to confer with the apostles, who determined that Gentiles did not need circumcision in order to become believers. After returning to Antioch, Paul and Barnabas decided to go on a second missionary journey, but when Barnabas wanted to take John Mark, he and Paul disagreed so sharply that Paul took Silas and Barnabas took John Mark and they parted ways.

The Cities of Paul's Second Journey
In addition to the cities Paul revisited, the New Testament mentions 12 other places Paul visited on his second missionary trip:

1. *Troas.* The name sounds like Troy and is only 10 miles from that famous city of ancient Greek history (today it is Hisarlik in modern Turkey). An important city in northeast Asia Minor in Paul's day, it was a port on the major trade route to Macedonia.

2. *Neapolis.* The first city that Paul visited in what is now called Europe, this town was Philippi's seaport. Located on the coast of Macedonia in northern Greece, it is believed to be near modern Kavalla.

3. *Philippi.* Located about 10 miles north of the Mediterranean Sea and Neapolis, Philippi was founded by Philip II of Macedon, the father of Alexander the Great. Here, in 42 B.C., Mark Antony defeated Brutus and Cassius, the murderers of Julius Caesar. Augustus made Philippi a Roman colony. The tradition that this was Luke's birthplace is supported by the fact that an important physicians' guild was located here. Though there is no significant settlement here today, Philippi was the first European city in which Paul preached the Gospel.

4. *Amphipolis.* Located 33 miles southwest of Philippi, Amphipolis was its rival and the capital of the region.

5. *Apollonia.* Like Philippi and Amphipolis, Apollonia was located on the famous Roman road called the Via Egnatia. It was 28 miles west of Amphipolis and 38 miles east of Thessalonica.

6. *Thessalonica.* The most important city in this part of Greece today, Thessalonica was founded by Cassander, the military officer who took control of Greece after the death of Alexander the Great, in 323 B.C. A consolidation of several small towns, it lay on both sea and land trade routes. Its sheltered harbor made it Macedonia's major seaport. Coins that have been excavated reveal it to have been a very prosperous city.

7. *Berea.* The origins of this small town on a branch of the Aliakmon River are unknown. It surrendered to the Romans after the battle

of Pynda in 168 B.C..

8. *Athens.* The well-known capital of Attica and educational center of all of ancient Greece, Athens was named after the goddess Athene. According to tradition, Cecrops of Egypt founded the city in 1556 B.C. Many of its best-known buildings were built during the days of its most famous leader, Pericles (461-429 B.C.). With a population of over a quarter of a million in Paul's day, Athens was situated on and around the Acropolis, a large, rocky hill four miles in from the Saronikos Bay. It was connected to its seaport, Peiraeus, by a street 250 feet wide, with high walls on both sides.

9. *Corinth.* Because Corinth is located on a narrow neck of land that joins the southern part of Greece, called the Peloponnesus, to the northern mainland, it became the most important city in the region. In addition, sailing around the south of the Peloponnesus was treacherous, so most sea traffic between Rome and the East passed through Corinth.

10. *Cenchrea.* Located east of Corinth, Cenchrea was its seaport.

11. *Ephesus.* The most important seaport along the west coast of Asia Minor in Paul's day, Ephesus was the center of the Artemis cult.

12. *Rhodes.* A city and island off the Asia Minor coast, Rhodes once rivaled Rome in wealth.

The Macedonian Call

ACTS 16:1-10

Synopsis
After Paul and Barnabas returned to Antioch from their first missionary journey, they remained there for some time. A controversy over circumcision took them to Jerusalem to confer with the apostles, who determined that Gentiles need not be circumcised to be saved. Back in Antioch, Paul and Barnabas decided to go on another missionary journey, but they disagreed about taking John Mark, so they separated. Paul took Silas, and Barnabas took John Mark. Paul and Silas went through Syria and Cilicia, retracing some of the steps Paul had taken earlier. But at Troas, Paul saw a vision of a man of Macedonia, asking Paul to come and help his people. Paul and Silas immediately left for Macedonia, arriving at last in Philippi.

The Roman Provinces of Asia Minor
Asia Minor in Paul's day was divided up into provinces. There were three basic types: senatorial provinces, imperial provinces governed

At the right is a coin of Macedonia from Bible times. The coastline of Macedonia, west of Philippi, is seen in the center. The photo below shows the coastline and ruins at Troas.

by consuls or praetors, and imperial provinces governed by procurators.

1. *Senatorial provinces.* Ten older, more stable provinces remained under senatorial control as they had been during the republic. Macedonia was one of these.

2. *Consular or praetorial provinces.* Twelve old provinces and all provinces added after 27 B.C., when Augustus reorganized the empire's political structure, were governed by the emperor's appointees, called legates, for one-year terms. Large frontier provinces requiring a military presence were given a consul, smaller ones a praetor.

3. *Provinces governed by procurators.* Provinces that were problematical were ruled by procurators, members of a military elite called equites, who were responsible both to the emperor and to the legate of the neighboring province.

Some ancient territories, such as the old kingdoms of Pergamum, Mysia, and most of Phrygia, were absorbed in larger units such as the province of Asia.

Macedonia

United by Philip II and head of an empire that stretched from India to Egypt under Alexander the Great, Macedonia then became a maelstrom of political struggle until Rome conquered it and built the Via Egnatia, an impressive road that went from west to east coast.

Silas

Greek writers often abbreviated names. Silas is probably short for Silvanus, from the Latin word for "wood." His name suggests he was a Roman citizen, probably with Hellenistic Jewish roots. Tradition says a Silas and a Silvanus became bishops of Corinth and Thessalonica.

The coin above is from Alexandria Troas, also called Troas. The name Alexandria Troas was for Alexander the Great, who founded the city. Troas was both a city and the territory around it.

Timothy's Family and Home

ACTS 16:1-4; 2 TIMOTHY 1:5

Synopsis

While Paul and Silas were on their second missionary journey, they met Timothy at his home in Lystra. He was the son of a Jewish mother, a devout woman, and a Greek father. Timothy joined Paul and Silas as they went on their way.

Timothy

Timothy's name means "one who honors God." He was raised in Lystra by a Christian mother and grandmother. Probably both Lois and Eunice became believers in Jesus as a result of Paul's preaching on his first missionary journey, when Timothy was still in his teens. By the time Paul made his second visit to the towns of Lycaonia, Timothy may already have been functioning as a prophet or elder (see 1 Tim. 4:14), though the existence of a group of elders suggests a more well-organized church than might have existed in A.D. 48. His natural talents and spiritual gifts appear to have been recognized by a prophet in the Christian community in Lystra or Iconium (see 1 Tim. 1:18) and he was enthusiastically approved by the Christians in both churches (Acts 16:2). His familiarity with the Old Testament from his childhood (2 Tim. 3:15), combined with his abilities and acceptance by the Christian community, made him an ideal choice for Paul's companion in his ministry for Christ, despite his youth.

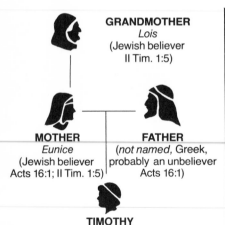

GRANDMOTHER
Lois
(Jewish believer
II Tim. 1:5)

MOTHER
Eunice
(Jewish believer
Acts 16:1; II Tim. 1:5)

FATHER
(*not named*, Greek,
probably an unbeliever
Acts 16:1)

TIMOTHY

Timothy, far right, was fortunate to have both a Christian mother and grandmother. His family relationships may be seen above. At the right, Lystra is seen in relationship to other cities which Paul visited. The countryside near Lystra is seen in the upper center.

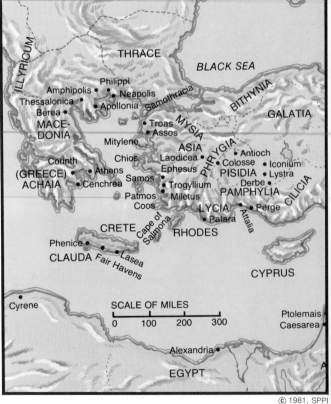

He is not mentioned in the stories of Paul's imprisonment in Philippi or Paul's work in Thessalonica. Perhaps Timothy was using his talents in other places such as Amphipolis and Apollonia, since he was known in Thessalonica (1 Thes. 3:1-2). The fact that he remained Paul's companion until his death, whereas Silas disappeared after the end of the second journey, suggests that Timothy's gifts as a preacher and leader were greater. Timothy took Paul's place in Corinth when Paul was in Ephesus, and sent his greetings to Rome when Paul wrote to the church there (1 Cor. 4:17; Rom. 16:21). As Paul faced death, he passed his responsibilities on to Timothy, his successor and "dear son" (2 Tim. 1:2), who had spent 20 years as his associate. The writer of Hebrews (13:23) mentioned Timothy's release from prison.

Later tradition tells us that Timothy became the bishop of Ephesus. Liberal scholars in the 19th century saw him as the author of Acts. Other Bible scholars suggest that he was the "angel" of Revelation 2:1-7.

Eunice and Lois
Both names, Eunice ("good victory") and Lois ("more desirable") are Greek. Tradition says both were widows.

Lydia Becomes a Believer

ACTS 16:11-15

Upper left: Lydia meets with Paul and Silas. Lydia was from Thyatira, now in Turkey, where she probably learned her trade in purple goods. Thyatira is pictured above, and is located on the map at the upper right. It was one of the cities of the seven churches to whom John wrote Revelation. Lydia's purple goods may have been dyed with a substance from the murex shellfish (above).

Synopsis

On his second missionary journey, Paul traveled through many of the same places he had visited on his first journey. But when he came to Troas, he saw a vision of a man of Macedonia, asking Paul to come over there to help. Paul and Silas went, arriving at Philippi. There they joined a group of women who met together for prayer. Lydia, one of these women, accepted Jesus as her Saviour.

Philippi

The women's prayer group Paul found probably gathered on the banks of the Ganga or Gangites River, a mile west of Philippi. Flanked on the west by the Strimon River and on the east by the Nestos-Mesta River and surrounded on all sides by mountains, Philippi

looked out over a broad plain. The Via Egnatia ran down its main street. On the south side in the center of the city was the forum or market-place in which Paul and Silas appeared before the city's two magistrates, called praetors or, more exactly, duumviri. This forum was excavated in the 1920s, when other buildings, temples, houses, and a theater were also found.

Settlers first arrived in Philippi from the off-coast island of Thasos to mine gold. Philip II of Macedon named the city after himself, built

a wall, and colonized it in 356 B.C. At the Battle of Philippi in 42 B.C. Cassius committed suicide here after Mark Antony defeated his army. Luke may have grown up and attended medical school here. The church at Philippi was Paul's favorite church.

Purple Cloth

The purple or crimson cloth so valued by the ancients as a sign of nobility and distinction came from either a shellfish called the murex, or "turkey red," a dye taken from the madder root. A dyer's guild was located in Thyatira.

Thyatira

Thyatira was a busy commercial center. Lydia probably learned her trade in one of its many guilds.

The forum at Philippi may still be seen, in ruins, today (far left). The river where Lydia and her friends met for prayer is at the left. Above it, a coin of Thyatira.

581

The Philippian Prison

ACTS 16:16-40

Synopsis

While traveling on his second missionary journey, Paul saw a vision of a Macedonian man, asking Paul and Silas for help. They went immediately, arriving in Philippi. There they joined a group of women who met for prayer, and Lydia, one of them, accepted Jesus as Saviour. But in that same city there was a girl who was used for sorcery. Paul commanded the evil spirit to leave the girl, and for that he and Silas were beaten and thrown into prison. But when the magistrates in town learned that Paul was a Roman citizen, they were frightened, for they had beaten him and imprisoned him without a trial. They begged Paul and Silas to leave town.

Roman Citizenship

Citizenship was a coveted honor in ancient Rome. The better emperors tried to expand the number of citizens, so that by the time of Claudius (A.D. 41-54) there were almost six million citizens, one of whom was Paul. Emperor Pompey may have granted Paul's Jewish ancestors their citizenship, over half a century earlier.

To be a Roman citizen involved certain rights and imposed certain duties. If a citizen felt he had been unjustly imprisoned, for example, as Paul did later on in his career, he had the right to appeal directly to Caesar. At one time a citizen had the duty of serving in the army and the right to vote, but both of these rights had gradually disappeared.

The Philippian jailer asks Paul and Silas what he must do to be saved (right). Above this painting is a coin of Philippi. Around the bust is an inscription, "Tiberius Claudius Caesar Augustus, High Priest, Tribunal Power, Emperor." Around the statues on the reverse side is the inscription "Colony of Julia Augusta of Philippi."

582

© 1981, SPPI

Paul saw Christians as citizens of God's kingdom ("conversation" or "conduct" in Phil. 1:27; 3:20).

Fortune-Telling

Can you imagine anyone thinking he could tell his future by looking at the liver of an animal? Perhaps not, but that method of determining an individual's future was once as popular as the horoscope is today—and just as foolish!

The slave girl who earned money for her owners by fortune-telling is an example of the age-old superstition that by natural or supernatural omens we can learn specific facts about our futures. The Greek text says she had "a python spirit." Python was the serpent or dragon that guarded the Delphic oracle in Greece, lived at the foot of Mt. Parnassus, and was slain by the sun god, Apollo. The slave girl's owners saw her as an instrument of Python, whose spirit was thought to live in her belly. Whatever its name, an evil spirit lived in her.

There were many other superstitious methods in the ancient world by which people thought they could foretell events. Soothsayers used omens from nature, such as earthquakes, a sneeze, and the flight of birds; and signs, such as dreams, star patterns, and casting lots. Diviners communicated with the gods through oracles. Mediums consulted the spirits of the dead. The reason Babylonians consulted animals' livers was that they believed the liver was the seat of life. Whenever God is abandoned, as He was in ancient Rome, astrology seems to become popular. The Bible opposes such practices (Lev. 19:26, 31; Deut. 18:9-14).

Stocks

Stocks are mentioned a number of times in the Old Testament, but only in Acts 16:24 in the New. In Paul's day they were iron bolts attached to wooden posts, through which the prisoner's hands and feet were attached.

At the top center are the remains of a prison at Philippi, presented today as the prison where Paul and Silas stayed. Philippi is located on the map at the left, among other cities which Paul visited. Stocks are pictured at the left. Paul and Silas were put into stocks such as these in the Philippian prison.

583

Paul at Thessalonica

ACTS 17:1-9

Synopsis

While at Troas, Paul had a vision of a man of Macedonia, begging Paul to come there to help. Paul and Silas went immediately, arriving in Philippi, where they joined some women who met for prayer. Lydia, one of the women, became a believer. While in Philippi, Paul commanded an evil spirit to leave a girl who was used for sorcery. For this her masters had Paul and Silas thrown into prison. When they were released, they went on to Thessalonica. Paul preached in the synagogue there, but jealous men stirred up trouble and Paul had to leave town.

Thessalonica

Still the largest city in the region once known as the capital of the Roman province of Macedonia, Thessalonica (today's Thessaloniki) is located on the Gulf of Salonika.

Coming from Apollonia to the east, Paul entered the city through the southeastern gate, called the Arch of Galerius. The famous Roman road, the Via Egnatia, went through the city and left through the only other opening in Thessalonica's walls, the Vardar Gate, which existed until its destruction in 1878. Many of the city's old buildings were destroyed by fire in 1917. The north and east sections of the wall can still be seen in ruined form.

There are two different accounts of how the city was founded. The most likely one is that Cassander, the son of Alexander the Great's regent and Alexander's successor as king of Macedonia, founded Thessalonica in 315 B.C. and named it after his wife, Alexander the Great's sister. The other explanation says it was founded by Philip II and named in honor of either his daughter or his victory over the Thessalians. Its formation united no less than 26 smaller towns and villages. Known as the leading seaport of Macedonia, Thessalonica assumed that reputation only after Pella, a short distance to the west, filled up with silt. When it was conquered by Rome in 167 B.C., it became the capital of one of four districts. Then in 148 B.C., when it was made a province,

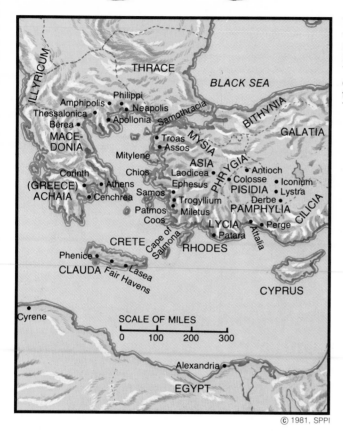

THRACE

BLACK SEA

ILLYRICUM

Philippi
Amphipolis
Neapolis
Thessalonica
Apollonia
Samothracia
Berea
MACE-
DONIA
Mitylene
Troas
Assos
MYSIA
BITHYNIA

GALATIA

ASIA
Chios
Laodicea
Antioch
Colosse
Iconium
PHRYGIA
Corinth
Athens
Ephesus
PISIDIA
Lystra
(GREECE)
Samos
Derbe
ACHAIA
Cenchrea
Trogyllium
PAMPHYLIA
Patmos
Miletus
Coos
LYCIA
Perge
Patara
CILICIA
Attalia
CRETE
Cape of Salmona
RHODES
Phenice
Lasea
CLAUDA
Fair Havens
CYPRUS

Cyrene

SCALE OF MILES

0   100   200   300

Alexandria

EGYPT

© 1981, SPPI

Thessalonica, which Paul visited, is pictured at the far upper left, looking from the high hills toward the sea. Thessalonica may be located on the map at the left. Above the map is a coin of Thessalonica.

it became the capital of the whole area. Octavian and Mark Antony made it a free city as a reward for its support against Brutus and Cassius. Its five or six governors, called "politarchs" (see Acts 17:6), formed the city council.

Jason

Jason of Thessalonica was a Jewish Christian who may have been one of the three relatives of Paul mentioned in Romans 16:21. His name, meaning "healing," was often used by Greek-speaking Jews instead of the names Jesus and Joshua. Paul and Silas probably stayed at his house during their stay in Thessalonica. After his trial in the marketplace Jason was freed, but six years later he may have accompanied Paul to Corinth. Tradition says he became bishop of Tarsus.

The Marketplace

The marketplace in Thessalonica was probably in the center of the city, north of the Via Egnatia. Unlike the ancient Near Eastern marketplace with its open bazaars and shops, the *agora* of the typical Greek city was like the Roman forum. A large square surrounded by beautiful columned buildings, statues, and temples, the agora was far more than just a place where slaves purchased food for their masters. It was also a political and social center. Here the aristocracy met to discuss current topics of interest, students and philosophers exchanged ideas, and the small group of politarchs sat to try people such as Paul and Silas. But when Paul preached in the agora in Athens he appeared more in the role of a philosopher who was presenting his view of life.

585

The Bereans Accept Paul

ACTS 17:10-14

Synopsis

In a vision, Paul saw a man of Macedonia begging him to come over and help. Paul and Silas went, stopping first at Philippi, where they joined a women's prayer group. One of the women, Lydia, became a believer. But Paul and Silas were imprisoned in Philippi for driving an evil spirit from a girl. When they were released, they went to Thessalonica, where jealous men stirred up trouble and Paul and Silas had to leave town, stopping next at Berea.

Berea

Berea lives in the minds of Christians as a town where believers searched the Scriptures. With a population today of 30,000, the small city, called Verria, is a ski resort. Twenty miles from the Thermaic Gulf on the Mediterranean coast, it is located 46 miles southwest of Thessalonica.

In New Testament times Berea was one of the largest cities in Macedonia, perhaps because it was just a few miles south of the famous Roman commercial and military road called the Via Egnatia. In normal circumstances Paul's next stop after Thessalonica would have been Edessa, but perhaps for safety reasons he chose a city off the beaten path. It is interesting that Cicero also mentions that a century earlier an unpopular Roman governor named Piso crept into Thessalonica at night but withdrew to Berea when the citizens rose up in protest. On the eastern slopes of a mountain in the Olympian range, the city gave Paul a beautiful view to the north, east, and west, including Dium, the seaport to which he probably fled to reach Athens. Today only a few ruins of the ancient

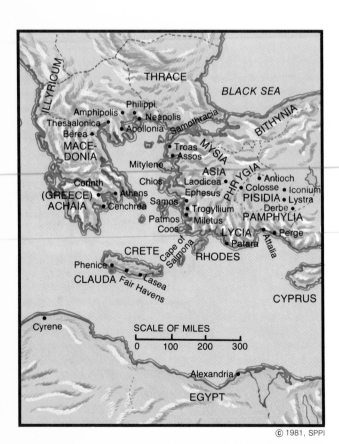

© 1981, SPPI

The modern city of Verria at the right is built over the ancient city of Berea, which Paul visited. The ancient coin of Berea is above the photo. Berea, is shown on the map at the left.

city remain. Behind the Hawaii (Chebaë) Restaurant near a mosque is a platform from which Paul is said to have preached to the Bereans. Sopater, one of Paul's associates, came from Berea, and Onesimus is said to have been Berea's first bishop.

The Jewish Diaspora

The word "diaspora" means "scattering." It refers to the voluntary settling of Jews outside Palestine. Large groups of Jews settled in Egypt, Syria, Mesopotamia, Asia Minor, Greece, and even Italy. Such Jews usually became enterprising merchants. Though Judaism was officially recognized by Rome, emperors such as Tiberius and Claudius persecuted the Jews. Many Gentiles were attracted to Judaism because of its high ethical standards and one God. The translation of the Old Testament into Greek, called the Septuagint, made it even easier for Gentiles to convert to Judaism, and probably many did so.

Diaspora Judaism (Jews scattered in other lands) was also a bridge for infant Christianity to cross into the Gentile world.

Many diaspora Jews made trips to Jerusalem at the time of the Passover, as Luke (Acts 2) indicates. Those who could not, contributed to the annual collection for the temple.

Paul at Mars Hill

ACTS 17:16-34

Synopsis
When Paul saw a vision of a man from Macedonia calling for help, he crossed over and began his work at Philippi. There a woman named Lydia became a believer. There also Paul and Silas were thrown into prison after they drove an evil spirit from a girl. When they were released, they went to Thessalonica, but troublemakers forced them to leave. Next stop was Berea, where people searched the Scriptures to check out what Paul said. From Berea, Paul went to Athens.

Athens
Draw a circle and imagine it to be the walls of ancient Athens. Now draw an upside-down T inside the circle. The tip of the stem is where the *agora* or marketplace was. The left arm of the T is where the Areopagus was, and the right arm is where the Acropolis was.

At one time, Athens was the cultural center of the world. Religion, philosophy, and education thrived. Magnificent buildings seemed to spring up overnight. By Paul's day however, the elegant city had lost much of its importance.

The Areopagus

Mars Hill, or Areopagus, originally referred to the large limestone hill, 375 feet high, that overlooked the agora (marketplace) from the south. Over time, the name also came to mean the court that met there. Earlier, this court had the power to judge all cases including murder. But in Paul's day it seems to have lost much of this power.

Though Athen's glory was declining, it was still a famous center of education and philosophy. Paul must have matched minds with some of the most brilliant men of his day. Apparently these "great thinkers" were not completely satisfied with their lives, for they were eager to listen to Paul's words.

Stoics and Epicureans

These were two groups of people (often called philosophers) that Paul met while in Athens. Both groups had unusual viewpoints toward life.

The Stoics believed that the world was run by some divine force. Since man could not control his own destiny, he had to accept both pain and pleasure as it came along, and feel no emotion.

The Epicureans sought after pleasure only, though not necessarily evil pleasures. For them, pleasure was the absence of pain. So they avoided anything that might cause pain to their body, mind, or heart. Religion, raising a family, and public office were avoided. You can see that speaking with these men must have been quite a challenge for Paul.

Paul reasoned with the men of Athens (far left). The coin of Athens at the upper center shows the head of Minerva and the owl, sacred to that goddess. Mars Hill is seen below the coin. It also is the focal point of the photo of Athens below. The ruins of the Acropolis may be seen at the bottom center.

Paul at Corinth

ACTS 18:1-4

Synopsis

When Paul saw a vision of a man of Macedonia, he went there to minister. His first stop was at Philippi, where he helped Lydia and a jailer become believers. From there Paul and Silas went to Thessalonica, but were forced by troublemakers to leave. At Berea, the people searched the Scriptures to test what Paul said. Paul went on to Athens, and then to Corinth, where he, Priscilla, and Aquila worked as tentmakers.

Corinth

The old city of Corinth was located three and one half miles southwest of the present city. With the Corinthian Gulf two miles to the north and Cenchrea (Kenchreai) seven miles to the east on the Saronic Gulf, Corinth was a very important trade center because ships preferred to use the paved stone passageway that linked the two gulfs rather than risk the treacherous waters around the Peloponnesus. The Acrocorinth Mountain to the south of the city was a steep, rocky fortress that was all but impregnable. Long walls joined the mountain and the city to the Corinthian coast. The Isthmian Games were held here every two years and further enhanced Corinth's reputation. At the peak of its glory it may have had 300,000 to 450,000 inhabitants.

In an age of moral decadence, Corinth had a reputation for its excesses, connected with the worship of Aphrodite, goddess of love and beauty.

The strategic location of this city is underlined by the fact that it has been settled since the fifth millennium B.C. A battle with one of its colonies led to the Peloponnesan War (431-404 B.C.). Some two centuries earlier Periander built the *diolkos,* or paved stone slipway, that carved out Corinth's future. (Today there is a canal about five miles northeast of Old Corinth). After Philip of Macedon became its leader it experienced two centuries of prosperity, but in 146 B.C. Rome razed it to the ground for siding with rebels, and it was not rebuilt until Julius Caesar made it the capital of Achaia, in 44 B.C.

Tentmaking

This is the only place in the Bible that mentions tentmaking. It could mean the weaving of tent cloth from goats' hair, or it could mean the cutting and sewing of tents. The latter is probably what Paul, Priscilla, and Aquila did. Paul's province of Cilicia was noted for the goats'-hair cloth, called *cilicium,* used in making tents.

But, some have asked, could the word mean "leatherworker"? The earliest Latin translators thought that the Greek word used by the author of Acts meant someone who made beds and the leather cushions to go on them. So many of the Latin and Greek church fathers call Paul a leatherworker.

But it is not likely that Paul's father, a strict Pharisee, would have allowed his son to work in a trade that Jews disapproved of. Thus, Paul probably was a tentmaker, not a leatherworker.

Paul worked as a tentmaker with Priscilla and Aquila (far lower left). The engraving to the right of this painting shows tentmakers still at work in the past century, much in the same way that Paul did his work. The ruins of the temple of Apollo may be seen at Corinth today (above). Below is a reconstruction of ancient Corinth. The top coin at the left is a silver stater of Corinth, with a helmeted head of Pallas on the front and winged-horse Pegasus on the back. The lower coin is of Autoninus, struck at Corinth. On the reverse is the inscription ISTHMIA.

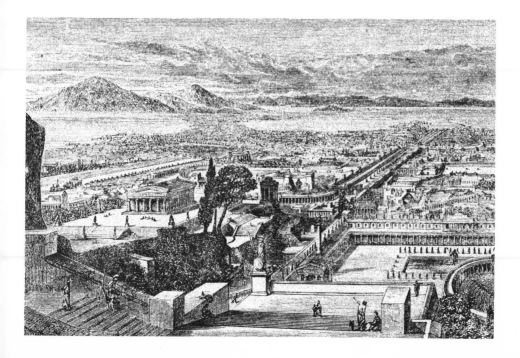

Gallio Judges Paul at Corinth

ACTS 18:5-17

Synopsis
After entering Macedonia, Paul visited Philippi, where Lydia and a jailer became believers. From there he went to Thessalonica, but was forced by troublemakers to leave. At Berea, the people searched the Scriptures to see if what Paul said was true. Paul traveled on to Corinth, where he worked as a tentmaker with Aquila and Priscilla. He remained at Corinth for a year and a half, during which time the synagogue ruler, Crispus, and many other Corinthians believed in Jesus. Many of the Jewish people of Corinth brought Paul to court, but Gallio, the proconsul, threw them out and refused to stop a crowd from beating Sosthenes, the synagogue ruler.

Gallio, Proconsul of Achaia
Lucius Junius Gallio Annaeus was proconsul, or governor, of the Roman province of Achaia in Greece during A.D. 52 and part of the year before or after. The son of a rhetorician named Marcus Annaeus Seneca and brother of Seneca, the millionaire tutor of Nero and well-known philosopher, he was born in Cordova, Spain as Marcus Annaeus Novatus. A wealthy friend, Lucius Junius Gallio, adopted him and trained him for political leadership.

From the foot of Acro-Corinth, one may look out over modern Corinth in the distance and the ruins of ancient Corinth in the foreground. The Roman coin above shows lictors, officers who cleared the way in public for the magistrates. These may have been the people referred to in Acts 16:38.

Archeologists have discovered an inscription that reveals that Gallio was proconsul *after* the 26th year of the acclamation of Claudius as emperor of Rome. That date is important for fixing the dates of Paul's ministry.

An unusually agreeable man, Gallio became ill in Corinth's climate and retired to Egypt when his one-year term of office was over to seek a cure for a lung hemorrhage. After returning to Rome, he joined his brother in a conspiracy to overthrow Nero. His brother was killed and, though he was pardoned, he shortly after committed suicide or was executed by Nero's orders.

Gallio's judgment seat has been discovered on the south side of Corinth's agora. Surrounded on the left and right by shops, the monumental platform, called a *bema,* was the place on which Roman officials stood and may have been the place where Paul appeared before Gallio. A Christian church was built over its ruins.

Synagogues

Though the exact origins of synagogue buildings are unknown, they probably began during the Jewish exile in Babylon after 586 B.C. The temple of Solomon had been destroyed, so local gatherings on feast days and Sabbaths arose to preserve the faith. The New Testament contains some of the earliest references to synagogues. Pharisees early became their leaders and by New Testament times the tradition had emerged that synagogues went back to the time of Moses (see Acts 15:21).

Everywhere Paul went in the Hellenistic world there were synagogues. Several have been excavated. The seven-pillared synagogue in Capernaum, where Jesus taught, has been discovered at Tell Hum and partially restored. The synagogue in Rome's seaport town of Ostia may date back to the first century.

Though worship played an important part in synagogue life, teaching was equally important. Had it not been for synagogues, it is questionable that Judaism could have survived, especially in the diaspora. The two leaders of each synagogue, the "ruler" and the *hazzan* (minister, attendant) who was his helper, supervised the worship, which included 18 prayers, readings from the Law and Prophets, and a sermon.

At the left are the ruins of the *bema,* where Gallio judged Paul at Corinth.

593

The ruins of the agora, the marketplace of Ephesus, may be seen above. The photo at the right shows a view of Ephesus, looking north from the theater where the people gathered during the silversmith riot (Acts 19:23-41). At the far right, Ephesus and other cities on Paul's journey may be identified.

Books of Evil Are Burned

ACTS 19:17-20

Synopsis

Paul visited Macedonia after he saw a vision of a man there, calling for help. In Macedonia, he visited Philippi, where Lydia and a jailer became believers. He moved on to Thessalonica, but troublemakers forced him out. Next he went to Berea, where people searched the Scriptures to test what he was saying. After that, Paul visited Athens, and then moved to Corinth, where he stayed for a year and a half, working as a tentmaker with Aquila and Priscilla. From Corinth, Paul traveled to Ephesus, and then concluded his second missionary journey, returning to Caesarea, and back to the home church at Antioch. Later Paul began his third missionary journey, traveling back to Ephesus. Mighty works happened this time as Paul remained there.

Ephesus

Ephesus is located along the west coast of Turkey, though today it exists only as a historical site. Located about seven miles inland because of the silt that has filled the ancient harbor, it sits on the plain of the Caÿster (Kuçuk) River. The ancient town was located on the slopes of the Coressus and Prion hills. The temple to the goddess Artemis (Diana to the Romans) was located a mile lower on the plain itself. The region is southeast of the present town of Selçuk. In biblical times Ephesus was a terminal of the great trade route from the east and linked it with the great western trade routes.

Settled by colonists from Athens, Ephesus was developed to replace Miletus, its rival to the south, which had silted up. The kingdom

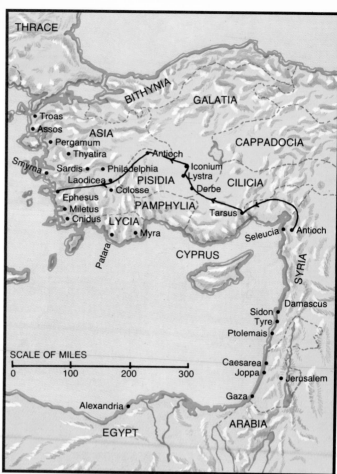

of Pergamum developed the harbor and Rome made Ephesus the seat of its proconsul. Coins call Ephesus "the Landing Place."

By New Testament times Ephesus too had begun to fade as a harbor. Silting is indicated even on some coins, which depict shallow-bottomed boats, not the deep-hulled merchant ships of the days of the city's glory.

Devotion to Artemis the Great and her temple produced a replacement for the city's declining naval importance, however. Founded by the son of the last king of Athens, Ephesus already had a shrine to an ancient Anatolian goddess whom the Greeks renamed Artemis. The fertility goddess was kept "alive," however, in the sexual orgies and prostitution connected with her rites. Through the years the temple became one of the wonders of the ancient world. It was once four times the size of the Parthenon in Athens. Today its ruins have been located in a marsh northeast of the ancient city. Paul was thus attacking a major fortress of paganism.

Scrolls

Paul's Ephesian converts who had been sorcerers burned their scrolls. A scroll was the ancient form of our modern book. Made of papyrus, leather, or parchment, sheets were joined together to form a sheet usually not more than 30 feet long and a foot high. A scroll was rolled up on wooden rollers and wound off the left and onto the right roller. Occasionally, though, enormous scrolls were made. One in Egypt was 133 feet long and 17 inches high. Written in capital letters with no breaks between words and with a very durable ink, scrolls contained columns with only narrow spaces between them. Writing at first went from right to left. Then the boustrophedon, rows alternating from right to left and then left to right, was introduced. But it was soon replaced by the practice we use, from left to right.

595

Diana of the Ephesians

ACTS 19:23-41

Synopsis
On his third missionary journey, Paul visited Ephesus, where he performed a number of miracles. While he was there, seven sons of a Jewish chief priest, Sceva, tried to drive out a demon in Jesus' name, but the man possessed by the demon jumped on them and beat them. As a result, fear spread among the believers, and many burned their books of sorcery. About this time, the silversmiths of Ephesus started a riot against Paul, angry because his ministry was hurting their sales of Diana's shrines. But the city clerk quieted the riot and sent the people home.

Artemis the Great, Diana of the Ephesians
The Artemis of Ephesus was quite different from the goddess of classical antiquity. That is not surprising, perhaps, because Artemis was the most widely worshiped and popular of all the Greek deities, especially among women. Homer portrays her as a virgin hunter, but she is also portrayed as a moon goddess, patron of maidens, and female fertility deity associated with childbirth. Ancient myths said she had given her mother, Leto, no pain at her birth. The daughter of Zeus, she assisted at the birth of her twin brother, Apollo! In Greece little girls would "play the bear" in

Above left: a column from the temple of Diana. The coin of Ephesus above refers to the town clerk. The heads are of Augustus and Livia.

596

front of her image, suggesting that she originally may have had an animal form. At Halae, south of Athens, blood was taken by sword from a man's neck, a vestige, perhaps, of human sacrifice connected with the worship of Artemis. This rite was brought by Orestes from the Tauric Chersonese of Crimea.

But in Ephesus Artemis was nothing like the gentle moon goddess. Here she was the lusty female fertility goddess said to have been worshiped by the warrior maidens of Asia Minor called the Amazons. Like them, the female slaves dressed in short skirts and bared one breast when they served in the magnificent temple to Artemis in Ephesus, one of the seven wonders of the world. The temple also had eunuch priests, called *megabuzoi,* and other chaste male attendants. Prostitution may not have been part of the rites of this temple, though it was of all other Anatolian fertility goddess temples.

The City Clerk
The Ephesian "city clerk" was more of a mayor than what we think of as a town clerk. The word, which appears in the Bible only in Acts 19, is difficult to translate exactly, since the functions and status of offices changed from place to place. However, Apollonius of Tyana around A.D. 100 refers to a high official in Ephesus and used the same word Luke used here in Acts. An important, wealthy Roman official of noble birth, he was president of the assembly, chaired meetings, and eventually became the chief executive.

The theater of Ephesus, where the rioting crowd gathered, is at the lower left, as seen today. At the bottom: the temple of Diana, with its floor plan at the bottom right. Diana's statue is at the right. The coins of Ephesus are, from left to right: Diana in a chariot, Diana of the Ephesians, and Diana's temple.

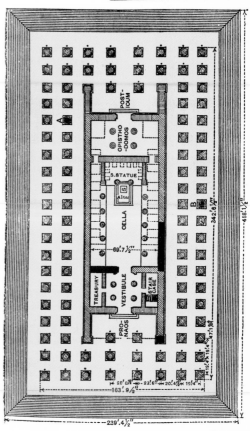

597

Eutychus

ACTS 20:6-12

Synopsis

On his third missionary journey, Paul went through Galatia and Phrygia, encouraging the believers in the churches there. When he arrived in Ephesus, he stayed for some time, performing miracles and teaching. Seven sons of a Jewish chief priest tried to drive out an evil spirit in Jesus' name, but the spirit-possessed man jumped on them and beat them. This brought a fear to the believers in Ephesus, and many burned their books of sorcery. About this time the silversmiths of Ephesus stirred a riot against Paul, whose preaching was hurting the sales of Diana's shrines. When the riot died down, Paul left Ephesus and traveled through Macedonia and Achaia, arriving at last at Troas.

Eutychus

The name Eutychus means "fortunate" or "lucky." It was common among slaves. Josephus mentions two people by that name. One, interestingly enough, was the charioteer who overheard Herod Agrippa tell Caligula he thought the latter would make a better emperor than Tiberius, and told Tiberius. The other, also a charioteer "of the green band faction," was a close friend of Caligula who said he would, after Caligula's murder, bring Claudius—or at least his head—to the soldiers.

Eutychus of Troas was probably an exhausted slave, hot from the oil lamps, and sleepy from all the talk and warm bodies in the room. William Jowett described a room where he stayed in 1818 that may have been similar to the room in Troas. The lower level was a storage area for olive oil. The second level was the family living quarters. But the third level, the area for guests and their company, was large and had projecting windows.

The lamps pictured on these pages are from the time of the New Testament. Oil was poured into the center hole and the wick burned in the hole at the end. Troas today is pictured at the bottom center. Paul's journey through Troas may be traced on the map at the upper right. The coin of Troas at the right shows a Roman soldier and the twin founders of Rome, Romulus and Remus, nursing from a wolf.

598

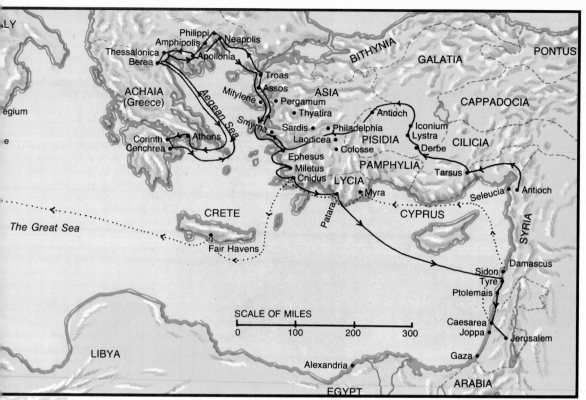

Divans went around the three sides of the window area. A second row of people could be placed behind and above those on the divan by placing cushions there, level with the windows that could be opened to let in air. A fall from such a window could be fatal. In such a large room Paul might have addressed the Christians of Troas, when Eutychus fell asleep.

Troas

Troas is 10 miles south of Troy. Near the present-day town of Hisarlik on the northwest coast of Turkey on the Aegean Sea, it lies at the mouth of the Dardenelles. A port opposite the Bozca Ada (Tenedos) Island, it was originally called Sigia. Renamed Antigonia Troas (Troas means "area around Troy") by Antigonus, one of the generals of Alexander the Great who took over parts of his empire on his death in 323 B.C., the city became Alexandria Troas, in 300 B.C. Troas stayed independent even during the height of power of the kingdoms of Pergamum and Rome. Julius Caesar, Augustus, and Constantine all thought of making Troas the capital of the empire. It was a large, important city in its day, but is now in ruins.

Paul Is Arrested

ACTS 21:17—23:11

Synopsis
When Paul went on his third missionary journey, he traveled through Galatia and Phrygia before arriving at Ephesus, where he stayed for a while. At Ephesus, he taught and worked miracles. Seven sons of a chief priest tried to work a miracle in Jesus' name, but the demon-possessed man involved beat them up. This brought fear on the believers, and many burned their books of sorcery. Many others became believers in Ephesus, and the sales of silver Diana shrines dropped. The silversmiths got angry and started a riot against Paul, but the city clerk stopped it. Paul then left Ephesus and traveled through Macedonia and Achaia to Troas, where Eutychus died from a fall and Paul brought him back to life. From Troas, Paul stopped at several places, then returned to Jerusalem. In the temple, Paul went through certain rituals to prove he had not deserted his Jewish past, but he was falsely accused and arrested anyhow.

The Roman Cohort Commander or Tribune
The commander, Claudius Lysias, was a chiliarch, the leader of a thousand men. A tribune later was the commander of a cohort, usually consisting from 360 to 600 men. Today he would be major or colonel.

The commander of the cohort stationed in the Tower of Antonia was in charge of soldiers in the nearby barracks. They were part of the Roman Tenth Legion, headquartered in Caesarea. Josephus tells us that at Herod Agrippa's death in A.D. 44 Rome had five cohorts stationed at Caesarea. A full legion consisted of 10 cohorts, and each cohort had 6 centurions, each in charge of 60 men.

Rome also organized an auxiliary army. The regular army was made up only of Roman citizens. But the auxiliary army, which was equal to it in size, consisted of soldiers from the provinces who were not citizens. Maybe

At the top left, a fourth-century jasper-agate with two civilian figures on a platform, each holding a palm branch and a knotted scourge, suggests whipping with scourges. Two Roman scourges are at the left center. At the bottom left, a Roman centurion. Tarsus today, at the right, and two coins of ancient Tarsus, far right. The diagram, upper right, shows the Antonia Fortress, where Paul was held prisoner.

the Antonia Fortress was staffed by auxiliaries.

The Antonia Tower where the commander or tribune was stationed was next to the temple. From the southeast, and tallest, of its four towers he could see all of the temple area. Should anything happen, the Antonia was joined to the temple by two stairways and an underground passageway. On Jewish feast days Rome may have increased its military forces to 2 cohorts up to 1,200 soldiers—a small part of the total force of 400,000 believed to have been in the regular and the auxiliary armies.

The Vow of Paul and His Associates

It is not easy to understand the vow the Jerusalem Christians asked Paul to make. Vows were usually religious pledges made in the hope that God would do something for you. But the vow Paul and his friends made does not fit the pattern of Old Testament vows. No reference is made to eating a vowed peace offering or even to making a money offering predetermined by age, sex, and wealth—unless it is the reference in Acts 21:24 to paying expenses. Instead there are references to shaving the head and a set number of days of purification (Acts 21:24, 26). This may have been a temporary Nazirite vow, a vow for safety (see Jonah 1:16), or a rite of purification after Paul's Gentile contacts.

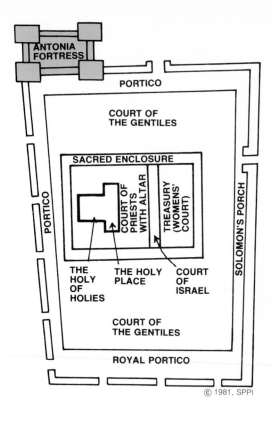

© 1981, SPPI

601

Paul's Nephew Warns Him

ACTS 23:12-35

Synopsis
Returning from his third missionary journey, Paul visited the temple in Jerusalem. There he tried to show the Jewish people that he had not deserted their traditions, but he was falsely accused and arrested. Some men plotted to kill Paul, but his nephew learned of the plot and told the Roman commander, who then transferred Paul through Antipatris to Caesarea.

Antipatris
Under the safety of no less than 470 soldiers Paul was taken to Antipatris. Antipatris was a *mutatio*, or military relay station, on the border between Judea and Samaria. Forty miles from Jerusalem downhill from the mountainous Aijalon Valley into the Plain of Sharon, it was located on the main coastal road 10 miles north of Lydda and 25 miles south of Caesarea, the capital of Judea at this time.

Antipatris was excavated by the Palestine

Above left: Paul's nephew warns him of a plot against his life. The two photos at the upper right show the Tower of Antonia, or Antonia Fortress, as reconstructed in a model. In the center are ruins of Antipatris. The Roman officer's cuirass above may have been worn by a centurion, such as the one who guarded Paul.

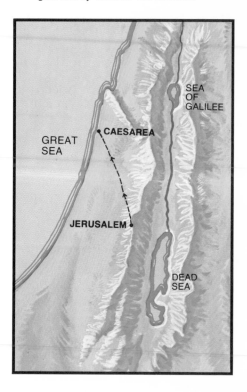

The map below shows the journey from Jerusalem to Caesarea, about 55 miles. To assure his safety enroute, Paul was guarded by at least 470 soldiers.

Department of Antiquities in 1946. The excavations revealed that Antipatris had been built above the older Philistine town of Aphek (2000 B.C.). Antipatris (accent the "tip") was rebuilt in 9 B.C. by the great builder Herod the Great and named in honor of his father Antipater, governor of Judea under Julius Caesar. Earlier, in about 85 B.C. Alexander Jannaeus, the Maccabean ruler of Israel, built a trench between Kefr Saba (Antipatris) and the shores of Joppa, and added a wall and wooden tower to protect himself against Antiochus X of Syria. But Antiochus promptly burned it to the ground!

603

The Procurators (Governors)

1. Coponius
About A.D. 6-9
Coin is a
bronze lepton.

2. Marcus Ambibulus
(Ambivius)
A.D. 9-12
Coin is a
bronze lepton.

4. Valerius Gratus
A.D. 15-26
Coin is a
bronze lepton.

3. Annius Rufus
A.D. 12-15
Coin is a
bronze lepton.

5. Pontius Pilate
A.D. 26-36
Sentenced Jesus
Coin is a
bronze lepton.

Paul Before Felix and Festus

ACTS 24:1—25:12

Synopsis

After returning from his third missionary journey, Paul went to the temple in Jerusalem. But he was arrested there and held prisoner. Paul's nephew learned of a plot to kill Paul, and told the Roman commander, who transferred him by night to Caesarea, where Paul remained prisoner for two years. While there Felix and Festus judged Paul.

Governor Felix (A.D. 52 or 53 to 60)

Antonius Felix, brother of Pallas, a favorite of Claudius, and a freedman from the house of Antonia, Claudius' mother, got his procuratorship of Judea through his brother's influence on the emperor. His term was marked by corruption, mismanagement, and near anarchy. Tacitus, the Roman historian, not always an impartial witness, is probably correct in calling him "a master of cruelty and lust who exercised the powers of a king in the spirit of a slave." His mismanagement is revealed in the fact that it required 470 men to convey Paul safely the 40 miles from Jerusalem to Antipatris.

Just when did Felix become governor of Judea? Tacitus and Josephus do not agree on this. Josephus says quite simply that Ventidius Cumanus became procurator in A.D. 48 and Antonius Felix after Cumanus' recall in A.D. 52. Tacitus says Cumanus was procurator of Galilee while Felix held the same office in Samaria and Judea.

Felix took Drusilla, the 15-year-old wife of Azizus, king of Emesa (a small principality northeast of Damascus), and made her his third wife. (He had also been married to the granddaughter of Mark Antony and Cleopatra.) Drusilla was also the sister of King Herod Agrippa II. She bore a son, Agrippa.

6. Marcellus
A.D. 36-44

10. Antonius Felix
A.D. 52-58
Judged Paul
Coin is a
bronze lepton.

7. Cuspius Fadus
A.D. 44-46

8. Tiberius Julius
Alexander
A.D. 46-48

11. Porcius Festus
A.D. 58-62
Judged Paul

9. Ventidius Cumanus
A.D. 48-52

Felix's tenure was marked by many uprisings, the murder of the high priest, and the slaying of 400 of the followers of an Egyptian Jew (see Acts 21:38). When Nero recalled Felix in A.D. 60, a large deputation of Jews brought charges against him. His cruelties triggered a war that broke out in A.D. 66.

Drusilla

Drusilla, Felix's wife, was the youngest of Herod Agrippa I's three daughters. She was probably named after the sister of Herod's friend, the young emperor Caligula. Drusilla had just died at the age of 22 when Herod's daughter was born, and Herod had been in Rome at the time, A.D. 38. By A.D. 53 she broke her engagement to Epiphanes, prince of Commogene (northeast of Tarsus), because he changed his mind about converting to Judaism, and married Azizus of Emesa. In 54, however, Felix persuaded her to leave Azizus and marry him. She was 20 when Paul spoke to her and her husband. Their son Agrippa

died later in the eruption of Mt. Vesuvius, A.D. 79. Drusilla, a widow by this time, may have died with him.

Porcius Festus (A.D. 60-62)

The two years before Festus became procurator are years of silence in Paul's life, unless he wrote some New Testament letters then.

We know nothing of Porcius Festus except for the brief time he was procurator of Judea. According to Josephus, he was a welcome contrast to his corrupt predecessor, Felix, and his equally corrupt successor, Albinus. Lawlessness had broken out throughout the land, foreshadowing the Jewish war that was to break out in A.D. 66. Festus had the difficult task of placating all groups in Judea. With near anarchy in Judea, Paul no doubt made the right decision when he rejected Festus' suggestion that he return to Jerusalem. Festus supported Herod Agrippa II in a controversy with the Jews and died before hearing from Rome on the matter.

605

For about two years, Paul was imprisoned at Caesarea. Ruins of Caesarea are pictured above and left. The aqueduct, lower right, carried water into the city. Caesarea was Palestine's Roman capital for about 500 years. Herod the Great built the city in 22 B.C. and named it to honor Caesar Augustus.

Paul Before King Agrippa

ACTS 25:13—26:32

Synopsis

After Paul was arrested in the temple in Jerusalem, he was held prisoner there. But his nephew discovered a plot against Paul's life and told the Roman commander in charge. Paul was secretly transferred to Caesarea, where he was held for about two years. During this time he was judged by two procurators, Felix and Festus, and by King Herod Agrippa II.

King Herod Agrippa II

Born in A.D. 27 the oldest of the first Herod Agrippa's five children, Herod Agrippa II was the brother of Drusus, Bernice, Drusilla, and Mariamne. His mother was the daughter of Herod the Great's nephew and daughter. When his father died in A.D. 44, Agrippa

was only 17. Emperor Claudius felt he was too young to be king of his father's territories and appointed Cuspius Fadus procurator of Palestine instead. For the next four years Agrippa used his influence to help the Jews. When he turned 21 he was appointed king of Chalcis, a region north of Caesarea Philippi and west of Damascus, which his late uncle had ruled. In A.D. 53, five years later, he exchanged Chalcis for his Uncle Philip's tetrarchy, including Abila. In A.D. 55 Nero added Tiberias and Taricheae in Galilee and Abilene in Perea with its 14 villages to Agrippa's territory. In appreciation Agrippa gave Caesarea Philippi the name Neronias. He built Jerusalem's "third wall." With his sister Bernice he tried to stop the Jewish war from starting, but was unsuccessful and was wounded by a slingstone at the siege of Gamala, east of the Sea of Galilee. A friend of Vespasian's son Titus, he sided with Rome throughout the war, and when Vespasian became emperor he confirmed

606

Agrippa in his territories and added unspecified others. Little is known of his later years except he corresponded with Josephus who wrote *The Jewish War*. He never married. He died about A.D. 100.

Bernice

Bernice was the oldest of Herod Agrippa's three daughters. Born in A.D. 28, she was married at 13 to Marcus, the son of Tiberius Julius Alexander the alabarch. On his death she married her uncle Herod, for which her father got the little kingdom of Chalcis, west of Damascus, and to whom she bore two sons, Berniceanus and Hyrcanus. On Herod's death in A.D. 48, she went to live with her brother, Herod Agrippa II. Rumors, apparently groundless, of incest resulted from their friendship and intellectual affinity. To squelch them she married Polemo II of Olba in Cilicia, about A.D. 65. Shortly thereafter she left him and returned to her brother's home, where she worked hard to prevent the outbreak of the Jewish war by confrontation with the procurator, Gessius Florus, and in other ways. Vespasian's son Titus fell in love with her during a stay in Caesarea and took her to Rome. But when Titus became emperor, A.D. 70, he sent her away. He died two years later. Bernice disappeared from history.

Bonds and Prisoners' Chains

Two different words are used for objects used to keep prisoners under control. The word used by Paul in his speech to King Herod Agrippa II is the more general word. It refers to any kind of instrument used to tie or fasten, a bond or a fetter. They were used to prevent persons from using their arms or legs, usually to keep prisoners under control. In such cases they were called shackles.

The more specific word, used to refer to Paul's chains or handcuffs (Acts 28:20 and elsewhere), refers to the handcuffs that attached a prisoner to his guard.

King Agrippa's Family

The "King Agrippa" before whom Paul appeared was a member of a powerful but evil family. This family of Herods ruled Palestine for many years. King Agrippa's great-grandfather, Herod the Great, tried to kill the infant Jesus at Bethlehem. The brother of Agrippa's grandfather (Herod Antipas) judged Jesus at His trial. Agrippa's grandfather, Herod Aristobulus, had three children, shown in the chart below—Herod of Chalcis, Agrippa I, and Herodias.

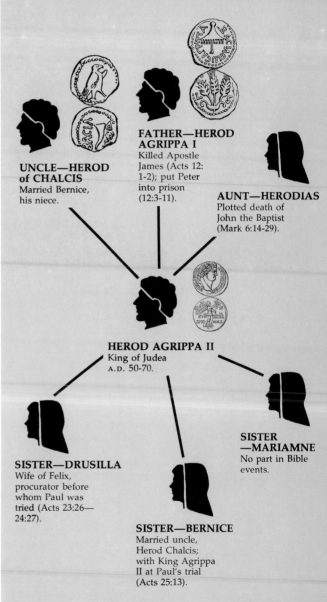

UNCLE—HEROD of CHALCIS
Married Bernice, his niece.

FATHER—HEROD AGRIPPA I
Killed Apostle James (Acts 12: 1-2); put Peter into prison (12:3-11).

AUNT—HERODIAS
Plotted death of John the Baptist (Mark 6:14-29).

HEROD AGRIPPA II
King of Judea
A.D. 50-70.

SISTER —MARIAMNE
No part in Bible events.

SISTER—DRUSILLA
Wife of Felix, procurator before whom Paul was tried (Acts 23:26—24:27).

SISTER—BERNICE
Married uncle, Herod Chalcis; with King Agrippa II at Paul's trial (Acts 25:13).

Paul's Journey Toward Rome

ACTS 27:1-8

Nero is pictured on the front of the coin at the right and a Roman grain freighter on the back. The ship drawing below was taken from a Roman monument from New Testament times.

Synopsis

After Paul had presented his case to King Agrippa, who was actually Herod Agrippa II, son of Herod Agrippa I, he appealed to have his case heard by Caesar. Paul had already spent two years in prison at Caesarea and he believed he would have a fair hearing in Rome. Under Roman law, a Roman citizen who appealed to Caesar had to be sent to Caesar to be judged. Paul was placed on a ship sailing from Caesarea, then transferred to another ship at Myra, a city in Cilicia, which is in present-day Turkey. But sailing was slow because of contrary winds. By the time the ship had reached Cnidus in early October, the dangerous autumn weather had set in, and the danger of shipwreck had increased.

The Ships

Two ships are mentioned. The first was a ship from Adramyttium, on the coast of present-day Turkey. The second was a Roman grain freighter based in the Egyptian city of Alexandria.

The Emperor

The Roman Emperor Nero was Caesar at this time. The term Caesar was, like the term Pharaoh, a title which meant supreme ruler. Rulers over small areas, sometimes cities, were called kings, so the rulers of empires wanted a more grand term to describe their greater powers. Nero had begun to reign in A.D. 54, nine years before Paul arrived in Rome. His early years as Caesar were peaceful and people were judged fairly. But in A.D. 64, the year after Paul was freed, Nero seemed to change. In that year much of Rome was destroyed by fire and it was thought that Nero was responsible. Paul spent two years (A.D. 61-63) waiting for Nero's trial. Four years later, in A.D. 67 Paul was arrested again and brought before Nero for trial. This time he died as a martyr.

608

Why Roman Ships Sailed from Alexandria

At first it seems strange that Roman ships based in Alexandria, Egypt were bringing grain to Rome. Why were Roman ships in Egypt? And why were they bringing grain to Rome? These ships transported the tribute of grain from Egypt, for Egypt was ruled by Rome at that time. There was a large fleet of these grain freighters. Alexandria was the port for Egypt. The average ship was about 350 tons but some were as large as 1,200 tons. Probably as much as 150,000 tons of grain were shipped to Rome each year from Alexandria during the first three centuries A.D..

The two photos above show the harbor at Fair Havens on the southern side of Crete. At the right is a model of a Roman grain ship, similar to the one on which Paul rode. Another similar ship, a Sidonian one, is at the bottom.

Anchors of the Ancient World

What we know about ancient anchors comes to us through drawings from monuments or wall paintings, coins, and actual anchors found by archeologists. The following pictures show some types of anchors common in the lands and times of the Bible.

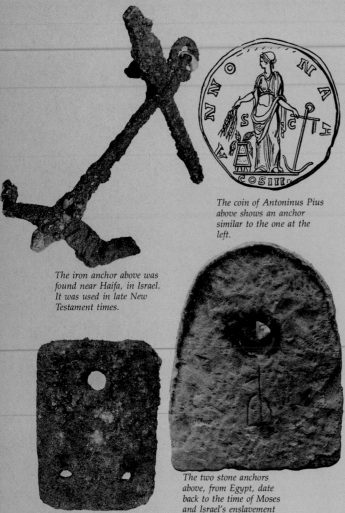

The coin of Antoninus Pius above shows an anchor similar to the one at the left.

The iron anchor above was found near Haifa, in Israel. It was used in late New Testament times.

The two stone anchors above, from Egypt, date back to the time of Moses and Israel's enslavement there.

610

Fragments of anchors have been retrieved from the sea, such as the parts of a crossbar, above.

Paul's Shipwreck

ACTS 27:27—28:10

Synopsis

When Paul was arrested in the temple in Jerusalem, some men plotted to kill him. His nephew discovered the plot and warned the Roman army commander. Paul was transferred to Caesarea, where he remained for about two years. During this time, he was judged by the two procurators, Felix and Festus, and by King Herod Agrippa II. During his trial, Paul appealed to Caesar to hear his case, and under Roman law, the procurators were obligated to send him to Rome. But on the way to Rome, Paul's ship was wrecked.

Ships in Paul's Day

There were two basic types of ships in the ancient world, the merchantman and the warship. The earliest Greek ship, the swift *pentekontor*, was manned by 50 oarsmen, 25 on each side, and was used for both trade and piracy. The heavy merchantman, a trading ship designed to travel day and night through stormy weather, was the type of ship on which Paul is said to have traveled on 13 occasions in Acts. There were no commercial passenger ships. Propelled by sails or long, heavy oars called sweeps, some ships were as long as 300 feet and could carry 600 passengers.

The top coin below, from Gadara, shows a Roman galley, with rows of oars. Below it is a coin of Malta, showing both front and back.

The most common of several types of Greek warship was the *trireme*.
It was a light, swift, slim ship with a distinctive high, hooked prow
that ended with a bronze ram and had an eye painted on each side to
ward off evil. The trireme received its name from the three rows of
oarsmen, one above the other. As many as 200 men could be crammed
into its tiny space. Its prows often ended in the bent neck of a goose,
and its stern with the head of Minerva or some other goddess.

The design of these ancient ships was so advanced it did not change
in its basic outlines over the next 18 centuries.

Malta (Melita)

The island of Malta lies 60 miles south of Sicily and 90 miles from its
capital, Syracuse. Since Syracuse was the Mediterranean's central
commercial port, Malta with its good harbors could not have been
more ideally located for trade. The island seems to have been settled
as early as 2000 B.C., but its historical beginnings date to 1000 B.C.,
when the Phoenicians colonized the island and built the city of Malta.

After three centuries of harsh domination by Carthage, Malta became a Roman *municipium*, a privileged town. Cicero mentions its
prosperous, wealthy people and the elegant houses of Malta.

Publius, Malta's "Chief"

Monument inscriptions indicate that Publius was known as "chief."
He may have been a Roman procurator or the leading native official.

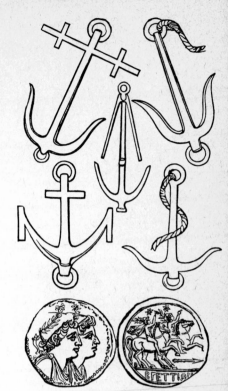

Above: a coin showing the
heads of Castor and Pollux
on one side and their figures
mounted on horseback on
the other. Above the coin are
drawings taken from ancient
monuments, showing Roman
anchors of New Testament
times.

At the left is a 19th-century drawing
of Paul's Bay, at Malta. Below it, a
drawing of the same era, showing
soundings in fathoms and a scale of
miles. The Roman ship below,
showing rudders and anchor rope,
is taken from a Roman monument.

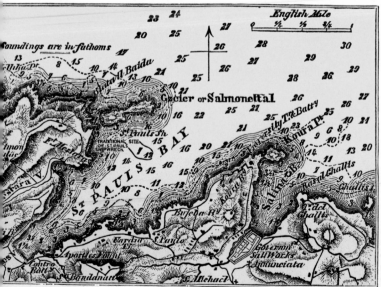

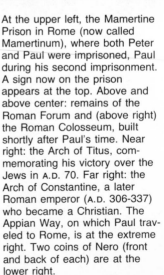

Paul at Rome

ACTS 28:11-31

Synopsis

For about two years, Paul was imprisoned at Caesarea, and was judged by two procurators, Felix and Festus, as well as by King Herod Agrippa II. While before Festus, Paul appealed to Caesar to judge him, so he was sent to Rome. But on the way, his ship was wrecked on the island of Malta. Then he resumed his trip to Rome, where he lived in a private home while waiting for trial.

The Sites of Paul's Journey

1. *Syracuse.* Founded by Greek colonists led by Archias in 734 B.C., Syracuse, on the east coast of Sicily below the "toe" of Italy, became second only to Carthage in importance in the fifth century B.C. Captured by the Romans, Syracuse became a colony under Augustus. Cicero called it the loveliest city.

2. *Rhegium* (today Reggio). On the seven-mile-wide treacherous Strait of Messina which separates Sicily from Italy, Rhegium may have gotten its name from the Greek word for "tear," since it looks as if Sicily had

At the upper left, the Mamertine Prison in Rome (now called Mamertinum), where both Peter and Paul were imprisoned, Paul during his second imprisonment. A sign now on the prison appears at the top. Above and above center: remains of the Roman Forum and (above right) the Roman Colosseum, built shortly after Paul's time. Near right: the Arch of Titus, commemorating his victory over the Jews in A.D. 70. Far right: the Arch of Constantine, a later Roman emperor (A.D. 306-337) who became a Christian. The Appian Way, on which Paul traveled to Rome, is at the extreme right. Two coins of Nero (front and back of each) are at the lower right.

612

been torn from the mainland of Italy at this point. In 280 B.C., 4,000 Roman soldiers, called in to protect Rhegium, slaughtered all its citizens and settled here themselves.

3. *Puteoli* (today Pozzuoli). A fashionable Roman resort, port, and spa on the Bay of Naples halfway between Rhegium and Rome, Puteoli was colonized from the island of Samos near Ephesus and made a Roman colony in 194 B.C. In Paul's day it was the most important commercial port for the receipt of imports from the east. Seneca, the Roman author, says the residents loved to watch the arrival of Alexandrian grain ships like the one Paul traveled on. Tradition says Paul stopped off nearby to visit the Latin poet Virgil's tomb.

4. *The Appian Way and the Forum of Appius.* The Appian Way was the first of the famous Roman paved roads. It went from Rome south to Brundisium in the "heel" of Italy, a total of 350 miles. Fifteen feet wide, the Appian Way was started by the man after whom it was named, Appius Claudius Caecus, in 312 B.C. Paul went 20 miles from Puteoli to Capua, where the road originally stopped, to reach the Appian Way, "the queen of the long roads." He then traveled 132 miles on it to Rome. The market town, called the Forum of Appius, was on the Appian Way 43 miles from Rome. It was a long day's journey for those Roman Christians who met Paul here.

5. *Three Taverns*, or, more accurately, *Three Stores*. A stopover for travelers, 33 miles from Rome and 10 miles from the Forum of Appius.

Castor and Pollux

Twin sons of Zeus according to mythology, they were the children of Leda, wife of Tyndareos, king of Sparta, and the patrons of mariners. They guided sailors through their positions as the two brightest stars in Gemini. Paul's ship had their figureheads on its mast.

Philemon

The Book of PHILEMON

Synopsis
While Paul was imprisoned at Rome, he came to know a runaway slave, Onesimus, who had come to Rome after leaving his master Philemon behind at Colossae. Onesimus must have become a believer under Paul's ministry and evidently helped him there in Rome. But in time Paul sent him back to Philemon with a letter. Paul asked Philemon to forgive Onesimus and receive him as a brother in Christ.

Colossae
The Letter to Philemon is usually associated with the city of Colossae. Colossae was located in southwest Asia Minor in the valley of the Lycus River. The Lycus (now called the Çuruksuçay) flows into the Maeander River not far from Laodicea, which is located about 10 miles west of Colossae. In its prime Colossae was a busy stopover on the main

Above: two coins of Colossae, home of Philemon and Onesimus. The Colossae area is pictured above, with the Lycus (Curuksucay) River in the foreground. Left: Onesimus returns to his master Philemon, who reads Paul's letter.

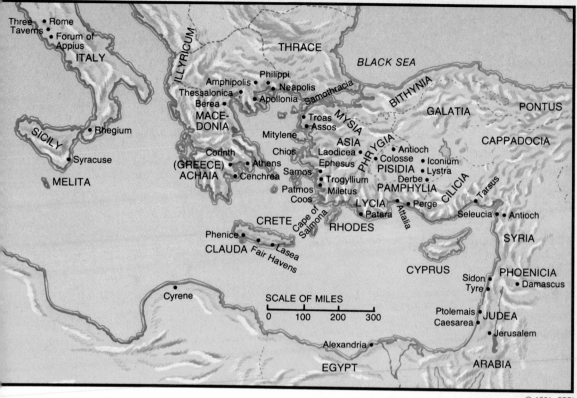

Map labels (clockwise / by region):

Three Taverns • Rome • Forum of Appius
ITALY
ILLYRICUM
THRACE
BLACK SEA
Amphipolis • Philippi • Neapolis
Thessalonica • Apollonia
Berea •
MACE-DONIA
Samothracia
BITHYNIA
GALATIA
PONTUS
SICILY • Rhegium
• Syracuse
MELITA
Troas • Assos
Mitylene
MYSIA
ASIA
PHRYGIA
CAPPADOCIA
Corinth • Chios
(GREECE) • Athens
ACHAIA • Cenchrea
Samos
Laodicea • • Colosse • Antioch
Ephesus • • Iconium
PISIDIA • Lystra
Derbe •
Trogyllium
Miletus
PAMPHYLIA
CILICIA
Tarsus
Patmos
Coos
LYCIA • Perge
• Patara
Attalia
Seleucia • • Antioch
CRETE
Cape of Salmona
RHODES
SYRIA
Phenice •
CLAUDA Fair Havens
• Lasea
CYPRUS
Sidon • Tyre •
PHOENICIA
• Damascus
Cyrene •
SCALE OF MILES
0   100   200   300
Ptolemais • JUDEA
Caesarea •
• Jerusalem
Alexandria •
EGYPT
ARABIA

© 1981, SPPI

road from the east to Ephesus. The road to Sardis and Pergamum to the north also branched off at this point. Today the highway and railroad still follow the Lycus Valley trade route.

During Rome's imperial days, however, Colossae declined in importance because the branch road to the north was moved to Laodicea and Laodicea became the more important city. Colossae, not Laodicea, appears to have been the more important center in the days of Xerxes and Cyrus because it is mentioned as a stopover for their armies as they traveled westward.

Today Colossae is an uninhabited ruins. Motorists' guides to Turkey point out Laodicea's ruins near the modern town of Denizli but do not even mention Colossae. William J. Hamilton located the site of ancient Colossae in 1835, but the spot has never been excavated.

Several of Paul's associates seem to have come from Colossae. Epaphras came from there (Col. 1:7), and Archippus too seems to have been active in Colossae (Col. 4:17).

Above: Colossae may be located near the center of the above map of Paul's day. Note from the scale of miles how far it was to Rome, from which Paul sent this letter. Note also the distance to other key places such as Jerusalem.

Onesimus

Onesimus, whose name means "useful," was one of the millions of slaves who kept the Roman Empire functioning. The brief letter that mentions him as its central subject leaves a lot of unanswered questions. Where was Paul when he met Onesimus, in Rome or in Ephesus? What did Onesimus do? What is Paul asking the recipient to do? Was the recipient Philemon or Archippus? The most common answers are that Paul was in Rome at the end of his life, that Onesimus had stolen money and run away, that Paul is asking the recipient to take Onesimus back as a Christian brother, and that Philemon is the recipient. But each question can be answered in different ways.

615

The Seven Churches

The Book of REVELATION

Synopsis
The first century was drawing to a close. The Emperor Domitian had banished the Apostle John to the island of Patmos. There John wrote the last book of the New Testament, part of which is addressed to the seven churches at Ephesus, Smyrna, Pergamum, Thyatira, Sardis, Philadelphia, and Laodicea.

The Emperor Domitian
No one expected the younger brother of Titus and younger son of Vespasian to become emperor. In fact, Titus was suspicious of him and deliberately gave him no governmental responsibilities.

Born Titus Flavius Domitianus in A.D. 51, Domitian was forced to flee Rome at 18 dressed in the habit of an Isis priest. When

the popular Titus died at 42, Domitian was only 30, a man embittered by his father's and brother's humiliation through the years. Around A.D. 85 he allowed himself to be worshiped as a god. After a revolt in Germany in A.D. 89, Domitian became increasingly suspicious and autocratic. With spies and informers all over Rome, he even came to suspect his niece and her husband, Flavia Domitilla and Flavius Clemens, the parents of his heir-apparent. Flavius was accused of godlessness and executed; Flavia, possibly a Christian, was exiled. He hated the aristocracy, and he persecuted the Christians, largely as part of his effort to enforce Nero's laws. In A.D. 96 his wife murdered him.

The Isle of Patmos

Shaped like the right half of a T, Patmos is located 37 miles southwest of Miletus off the coast of Asia Minor in the Icarian Sea. A mountainous island covering only 15 square miles, it is 10 miles from north to south and only 6 miles at its widest point in the north. Today it is part of "12 Islands," actually a group of 14 islands with local government and a capital in Rhodes.

During Roman times Patmos was a place of political banishment. John was banished here in A.D. 95 by Domitian. Per tradition he was released 18 months later under Nerva, Domitian's successor. John was head of the Ephesus church. The seven churches mentioned in Revelation 2 and 3 were all located in the area around Ephesus and may have been founded by the mother church in that city.

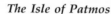

Below: the cities of the seven churches may be located. Their locations, and their ancient coins are: far left, top to bottom, Ephesus, Smyrna, and Thyatira. Center, top to bottom: Pergamum and Laodicea. Coins and photos on this page, top to bottom: Sardis and Philadelphia.

© 1981, SPPI

Index

The format of this volume is story by story, through the Bible. Topics are indexed below in alphabetical order. With each topic are phrases which tell specifically what you will find concerning that topic on certain pages.

618

619

625

628

629

637

639

Typesetting and engraving:
Custom Composition Company
A Division of York Graphic Services
York, Pennsylvania

Printing and binding:
R. R. Donnelley and Sons Company
Willard, Ohio

Type: 9 on 10 pt. Palatino
Text stock: 60# Mead Publishers Matte
Case materials: Holliston Mills, Inc., Roxite B

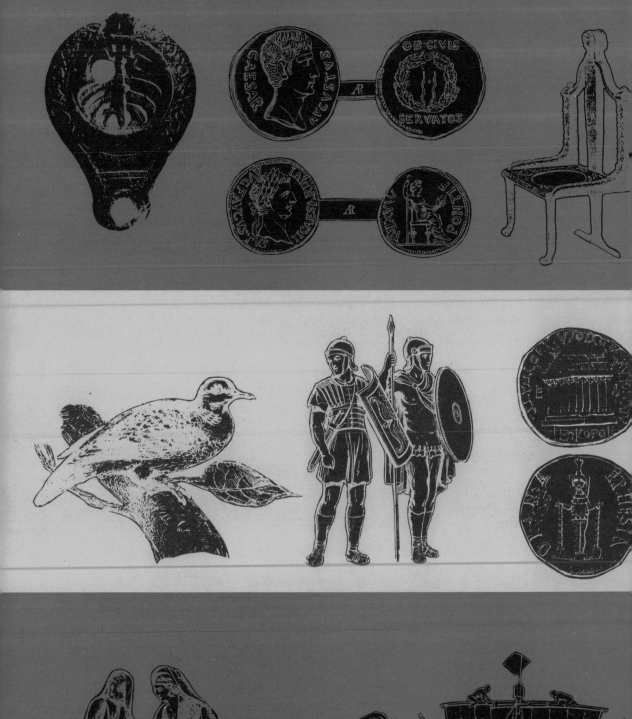